Dispensing Justice in Islam

Dispensing Justice in Islam

Qadis and their Judgements

Edited by

Muhammad Khalid Masud
Rudolph Peters
David S. Powers

BRILL

LEIDEN • BOSTON
2012

Library of Congress Cataloging-in-Publication Data

Dispensing justice in Islam : Qadis and their judgments / edited by Muhammad Khalid Masud, Rudolph Peters, and David S. Powers.
p. cm. — (Studies in Islamic law and society, ISSN 1384-1130 ; 22)
Includes bibliographical references and index.
ISBN 90-04-14067-0 (alk. paper)
1. Judges (Islamic law) I. Masud, Muhammad Khalid, 1939- II. Peters, Rudolph. III. Powers, David Stephan. IV. Series.

KBP1610.D57 2005
297.1'4—dc22

2005047139

This paperback was originally published in hardback under ISBN 978 90 04 14067 7 as volume 22 in the series *Studies in Islamic Law and Society.*

ISBN 978 90 04 22683 8

Copyright 2006 by Koninklijke Brill NV, Leiden, The Netherlands.
Koninklijke Brill NV incorporates the imprints Brill, Global Oriental, Hotei Publishing, IDC Publishers, Martinus Nijhoff Publishers and VSP.

All rights reserved. No part of this publication may be reproduced, translated, stored in a retrieval system, or transmitted in any form or by any means, electronic, mechanical, photocopying, recording or otherwise, without prior written permission from the publisher.

Authorization to photocopy items for internal or personal use is granted by Koninklijke Brill NV provided that the appropriate fees are paid directly to The Copyright Clearance Center, 222 Rosewood Drive, Suite 910, Danvers, MA 01923, USA.
Fees are subject to change.

This book is printed on acid-free paper.

CONTENTS

Preface ix
List of Contributors xi

Chapter One Qāḍīs and their Courts: An Historical Survey 1
Muhammad Khalid Masud, Rudolph Peters, David S. Powers

PART I

JUDGING

Chapter Two Settling Litigation without Judgment: The Importance of a *Ḥukm* in *Qāḍī* Cases of Mamlūk Jerusalem 47
Christian Müller

Chapter Three A New Judge for Aintab: The Shifting Legal Environment of a Sixteenth-Century Ottoman Court 71
Leslie Peirce

Chapter Four Broken Edda and Marital Mistakes: Two Recent Disputes from an Islamic Court in Zanzibar 95
Erin Stiles

Chapter Five Fairness and Law in an Indonesian Court 117
John R. Bowen

Chapter Six The Practice of Judging: The Egyptian Judiciary at Work in a Personal Status Case 143
Baudouin Dupret

Chapter Seven The Constitution and the Principles of Islamic Normativity against the Rules of *Fiqh*. A Judgment of the Supreme Constitutional Court of Egypt 169
Baber Johansen

Chapter Eight Commercial Litigation in a Sharīʿa Court 195
Brinkley Messick

Chapter Nine The Re-Islamization of Criminal Law in Northern Nigeria and the Judiciary: The Safiyyatu Hussaini Case 219
Rudolph Peters

PART II

ORGANIZING LAW

Chapter Ten Law in the Marketplace: Istanbul, 1730–1840 245
Engin Deniz Akarlı

Chapter Eleven On Judicial Hierarchy in the Ottoman Empire: The Case of Sofia from the Seventeenth to the Beginning of the Eighteenth Century 271
Rossitsa Gradeva

Chapter Twelve Islamic Judicial Councils and their Sociopolitical Contexts: A Trans-Saharan Comparison 299
Allan Christelow

PART III

APPLYING DOCTRINES

Chapter Thirteen Ill-treated Women Seeking Divorce: The Qurʾānic Two Arbiters and Judicial Practice among the Malikis in al-Andalus and North Africa 323
Maribel Fierro

Chapter Fourteen The Award of *Matāʿ* in the Early Muslim Courts 349
Muhammad Khalid Masud

Chapter Fifteen Four Cases Relating to Women and Divorce in al-Andalus and the Maghrib, 1100–1500 383
David S. Powers

Chapter Sixteen The Application of Islamic Law in the Ottoman Courts in Damascus: The Case of the Rental of *Waqf* Land 411
Abdul-Karim Rafeq

Chapter Seventeen The *Waqf* in Court: Lawsuits over Religious Endowments in Ottoman Aleppo 427
Stefan Knost

Chapter Eighteen Shopping for Legal Forums: Christians and Family Law in Modern Egypt 451
Ron Shaham

PART IV

RECORDING PROCEDURES AND EVIDENCE

Chapter Nineteen Twelve Court Cases on the Application of Penal Law under the Almoravids 473
Delfina Serrano

Chapter Twenty *Shahādat Naql* in the Judicial Practice in Modern Libya 495
Aharon Layish

Chapter Twenty-One Pakistan's Evidence Order ("Qanun-i-Shahadat"), 1984: General Zia's Anti-Islamization Coup 517
Lucy Carroll

References 543
Index 571

PREFACE

The qāḍī or judge has been a key figure in Muslim societies across the globe for over 1400 years. Sometimes a trained scholar, sometimes not, the qāḍī performs judicial, administrative, and symbolic functions. To the qāḍī belongs the often tumultuous domain of resolving legal disputes by hearing complaints, applying rules of procedure, soliciting and assessing witness testimony, and issuing and enforcing binding judgments. In many Muslim communities, the qāḍī also serves as an administrator and an intermediary between the state and its subjects, executing the ruler's decrees and collecting his taxes. The qāḍī is frequently a revered figure whose office is a symbol of the *shariah* or Divine justice. He is responsible for the general welfare of both Muslims and non-Muslims, the safety and security of travel, ensuring that people are accorded their rights, and promoting respect for Islam and its adherents.

As he carries out his judicial functions, the qāḍī often works closely with the *muftī* or jurisprudent, who operates in the more abstract domain of legal thinking and reflection, as embodied in the *fatwā* or advisory legal opinion. The relationship between the qāḍī and the *muftī* is close and intertwined, and any treatment of Muslim courts that considers one to the exclusion of the other will perforce be one-sided and incomplete. The complex modes of thought and reasoning that characterize the activity of the *muftī* have been treated in Muhammad Khalid Masud, Brinkley Messick, and David S. Powers (eds.), *Islamic Legal Interpretation: Muftis and their Fatwas* (1996). The present volume, devoted to qāḍīs and their judgments (*aḥkām*, sg. *ḥukm*), is designed to complement the *muftī* volume.

In September 2000, Muhammad Khalid Masud, Academic Director of the International Institute for the Study of Islam in the Modern World (ISIM) in Leiden, circulated a call for papers for an international conference devoted to "The Application of Islamic Law in Courts." The call for papers specified that the essays should be constructed around one or more court judgments, include a translation of an exemplary legal document, and/or focus on the qāḍī's application of legal doctrine (*fiqh*) in the daily practice of judging. The selection process was designed to achieve thematic consistency and a balance of discipline, period, region, school of law, language, and legal subject matter. The resulting conference, held in Leiden on October 26–28, 2001, brought together twenty-three scholars from the disciplines of history, law, anthropology, and sociology. The chronological range of their essays extended from the eighth to the twentieth centuries and their geographical scope included the regions that are today the states of Bulgaria, Portugal, Spain, Morocco, Algeria, Libya, Egypt, Nigeria, Zanzibar, Jordan, Syria, Yemen, India, and Indonesia. Following the conference, Khalid Masud, David Powers, and Ruud Peters selected for publication those essays that fit the mandate of the project and sought to fill in gaps in coverage by soliciting a handful of essays from scholars who had not participated in the conference.

We hope that the present volume will serve as a sourcebook of Islamic legal practice and qāḍī judgments. In the first chapter, we survey the state of the field in the study of qāḍīs and their judgments, sketching the history, structure, and modern transformation of this institution. The twenty chapters that follow are grouped thematically in four sections. Section I, "Judging," deals with the nature and functions of the judgeship and its development over time. Section II, "Organizing Law," examines the structure of the judicial apparatus; Section III, "Applying Doctrines," highlights the application of juristic thought and reasoning to specific cases in selected areas of the law; Section IV, "Recording Procedure and Evidence," treats judicial procedure and the different forms of evidence.

As this project draws to a close, we gratefully acknowledge the generous financial support received from ISIM, the University of Amsterdam, and the Society for the Humanities at Cornell University. We also thank Ron Shaham and Nurit Tsafrir for helpful comments on a draft of the Introduction and Robert Mory for his invaluable editorial assistance.

Muhammad Khalid Masud
Rudolph Peters
David S. Powers

LIST OF CONTRIBUTORS

ENGIN DENIZ AKARLI is the Joukowsky Family Professor of Modern Middle East History at Brown University. He has taught at several universities, serves on the editorial board of *Islamic Law and Society*, and is the author of *Political Participation in Turkey* (1974), *Belgelerle Tanzimat* (1977), and *The Long Peace: Ottoman Lebanon, 1861–1920* (1993).

JOHN R. BOWEN is the Dunbar-Van Cleve Professor in Arts & Sciences at Washington University in St. Louis, where he directs the Program in Social Thought & Analysis. His most recent book on Indonesia is *Islam, Law and Equality: An Anthropology of Public Reasoning* (Cambridge U.P., 2003), and he currently is working on Islam in France.

LUCY CARROL is an independent scholar who has written extensively on Islamic law in South Asia.

ALLAN CHRISTELOW is professor of history at Idaho State University. His research has focused on Muslim law courts in both Algeria and northern Nigeria, and on modern Islamic thought in Algeria.

BAUDOUIN DUPRET received his Ph.D. and Habilitation à diriger des recherches in Political Sciences from the Institut d'Etudes Politiques de Paris, France. He is currently research fellow at the French National Centre for Scientific Research (CNRS) and was based for several years at the Centre d'Etudes et de Documentation Economique, Juridique et Sociale (CEDEJ) in Cairo, Egypt. He is now based in Damascus, Syria, at the Institut Français du Proche-Orient (IFPO). He is co-editor of several volumes, including *Legal Pluralism in the Arab World* (Kluwer Law International, 1999), *Egypt and its Laws* (Kluwer Law International, 2002), and *Standing Trial: Law and the Person in the Modern Middle East* (Tauris, 2004). He is the author of *Au nom de quel droit. Répertoires juridiques et référence religieuse dans la société égyptienne musulmane contemporaine* (Paris 2000) and *Le Jugement en action. Ethnomethodologie du droit, de la morale et de la justice en Egypte* (2005).

PROFESSOR MARIBEL FIERRO is Scientific Researcher at the Consejo Superior de Investigaciones Cientificas (Higher Council for Scientific Research) in Madrid. Her main fields of interest are the history of al-Andalus, Maliki law and religious trends in premodern Muslim societies. She is Sectional Editor for religious sciences for the *Encyclopaedia of Islam* (3rd edition) and is presently editing volume two of the *New Cambridge History of Islam.*

ROSSITSA GRADEVA is a Research Fellow at the Institute of Balkan Studies at the Bulgarian Academy of Sciences. Her research interests include the functioning of the Ottoman kadi court and administrative system, the status of the non-Muslims, Islamic culture and the time of secession in the Ottoman Balkans in the pre-nationalist period.

BABER JOHANSEN received his Ph.D. in Islamic Studies and Sociology (1965) and Habilitation in Islamic Studies (1972) at the Freie Universität Berlin, where he was Professor of Islamic Studies from 1972 to 1995. From 1995 to 2005, he was *Directeur d'études* (*Structures normatives et histoire en Islam*) at the Ecole des Hautes Etudes en Sciences Sociales (Paris). In July 2005, he became Professor of Islamic Religious Studies at the Harvard Divinity School. Johansen is executive editor of *Islamic Law and Society* and a member of the editorial board of *Arabica* and of the scientific committees of *Revue des mondes musulmans et de la Méditerranée* and *Mélanges de l'Université Saint-Joseph.* He is the author of numerous articles and several books, including *Contingency in a Sacred Law: Legal and Ethical Norms in the Muslim Fiqh* (1999), *The Islamic Law on Land Tax and Rent* (1988), and *Muhammad Husain Haikal—Europa und der Orient im Weltbild eines ägyptischen Liberalen* (1967).

STEFAN KNOST, Ph.D. is a research fellow at the *Institut français du Proche-Orient,* Damascus and at the German *Orient-Institut,* Beirut. His research focuses on the history of *waqf*-administration in Ottoman Aleppo.

AHARON LAYISH, Ph.D. Professor Emeritus of Islamic Studies, received his degree from the Hebrew University of Jerusalem in 1973. He has published extensively on Islamic, customary and Druze law, including *The Reinstatement of Islamic Law in the Sudan under Numayri*

(2002). He is Executive Editor of *Islamic Law and Society*, and chairman of The Israel Oriental Society.

MUHAMMAD KHALID MASUD is former academic Director, International Institute for the Study of Islam in the Modern World, Leiden, The Netherlands (1999–2003). He is also a student of religion, law and social change in Muslim societies. His publications include *Shatibi's Philosophy of Islamic Law* (1995), *Iqbal's Reconstruction of Ijtihad* (1995), *Islamic Legal Interpretation: The Muftis and their Fatwas*, (co-edited with Brinkley Messick and David Powers, 1996), *Islamic Laws and Women in the Modern World* (Editor, 1996), *Travelers in Faith, Studies on Tablighi Jama'at as a Transnational Movement for the Renewal of Faith* (Editor, 2000), and *Muslim Jurists' Quest for the Normative Basis of Shari'a* (2001).

BRINKLEY MESSICK is Professor and Chair of the Department of Anthropology at Columbia University. He is the author of *The Calligraphic State* (University of California, 1993), and coeditor of *Islamic Legal Interpretation* (Harvard, 1996). He is completing a work on doctrine and cases from mid-20th-century Yemen.

CHRISTIAN MÜLLER Ph.D. (1997) in Islamic Studies, Free University of Berlin, Junior Fellow at the Institute of Advance Study in Berlin, 1998–99, recipient of Feodor Lynen-Research Grant of the Alexander von Humboldt Foundation, 1999–2001. He is chargé de recherche at the Institut de Recherche et d'Histoire des Testes in Paris. He works on judicial and legal practice in the Mamluk era.

LESLIE PEIRCE teaches at Berkeley in the departments of History and Near Eastern Studies. She received her Ph.D. from Princeton in 1988, and taught at Cornell University for ten years before moving to Berkeley. She is the author of two books, *Morality Tales: Law and Gender in the Ottoman Court of Aintab* (2003) and *The Imperial Harem: Women and Sovereignty in the Ottoman Empire* (1993).

RUDOLPH PETERS teaches Islam and Islamic law at the University of Amsterdam. From 1982–87 he was the director of the Netherlands Institute in Cairo. In 2001 he conducted research for the European Union on the human rights aspects of the re-Islamization of criminal law in Northern Nigeria.

DAVID S. POWERS Professor of Islamic History at Cornell University, is the author of *Studies in Qur'an and Hadith: The Formation of the Islamic Law of Inheritance* (1986); *Law, Society, and Culture in the Maghrib, 1300–1500* (2002); coeditor of *Islamic Legal Interpretation: Muftis and their Fatwas* (1996); and Editor of the journal *Islamic Law and Society*.

ABDUL-KARIM RAFEQ is William and Annie Bickers Professor of Arab Middle Eastern Studies at the College of William and Mary in Virginia. He was formerly Professor of modern Arab history and chairman of the Department of History at the University of Damascus. He has written numerous articles. His books include *The Province of Damascus 1723–1783* (paperback ed. 1970), and, in Arabic, *The Arabs and the Ottomans (1516–1916)* (Damascus, Atlas, 2nd ed. 1993) and *Studies in the Economic and Social History of Modern Syria* (Damascus 2002).

DELFINA SERRANO is tenured researcher at the Consejo Superior de Investigaciones Cientificas in Madrid. Her current research focuses on Maliki law, Ashʿari *kalām* and the history of al-Andalus. She has translated and studied the collection of legal cases of Muḥammad b. ʿIyâḍ, *Madhāhib al-ḥukkām fī nawāzil al-akḥām*. She is the author of several articles on the application of Māliki doctrine in al-Andalus.

RON SHAHAM, Ph.D. in Islamic Studies, the Hebrew University of Jerusalem, is a senior lecturer at the Hebrew University. He was a visiting scholar at Cornell University (1993–94) and at Princeton University (1999–2000). He is the author of *Family and Courts in Modern Egypt* (1997). He has published extensively on the shariʿa courts and qadis in modern Egypt, on Egyptian family law reform, and on the legal status of non-Muslims in modern Muslim societies.

ERIN STILES is Assistant Professor in the Department of Humanities and Religious Studies at California State University, Sacramento. She received her Ph.D. in Cultural Anthropology from Washington University in St. Louis in 2002; and was a postdoctoral research fellow in the Institute of African Studies at Columbia University in 2002–03.

CHAPTER ONE

QĀḌĪS AND THEIR COURTS: AN HISTORICAL SURVEY

Muhammad Khalid Masud, Rudolph Peters,
David S. Powers

> Know that the cadi's office enjoys in God's sight an importance exceeding any other. This is because it is God's balance, by means of which the affairs of everything in the world are regulated. When justice prevails in the cadi's office and in the execution of his decrees, the subjects' welfare is assured, the highways are kept safe, those who have been wronged are given just recompense, people receive their due rights, life becomes pleasant, rightful obedience is freely vouchsafed, God gives provision for happiness and preservation of life, religion is firmly maintained, the norms and customs (*sunna*) and the religious law are put into practice, and, on the basis of their effectiveness, truth and justice are successfully achieved.
>
> Ibn Abī Ṭāhir al-Ṭayfūr (1949:30–1); Engl. trans. by C.E. Bosworth (1970:36–7)

Literature Review and Themes

E. Tyan's masterly *Histoire de l'organisation judiciaire en pays d'Islam*, published in 1938 and reprinted in 1960, remains the most comprehensive survey in a Western language of the organization of justice in Muslim societies. Subsequently, scholars in a wide range of disciplines have produced a substantial body of knowledge that has sharpened our understanding of the manner in which the qāḍī and his court have functioned in Muslim societies throughout history. In what follows, we will provide a brief sketch of some of the most significant achievements, with special attention to the challenges and opportunities posed by the changing nature of available sources for different periods of Islamic history.

Apart from scattered references to qāḍīs in the surviving papyri (Sijpesteijn 2004), our knowledge of judicial practice during the formative period of Islamic history—roughly 600–1000—is based largely on literary sources: biographical dictionaries of qāḍīs, treatises devoted to *adab al-qāḍī* or "the etiquette of judging," historical texts, and belles-lettres. Of these sources, biographical dictionaries are especially important, and we are fortunate to have at least three such works that treat the regions of Egypt, Iraq, and Syria. The *Akhbār al-quḍāt* of Wakīʿ (d. 306/918) is arranged regionally according to garrison towns and chronologically by qāḍī within those regions. Some of the entries contain lists of judicial rulings that can be used to reconstruct the earliest stages of Islamic judicial practice. Published in 1950, this text has recently been the subject of renewed attention by M.K. Masud (1994 and this volume) and others (Schneider 1990; Zuhaylī 1995; Johansen 1997c). Another important text, composed about fifty years later, is the *Kitāb al-wulāt wa-kitāb al-quḍāt* of al-Kindī (d. 362/972), which contains information about qāḍīs and judicial practice in early Islamic Egypt. For Syria at a later period, we have the *Quḍāt Dimashq* of Ibn Ṭulūn (d. 953/1546).

Scholars interested in the period between 1000 and 1500 also must rely largely on literary sources such as *fatwā*s and manuals of legal formularies (*wathāʾiq*). Such texts are plentiful for al-Andalus and the Maghrib. For example, *al-Aḥkām al-kubrā*, compiled by the qāḍī Ibn Sahl (d. 1093), is a *fatwā* collection that was designed to serve as a textbook for the training of judges and *muftī*s. The text is noteworthy because Ibn Sahl wrote summaries of the court proceedings that led to the issuance of the *fatwā*s themselves, and it has recently been exploited by C. Müller (1999, 2000) to reconstruct the activity of the chief qāḍī of Cordoba in the middle of the eleventh century. Another important text for a slightly later period in the history of al-Andalus and the Maghrib is the *Madhāhib al-ḥukkām fī nawāzil al-aḥkām*, a collection of legal cases (*nawāzil*) compiled by Muḥammad b. ʿIyāḍ (d. 1179), son of the famous Qāḍī ʿIyāḍ (d. 1149). These cases, which took place in Ceuta, shed light on a wide range of judicial activities, e.g.: the composition of the court, the unfolding of a litigation, the outcome of court activity in the form of *fatwā*s and judgments, court practice (*ʿamal*), the jurisdiction of qāḍīs, judicial review, and the use of law by jurists and laymen (Serrano 2000).

Systematic archives are unavailable for the period prior to 1500, even though we know that qāḍīs kept records of the activities that transpired in their courts. The most likely explanation for the disappearance of the majority of these records is that they were passed from one qāḍī to his successor and that there was no central repository for their preservation (Hallaq 1998). Be that as it may, smaller caches of qāḍī records have survived in different parts of the Muslim world, the most prominent example being the Ḥaram documents discovered at the Islamic Museum in Jerusalem between 1974 and 1976. This is a collection of approximately 900 documents, a large number of them issued by a single Shafiʿi qāḍī during the last decade of the fourteenth century. These documents have been systematically studied by Little (1984), Lutfi (1983) and Müller (this volume).

Documents similar to those discovered in the Ḥaram collection are also preserved, albeit second-hand, in *fatwā*s, or, more precisely, in *istiftā*ʾs, or requests for a *fatwā*, many of which were composed by qāḍīs confronted by difficult or politically sensitive cases. The *istiftā*ʾ may include the qāḍī's self-description of the work that he performed as a particular case unfolded in his court, and, on occasion, he was careful to provide a more or less complete transcription of one or more documents that were brought to court by the litigants, e.g., bequests, endowment deeds, marriage contracts, deposits, appointments of agency, and judicial certifications. These transcriptions are precious artifacts of the practice of qāḍī courts prior to 1500. One *fatwā* collection that is especially rich in such documents is the *Miʿyār* of al-Wansharīsī (d. 1508), examined by Powers (2002) in an effort to shed light on the workings of the qāḍī and his court and the manner in which law, society, and culture interacted with each other.

The nature of the sources available for the study of qāḍīs and their courts changes dramatically with the Ottomans (1517–1924), who kept systematic records (*defters*) of court activity in regions that are today Turkey, Syria, Lebanon, Egypt, Greece, and Bulgaria. A typical volume of Ottoman court records contains *inter alia* documents formulated in the local court by the judge, e.g., summary accounts of cases, transcriptions of contracts, inheritance records, divorce documents, and documents relating to maintenance and guardianship. Whereas the first generation of Ottoman historians used this massive and seemingly inexhaustible source to examine social, political, and economic issues, a younger generation of scholars is currently studying it to better understand the workings of the Ottoman legal system between the end of the fifteenth century and the demise of the empire in 1924. The availability of continuous series of *defters* for individual towns and cities scattered across the Ottoman realm has made it possible for scholars to produce microlevel studies of the daily application of law in local contexts. These studies reveal how justice was dispensed in various parts of the empire and the role played by the qāḍī in that process (e.g., Jennings 1975, 1978, 1979; Gerber 1981a, 1994; Peirce 2003; Akarli, this volume). Writing about the Anatolian towns of Çankırı and Kastamonu in the seventeenth century, for example, Ergene (2003) concludes that the function of the local qāḍī was not limited to the resolution of disputes but rather extended to the administration of the district in which he served, the execution of decrees and orders sent from Istanbul, and the collection of taxes.

The source material changes once again when we turn to the modern period and, especially, the rise of the nation-state in the twentieth century. In many countries of the Arab-Muslim world, court records are now published or preserved in archives. As the chronological gap closes between modern scholarship and the object of its investigation, it becomes possible for scholars to examine and analyze records of the present and the recent past. Thus, Islamicists and legal historians have written monographs and articles on qāḍī courts in various parts of the Arab world, including Saudi Arabia (Vogel 2000), Egypt (Shaham 1997; Peters 1990, 1997, 1999), Palestine (Welchman 2000), and Israel (Layish 1975), to name just a few. Anthropologists, who have the opportunity to engage in the direct observation of qāḍī courts in far-flung regions of the Muslim world, are increasingly turning their attention to the observation and analysis of modern courts, the study of which has become a subfield in the discipline. Case studies of qāḍīs and their courts have been written by anthropologists about Kufr al-Māʾ, Jordan (Antoun 1980); Ibb (Messick 1993) and Sanʿaʾ (Würth 2000) in the Yemen; Bodrum, Turkey (Starr 1992); Sefrou, Morocco (Rosen 1989, 2000); Mombasa and Malinde, Kenya (Hirsh 1998); Mkokotoni, Zanzibar (Stiles, this volume); Rembau, Malaysia (Peletz 2002); and Takengen, Indonesia (Bowen 2003). We also have three important studies of Egyptian courts, one by a sociologist (Dupret 2000) and two by political scientists (Hill 1979; Brown 1997).

A distinctive feature of recent scholarship is a shift of focus from jurisprudence (*uṣūl al-fiqh*) and legal doctrine (*fiqh*) to local practice, from an idealized model of Islamic law to its manifold instantiations in specific times and places. Unlike an earlier generation of scholars who tended to view "Islamic law" as an unchanging and timeless essence (with the important consequence that changes in modern times were treated as deviations from this ideal type), the current generation of scholars looks to local manifestations of Islamic law and attempts to situate the application of jurisprudence and legal doctrine in local and time-bound contexts.

This shift is reflected in another major theme of Western scholarship on Islamic law for over a century, namely, the attempt to characterize the nature of the qāḍī's work and to determine whether the dispensation of justice in Muslim societies is governed by revelation or reason—or perhaps a mixture of the two. Some eighty years ago the German sociologist Max Weber (1864–1920) posited that Islamic law is irrational in two important respects: *procedurally*, because the tools employed to determine its legal norms (oaths, curses, and appeals to divine authority) are not subject to human reason; and *substantively*, because qāḍīs reportedly decide cases according to ethical, political, personal, or utilitarian considerations, not according to an established body of legal doctrine. Weber defined *kadijustiz* as a legal system in which judges are empowered to decide each case according to what they see as its individual merits, without referring to a settled and coherent body of norms or rules and without employing a rational set of judicial procedures.

Based upon his study of judges in the town of Sefrou, Morocco, in the 1960s and 1970s, Rosen has attempted to refine and qualify Weber's thesis by detaching the notion of doctrine from that of consistency. Like Weber, he argues that Muslim judges do not focus on substantive legal doctrines or on the similarities to, and differences from, the facts of prior cases; do not emphasize antecedent concepts; and do not employ a mode of judicial reasoning that would result in increasingly refined methods of legal analysis. Unlike Weber, Rosen contends that Islamic law is nevertheless rational and consistent, although dependent in these respects on the skill with which the qāḍī analyzes and interprets witness testimony, assesses competing social interests, and exploits local knowledge. He concludes that the qāḍī's primary goal is to return people to a position in which they can negotiate their own permissible relationships outside of the legal realm. Only secondarily and incidentally does the qāḍī seek to enforce individual rights or impose a resolution to a dispute (Rosen 1989, 2000).

Rosen's thesis, whatever its merits, suffers from three flaws: His perspective is ahistorical—he disregards important differences between the modern judicial system within which the contemporary qāḍī operates and the traditional system within which the qāḍī of the past operated; it is essentialist—he generalizes from his observations of twentieth-century qāḍīs in the town of Sefrou to qāḍīs in all times and places; and he largely ignores the role of the *muftī* in the judicial process and his close relationship with the qāḍī.

Recent scholarship suggests that the work of the qāḍī involved *both* the invocation of underlying sociocultural norms and the application of legal norms and procedures; that qāḍīs sought to ground their decisions in reliable knowledge and in the authority of Islamic legal doctrine; and that Muslim communities placed a high value on the *reasoned* justification of judicial decisions (Powers 2002). Be that as it may, the question remains open and, in the future, scholars may want to focus greater attention on the work of the qāḍī and the process of judicial decision-making.

To better situate the specific historical contexts addressed by the contributors to this volume, we (1) survey the history of the qāḍīship between 622 and 1798; (2) present a synthetic guide to the workings of qāḍī courts; and (3) examine changes in the institutional framework within which the *shariah* has operated in modern times.

Historical Survey

The Period of Prophecy and Revelation (610–32)

For Muslims, the Qur'ān is the word of God as revealed to the Prophet Muḥammad and collected and arranged by his followers in the years immediately following his death. Islamic tradition teaches that the Qur'ān was revealed seriatim over a period of twenty-three years. The content of the revelations changed dramatically between 610, the year in which Muḥammad received his first revelation in Mecca, and 632, the year of his death in Medina. The Meccan verses deal primarily with theological and ethical issues (e.g., the oneness of God, reward and punishment in the Hereafter, and the last judgment) and only secondarily with legal issues and ritual matters (e.g., prayer, fasting and pilgrimage). In 622, however, Muḥammad was invited to Medina by representatives of the two major Arab tribes of that city to serve as their arbitrator (*ḥakam*) and to settle their disputes on the basis of tribal custom. The resulting *hijra* or migration was a watershed event in the career of the Prophet; indeed, it marks the beginning of Islamic history, properly speaking. In Medina, Muḥammad became the head of a religiopolitical community (*umma*) that accepted God and His Prophet as the ultimate sources of authority not only for human belief but also for human action, and the revelations that were "sent down" during the Medinan period increasingly address issues such as personal status, crime and its punishment, and trade and commerce.

The Qur'ān contains two linguistic forms that would come to characterize the activity of judging in Muslim societies, one derived from the root *ḥ-k-m*, the other from the root *q-ḍ-y*. Muḥammad attached great importance to his role as an arbitrator in the young Muslim community, and whenever the Qur'ān mentions his judicial activities, it uses the verb *ḥakama* and its derivatives (e.g., Q. 4:65 and 105; 5:42 and 48–9; and 24:48 and 51). Although the Qur'ān does not use the term *qāḍī*, the verb *qāḍā* does occur frequently in the sense of a sovereign ordinance of God or his Prophet or in connection with the Day of Judgment. In Qur'ān 4:65, the two verbs occur in parallel, with *ḥakkama* referring to the Prophet's role as an arbitrator and *qaḍā* referring to the authoritative character of his decision.

> Indeed, by your Lord, they will not believe till they make you adjudge (*yuḥakkimūka*) in their disputes between them and find no constraint in their minds about your decisions (*mimmā qaḍayta*), and accept them with full acquiescence (trans. of Ahmed Ali).

As the leader of the *umma*, Muḥammad was called upon to resolve disputes and, when he did so, he acted in his capacity as God's messenger, *rasūl allāh*. His actions in this regard, as remembered by posterity, established a model for the ideal judge. For example, it is reported that the brother of a man who had been slain apprehended the murderer and brought him to the Prophet to decide the case. The murderer confessed to his crime, whereupon the Prophet asked if he or his relatives could pay the blood money (*diya*). When he replied in the negative, the Prophet gave him to the person who had apprehended him, saying, "He is yours." As they were leaving, the Prophet said, "If he kills him, he will be no different than the murderer." Upon hearing the Prophet's explanation, the man returned and released the murderer (Muslim 1998:744). Here Muhammad used his position as the Messenger of God to temper the application of tribal justice and to produce an outcome that was acceptable to both parties.

The Four Righteous Caliphs (632–61) and the Umayyads (661–750)

The first four caliphs inherited the judicial powers exercised by the Prophet during his lifetime and served as arbitrators of disputes. The early Umayyad caliphs reportedly held their own courts, responded to requests from qāḍīs for their opinions in difficult cases, and sent written instructions to qāḍīs in the provinces of the empire.

The emergence of the qāḍī's office is directly linked to the establishment of garrison towns in Kufa, Basra, and Fustat, where the conquering Arab tribesmen lived with their families and other members of their tribes. The earliest qāḍīs may have been appointed directly by the first caliphs—although the point is contested in the sources—and were subject to their authority.[1] Many of these men, recruited from the ranks of pre-Islamic arbitrators, lacked formal training and were illiterate. Their duties included the resolution of disputes among the conquering tribesmen in the garrison towns. It stands to reason that many of these disputes related to the details of nascent Islamic ritual practice, family matters such as marriage, divorce, and inheritance, and crime—all topics on which the Qur'ān has something to say. To the extent that the Qur'ān contains clear and detailed guidance on a particular topic, as is the case with inheritance, the qāḍīs no doubt resolved such disputes in accordance with their understanding of the regulations contained in the Book of God. Otherwise, they exercised personal discretion and relied on ad hoc reasoning; it is noteworthy that the solutions to some of the earliest cases reported in the sources run counter to the principles of what would become mature legal doctrine. Until the third quarter of the first century A.H., the jurisdiction of the qāḍīs was limited to the garrison towns and to the resolution of disputes among Arab tribesmen and their families and clients; it did not yet extend to the surrounding countryside or to the towns and cities inhabited by Christians, Zoroastrians, Jews and others (Hallaq 2004:29ff.; Masud 1999:393–9).

[1] Some sources report that the first four caliphs sent out *muftīs* and *ḥakam*s (not qāḍīs) to serve as their judicial agents, while other sources report that the Prophet and the first four caliphs delegated their judicial authority to qāḍīs who were appointed in the major towns and cities of the expanding Muslim state. Alternatively, it is reported that Muʿāwiya was the first caliph to appoint qāḍīs in the newly formed garrison towns.

The qāḍīship became firmly established under Muʿāwiya (r. 661–80) and the early Umayyads.[2] Upon his accession to the caliphate, Muʿāwiya took the title of God's caliph (*khalīfat allāh*) and delegated his authority to qāḍīs and other agents in the garrison towns. Later, the power to appoint and dismiss qāḍīs was exercised by Umayyad provincial governors. The earliest qāḍīs not only resolved disputes but also performed non-judicial functions, serving as governors, tax collectors, military commanders, leaders of prayer, and supervisors of the Public Treasury and the land tax. The *qāḍī al-jund* was a judge who exercised authority over the Muslim soldiers organized according to military units in the garrison towns. Under the Umayyads, the functions of criminal enforcement (*shurṭa*) and the judgeship were often united in the hands of a single individual who was responsible for both criminal matters and other areas of the law. In their capacity as *ʿarīfs* or experts in customary matters, qāḍīs were responsible for distributing stipends to soldiers among the members of their respective tribes, guarding the interests of orphans within a particular tribe, or serving as an assistant to the market inspector (Bligh-Abramski 1992:43–5, 48).

Most of the early qāḍīs were Arabs and a high percentage of them were Yamanīs. Many qāḍīs trained their sons to follow in their footsteps, and there was a tendency for the office to be transmitted from father to son. We know that many qāḍīs were active in trade and commerce, either because they sought to supplement their salaries as judges, or because they refused to accept money for their judicial activities and needed to support themselves by other means (Bligh-Abramski 1992:53–5).

Although the earliest qāḍīs lacked formal training, many of them were familiar with the Qur'ān and had knowledge of the precedents established by Muḥammad and the first four caliphs. Many of these men were also storytellers (*quṣṣāṣ*, sg. *qāṣṣ*) who explained the significance of the Qur'ān to members of the community at the conclusion of Friday prayers and also cursed the "enemies of Islam" after morning

[2] The transition from tribal arbitration to the qāḍīship may be related to the dispute that arose between Muʿāwiya and ʿAlī over the murder of ʿUthmān and the question of retaliation (*qiṣāṣ*); the Muslim community responded to this dispute by appointing two *ḥakams* or arbitrators, one for each of the two parties to the conflict. The inability of the two arbitrators to reach a mutually satisfactory agreement may have highlighted the shortcomings of tribal arbitration and contributed to the rise of the qāḍīship (Masud 1999:393–9).

prayers. The religious character of the qāḍī's office is evidenced in a letter in which ʿUmar b. al-Khaṭṭāb (r. 634–44) appointed Abū Mūsā al-Ashʿarī as qāḍī of Kūfa; the letter begins, "Now, the office of judge is a definite religious duty" (Ibn Khaldūn 1958, 3:452–6). Under ʿAbd al-Malik (r. 685–705), many qāḍīs were involved in teaching and disseminating information relating to the life of the Prophet; over time this material developed into a distinctive genre of oral reports, separate from precedents established by the first four caliphs and other Companions (Hallaq 2004:39).

During the last quarter of the first century A.H., the judicial apparatus expanded outwards from the military garrisons and embraced major towns, such as Alexandria, Homs, and Rayy, in which Muslims were as yet only a minority of the population. The rapid expansion of the Arab empire and the growing complexity and sophistication of the state apparatus led to the development of the judgeship (*qaḍāʾ*) as a professional office. In the last decade of the first century A.H., the functions of the qāḍī came to be limited to the resolution of legal disputes and the administration of the emerging judicial apparatus. Beginning with Sulaymān b. ʿAbd al-Malik (r. 715–17), judges were appointed directly by the caliphs from the capital in Damascus (Hallaq 2004:57–8).

The Umayyads employed important and influential religious figures as qāḍīs, using them to disseminate their ideology and promote the popularity of the regime. The jurist al-Shaʿbī (d. 721), who served as a tutor to the sons of ʿAbd al-Malik, was sent on a diplomatic mission to the Byzantines and served as qāḍī of Kufa during the caliphate of ʿUmar II (r. 717–20). Al-Ḥasan al-Baṣrī (d. 728) counseled both ʿAbd al-Malik and ʿUmar II and served as qāḍī of Basra during the latter's reign. Al-Zuhrī (d. 741–2), who served as judge under Yazīd II and tutored the sons of Hishām, was known for circulating pro-Umayyad traditions (Bligh-Abramski 1992:62–5).

From the outset, however, the relationship between the Islamic state and candidates for the office of qāḍī was marked by tension. The caliphs used the qāḍīship as a form of patronage. Although there was no lack of qualified candidates to fill these posts, many potential candidates either refused to accept such appointments or had to be cajoled to do so, presumably because they were reluctant to associate themselves with a state regarded as unjust or impious. This tension is reflected in a number of vivid statements attributed to the Prophet Muḥammad, e.g., "a person who is appointed qāḍī is slaughtered without a knife" (Ibn Ḥanbal 1969, 2:230, 265) and "two out of every three qāḍīs are in hell" (Wakīʿ 1947, 1:13ff.).

The qāḍīs who held office during the first century A.H. made an important contribution to the formation of Islamic legal doctrine. The judgments that they issued were based upon their understanding of the Qurʾān, *sunna*, and local custom; for most of this century, however, the major source of legal reasoning employed by qāḍīs was *raʾy* or personal discretion. In this manner, the early qāḍīs established the foundation for what would become the mature legal doctrine of the classical schools of law (*madhāhib*, sg. *madhhab*).

The ʿAbbāsid period (750–1250)

In Umayyad and early ʿAbbāsid times, the jurisdiction of the qāḍī was limited to the town over which he was appointed. At first, the qāḍī was usually a local representative of the inhabitants of a town who was familiar with many of the town's residents and responsive to public opinion. Candidates for the office were invited to appear before the caliph or governor, who attached great importance to popular sentiment in making a decision to appoint—or dismiss—a qāḍī. The residents of a town might oppose a candidate for the office either because he represented a legal tradition different from that of the majority of the townsmen or because they feared that his appointment would have adverse consequences on their economic status (Tsafrir 2004:37).

An important step in the consolidation of state control over the judiciary was taken by the ʿAbbāsid caliph al-Mahdī (r. 775–85), the first caliph to arrange for the regular hearing of petitions and complaints in the forum that came to be known as the *maẓālim* or courts of complaint (the singular form, *maẓlima*, signifies an unjust or oppressive action). This was the institution by means of which the state assumed direct responsibility for dispensing justice and for responding to complaints regarding administrative and judicial abuses. This court, which was the personal responsibility of the caliph or one of his governors, was composed of a qāḍī, guards, jurists, scribes, and notaries. Although the primary function of the court was to hear and respond to complaints about the abuse of official powers, it also served as a court of appeal against the decisions of qāḍīs and played a role in the allocation and confiscation of *iqṭāʿ*s or land grants. The rules of judicial procedure applied in these courts were not as strict as those applied in qāḍī courts, and the *maẓālim* courts had the power to compel litigants and witnesses to appear before them, using force if necessary. Over time, the *maẓālim* courts were incorporated into the state bureaucracy, and procedures for the presentation and treatment of petitions became increasingly formalized (Nielsen 1991).

Another important step in the consolidation of state control over judges was taken by Hārūn al-Rashīd (r. 786–809), who created the office of *qāḍī al-quḍāt* or chief qāḍī, appointing Abū Yūsuf (d. 798) as its first incumbent. The chief qāḍī, the caliph's deputy in all matters relating to justice, was empowered to appoint, supervise, and dismiss qāḍīs and other judicial officials throughout the empire. Abū Yūsuf and his immediate successors counseled the caliphs on the appointment and dismissal of judges in the different provinces of the empire. Eventually, it became customary for the chief qāḍī to nominate the main provincial judge who, in turn, delegated his judicial powers to one or more local agents (*nuwwāb*, sg., *nā'ib*). Some of these agents were empowered to hear specific types of disputes (e.g., inheritance or criminal cases), while others had jurisdiction in all fields in a limited geographical district (Bligh-Abramski 1992:56–9).

According to Islamic political theory, the caliph retains the power to adjudicate cases even though, in practice, he generally assigns this power to qāḍīs who serve as his agents. In most Muslim polities the caliph (or sulṭān) and executive officials exercise general, albeit not exclusive, jurisdiction over criminal cases. This type of justice is called *siyāsa* (literally: "discipline"), a term that signifies both "state policy" and "the right of the ruler and his agents to impose discretionary punishments." Muslim jurists, who treat *siyāsa* as an administrative supplement to *fiqh* doctrine, recognize its validity for the sake of the general interest of the polity.

Like the Umayyads, the ʿAbbāsids also used qāḍīs to disseminate their religious ideology and to increase the popularity of the regime. ʿAbbāsid qāḍīs, in turn, advised the caliph on how best to manage affairs of state. ʿUbayd Allāh b. al-Ḥasan al-Anbārī (d. 784) wrote a letter to al-Mahdī in which he advised the caliph to appoint judges who were pious, shrewd and capable of exercising their independent reasoning in order to establish certain judicial regulations. Abū Yūsuf wrote his *Kitāb al-kharāj*, which treats public finance, taxation, and criminal justice, for his patron Hārūn al-Rashīd (Bligh-Abramski 1992:62–5).

The failure of the *miḥna* or Inquisition in 849 led to major changes in the judicial administration. The caliph no longer attempted to impose religious uniformity, and, as a consequence, the status of the chief qāḍīship declined. By the time of al-Muʿtaḍid (r. 892–902), the vizier had replaced the chief qāḍī as second-in-command to the caliph. Henceforth, it was the vizier who appointed the chief qāḍī and, on occasion, provincial qāḍīs as well (Bligh-Abramski 1992:69).

The qāḍīship itself was transformed. A critical consideration in the nomination of a qāḍī was his loyalty to the caliph and willingness to implement the ruler's policies in the district in which he served. By accepting the office of qāḍī, a man acknowledged his support for the caliph's policies and readiness to implement them. All of these changes were part of a concerted effort by the central government to centralize the legal system and to strengthen the government's control of it (Tsafrir 2004:90–1).

By the middle of the ninth century, the men who received appointments as qāḍīs increasingly were people of high standing at the ʿAbbāsid court without ties to the towns over which they were appointed; and they were appointed from Baghdad rather than by local governors (Tsafrir 2004:37). The jurisdiction of a single qāḍī now might include as many as three or four towns and their surrounding districts, although the range of legal issues over which he exercised control was further limited. The qāḍī was no longer a local individual who had distinguished himself as a leader by virtue of his scholarship and broad base of popular support, but rather an outsider whose authority was confined to legal issues. This new type of qāḍī often did not reside in the town over which he was appointed. The qāḍī of Basra, for example, usually lived in Baghdad and appointed agents who carried out his work in the area of his appointment. In short, the qāḍī had become a state functionary whose authority emanated from, and was dependent upon, his nomination by the caliph (Tsafrir 2004:37, 90–1).

The qāḍī carried out his judicial activities in his *maḥkama* or court, where he applied the fully developed legal doctrine of a specific law school (*madhhab*). In theory the qāḍī's jurisdiction was general and included both civil and criminal cases;[3] in practice most criminal

[3] Although the terms *civil* and *criminal* are modern, classical Muslim jurists distinguished between cases relating to property (*māl*) and those relating to crimes (*ḥudūd*), which is essentially the distinction between what we call civil and criminal law. Throughout the Introduction, we use the terms *civil* and *criminal*, for convenience, although it must be emphasized that they are not exact equivalents of their Arabic counterparts.

cases were handled by the police and military governors. Qāḍīs also performed important extrajudicial functions, such as the administration of charitable endowments, supervision of funds earmarked for orphans, and, especially in later periods, collection of the alms tax and poll tax (Bligh-Abramski 1992:57, 69–70). The city of Baghdad was divided into three jurisdictions, two on the western side of the Tigris and a third on the east bank. Although each jurisdiction usually had its own qāḍī, it sometimes happened that one qāḍī was put in charge of two of these areas or all three. The chief qāḍī's office was separate from the qāḍīship of these three jurisdictions, although he occasionally held the post of qāḍī in one or more of them (Tsafrir 2004:40–1).

May a ruler (*imām*) appoint a qāḍī on the condition that he issue his judgments on the basis of the legal doctrine of a specific *madhhab*? No, he may not, according to the Shafiʿis, Malikis, and Hanbalis, at least in the case in which the qāḍī is a *mujtahid.* Such an appointment is void—or the appointment is valid but the stipulation is inoperative (Wizārat al-Awqāf 1986, 33:300; Ibn ʿĀbidīn, 1889, 4:464–5]. Likewise, if the ruler commands or forbids a qāḍī to follow a certain *madhhab* in a specific case, the command or prohibition is void. (The jurists compare this issue to a stipulation that is added to a nominate contract, in which case it must be determined whether or not the stipulation is valid and/or vitiates the contract.) For these three schools, the only way for the state to influence the administration of justice is to prohibit the qāḍī from hearing certain types of cases.

According to the early Hanafis, however, the ruler may appoint a qāḍī on the condition that he issue his judgments on the basis of the legal doctrine of a single *madhhab*, but only if the nominee is himself affiliated to that *madhhab*; if he issues a judgment according to the doctrine of a *madhhab* other than the one to which he is affiliated, that judgment is void, since it is presumed that he was motivated by arbitrary personal biases (*hawā bāṭil*). Later Hanafi jurists asserted that a qāḍī who is a *muqallid* must issue his judgments on the basis of the 'correct opinion' of the school (*ṣaḥīḥ al-madhhab*) and that the sultan may require him to do so (Ibn ʿĀbidīn 1889, 4:164–5); if he issues a judgment that is not based on the correct opinion of his school, he thereby exceeds his competency, and his judgment is therefore ultra vires.

In those areas of the Muslim world that were independent of central control, local rulers introduced variations on the above patterns. In Cordoba, the Umayyad Caliph ʿAbd al-Raḥmān (r. 756–88) manifested his independence from the ʿAbbāsids by designating his military judge as *qāḍī al-jamāʿa*, a term that came to be used throughout al-Andalus and the Maghrib. After conquering Egypt in 969, the Fāṭimids (909–1171) established a chief qāḍī in Cairo, and the holder of this office exercised his authority in the name of the Imām. Between 969 and 1517, there were two chief qāḍīs in Islamdom, one in Baghdad, the other in Cairo. Under the Mamlūks (1250–1517), the chief qāḍī of Cairo delegated his authority to chief qāḍīs in the major cities of the empire, so that there were several chief qāḍīs scattered throughout the realm. The Mamlūks also appointed a chief qāḍī for each of the four *madhhab*s.

The qāḍī system developed by the ʿAbbāsids continued to operate under the Mughals in India (1526–1858), the Safavids in Iran (1501–1722) and the Ottomans in the Middle East (1512–1918). The Ottomans, however, revamped the judiciary. In an effort to exercise greater control over the provinces, Selim I (r. 1512–20) and Süleyman I (r. 1520–60) created a hierarchical judicial structure headed by the military judges (*qāḍī ʿaskar*s) and the *Shaykh al-Islām* or state mufti. Below them were the qāḍīs of the *mewlewiyet*s, i.e., of the major towns and cities; below them were local qāḍīs whose jurisdiction was restricted to a district (*qaḍāʾ*) or sub-district (*nahiye*) (Gradeva, this volume).

Qāḍīs played a key role in the administration of the empire. Important sultanic decrees were sent to local qāḍīs for promulgation in their district. If an individual (or group) wished to present a petition to the central government, he usually acted through the good offices of a local qāḍī. Qāḍīs also performed local administrative duties such as supervising guilds and the suitability of buildings, securing the availability of foodstuffs, and enforcing economic regulations (Akarli, this volume). The jurisdiction of qāḍīs and of local officials was defined by legislation (*qānūn*), and the powers of qāḍīs and executive officials were defined in such a way as to keep one another in check. The local qāḍī monitored the lawfulness of the acts of other officials involved in *siyāsa* justice, thereby ensuring the proper conduct of criminal proceedings, including the interrogation and detention of anyone accused of a crime. The conduct and behavior of the qāḍī was, in theory, the responsibility of the Sultan, although in practice he delegated this responsibility to the local governor, who was empowered to open an investigation into a qāḍī's actions and, if necessary, to dismiss and/or imprison him.

Another change instituted by the Ottomans was to designate the Hanafi *madhhab* as the 'official' *madhhab* of the empire. Qāḍīs were instructed to follow the most authoritative opinion within the Hanafi school, i.e. that of Abu Hanifa, although the sultan might instruct qāḍīs to follow the opinions of other Hanafi jurists, if that was politically or socially expedient. Any judgment issued contrary to these instructions was null and void and would not be enforced by the executive authorities.

Adab al-Qāḍī

The genre of literature known as *Adab al-qāḍī*, literally, "the etiquette of judging," deals with the judgeship (*qaḍā'*) and its regulation. This genre has served as an important source for many modern studies of the administration of justice in Muslim societies (e.g., Nakadī 1923, Ibn 'Arnūs 1984 [1934], Mubārak 1977, Zaydān 1983, Azad 1987, and Fuḍaylat 1991).

To date, the only comprehensive study of this genre is that of Schneider (1990), who, using *adab* texts composed between the eighth and the thirteenth centuries, surveyed the literature, with special attention to the qualifications of a qāḍī, his appointment and removal, court procedure, and the qāḍī's relationship to the ruler. In addition, at least two scholars, Fyzee and Ziyada, have studied individual *adab* texts,[4] although they disagree over the value of these texts for the purposes of historical investigation. Whereas Ziyada (al-Khaṣṣāf 1978, Introduction) treats *adab* texts as a valuable source of information about actual court procedure, especially witness testimony and evidence, Fyzee (1964:120)—like Tyan (1960:9) before him—treats them as ideal codes of conduct for qāḍīs, similar in certain respects to British "etiquette of the Bar and profession." We concur with Fyzee and Tyan on this point: although the *adab al-qāḍī* texts

[4] Fyzee (1964) analyzed the chapter on *adab al-qāḍī* in *Da'ā'im al-Islām* of the Ismā'īlī Qāḍī Nu'mān; Ziyada edited the *Adab al-qāḍī* text of the Hanafi jurist al-Khaṣṣāf (1978).

contain important information *about* court practice, they are not reports *of* court practice and therefore must be used with caution.

Most doctrinal law books contain, in addition to chapters on court procedure and witness testimony, a chapter devoted to *adab al-qāḍī*. The etiquette of judging is also discussed in works on statecraft, such as al-Māwardī's (d. 1058) *al-Aḥkām al-sulṭāniyya*, and in style books for chancery scribes, such as al-Qalqashandī's (d. 1418) *Ṣubḥ al-aʿshā*.

According to Ziyada, the Hanafis were the first to write on the subject, and he identifies Abū Yūsuf (d. 798) as the author of the first *Adab al-qāḍī* treatise, no longer extant. In the ninth century, Ibn Samāʿa al-Tamīmī (d. 847; on him see al-Nadim 1970, 2:508), al-Khaṣṣāf (d. 874), and al-Qaysī (d. 891) also wrote on the subject. Schneider, however, regards the chapter on *adab al-qāḍī* in the *Umm* of al-Shāfiʿī (d. 820) as the first *adab* treatise. Ḥājjī Khalīfa (1893, 1:22–3) mentions at least five books on *Adab al-qāḍī* by Hanafi jurists and thirteen by Shafiʿis. Of the numerous texts in this genre, the most popular are al-Māwardī, *Adab al-qāḍī*, Ibn Abī al-Damm (d. 1244), *Kitāb adab al-qaḍāʾ*; Ibn Farḥūn (d. 1358), *Tabṣirat al-ḥukkām*; and al-Ṭarābulusī (d. ca. 1440), *Muʿīn al-ḥukkām*. It is noteworthy that both al-Māwardī and Ibn Abī al-Damm were themselves qāḍīs.[5]

The following summary is designed to provide the reader with a general idea of the structure, scope and content of the *adab al-qāḍī* literature between roughly the ninth and the fifteenth centuries, drawing primarily on the Hanafi jurist, al-Khaṣṣāf, but with attention to the positions of other schools, as appropriate. We will examine six topics: (1) the judgeship, (2) the court, (3) litigation, (4) procedure, (5) judgment, and (6) successor review.

Al-Khaṣṣāf

If the existence of multiple commentaries is a mark of a book's prominence, al-Khaṣṣāf's *Adab al-qāḍī* stands out among treatises on the subject by Hanafi jurists.[6] This treatise, written during the reign

[5] Other common titles in this genre are: *Adab al-qāḍī, Adab al-qaḍāʾ* and *ādāb al-qaḍāʾ; Tuḥfat al-ḥukkām, Muʿīn al-ḥukkām,* and *Tabṣirat al-ḥukkām.*

[6] Ziyada (al-Khaṣṣāf 1978) draws attention to commentaries on this work by the following prominent Hanafi jurists: Abū Jaʿfar al-Hinduwānī (d. 972), Abū Bakr Aḥmad b. al-Jaṣṣāṣ (d. 980), ʿAbd al-ʿAzīz al-Ḥalwānī (d. 1062), ʿAlī b. Ḥasan al-Ṣughdī (d. 1068), Muḥammad b. Aḥmad al-Sarakhsī (d. 1090), Muḥammad Khwāhir Zādeh (d. 1090), and Ḥusām al-Dīn al-Ṣadr al-Shahīd (d. 1141).

of the ʿAbbasid Caliph al-Muhtadī Billāh (r. 864–870), soon became an authoritative source on not only the conduct of qāḍīs but also Hanafi legal doctrine. The text is currently available in two editions (1978, ed. Ziyada; and 1987–2001, trans. Aḥmad), each accompanied by a commentary, the former by al-Jaṣṣāṣ (d. 980), the latter by al-Ṣadr al-Shahīd (d. 1141) (hereinafter all references are to the 1987–2001 edition). Typically, a commentator will distinguish between text and commentary by inserting the word *qāla* ("he says") before the text itself; and by inserting the word *qultu* ("I say") before his comment. Unfortunately, neither al-Jaṣṣāṣ nor al-Ṣadr al-Shahīd used this rhetorical device, and it is therefore impossible to distinguish between al-Khaṣṣāf's text and the commentaries on it. This is not a problem here, however, because we are not concerned with the history of the text, but rather with the general contours of the genre in the middle period of Islamic history.

Al-Khaṣṣāf opens his book by raising two controversial questions: Is a qāḍī required to have the capacity to exercise independent reasoning (*ijtihād*); and is a person required to accept the qāḍīship, if the ruler offers it to him. In response to the first question, he explains that a candidate for the position must have the capacity to exercise independent reasoning, in addition to possessing knowledge of the Qurʾān and the Sunna. And he must also be *ʿādil*, that is to say, he must have a sense of justice and professional integrity. If he possesses all of these qualities, then his appointment is valid, even if the appointing authority is an unjust ruler. A just ruler, on the other hand, can validly appoint a qāḍī who lacks these qualifications. In response to the second question, al-Khaṣṣāf emphasizes that the qāḍī's office carries a heavy responsibility, and he advises potential candidates to avoid accepting it, if possible.

Al-Khaṣṣāf treats a range of issues relating to the qāḍī's office, albeit unsystematically. References to the work of the qāḍī, to evidence and to witness testimony are scattered across several chapters. He begins each chapter with a relevant saying of the Prophet or one of his Companions. Because the treatise is primarily a collection of Hanafi doctrine, al-Khaṣṣāf mentions the opinions of jurists affiliated to other law schools only to explain that those views were not acceptable in his time. If no Hanafi position was available, the author offers his own opinion.

In addition to the qualifications for the qāḍīship, al-Khaṣṣāf addresses the following topics: the procedure to be followed when a qāḍī assumes office; how a court session (*majlis*) should be conducted; the composition of the court, its personnel and the place in which it should be held; procedures for receiving complaints and for conducting a judicial hearing; evidence, proof, judgment, oath, guarantee and court records; correspondence between qāḍīs, the transfer of records from an outgoing qāḍī to his successor; successor review; the legal status of a judgment issued by a qāḍī who has been dismissed; qāḍī error; legal representation or agency; and, finally, cases relating to specific legal topics such as preemption, arbitration, acknowledgment, marriage, divorce, paternity and the ownership of property.

The Judgeship (Qaḍāʾ)

Qaḍāʾ is a right of God the fulfillment of which is a collective duty upon the community as a group. The judgeship is a public office, and the qāḍī is therefore appointed by the caliph or sultan or his deputy. The ruler may limit the qāḍī's authority in administrative matters; and he may instruct a qāḍī not to issue a judgment but rather to send him, the ruler, his recommendation, which may or may not be accepted. A qāḍī may not appoint himself. As noted, his jurisdiction, in theory, is general, encompassing both civil and criminal cases. A qāḍī may appoint a deputy, conditional upon approval of the ruler.

As a representative of the general community, the qāḍī remains in office even after the death of the caliph or governor who appointed him. A qāḍī is encouraged to consult with a *muftī*, although it is the qāḍī's assessment that prevails in the event of disagreement between the two, even if the *muftī* is more learned than he is. (In al-Andalus, the practice of soliciting the opinions of expert jurists became mandatory by the ninth century, and it was standard practice for every court to have two advisory jurists, known as *mushāwars*) (Serrano, this volume).

For most of the seventh century, qāḍīs received administrative stipends from the Public Treasury (*bayt al-māl*), but by the eighth century they received regular salaries. In the eighth century, the average salary of an Egyptian qāḍī was 30 dinars per month (three times the income of an artisan or craftsman). As the judiciary became more professional, qāḍī salaries increased dramatically. By the end of the eighth century, the qāḍī of Fustat reportedly earned 168 dinars per month. Although this salary was unprecedented at the time, it soon became standard. By the end of the ninth century, the office was highly coveted and, therefore, a potential source of corruption (Hallaq 2004:97–8). It is no coincidence that al-Khaṣṣāf states that qāḍīs are forbidden to accept bribes or gifts.

It is the obligation of the qāḍī to do justice by insuring that people are accorded the rights to which they are entitled; he also seeks to promote social harmony and to reconcile people who are in conflict (Akarli, this volume). His duties include the supervision of his staff and of the properties over which he exercises control, and the investigation of witnesses. At the time of his appointment, the qāḍī receives the registers of his predecessor and other court documents. He also takes charge of prisons and documents relating to detainees, which include each individual's name, crime, and the terms of his or her detention. He may release a detainee after personal investigation into his or her complaint. Similarly, he also takes charge of the properties under the supervision of the court, including deposits, endowment property, property belonging to widows and orphans, and other real estate. In property disputes, the qāḍī is empowered to imprison a person or to restrict his rights.

Qualities of a Qāḍī. A qāḍī must be a Muslim, an adult, and male. Exceptionally, the Hanafis allow a female to serve as a qāḍī, although they limit her jurisdiction to civil cases. A qāḍī should be wise, patient, honest, humble, learned and inquisitive. According to the Malikis, Shafiʿis and Hanbalis and a minority of the Hanafis (including al-Khaṣṣāf), he must have the ability to exercise *ijtihād.* Al-Khaṣṣāf suggests that the scope of a qāḍī's independent reasoning is limited to the doctrine of the law school to which he is affiliated. He must be knowledgeable about the local population and their customs and familiar with the trustworthiness and integrity of local persons before they appear in his court. If he does not have all of these qualities, his judgment is nevertheless enforceable, on the condition that he was appointed by the ruler or his agent.

As noted, the earliest qāḍīs received no formal training. By ʿAbbasid times, however, candidates for the office often served an apprenticeship in court prior to their appointment.

The Court

Al-Khaṣṣāf mentions only one type of court, the qāḍī court—he does not discuss the *maẓālim* (see above). The qāḍī court is a single judge court, although, as noted, qāḍīs were encouraged to seek the advice of learned jurists or *muftī*s. Court sessions should be held in a location that is easily accessible to the public. Some jurists opposed the holding of a court session in a mosque because, *inter alia*, a mosque is not accessible to *dhimmī*s or "protected people."

In addition to the qāḍī, court personnel included several assistants, including a scribe (*kātib* or *amīn*), chamberlain (*jilwāz*), and witness investigator (*ṣāḥib al-masā'il* or *muzakkī*). The scribe was required to be pious, just, knowledgeable in the law, and skilled in the art of writing. It was his responsibility to record all claims, counterclaims and depositions of the litigants, to draft legal documents, and to schedule cases. The chamberlain ensured discipline at the court and meted out punishment; he was expected to be present in court but to remain out of earshot of the litigants. The witness investigator assessed the integrity and reputation of witnesses and kept a record of men who, by virtue of their upright character, qualified as witnesses. The qāḍī's staff should sit where he can keep an eye on them.

The qāḍī's *dīwān* or archive includes all of the records kept by a judge, filed in a book case. The two primary components of the *dīwān* are *maḥḍar*s and *sijill*s. The *maḥḍar* is a record of the actions of, and claims by, litigants, made in the presence of the qāḍī, as recorded by his scribe. For purposes of authentication and completeness, the qāḍī customarily signs the *maḥḍar* in the presence of witnesses. The term "*maḥḍar*" also refers to a written record of the testimony of witnesses to the effect that a certain legal action—e.g. pledge or sale—has taken place. The qāḍī bases his judgment on the contents of the *maḥḍar*.

The *sijill* is the witnessed record of the contents of each *maḥḍar*, together with the qāḍī's judgment in each case, i.e., it is a collection of the *maḥḍar*s of individual cases. In addition, the qāḍī's *dīwān* includes: a record of witnesses whose character and integrity had been confirmed by the witness investigators; a register of individuals appointed as endowment supervisors, guardians of orphans, divorcées, and widows; a list of endowment properties, account sheets, and the names and salaries of endowment supervisors; a register of bequests; copies of written instruments (*ṣukūk*, sg. *ṣakk*), e.g., contracts, pledges, acknowledgements and gifts; and copies of letters sent to and received from other qāḍīs (Hallaq 2004:93–4).

The qāḍī must have his personal seal and a bag for current documents. If a qāḍī is dismissed from office, his successor must receive these documents in the presence of the outgoing qāḍī and his court officials.

Litigation (khuṣūma)

The qāḍī's scribe receives and collects petitions submitted to the court and presents them to the qāḍī for scheduling, after making a notation that should include the full name of the plaintiff and the defendant. If all of the petitions cannot be handled in a single day, the scribe selects the first fifty and presents them to the qāḍī.

A qāḍī should hold court as often as necessary; if fewer than seven court sessions per week are needed, the preferred number is three and the preferred days are Saturday, Monday, and Thursday (Māwardī 1994, 16:28). The order in which cases are heard is determined by the drawing of lots. The qāḍī should keep a record of the cases that have been scheduled in his personal notebook. Once the day's schedule has been determined, the scribe or chamberlain summons the parties in the first case to be heard and instructs them to present their witnesses.

Both parties to a dispute must be summoned to the court and both parties are normally present in court at the time of the hearing. However, if the defendant is unable to appear in court, the qāḍī should solicit a written statement from him before proceeding with the hearing (Powers, this volume). If a defendant fails to appear in court, Maliki, Shafiʿi, and Hanbali jurists allow a qāḍī to pronounce judgment against him, on the condition that the plaintiff has presented valid evidence (Zuḥaylī 1996, 6:511).

After listening to the claim and any counterclaim, the qāḍī must determine which of the litigants is the plaintiff (*muddaʿī*) and which is the defendant (*muddaʿā ʿalayhi*). Usually, the plaintiff is the person who initiates the claim and the defendant is the person who denies it. According to the rules of procedure, the burden of proof rests upon the plaintiff (*al-bayyina ʿalā al-muddaʿī*), who must support his claim with witness testimony or some other form of evidence. But the roles of the litigants as plaintiff or defendant may change during the course of the hearing. For instance, A approaches a qāḍī with a claim against B; here A is the plaintiff and B is the defendant and the burden of proof is on A. If B, in his defense, makes a counterclaim against A, the roles of the litigants change: B is now the plaintiff, who bears the burden of proof, and A is the defendant.

The qāḍī is instructed to treat litigants impartially and he should give each party an equal opportunity to present its case. After assigning the roles of plaintiff and defendant, the qāḍī asks the plaintiff to present his evidence. During the plaintiff's presentation of the evidence, the qāḍī may interrogate him about specific details relating to the dispute. For instance, in a dispute over property that has been stolen or the ownership of which is disputed, he may ask questions about the size, color, quality, value, and quantity of the property in question. The scribe keeps notes of this investigation in a *maḥḍar*, and the qāḍī signs his name at the bottom of each page of notes. When the qāḍī has finished with the plaintiff, he summons the defendant. After advising the defendant that the case will be decided against him if he does not respond to the claim or fails to present a counterclaim, the qāḍī interrogates him or her about the plaintiff's claim.

If the defendant acknowledges the plaintiff's claim, the qāḍī asks his scribe to record the acknowledgment, and the case is decided in favor of the plaintiff. If the defendant denies the claim, the qāḍī asks the plaintiff to submit evidence in support of his claim.

Agency (Wakāla). A litigant may not appoint an agent (*wakīl*) to represent him in court without the prior consent of the other party, unless he is ill or if circumstances make it impossible for him to be present at the hearing, in which case he may appoint an agent without the consent of the other party. The agent must satisfy all the conditions required of a witness.

Agency is not allowed in a case that involves a *ḥadd* crime (theft, highway robbery, consumption of alcohol, illicit sexual relations, and false accusation of illicit sexual relations) or in a case that involves retaliation (*qiṣāṣ*). This is because the accused in such cases enjoys the benefit of doubt, which may not be transferred to a third party.

Women. The court reserves a special day for complaints initiated by women. A woman may present her case directly to the qāḍī orally, if this is more convenient for her than dictating it to a scribe. In court she should be called by her agnomen (e.g., Umm Qāsim), not by her personal name (e.g., Fāṭima).

Protected People (Dhimmīs). *Dhimmīs* or protected people (e.g., Jews, Christians, and Zoroastrians) may conclude marriages and settle their disputes among themselves. However, if two non-Muslims ask a qāḍī to resolve a dispute between them, he cannot refuse to hear the dispute or issue a judgment. *Dhimmīs* who bring to a qāḍī court a dispute relating to an inheritance, sale or criminal offense are treated in accordance with the doctrine of the law school to which the qāḍī is affiliated. But the qāḍī may not apply this doctrine to the formation of marriage between non-Muslims; nor may he apply it to disputes involving the possession or consumption of pork or wine, because the Qur'ānic prohibitions of these substances apply exclusively to Muslims.

Out-of-Court Settlement. The litigants, by mutual agreement, may agree to allow a third party to arbitrate their dispute, but the arbiter's decision is not enforceable by the court. When an arbiter's decision is referred to a qāḍī, he should treat it as a private agreement, unless he finds it contrary to the general principles of his law school, in which case he may annul it. Arbitration is not allowed in *ḥadd* cases because these involve rights of God (*ḥuqūq Allāh*) with respect to which only the Imām or head of state can make a final decision (for modern developments in this regard, see Bowen, Christelow, this volume).

Procedure

Judicial procedure involves determining the roles of plaintiff and defendant, establishing the facts of the case, and insuring the veracity of witness testimony and other evidence (Messick, Powers, this volume). The primary methods of establishing the veracity of a statement or occurrence are acknowledgment (*iqrār*), witness testimony (*shahāda*), oath (*yamīn*) and, in certain circumstances, a letter written by a qāḍī (on developments in this regard in modern times, see Carroll, this volume).

Acknowledgment and Confession (Iqrār). To be valid, an acknowledgment must be made in court in the presence of a qāḍī; no witnesses are required. An acknowledgment has the same legal value as does the personal knowledge of a qāḍī and thus is limited to civil cases.

A confession (also called *iqrār*), is binding and irrevocable in criminal cases involving the rights of men (e.g., retaliation). In *ḥadd* cases, which, by definition, involve the rights of God, a confession may be withdrawn at any time prior to the moment at which the punishment is imposed. If a person is accused of engaging in illicit sexual relations (*zinā*), his or her confession is acceptable on the condition that it is made during four separate sessions in the presence of a qāḍī. As noted, if the defendant acknowledges the plaintiff's claim, the case concludes in favor of the plaintiff. A defendant's silence in the face of a claim against him by a plaintiff does not constitute an acknowledgment.

Witnesses. Normally, two male witnesses are required, as suggested by Qur'ān 2:282. In addition, *ḥadīth* reports stipulate that a witness must see the event in question as clearly as he sees the sun (Zuḥaylī 1996, 6:556). A witness who has knowledge that is relevant to a case is required to appear in court only if the other witnesses fail to appear; in *ḥadd* cases, the appearance of a witness in court is voluntary (Zuḥaylī 1996, 6:556). The testimony of a witness is valid only if it is made in the presence of a qāḍī during the course of a litigation.

Witness testimony is of two types: (1) eyewitness testimony (*muʿāyana*) by someone who was present at the event and witnessed (*shahida*) the action with his or her own eyes; (2) hearsay testimony (*shahāda bi'l-khabar*) by a witness who testifies to a statement made by someone who is not present to testify in court.

Hearsay testimony may be sufficient to verify a fact or occurrence in claims relating to marriage, paternity, manumission, and death. In property claims, hearsay testimony establishing or confirming general information about the property in question is not sufficient; in addition, an eyewitness is also required, as suggested by Qur'ān 43:86: ". . . only he who bears witness to the truth, and with full knowledge," by Qur'ān 12:81: "We bear witness only to what we know," and by the *ḥadīth*: "You should bear witness only to what you have seen clearly, like the sun."

In property cases, only a person who has seen both the property and the owner with his or her own eyes is acceptable as a witness, unless ownership of the property is widely known, in which case the Hanafis, exceptionally, accept the testimony of a person who has seen the property but not the owner. As for testimony about a written document, a witness may testify to the authenticity of the document only if he or she was present when it was indited and can verify its authenticity and accuracy.

As noted, before a witness may testify, it must be determined that he or she is a person of personal integrity and has not been convicted—or accused—of slander. Every Muslim is presumed to be qualified as a witness until it becomes evident that he or she is a sinner (*fāsiq*). Thus, it is not necessary to initiate an investigation into the possible sinfulness of a witness—unless the defendant makes such a claim, except in criminal cases, in which prudence dictates that all witnesses be investigated for sinfulness. Excluded as witnesses are the following: a slave, a blind man or woman; a person whose objectivity may be affected by tribal ties to one of the litigants; a person who has committed a *ḥadd* crime; and a person whose integrity has been impugned by the performance of an undignified act, such as listening to music or engaging in illicit sexual relations. A woman may appear as a witness but only together with a man.

Al-Khaṣṣāf stipulates the following conditions for the validity of witness testimony:

1. The witness must know the facts of the case beyond doubt;
2. a father and son cannot testify on behalf of one another (because of the strength of the blood tie), although brothers may do so (presumably because they do not have the same feelings for one another as a father and son do);
3. the witness must have attained legal majority;
4. he will derive no benefit from his testimony nor will his testimony avert any harm from him;
5. he is not a product of illegitimate sexual relations;
6. a non-Muslim cannot testify for or against a Muslim, but one non-Muslim may testify for or against another non-Muslim.

Although two male witnesses are normally required, two female witnesses may testify alongside a single male witness. In cases involving a charge of illicit sexual relations, there must be four eyewitnesses to the act; if there are three or less, no crime is established, and any witness who does testify will be charged with false accusation of illicit sexual relations (*qadhf*), which carries a punishment of eighty lashes.

Al-Khaṣṣāf also discusses the phenomenon of a witness who withdraws his testimony during or after the court session. Such a withdrawal, he explains, cannot be treated as new testimony because it amounts to a denial of previous testimony, which constitutes an admission of mendacity. Similarly, a withdrawal followed by a new statement that differs from the first cannot be treated as a valid declaration, again, because a person who admits to giving false testimony effectively disqualifies himself as a witness. Thus, his revocation is not acceptable and it does not affect the judgment.

The underlying principle is that a person is not guilty unless his offense is established with certainty. If the defendant denies the plaintiff's claim, he is presumed innocent unless and until the plaintiff produces legally valid evidence.

The Oath. The principle that "the person who denies the claim must take the oath" (*al-yamīn ʿalā man ankara*) establishes the oath as a method of proof. According to Mālik, if the plaintiff cannot produce witness testimony or other evidence, the qāḍī may dismiss the case after asking the defendant to take the oath. If the defendant refuses, the qāḍī may ask the plaintiff to take the oath and, if he complies, settle the dispute in his favor (Zuḥaylī 1996, 6:490). The majority of jurists allows this procedure in property cases. In *ḥadd* cases the defendant is not required to take the oath, except in cases involving theft, in which he may be asked to swear an oath if the plaintiff demands it; if the defendant refuses, the plaintiff's right is established.

If only one witness is available in a civil case, most jurists—with the notable exception of the Hanafis—allow the substitution of one witness by one oath (Zuḥaylī 1996, 6:526; Serrano, this volume; Masud 1999).

Letter of a Qāḍī (Kitāb al-qāḍī). One qāḍī may communicate with another in writing, and the contents of such a letter (called *khiṭāb*) are admissible as evidence in court. The Malikis call such a document *shahādat al-naql,* i.e., testimony relating to the conveyance of evidence (Layish, this volume).

In addition, a qāḍī may compose a letter about a specific claim, and the contents of that letter (called *kitāb*, perhaps to distinguish it from a normal letter, *khiṭāb*) are admissible as evidence in another court, under prescribed conditions. For example, A approaches a qāḍī stating that he has a claim against B in another city. He asks the qāḍī to attest to his claim and to write a letter to the qāḍī in the other city. Since B is not present, the qāḍī may not decide the case nor may he issue a judgment; he merely records A's claim and stamps it with his personal seal in the presence of two witnesses, who then convey the letter to the qāḍī in the other city, before whom they testify that the letter was sealed in their presence. (The witnesses do not testify to the *contents* of the letter.) The second qāḍī accepts this letter as an attested statement of the claim. Such a letter has the same legal value as a normal letter (*khiṭāb*) written by one qāḍī to another.

Circumstantial Evidence (Qarīna). Circumstantial evidence may be strong or weak and its acceptability varies according to the type of case, with differences from one school to the next. For instance, if someone, holding a knife smeared with blood, is found near the body of a man or woman who has been stabbed to death, the bloody knife constitutes strong circumstantial evidence (called *lawth*) that a crime has been committed, whereas the alleged murderer's hostility to the victim is a weak form of evidence. In such a case, the collective oath of compurgation (*qasāma*) is admissible as evidence according to all schools except for the Hanafis.

Most jurists reject a judgment based on circumstantial evidence in *ḥadd* cases, although the Malikis treat pregnancy as circumstantial evidence of adultery and the smell of alcohol on a man's mouth as evidence of wine consumption. It is reported that Mālik, Aḥmad b. Ḥanbal and Abū Ḥanīfa all accepted as valid circumstantial evidence that is obvious and credible (Zuḥaylī 1996, 6:782). In property cases, Maliki jurists use the term *tuhma* to signify suspicion in a general sense, which may be circumstantial, e.g., the presence of stolen goods in a person's home, or based on hearsay. All of the schools recognize *tuhma* as grounds for the imposition of a discretionary punishment (*taʿzīr*) (Serrano, this volume).

Although it is often asserted that written documents are not admissible as evidence in Muslim courts, this is not accurate. Initially, written documents were viewed with suspicion—for which reason witness testimony was required for confirmation of authenticity. Over time, however, documents proved to be indispensable as a form of evidence, e.g., in disputes over family or public endowments (Bowen, Akarli, and Layish, this volume).

Judgment (Ḥukm)

The order or action of a qāḍī must be distinguished from his judgment (*ḥukm*). A large number of disputes are resolved by means of the issuance of a court certification (*thubūt*) that serves to confirm one or more existing legal facts. A qāḍī is not obligated to issue a judgment unless specifically asked to do so by the plaintiff (Müller, this volume). As noted, only a qāḍī who has mastered the doctrine of his school and is aware of juristic disagreement over the legal norms is qualified to issue a judgment.

In a criminal litigation, if a qāḍī determines that the appropriate punishment for a crime is amputation (for theft) or execution (e.g., for illicit sexual relations), he customarily will refer the case to the appointing authority, e.g., caliph, sultan, governor or chief judge.

As noted, school doctrine encourages a qāḍī to consult with other jurists, especially in cases that may require bodily punishment, raise a difficult point of law, or are politically sensitive. In al-Andalus, two judicial advisors were attached to every court; elsewhere, qāḍīs solicited *fatwā*s or legal opinions from *muftī*s or expert jurists (Powers, Serrano, this volume). In either case, the qāḍī was expected to issue his judgment on the strength of what he determined to be the truth of a matter. He was also expected to abide by the consensus (*ijmāʿ*) of the jurists and to limit his exercise of *ijtihād* to matters on which no consensus had emerged. A qāḍī who is qualified to exercise independent reasoning is bound by his own *ijtihād*, and he should not follow the recommendation of his advisors—even if their juristic qualifications are stronger than his.

A qāḍī who is a *mujtahid* should exercise his independent reasoning within the boundaries of his law school. The authoritative sources of *ijtihād*, in order of importance, are: Qur'ān, Sunna, the consensus of the Companions and Successors, and the agreed views of the jurists. A Hanafi qāḍī may exercise *ijtihād* only on matters upon which there is a disagreement between Abū Ḥanīfa, Abū Yūsuf and/or Muḥammad al-Shaybānī; he may not exercise *ijtihād* on a matter upon which they are in agreement.

Although qāḍīs based their judgments on school doctrine, they also took into consideration established court practice, local custom and socioeconomic norms and conventions. The high value that Islam places on the notion of fairness helped to harmonize school doctrine with local custom and to integrate custom into the legal system. It was through the process of judicial reasoning that legal principles, norms, and concepts were adapted to local contexts (Bowen, Dupret, this volume). At the same time, however, the position of a renowned jurist or a particular school doctrine was not always normative, and, in exceptional cases, qāḍīs did cross *madhhab* boundaries in the search for justice (Johansen, this volume).

Al-Khaṣṣāf distinguishes between a qāḍī's personal opinion based on his *ijtihād* and his personal knowledge about the facts of a case. Generally speaking, Hanafi, Maliki, and Hanbali jurists do not allow a qāḍī to decide a case on the basis of his personal knowledge. Al-Khaṣṣāf makes an exception in cases relating to slander and false accusation of illicit sexual relations, in which a qāḍī's personal knowledge of the character of a litigant may be decisive. Shafiʿi jurists allow a qāḍī to decide a civil—but not a criminal—case on the basis of personal knowledge (Zuḥaylī 1996, 6:490).

If a qāḍī commits an error in a case that concerns a right of God, his judgment should be implemented, but anyone who is wrongly punished should receive compensation from the Public Treasury. If the error concerns a right of men (*ḥaqq ādamī*), as in a property dispute, the judgment should not be implemented. If the error was unintentional, the qāḍī is not liable for damages; if it was intentional and unjust, then the qāḍī should be punished and dismissed (Rebstock 1999). Muslim jurists also distinguish between the formal legal validity (*ẓāhir*) of a qāḍī's judgment and its moral value (*bāṭin*). With the exception of Abū Ḥanīfa, who held that a qāḍī's judgment is always binding—both legally and morally—most jurists held that an erroneous judgment, although legally binding, is not morally binding, even if it is formally sound (Zuḥaylī 1996, 6:488).

Successor Review

Schacht's assertion (1964) that "there is no means of reversing an unjust judgment, because strict Islamic law does not recognize stages of appeal" requires qualification. It is true that the law schools are in general agreement that if a judge bases his decision upon the proper legal texts and follows the requisite judicial procedures, the judgment is binding and may not be reversed. It should be noted, however, that this formulation leaves open the possibility of reversing a decision that *fails* to meet these conditions.

The specific circumstances in which a judicial decision may be reversed are discussed by al-Khaṣṣāf in a chapter devoted to a later qāḍī's responsibility in dealing with a decision issued by an earlier qāḍī. Here al-Khaṣṣāf adds two significant qualifications to the holding that a judicial decision is, in principle, binding: First, a decision may be reversed if the pronouncing judge was not legally competent to pass judgment. Such would be the case, for example, if he were a sinner, or he had been punished for unlawful slander, or he did not possess the requisite qualities of moral uprightness. (An Anglo-American jurist would refer to these as *jurisdictional* grounds for appeal.) Second, a judicial decision also may be reversed if a judge who is legally competent nevertheless engages in the improper use of independent reasoning; for example, if his judgment contradicts a Qur'ānic text about whose plain meaning there is universal agreement, or it contradicts a widely transmitted *ḥadīth*, or opposes the consensus of Muslim jurists. (An Anglo-American jurist would interpret this to mean that an appeal will be considered if it raises a question of law but not if it raises a question of fact). Thus, if a judge is not legally competent or if a legally competent judge engages in the improper use of independent reasoning, his judgment may be nullified by another judge; this is the common doctrine of both the Sunni and the Shiʿi law schools. Conversely, the general position of all the schools is that a judgment issued by a competent judge that is based upon sound *ijtihād* may not be reversed under any circumstances.

Al-Khaṣṣāf's discussion signals the existence in Islamic law of what has been called *successor review*. For example, the thirteenth-century Hanbali jurist Ibn Qudāma (d. 1223) addresses the question of how a succeeding judge is to treat judgments issued by his predecessor. In the absence of evidence to the contrary, the general presumption is that the former judge was qualified to hold office and that his judgments are therefore legally valid and correct. For this reason, the new judge is not required to investigate his predecessor's rulings, but he nevertheless has a discretionary right to do so, either in response to a request by a defeated litigant or on his own initiative. In the event that he does exercise this right, the primary factor to be considered is the jurisdictional issue of whether the former judge was qualified to hold office. If it can be determined that he was not qualified to hold office, then his judgments are unsound and may be treated as if they do not exist. In that case, the succeeding judge must examine all of his predecessor's rulings and determine which are legally sound and which are not. Those judgments that he determines to be sound are allowed to stand because justice has been served, willy-nilly, and nullification would serve no purpose. Those judgments that he determines to be unsound, including those based on the former judge's attempt to exercise his independent reasoning, are to be nullified (Ibn Qudāma 1964, 10:144).

If the former judge was qualified to hold office, only those of his judgments that can be demonstrated to have been in conflict with a clear text of the Qur'ān, a prophetic *sunna*, or a juristic consensus are subject to reversal. Here Ibn Qudāma reiterates the principle previously announced by al-Khaṣṣāf that there can be appeal on questions of law but not on questions of fact. To this principle Ibn Qudāma adds a further qualification based on a distinction that Muslim jurists draw between public and private claims: a judgment relating to a public claim—in which category he includes the manumission of slaves and divorce—must be overruled by the succeeding judge on his own initiative, even if the defeated litigant does not demand its reversal; a judgment relating to a private claim may be reversed by the succeeding judge but only in response to a request from the defeated litigant (Ibn Qudāma 1964, 10:144).

The Qāḍī in the Modern Period

Although there are no comprehensive studies of judicial reform in the Muslim world during the nineteenth and twentieth centuries, we do have studies of the judiciary and the administration of justice in individual countries and even in specific courts. To date, scholars have focused greater attention on substantive law and its modernization than on judicial reform. Below, we outline changes in the institutional framework of the application of the *shariah* from the early nineteenth century until the present. The most salient features of these changes are as follow:

1. The abolition of *siyāsa* or discretionary criminal justice—in the interest of the state and public order—and the promotion of respect for the rule of law;

2. bureaucratization of the shariah courts;
3. codification of the shariah;
4. the emergence, in most countries, of a dual judiciary composed of (a) secular, national courts that apply Western-style legal codes; and (b) shariah courts that apply Islamic legal doctrine in fields such as family relations and inheritance;
5. the gradual integration of the shariah court system into the national court system.

In the wake of Western economic and political expansion into the Muslim world during the nineteenth century, most Muslim majority countries gradually and selectively adopted western legal codes and institutions. This did not immediately affect the qāḍī courts because independent states (e.g., the Ottoman Empire, Egypt, which was largely autonomous, and, later, Iran) made use of *siyāsa* (see above) to create institutions for implementing Western laws that operated in tandem with the qāḍī courts. Although informed by Western notions and ideas, law reform in these countries was carried out by independent governments. However, in some regions of the Muslim world, colonial rulers transformed the legal system and carried out extensive reforms of the qāḍī courts.

Let us examine judicial reform in independent Muslim countries—taking the Ottoman Empire as our model, and under colonial rule—using India and Nigeria as examples. Reform in the Ottoman Empire not only served as an example for other countries, such as Egypt and Iran, but also had an influence in those regions of the Middle East that remained under Ottoman rule until World War I. Colonial India is of interest because the specific and unique way in which the shariah is currently implemented in Bangladesh, India and Pakistan is, to a large extent, the result of British colonial reform. Nigeria is important because it provides a fine illustration of how the British colonizers institutionalized legal pluralism by setting up "native courts" to enforce customary law under British control. Maliki legal doctrine was then applied under the guise of customary law. This model was followed in many other British colonies in Africa.

Modernization of the Judiciary

Independent Countries: The Ottoman Empire[7]

The Ottomans took three crucial steps on the road to legal modernization of the empire. First, in 1838 the Supreme Council of Justice (Meclis-i Vālā'i Aḥkām-i ʿAdliye) was established to serve as both a legislative body and a high court. Second, in 1839 the famous Gülhane Decree proclaimed the end of arbitrary and secret criminal procedures connected with *siyāsa* or state justice, chiefly criminal, administered by executive officials. The Decree added that henceforth laws would be enacted for the protection of life, property and honor. It declared:

> Thus, from now on, the cases of those persons [suspected] of [having committed] offenses shall be publicly examined in accordance with enacted laws that are consistent with the shariah (*qawānīn sharʿiyya*), and without a sentence pronounced by a court of law no one may be secretly or publicly put to death, by poison or by any other means.

Third, in 1840, the Ottomans established provincial councils (*mecalis*) that exercised both judicial and administrative functions. These councils, membership on which was open to Christians, were charged with enforcing the newly enacted laws, the first of which was the Penal Code of 1840. By subjecting *siyāsa* to the rule of law, these three measures sought to put an end to the arbitrary and often secret exercise of *siyāsa* justice by the Sultan and high state officials.

These steps heralded the beginning of a process of legal reform that was part of a wider reform movement, the main objectives of which were the centralization and modernization of the empire. This required the creation of a bureaucracy that operated according to enacted laws through objective procedures. To this end, the jurisdictions and powers of the various bureaucratic and judicial organs of the state had to be defined clearly so that, in theory, identical procedures would be followed throughout the empire. The law, therefore, was to be enforced impartially, without regard for the social, economic, or religious status of the litigants. Legal predictability, a major objective of law reform, was to be achieved by limiting the ability

[7] This section is based mainly on Cin and Akgündüz (1989, passim); Inalcik (1991); Findley (1990); and Starr (1992:21–41).

of persons sitting on judicial councils—mostly state officials but also qāḍīs and *muftīs*—to use their personal discretion to decide cases.

Special courts and councils were established and new codes were enacted in the fields of criminal and commercial law. The provincial councils established in 1840 were replaced in 1864 by Niẓāmiye courts, a nonreligious court system with four levels or instances staffed by both Muslims and non-Muslims. The Niẓāmiye courts exercised jurisdiction in criminal cases governed by the French inspired Penal Code of 1858 and in civil litigation between non-Muslims. For trade disputes, specialized commercial tribunals applied the 1850 Code of Commerce, a translation into Turkish of the French *Code de Commerce.* However, if the parties agreed to submit their commercial litigation to a shariah court, they were entitled to do so. With the introduction of the French inspired 1879 Code of Civil Procedure, the Niẓāmiye courts were also given jurisdiction over commercial disputes, in addition to their competence in criminal and civil cases. Beginning in the 1840s, mixed courts were established for commercial and criminal cases in which one of the parties was a foreigner. Half of the judges on these courts were Christians selected by foreign embassies.

The newly created secular courts did not replace the qāḍī courts, which continued to function much as they had done before, although they were now subjected to a process of bureaucratization. The appointment of a qāḍī was made conditional upon passing an entrance examination, and a stream of government decrees regulated the various ranks of qāḍīs, the duration of their service, and their salaries. Other decrees defined the jurisdiction of the various courts, the fees that they could collect and the possibility of appeal. A major reform was that shariah courts were instructed to adjudicate certain types of cases on the basis of law codes rather than with reference to the standard *fiqh* texts. Between 1870 and 1877 the Hanafi law of obligations, personal property and procedure was brought together in a law code called *Mecelle,* to be applied by both the shariah and the Niẓāmiye courts. A family law code was enacted in 1917.

The shariah courts continued to exercise unlimited general jurisdiction until 1886, when the Ministry of Justice issued instructions to limit their jurisdiction to lawsuits relating to personal status and family law, inheritance and, in cases of homicide and wounding, to claims involving retaliation and blood money. Other civil cases were heard by the Niẓāmiye courts, unless the parties agreed to submit their dispute to a shariah court (Berkes 1998:170). In homicide cases, Niẓāmiye and shariah courts shared jurisdiction. The Niẓāmiye courts were empowered to sentence a guilty party to imprisonment, whereas the shariah courts, at the request of the victim's heirs, could examine whether or not there were grounds for capital punishment or, alternatively, the award of financial compensation. As of 1876, court practice was governed by the last three chapters of the Mecelle dealing with procedure, evidence and sentencing. In 1917, these chapters were repealed and replaced by a new law on procedure for the shariah courts.

After the foundation of the Republic of Turkey in 1923, the qāḍī courts were abolished and a new legal system—unified and entirely secular—was introduced. However, the Ottoman legal system continued to function in those regions of the empire that had become mandates of Great Britain and France after World War I.

Ottoman legal reform produced a dual system in which litigation relating to family matters and inheritance fell within the jurisdiction of the shariah courts, whereas all other cases were subject to the jurisdiction of statutory courts that applied laws enacted by the state. Moreover, the Ottoman Empire was the first Muslim state officially to codify parts of the shariah in an effort to facilitate the process of law finding for judges. These features continue to form the basis of the legal systems of most states in the Middle East that were formerly under Ottoman rule.

Under Colonial Rule

In most regions that came under colonial rule, laws based on those of the metropolis replaced whatever *madhhab* doctrine previously had been in force. For the implementation of these laws, new courts were established to hear criminal, civil and commercial cases. In addition, separate and parallel court systems were often set up to hear lawsuits involving citizens of the colonial power (and frequently other Europeans as well). As a result, the jurisdiction of the qāḍī courts was restricted to family law and inheritance, and, sometimes, the law of contracts and personal property. The qāḍī courts also were subjected to supervision and control by the colonial authorities. This happened in Muslim majority countries under French rule (Algeria and Tunisia), under Dutch rule (Indonesia) and under Italian rule (Libya). After these countries achieved independence, their legal systems and the position of the shariah within them came to resemble those of the countries of the former Ottoman Empire. Typical features of these legal systems were the juxtaposition of a secular, national judiciary alongside qāḍī courts and the restriction of *sharʿī* jurisdiction to family law and inheritance.

A different course was followed in colonial India and Nigeria, where the British, in principle, recognized and applied local laws insofar as they did not conflict with "natural justice, good conscience and equity." The most salient feature of nineteenth-century Indian legal history is that shariah justice was administered by British judges sitting on shariah courts. British courts exercised general jurisdiction and, unlike other colonies, India did not develop a dual judiciary with secular and shariah courts.

After the British East India Company acquired authority over the department of finances of Bengal in 1765, the British extended their control over other branches of government, including the administration of justice.[8] Legally, Bengal remained part of the Mughal Empire, and the legal system was essentially Islamic and based on Hanafi law. According to the terms of their treaty with the Mughals, the British could not change the position of the shariah as the law of the land, although in 1772 they began to reform the judiciary by establishing criminal and civil courts staffed by British judges, assisted by local law officers called *maulvis* (experts on Islamic law) and *pundits* (scholars versed in Hindu law). The courts of first instance heard both criminal and civil cases. In criminal cases, the court of the Mughal governor of Calcutta was transformed into a high court for purposes of appeal (Niẓāmat-i ʿAdālat, or, according to then current British orthography: Nizamut Adaulut). These criminal courts applied Hanafi law, enforced by British judges on the basis of *fatwās* issued by law officers, called qāḍīs and *muftīs*, titles that evoked the former position of Muslim religious authorities under Mughal rule.

In an effort to eliminate certain harsh features of Hanafi criminal law, the British issued regulations instructing the courts to commute to imprisonment any judgment that required amputation of a limb or stoning. Otherwise, however, the British regarded Hanafi criminal law as too lenient, because the application of capital punishment

---

[8] Our discussion of British India is based mainly on Pearl (1987:21–41); Rahim (1968:37–48); and R. Peters (forthcoming/a: ch. 4.2.1).

was difficult and the shariah offered many possibilities of avoiding punishment to persons accused of serious offenses such as manslaughter, rape, and theft. The British therefore issued new regulations aimed at bringing Hanafi criminal law more closely into line with the stricter and more severe British notions of justice. In an attempt to eliminate *sharʿī* loopholes, the law officers were instructed to issue their *fatwā*s on the basis of hypothetical presumptions. In manslaughter cases, for instance, the British considered it unacceptable that the punishment of a murderer should depend on the willingness of the victim's heirs to accept financial compensation in return for waiving a claim to retaliation. Therefore, *fatwā*s in such cases were issued on the presumption that all of the victim's heirs had demanded the death penalty. Such regulations gradually modified shariah criminal law.

Not until 1861, however, was the theoretical primacy of the shariah in criminal cases abolished by the introduction of the Indian Penal Code and the Code of Criminal Procedure. And in the field of civil law, the courts continued to apply the shariah unless otherwise directed by statute, e.g., the 1864 Contracts Act. If neither the shariah nor statute law contained provisions pertaining to a case, the courts were to act according to "justice, equity and good conscience," which, in practice, meant that they would implement English law. Initially, court practice was also governed by the shariah, but it was gradually modified by statute law, such as the 1864 Evidence Act. In 1858, after the demise of the Mughal Empire and the transfer of power from the East India Company to the Crown, the court system in the various provinces was unified, and the Privy Council in London became the highest court of appeal. In 1864 the position of the native law officers was abolished, and, henceforth, British judges had to find the relevant rules of the shariah themselves. Not until 1908 was a Code of Civil Procedure introduced.

In cases relating to family relations, inheritance, endowments and gifts, the courts applied the law of the litigants and, in disputes between litigants who were not co-religionists, the law of the defendant. The courts were not required to follow one particular *madhhab*, and they generally ruled according to the *madhhab* of the litigants. This meant that the civil courts enforced both Sunni (mainly Hanafi) and Shiʿi doctrine. The British rarely interfered by enacting legislation. In 1850 they introduced the rule that conversion to another religion does not affect one's inheritance rights (Caste Disabilities Removal Act). Other examples of laws reform-ing the shariah, such as the 1913 Wakf Act and the 1939 Dissolution of Muslim Marriages Act, were adopted at the specific request of Muslim organizations.

British judges adopted different approaches to the application of Islamic law. In those legal fields in which they were explicitly instructed to apply the shariah (e.g., family law and inheritance), they closely followed the interpretations of the classical *fiqh* books, which they consulted in translation. Thus, the validity of a repudiation pronounced under duress was upheld in court, in accordance with classical Hanafi doctrine. However, in other fields, such as property rights, if both litigants were Muslims, the shariah was enforced not on the basis of an express instruction to the courts, but as a principle of "justice, equity and good conscience." Here the judges had greater discretion and they sometimes deviated from the provisions of the shariah, again for reasons of "justice, equity and good conscience."

The implementation of Hanafi substantive law by British judges, based on translations of classical texts and under the supervision of the Privy Council in London, resulted in the emergence of a novel and unique form of Islamic law, called *Anglo-Muhammadan Law*, which to this day remains in force in India, Bangladesh and Pakistan. The distinctive feature of the judicial organization of these three countries is that Islamic law is applied by national, regular courts and not by specialized shariah courts, as it is in most other parts of the Muslim world.

In colonial Nigeria, Maliki legal doctrine was applied in a different institutional context. Whereas in India, British courts and judges took over the administration of Islamic law, in Nigeria, the British colonial rulers left the qāḍī courts as they were but integrated them into a nationwide system of Native Courts that issued judgments and settled disputes according to local customary law, so long as that law was not incompatible with any enacted law or with "natural justice, equity and good conscience."[9] This feature of the British policy of indirect rule was applied in many parts of Africa. In northern Nigeria the British exercised control through the existing administrative and

---

[9] Our discussion of Nigeria is based mainly on Obilade (1979:17–55); Anderson (1954:195–204); Karibi-Whyte (1993); Keay and Richardson (1966); Tabi'u (1991: 53–76); and Mahmud (1988).

judicial structures: the emirs or local rulers governed and *alkalis* (Hausa, derived from Arabic *al-qāḍī*) staffed the local court system. British colonial officials and courts supervised the qāḍīs and their courts to ensure that they pronounced no judgment repugnant to "natural justice, equity and good conscience." The Native Courts Proclamation of 1900 (subsequently replaced by the Native Courts Ordinance of 1933) was based on this principle: The British Resident (i.e., the provincial governor), with the consent of the emir, could establish native courts with full jurisdiction over the native population in civil and criminal matters. The British used this power to confer official status on the existing courts of the emirs (Christelow, this volume) and the *alkalis*, who applied Maliki legal doctrine. Judges were appointed by the emir with the approval of the British Resident, who had extensive powers: he could enter and inspect the courts; suspend, reduce and modify judgments; order a rehearing of a trial before another native court; or order a transfer to a provincial court that applied English common law.

In *ḥadd* cases, if the qāḍī court sentenced a defendant to a penalty of amputation or death by stoning, the British authorities charged with the execution of judgments routinely commuted such sentences to imprisonment. The application of Maliki law by the native courts in the North extended to judicial practice and procedure. The British authorities gave these courts much latitude. For example, according to the Maliki *qasāma* procedure, if a person is suspected of manslaughter, and evidence is available but is insufficient to convict, the accused may be sentenced to death if the victim's male next of kin swear fifty oaths against him. In 1930, this procedure was recognized by the West African Court of Appeal, at that time the highest appeal court for the British colonies in West Africa. The Court of Appeal explained its position as follows:

> There is no desire to interfere with decisions which are in accordance with native law, the principle has been that the verdict and sentence of a Native Court which is an integral part of our judicial system carried out in accordance with procedure enjoined by native law and not obviously inequitable will be accepted even though the procedure is widely different from the practice of English Criminal Courts.[10]

[10] Abdullahi Kogi and others vs Katsina Native Authority (1930) 14 NLR 49, as quoted in Karibi-Whyte (1993:162–4). See also Mahmud (1988:18).

In subsequent years, there have been only a few instances in which the Nigerian Supreme Court has set aside a provision of the shariah when called upon to determine whether a certain rule of Maliki law is repugnant to justice, equity, and good conscience. In two such cases, injunctions of the shariah were set aside because they infringed upon freedom of religion (by excluding a person from inheriting on the ground of his conversion to another religion) or discriminated on the basis of religion (by refusing to accept the testimony of a non-Muslim in court).

The native courts of the northern region of Nigeria closely followed (and still follow) Maliki substantive law and procedure. This was also true in criminal cases, as we have seen, until the Penal Code for the Northern Region was passed in 1959 and enacted in 1960. Maliki legal doctrine remained uncodified and the courts continued to cite the standard books of Maliki *fiqh*. What is perhaps most interesting about the situation in northern Nigeria is that here we have one of the very few examples in which the shariah was and remains the law of the land and is applied in most fields, including procedure, first under colonial rule and then, after Nigeria became independent in 1960, within the framework of a secular and multi-religious state.

Shariah Justice Today

With the exception of Turkey and Albania—the only two Muslim majority states in which the law is completely secular and the shariah is not implemented—the shariah is part of the national legal system of all Muslim countries. Typically, the law of the land is Western in its orientation, and the implementation of the shariah is limited to specific legal domains. This is also true of countries in which the shariah is applied to a Muslim minority, as in India and many African states. In some Muslim majority countries, such as Saudi Arabia and Iran, the shariah dominates the legal system: the shariah is the law of the land and statute law must be compatible with it. Since the position of the shariah within a national legal system affects the way in which it is implemented by the judiciary, we will discuss, first, legal systems in which the shariah is enforced within the framework of an essentially Western legal system and, second, systems in which the shariah is dominant.

In Muslim countries with a Westernized legal system, the shariah is usually applied by special courts whose jurisdiction is limited to disputes involving the law of persons (e.g., legal capacity), family law (marriage, divorce, paternity), guardianship, inheritance and endowments. In some countries disputes over gifts, certain aspects of the law of real property (such as *shufʿa* or preemption) and financial compensation for homicide are also decided under the shariah. Frequently, those aspects of the shariah that are applied in courts have been codified, which means that the judges need not consult the classical legal treatises, except in cases not covered by the law codes. As a result finding the law has been simplified and can be accomplished by jurists trained in modern law who have not received a traditional *madrasa* education. At present, the shariah tribunals are integrated into the national court systems, although the degree of integration varies. In some countries it is possible to appeal a case from a shariah court to a non-shariah national court of appeal, whereas in other countries there are separate shariah courts of appeal. Almost everywhere shariah justice is controlled by a national supreme court in order to ensure uniformity in the implementation of the law. This is the case, for instance, in Indonesia, where, as Bowen (this volume) mentions, there exists, alongside the regular courts, a parallel system of Islamic courts, both of which are subordinate to the Supreme Court. The same is true in Zanzibar, which forms an autonomous part of Tanzania. Unlike the rest of the country, where Islamic law is applied by common, nonshariah courts, Zanzibar, which is almost entirely Muslim, has special qāḍī courts (Stiles, this volume). Judgments issued by these courts can be reviewed by the Tanzanian Court of Appeal, which is the highest national court.

However, in India, Pakistan, and Bangladesh, whose legal systems were shaped by the experience of British colonialism, shariah justice is not entrusted to special shariah courts but rather is enforced by the national court system. In India this means that the shariah is applied by judges irrespective of their religion, as under colonial rule, whereas in Pakistan and Bangladesh, which define themselves as Islamic states, the judges are Muslims. In Pakistan the Federal Shariat Court was established in 1980, and although this court appears to restore special shariah jurisdiction, this is not in fact the case; the court was created to supervise the Islamization of the legal system, not to adjudicate disputes in accordance with the shariah. In other countries, the state has attempted to do away with a special shariah court system more or less separate from the national court system, and shariah tribunals have been abolished in Egypt (1956), Tunisia (1956), and Algeria (1975) in order to unify the judiciary. Cases previously heard by shariah courts are now adjudicated by special benches or divisions within the national courts.

The shariah remains dominant in Saudi Arabia and in countries that are experiencing Islamization. In Saudi Arabia, the shariah has always been an essential part of the legal system, and shariah courts retain general jurisdiction, although other courts or judicial bodies have been established to enforce certain codes, which, however, must be compatible with the shariah and are regarded as complementing it. In Sudan and Pakistan, where Islamist regimes have taken power, and in Northern Nigeria, where shariah has been reintroduced under popular pressure (Peters, this volume), western codes regarded as inconsistent with the shariah have been replaced to some extent by shariah codes. In such countries, the entire legal system is now technically Islamic, and there is no longer any justification for special shariah courts, which were abolished in Libya (1973), Iran (1979) and Sudan (1983), where their functions have been taken over by common, national courts that now have become shariah courts. The extent to which court practice, e.g., the law of procedure and evidence, is governed by the shariah varies from country to country. For practical reasons the new shariah courts often continue to follow the previous Western style procedure codes.

A typical development associated with the re-Islamization of a legal system is the judicial review of laws proposed by the legislature in order to determine whether or not they are in conformity with Islam and the principles of the shariah. We find this in Pakistan, where the Federal Shariat Court, established in 1980 in the wake of Islamization measures, is charged with testing statute law for repugnancy to "injunctions of Islam, as laid down in the Holy Qur'an and the *Sunnah*." In other countries, like Egypt, the government has made minor concessions to Islamization of the law by adding a clause (Art. 2) to the Constitution stating that the "principles" of the shariah are "the" main source of legislation. The Supreme Constitutional Court (SCC) is empowered to examine legislation enacted after the adoption of the new constitutional provision in 1980 and to determine whether or not it is in agreement with these principles. The SCC does not regard the legal rules of the Hanafi *madhhab* as identical with these "principles"; rather, it regards as "principles" of the shariah only rules embodied in univocal revealed texts that have been interpreted in the same manner by all qualified jurists (Johansen, this volume). This is a restrictive standard, and, to date, no laws have been nullified on the grounds of being repugnant to these principles.

PART I

JUDGING

CHAPTER TWO

SETTLING LITIGATION WITHOUT JUDGMENT: THE IMPORTANCE OF A *ḤUKM* IN *QĀḌĪ* CASES OF MAMLŪK JERUSALEM[1]

Christian Müller

The adjudication of legal cases is the principal task of the *qāḍī* who, when establishing legal facts that serve as the basis of his ruling (*ḥukm*), is bound and guided by procedural law. From early on, Muslim jurists have discussed what is, and what is not, a final court decision.[2] They consider a judicial certification (*thubūt*) to be different from a court decision, with either the same or different legal consequences. Beyond these well-documented general norms, we know very little about how *qāḍī*s decided cases in periods before the Ottoman court registers begin to appear in the 10th/16th century. The rich historical and legal sources written in Arabic during the middle period offer little information on actual court decisions.

Mamlūk chronicles abound with anecdotes about punishments inflicted on people, but they are not concerned with legal aspects of these cases. Moreover, Muslim jurists produced a rich literature, not only on legal doctrine but also on various legal problems and cases. Only a few of these texts, however, make any reference to the decision taken by the judge at the outcome of a litigation. Legal manuals do mention cases in which *qāḍī* decision differed from legal doctrine, but only rarely. And the richly documented *responsa* literature (*fatāwā*) is not concerned with the judge's decision on a case. This lack of information is one of the reasons why legal historians, until recently, considered *fiqh* to be a set of moral and legal duties produced by private scholars rather than Islamic law applied in courts. Such a view would explain why intensive discussions on legal problems,

[1] I want to thank Baber Johansen and David Powers for their comments and suggestions.

[2] On the juridical status of the judgment, see Johansen (1990); and for the position of al-Shāfiʿī, see Johansen (1997c:1045–55).

like the conditions of a final judgment (*ḥukm*), did not lead to court decisions being reported in the sources. There is one problem, however: this view of the law does not conform to our present knowledge. Increasingly, studies on the doctrinal development of Islamic law emphasize its vitality and responsiveness to social change, largely due to its application in court. Why then do we have so few records of court judgments?

It has been argued that the jurists did not transmit *qāḍī* judgments because they were critical of them. Surely, another reason for the absence of court decisions in the juridical literature is their legal status: the court decision did not create precedent as it did in Anglo-Saxon case law. There was no reason for a jurist to refer to an earlier judgment that was valid only for the specific case for which it was issued. The fact that the *fatwā* literature transmitted legal opinions on individual cases, but not the *qāḍī*'s decision on the same case, is due to the legal distinction between *qāḍī* and *muftī*. The *muftī* based his legal opinion on accounts of facts that were communicated to him by the *qāḍī*, irrespective of whether or not they corresponded to the facts presented in court. The validity of his opinion did not depend on the facts, and for this reason such a normative legal response might make its way into legal literature. The *qāḍī*'s assessment of the facts and adjudication of individual rights, on the other hand, was not a matter of interest beyond the parties concerned, and therefore was not transmitted.[3]

To historians of the judicial system, however, the *qāḍī*'s decision-making is of primary importance. Was the *qāḍī* a kind of notary, whose judgment was bound to legal facts as presented by witness evidence (*bayyina*), but who did not decide litigations (*khuṣūmāt*) without legal proof? Or could he adjudicate such litigations without issuing a formal judgment (*ḥukm*) and, if so, what was the result of such a decision? What was the function of a judicial certification as opposed to that of a judgment? In posing these and related questions, we are confronted with an epistemological dilemma: because there were so many reasons for excluding a court's decision and its judicial assumptions from any literary account of the case, we may never know whether or not the *qāḍī* issued a *ḥukm* or chose to resolve the case in some other manner. Although one can reconstruct judicial cases

[3] B. Johansen (1993:35).

from literary sources, as the contributions to this volume demonstrate,[4] these sources rarely tell us if the *qāḍī* resolved the case in a form other than a judgment. There are indications that jurists were opposed to a *ḥukm* by the *qāḍī* in specific cases,[5] but we do not know what the *qāḍī* was supposed to do instead of issuing a *ḥukm*. One way to resolve this problem is to study cases on the basis of original documents in which we may follow "court procedure"—actions of legal relevance that happen in court—until the case results in a decision, if any. Original court documents reflect judicial practice in a very immediate manner. But they have shortcomings; apart from the difficulty of deciphering them, court documents were not, at least in the period that concerns us here, systematically archived, or these archives did not survive the ravages of time. Under these circumstances, the preservation of documents was a result of historical coincidence rather than legal consideration. Therefore, surviving specimens are not always the most instructive ones. And judicial documents are not always easy to interpret and may not tell us everything that we want to know. However, they are our best available source for determining whether and how a *qāḍī* decided litigations and certified legal deeds without passing a judgment.

The collection of some 900 Mamlūk documents discovered at the Ḥaram al-Sharīf in Jerusalem between 1974 and 1976 offers a unique opportunity to answer some of the questions raised above.[6] Several documents record court cases presented to a *qāḍī*. The majority of the documents were issued in Jerusalem during the last decade of the 8th/14th century in connection with the Shāfiʿī court of the city. All cases discussed here, unless stated otherwise, were presented to the Shāfiʿī *qāḍī* of the city, Abū 'l-Rūḥ al-Anṣārī (d. 797/1395).[7] Any differences in the style or content of these documents, therefore, reflect a legal concern that was not caused by geographical or temporal differences or by the judge's adherence to a different legal school.

On the following pages, I will link the evidence from the Ḥaram documents with juridical norms discussed in contemporary legal

[4] See also, e.g., the articles of D. Powers on judicial cases in North Africa, based on the *Miʿyār* of al-Wansharīsī, in Powers (2002).

[5] For cases in eleventh-century Cordoba in which jurists objected to a *ḥukm*, see Müller (1999:280, 296, 397).

[6] On this collection, see D. Little (1984) and the editions of various documents prepared by D. Little, K.J. ʿAsalī, H. Lutfi and others.

[7] On him, see D. Little (1982) and the introduction to Little (1984).

manuals: Those documents that mention a formal court judgment (*ḥukm*) may help us to determine the legal characteristics of a *ḥukm*, as reported in the Mamlūk period. Once we have identified the legal characteristics of a *ḥukm*, we can better isolate and analyze cases that were settled in court without a formal *ḥukm*. These will be discussed on pp. 58ff. Since contemporary judicial practice distinguished a judgment (*ḥukm*) from a judicial certification (*thubūt*), I hope to determine the legal character of each court decision reported in the documents. In the conclusion, I will argue that those cases in which facts were certified in court without a final *ḥukm* were treated, in effect, as cases in which there was a final *ḥukm*: The decision of whether or not to issue a *ḥukm* depended on the differing legal aspects of the litigation, and was not a question of how well or poorly the jurisdiction functioned.

The Judgment (Ḥukm) *in the Ḥaram Documents*

We begin by examining documents that do mention a *qāḍī* judgment. Fortunately, the term *ḥukm* is recorded several times in different contexts in the Ḥaram documents. They are the following:

1. Two sale deeds of houses specifically mention the necessity of a *ḥukm*.[8]
2. Several orders, issued by a judge to certify the legal content of a document, mention a *ḥukm*. These orders, called *tawqīʿ*, are followed on the verso by *ishhād* documents which mention the term *ḥukm* as well.
3. Among the two dozen documents describing events in court (the "court records"), only three specimens mention the term *ḥukm*.

The first two groups concern judgments issued in corroboration of a legal claim. We will deal with them at the end of this section. The third group involves litigation between adversaries. I will begin with a short summary of each of the three cases in this group in order to identify the legal and judicial characteristics of the *ḥukm*.[9]

---

[8] These are documents nos. 39 and 853.

[9] A fourth document on the certification of a *waqf*, no. 606, mentions a *ḥukm* document by another judge. Since no *ḥukm* was mentioned to qualify the decision of the Jerusalem *qāḍī*, this case will be presented below.

These cases are all reported in a single document that begins with the same formula: "On the date . . . appeared at the court session of the Shāfiʿī judge in Jerusalem the person. . . ." (*bi-ta'rīkh kadhā wa-kadhā ḥaḍara majlis al-ḥukm al-ʿazīz al-fulānī al-shāfiʿī al-ḥākim bil-Quds al-sharīf* . . . *fulān*). Despite their appearance, these "court records" not only report on the session held on the date indicated at the beginning, but also summarize the legal content of a litigation, as attested by the witnesses.[10]

> On 25 Shawwāl 794, testimony was given in the Shāfiʿī court of Jerusalem that a claim had been forwarded, in the name of the beneficiaries of the foundation of al-Khānqāh al-Ṣalāḥiyya, to end the contract of a lease of land because the leaseholder had died prior to its termination. However, the defendant, one of the leaseholder's heirs, insisted that the contract be continued, since its term had been set for thirty years and was not linked to the life of the original leaseholder. There was no reason to terminate the contract since the claimants would receive all outstanding payments from the estate of the deceased. The *qāḍī* Abū 'l-Rūḥ ruled accordingly and had his *ḥukm* certified and ratified.[11]

In this first case, the initial pattern between the parties changed: the original claimant on behalf of the foundation of al-Khānqāh al-Ṣalāḥiyya lost the case against the original defendant, a representative of the leaseholder's heirs. The latter, in the end, obtained the judgment in his favor.

> On 5 Dhu'l-Qaʿda 795, testimony was given at the Shāfiʿī court of Jerusalem that a divorcee claimed 1000 dirhams from her ex-husband. He refused to pay since he had already paid her *ṣadāq* some months earlier. She claimed, however, the alimony (*mutʿa ṭalāq*) that was due after divorce. After questioning the husband on his financial situation, the judge Abū 'l-Rūḥ passed his *ḥukm*: he awarded 300 dirhams to the wife. On the back of this piece of paper, in a separate document written during the same month, the wife acknowledged receipt of this sum.[12]

---

[10] This is made clear, e.g., in the second case discussed here, nos. 31, 32, and 650: one of the claimants, a slave, who is reported to have attended the court session (and he may well have been present at the beginning of the case), had fled to Damascus and was certainly not present when the reported court session deliberated whether the price received for selling the slaves was adequate or not. For the case, see below.

[11] Document no. 334, edited by ʿAsalī (1983–85, 2:22ff., no. 2). The transcriptions of this and all other cases in this essay are summaries, not word-for-word translations.

[12] Document no. 653, edited by ʿAsalī (1983–85, 2:19ff., no. 1), without the acquittal on the back.

After deliberation, the judge settled this litigation with a judgment, although the wife, inexplicably, was not obligated to produce witness evidence regarding her husband's financial situation.

> On 19 Muḥarram 797, testimony was given at the Shāfiʿī court of Jerusalem that the claim of some slaves regarding their emancipation by their late master had been denied by a judgment of Abū 'l-Rūḥ, following a counterclaim by a "legal claimant." According to this unnamed person, at the time of the emancipation, the former master had attained puberty, but not the age of discretion (*rushd*), making the emancipation invalid—although it did not invalidate the deceased's legacy (*waṣiyya*) to the Ṣāliḥī Hospital. The document goes on to describe the public auction and the sale of the slaves by order of the judge.[13]

All documents in these three cases summarize court procedure in a litigation that was resolved by the *qāḍī*'s judgment (*ḥukm*). Since the judge was confronted with contradictory claims in all three cases, none of his judgments certified an existing legal situation. In the second and third case, we are informed about the consequences of the judgment: the divorced wife received the money awarded to her; and the slaves were sold after it was determined that the manner in which they had been emancipated was invalid.

What kind of documents were these and what was their function in judicial practice? The first two documents (no. 334 and no. 653) may well represent an "act of judgment," but this cannot be said of the documents in the third case, since they mention legal actions posterior to the judgment. In order to answer these questions, we need to determine not only the conditions for a *ḥukm* as discussed in the legal literature,[14] but also the features of a *ḥukm* when notarized by contemporary notaries. For Mamlūk legal practice, the 9th/14th century *shurūṭ* manual, *Jawāhir al-ʿuqūd*, by Shams al-Dīn Muḥammad al-Manhājī al-Asyūṭī, is highly instructive.[15]

Asyūṭī's manual contains several examples of a final judgment (*ḥukm*) that settled a claim (*daʿwā*). Once the hearing of evidence and

---

[13] On this case, see the three nearly identical documents, nos. 31, 32, and 650, the latter edited by Little (1982:30–5) and commentary, and no. 32, edited by ʿAsalī (1983–85, 1:221–3, no. 26). One slave "withdrew" to Damascus and was not sold. Thus he could not have been present in Jerusalem on the date of the document.

[14] For the period under consideration, see for the Shāfiʿī school of law: Ibn Abī al-Dam al-Ḥamawī (1982).

[15] Asyūṭī (n.d.).

court procedure was concluded, the claimant asked for a judgment. The request is described in a stock phrase that appears in the manual, "The aforementioned claimant asked the judge to whom reference has been made . . . and for a [corresponding] judgment" (*saʾala al-muddaʿī al-madhkūr min al-ḥākim al-mushār ilayhi . . . wa-l-ḥukma bi-. . . .*).[16] Thereupon, the *qāḍī* "asked God for right inspiration and took Him as guide and advisor" (*fa-istakhāra Allāha kathīran wa-ittakhadhahu hādiyan wa-naṣīran*) (ibid.). The *qāḍī* then imposed a certain ruling on the defendant (i.e., loss of possession of a piece of land), and then issued his judgment. In juridical terms, the *ḥukm* is characterized as a "legal judgment completing [the conditions set by] his school of law and his doctrine, being aware of [existing] dissent (*ḥukm . . . ḥukman sharʿiyyan li-muwāfaqat dhālika madhhabahu wa-muʿtaqadahu maʿa al-ʿilm bi-l-khilāf*).[17] The second half of the formula ("being aware of [existing] dissent") was dropped if there was no disagreement concerning the relevant legal norms in the case. Thus, the *qāḍī* declares that he asked God for proper guidance and that his judgment conforms to the doctrine of his school of law. We are not concerned here with an analysis of the legal technicalities of this formulation. Its application, however, was necessary for the legality of any judgment and determined its validity in the eyes of succeeding judges.

Those Ḥaram litigation documents that mention a judgment (concerning three different cases) do not contain the same stock phrase concerning the *ḥukm*. Since they were drafted at different phases of a litigation and cover different aspects, this is not surprising. All of these documents mention that the judgment had been solicited (on this, see below). "Asking God for guidance" is mentioned only in nos. 650 and 653. The formula of issuing the judgment and its conformity to the law is different in each document. We will examine in detail the formulas pertaining to the *qāḍī*'s *ḥukm*: the three specimens recording the judgment to annul the emancipation of slaves (nos. 31, 32, and 650) continue by explaining the execution of this judgment. Evidently, these documents were drafted to explain the sale of the slaves that was ordered by the judge, not to justify the soundness of his earlier judgment. These documents, therefore, are not "acts of

---

16 Ibid., 2:512, l. 23–513, l. 3.

17 Asyūṭī (n.d.), 2:513, ll. 4–5. Compare similar phrases in ibid., 287, l. 19; 409, 460, 510, 527; cf. Little (1982:43) as well as Ibn Abī al-Dam (1982:556).

judgment" but court records. They make only brief mention of the *qāḍī*'s judgment: "Someone, who is legally qualified to ask, asked [the *qāḍī*] for the judgment . . . and he accordingly issued his judgment in a sound and legal manner." (*thumma sa'ala sā'ilun sāgha lahu al-su'āl sharʿiyyan al-ḥukma bi- . . . fa-ḥakama [al-qāḍī] bi- . . . dhālika ḥukman ṣaḥīḥan sharʿiyyan.*)[18] Even document no. 650, which does mention the request for God's guidance, is very brief with regard to the other aspects of this judgment. The appeal for divine guidance is essential only when the judge issues the judgment, and documents that record a later stage in the legal process do not attach the same importance to this act. Since the appeal for divine guidance concerns the *qāḍī*'s *forum internum*, this act loses importance as the case continues and may later be dropped. Whenever a judge records an ongoing case with regard to a judgment passed days or weeks earlier, he usually does not include the formula in which he asks for God's guidance.

Document no. 334 is different. Here, the *qāḍī* issues a judgment not to terminate the term of a lease contract with a *waqf*, using the following phraseology for passing the judgment: "The aforementioned claimant asked the judge to whom reference has been made for a corresponding judgment . . . and he accordingly issued a judgment, being aware of [existing] dissent [between the schools of law], in a sound and legal manner." (*fa-sa'ala al-muddaʿī al-madhkūr al-ḥākim al-mushār ilayhi* [l. 12] . . . *al-ḥukm bi- . . . fa-ḥakama [al-qāḍī] bi-dhālika maʿa al-ʿilm bi-khilāf ḥukman ṣaḥīḥan sharʿiyyan* [ll. 14–15]). We note the absence of the appeal for divine guidance, the notion of conformity with the school of law, and a short legal qualification of the *ḥukm*. This document continues: "The judge had this judgment established as proven fact, authorized it, and made it binding, as requested." (*thabatahu wa-amḍāhu wa-alzamahu bi-muqtaḍāhu mas'ūlan fī dhālika*, l. 15). Next, witnesses attested to these procedures on the date on which the document was drawn up. Thus, this document fulfilled another legal requirement of a valid judgment: its attestation by upright witnesses prior to the conclusion of the court house session. At the bottom of document no. 334 we find the signatures of two witnesses who attest to their presence in court and to the judge's actions, as

---

[18] For documents nos. 31, 32, see ʿAsalī (1983–5, 1:222, ll. 11ff.); no. 650, which reports the same events, integrates the formulation *fa-istakhāra allāha kathīran wa-ittakhadhahu hādiyan wa-naṣīran*, l. 9; cf. Little (1982:32–3).

described in the document (*bi-mā nusiba ilayhi fīhi*). In a final step, the judge authorized the document with his personal formula of authorization (*ʿalāma*), here "*al-ḥamdu li-Llāhi wa-asʾaluhu al-tawfīq*," the motto of the *qāḍī* Abū 'l-Rūḥ.[19] All this serves to indicate that this document is in fact the written formulation of the *qāḍī*'s judgment, a real *ḥukm* document (*Urteilsurkunde*), probably the only one of its kind in the Ḥaram corpus.

Only one document, no. 653, lines 15–18, contains the complete formula with its three constituent elements, that is, "the request for a judgment, the *qāḍī*'s seeking God's guidance and the issuance of a sound legal judgment": *saʾalat sayyidanā al-ḥākim al-mushār ilayhi . . . al-ḥukma ʿalayhi bi-mā yaqtaḍīhu madhhabuhu al-sharīf min . . . fa-istakhāra Allāha kathīran wa-ittakhadhahu hādiyan wa-naṣīran wa-ḥakama lahā ʿalayhi bi . . . ḥukman ṣaḥīḥan sharʿiyyan muqarran murḍiyan baʿd suʾālihā dhālika ʿalā al-wajh al-sharʿī . . .*[20] Not mentioned in this document, however, are the *ḥukm*'s conformity to the judge's school of law and the judge's knowledge of legal *ikhtilāf* (see above). It is possible that the judgment in this case, which involved determining the sum to be paid to the divorcee in accordance with the husband's financial situation, was not regulated by the school's norms and therefore did not require these elements. This document, unlike no. 334, does mention that witnesses were summoned to attest to its content (*ishhād*), but not to its authorization (*imḍāʾ*) by the judge. Accordingly it does not bear the judge's motto (*ʿalāma*), but rather a notice, written by the *qāḍī* in the space where the *ʿalāma* normally is found, to the left of the *basmala*: "This took place in the manner described" (*jarā dhālika ka-dhālika*). We regard this document as either a later record of the judgment, which may have served as confirmation of the fact that the divorcee received the money from her former husband, as documented on its reverse side, or as the nonauthorized copy of the judge's *ḥukm* in a case in which authorization was not considered necessary.

These examples show that the *qāḍī*'s "appeal for God's proper guidance" to issue the *ḥukm* was not used to qualify his judgment at all stages of its documentation, despite its frequent use in the *shurūṭ* literature as part of a stock phrase.

---

[19] I will deal with the procedure of judicial ratification in a study on jurisdiction in Mamlūk Jerusalem, currently under preparation.

[20] ʿAsalī (1983–5, 2:19–20, ll. 15–8, no. 1).

The Request (su'āl) *for a Judgment*

Whereas the notion of "God's proper guidance" is not always mentioned in connection with the *ḥukm*, another legal detail is always recorded, even if only briefly: the fact that the claimant asked for the judgment. The legal requirement to ask for the *ḥukm* is made clear in document no. 653 by accentuating the judgment's conformity with the law: the judge issued the judgment in her favor after she had asked for it "in the legal manner" (*wa ḥakama lahā . . . baʿd suʾālihā dhālika ʿalā al-wajh al-sharʿī*, l. 18). All Ḥaram court records that contain a *ḥukm* mention this request. Sometimes this request is mentioned in a separate sentence, at other times it is signified by a passive participle indicating that the judgment was "*masʾūl*," requested.[21] Asyūṭī's manual for notaries also mentions the claimant's request for a *ḥukm* (*wa-saʾala al-khaṣm al-muddaʿī al-ḥukm*).[22]

The wording of the claimant's request for the *ḥukm* was certainly a stock formulation. This does not imply, however, that the request was a mere formality without consequences, as is clear in one claim regarding a sale of land, recorded by Asyūṭī: a first document ends with the transfer (*taslīm*) of the land to the new owner.[23] The claimant took possession of the land, thereby indicating that the claim had reached its objective. In addition, the transfer may be corroborated by a judgment on the basis of established legal facts, "if the buyer wishes." In this case, the scribe continues as follows, "Upon this act [of transfer] the above-mentioned buyer asked the judge to whom reference has been made to certify the testimonial evidence given in his presence and to issue a judgment with regard to it." (*fa-in ṭalaba al-mushtarī min al-ḥākim thubūt dhālika wa-l-ḥukm bi-mūjibihi kutiba baʿd dhikr al-taslīm "fa-ʿinda dhālika saʾala al-muddaʿī al-madhkūr min al-ḥākim al-mushār ilayhi bi-thubūt mā qāmat bihi al-bayyina al-sharʿiyya ʿindahu fīhi wa-l-ḥukm bihi."*)[24] Only then, in preparation for the judgment, was the other party, the defendant, summoned to make a deposition con-

---

[21] See document no. 32 in ʿAsalī (1983–5, 1:222, l. 7–8) and document 650 in Little (1982:11ff.) (*thumma saʾala . . . al-ḥukma bi- . . . fa-ḥakama [al-qāḍī]*). See as well document no. 334 in ʿAsalī (1983–85, 2:22–3) (*ḥakama . . . masʾūlan fī dhālika* [ll. 14ff.]).

[22] Cf. Asyūṭī (n.d.; 2:506, 508, 7f., 511 last line, and the last sentence of 512 to 513), as well as Ibn Abī al-Dam (1982:558).

[23] Asyūṭī (n.d., 2:505–6, until l. 3).

[24] Ibid., 2:506, ll. 4–6.

cerning the plaintiff's claim and evidence (*iʿdhār*). This act is represented in the sentence that follows the request for a judgment: "The above-mentioned defendant was summoned and he legally acknowledged (*iʿtarafa*) that he had no counterclaim, contestation, or anything else. This was legally certified." (*fa-aʿdhara lil-muddaʿā ʿalayhi al-madhkūr fa-iʿtarafa bi-ʿadam al-dāfiʿ wa-l-miṭʿan li-dhālika wa-li-shayʾ minhu al-iʿtirāf al-sharʿī wa-thabata iʿtirāfuhu bi-dhālika ladayhi thubūtan sharʿiyyan.*)[25]

We can now turn to the central concern of this essay. If a *qāḍī* issues a judgment (*ḥukm*) only after being asked to do so by a claimant,[26] and was not obligated to do so by his office, might he decide other litigations without issuing a *ḥukm*? Yes. Legal doctrine makes a clear legal distinction between an order (*amr*) or action (*fiʿl*) of a *qāḍī*, on the one hand, and his judgment (*ḥukm*), on the other. The judgment is binding only when he explicitly pronounces "*ḥakamtu bi-kadhā*".[27] If the *qāḍī* fails to pronounce this phrase, then the legal consequences of this action are not the same. In some legal domains, e.g., pronouncing the *talio* punishment (*qiṣāṣ*), it is forbidden to decide a case without giving a *ḥukm*; in others the omission of a *ḥukm* does not pose legal problems.[28] It is permissible, for example, for a creditor to accept money from his debtor on the simple order of the judge; no judgment was needed (*lā yakūn ḥukm*).[29]

Islamic legal literature in the Ayyubid and Mamlūk period cites many cases and decisions in which there is no mention of a *ḥukm*.[30] As noted, these examples cannot serve as decisive proof of the absence of a judgment, unless stated explicitly, since the compiler may have omitted the *ḥukm* for one reason or another. That *qāḍī*s settled disputes without issuing a *ḥukm* can be established beyond doubt by original documents. Two formal elements may help us determine if a case was decided without the passing of a judgment: first, the above-mentioned

---

[25] Ibid., ll. 6–8.

[26] Cf. also Veselý (1972:312–43, esp. 328 note 80).

[27] For the period that concerns us here, compare Ibn Abī al-Dam (1982:118ff.).

[28] Ibn Abī al-Dam (1982:119). On the requirement to issue a *ḥukm* in cases of *talio*, see the sample document in Asyūṭī (n.d., 2:287); the order to receive the blood money, on the contrary, is not declared as a *ḥukm*, ibid., 2:286. Cf. also Powers (1994:332–66, esp. 357). The document shows that there was no need for a *ḥukm* declaring the claimant's freedom.

[29] Ibid.

[30] Cf., e.g., Asyūṭī (n.d., 2:505), or Ibn Abī al-Dam (1982:562–5), where the *qāḍī*'s order, after witness evidence, to hand over the estate to the claimant, is not qualified as a *ḥukm*.

obligation for the *qāḍī* explicitly to pronounce the act of adjudication (*ḥakamtu*), and, secondly, the requirement to certify his *ḥukm* immediately afterwards. That is, legal doctrine regarded a judgment as valid only if the *qāḍī* summoned witnesses to attest to his judgment prior to the termination of the court session—his word regarding the judgment is not accepted after the fact.[31] This legal doctrine was applied strictly in the Ḥaram documents. As a consequence, we can be sure that documents lacking these formal elements—mention of a judgment and its attestation by witnesses—do in fact involve cases in which no *ḥukm* was issued.

Court Decisions Without Ḥukm*s—Do They Exist?*

Having established that a court decision without a binding judgment is theoretically possible, we will now try to identify some of these cases in the Ḥaram collection. Let us begin our enquiry with documents that contain reports on court proceedings in the *qāḍī*'s tribunal. In his *Catalogue*, Donald Little calls them—among other things—"court records" (Little 1984:262–70). The second group of his "court records," entitled "Proceedings initiated by Mamlūk officials" (ibid., 270–3), do not, with one exception (no. 645), report cases dealt with by the *qāḍī* in his capacity as judge.[32] For our purposes, we want to exclude from the present inquiry all "court records" that do not mention any intervention by the *qāḍī*, since we will never know whether or not the *qāḍī* settled these cases.[33] Among the group of "court records" that in fact report on court proceedings in the *qāḍī*'s tribunal, I will first present those cases with litigations over conflicting claims. These documents on litigations seem to be more

---

[31] Ibn Abī al-Dam (1982:178).

[32] Document no. 335 records a court session by the Mamlūk Viceroy of Jerusalem (*nā'ib al-salṭana*) in the presence of the *qāḍī* Abū 'l-Rūḥ and a police officer. Document no. 30 is a written testimony, issued in response to the request of a Mamlūk police officer to the *qāḍī* for sending his court witnesses to inspect the victims of a murder that was allegedly committed in the course of a village feud. Similar to this, document no. 642 concerns the inspection of a wounded person by witnesses sent from the *qāḍī* court. Document no. 706 describes royal orders and legal procedures to send the estate of the Damascene chief *qāḍī*'s son from its depository at the al-Aqṣā-Mosque to Egypt. Document no. 223 attests to obligations by village chiefs vis-à-vis the waqf administration (*majlis naẓar al-awqāf al-sharīfa*).

[33] Documents nos. 219, 455, 488, 500, 628, 671, and 698.

relevant to our inquiry than other "court records," in which the *qāḍī* did not have to choose between conflicting rights, but brought the court procedure to an end by certifying certain legal facts.[34] In the following, I summarize these litigations, focusing on how they were settled and on the decisions taken by the court.

In the first two cases, neither a woman contemplating death nor an heir had disclosed the entirety of the estate, in order to prevent the division of certain properties according to inheritance rules. Both litigations were based on information presented by unnamed persons that cast suspicion upon the parties and their witnesses, who were duly punished:

> In the first case, on 16 Ramaḍān 796, testimony was given at the Shāfiʿī court in Jerusalem: with the *qāḍī*'s permission, an unnamed person informed [the court] that when Zaynab, who was weak (*ḍaʿīfa*), entered the Ṣalāḥiyya Hospital of the city, she did not mention (*dhakarat*) all of the property that belonged to her. Some items belonging to her, including 100 dinars, were now in the possession of a Muḥammad al-Miṣrī. In response to an order by the *qāḍī*, the witnesses testifying in the document proceeded to meet Zaynab. When asked, she mentioned (*dhakarat*) that the designated items were indeed in the possession of Muḥammad. He was summoned to the tribunal. After denying possession at the beginning of the interrogation, he acknowledged (*iʿtarafa*) possession when threatened with incarceration. [The witnesses] made their way to his dwelling in Jerusalem and found many objects, all itemized in the document. Muḥammad's breach of law was proved to the *qāḍī*. This resulted in his loss of integrity (*ʿadāla*), trust (*amāna*) and trustworthiness, and the necessary legal measures were taken against him. The *qāḍī* certified the content of this document.[35]

As a result of the information given to the court by the unnamed person, those items not specified by Zaynab when she entered the hospital were declared as belonging to her and thus became part of her estate which, if she had no heirs, went to the Public Treasury.

---

[34] The following "court records" do not concern litigation and will not be presented in detail: in document no. 75 the claimants declare their claim of blood money and exclude the *talio*. No decision of a *qāḍī* is mentioned. Document no. 620 is the draft of a court report. One person accepts the nomination of another as *shaykh* of a *khānqāh* and takes the oath to abstain from any claim. A court decision is not mentioned, nor was it necessary. Document no. 847 attests to the declaration and oath of village chiefs that they had paid their taxes in arrears, a fact attested to by witnesses.

[35] Document no. 615 (my summary). The document is briefly described in Little (1984:266).

In this document, all actions taken by the informant and the witnesses were sanctioned or ordered by the *qāḍī*, without any mention of a *ḥukm*. Muḥammad al-Miṣrī's behavior, classified as a "breach of law," was sanctioned, although the terms of his punishment were not of interest to the scribe, who also does not specify whether the punishment was based on a *ḥukm*—a possibility that cannot be excluded.

The second case involved a woman who died leaving her mother and the Public Treasury as heirs. The succession was carried out during several court sessions spanning a period of time.

> On 16 Dhū 'l-Qaʿda 793, the following testimony was recorded: The Shāfiʿī *qāḍī* in Jerusalem had been informed by the *ustādār* of the Viceroy of Jerusalem in a letter that the mother had hidden some precious items belonging to her daughter and had not declared them as part of the estate. When first summoned to court, the mother claimed that her daughter had sold those items in Damascus before her death, but she could not provide evidence for this. A few days later, the mother declared in court that the items had been stolen on her way from Damascus to Jerusalem. However, one witness declared that he himself had traveled with the caravan in question, but neither the deceased woman nor her mother participated in the journey. Thereupon, the mother presented to the Mamlūk Viceroy a bundle of precious cloths and declared that they belonged to her. She produced two witnesses to this effect who attested to the fact that the property belonged to her. When asked by the *qāḍī*, the first witness declared that he followed the testimony of his companion, and the second witness attested that the mother had purchased these items in Cairo. The mother, on the other hand, declared that she had inherited these items from her own mother. Confronted with this contradiction, which made the *qāḍī* invalidate the witnesses' testimony, the mother finally acknowledged that the items did in fact belong to the deceased woman, her dead daughter. This was certified by the *qāḍī* and attested to by court witnesses. The two witnesses were punished and imprisoned by the *qāḍī* for false testimony (*amara bi-taʿzīrihimā wa-ḥabbasahumā*). No judgment is mentioned.[36]

The next case was a litigation over money:

> On 18 Dhū 'l-Qaʿda 796, testimony was given at the Shāfiʿī court of Abū 'l-Rūḥ that one *shaykh* from Ramalla claimed 420 dirhams from a reciter of the Qur'ān in Jerusalem. When the defendant denied the

[36] Document no. 645, edited by ʿAsalī (1983–5, 2:129ff., no. 46).

> claim, the claimant demanded that he swear an oath to this effect. The judge gave the written order for this oath (*rasama bi-taḥlīf*), and the witnesses to the document proceeded, accompanied by the claimant and the defendant, to the al-Aqṣā Mosque, where the witnesses asked the defendant to swear the oath. He swore in their presence that he did not owe the claimant 420 dirhams, and they attested to this.[37]

In this case, the claimant did not have witness evidence to support his claim. The *qāḍī* accepted the claim but required the defendant to take the oath. This order is not called a *ḥukm*, but a *marsūm* (decree, from *rasama*). Unless he could produce evidence in support of his claim, the claimant had no further legal recourse, and he certainly was not interested in having this situation established as a *ḥukm*. The defendant, on the other hand, might demand the issuance of a judgment on the basis of his oath in the form of a *qaḍāʾ tark* (temporary judgment),[38] but there is no indication to this effect on the document.

Another document records a request to sell chattels from the estate of minor heirs:

> On 11 Dhū 'l-Qaʿda 793, testimony was given at the Shāfiʿī court in Jerusalem that a "legal claimant" (*muddaʿī sharʿī*) requested that several slaves and a mule be sold from the estate of the late al-Badrī, Confidential Secretary in Damascus, who had left minor children. According to the claimant, the sale would be in the interest of the minor heirs because of the expenses involved in maintaining the chattels and the risk that they might die. The judge required witness evidence and its court certification. This took place, and our document enumerates the witnesses' names and their testimony in court. The judge listened to and accepted them as witnesses. Then he had the court witnesses attest to the certification of his court session, as well as to his permitting (*idhn*) the sale to the highest bidder.[39]

The *qāḍī*'s decision to allow the sale of the slaves and the mule, once the required witness testimony had been established, is characterized as his "permission" (*idhn*, 1.18), not as a "judgment" (*ḥukm*). Since the court procedure was completed, and the document was signed by witnesses and ratified by the judge, we assume that this

---

[37] Document no. 648, edited by ʿAsalī (1983–5, 2:28, no. 4).

[38] See Johansen (1990:15f.).

[39] Document no. 649, edited and translated by Little (1982:18–21, and by ʿAsalī (1983–5, 2:25, no. 3). See photograph on p. 69.

file was finished. We would not expect a *ḥukm* in this case.[40] Clearly, the *ḥukm* of the *qāḍī* was not required to allow the sale of chattels from the estate of minors.

The following record deals with a claim for transferring the estate of a deceased person to the guardian of his minor children. This estate included debt certificates by people who owed money to the deceased.

> On 5 Ramaḍān 795, testimony was given at the Shāfiʿī court in Jerusalem [confirming] that Jamāl al-Dīn ʿAbd Allāh, guardian of the estate of his late brother, had presented a judicial decree (*marsūm*) issued and certified in Damascus concerning the bequest of his brother. He asked the judge Abū 'l-Rūḥ to place the property of his brother's children under his control, in accordance with the bequest and the Damascene decree. This being in the orphans' interest, the *qāḍī* Abū 'l-Rūḥ gave his written permission in the month of Rajab, but asked for a court certificate of the deceased's legal competence (*ahliyya*) and [financial?] situation (*ḥāl*). In response to this request, the claimant produced a *maḥḍar*, issued by the former *qāḍī* of Jerusalem, Taqī 'l-Dīn, which was then certified by Abū 'l-Rūḥ. Thereupon the *qāḍī* ordered the delivery of the orphans' money and debt certificates, which had been kept by the deputy judge (*khalīfat al-ḥukm*), to the claimant. The document specifies that the guardian, ʿAbd Allāh, had in fact received everything, and it then lists the names of all debtors and the amount of the debts.[41]

Neither the decree by the Damascene judge nor the permission of the *qāḍī* Abū 'l-Rūḥ to deliver the estate to the orhans' uncle is qualified as a *ḥukm*. The file ends with the handing over of the estate, previously deposited with a fiduciary, to the orphans' guardian. It seems that the debt certificates (*masāṭir sharʿiyya*) were not paid immediately and remained in the form of obligations. The *qāḍī* Abū 'l-Rūḥ noted at the top of the document that the procedure was carried out as described. Now, one may object that court records do not mention whether or not a nonlocal *qāḍī*'s decision was a judgment (*ḥukm*). This objection, however, is not valid, as court record no. 606 illustrates regarding a confirmation of a *waqf* in Jerusalem: this record mentions that the claimant presented a parchment document containing the *ḥukm* of a Damascene deputy judge regarding the validity of the *waqf*.[42]

Thus, some of the "court records" from the Ḥaram collection end

---

[40] In his summary of the case, Little (1982:22) states that he "gave his judgment."
[41] Document no. 709, not edited; cf. Little (1984:269).
[42] Document no. 606, l. 12, not edited; cf. Little (1984:265–6).

with a final court decision that is not qualified as a *ḥukm*. Documents 648, 649, and 709 record cases that did not require any further decision in the form of a *ḥukm*.

Other documents in the Ḥaram collection indicate that litigations might end without a *ḥukm*. I will limit my attention to two specimens that record separate procedures relating to one case in several distinct documents on the same piece of paper. Both specimens begin with the petitioner's solicitation (*su'āl*) of the judge for a court audience and the drafting of a "*maḥḍar*."[43] In these and other examples, the solicitation (*su'āl*) is accompanied by a document, as demanded by the petitioner, and, also by its judicial certification on the *verso*. By comparing all documents issued as a consequence of the *su'āl*, we learn that the term "*maḥḍar*" here was understood in the narrow sense of Mamlūk chancellery usage, as defined by Ibn Abī al-Dam: The scribe attests that those [witnesses] who record their testimony (at the end of the document) know the person, and that he did such and such. As a special form, this *maḥḍar* may also concern a *qāḍī* and his action in court.[44]

The first example concerns a lost camel.

> The petitioner reports that he lost a camel that he subsequently found in the possession of a man named ʿUmar b. Abī Bakr. He can prove this and asks for a *maḥḍar* to this effect. The *qāḍī* granted his request and, in a second document on the same piece of paper, dated 18 Muḥarram 794, we find witnesses attesting to their knowledge of the claimant, a Bedouin from Karak, who owned a herd of camels and had lost one of them. The witnesses knew that this camel had been found in the possession of the thief ʿUmar. When summoned to court, ʿUmar claimed to have purchased the camel from a criminal companion and that his companion's possession of the camel was illegal (*ghalaṭ*). The sale of the camel to ʿUmar was unknown to the witnesses of the document. The same witnesses testified to all this in the presence of the judge, except for the assertion that the camel had been purchased by ʿUmar. The text then mentions that this document was written with the *qāḍī*'s permission. On the left column of the *verso*, the *qāḍī* had his court witnesses attest to the testimonial evidence on the *recto*, and on the right column of the *verso*, witnesses attested to the fact that the petitioner had received the camel described in the document.[45]

[43] See Little (1984:44ff.).

[44] Ibn Abī al-Dam (1982:553). The other, larger usage of *maḥḍar* in the general sense of describing court procedure, that is a court record, is called "*mithāl sharḥ al-majlis*" by this 7th/13th century author, ibid., 561ff. On the *maḥḍar* issued under the supervision of a *qāḍī*, see also Veselý (1972:326).

[45] Document no. 718, not edited; cf. Little (1984:48f.).

The first decision by the *qāḍī* was to accept the claim and to draw up a *maḥḍar* concerning the claimant's evidence. The *qāḍī* must have questioned the defendant, who tried to give a legally valid explanation for his possession of the camel. Thereupon the *qāḍī* ordered the writing of this complex *maḥḍar*, which also described the events in court. It is not mentioned anywhere that the judge passed a *ḥukm*. Apparently, the drafting of this *maḥḍar* and its subsequent certification (*thubūt*) were sufficient to solve the problem: only one day after the court session, the claimant received his lost property. Whether or not the thief, either the defendant or his companion, was punished, and how, is not addressed in the document.

The second case concerns the recovery of deposited items.

> The petitioner reports that he had deposited certain items with the late Yaḥyā, *shaykh* of the *zāwiyā* of Muḥammad Bāk, which he now wants to reclaim. He has witness evidence for this and he asks the *qāḍī* to listen to his case and to write it down. The *qāḍī* grants this request and, in a second document, beneath the request, witnesses attest, during the middle ten days of Dhū 'l-Ḥijja 793, with the *qāḍī*'s permission, that the petitioner had deposited with the deceased five new saddlebags (*khurj*, pl. *khirja*), a sword, eleven Florin and 105 dirhams. Following the order (*tawqīʿ*), it is reported in a third document, dated 20 Dhū 'l-Ḥijja, that the petitioner swore an oath confirming the testimonial evidence, that he was entitled to receive these items, and that he had not reclaimed them at an earlier date. A separate notice attests that, on the same day, the "officer of inheritances" (*shādd al-mawārīth*) had been summoned to court (*iʿdhār*), but had offered no objection. On the same day, the *qāḍī* Abū 'l-Rūḥ had all these procedures attested: the certification of witness testimony in court, the petitioner's oath, the officer's lack of objections and his summoning of witnesses (*ishhād*). As a result, the items were handed over to the claimant.[46]

Here the *qāḍī* accepts the request, orders the plaintiff to swear an oath, and listens to the officer of inheritances, whereupon he has all this certified and attested. Without any mention of a *ḥukm*, the claimant receives his property. A special *ḥukm* to confirm this legal fact is not necessary. Document no. 616[47] deals with a similar case, except that no "officer of inheritances" is summoned to give his *iʿdhār*. Here also, no *ḥukm* is issued. The court procedure used to re-

---

[46] Document no. 719, not edited; cf. Little (1984:49f.).
[47] Edited in Little (2001:179–81 and 185–7).

solve these litigations was limited to the judicial certification of established facts (*thubūt*)—without passing a *ḥukm*.

Nowhere in the Ḥaram petitions to a judge soliciting the hearing of a case, nor in the resulting *maḥḍar*, does the solicitation (*su'āl*) mention a request for a *ḥukm*, nor was a *ḥukm* mentioned in the resulting judicial certification.[48] May we conclude from this that this kind of court petition did not result in a *ḥukm*? Six documents do not allow a definite answer. It is conceivable that the *qāḍī* issued a *ḥukm* when circumstances required a judgment. Possibly, however, a *ḥukm* in such cases was not certified together with the court petition, but on a new document.

Does the judicial certification of legally established facts (*thubūt*) constitute a judgment (*ḥukm*)? We have already noticed the importance of the *thubūt*, not only for the passing of a judgment, but also in litigations that ended without a judgment. The judge issued his orders concerning court procedure in a certain generally accepted way. In the complex specimens of court petitions and records, the *qāḍī* demanded that his witnesses attest to the established facts (*li-yushhad bi-thubūtihi*). This order, called *tawqīʿ*, was, in the case of the Ḥaram documents, always written in the right-hand margin of the document, upside down. Thereupon court witnesses attested to the certification of facts established in court. This certification document usually began with the stock phrase "Our lord and master summoned me to testify" (*ashhadanī sayyidunā wa-mawlānā*) and was written on the back of the record that was being certified. It named the judge's ascendants up to the third generation (to eliminate confusion between different judges), followed by what he established as fact (*annahu thabata ʿindahu*).

As already stated, some of these *tawqīʿ* notations mention the attestation not only of the established facts but also of the *qāḍī*'s binding judgment (*ḥukm*): *li-yushhad bi-thubūtihi wa-l-ḥukm bi-mūjibihi*.[49] This formulation was used by several different contemporary judges. Whenever the *qāḍī* ordered, through his *tawqīʿ*, the attestation of a *ḥukm*, the resulting certificate on the *verso* also contained, next to

[48] See also documents nos. 279, 654, and 719 (my copy of no. 368 is too defective to be read completely).

[49] See Ḥaram documents nos. 39, 209, 210, 211, 315, 355, and 853. It is interesting to note that none of these *tawqīʿ* orders that mention a *ḥukm* were delivered by the *qāḍī* Abū 'l-Rūḥ.

the established facts, the mention of a *ḥukm*. The attesting witnesses followed the judge's order exactly, as expressed in the *tawqīʿ*. The *tawqīʿ* notation was, by the way, written by the judge himself, and not by the scribe who wrote the *maḥḍar* or the certification document. This is established by comparing documents nos. 210 and 315, both written on the same day by different scribes. However, they represented claims to the same (Ḥanafī) judge, who responded with a judgment: the *tawqīʿ* notation by the same judge is identical in both cases!

Does the *tawqīʿ* notation attesting to a *ḥukm* apply to a judgment that the judge has just issued on the basis of facts established in the current court session; or does it refer to any *ḥukm* that had been passed during a litigation, even at earlier stages, and which may have resulted in further legal steps, as in the annulment of the emancipation of slaves and their subsequent sale, cited above? In some cases one can make the following point: some legal documents that the judge orders to be certified do not mention a *ḥukm*. In these cases, the *ḥukm* whose attestation the *qāḍī* requests must be the one that he issues in the course of the current court session.[50] Other specimens, in which the *qāḍī* orders the attestation of a *ḥukm* by his *tawqīʿ*, mention the necessity of a judgment in the text of the document. The sale contract for a house in the possession of the Public Treasury required a *ḥukm* to legalize transfer of the property to the purchaser.[51] The division of an estate that involved a deposit for absentees also required a *ḥukm*.[52] In these cases, a *ḥukm* was necessary for the intended legal result. Therefore, the document itself mentions the request. The documents in the first group, which do not mention a *ḥukm*, all concern a legal acknowledgment (*iqrār*), which does not require a *ḥukm* to be valid. In these acknowledgment documents, the *ḥukm* seems to result from a desire for additional security against contestation in the future.

The Ḥaram documents thus indicate a distinction between a *ḥukm* and the certification of established facts (*thubūt*). However, the legal literature discusses whether or not a *thubūt* is equivalent to a judgment (*ḥukm*), even if the judge does not say, "I ruled" (*ḥakamtu*). One

---

[50] See document nos. 209, 210, 211, and 315.

[51] Document no. 39, l. 13, mentions the *ḥukm*. No. 853 seems to be a similar case, although here the buyer acts on behalf of the minor children of his brother.

[52] See Little (1998:127–34).

opinion holds the *thubūt* to be a *ḥukm*, the other does not.[53] This was not merely an academic discussion among jurists. The opinion adopted might have serious consequences if the *qāḍī* wanted to revoke the *thubūt*, if a witness retracted his testimony, or if a claim were made against a dead person or an absentee.[54] Although it is clear that *ḥukm* and *thubūt* were not the same procedure in the Ḥaram documents (otherwise it would have made no sense to demand the attestation of the *ḥukm* and the *thubūt* in one case, but not to demand it in another), we may not rule out the possibility that both, despite differences in content and function, carried more or less the same legal status. Here more research needs to be done. The fact that not just some, but the majority, of *tawqīʿ* orders in the Ḥaram documents do not mention a *ḥukm* may indicate that the claimant did not request a *ḥukm*. Perhaps legal evidence was equivocal and prevented the issuance of a final judgment; or perhaps a *ḥukm* was expensive to obtain.

The study of documents from the Ḥaram collection has made it possible for us to analyze the distinction between judgment and certification in several specific cases. Sometimes, the *qāḍī*'s judgment created a new legal situation that was recorded on the document. Only one record ends with the passing of a judgment, while others mention subsequent events or the ratification of a *ḥukm*. Apparently, the *qāḍī* issued a judgment only if this had been requested by the claimant. Such a request was always mentioned in conjunction with the *ḥukm*. In some cases, but not all, the judge's *tawqīʿ* instructed his court witnesses to attest to the certification of established facts, as described in the text of the document, and to his judgment. The judgment referred to had been issued during the current court session by the judge himself.

Other litigations or claims were resolved through judicial certification (*thubūt*) without the expectation that a judgment might be needed to settle the dispute in the future. Legal theory allowed the *qāḍī* to resolve legal conflicts without passing a judgment, as his order (*amr*) or action (*fiʿl*) was distinguished from his judgment (*ḥukm*). As a consequence, not every case resulted in a judgment. This leaves one final consideration: if, as demonstrated here, an effective *qāḍī*

---

[53] Ibn Abī al-Dam (1982:161).
[54] Ibid., 161f., with a discussion of the consequences.

jurisdiction did not need to issue a *ḥukm* in every case, our perspective on the *ḥukm* as an indicator of historical facts changes. The mentioning of a *ḥukm* in historical sources is not the sole indicator of the efficacy of *qāḍī* jurisdiction. The issuance or nonissuance of a *ḥukm* may have been due to the specific content of the cases. The *ḥukm* was essential in some legal fields, like *talio*, and it was often used to protect long-term contracts, but it was not required in other domains of the law, e.g., the restitution of stolen goods.[55] A court certification (*thubūt*) not only served to affirm already existing legal facts, but also constituted an instrument to resolve legal conflicts that did not require a formal *qāḍī* judgment.

[55] Document no. 75 attests to the claimant's choice for blood money instead of *talio*. It does not mention a *ḥukm*, which is only essential if the *talio* was to be executed—see above. Asyūṭī (n.d., 2:505) gives an example of agricultural land requiring a *ḥukm*.

بسم الله الرحمن الرحيم

Ḥaram Document no. 649, published with kind permission of the Museum of al-Ḥaram al-Sharīf in Jerusalem.

CHAPTER THREE

A NEW JUDGE FOR AINTAB: THE SHIFTING LEGAL ENVIRONMENT OF A SIXTEENTH-CENTURY OTTOMAN COURT

Leslie Peirce

On June 23, 1541, a new judge, one Hüsameddin Efendi, arrived in the provincial city of Aintab. A month before his arrival, news of his appointment by the Ottoman regime had been hailed in the daily register of the city's court. Three days after Hüsameddin Efendi took up his post in person, the judicial residence was physically expanded. Larger official quarters suggested a judge of greater stature than his predecessors. Indeed, that Hüsameddin Efendi was endowed with expanded authority was immediately made clear to the court's constituents. Why a powerful judge appeared at this moment in the city's history and how his authority was received or rejected by the people of Aintab is the subject of this essay.

Located in the transition zone between southeastern Anatolia and northern Syria, Aintab can best be characterized as a regional economic and cultural center. The city had surrendered to Ottoman forces in 1516 on the eve of the Ottoman conquest of the Mamluk empire. Although the Ottoman regime paid immediate attention to the metropolitan centers of its newly conquered domain—Cairo, Damascus, and Aleppo—by appointing Ottoman judges and, in the case of Cairo at least, expanding the number of "courthouses," it was only some twenty years later that the regime began to pay attention to smaller provincial capitals such as Aintab.[1] It is this process of grass-roots imperialization of the legal system that forms the backdrop for this essay, which is based on study of a thirteen-month

[1] For the appointment of judges, see M.A. Bakhit (1982); on the proliferation of court-houses and on the systematic aspects of sixteenth-century Ottoman legal innovations in general, see Hanna (1995).

period in the life of the Aintab court.[2] Of particular interest is the dialogue between local residents and the new sovereign via the judge over the place and meaning of law in daily life. Indeed, the local court was a critical venue where sovereign and subject negotiated mutual claims to the legitimacy of their views on law and society.[3]

Beginning in the mid-1530s, there were numerous signs that Aintab was undergoing integration into the empire's fiscal, military, and legal systems. In 1536 and 1543, extensive cadastral surveys—the famous, and in the eyes of some, notorious, Ottoman inventories of local taxpayers and taxable revenues—were ordered for Aintab province. The 1536 survey was accompanied by the first provincial law code for Aintab issued by the Ottoman regime. This simultaneity of survey and law code demonstrates the intimate connection between uses of the land for fiscal purposes and the legal regime of the Ottoman state. As for judicial administration itself, a major sign of change stimulated by the imperializing thrust of the Ottoman regime in Aintab was the inception of a public court record. The practice of keeping the written protocols of judges as a *public* record seems to have been an Ottoman innovation. The question is not the keeping of written records per se, but rather requiring that records "should be deposited in a public domain," to use Wael Hallaq's formulation (Hallaq 1998; Mandaville 1966:311). Although Aintab undoubtedly had a well-established court before the 1530s, it is only from that decade on that records began to survive.

Another sign of the Aintab court's absorption into an empire-wide

---

[2] The records from the year studied here are contained in two registers: the first, numbered 161 in the series of Aintab registers, covers the period from September 15, 1540, through May 19, 1541 (in the Islamic calendar, 12 Cemaziülevvel 947 to 22 Muharrem 948); the second, numbered 2, from May 25, 1541, to October 3, 1541 (29 Muharrem 948 to 11 Cemaziülaher 948). These registers are the second and third in the series of some 180 registers comprising the court records of Aintab (today's Gaziantep); the first register was unavailable to scholars when I was doing my research (with the exception of Istanbul, the court records from cities in the Republic of Turkey are housed in the National Library in Ankara). The earliest Aintab records reportedly date from 935 H (1528–29), and the latest from 1327 H (1918–19).

I have abbreviated references from the Aintab court records as follows: AS stands for Aintab Sicili; AS 161:132c, for example, cites the third entry (*sicill*) on page 132 of the register numbered 161 in the series of Gaziantep court registers.

For making my research in the court records both possible and pleasant, I would like to thank Dursun Kaya and the staff of the Ibni Sina Manuscript and Rare Books division of the National Library.

[3] For further development of the themes of this essay, see Peirce (2003).

legal system was the appointment from Istanbul, capital of the empire, of the new judge, Hüsameddin Efendi. As noted above, three days after the new judge's arrival in the city, the judicial compound was physically expanded through the donation of an adjoining property.[4] Enhanced authority and enlarged space were immediately reflected in the legal life of the province. The court's case load in the next few months was twice what it had been in preceding months, and new kinds of cases were brought before the judge. It is not difficult to imagine a range of transformations proceeding from Hüsameddin Efendi's reorganization of his jurisdiction: the more efficient processing of petitioners and suspects through the judicial compound, instructions to police authorities to be alert for previously unmonitored offenses, and the correspondingly adjusted legal strategies of the court's local users.

I want to explore the meanings of these changes in Aintab's legal status by looking at one case that came before the new judge in the summer of 1541. This case takes us into a social domain that became increasingly conflicted as a result of the new legal developments: the question of proper contact between the sexes. In state law of the period, that is, in the imperial law book that was periodically updated and re-issued by the Ottoman sultans of the fifteenth and sixteenth centuries, social intercourse between adult females and males who were not closely related was increasingly criminalized. Of central significance to this essay, the law book, or *kanunname*, of Sultan Süleyman (r. 1520–1566) is thought to have been issued some time between 1539 and 1541.[5] In the section in Süleyman's law book "On illicit sex and related matters" (*der beyan-ı zina ve gayri*), many penalties were introduced that had not appeared in the law books of his father or grandfather.[6] As for Aintab, the rise in cases involving male-female contact in the court of Hüsameddin Efendi suggests that these new rules went into application immediately upon his arrival. In other words, Hüsameddin Efendi may in fact have been responsible for introducing the sultan's new law book to the province of Aintab. The case examined here, in which the woman Ayşe was seen emerging from the house of her neighbor, Saadeddin, in the early hours

[4] AS 2:50d.
[5] On the dating of Süleyman's law book, see Heyd (1973:24–7).
[6] For the criminal penalties in Süleyman's law book, see Heyd (1973). For Beyazid II, see Akgündüz (1990), and for Selim I, see Pulaha and Yücel (1995).

of the morning, is one in which the suspects successfully defended themselves. Other cases, however, did not have as benign an outcome.

The case of Ayşe and Saadeddin most probably would not have come to court before the arrival of the new judge in June 1541. In other words, their conduct would not have constituted a prosecutable offense. The larger point of this essay is to emphasize that the local court operated within a set of shifting frames—the political, the social, the religiolegal—that placed limits on the autonomy and predictability of the legal process. In other words, normative law in action was deeply conditioned by local contingencies. This may seem a banal statement, but it is a point that is often overlooked in the study of Islamic legal institutions and practices. The following discussion looks closely at legal events in Aintab during the summer of 1541 in an attempt to demonstrate the interactive process that gave meaning to legal rules and the quotidian nature of socio-legal change.

The New Judge

The appointment of Hüsameddin Efendi to the judgeship of Aintab had an impact on the court that is immediately discernible in its written records. Shortly after the new judge took up office, new kinds of legal problems began to be aired at court. For example, murder cases started to be adjudicated under the judge's oversight, and women now brought property claims against male family members, something they had not done in the preceding nine months. And, as mentioned above, sexual misconduct was increasingly prosecuted under the auspices of the court as scrutiny of male-female contact in public spaces, and even in private spaces, intensified. This broadening in the scope of the court's work led to an expanded case load: the court now averaged twice as many cases per week as it did during the preceeding eight months.[7]

In and of itself, the new judgeship represented a significant shift in the legal politics of Aintab. But the appointment of Hüsameddin Efendi was only one of a cluster of events occurring in May and June of 1541 that suggest a major intervention of imperial author-

[7] Records comprising the first eight months of this study are contained in Aintab Sicili 161, where a week's work took up an everage of 10.3 folios. The remaining four months, contained in Aintab Sicili 2, averaged 20.1 folios per week.

ity in the management of the province's affairs. In late May, a government-appointed agent (*havale*), Gulamşahi Ahmed Çelebi, appeared in Aintab with the assignment of disciplining errant tax-farmers—in particular, one prominent tax-farmer who belonged to one of the three notable families (*ayan*) of Aintab. It was during the four-week stint in Aintab of Ahmed Çelebi, whose work suggests that he was a kind of special prosecutor, that the court's pace began to pick up (his work ended just as the new judge arrived). Other innovations were also evident: for example, the work of the market inspector (*muhtasip*) began to be carried out under the auspices of the court, with instances of poor workmanship and defective products now recorded in the court's register.

It is surely not coincidental that the prosecutor began his investigations just as Aintab received the news of Hüsameddin Efendi's appointment—indeed, he may have been the bearer of the appointment letter to the city. And on June 18, five days before the new judge arrived in Aintab, a new provincial governor was appointed to the province, one whose rank outclassed that of his predecessor.[8] Aintab, it would seem, was coming under invigorated government scrutiny in the early summer of 1541. It was also being upgraded as a provincial administrative center.

What gave the new judge his ample authority? It seems likely that Hüsameddin Efendi was among the first judges—perhaps the very first—to be appointed to Aintab by the Ottoman government. In the traditional practice of Muslim states, followed by the Ottoman sultanate, judges were appointed by the ruling authority. But this normative practice was not always observed or even observable. For example, we need to be careful about assuming that the practice was applied immediately in the vast heartland of the Middle East following its conquest in 1516–1517. Naturally, the Ottoman regime moved swiftly to control the metropolises of the newly conquered territories. The sultan Selim I appointed a governor, a judge, and a treasurer for Aleppo right after his decisive victory over Mamluk forces in August 1516, before the Ottoman army moved on to take Damascus and Cairo.[9] But it took time for the regime to turn its attention to

---

[8] AS 2:93a.

[9] Feridun Beg (1880–81:399). The governor was Karaca Paşa, the judge Çömlekçizade Kemal Çelebi, and the treasurer was the former *timarlar defterdarı* of Rumeli, Abdülkerim Beg.

the full administrative assimilation of lesser provincial cities like Aintab.

This is not to say that the judges preceding Hüsameddin Efendi were weak or incompetent. The records of 1540–1541 give every sign that Aintab's was a well-functioning court. Court users in 1540–1541 sometimes brought copies of judicial decrees issued in earlier years to support their suits, demonstrating that the practice of "anticipating consequences," which rested on the assumption of the court's continuing effectiveness, was not new.[10] Rather, what I want to suggest is that previous judges may have been local in origin. In the period of relative political insecurity preceding the Ottoman conquest, the cosmopolitan networks of training and appointment of religious officials characteristic of more settled times were breaking down. Jon Mandaville has shown that judicial offices in the Syrian cultural and administrative center of Damascus were becoming the monopoly of a closed corporation of local families (Mandaville 1969:20–23). The same was likely to have been true of Aintab, which may have drawn on its own educational resources and those of nearby urban centers.

Who was this new judge, Hüsameddin Efendi, who assumed the Aintab judgeship in June 1541? It would be wonderful to know, since the mentality and even the personal quirks of provincial judges were critical not only to the practice of law but also to the quality of civic culture in the cities and towns in which they served. Despite the apparent significance of Hüsameddin's tenure as Aintab judge, we know his name only because his appointment was conspicuously hailed in the court register on May 25, 1541, with the following notice on its opening page:

> The news came that the judgeship of Aintab, the well-protected, has been granted to Hüsameddin Efendi, may his virtue increase; read at the sitting of the court and inscribed on the 29th of the month of Muharram in the year 948.[11]

[10] One of many examples is a case in which Hasan sued Ismail to recover three years' worth of child support that Ismail had contracted to pay for his small daughter, engaged to Hasan's son and living in Hasan's home (AS 2:185b). Hasan won because "he produced a copy of the decree of the former judge, which had been written in the month of Şaʿban in the year 944 (January 1538); it was found that the sum of 1.5 akçes per day had been decided upon."

[11] AS 2:1a.

But nowhere else in the 330 pages of the register was this judge named again, although on June 23 a brief line was penned announcing "the arrival of His Honor" in Aintab. No similar announcement of the judge (or judges) who served during the preceding nine months studied here is evident in the records. The names of some former judges of Aintab—Küçük Ali, Seyyid Cafer, Pir Mehmed—can be determined because litigants occasionally dated a previous court appearance by stating who had been in office at the time; the terms of service of these individuals, however, cannot be dated.[12]

Although clearly a pivotal element in the court's work, judges are only dimly present in the written record. Unlike Ottoman courts in some other places and times, judges in the 16th-century Aintab records did not sign their rulings.[13] Their personal decision-making role is revealed only indirectly in the phrase "it was ruled" (*hükm-olunub* . . .). In other words, if one knew nothing about the structure of the Ottoman legal system, one could not tell from the court records that there was in fact a judge presiding. Litigants, witnesses, arbitrators, and police agents bringing cases to court—all these individuals are named and verbally present in the court record, but the judge, situated at the nexus of religion, state, and community, is, as an individual, virtually nameless and textually silent.

What sort of a person was Hüsameddin Efendi? Ideally, it is essential to a study of this sort to know the identity of the provincial judge, the quality of his education, and the trajectory of his career. But biographies of religious officials of this period, contained in collective works composed in the sixteenth and seventeenth centuries, rarely include men who made their mark as provincial judges. The biographic encyclopedia was a historically common Islamic literary genre, but it focussed on the life stories of scholars, teachers, jurists, and more prominent judges.[14] The Ottoman compendia reflect the

---

[12] These judges are named in AS 2:25b, 76b, 206b, 302b.

[13] For example, in Jerusalem court records dating from the 1550s onward, the judge was named in the first line of each entry; see Cohen and Simon-Piqali (1993: nos. 325, 353).

[14] The major Ottoman biographical compendia for the sixteenth century are Ahmed Taşköprüzade's *Al-Shaqā'iq al-nu'mānīya,* of which an expanded Turkish translation was done by Mehemmed Mecdi, *Hada'ik ul-şaka'ik,* which includes biographies of religious figures through the middle of Süleyman's reign; picking up where these works leave off is Nev'izade Ata'i's *Hada'ik ül-haka'ik fi tekmilet üş-şaka'ik.* On these works, see Repp (1986:3–7).

typical bias against provincial judges. They also exhibit a bias toward the imperial core of the empire, that is, toward figures whose careers circulated around Istanbul and the two former capitals, Bursa (in northwest Anatolia) and Edirne (in European Thrace). Despite the fact that judges, jurists, and scholars studied the same curriculum in religious sciences, the stereotype held that judges were inevitably compromised in their pursuit of a religious career by going on the payroll of the state and by having to make worldly concessions in their official judgments. Judges who made it into the major biographical encyclopedias were therefore likely to have made their principal mark as scholars and teachers. In short, the provincial judge had a harder time creating a reputation that was thought worthy of being memorialized. But the reality was that many sixteenth-century products of Ottoman educational institutions who began their professional lives as teachers soon opted for the career of provincial judge because the salary of a judge was higher than that of a scholar in the short run, although the ladder of opportunity was considerably shorter in the long run (Repp 1986:55–6).

As for Aintab, the biographical compendia yield no matches for the Aintab judges who preceded Hüsameddin. There is, however, a Molla Hüsameddin whose brief biography in the compendium composed by Nevʿizade Ataʾi, *The Gardens of Truth*, makes him a possible candidate for the judgeship of Aintab in 1541 (Ataʾi 1851–52:11–12). (Molla was a title for individuals with a religious education and employment as judge, teacher, or jurisconsult; all the judges of Aintab carried the honorific title "Efendi" after their given names—e.g., Molla Hüsameddin Efendi.) The Hüsameddin described in *The Gardens of Truth* was clearly a successful provincial judge who may have originally wished for the preferred career of scholar/teacher. Born and apparently educated in central Anatolia, Hüsameddin devoted himself to the career of judge shortly after beginning his professional life in 1523 with a brief stint as teacher. He had begun his career in the not untypical pattern of acquiring a patron; in his case, he entered the personal service of a retired judge of Edirne. When the latter died, Hüsameddin received an entry-level teaching post, but shortly thereafter resigned to become a judge. According to his biographer, he served in a great many choice assignments until his death in 1554, making him "an envy-inspiring high-ranking molla."

Ataʾi, however, gives no specifics about where Hüsameddin actually served, perhaps because, composing his work in the seventeenth century, he recorded only what was remembered about this figure from a century earlier. Whatever the case, Molla Hüsameddin was recalled as a stern and dignified individual, "notorious for his firmness and integrity in the performance of his office, counted among judges as grave and well-mannered, a dread-inspiring, venerable magistrate." Given his reputation for toughness, he was well named, for Hüsameddin means "the sharp sword of religion." Ata'i's Hüsameddin appears to be a judge's judge, a knowledgeable, experienced, and decisive individual. It seems that the molla's appearance was as impressive as his demeanor, for he was nicknamed Papas ("the priest") Hüsam "because of the thickness of his beard, which had an extraordinarily noble and pleasing appearance."

This is not to claim that the Hüsameddin of Ata'i's compendium was the individual dispatched to Aintab in the summer of 1541. We have only plausible dates, Anatolian origins (Hüsameddin's patron was also from central Anatolia), and a personality that could explain the increased rigor observable in the court during the summer of 1541. But even if the biographied individual was not the judge who came to Aintab in 1541, he serves as an example of what the historical record can tell us about provincial judges of the sixteenth century. If, on the other hand, the Hüsameddin of the biography should happen to be our man, his appointment to Aintab tells us that the Aintab judgeship ranked as a relatively important provincial post. According to *The Gardens of Truth*, Hüsameddin was a "300-akçe judge", that is, a middle to high rank for provincial service.[15] That Aintab was an important provincial post is confirmed for the mid-seventeenth century by the famous Ottoman courtier and traveller, Evliya Çelebi, who noted that it was by then a 500-akçe judgeship (Çelebi 1935:353).

Surveillance and Slander: Monitoring Male-Female Contact

On July 20, Hüsameddin Efendi heard the case of the suspect neighbors. In this incident, the man Saadeddin, the woman Ayşe, and

[15] These terms should not be understood as indicating actual incomes received by judges. On the meaning of the ranking of judgeships as "500-akçe," "300-akçe," etc., see Uzunçarşılı (1988:87ff.); Repp (1986:33ff.).

her husband Haci Mehmed were brought to court by a local police official on the grounds of suspected illicit association between Ayşe and Saadeddin. This hearing was then followed by a second, which grew out of Ayşe's cursing one of the two men who informed against her. The affair of Ayşe and her accusers is an obvious case of social surveillance by members of the community. Its context was in part the legal climate generated by the new judge, who had been in office for a month when the neighbors came to court. But the case is also one of resistance by the surveilled, who asserted that the neighborly contact was just that—neighbors helping neighbors. Ayşe's attack on the informant Cuma (she called him a pimp) can be read as her way of restoring her honor by slurring the reputations of the informants.

Here is the full record of the affair, entered into the court register as two separate cases, or *sicill*s:

> *the first sicill*
> Arab, Chief of the night watch, came to court and summoned the individuals named Saadeddin son of Haci Süleyman and Ayşe daughter of Halil and her husband Haci Mehmed, and said: "This woman was seen coming out of Saadeddin's house at daybreak. They are not closely related. What business does she have in his house?" When the aforementioned Saadeddin was questioned, he answered: "I owed her 90 silver pieces; she came to ask for it. Also, my little son was sick. The previous evening I had sent my little son to ask for a [nugget of sandalwood];[16] I thought perhaps she had come to bring it." When Haci Mehmed was asked the question "What business did your wife have in his house?", he said: "It was I who sent my wife; I told her to go get the money." What occurred was recorded.
>
> [Note appended to the record:] It was recorded that Haci Derviş and Cuma son of Derviş Mehmed said: "We saw the said woman coming out of Saadeddin's house during the day.... He owed us some money, we had come to collect the debt...."
>
> Witnessed by: Bozoğlan son of Abdullah; Ibrahim son of Ali; Mansur son of Neccar
>
> *the second sicill*
> Cuma son of Derviş Mehmed came to court and summoned Ayşe daughter of Halil, and said: "This woman slandered me by calling me

[16] The meaning of the phrase *sandal taşı* is unclear, although the context suggests it has something to do with curing the little boy. One meaning of *sandal* is white sandalwood (bot., *santalum album*), whose oil is used for medicinal purposes. I am grateful to Dr. Xingning Zhao of Ithaca, New York, for informing me that white sandalwood is used in traditional Asian medicine to treat a variety of illnesses; it is administered primarily in the form of an infusion.

> a pimp [*gidi*]." When the woman was questioned, she denied [the allegation]. When Cuma was asked for proof, the individuals named Bozoğlan son of Abdullah and Ali son of Mehmed testified as follows: "The said woman slandered Cuma by calling him a pimp." Upon acceptance [of their testimony], the foregoing was recorded at the request of Arab, Chief of the night watch.
> Witnessed by: Haci Derviş son of Ali Haci; Haci Ali b. Abdulrahman; Haci Mahmud the steward[17]

In order to locate this incident in the shifting frames of politics, social practice, and local legal culture, let us look at these two records in the context of legal principles operative in the mid-sixteenth century. The first of the two cases hinges on the prohibition of contact between males and females outside the degrees of kinship permitting men and women to mix freely. Such contact was forbidden in the view of religious law and of sultanic statute, but not, obviously, in the view of our protagonists: Ayşe, her husband Haci Mehmed, and their neighbor Saadeddin. Here is the relevant clause in Süleyman's law book, in which the term *zina* includes both adultery and fornication:

> If a woman is publicly spoken ill of in connection with a man, and people see them together in a secluded spot and testify [to that effect], the judge shall chastise them [*ta'zir ide*]. They shall collect the normal fines for *zina* [adultery/fornication].[18]

Additionally, the law book contains two variant provisions on the penalty imposed on a married woman guilty of adultery: first, that she pay the same fine as a male guilty of adultery, and alternately, that her husband pay her fine, and, should he fail to divorce her for her dishonorable conduct, a cuckold tax as well.[19] In other words, if Ayşe and Saadeddin's contact were to be judged illicit on the basis of the informants' testimony, strict application of the statute could result in fines for adultery imposed on both Ayşe and Saadeddin as well as pressure on Haci Mehmed to divorce Ayşe. This assimilation of mere association with no proven sexual contact to the crime of zina was an innovation of Süleyman's law book and absent from

---

[17] AS 2:114a,b.

[18] Heyd (1973:61, 99). (I have made some changes to Heyd's translation of the Turkish.)

[19] Heyd (1973:57–8, 96–7). (Again, I have slightly altered Heyd's translation of the Turkish.)

that of his father Selim, the previous sultan. This change demonstrates a tightening up of rules on gender contact and, consequently, an expansion of prosecutable conduct.[20]

Did the informant Cuma deserve Ayşe's curses? While the statute cited above makes prosecution dependent upon the testimony of observers, Süleyman's law book also states that an observer of an act of illicit sexual behavior is under no compulsion to report the incident, although an instance of theft, by contrast, must be reported or a fine of ten silver coins will be imposed:

> If a person knows of an instance of fornication/adultery and does not go to the judge and inform him, there is no fine. If he knows of an instance of theft and does not speak, a fine of 10 akçes should be taken.[21]

If opinion in Aintab matched the view at the center on this matter, Haci Derviş and Cuma were liable to be seen as busybodies and mischiefmakers. Other cases in the Aintab record suggest that accusations of illicit association were a way of calling down the authorities on a person against whom one bore a grudge or toward whom one felt antagonism (in our case, Saadeddin's financial dealings with both parties may be an issue).

It was no doubt useful to have the authorities on one's side in such an accusation, since the structure of sexual crime in both Islamic legal discourse and sixteenth-century Ottoman practice frequently protected those accused of illicit conduct at the expense of their accusers. The principal means of protection was the punishment imposed for "slander" (*kazf*), that is, an unsubstantiated accusation of illicit sexual behavior against another. Inducing the "people of authority" to act as conduit for the accusation provided one with a screen against potential punishment for slander.

On the other hand, we should not dismiss the possibility that Haci Derviş and Cuma were motivated by genuine moral scruples.[22] The

[20] For further discussion of this point, see Peirce (1998).

[21] Heyd (1973:63, 102). (Again, I have slightly altered Heyd's translation of the Turkish.)

[22] In this regard, the fact that both informants appear to have dervish affiliations calls for consideration. The prominent role in local affairs played by the heads of well-endowed dervish lodges in Aintab suggests that the local dervish community, or some elements within it, enjoyed an "establishment" position within the community. An attitude of strict moral rectitude was not, as is sometimes assumed, incompatible with dervish allegiance.

role of local residents in the prosecution of crime was substantial. On July 20, the date on which Ayşe and Saadeddin's case came to court, the business that dominated the day's work at court was also the result of community surveillance. This was a complex murder case the genealogy of which was now being formally heard by the judge and sorted out into four *sicill*s.[23] The actual murder—of two Christian merchants robbed and killed by their caravan escort, one of whom was from Aintab—was not local, since it occurred on the road from Erzincan to Diyarbakır, east of Aintab. What exposed the crime locally was a citizen's arrest of the Aintab suspect's brother, who was held as a kind of bondsman in lieu of his absent sibling.

Community surveillance, in fact, was built into the legal process. People had a real stake in how others conducted themselves, since they could be implicated in legal responsibility for criminal acts. Several clauses in the law book of Süleyman held individuals, urban neighborhoods, or whole villages liable for compensation for crimes committed on their property if the guilty party could not be found.[24] The corollary to collective liability was the collective right of neighborhoods to protest against and even expel residents known to have criminal reputations (in particular, thieves and harlots) (Heyd 1973:92). There was, in other words, a thin line between legitimate scrutiny of one's neighbors and surveillance that bordered on harrassment.

As we see, our protagonists resisted the informants' implication that their behavior was improper. The explanations offered to the court for Ayşe's presence in Saadeddin's house demonstrate a comfortable freedom of movement in the neighborhood, or at least between the two households. Their contacts included neighborly assistance—lending a hand in illness. Ayşe's loan to Saadeddin may have been another instance of neighborly assistance, although given the frequency of loans among members of the Aintab community, it could just as well have been a business dealing. The small window that this case provides onto the physical interaction between the two households suggests that if family honor was at all at stake, what was being upheld in this neighborhood was the dignity of men, who sent their wives and children into the streets to do their bidding.

---

[23] AS 2:116a,b; 117a,b.

[24] Heyd (1973:106ff.; clauses 44, 76–9, 80, 83, 84, and 117). Watchmen and guards were also liable for compensation for theft or damages occurring on premises under their supervision.

In this incident, as in many cases aired before the Aintab judge, the court appeared to act as a forum for weighing the merits of allegations of improper or criminal behavior. In other words, through the auspices of local policing agents and especially the court, discordant voices were modulated. The court took the voices on both sides of this case seriously. On the one hand, it honored the informants' allegation by treating it as more than barbed gossip and allowing it to be heard by the judge. On the other hand, in its written summary at least, the court framed the challenge to the neighborhood residents in such a way as to give them the benefit of the doubt, that is, to imply that there was no problem if it could be shown that Ayşe had constructive business in Saadeddin's house. In the official's question, "What business [*maslahat*] does she have in his house?", the word *maslahat* carried overtones of socially or communally beneficial activity. The structure of the case record, leaving the neighbors' defense of their conduct unchallenged, suggests that Ayşe and Saadeddin were not fined or otherwise punished.

We cannot help but note, however, that Ayşe's voice is absent from the first of the two entries in the court record concerning this case. She was the one "out of place," but her own account of her movements was not deemed necessary of inclusion in the case record. That Ayşe was not a subdued or silenced female in this affair is evident from her cursing; she was silenced only in the written summary, and perhaps also in the formal proceedings. The privileging of the men's voices at court stemmed from the practice of holding male heads of household legally responsible for the family's reputation, and thus for their wives' conduct. As husband, Haci Mehmed's statement that he was the instigator of the allegedly illicit contact was enough to clinch the case in favor of the neighborhood residents.

The second stage in this double case was the aggravated encounter between Ayşe and the informant Cuma. When and where she called him a pimp is not clear—probably in the course of their encounter at court. The cursing was actionable because, in the view of the Aintab court at least, it constituted slander, and indeed, Cuma chose to take legal action against Ayşe. (This may account for the uncharacteristic note added to the first case summary; had Cuma not taken action, it is possible that the identity of the two informers would never have been entered into the record—a contingency that reminds us of how court records are only partial reconstructions of events in real time.) The written summary of this second stage of the affair, with its endorsement of the two witnesses' support of the slander accusation, suggests that Ayşe was fined for slander if the penalties outlined in Süleyman's law book were applied.

But did Ayşe's cursing backfire? Was she done in by legal rules? Not necessarily: she was erased from the written summary but, even with the risk of punishment, she voiced her view of the affair publicly. Indeed, Ayşe perhaps felt compelled to speak out for her own honor, since the court paid her no heed while devoting its attention to restoring the moral integrity of her husband. By labelling Cuma a moral reprobate, she suggested that dishonor lay with him, not with herself. Calling Cuma a pimp suggested that he was complicit in his own wife's sexual immorality, that is, that Cuma's wife was in fact the adultress, not Ayşe, and that Cuma was a cuckold, not Haci Mehmed. In other words, through her cursing, Ayşe displaced the onus of sexual misconduct onto her accuser.

Judicial Discretion

The case of Ayşe and Saadeddin was only one of several instances of suspect social contact that were reviewed by the court subsequent to the arrival of the new judge. During the summer of 1541, a number of cases were recorded where people were summoned to court to question their presence on the streets at night or in the early hours of the morning. With the exception of Ayşe, however, all were men.[25] In one case, a baker who was apprehended in a dead-end street in front of the house of a woman (a widow?) claimed he was on his way to work.[26] In a case from Arablar, one of Aintab's villages, two men accused a third of being on the roof of a certain Ali's house in the early hours of the morning when Ali was absent; the man claimed he had gone to Ali's house to get a drink of water.[27] It is noteworthy that all these cases occurred under the judgeship of Hüsameddin Efendi; that is, the court register for the previous nine months recorded no such incidents. In other words, movement in the streets that might conceivably have a sexually illicit purpose was now being surveilled under the aegis of the court.

---

[25] AS 2:137a, 205b, 279a, 307c, 323b.
[26] AS 2:205b.
[27] AS 2:279a.

A key figure in these cases was the police agent who brought instances of potential sexual offense to court—the *asesbaşı*, or chief of the night watch. The asesbaşı reported to the local governor (*sancakbegi*), and his office was purchased from the governor at auction as a tax-farm. The asesbaşı, in other words, was a member of the local community. The office of asesbaşı was not the only policing agency attached to the provincial governor's office, however. The latter's principal arm of law enforcement was the office of *subaşı*, or "police chief", an official who was directly appointed by the governor and perhaps part of his permanent suite. In the hierarchy of local law and order, the asesbaşı reported to the subaşı, who reported to the provincial governor, the local delegate of imperial authority.

In the Aintab court records of 1540–1541, the asesbaşı appears to be a morals police, his duties comprising part of the domain that classical legal-administrative texts had assigned to the muhtasip. Typically, the asesbaşı in Aintab brought to court instances of drinking, blasphemy, brawling, and pickpocketing (his role in rooting out alcoholic consumption by Muslims was particularly noteworthy). After the arrival of Hüsameddin Efendi, sexual misconduct and sexually slanderous cursing were added to the roster of immorality that the asesbaşı was responsible for exposing. Sexual slander, illicit sex, drinking—these of course are three of the five *hadd* crimes—crimes, that is, explicitly penalized in the Qur'an. It is no coincidence that it was a local delegate of sultanic executive authority who monitored the Aintab community for offenses in these areas of conduct. Regarded as offenses against God rather than against a particular individual, *hadd* crimes were not allowed to stand unprosecuted; the duty to investigate and to punish if necessary rested with the sovereign, who acted on behalf of God.[28] This prosecutorial responsibility of the governing regime for *hadd* crimes explains why the first sections in the penal regulations of Ottoman imperial law books were sexual offenses (including sexual slander) and drinking. It also explains why this essay concentrates more on sultanic kanun than on contemporary shariah

---

[28] In the words of the twelfth-century Hanafi jurist al-Marghinani, popular among the Ottomans, "This right is to be exacted by the prince, as the deputy of the law, or by the judge, as the deputy of the prince." (al-Marghinani [1957, 2:13–14]). For a useful discussion of this subject, see Johansen (1981:197–303).

discourse in analyzing the normative legal frame for the case of Ayşe and Saadeddin.

It may be that male-female interaction was tracked by the asesbaşı *before* the new judge took up office, with the difference that offenses were not customarily reported at court. If so, the responsibility of the asesbaşı in the matter of contact between the sexes was similar to the responsibility of the muhtasip in monitoring market practices: the fact that their work only began to be registered at court *after* the arrival of the special prosecutor and the new judge doesn't mean that their duties had not previously extended to these areas of social and economic behavior. What it does mean is that the Ottoman regime was insisting on *public* scrutiny of these domains of communal life.

In other areas of sexual crime too, shifts are evident. It was only after Hüsameddin Efendi's arrival that instances of sexual slander and homosexual rape appeared in the court record. Such cases were no doubt the result of increased surveillance and enforcement rather than new fashions in offensive behavior. "Hard-core" sexual crime—actual instances of illicit sex and accusations of rape or illegal entry—occurred throughout the year. In other words, it did not take the expanded authority of the court that is apparent in the records from June 1541 onward for the traditional definition of sexual crime—of zina—to be prosecuted. What was new was the stepped-up regulation of male-female contact, the assimilation of sexual slander to the crime of false accusation of zina, and the prosecution of homosexual rape and slander. Regulation of male-female contact and the inclusion of homosexual contact under the rubric of zina were matters that did not appear in the law books of Süleyman's ancestors; hence they represented practices newly criminalized in kanun.

Some Aintabans actively resisted the new practice of policing neighborhood traffic under the aegis of the court. In the context of stepped-up scrutiny of both the work of local officialdom and the conduct of local residents, policing might now threaten to become more than the familiar authority of the night watchman. It might also open the door to an increase in "accusationism" among ordinary residents of Aintab. The narrow line between legitimate surveillance by civilians and potential harrassment is demonstrated in a case from the village of Sam:

> Ümmet b. Kara, from the village of Sam, summoned Ramazan b. Karaca to court, and said: "This Ramazan slandered me by saying 'A man

> entered your house at night'." When Ramazan was questioned, he answered: "I had gone for a walk at night. I saw that two people were coming along the street. I said to myself, 'Let's see what they're doing.' While I waited, one of these two people entered Ümmet's house and one kept on going." His statement was recorded at Ümmet's request.[29]

Here, Ümmet has apparently preempted an assault on his honor by accusing Ramazan of slander. One has to wonder if going for a walk was itself sufficient justification for being on the streets at night. Indeed, all cases of civilian surveillance raise the question of how the surveillers justified their own presence on the street!

Surveillance of male-female conduct may have been on the increase, but it did not necessarily lead to punishment. In other words, as translated through the court, stricter imperial laws did not necessarily constitute a regime of legal repression and imposed social conformity. As Ayşe's case suggests, the court was willing to listen to the accused as they attempted to justify their actions. Hüsameddin Efendi did not give the imperial law book the narrow reading that it might theoretically have supported (recall the scenario envisioned by the statute: "If a woman is publicly spoken ill of in connection with a man, and people see them together in a secluded spot and testify [to that effect] . . ."). Ayşe and Saadeddin *were* observed together in a secluded spot, and testimony to that effect *was* provided. But by accepting the account of affairs offered by Saadeddin and by Ayşe's husband, Hüsameddin Efendi apparently regarded the contact between the neighbors as tolerable by local standards. Assuming that he used Süleyman's law book as a standard of judgment (which we can only hypothesize), he may have satisfied himself that Ayşe had not previously been "publicly spoken ill of" in connection with Saadeddin, or, in other words, that she had no prior record of sexual indiscretion that might render Haci Derviş's and Cuma's accusation plausible. Like all local judges, Hüsameddin Efendi was charged not only with applying legal rules but also with preserving social order. The latter would be impossible if a rigid yardstick of judgment were applied to a socially complex community such as Aintab, which was made up of a number of different microcultures with different views of what constituted unacceptable behavior.

---

[29] AS 2:137a.

The court records of 1540–1541 make it clear that this complex community accepted no single standard of conduct for interaction between males and females. Only the very elite of Aintab seem to have practiced strict segregation between men and women, while the lower classes, who lacked slaves and servants to perform the routine interactions of daily life, necessarily tolerated a greater degree of contact. People might agree on the outer boundaries of acceptable behavior but they actively disagreed over the details. The code of conduct in Ayşe and Saadeddin's neighborhood, where it was acceptable for women to be on the street doing family business, clearly would not have met the approval of all Aintabans. If there was a rule of thumb guiding non-elite Aintabans in the matter of male-female interaction, it would seem to depend on the motivation for contact. The court records suggest that people made a distinction between contacts with legitimate purpose (business dealings, use of the court, neighborly assistance) and idle contact (loitering on the street, peering out a window into the next-door courtyard, dropping in spontaneously to another's home).

Broadening the Frame

The increasing criminalization of male-female contact in state law—specifically, in the imperial law book of Süleyman—would seem to be the thrust behind the sudden appearance of court-monitored surveillance of movement in the streets of Aintab. However, the law book was clearly not reflective of patterns of conduct among all Aintabans, although the fundamental notion that unwarranted contact between the sexes was immoral and dishonorable was shared at all levels of society. Rather, the standard of conduct endorsed in the law book reflected the stricter separation of the sexes in upper-class social practice. The same endorsement of "elite" models of behavior can be found in fatwas issued by the prominent jurists Ibn Kemal (d. 1534) and Ebu Su'ud (d. 1574), both of whom served Süleyman as chief mufti of the empire.[30] But as this essay hopefully makes clear, people argued back as the state's norms shifted. Mediating between the different views of proper social behavior was the job of

---

[30] On Ebu Su'ud's pronouncements, see Peirce (1999).

the judge, who interpreted normative laws in the context of local moralities and local socio-economic constraints.

What was the cause of this "conservative" move on the part of the Ottoman regime in the matter of social intercourse between the sexes? Was Süleyman getting into the business of social engineering through the auspices of the empire's local judicial arm? In the light of Foucauldian perspectives on surveillance by the state, we might also ask whether surveillance with the ostensible purpose of promoting sexual morality helped advance other more covert aims of the regime in scrutinizing the activities of its subjects. Let us now look at the case of Ayşe and Saaddedin in a broader frame.

Despite the tenacious view in Ottoman historiography of Süleyman's reign as the Ottoman golden age, 1540 was not a time marked by social harmony. Order is not something that should be taken for granted or assumed as the default state of affairs in our region and period. Indeed, if there was a state of relative security in 1540, it had been hard won, and won only recently. Conquest did not mean pacification, and it was only the critically important two-year military offensive against Safavid Iran in 1534–1536—the much celebrated "campaign for the two Iraqs"—that put an end to nearly twenty years of Ottoman struggle to gain control over Anatolia and northern Syria. Resistance can be documented throughout these years, during which numerous military expeditions were sent to quell large-scale uprisings in central and southeastern Anatolia. In securing social and legal order, the Ottoman regime was faced with troubles from two directions: on the one hand, challenges to its sovereignty from tribal groups, and, on the other, the lawless, and sometimes rebellious, conduct of its own soldiers and officers. Even though the region in which Aintab was located had been largely pacified by 1540, not all subjects were reconciled to their Ottoman overlord. The historian Ahmet Yaşar Ocak has characterized the atmosphere surrounding resistance to the regime's policies as "a general discontent and a state of despair among the population, especially around the year 1540" (Ocak 1991).

Building up the court of Aintab was only one small example of the attention that the Ottoman regime paid to invigorating its legal system in these years. Local courts were clearly an instrument in the achievement of local order. But, as Ayşe's case suggests, the regime did not baldly use its network of provincial judges to enforce a set discipline. The justice purveyed by the regime had to be flexible and adaptable if it was to work across the varied landscape of this Eurasian empire and to induce subjects to bring their legal problems into its orbit. The doubling of the Aintab court's case load in the summer of 1541 was in part a result of heightened police surveillance, but only in part. A strong court could also be an instrument in the socio-legal strategies of local residents. As we have seen, they were "talking back" and "talking out" in ways that suggested that they not only grasped the potentially punitive elements in the shifting climate of the court but also the opportunities it opened up for individuals to manipulate the legal process to their own advantage.

In this regard, the broader framing of the affair of Ayşe and Saadeddin and other cases like it must include another key aspect of law and order: the matter of punishment. The law-enforcement aspect of legal practice is, in my opinion, too often omitted when we study Islamic law in theory and practice. At least for mid-sixteenth-century Aintab, the story of how the court acted to further social order becomes more complex when the matter of policing and punishment is brought into the picture.

One reality of the times was corruption in law enforcement. Contemporary sources accused police and other enforcers of criminal penalities of imposing excessive punishments (mainly excessive fines), accepting bribes, and even arresting and punishing the innocent.[31] All this was part of the breakdown of the old pre-Ottoman order and the chaotic aftermath of conquest. That the Ottoman regime was concerned about corruption in local legal administration is evident in its law books, both imperial and local, where we find repeated emphasis on the need for trial by a judge before punishment is imposed; for example:

> Officials may not interfere with a person or impose a fine with nothing being proved in accordance with the shariah and merely on suspicion of misconduct. If they do exact [a fine], the judge shall give an order and recover it (Heyd 1973:127).

The 1536 law book for Aintab established the imperial law book as the referrent for deciding punishment and warned against excessive fines:

---

[31] See the petition to the sultan and grand vezir from one Musa, governor of the central Anatolian province of Bozok, complaining of abuses by local officials (Başbakanlık Osmanlı Arşivi, DBŞM 1/30, formerly classified as Fekete 89). This document is discussed by Heyd (1973:51–2); Heyd placed it between the years 1529 and 1536 because of its reference to the grand vezir Ibrahim Pasha as *serasker*.

> For every finable crime which occurs, great or small, the Ottoman Kanun shall be consulted and [the fine] exacted; force shall not be used to exact anything more than that.[32]

Expanded jurisdiction of the local court, such as we have seen in Aintab, and a strong system of interlinked courts—both Ottoman legal reforms of the times—established a system of checks and balances that offset the chain of command from governors to subaşıs, asesbaşıs, and other local police. Such division of local authority not only gave the Ottoman regime a dual legal presence in the province but also provided a source of legal protection to subjects. Specifically, insistence on a hearing by the judge prior to the imposition of criminal penalties protected the innocent from harassment and the guilty from excessive punishment. This regulatory rigor is all the more significant when we remember that in the sixteenth century, fines for criminal infractions typically were part of the revenue assigned to local officials, from the provincial governor down to the petty police officer serving as a member of his staff.

Trial by the judge had the additional advantage of furnishing a forum where people might legally resist or reinterpret norms of conduct promoted by the state. The dialogue at court among the judge, the asesbaşı, the three neighbors, and their two accusers was in effect a negotiation over the applicability of a legal rule. It was the sum of thousands of such instances of negotiation that allowed the imperialization of the legal system to have a local face. Choreographing negotiation was perhaps the most important function performed by the hundreds of nameless judges working throughout the empire.

People were not always successful in imposing their reading of events on the court, however. Two weeks before Ayşe and Saadeddin were summoned before him, Hüsameddin Efendi imposed the severe punishment of banishment on a female teacher and her male associate for mixing the sexes in their classes, despite the teachers' ardent and articulate self-defense in court.[33] Yet the very fact that the court record preserved their self-defense in full and even persuasive detail is noteworthy—indeed, it is remarkable in view of the routine brevity

---

[32] For the Aintab kanunname of 1536, see Tapu Tahrir Defteri 186, folios 4–5 (housed in the Başbakanlık Osmanlı Arşivi in Istanbul); for a facsimile and transliteration, see Özdeğer (1988:201–3).

[33] For a full treatment of this case, see Peirce (2003): "Haciye Sabah's Story."

of entries into the court register. Similarly, the court and its records provided other Aintabans who were clearly guilty with a stage upon which to give moral justification to their acts or at least to plead extenuating circumstances. Ayşe's cursing may be such a deliberately staged act. We cannot know for sure if she meant for her voice to enter the court record or if she was simply a hapless victim of her loose tongue. But other cases in the Aintab court records suggest that some women, especially those accused of dishonor, intentionally used the court as an arena to address their fellow citizens as they attempted to rehabilitate their reputations. Its enhanced stature and the new public status of its records may have made the court an increasingly attractive arena in which to speak. Perhaps paradoxically, perhaps not, it was the imperializing thrust of the Ottoman regime in legal administration that created the public record of local voices that allows us to retrieve some knowledge of Aintab's past.

CHAPTER FOUR

BROKEN EDDA AND MARITAL MISTAKES: TWO RECENT DISPUTES FROM AN ISLAMIC COURT IN ZANZIBAR

Erin Stiles

This essay examines two recent cases from an Islamic court in rural Zanzibar to demonstrate how family law issues are understood and discussed by litigants and court personnel. The way in which cases are categorized and framed throughout the legal process shows how different parties interpret Islamic law with respect to Zanzibari norms concerning marriage and divorce. Specifically, I consider how the differences between lay and professional notions of divorce and maintenance are played out in court procedure and judicial reasoning. I take into account the roles and legal understandings of the litigants, court clerks, and judge—called the *kadhi* in Kiswahili. When are certain cultural practices understood as properly "Islamic" or "religious," and by whom? Does the kadhi uphold practices or events that he does not consider properly religious? If so, under what circumstances?

The cases are two that I studied during eighteen months of ethnographic field research in Zanzibar in 1999 and 2000. This analysis combines ethnographic data with a study of the various documents produced by the court. Using both kinds of information together proves beneficial. While prepared documents and records reveal how the record-keeper—most often a clerk in Zanzibar's courts—understands a case, the documents often differ significantly from what the claimants or the kadhi perceive as the essential legal issues of a dispute.

Throughout the paper, I use the Kiswahili form of religious and legal terms, though many are similar to the Arabic: for example *kadhi* and *qadi*, *sheria* and *shariʿa*, or *mahari* and *mahr*. The translations of the Kiswahili court documents are my own, and I have changed most of the proper names of people and villages.

Zanzibar's Islamic Courts Today

Zanzibar is a semiautonomous island state of Tanzania with its own president, parliament, and semi-independent legal system. The population of about one million is over 95% Muslim, and Islamic courts are part of the state legal system at both the primary and appellate levels. They are most recently established in the 1984 *Kadhi's Act.* There are nine primary Islamic courts on the two major islands of Unguja and Pemba, and all primary decisions may be appealed to the Chief Kadhi in Zanzibar Town, on the southernmost island of Unguja. My research took place in the court at Mkokotoni, which serves the northern district of Unguja—a rural region of about 70,000 people who subsist primarily by farming, fishing, and running small businesses.

The jurisdiction of the Islamic courts is limited to family and personal status matters, and Zanzibari Muslims may bring such disputes only to these courts. Although the courts handle a range of problems concerning marriage and divorce, child custody, and inheritance, the vast majority of cases opened concern marital disputes.[1] Among these, divorce suits, maintenance claims, and pleas for the return of missing wives are common. Of the seventy-seven cases opened in the Mkokotoni court in my research period, between January 1999 to July 2000, seventy concerned marital disputes. These numbers are fairly typical of the last ten years in Mkokotoni—on average, about forty cases are opened per year, and about 90 percent of these are marital disputes. The majority of cases in Zanzibar are opened by women; of the seventy-seven cases opened in my research period, women were the plaintiffs in fifty-eight.

Divorce is very common in Zanzibar today, and has been since the recent past; J.N.D. Anderson noted in the mid-twentieth century that a Shāfiʿi kadhi told him that only about 20 percent of Zanzibari marriages did *not* end in divorce (1970). Today, Zanzibari men have the unattenuated right to divorce their wives unilaterally through repudiation. Women may file for divorce in court and are granted it on a variety of grounds, the most common being desertion and

[1] Marital disputes in which physical abuse is the primary complaint are handled as secular criminal cases; those inheritance disputes in which the problem concerns property itself rather than determining proper heirs or the proper division of property are handled in the secular courts.

lack of maintenance. However, divorce happens most often out of the court through repudiation or local variations on *khulʿ/khuluu* (Arabic/Kiswahili).[2]

All of the kadhis in Zanzibar's primary courts are appointed by the state. The kadhi of Mkokotoni is Shaykh Haji who has presided over the court for about six years. Before his appointment, Shaykh Haji taught religion in the government school in his village on the tiny island of Tumbatu, located off the northern tip of Unguja. There is neither standard training for kadhis nor educational prerequisite for achieving the post. Rather, they are appointed on the basis of their reputation as religious scholars and as a result, have fairly diverse educational backgrounds. Shaykh Haji was trained in Zanzibar and in the city of Tanga on the Tanzanian mainland. Others were educated as far afield as Saudi Arabia and al-Azhar in Cairo. Although all of the state-appointed kadhis follow the Shāfiʿi *madhhab*, many claim to make provisions for disputants from other *madhhab*s when and if they appear in court.[3] It should be noted that avowed followers of other *madhhab*s are few in Zanzibar, and are especially rare in rural areas.

Shaykh Haji comes to the court every Monday through Thursday. He arrives at about eight o'clock in the morning and hears or researches cases until the early afternoon. Opening a case in a Zanzibar kadhi's court follows a regular procedure. Perhaps the most interesting precondition is a mandatory reference letter from a local community leader, or headperson, called a *sheha*. *Sheha*s preside over groups of villages in the rural areas and over urban neighborhoods in towns, and their role is an interesting one in the recent history of Zanzibar. Although in the past local elders selected them from within their communities, today they are appointed by the government and are thus most often acknowledged supporters of the ruling political party. Though they have no formal training in either religious or secular law, *sheha*s are in principle responsible for all types of community dispute resolution. People with family or marital problems are required to bring their issues to the *sheha* before opening a case in the kadhis court. For such matters, the *sheha* is popularly considered the second

[2] A *khuluu* divorce is one in which a wife compensates her husband financially for a divorce. In Zanzibar, the court often orders khuluu.

[3] Although Ibadi kadhis were common in the past, most kadhis have been Shāfiʿīs since the 1964 revolution and Zanzibar's union with Tanganyika.

step in the dispute resolution process; the first is the family elders, the *wazee*, and the last is the state-appointed kadhi.

Although only the kadhi may decide cases and write judgments, *hukumu*, clerks have a very important role in court procedure. The most senior clerk at Mkokotoni is Fumu Mwadini, a man in his late thirties who has worked there for about ten years. Once a claimant has a referral letter from her *sheha*, she presents her problem to the clerk(s). The clerk then determines whether the issue is suitable for the kadhi's court. If a case is opened, the clerks aid in the preparation of the plaintiff's official claim, *madai*, and the defendant's counter-claim, *majibu ya madai*. They also schedule court dates, manage case files, write summons, and explain procedure and rulings to litigants, their families, and witnesses. There are usually between two and four clerks working in each primary court and they assist the secular judge as well as the kadhi. Although they are not required to have any special religious or legal training, most clerks have finished secondary school and have achieved a relatively high level of education.

The Cases

Case One: Broken Edda

Bwana (Mr.) Machano v. Bibi (Ms.) Aisha

A middle-aged man named Machano opened the first case in February 2000. On his first day in court, Machano brought a letter from his *sheha* and explained his problem to Fumu, the senior clerk. He said that he had divorced his wife, but shortly after decided he wanted her back. He explained that he went to her family home to take her back,[4] but that she refused because she had already married someone else. The clerk asked Machano how much time had passed between the date on which he divorced his wife and the date on which he went back to her. He replied that only two weeks had elapsed since the divorce, and argued that she could not possibly have maintained *edda*—the mandatory waiting period of three menstrual periods before remarrying after a divorce. Therefore, he said, she had unlawfully remarried.

[4] Zanzibari women return to their family home when they are divorced or widowed.

A debate ensued between the clerks about whether this was a criminal or civil case: if his wife had married before she completed the waiting period, then it would be a criminal case. There was much discussion about exactly how many days had passed since the divorce and whether a woman could menstruate three times in that time period.

Eventually, Fumu asked Machano what exactly he wanted to accomplish by coming to the court. Machano replied that he wanted his wife back, and Fumu decided that Machano should open a case in the kadhi's court since he wanted more than simply prosecuting her for violating *edda.* Demanding the return of a missing wife is by far the most common claim in cases where the plaintiff is male, and Machano's *madai* (the plaintiff's claim) was framed as such. As in all opened cases, Fumu prepared the *madai* document with Machano by asking him specific questions, typing the claim in the standard format, and reading it aloud for Machano's approval.

The *madai* was written as Machano's demand for the return of his wife, and was very similar to the *madai* of other cases opened by men. Although the alleged violation of *edda* was not mentioned, it was noted that the plaintiff claimed that the defendant married another man while still his wife.

MADAI: THE PLAINTIFF'S CLAIM[5]

1. Plaintiff, male, age 45, Mtumbatu (ethnicity), from Mcherani village.
2. Defendant, female, age 30, Mtumbatu, from Chombo village.
3. They have been married for twenty years, have had nine children, two of whom died.
4. The plaintiff claims that he divorced his wife on the twenty-fifth of the month of *mrisho* 1999 and he returned to her to take her back around the tenth of the month *mfunguo mosi* 2000; he went to her elder brother.[6]
5. The plaintiff claims that the defendant refused to return to him when he asked her to. By the twentieth of *mfunguo mosi*, the defendant was married to another husband.

---

[5] Mkokotoni Court Case No. 13–00.

[6] In the Zanzibari calendar, the month of *mrisho* is Ramaḍān, and *mfungou mosi* is Shawwāl.

6. The plaintiff demands that the defendant return to him because he is indeed her true husband.
7. This claim began with a complaint that the defendant married another man while she was the wife of the plaintiff.
8. The claim and the plaintiff originate from Mcherani, Northern A district.
9. The plaintiff begs the court:
   a. To order the defendant to return to him immediately.
   b. To pay all relevant court fees.
   c. Follow any other obligations incurred.

The defendant, Aisha, was summoned and came to court with her new husband, Kassim, the following week. The clerks read the *madai* to her, and proceeded to question her. Kassim, who was an active participant in all of the court proceedings, informed the kadhi that although Aisha was lawfully divorced and had paid Machano for it, Machano would not give her a divorce paper, *karatasi.* The kadhi assured him that Machano would be required to produce the paper. Aisha asked how the case would proceed, and Shaykh Haji told her that since she had paid money, it seemed that her divorce was an instance of *khuluu,* which a woman compensates her husband financially for a divorce she desires. Shaykh Haji asked Aisha specifically about the *edda* and when she had married Kassim. She answered that she had completed the waiting period, and that she married Kassim on the nineteenth of *mfunguo mosi,* the first month of the Islamic calendar—the same date that Machano had cited.

When I interviewed Aisha, I learned that she was about forty years old and did not have any formal education except for a bit of Qur'an school when she was a child. She had been married to Machano for many years and over the course of their marriage he had divorced her twice. He asked her to return after the first divorce and she agreed. They stayed together until recently, when he divorced her for a second time. Aisha explained that when he asked her back after the second divorce he did not come to their home, as he said, but rather asked her to return when they met farming in the fields. She did not want to return to him, so he asked for money, indicating the return of her marriage gift, *mahari.*

Aisha and Kassim explained that Machano divorced her on his own initiative, and then asked for money when she refused to return to him. They said that she paid him 50,000 Tanzanian shillings (about forty-five US dollars), which was more than her *mahari,* though she could not remember the exact amount. Aisha told me she knew that Machano opened the case because he thought she had violated the *edda*, but she counted out the days and assured me that she had observed the full waiting period. She explained, however, that she got married right away after waiting because "Life is difficult for a woman without a husband. I'm not going to remain a divorcee!" Her counterclaim, the *majibu ya madai*, was prepared on the same day with Fumu's aid.

MAJIBU YA MADAI: DEFENDANT'S COUNTERCLAIM[7]

1. The defendant agrees with points 1, 2 and 3.
2. The defendant does not agree with the explanation of the plaintiff in section 4. After she was divorced by the plaintiff, he did not return to her like he said. Rather, she remembers that one day she went to farm her potatoes and there they met each other; the plaintiff then told her that he wanted her to return to him, "I told him that I would not return because I was tired of his behaviour, and it is not true that he went to my elder brother because he is not at all nearby—he lives far away."
3. The defendant agrees with section 5 that she married another man on the nineteenth of *mfunguo mosi* but it was not like he claims: she married because she had already given the defendant the money that he wanted in the amount of 50,000 Tanzanian shillings; indeed, he received it, "I then decided to remarry another husband."
4. The defendant does not agree with section 6; she explains that she cannot return to the home of the plaintiff because he is not her husband and she is lawfully married to another man.
5. The defendant does not agree with section 7; she explains that she is no longer the wife of the plaintiff and she has been lawfully married to another man.
6. The defendant agrees with section 8.
7. The defendant begs the court:
   a. To throw out the claims of the plaintiff because he has no foundation on which to base these claims as she has lawfully married another man.
   b. That the plaintiff pays all court fees.
   c. Any other orders the court gives to reach an agreement.

---

[7] Mkokotoni Court Case No. 13–00.

Machano and Aisha came to court together some days later, when the *sheha* of their community was called to give his testimony. Because *sheha*s are expected to be familiar with the happenings of their communities, they are often called in by the kadhi as supplemental witnesses. The sheha's statement in this case, however, did not indicate much knowledge of the situation. He said that he did not know anything about their problems: he had not heard that they had divorced or that Aisha had remarried.

Witnesses were called, and a few days later the case resumed. Machano's witness, one of his older male relatives, explained that he knew about the divorce and claimed that he himself had told Machano not to divorce Aisha and not to take her money. He said he knew about Aisha's new marriage, but did not know who gave her permission to marry.

At this, Aisha protested that the testimony was irrelevant because the witness did not know enough about their circumstances. The kadhi considered her complaint, and noted to Machano that it would be helpful in the future to bring witnesses who knew more about the case. However, he also assured Aisha that in fact the testimony was relevant because the witness said that he knew about the divorce, and knew that Machano wanted Aisha back. This comment was significant because it was the first time Shaykh Haji emphasized the need to establish the actual circumstances of the divorce. He kept the witness for some time, and asked more questions about the divorce event. He specifically tried to determine whether Machano had expressed his desire to go back to his wife and when he had done so. He also wanted the witness to confirm that Machano had asked Aisha for money and received it from her. The witness said that Machano did so, although he reemphasized that he himself had advised Machano not take her money.

Aisha's witness was a local Qur'an teacher called *Mwalimu* (teacher) Simai, who was highly respected in the community for his religious knowledge. As was his usual practice when a respected elder came to court, Shaykh Haji explained to Mwalimu Simai that he had been called in to help solve the couple's problem. With less prestigious and younger witnesses he simply asked them to explain their relationship to the couple and their knowledge of the problems at hand. Mwalimu Simai explained that although he himself had contracted the marriage between Aisha and Kassim, he knew only a little about the case. When Shaykh Haji asked him if they brought him an *alama* (sign) that they could lawfully be married, Mwalimu Simai answered that although they did not bring him anything, he believed Aisha when she said that she had observed *edda* and could remarry. Aisha interjected to explain once again that she thought it better to remarry and so waited for the *edda* period and then married again right away.

At this, Shaykh Haji said to Machano, "You heard her: she says you divorced her, she waited, and then she got married again." Machano nodded his understanding, and the kadhi continued.

"You said you divorced her, then you returned to her, then you asked for money, and then she gave it to you. Correct?" Machano agreed, and stated that he had received 50,000 shillings from her. After this, the party left the court.

Shaykh Haji decided the case the following week, in early April, ruling that Aisha had been validly divorced through *khuluu* and was legitimately remarried to her new husband. He explained the decision and read it aloud. Aisha and Kassim were pleased with the ruling but Machano was very unhappy and tried to steal a piece of Aisha's clothing as they left the courtroom.

In the written judgment, *hukumu*, Shaykh Haji emphasized the testimony of the witnesses and ruled that Aisha had been validly divorced through *khuluu*, "according to the laws of Islam."

HUKUMU, JUDGMENT, April 4, 2000[8]

> After listening to the plaintiff and the defendant and investigating their claims, the court has made a decision. The defendant has not erred because the plaintiff stated himself that she paid 50,000 shillings [for the divorce] and that he was given it. And indeed the plaintiff received it. He agreed that he divorced his wife. The court recognizes that he received it after he divorced his wife.
>
> The days of *edda* were completed. Therefore the defendant, Ms. Aisha, is not the wife of the plaintiff Mr. Machano.
>
> "And if ye fear that they may not be able to keep the limits of Allah, in that case it is no sin for either of them if the woman ransom herself."[9]
>
> And he divorced her by means of *khuluu* according to the laws of Islam. And the plaintiff does not have the right to harass his [ex] wife because she is already married to another man. This case is closed.

---

[8] Mkokotoni Court Case No. 13–00.

[9] Qur'an IV v. 229. Muhammad Marmaduke Pickthall translation.

I find this case interesting because of the range of legal issues emphasized by the litigants, clerks, and kadhi. Machano opened the case because he thought Aisha had violated the law by remarrying before completing *edda*. On his first day in court he stressed this as the essential issue. Only later did he state his desire to remarry her. The clerk, however, advised him to open a case in the religious court because he deemed the important issue to be Machano's request for his wife back—not the violation of *edda*. In his first hearing with the kadhi, Machano explained the *edda* problem even though the prepared *madai* emphasized his desire for her return. The kadhi acknowledged his anxiety about the waiting period, but considered it settled with Mwalimu Simai's testimony. A religious authority married Aisha and Kassim, and this sufficed as evidence of her legal status to remarry—no other proof of her having completed the waiting period was requested or expected.

Instead, Shaykh Haji emphasized the validity of the divorce that had taken place, which he had ascertained through questioning the litigants and witnesses. The validity was established through determining that Machano had indeed tried to return to Aisha, and her refusal indicated her desire to be divorced from him. According to Shaykh Haji, valid *khuluu* means that a divorce is desired by the woman who compensates her husband financially for it.

Shaykh Haji's attempt to validate *khuluu* was not unique to this case. He often tried to determine the nature of a divorce even when the litigants or clerks prioritized another legal issue. I believe this is because of the frequency of a divorce practice among lay people called "*writing* for money," which Shaykh Haji and other legal scholars in Zanzibar consider a misinterpretation of Islamic divorce. What is called *khuluu* in court is referred to as *kununua talaka* by ordinary Zanzibaris, meaning literally "to buy a divorce." This is locally understood to be a situation in which a woman compensates her husband for a divorce she desires, much like Haji's understanding of *khuluu*.

However, out-of-court divorces also take place through a process known in the vernacular as "writing for money," or *kuandikia pesa*. This occurs when a man, usually via a written request, asks his wife to pay him to divorce her on his own initiative without her request. It is therefore somewhat like a man being paid by his wife to repudiate her. Although fairly common, it is considered unlawful by those with religious knowledge, and is neither ordered nor recognized by the kadhi and other religious experts in Zanzibar. Caplan has described a similar practice on Mafia island, a Tanzanian polity to the south of Zanzibar, where husbands "ask their wives to 'buy' their *talaka*"—the unilateral repudiation (1995).[10]

Shaykh Haji's quick dismissal of the *edda* problem also indicates how the important role of local elders and scholars is upheld in the court. Shaykh Haji considered the question of *edda* settled because a noted religious authority said that he had lawfully married them. Shaykh Haji's normal deference to elders and religious scholars in the courtroom complements what people told me in interviews and discussions about the importance of elders and "local kadhis"—*kadhi wa mtaa*—in community life and especially dispute resolution. The state-appointed kadhi often deferred to the opinions of the "unofficial" community kadhis when they were present in the court and occasionally summoned them for help in difficult cases.

Case Two: "They have both made many mistakes"
Bibi Mosa v. Bwana Juma

A woman in her fifties named Mosa opened the second case in October 1999. She complained that her husband, Juma, did not provide adequate maintenance for herself and her children, some of whom were from a previous marriage. Specifically, she noted inadequate food and inadequate money for the children's school fees. The first time Mosa came to court, she explained these maintenance problems and mentioned the possibility of filing for divorce. However, the kadhi and clerks told her to claim simple maintenance instead.

In the first of our discussions of her case, Mosa told me that Juma was her second husband and they had four children together, one of whom died. She had four additional children from her first marriage. Mosa had no profitable work other than farming, and she told me that Juma also did not work or farm. She explained to me that she came to court because of maintenance, emphasizing that she did not have a house to live in and that Juma refused to support the children from her first marriage. Although she specifically stated that

[10] Differences in interpretation of *khulʿ* are of course not unique to Zanzibar and Tanzania. Layish, for example, discusses variations on *khulʿ* evident in Libyan *sijill* (1988), which he calls "customary *khulʿ*." Layish's data indicate the qadis' support of local definitions of *khulʿ*. Anderson noted similar variations in parts of sub-Saharan Africa (1970).

she had not asked him for a divorce, she said that Juma had previously "written her for money."

Her *madai* was prepared with Fumu, and Mosa stressed again that she had *not* asked for a divorce. While preparing the document, Fumu asked if she and her husband got along, and gave examples of the kind of strife they might have—foul language, arguing, and rudeness. Although Mosa listened carefully and agreed that they did not get along well, she continued to emphasize that her main problem was the house, food, and the fact that Juma refused to support her children by a previous marriage. In the *madai*, however, Fumu highlighted their inability to get along and Juma's bad language as her major complaint.[11] The document referred to maintenance problems only in a general way: it stated that one of Juma's bad habits was that he did not support her. Her demands were that he support her in the "normal manner."

Later, Fumu told me that a man is responsible only for his own children and that therefore Mosa did not have a strong maintenance claim. The emphasis on verbal abuse can be read as his effort to make Mosa's claim more compelling.

MADAI: PLAINTIFF'S CLAIM[12]

1. Plaintiff, female, 44 years old, Shirazi (ethnicity), from Kifaa village, Zanzibar.
2. Defendant, male, 50 years old, Mtumbatu, from Kifaa village, Zanzibar.
3. The plaintiff and the defendant are man and wife and have been married for the past 18 years; they had four children, one of whom died.
4. The plaintiff claims that she does not get along with the defendant and he abuses her with bad language and does not fulfil the requirement of lawful maintenance for her.
5. The plaintiff demands that the defendant correct his habits of not supporting her and of abusing her with foul language for no reason; if the defendant is unable to stop these bad habits then she demands he give her a divorce.

---

[11] The inability to get along with their husbands was a frequent complaint of women coming to court.

[12] Mkokotoni Court Case No. 33–99.

6. The plaintiff begs the respected court of the kadhi to listen to this claim stemming from the village of Kifaa Kubwa in the Northern A district in the region of the northern Unguja where the court has the authority to listen to these claims.
7. The plaintiff begs the respected court to rule that the defendant follow the terms below:
   a. The court orders the defendant to support his wife in the normal manner of wife and husband.
   b. If the defendant fails to stop his habit of verbally abusing the plaintiff, then he must divorce her.
   c. The defendant should pay the court fees.

Juma was summoned and he came to court the next week. After the *madai* was read to him, he argued that he himself had done nothing wrong and that their marital problems stemmed from Mosa leaving him for no reason. His counterclaim was prepared with Fumu, and stated that he was without guilt, had not verbally abused Mosa, and that she blamed him for negligence to hide the fact that she had left him. He claimed that she left him without his permission or a reason, and that he wanted her back.

MAJIBU: DEFENDANT'S COUNTERCLAIM[13]

1. Concerning points 1–3 of the claim, the defendant agrees with the plaintiff's explanation.
2. Concerning point 4, the defendant does not agree with the explanation and he answers that he is able to get along with the plaintiff although the plaintiff indeed left his home without his permission.
3. Concerning point 5, the defendant answers that he has not verbally abused his wife but the defendant gives this reason to hide her own faults of leaving her husband without his permission.
4. Concerning point 6, the defendant answers that he has objections to being with his wife, and asks that the court listen to his claim.
5. Concerning point 7a, b, and c the defendant does not agree with these requests and answers that the court should throw these demands out because, indeed, the plaintiff left the defendant without a reason.

[13] Mkokotoni Court Case No. 33–99.

6. Finally, the defendant begs the respected court to rule that the plaintiff follow the terms below:
   a. The court order the plaintiff to return to the home of the defendant.
   b. The court fees are the responsibility of the plaintiff.
   c. The plaintiff obey any other orders the court gives to reach an agreement with the defendant.

One week later they appeared in court together to give their testimonies. Mosa explained to the kadhi that when Juma asked her to marry him, she told him that because she already had children and he had another wife, marriage might be imprudent. They were married anyway and she received 7000 shillings (about ten dollars) for her marriage gift, the *mahari*. Mosa explained that she continued to live at her family home after the marriage because she was taking care of her children. This was unusual, as newly married couples in Zanzibar are most often virilocal. Eventually, she moved in with Juma.

Shaykh Haji asked about her marital problems and Mosa answered that she did not receive any clothing and that the food that Juma provided was not sufficient to feed all of her children. She added that Juma had "written her for money" for a divorce last year when she was in town visiting a relative. He had asked her for 70,000 shillings—ten times her *mahari*—and she told the kadhi that she did not know why he thought she had so much money. She said that she did not pay him and eventually they reconciled and lived together for the next year. When Shaykh Haji asked her if there were other problems, she said that Juma had promised to build a new house for her but had not yet done so. In his testimony, Juma explained that they began having problems when Mosa left him without an explanation. He said that eventually he went to her elder brother and found out that she left because his house was *mbovu*, rotten. Juma claimed that he had problems with her children, saying that they were all disrespectful and foul-mouthed, and that her daughters brought their lovers back to the house. When the kadhi asked him about the 70,000 shillings he requested, Juma replied that he had indeed written for money because she was away for such a long time, but that now he no longer had a desire for a divorce.

One week later, Shaykh Haji heard witnesses for both parties. Juma's witness, a male relative, testified that he knew that Juma had "written for money" and that he had had problems with Mosa's children. Mosa's witness was her daughter Fatuma, who had accompanied her to court many times. Fatuma unceasingly and vehemently supported everything her mother said, and testified specifically that Juma did not support her mother properly.

Shaykh Haji decided the case the following week. He told Mosa that both she and Juma had made mistakes, and ruled that because they had lived together peacefully until they brought their problems to court, they must try living together again and to uphold their respective marital duties. His written judgment was in the form of terms, *masharti*, that each of them must follow, which was typical of cases in which the kadhi thought the couple capable of reconciliation. Juma was not ordered to support Mosa's children from her previous marriage, and after reading the decision aloud, Fumu reminded me that men were only required to support their own children.

JUDGMENT[14]

Terms for the plaintiff
The plaintiff has children, who have been disrespectful to their elders, therefore, the plaintiff must teach her children good language and manners. She should share her life with her husband and leave behind her harsh words and behavior. She must respect the marriage because it is an order of God. She must follow these orders of marriage because if she does not she will break the law of Islam. If she makes any mistakes, then she must buy her divorce from her husband.

Terms for the defendant
The defendant must recognize that he is the provider for his wife. He is expected to get along with her and use good language, to live well with her children, to support her with food, clothing, and a house, and he must give her money for household necessities such as hair oil, perfume, etc. He must fulfill all these terms and if he does not, he must divorce his wife if she brings in witnesses and a letter from the *sheha* attesting to his misdeeds.

---

[14] Mkokotoni Court Case No. 33–99.

Terms for both
Both the plaintiff and the defendant must give a report of misdeeds to the *sheha.*

Three months later, Juma came to court claiming that Mosa was not fulfilling her terms. He brought a letter from the *sheha* stating that he himself had tried to live by the agreement but that Mosa was not upholding her end of the bargain.

Mosa came to court by herself two days later, claiming that Juma only brought food in the afternoons, that he did not give her soap, oil or money for the children's schooling, and that the house was still not adequate. The kadhi listened, but reminded her that she must first go to the sheha if she had marital problems, as it was set out in the judgment. On her way out, Mosa told me that she felt shy about going to the *sheha* because she was an adult who already had great grandchildren. "I am embarrassed to go to the *sheha* every day to complain about my husband!"

One week later, Mosa and Juma came to court together. Shaykh Haji asked Mosa directly if she had fulfilled the terms of the judgment. She said that she had. He asked her why then she was not living with Juma as ordered. She answered, "Because he has no house!" Shaykh Haji was surprised, and told her again to go to the *sheha* to register the problem. When he questioned Juma about the house, Juma said that he did have a house, but that she would not stay there because it was "a bad one." Mosa also complained that Juma was not giving her adequate food. Juma responded that he brought food regularly, but agreed that it was not enough for all of her children.

After hearing their complaints, Shaykh Haji reminded the litigants that they had "two laws" to fulfill: maintaining the terms set by the court and going to the *sheha* if they had problems. He explained again that when the court issues terms, both disputants must go the *sheha* if the other party breaks the terms. He added that failure to do so was a violation of court procedure and thus they had violated the law both by not going to the sheha and by not fulfilling the terms of the ruling. Shaykh Haji very often stressed the importance of proper procedure in cases like this one where he issued terms as part of the judgment.

Shaykh Haji explained that Mosa would have been able to easily dissolve her marriage only if Juma had not fulfilled his obligations. However, she had also erred. He noted that they "were not sleeping in the same place," that Mosa did not return with him to his home, and that she did not go to the *sheha* to report the problem. Shaykh Haji decided that they must try to live together one more time, and that if Mosa could not bring herself to live with Juma, she must buy her divorce in a court-ordered *khuluu*. At this, he sent them home.

Two weeks later, Juma came to court, again complaining that Mosa would not live with him. They came, together, a few days later, and Shaykh Haji immediately ordered Mosa to buy her divorce. She agreed without argument. However, much debate ensued about how much she would pay. Juma demanded 70,000 shillings, just like he wrote for money before, but the kadhi told him that he was breaking the law by asking for more than he paid in *mahari*. Nevertheless, he permitted them to negotiate the amount outside of the courtroom and eventually the sum was set at 25,000 (about thirty dollars)—still greater than the original *mahari* of 7000 shillings.

I asked Shaykh Haji why he allowed this, since he had told Juma it was unlawful to pay more in *khuluu* than was given in the marriage gift. He explained that although Mosa was the plaintiff, they had both caused significant problems in the marriage. Juma still wanted her, but she did not want him and she was not without blame in the marital strife; therefore, she must buy her divorce from him. Because she no longer wanted to be married to Juma she must buy the divorce in *khuluu*, and since she had caused problems in the marriage she could pay more than her *mahari* if the litigants agreed on an amount outside of the court.[15] Shaykh Haji's explanation seems similar to what Layish found in Libya and Israel, where qadis accommodated voluntary agreements that were made between litigants outside of the court: "This attitude of the qadis [in Libya] towards customary *khuluu* is strikingly in line with the declared attitude of Muslim qadis in Israel on the same issue, according to which the court does not interfere in voluntary agreement, holding that 'mutual agreement is stronger than the qadi'" (Layish 1988:29).

In the final ruling, given in late March, Shaykh Haji explained that Mosa agreed to buy her divorce in a *khuluu* fashion because she

[15] There are considerable differences of opinion among Zanzibari kadhis and religious scholars on this subject. While Shaykh Haji allowed a negotiation of financial compensation in court-ordered *khuluu* divorce, others did not. Among others who thought it permissible, there were different reasons given for why it was so.

did not want to return to Juma. Mosa would be required to buy her divorce not only because she bore some responsibility for the marital discord, but also because she failed to see the *sheha* and thus violated procedural regularities. Interestingly, although he took time to explain this to the litigants, he did not specify it in the written statement.

> March 28, 2000.[16] In the court of the kadhi of Mkokotoni, the defendant says that from the day they were given the court's contract until today, "my wife has not agreed to follow me to my home and every day I go to her home to call her but she does not want to come. She was also called by the *sheha* but she did not go. This is indeed my explanation."
>
> The plaintiff says, "I will not go to his home because I do not want him and he has no place to keep me and I will follow the terms of our agreement by buying my divorce from him according to the law."
>
> The defendant agrees. The plaintiff begged for a delay to bring the money to buy her divorce. After the agreement of the plaintiff and the defendant, the court read the hadith of the Prophet Mohamedi concerning *khuluu* divorce. And the *aya* of the Qur'an which explains the process of *khuluu*. After this, the court wants the plaintiff to pay the amount with which she was married [*mahari*]; 25,000 shillings. She has until April 3 to bring it to the court.
>
> April 3, 2000. The plaintiff and the defendant have arrived at the court. The plaintiff paid 25,000 shillings to buy her divorce from the husband. The defendant has received the money, divorced his wife, and the divorce paper has been written. This case is closed, and the plaintiff and defendant are now divorced.

In our follow-up discussions, it was evident that Shaykh Haji ruled in this way because he considered Mosa at fault in their marital problems. Although Juma was ordered to improve his behavior and support her according to the law, the court never established that he was not supporting Mosa or their children adequately. Also, because he had no legal responsibility to support her children from a previous marriage, that claim was not seriously considered. Shaykh Haji also stressed that by refusing to go to the *sheha*, Mosa did not follow proper procedure. Further, since it was determined that her husband did indeed have a house, albeit not a nice one, she should have returned to him.

---

[16] Mkokotoni Case No. 33–99.

Discussion

A close look at these cases shows what various court players consider the essential legal issues in them and how different understandings of law and legal activity play out in courtroom practice. The analysis demonstrates the benefit of combining ethnography with documentary study. While a study of documents like the *madai* and *majibu* shows how the clerks present legal issues in a formulaic way, and the *hukumu* shows the way in which a judge writes his decision, court ethnography reveals the variation in the legal understandings of the different parties to a case and shows how documents may not tell the whole story.

The clerks, for example, played a significant role in all of the Mkokotoni cases. Their duty of rendering the jumbled grievances of a claimant into a coherent case for the judge is certainly not unique to Zanzibar. As elsewhere, it is common for the clerks to file cases into familiar categories.[17] However, the two cases discussed here illustrate the clerks' role as translator between differing understandings of Islamic law.[18] In Machano's case, Fumu determined that the plaintiff wanted his wife back more than he wanted to prosecute her for violating *edda*, which would have been a matter for the criminal courts, and he therefore told Juma to open the case in the kadhi's court and subsequently framed it as a familiar "missing wife" problem. In Mosa's case, the clerks also framed the claim differently from the way that she initially presented it. In addition to providing her with a house, Mosa thought that Juma was responsible for the maintenance of all of her children, including those from another marriage. However, Fumu knew the kadhi would not require Juma to support children who were not his own, and so emphasized Juma's bad behavior in her *madai*.

Many scholars studying Islamic legal practice today are interested in the interaction of various norms in court activity, legal understandings, and dispute resolution (see Bowen 1998, 2000, Caplan

[17] See, for example, the work of Merry (1990) and Yngvesson (1993) on courts in the United States.

[18] Brison's discussion on village magistrates' role as intermediaries between the "village and outside powers" in Papua New Guinea seems to be an interesting parallel to the position of the clerks and also the shehas' role in dispute resolution—as links between the communities and the state (Brison 1999).

1995, Hirsch 1997, Layish 1988, Messick 1990, Rosen 1989, 2000). These cases show how certain Zanzibari cultural norms of marriage and divorce, both considered technically unlawful, are either supported or contested in Shaykh Haji's rulings depending on how he attributes fault in marital disputes. To this aim, in both cases Shaykh Haji looked beyond what was presented in the *madai* and *majibu*. He made a point of questioning the legality not only of the defendant's actions, but also those of the plaintiff.

Conflicting ideas about divorce are evident in Machano's case. Shaykh Haji often stressed how and under what terms alleged divorces took place outside of the court. In this case, he accepted the testimony of a noted religious authority that Aisha was legitimately married to Kassim, yet questioned whether Machano had validly divorced her in a *khuluu* fashion. On more than one occasion, Shaykh Haji told me that he believed the average person did not understand much about the law; thus, he regularly aimed to establish the validity of out-of-court divorces. Here, his concern with establishing that the divorce was a valid instance of *khuluu* and not an episode of "writing for money" shows that the latter is a practice he considers a common misunderstanding of divorce, and one that he cannot condone in the courtroom. A woman should pay only if she is at fault or desires a divorce that her husband does not want. Aisha did not want to return to Machano, which indicated her desire to be divorced and legitimated her payment to him.

Mosa's case was similar to Machano's in that Shaykh Haji questioned her (the plaintiff) own behaviour in the recent history of the marriage. However, her case shows his support and legal justification of a local practice that he considered technically unlawful. He concluded that Mosa must buy her divorce because she had violated her marital obligations *and* the terms and procedural obligations set by the court. Juma was allowed to receive more financial compensation than he paid in *mahari* because Mosa broke procedural regularities and was at fault in the marital problems because she left him and allowed her children to misbehave. He allowed this kind of negotiation in a number of other cases as well, and justified it in the same way. Other kadhis and scholars handled this type of situation differently, however. Some did not allow negotiation at all, and others justified the negotiation religiously. Shaykh Haji, however, often told me that a Zanzibari kadhi was not able to apply religious law in full, and that although many scholars rejected the position of kadhi when offered it, he himself had accepted with knowledge of that aspect of the job.

Finally, it is interesting that in addition to encouraging the litigants to reconcile, in Mosa's case Shaykh Haji stressed the importance of following proper procedure as established by local norms and state-level directives. Although *shehas* and elders are not considered to have any special knowledge of religious or legal matters, their role in the dispute resolution process is upheld and promoted by the kadhi. This was evident in his repeated insistence that Juma and Mosa see the *sheha* to report problems in the marriage or violations of the *masharti*.

CHAPTER FIVE

FAIRNESS AND LAW IN AN INDONESIAN COURT

John R. Bowen

Introduction

Recently, historians, sociologists, and anthropologists (Dupret 2000; Libson 1997; Moors 1995; Powers 1994; Tucker 1998) have addressed the ways in which Islamic court judges draw on broad social norms in making their decisions. In the general spirit of this enterprise, in previous works (Bowen 1998, 2000, 2003) I sought to identify the social norms underlying legal reasoning by Indonesian judges. Here I shall focus on the language of justification employed by judges in deciding inheritance cases, taking as my examples several recent decisions from the Islamic court (*Pengadilan Agama*) of Central Aceh, in the highlands of Sumatra.

Indonesia has a nationwide system of Islamic courts that runs parallel to its system of civil courts (*Pengadilan Negeri*). In each of these two legal systems, one may appeal from a court of first instance to the provincial appellate court. The Supreme Court may review cases from either an Islamic or a civil appellate court. The jurisdiction of the Islamic courts is limited to matters of marriage, divorce, and inheritance in cases involving Muslims. (Jurisdictional conflicts in cases involving a mixed-religion couple do arise and have not been definitively resolved.) To a great extent, the organization, procedures, and the language of decisions in the Islamic courts are modeled after the Western-style civil courts (see Lev 1972).

The judges who serve on the Islamic courts are appointed by the Indonesian government, and they are rotated from one post to another during their careers. Most current judges graduated from one of Indonesia's state Islamic institutes, the IAIN (*Institut Agama Islam Negeri*), where they specialized in *sharīʿa.* Some judges also obtained a law degree from a general university, and all chief judges now are required to have done so. At the IAIN, they learn the basics of *uṣūl* al-fiqh, details of the substantive law areas in which they will be ruling (marriage, divorce and inheritance law), legal procedures, and relevant bodies of Indonesian state law. Since the mid-1990s they also have learned the state Compilation of Islamic Law in Indonesia. They are responsible to two distinct bodies; as civil servants they work for the Ministry of Religion, but the Supreme Court oversees their competence as judges.

As with many other Indonesian courts, the Islamic court in the town of Takèngën, Central Aceh, developed out of older Islamic law institutions. During the Sukarno years (1945–65), the court was staffed by local men, some of whom had no formal legal training. Some of these early judges served on the court for decades. Under President Suharto (1966–98), efforts were made to rotate judges more frequently and to demand a more uniform legal training. In the 1980s and 1990s, the province-level appellate court in Aceh exercised increasing degrees of control over local courts by overturning decisions and by summoning local judges for frequent "upgrading" sessions, where they were informed of new legal developments and sometimes upbraided for incorrect judicial decisions.

The legal and political situation has changed rapidly, and often violently, over the past ten years. In 1991, Suharto proclaimed that a newly written Compilation of Islamic Law was to be the sole source of law for judges serving on the Islamic courts (as well as for other civil servants). Since 1991, judges have justified their decisions in terms of the Compilation. In Aceh, the escalation of violence in the 1990s and early 2000s led many judges to flee the province. In 2001, a new set of laws for Aceh province, now renamed Nanggroe Aceh Darussalam (The State of Aceh, the Abode of Peace) to capture resonances of its past as an Islamic Sultanate, promised that "syariah" will be the basis for laws and that the courts will now be called Mahkamah Syariah—although what the courts will look like is as yet unclear. In the meantime, the battles between the Indonesian Army and the Acehnese continue, placing judicial reform on hold.

A Sketch of the Islamic Court

The court hears cases from throughout the district of Central Aceh, an area with about 200,000 people. Takèngën is the largest town both in the district and in the Gayo highlands, a larger area comprising Central and Southeast Aceh districts. Although the majority of highlands residents speak the Gayo language, considerable numbers of Acehnese (the majority people in the province) and Javanese also live there—the Acehnese mainly as traders, and the Javanese as farmers, brought to the area through the government resettlement program called transmigration. Acehnese domination in provincial politics and economics long has been an irritant to many in the highlands, and at present there is considerable support in the highlands for the creation of a separate province, to consist of the non-Acehnese areas.

Takèngën has a civil court and an Islamic court. Since the 1970s, civil court judges have come from outside the province, and have looked at Takèngën as a way station in a series of short-term appointments. Many of the Islamic court judges, however, were born in the highlands, speak the Gayo language, and are knowledgeable about Gayo social norms (*adat*). In court these judges play the role of the wise counselor, and often correct witnesses who mistakenly describe a rule of Gayo *adat*. Many Islamic judges served for long periods because the Indonesian government had trouble recruiting enough judges to staff the court. The court should have nine judges, but at the very least it must have three judges in order to hear cases involving disputes over property transfers (inheritance, gifts, and bequests). In order to reach even that minimum number, the provincial government approved the appointment as judge of a local man, Aman Arlis, who had served as chief clerk in the 1950s and 1960s and did not have a law degree. By the late 1990s, the court had been fully staffed with three Gayo judges, two Acehnese judges, one Malay man from the city of Medan who had lived for a long time in North Aceh, and three Javanese judges. (The three Javanese judges fled the highlands in 1999 to escape violence that was directed against Javanese settlers.) For a period of a few months in 1988, a woman judge (from West Sumatra) had served on the bench.

The court meets in a one-story wooden structure on a quiet residential street in the center of town. The court is near shops, primary schools, the mosque, and the district administrative offices. Two large buildings are joined by an open walkway. During court hours people mill about in the front courtyard, most of them relatives or supporters of someone appearing before the court that day. The scene is chatty and informal; people sit and openly discuss the cases at hand with much less animosity than I expected to find. Even in 2000, as violence was increasing in the highlands, the court was busy.

A man or woman coming to the court for any of these reasons first visits the clerks' building, which in the 1990s housed about a dozen male and female court clerks. Some clerks already have their law degrees and are waiting for judicial appointments; others have completed only high school. A clerk will interview the petitioner, usually in an effort to persuade him or her to settle the matter privately. Failing that, the clerk will help prepare the paperwork for the case and often give advice about how the petitioner should present his or her case, for example, suggesting which of many possible complaints about marital life are legitimate grounds for divorce.

An informal division of labor operates among the clerks. Some clerks do most of the initial interviewing, while others travel to villages to survey land under dispute. In the mid-1990s, three men shared duties as court reporter, sharing also a single dark sport coat that they would don before entering the courtroom. One clerk usually is charged with filing current cases, law books, and copies of the official Ministry of Religion journal *Mimbar Hukum*, and another with trundling older cases into the archives, a small back room with dusty, nearly forgotten files dating back to the 1940s.

Next to their large, shared work area is the office of the chief clerk, the Panitera, who supervises the stream of paperwork flowing between clerks and judges. There is also a small, one-judge courtroom. The second court building contains a larger courtroom, in which all cases tried by a panel of judges are heard, and two judges' offices: one for the chief judge and another shared by the remaining judges. Each office has a back door, which permits the judges to enter the larger courtroom without first exiting the courthouse.

Most of the clerks who had been working at the court in the early 1990s were still at their jobs in mid-2000 when I next visited the highlands. In one room three clerks were typing up documents on resounding manual typewriters. One woman had become the informal leader of the clerks, and it was to her that most court visitors first addressed themselves. Dressed in a white headscarf and a long print dress worn over trousers, she addressed everyone, judge, supplicant, or colleague, in the same friendly and direct manner. On a June day in 2000 she was busy typing up divorce papers for a Javanese couple in their late teens, lamenting to all who could hear, "Oh, you're so young and you're divorcing! Well, I guess you're no longer meant to be together (*tidak jodoh lagi*)." She asked them if they had children, and if the wife was pregnant, maintaining an informal tone with the couple. In another room a senior clerk was dealing with a large group involved in an inheritance case. A young man was visibly fuming about the fact that his adversary was occupying the house and selling goods from it even while the suit was in progress. The clerk kept urging him not to take matters into his own hands (*main hakim sendiri*), i.e., not to turn a civil suit into a criminal matter.[1]

The jurisdiction of the Islamic court is strictly limited to certain types of cases; all others are heard at the civil court. The Islamic court hears cases regarding marriage or divorce, as well as matters directly related to marriage and divorce, such as the reconciliation of a couple or the custody of children. As in all provinces of Indonesia, marriage and divorce cases involving Muslims may be brought only to the religious court. The court also hears demands to determine the rightful heirs to an estate, to adjudicate disputes over a gift or bequest of property, and to divide marital property as part of (or following) a divorce. In theory, disputes heard by the Islamic court may involve non-Muslims, if, for example, the heirs to an estate include people of more than one religion, or if a wife has converted to Christianity and then is sued for custody of her child. Such cases rarely if ever arise in Aceh, where all Acehnese or Gayo are Muslim, but they sometimes receive considerable popular attention when they arise elsewhere in Indonesia.

The frequencies of different types of cases have changed markedly through the years. In its first few decades (1945–1970s), the Islamic court in Takèngën heard a relatively small number of cases per year. Most of these cases involved either a request to register a marriage or a dispute over the ownership of land. By the 1980s and 1990s the court heard a large number of divorce cases each year and fewer cases in other categories. The cases involved requests for permission to take a second wife, demands that a husband meet his obligations to support his wife, petitions for divorce, requests that the court formalize the reconciliation of a divorced couple, and requests to determine the proper division of an estate. The table below lists the cases decided in the calendar years 1992 and 1993, and during the first half of 1999.

[1] Given that both the civil court and the town jail had shut down because of the extreme violence, and anyone arrested was promptly released, the cautionary remark was more of a moral nature than a physical threat.

Table 1. *Number of cases decided in the Central Aceh Islamic court, 1992, 1993, and January–July 1999, by type (source: court records)*[2]

Type of case	*Number of cases decided in:* 1992	1993	Jan–July 1999
Marriage			
validation of marriage	28	25	0
petition for polygamy	11	4	1
petition for husband's support	3	2	0
Divorce			
husband's petition	110	99	80
wife's petition	95	102	91
child custody	2	0	0
Property division			
after divorce	0	3	4
inheritance	12	5	3

Cases involving marriage occupy a small part of the court's time. People may request a marriage certificate if they either lost the original or were married before such certificates were routinely issued. These cases were numerous in periods of social upheaval, and again in the years after the passage of the 1974 marriage law, but there were no such requests in early 1999. Few requests were made for the court to approve taking a second wife. Divorce cases are the most numerous, and the number of such cases doubled during the 1990s. Inheritance cases are far fewer in number, but because they often require numerous witnesses (some of whom fail to appear the first time they are called), as well as trips to measure disputed plots of land, these cases usually stretch out over weeks or months. About half of the inheritance hearings I attended in 1994 lasted less than a quarter of an hour because a witness had failed to appear or one of the parties had failed to produce a document required for the hearing.

The cases are spread evenly throughout the year (including the fasting month of Ramadhan). The court hears cases each Monday through Thursday, from about nine o'clock in the morning until

[2] If marital property was divided as part of a divorce settlement, as often is the case, then that division is not recorded separately. Therefore, court divisions after divorce are much more common than is suggested by these figures.

about two in the afternoon. A blackboard lists the cases scheduled for each day, along with the judges and clerk assigned to each. The court usually hears inheritance cases on Mondays, after each judge has finished hearing his assigned divorce cases and three judges are free to make up the judicial panel. No hearings are held on Fridays, when the judges and staff spend a few hours catching up on paperwork, and then drift off to play badminton. Clerks set up ping-pong tables in the large courtoom and play until it is time to attend noontime congregational worship in the town mosque.

One judge suffices to hear a divorce case or to legalize a marriage (although by 2000, with what in theory was a larger staff, three judges had begun to hear divorce cases). Three judges must sit as a panel to hear an inheritance case. In 1994, twenty to thirty people would show up for the inheritance cases, fewer for divorce cases. Farmers for the most part, they dress up for the occasion. The women wear long batik wrap-around skirts (rather than the everyday India-cloth kind), dressy shirts called *kebayas*, and headscarves. The men wear good shirts, trousers, decent sandals, and black caps. One or two men don sport coats.

The larger courtroom can hold forty people if they sit close together on the long wooden benches. Witnesses sit on folding chairs, toward the front of the room, facing the judges. The three judges sit behind a table on a raised dais, with the court reporter to their right and slightly behind them. The judges wear robes with maroon fronts and black sleeves, with a white ascot tied around their necks. They wear the same black caps worn by all other local men. Although the court has a permanent chief judge, in the courtroom the judges take turns presiding.

When a case is ready for hearing, the presiding judge rings a bell, and a clerk calls for the parties to enter the courtroom. The judge calls the session to order by pronouncing the *Basmala* (In the Name of God, the Merciful, the Compassionate), and proceeds to business. When the session is over he says so, pounding his gavel once to emphasize closure. The inheritance hearings are entirely open to all visitors, as are the initial hearings in divorce cases, when the judge tries to reconcile the parties. If, however, efforts to reconcile fail, then the judge continues in closed session.

Plaintiffs always sit to the judges' right and defendants to their left. At the beginning of the session, the witnesses are asked to leave at the beginning of the session so as not to be influenced by others' testimony. They are then called in one by one to testify. After giving testimony each witness joins the others on the long benches.

Between sessions each judge sits in an office, reads new or pending cases, listens to the radio, and fields requests from petitioners. As I sat in the chief judge's office one day in 1994, a steady stream of people knocked on his door and entered. One woman came to request a divorce. The judge posed some questions to determine the grounds for her claim (her husband had taken her to her parents and not returned for fourteen months) and then gave her the right form to fill out. Other people came with various bits of paperwork to be filled out by the judge.

Judicial procedure follows a colonial-era version of European civil law. Plaintiffs and defendants introduce written statements, replies, and counter-replies, which are handed to the judges and entered into the court record. Attorneys rarely are involved in any way. After questioning the parties and their witnesses, judges write a decision in which they outline the arguments and testimonies offered by each side and present the legal considerations relevant to the case, followed by their decision.

At the appellate level, the judges reiterate lower court proceedings and then issue a judgment. Generally they work only from the documents forwarded to them. The appellate court might overturn, affirm, or send back the case for further evidentiary hearings at the first-instance level. From time to time it will set aside the lower court's decision, and issue a new ruling. The Supreme Court has the same options, but it generally restricts itself to the question of whether or not the lower court interpreted the law correctly, and avoids weighing claims about evidence, or considering arguments not already introduced at a lower level. A published account of a case that has been heard by the Supreme Court includes the decisions of the first-instance and appellate courts, and thus allows the reader to follow the arguments and legal reasoning presented at all stages.

Two types of family property cases showed up most frequently in a sample of cases drawn from the court's archives: requests to divide estates and marital property suits.[3] In the first type of case, a plaintiff

[3] I drew my sample of cases from the archives of the two courts during fieldwork conducted in July 1985, June–August 1994, and June 2000. For each court, I selected blocks of years, beginning in the late 1940s and including all available cases from the 1990s. For each sample I read all cases with a bearing on issues of family property.

asks the court to divide an estate according to Islamic law. The defendant is a sibling, cousin, or other close relative who has refused to divide the property. In some of these cases, the defendant does not contest the request, and the court divides the property. In other cases the defendant makes the counterclaim that he or she had received some of the estate as a *hiba*, gift from the deceased. The court either accepts or rejects the counterclaim, according to the proof offered by the defendant and the burden of proof required by the court. Marital property suits first were brought to the court in the 1970s. In these cases, the plaintiff, an ex-wife, asks for her share of marital property.

Women have benefited more from the court's actions than have men. For the forty-nine cases for which I have complete information concerning the litigants, women were the plaintiffs in thirty-one cases, usually against men, and they won significantly more frequently than did male plaintiffs. As has been reported elsewhere (Hirsch 1998; Tucker 1998), women often perceive Islamic courts to work in their interest, not because the substantive rules constitute an improvement over traditional rules, but because the courts can offer property divisions relatively quickly. In the case of the Central Aceh Islamic court, moreover, judges increasingly have added purported gifts and testaments back into the estate pool, thereby increasing the absolute size of the shares received by daughters (Bowen 1998, 2000).

The Form of Court Decisions

Islamic court documents are almost identical to documents produced in the local civil court. Each case has a number indicating the year it was introduced. Each time a court decides a case it issues a document called a "Decision" (*putusan*). It is written in Latin-script Indonesian; quotations from Qur'ān or hadīth are written in Arabic and then translated into Indonesian.

In a typical inheritance dispute, the Decision consists of three major sections. In the first section, called *Tentang duduk perkaranya* (Concerning the dispute in question), the judges summarize the statements and testimony presented by the two sides during the course of the trial. The judges first list all plaintiffs and defendants in the case; when needed, they assign each a number (e.g., "Plaintiff 3"). The substance of the case is presented as a list of propositions claimed by one side or the other and findings of fact by the court, all written as a series of phrases of the form "Considering that x. Considering that y." These phrases are grammatically subordinate to the final section in which the judges reveal their decision. This series of claims extends over most of the Decision, including the presentation of both parties' positions and replies, the evidence introduced by each side, any findings of fact by the court (such as the size of land parcels under dispute), and the testimony of witnesses. The court may also cite a verse of the Qur'ān or a hadīth as one such "consideration."

In the second major section of the Decision, *Tentang hukumnya* (About the Law), the judges restate the problem before them, evaluate each piece of evidence as strong or weak, make additional findings, most commonly concerning the identity of legitimate heirs to the estate, and cite the relevant Qur'ānic verses, hadīth, or articles from the Compilation of Islamic Law. Sometimes the court will also specify the amount of land or money due each heir according to Islamic law. It is, however, in the third and final section, entitled *Mengadili* (Judges or To Judge), where the court declares its judgment, including the division of land and other objects, the payment of court costs, and the names of the judges presiding in the case. (I will label the three sections "Claims," "Law," and "Judgment.")

The Decision, then, is a long statement, conceptually a single sentence, collectively authored by a panel of judges, which presents a smooth, continuous process of legal reasoning. The court presents all the evidence as grammatically and logically subordinate to a main clause, containing its finding, which comes only at the very end of the document. The form of the Decision represents the legal process as one of, first, evaluating the evidence and, secondly, deducing the judgment from the relevant laws.

These formal representations of the legal process derive from the European civil law tradition, as transformed by the Dutch colonial administration, applied in the colonial civil courts, and then adopted for the new, postindependence civil and Islamic courts. This resemblance between Islamic and civil court processes probably will increase, as Islamic court judges more frequently graduate from law faculties as well as from the State Islamic Institutions (IAINs). In parallel fashion, the sources cited by Islamic court judges in their decisions increasingly resemble those cited by their civil court counterparts. Islamic court decisions written in the 1950s and 1960s referred to Arabic-language books of Islamic jurisprudence as well as to the

Qur'ān, but never to state law. The 1974 Marriage Law significantly modified the content of marriage law and expanded the competence of the courts. Judges began to cite this law shortly after it was signed into law. By the early 1990s, the Compilation of Islamic Law, declared binding on judges by then President Suharto, began to appear as a major and sometimes sole justification for a decision (see Bowen 1999), although some judges continued to cite the older books of *fiqh*.

In the ways in which they represent their processes of legal reasoning, then, Islamic court judges in Indonesia highlight processes of deductive reasoning, and rely increasingly on positive law. Even if they hold a dissenting view on the matter, the appellate process and the top-down supervision of judges together have compelled judges to reason publicly by following a civil law tradition model of law. Elsewhere (Bowen 1999), I consider difficulties with the state's efforts to make *fiqh* and state law appear as perfectly compatible, particularly with regard to agency in divorce (who makes a *ṭalāq* happen?) and legality of marriage (which acts constitutes marriage?). Here I wish to look at the way judges bring other norms to bear in their decision-making.

Was There an Agreement? The Anatomy of an Inheritance Case

I present here a case decided in 1998 involving a disputed inheritance division. The case is one of many in which the court has had to sort out conflicting claims made by the parties concerning bequests (*wasiat*), consensual agreements (*musyawarah*), and division according to Islamic law (*farā'iḍ*). In this case, as well as in others heard during the 1990s, the judges drew on nonlegal social norms to make up their minds, but couched their decision in terms of such issues as the burden of proof, state law, and the rules of Islam governing the division of an estate. In these cases, the two parties do not differ on the relevant substantive Islamic law. The major issues facing the court have to do with the intentions of the parties and the fairness of any prior divisions of an estate.

The case at hand (PA TKN/159/1998), which for convenience I shall call *Inen Maryam v. Aman Mas* (there were in fact four plaintiffs and three defendants), is representative of inheritance disputes heard in Takéngën during the past two decades with respect both to the form of the case itself and to the direction of the legal reasoning carried out by the judges. At issue was not how to interpret the law, whether it be *fiqh* or state law, but whether agreements made by the parties superseded legal rules.

In the case, four of six sisters asked the court to redivide their parents' estate. These sisters were daughters of Abdul Kadir Aman Siti Esah (Abdul Kadir Father of Siti Esah), and his wife Letifah Inen Siti Esah (Letifah Mother of Siti Esah). The father had died in 1971, the mother in 1986. The estate consisted of several plots of land, a house, and other property, and most of it was in the hands of the only son, Aman Mas. The plaintiffs claimed that there never had been a meeting (*musyawarah*) to decide how to divide the land. Aman Mas said there had been such a meeting and that it had led to an agreement about the division. The two remaining daughters, who were listed as codefendants in the case, agreed with his version of the events. In 1998 the Court ruled in favor of the plaintiffs and ordered the land divided among all the heirs. The defendants appealed to the Islamic High Court in Banda Aceh, which affirmed the decision in August 1999. In January 2000, the defendants asked the Supreme Court to quash the decision; as of June 2000 the case was waiting a hearing.

Claims

In their arguments, the plaintiffs claimed that Aman Mas had held on to more than his share of the estate. They said that their father had instructed Aman Mas to give a particular plot of rice land to one of the plaintiffs, Halimah, because she had been the one initially to clear the land. In their Decision the court quoted (in Gayo, without translation) the plaintiffs' version of the father's oral commission (*manat*) on this matter to Aman Mas, which included the threat to haunt him from beyond the grave if he did not comply. The plaintiffs said that Aman Mas had promised to give his sisters some land, but that he had added that they should take it or leave it, because as the son he was the one who could rightfully determine what happened to their parents' estate.

In his reply to these charges, Aman Mas stated that after their parents' deaths each of the children had enjoyed use-rights over portions of the land. In 1986 they had held a meeting governed by the norms of consensus, a *musyawarah mufakat*, and at this meeting all the children agreed that Aman Mas had rightfully received some land as a bequest (*wasiat*).[4] According to him, the heirs agreed that they would divide the remaining land by lottery, and that they were all satisfied "and would not demand anything more." Although the subsequent division of the wealth was done by lottery, in his testimony Aman Mas frequently used the verbal form *difara'id* (to be divided according to Islamic rules) to refer to the division, seeking to suggest that it was in accord with Islam. The two codefendant sisters sided with Aman Mas regarding his claim that their father had bequeathed him a plot. When asked their opinion by the presiding judges, they agreed that there had been a consensual agreement among all the heirs.

After each side had presented its initial position statements, each had the opportunity, after a delay of some weeks, to submit replies: a *duplik* from the defendants, followed by a *replik* from the plaintiffs. At this point the two sisters who had sided with Aman Mas played an important role. Because they had not received large portions of the estate, one would have expected them to join their sisters in calling for the land to be redivided. However, they agreed with their brother that all the land had been "difaraid" forty-two days after their father's death. By this term the sisters meant to say that the land had been divided in a way that gave to each party ownership of a share. They did not imply that the land had been divided according to the Islamic rules of division. Indeed, they went on to say that the division had been carried out according to a lottery.

In their reply to the initial statement of the defendants, the plaintiffs conceded that there had been a lottery, but complained about how it had been carried out. They explained that Aman Mas had first selected which plot was to be his own, and then held the lottery on his own. Only afterwards did he call them to his house and point out to each sister her plot. Each side offered witnesses. Among them was the village headman, who said that the division indeed had taken place in 1986, but that several years later two of the plaintiffs had come to him, saying it was not fair. At that time, he reported, Aman Mas had given them a house in return for "a promise that they would not ask for any more" from the estate.

[4] Although bequests to heirs are invalid if contested by an heir, if all parties agree to them they are valid.

Law

The judges then presented their analysis of the issues and the relevant law. First, they enumerated those claims that had not been rebutted. The two parties agreed that the disputed land plots were part of their father's estate, and that there had been a lottery to divide the land. These claims could be set aside for the moment. They then considered claims that were yet to be resolved. For each such claim they focused on the credibility of the claim and the appropriate burden of proof.

The matter of allocating the burden of proof is of considerable importance in these cases. Very often the testimony offered by one side is countered by rebuttals from the other. Even written documents attesting to an estate division can be said to have been produced under duress or without all signers fully understanding the meaning of the document, as in a case discussed below. As a result, if the burden of proving the case falls squarely on one side, that side is highly likely to lose. The effect of assuming the burden of proof increased during the 1990s, as the court began to demand higher standards of proof.

The judges do have a certain amount of room for maneuvering with regard to the burden of proof. They can assign the overall burden to the plaintiffs, on grounds that the plaintiffs have made a claim that has been denied by the defendants. They can rely on a notion of the preponderance of the evidence, handing the decision to the party whose proof is stronger with respect to a particular factual claim, such as the date when a plot of land was purchased. (This fact may be relevant to deciding whether land is part of the family estate or the property of one party.) In cases such as the one at hand, in which the plaintiffs request a division of the estate, and the defendants counterclaim that a division already had taken place, the judges might rule differently. They can claim that it is up to the defendants to prove the case, because they are the party making a "positive claim," i.e., a claim about an event that took place in the past. My conversations with judges has led me to believe that sometimes they first decide who is telling the truth about a key matter of fact in the case, and then they assign the burden of proof to the other party.

The case involving Aman Mas fits into the third category of proof, that in which the burden falls on the defendants. The judges cited an article of the colonial-era civil law code stating that whoever makes a positive claim thereby assumes the burden of proof. In this case the defendants had claimed that the land already had been properly divided among the heirs. The burden of proof therefore fell on them to show that the land had indeed been divided in accordance with Islamic law. The key passage begins as follows (pp. 20–21 of PA TKN/159/1998):

> Considering, that in court the Plaintiffs stated that the wealth left by the deceased had not yet been divided. It is true that by means of a lottery the female heirs were allotted shares, but the Defendant had already taken his share beforehand, and in any case the daughters were given shares not through a division, but by the Defendant designating plots as he wished.
>
> Considering, that according to article 283 of the civil code, the burden of proof follows the system of positive proof. In this case, because the Plaintiff claims that the disputed items had never been divided among all the heirs, it is the Defendants, not the Plaintiff, who assume the burden of proving that the disputed wealth had been divided (difaraid) among all the heirs.
>
> Considering, that the Defendants have offered witnesses, and we find that the second witness's testimony may be heard even though he is the husband of the second co-defendant.
>
> Considering, that the second witness just referred to explained that before the division of wealth among the six female heirs, the Defendant took out his share. This testimony corroborates the admission of the Defendant. The Court (*Majelis*) is of the opinion that the division by lottery should have been held for all the heirs, male as well as female. However, this lottery was only used to distribute shares to the female heirs, such that there arose dissatisfaction among the heirs, and the Defendant later gave two of them, Plaintiffs III and IV, additional wealth in the form of a house.
>
> Considering, that in these facts clear indications can be seen that the Defendant's share was much larger than the share he should have received, a point strengthened in the Defendant's own conclusions by his statement that the daughters each received 15 bamboo measures of land, plus a house to share among them, whereas the Defendant received 6 1/2 kaleng measures of land.
>
> Considering, that despite the testimony of the Defendant's first and second witnesses that the disputed items had been divided following a *musyawarah*, the witnesses (supported by the Defendants) also stated that after the division there arose dissatisfaction among the Plaintiffs because the gap between their shares and that of the Defendant was too great and unbalanced, such that from the Defendant's share an additional house was given to Plaintiffs III and IV. These events were confirmed by the third defense witness.

Now, the division of the estate clearly had not been along the lines stipulated by the "science of shares": the son had taken much more than twice the share awarded each daughter. His claim that the court ought to ratify the earlier division rested on the claim that all the heirs had agreed both to the lottery and to the bequest of land to him by their father. The court does indeed regularly affirm agreements reached by parties and considers such findings to be a matter of Islamic law, a proposition strengthened by the Compilation of Islamic Law (Article 183). The court could have restricted their findings to an assessment of the evidence offered by the defendants that all parties had agreed to the division and to the bequest.

But the judges did not so restrict themselves. Instead, they made claims about the fairness of the division and the probable states of mind of the daughters. Although they did not object to a lottery qua lottery, they stated that the lottery should have been held for all the heirs rather than only for the daughters. Thus, the court did not object to the manner of division per se, to the absence of a reference to Islamic law, but to the control exercised by the son over the process. The fact that the son later added a house to the daughters' shares only confirmed in their minds that the daughters had been dissatisfied and that the son had recognized, if not the legitimacy of their complaint, at least its potential strength.

The judges then addressed the claims that the division had been made according to a *musyawarah.* In the Indonesian political-cultural context, the term *musyawarah* indicates more than a meeting; it implies that the participants reached a consensus on their topic of deliberation. The term is part of the state ideology, Pancasila, and its cognates appear in local ways of talking about dispute resolution in many parts of the country (Bowen 2000). To the defendants' claims that a *musyawarah* had settled the division, the court replied that witnesses had testified to the effect that the plaintiffs subsequently were unhappy with the division because of its unfairness. The judges concluded on the basis of the testimony that the defendant had failed to prove his case and that the *musyawarah* had not obtained the free agreement of the daughters. "Considering, that from the facts presented at the hearing, the court (*Majelis*) is of the opinion that the division of the disputed wealth carried out by the Defendant on the 44th day after the death of the deceased Letifah was not based on agreement and consensus (*kata sepakat dan mufakat bulat*) among all the heirs, but was dictated by the Defendant's own desires, this division therefore has no legal value and must be put aside" (p. 22 of PA TKN/159/1998).

The court then took up the Defendant's claim that their father had left to him by bequest (*wasiat*) a plot of land. "The Defendant did not offer any proof in the matter, and according to the Compilation of Islamic Law, article 195(3), bequests to heirs are valid [only] if they are agreed upon by all the heirs. In this case, however, the Plaintiffs said that they did not agree to it, and the court is therefore of the opinion that this *wasiat* never took place, and that it must be stated that the disputed objects are part of the deceased's estate and must be divided among the heirs" (ibid.). Here, too, the court reached a conclusion about the state of mind of the daughters at the time of the bequest based on their current testimony in court.

Judgment

Most of the decisive judgments in fact had been made in the Law section, leaving to the final Judgment only the statement of the heirs and their shares. "Considering, that the heirs are the Plaintiffs and the Defendants, consisting of six daughters and one son. Because there are no other heirs with rights to receive the deceased's wealth, the division of the deceased's estate is based on the stipulation in the Qur'ān Surat an-Nisa Ayat 11." Written below this statement in longhand is the Arabic of the verse followed by its Indonesian translation as: "God has ruled (*mensyari'atkan*) that the share of a son is twice the share of a daughter" (p. 23 of PA TKN/159/1998).[5] Article 176 of the Compilation of Islamic Law is cited as the second basis for the decision; this article restates the ratio of shares to sons and daughters.

The plaintiffs had presented the court with estimates of the monetary value of each plot of land, and because these estimates were not contested by the defendants, they were accepted. The values were added up to produce an estimate of the total monetary value of the estate, and the shares awarded to each heir were stated in rupiah. Typically, the court would stop at that point in its calculations, but in the mid-1990s the appellate court began to insist that it also specify which plots each heir would receive. Accordingly, the

[5] I translate the Indonesian gloss given in the text of the decision; the Arabic of the first part of the verse is "God commands you concerning your children."

court assigned a certain area to each heir in this case, awarding, for example, Siti Esah and Saunah each 4,479 square meters of plot 1. (The judges told me that they did not expect the siblings to take control of the land exactly as prescribed, because it made more sense for one party to sell to another.)

The court concluded by assigning court costs to the defendants and identifying themselves. The judge who presided over the case also wrote the decision: a Gayo judge, Dr. M. Anshary, SH (*Sarjana Hukum*, a degree only awarded by law faculties). Judge Anshary, who studied at an Islamic Institute (IAIN) as well as at a law school, had been acting as Chief Judge of the court for much of the previous three years. Two other judges sat on the panel, Dr. Jumaidi (from Java) and Dr. M. Ihsan (from Medan), both of whom graduated from an IAIN, where they specialized in *sharīʿa*, not from a law faculty.

Appeal

Later that year, Aman Mas, dissatisfied with the decision, appealed to the higher Islamic court in Banda Aceh, the provincial capital. The estate had been divided by *musyawarah mufakat* in 1986, he complained, "such that the defendant/appellant is surprised and startled that after more than ten years, suddenly there arrives a lawsuit." The Takèngën court's decision was wrong, he added, because it had overturned a *musyawarah mufakat*, and so doing "clearly invites social conflict, and it upsets our deceased parents (*Almarhum dan Almarhuma*) in the otherworld (*alam Barzah*)." Furthermore, he continued, property divisions carried out through *musyawarah mufakat* have a firm foundation in Islamic law because God said, "Consult among yourselves in all your affairs." (*Bermusyawaralah dalam segala urusan.*) After the appellate court affirmed the earlier decision, Aman Mas and the two daughters requested cassation from the Supreme Court. In each of these appeals, the original defendants, now called "the party requesting review/cassation," submitted a *memorie* outlining their argument, to which the original plaintiffs, now "respondents," submitted a *kontramemorie*. In these and other cases, both sides sometimes make strategic use of the original court's arguments and rhetoric when formulating their memoranda. In this case, the four sisters, now in the position of respondents, quoted the husband of one of their opponents as admitting that Aman Mas had taken his share out of the estate before the lottery was conducted. To this quotation, which had been cited in the original testimony before the Takèngën court, the authors of the memorandum now added that "he did this without *musyawarah*," emphasizing the point made by the court.

When Do People Really *Agree?*

In June 2000, as I sat in the courtroom reading through the typescript Decision of this case, Judge Anshary, its author, walked up to me and peered over my shoulder. I asked him how the judges had decided that the heirs had not freely consented to the division at the *musyawarah*. His answer linked the *inequality* of the division to the intentions of the heirs. "In that case, when we went to inspect the plots of land, we saw that the daughters had small plots of land, maybe 1/2 hectare for all six daughters, while the son had two hectares all to himself. We asked about each parcel whether it had been bought, and for each they said no, that it had been left by their father for them. The difference in the size of the parcels assigned to the brother and the sisters was so great that it was clear that they had not agreed on the division. At that time people would divide by just pointing to parcels, but that is not valid. The men dominated and the women could not say anything, although as soon as there was an opportunity to go to the court, they would do so." In other words, a true *musyawarah* had not been held.

The judge distinguished between overt acts of agreement to a division of property, and true, sincere agreement. Yes, there had been a meeting at which all parties had come to a conclusion, and there was no evidence that anyone objected to the meeting at the time. It was only several years later, according to the village headman, that some daughters had complained that the division was unfair, and twelve years passed before they brought suit. Did their earlier participation in the meeting mean that they had once agreed and later changed their minds? And regardless of the answer to that question, could they contest the earlier division on the grounds that it did not correspond to the Islamic "science of shares"?

In the 1960s and early 1970s, the Takèngën court routinely said "yes" to the first question and "no" to the second question. In cases adjudicated in the 1960s, the court said, "We should not keep redividing property." Once a settlement had been reached, the court was reluctant to change it. Indeed, the civil court, to which, until the rules of jurisdiction in Aceh changed in 1970, one could also bring inheritance cases, invented a legal category of "elapsed claims" and used it to disallow such requests to redivide property. The judges treated as irrelevant the objection that sons had coerced daughters into agreeing to the settlement, on the grounds that a settlement had been reached, and Islam supported agreements among heirs. In some cases the judges also accepted defendants' arguments that, according to Gayo social norms (*adat*), once a daughter married out of her natal village, she lost her right to make future claims on the family estate.

By the early 1990s the court had changed its position on this issue. It now could do so, because it was politically stronger than before—it had a firmer foundation in statutory law, it had the backing of an authoritarian government, and it now operated under conditions of relative stability (which were, however, to change). Moreover, the judges had changed their views on what women and men thought about rights and rules. Judges now assumed that all daughters, regardless of where they married, considered themselves to have rights under Islamic law.

Even in cases in which a purported *musyawarah* had led to the signing of an agreement, the objective inequality of the division sometimes led the judges to declare that the daughters *could not have* freely consented to the arrangement. In the 1987 case *Samadiah v. Hasan Ali* (PA TKN/381/1987), for example, a daughter who had received nothing from her parents' estate demanded the share due her according to Islamic law. The other children acknowledged that they had all quarreled over the disposition of these lands in 1969, but said that they had settled the dispute in a large village meeting that same year. They also said that their father had left a bequest stipulating that whoever took care of him would get certain lands, and that it was one of the sons, a man named Egem, who had done so. They noted that the bequest and the transfer of those lands to Egem had been made publicly at a meeting and had been approved by all the children. They produced a document attesting to the bequest that had been declared valid by the Takèngën civil court in 1970.

The practice of leaving land to the child who cares for his or her parents is widely followed in the Gayo highlands. Such bequests, called *pematang*, are generally considered to be the privilege of the parents. A parent's bequest is *ipso facto* valid; its authority comes from the right of the owner to dispose of the wealth, not from the consent of the other children. Bequests can be, and indeed are, challenged as contrary to Islamic law ("no bequest to an heir" unless all heirs agree to it). Indeed, the Compilation of Islamic Law, article 195(3), follows general Indonesian interpretations of *fiqh* in allowing bequests to heirs only if such agreement is produced (a rule cited by the court in the case described earlier).

In *Samadiah*, the Islamic court ruled that despite the document, the very fact that some heirs now contested the case was a sign of the absence of consensus. (Although the judges made no mention of this to me, they may have disregarded the general court's finding as having been tainted by bribery.) Furthermore, the judges argued that even according to Gayo *adat*, bequests must be agreed to by all the heirs. "*Pematang*, according to the Gayo *adat* that is still held to and approved of by the people, is considered valid only if all Wahab's children accept and approve of the declaration (of the agreement)," explained one of the judges who ruled in the case (interview, 1994). The judges ruled that because the plaintiff and two of the defendants said they knew of no such declaration, the bequest could not be approved. The judges ordered all the wealth divided.

The defendants appealed the case to the Aceh appellate court, insisting that the document proved that all the heirs had agreed to the division. The higher court, which heard the case in 1990, returned the case to the Takèngën court, ordering them to take a second look at the document. The lower court did as they were told. "We still thought the daughters were pressured, but we followed instructions," Judge Kasim commented to me. In 1992 they sent the case back up, unchanged, to the court in Banda Aceh, which set aside the decision and ruled in favor of the plaintiffs. (The case was appealed to Jakarta, and has yet to be settled.)

On what grounds did the judges determine that consensus had not been reached despite the existence of a document attesting to the contrary? Judges Hasan and Kasim explained to me in 1994 that the other heirs, principally the two daughters, could have sincerely accepted the 1969 agreement only if it had been in accord with their Islamic rights. That agreement clearly was in contradiction with the contents of the Qur'ān, however, because it did not award them their rightful shares. It therefore could not have been the product of consensus. Judge Kasim stated that he and the other judges had felt that the two daughters had been pressured into signing the 1969 document, even though such pressure could not be proven. Because no daughter would freely sign such an agreement if it were clearly against her interests, he reasoned, there must have been pressure.

Judge Kasim's statement also helps clarify the first case we considered, *Inen Maryam v. Aman Mas*. In both cases, the judges concluded from the objective unfairness of an earlier settlement that the plaintiffs could not have sincerely accepted the settlement, a conclusion based on the assumption that all parties knew and accepted the social norm that estates ought to be divided according to Islamic law, and not according to Gayo *adat* or any other arrangement. This assumption concerns the normative knowledge of the population, and not the law itself.

In this case, however, the judges went one step further. Not only did they find the bequest invalid because Islamic law requires a true consensus to have been reached, but they also claimed that Gayo *adat* requires such a consensus. In years of work in Takèngën and nearby villages I have never heard anyone characterize the rule concerning bequests in this way. The court in effect recategorized the Islamic rule regarding bequests as "local custom." They did not need to do so in order to rule as they did, because the Islamic law on the matter is clear. Their invention made it possible for them to base their ruling not only on an Islamic rule, but also on an agreed-upon local social norm. This claim made the decision not a matter of enforcing *adat* over Islam, but of enforcing a rule found in both *adat* and Islam.

In 1994, Judge Kasim discussed with me a similar case that was awaiting review by the Supreme Court, *Syamsiah binti Mudali v. M. Aji Aman Sarana* (PA TKN/180/1991). "A father had a son and four daughters," he explained:

> The father gave a lot of his rice land to the son and the son's wife; the son also received a large bequest. He gave very little to the daughters. In the 1970s, he drew up a document and had everyone sign. He even sent one of his grandchildren to persuade a daughter who had been reluctant to sign, and she signed. She was not satisfied, though. Later a second document, probably drawn up by the son, but written as if it were from the father, stipulated that the bequest was made officially to the son, and the son's portion of the remaining lands was increased! Each daughter, who should have received 2.5 tem measures of land [under a hectare], received only 0.5 tem!
>
> This was going too far, it deviated too far from justice. There is a *hadîth* that says that, although gifts should be given fairly, they can still be valid even if they are not fair. But this is going too far. Finally, after the father died, the daughter petitioned the court. She was joined by his other daughters, but at least one daughter sided with the son.

> The defendant based his case on the first document, but we said it was going too far. They appealed and lost, and the case is now with the Supreme Court. We are very interested in seeing whether the Court can support our judgment, because it introduces a sense of justice [*rasa keadilan*] into the court. Now, no one is totally fair—just look at the fingers on one hand: they work together but are all different lengths. And so it is with children: some will taste sweet, some rich, some bitter. But there are limits.

Observe in this case how easy it would have been for the judge to say that the agreement was valid. After all, all the interested parties had signed the letter of agreement, and no proof was offered of coercion. But the judges said that they disbelieved these documents. Here again the judges contrasted sincere (*ikhlas*) agreement, which could only be obtained if the division had been fair, with mere procedural correctness.

In 2000 I was able to see the case in the court files. The Takèngën court's ruling indeed had been appealed to the Supreme Court.[6] The father's document had stipulated that the daughters could not sell the land they had received to anyone but their brother, the defendant, because the land was *tanah pusaka* (heirloom land); this was their father's "final *wasiat*" to them.[7] The land was divided at a meeting held in the presence of the village headman. However, the headman announced at the meeting that the division was conditional, saying to the recipients that "if you sell the rice land, then one-half of your land will go to the defendant."

In their written decision, the Court, with Judge Kasim presiding, stated that they doubted the validity of the letter, adding that "the division is far from being just, and is 'tied' [*mukhait*, referring to the restrictions on selling the land], leaving the rights of the heirs unclear; therefore this exhibit [the document] is not accepted." Unfairness both in the division and in the power wielded by men over women rendered the settlement invalid despite the presence of a contract.

[6] Case No. 180, 1991, heard and rejected by the Supreme Court in 1995. Aman Sarana then had asked for a judicial review of the case (*peninjauan kembali*) and engaged a lawyer, an action that still is rare in Takèngën. As of June 2000 the file ended at that point.

[7] The document was signed in ways that shed light on the probable participation of the various parties in its drafting: the father, Aman Aji, signed "Aman Aji" in Arabic script; his wife, Inën Aji, just made a thumb print. Aji, the defendant in this case, signed in Latin script. Two sisters also signed: Jemilad made a thumb print, and Inën Lukman painfully printed IL. All documents are in Latin script, and by that time, the late 1980s, Arabic-script signatures were rare in the Takèngën area.

Conclusion

In all three cases, the judges found in favor of daughters who had demanded that estate divisions be redone to give them their rightful shares. The judges drew on two kinds of social norms to reach their decision: their own ideas of equality and fairness, and their assumptions about ideas held by the daughters at the time of the earlier division. In the course of developing a mode of reasoning that would support their conclusions, the judges rejected a written agreement that had been validated by the civil court, and they invented a rule of Gayo *adat* that would correspond both to their own norms and to Islamic law.

The judges might have reasoned otherwise within an Islamic legal framework. Indeed, their predecessors had done so (Bowen 2000). In two of the cases, *Samadiah* and *Syamsiah*, they might have fallen back on the strength of the written agreement as a contract binding on all parties. In *Inen Maryam*, even without a written agreement the testimony of the village headman could have served as a basis for a ruling that the heirs had in fact reached an agreement. In all three cases, the judges might have argued that unless the plaintiffs could prove that they had been coerced (thereby shifting the burden of proof), there was no compelling reason to place that agreement in question.

That they found as they did, then, is illustrative both of the capacity of judges to reach a range of decisions in what is formally and substantively "the same" judicial framework, and of the importance of their moral and social ideas in shaping their decisions. From where did the judges derive these ideas of equality and fairness? One can find such ideas in the traditions of Islamic jurisprudence, in norms of Gayo *adat*, and in the general values of gender equality that have served as a ground for a number of Indonesian reinterpretations of Islamic law (Bowen 1999). Moreover, the Indonesian Supreme Court long has urged lower courts to overturn property settlements when those settlements disproportionally favor men (Lev 1972). In other words, the judges may have drawn on one or more of several distinct normative frameworks in arriving at the conclusions they did.

The judges themselves did not justify their stance in legal terms; they did not refer to Islamic sources, to specific rules of *adat*, or to Indonesian statutes or court decisions. Instead, they referred to what we might call a common sense version of *adat*: not a body of law-like rules (the *adatrecht* constructed by the Dutch and taken over into Indonesian jurisprudence), but a set of everyday principles. In the explanation quoted above, Judge Kasim referred to the kind of equality that we can see in the fingers of the hand, with each finger performing different functions, but each one just as important as the others. This and other concrete images of equality draw from the Gayo poetic tradition of *didong* (Bowen 1991), in which concrete images are described at length as ways of talking about social life.

In its appeal to common sense and mundane life, this language has much in common with a style of reasoning about Islamic law that I frequently encounter in Takèngën and Jakarta, in which everyday social practices provide a normative ground for rethinking law (Bowen 1998). That village men and women work together in the fields, sharing equally the burdens and the fruits of their manual labor, offers concrete proof that equality and fairness are socially appropriate bases for choosing among alternative interpretations of the law. Takèngën judges (and, I would argue, most Indonesian Islamic judges and jurists) reason much as do judges and jurists everywhere, in striving to make the law fit with the norms of social life, and social life with the norms of the law.

CHAPTER SIX

THE PRACTICE OF JUDGING: THE EGYPTIAN JUDICIARY AT WORK IN A PERSONAL STATUS CASE

Baudouin Dupret
CNRS/CEDEJ (Cairo)

Introduction

It is commonly assumed that personal status is, in Egypt and in many other Arab countries, the last stronghold of Islamic law. Whereas in other legal domains law is supposed to have been secularized and mainly imported from Western countries, the domain of personal status is held to have remained true to the *sharīʿa*, to the point that one should speak of Islamic personal status law as applied in Egypt, not of Egyptian personal status law. However, I contend that, when attempting to determine the extent to which this or that part of the law is Islamic and whether this or that part of the law can or cannot be attributed to some historical development of Islamic law, one imposes a structure on the legal phenomena and activities instead of trying to discover the manner in which they operate. This is mainly because most scholars start with strong assumptions about the general model of which a given legal system is a sample. Thereby, research misses the phenomena it seeks to document. Central to these phenomena are the ways in which people understand and manifest their understanding of what any given situation is about, orient themselves to any given setting and its constraints, and behave and act in a more or less orderly manner within such a spatially and temporally situated context. This is not something that can be observed from any predetermined standpoint; rather, it must be documented by the close scrutiny of how people actually and situationally understand their environment, make sense of it, try to find their way within its constraining framework, and produce, reproduce, and transform the social order. In other words, the *a priori* characterization of personal status law in Egypt as Islamic law does not provide access to what people do in the Egyptian judicial setting when dealing with personal status questions. Such access can only be acquired by describing people's practices outside any preconceived interpretive framework.

In the first section of this essay, I examine literature that focuses on the notion of harm (*ḍarar*) as a grounds for divorce. I argue that it relies on the assumption that, e.g., Egyptian law belongs in the field of personal status to the family of Islamic law and, as such, must be read against its theoretical, formal, transhistorical and transgeographical background. However, my contention is that this literature never addresses the practice of Egyptian personal status law as it unfolds during the many steps that precede the production of a formal ruling. I conclude the section by sketching the main lines of the praxeological respecification I suggest in order to analyze the activity of judging in its fine-grained details. In the second section, I use some material from one recent Egyptian case involving judicial divorce issued on the grounds of harm caused to the wife to show how the notion of harm is dealt with in a practical, unproblematic, routine, and commonsensical way. First, I concentrate on the participants' orientation to procedural correctness. Second, I examine the production of legally relevant categories.

Causing Harm (ḍarar) *as a Ground for Granting Judicial Divorce in Egyptian Law: A Substantial Account and its Praxeological Re-Specification*

In his excellent account of Egyptian personal status law as applied in *sharīʿa* courts in the first half of twentieth century, Ron Shaham devotes one chapter (chapter six) to judicial divorce on the wife's initiative.[1] From the very first sentence, the reader gets the impression that social phenomena take place against the immutable background of Islamic law and Islamic legal doctrines.

> In Islamic law a marriage may be dissolved either through *ṭalāq* or through *faskh*. Each method of dissolution has specific legal and financial consequences, and each may be carried out either judicially or extra-judicially. Muslim jurists differentiate between *ṭalāq* and *faskh* on the basis of the grounds on which a dissolution is sought, about which there is considerable disagreement among the schools (Shaham 1997:112).[2]

---

[1] Shaham (1997:113ff.).

[2] Thus formulated, it becomes difficult to account for the provisions on *khulʿ* in

However, when discussing the different conceptions of *faskh* and *ṭalāq* according to the various schools of law, Shaham himself illustrates the weakness of the distinction between legal concepts and interpreting practices: Shāfiʿīs and Ḥanbalīs consider *faskh* the rule and *ṭalāq* the exception; Mālikīs do the opposite; Ḥanafīs do not care (ibid., 112). However, no sooner has the door to a sociological perspective on legal practices been opened than it is closed again. Shaham writes, "[B]eyond [the limited cases in which the Ḥanafīs allow a woman to apply for a judicial dissolution of her marriage], she has no means of freeing herself from a prejudicial union, apart from negotiating a divorce by mutual agreement" (ibid., 112–3). It is clear that Shaham speaks of doctrine and not practice, and this is precisely my point: why should practice be considered against the backdrop of legal doctrine? The production of legal doctrine is an interesting topic *per se*, but it creates confusion when the study of doctrine serves as a framing device for the study of practice.

The codification of personal status law—the laws of 1920 and 1929—is presented as the culmination of the modernist call to offer women additional grounds for the dissolution of marriage (ibid., 114). Although this can be considered a historical fact, one wonders why nothing is said about the considerable technical and procedural consequences involved in this codification process. Without prejudging the net result of such transformations, it can safely be said that they must have changed the ways in which facts, evidence, and legal arguments are presented, the procedural constraints that affect people when appearing before a court, and, hence, the practice of personal status.

Shaham proceeds to review the four additional grounds for a judicial divorce that have been accorded to women in the new laws: defects and diseases of the husband, nonprovision of maintenance by a husband, absence of the husband, and injury (p. 114ff.). His argument follows a general pattern. For instance, Shaham states, with regard to defects and disease, that "these articles were based

Law No. 1 of 2000. *Khulʿ* cannot be considered a repudiation, i.e., a unilateral divorce by the man, nor a judicial divorce (the judge has no power of appreciation), nor a ground for the nullification of the marriage. With such a model of Islamic law as a backdrop, legal transformations must necessarily be considered as conforming to, or deviating from, the "pure paradigm." However, this way to proceed leaves totally unaddressed the question of what people do and say when confronted by *khulʿ*.

on a minority opinion of the Ḥanafī school (that of Muḥammad al-Shaybānī, d. 805 CE) and the majority opinions of the three other schools" (ibid., 114). Although this statement seems true from a retrospective look at the historical development of Islamic law, it is also symptomatic of the dynamic of legal orientalism. Shaham's statement assumes that law is constructed along the same lines according to which the scholarly discourse on law is constructed. In this case, Shaham states that provisions for judicial divorce on the ground of a defect or disease of the husband are accepted by a few Ḥanafī scholars and most other scholars. From this, he infers that the provisions of the Law of 1920 are based on this shared acceptance. This suggests, however, that despite all possible practices, Egyptian personal status law is the mere replication (with some methods for selecting preferred solutions) of the substantive body of preexisting Islamic legal rules. But the matter may not be as simple as that. Moreover, this approach has the potential effect to invert the practical modes of reasoning that were followed in the drafting of the laws. Instead of assuming that the Islamic provisions existed first and that subsequently the drafters of the law made their choice among the many possibilities Islamic law offers, we might argue that these drafters first determined their preference and only then looked back at the corpus of *fiqh* to find legitimate justifications. Be that as it may, once again, something is lost in this quest for the historical and religious "roots" of legal provisions: namely, the sense of what is done when drafting or practicing Egyptian personal status law.

With regard to the fourth ground for judicial divorce—*ḍarar*, which Shaham renders as "injury" and which I prefer to translate as "harm"—his demonstration follows the same scheme. First, he states that Ḥanafī law "does not recognize injury caused to the wife by her husband as a ground for dissolution" (ibid., 116). Second, he provides us with the formulation of Art. 6 of the 1929 Law. Third, he states that, according to the explanatory memorandum, this reform was necessitated by public interest. Fourth, he explains that, because of the imprecision in the definition of what constitutes *ḍarar*, "the *qāḍī*s [were obliged] to consult the Mālikī literature, where *injury* is interpreted liberally in favor of the wife" (ibid., 117). Finally, Shaham wonders "whether or not the intent of the legislation was to apply the Mālikī understanding of judicial dissolution" (ibid., 118), although he permits himself to use the term "judicial divorce" because "the legal consequences of the Egyptian legislation correspond to those of the Mālikī school, and also because the legislator often uses the phrase, '[the *qāḍī*] *ṭalāqa 'alayhi*'—that is, the *qāḍī* divorced the wife on the husband's behalf" (ibid.).

One may wonder about the utility of establishing genealogical connections between, on the one hand, Egyptian personal status law as codified in the laws of 1920 and 1929 and subsequently amended in the laws of 1985 and 2000, and, on the other hand, the provisions of the different opinions of the different schools of Islamic law. Although these connections are in some way obvious, there is no practical gain in scrutinizing their precise origins. Worse, this approach threatens to create confusion. First, to posit a connection does not imply that there is a relationship of causality. As mentioned above, the line of argument may easily be reversed: Mālikī law was not the source from which the new legislation proceeded but the resource used to justify the new orientation of the law. Second, Shaham's presentation suggests that legal change can occur only in some interstitial space left open by the imprecision of the law. For instance, the interpretation of *ḍarar* in favor of the wife, along the lines of Mālikī doctrine, was made possible only by the ambiguity of the law of 1929. However, Shaham argues, the inclusion of *ḍarar* in Egyptian law was already an innovation grounded in Mālikī law. Still, the Egyptian judges' reading of the Mālikī sources (e.g., by not recognizing a second or subsequent marriage of the man as a source of harm) did not correspond to the Egyptian legislature's reading of the same Mālikī sources (recognizing in Law No. 100 of 1985 that this second or subsequent marriage may constitute a possible source of harm, if demonstrated by the wife). Nevertheless, Shaham invokes the general model of Islamic law and its many schools, despite the ambiguities of the various sources and of the references to these sources, as the background against which the notion of *ḍarar* must be evaluated in Egyptian personal status law. I maintain that the net result of this quest for the origins is not only of limited value, but, moreover, it diverts our attention from the examination of what people do when practicing personal status law.

In the sections following the above discussion, Shaham proceeds to address the practical content of adjudication in personal-status matters in pre-revolutionary Egypt. He offers a wonderful review of the many circumstances in which a woman may ask a judge to be judicially divorced from her husband on the grounds of harm and the circumstances in which the judge did or did not grant such a divorce. Unfortunately, Shaham presents these cases, for the sake of comprehensiveness, in a way that abstracts them from the actual circumstances in which they developed and were reported and treated by the courts. In other words, he produces a kind of compendium of case-law principles similar to the compendia that summarize rulings issued by the Court of Cassation (*Majmūʿat al-aḥkām allatī qarrarathā maḥkamat al-naqḍ*). These compendia, used as practical guides for the interpretation of statutory legal provisions, constitute the basis on which precedents of the Court of Cassation are constituted, referenced and referred to. In my view, however, the task of social scientists is, in addition to designing operational legal categories, to analyze the categorization process itself. To put it differently, legal researchers appear to be still ensconced within the scheme of the legal syllogism, according to which facts are presented to judges who, in a mechanical way, must identify the applicable law and apply this law to the facts. However, things happen differently. Facts are never raw facts, applicable law is itself an object of interpretation, and the legal characterization of facts is not an abstract and objective operation. This does not mean that everything is pure construction, since, as argued before, people (including judges) tend to objectify facts and legal categories. As David Sudnow has proposed, we must consider these categories "as constituting the basic conceptual equipment with which such people as judges, lawyers, policemen, and probation workers organize their everyday activities."[3] However, this means that we cannot be satisfied with the mere identification of the categories: we still need to examine how people practically orient themselves to them. Sudnow's study on plea bargaining shows that actual legal encounters often result in the coselection of lesser offenses (in exchange for pleading guilty) that are neither statutorily nor even situationally included in the more encompassing offense, but that are routinely associated by professionals with the crime as it is normally committed according to prevalent social standards.

If we are to draw a parallel between Sudnow's approach and that of Shaham, we reach the conclusion that what we miss in the latter is the practical operation by which Egyptian judges substantiate the concept of harm as a ground for granting judicial divorce. Apart from its formal definition, we fail to understand properly the con-

[3] Sudnow (1976:158).

cept of harm. For instance, we know that some judges interpreted Article 6 of the Law of 1929 by referring to Mālikī sources, "because the article does not explain in detail which types of injury make a divorce mandatory."[4] However, this suggests that judges, in their attempt to define the notion of harm, are constrained by its formal definition in the Mālikī legal sources. This may be partly the case, although we have no means of knowing it for sure. But it is only partly the case, for the features relating to the case at hand and the routine of the judges' work certainly contribute to the definition of what counts as "normal harm." Here again, if we follow Shaham, the judge seems to proceed syllogistically from the broad Mālikī definition of harm to the facts of the case, although everything that normally, routinely and situationally counts as harm in these many Egyptian legal settings is hidden behind the judge's quest for a satisfactorily formal justification of his decision. Sudnow has successfully shown, however, that it is not the statutorily conceived features of the harm but its socially relevant attributes that give it its status as a feature of the class "normal harm."[5]

Following Sudnow, we advocate a praxeological respecification of the study of law. Praxeology, in the form of ethnomethodology and conversation analysis, has, from its inception, regarded law and courtrooms as a privileged standpoint from which it is possible to observe language and action in context. The goal is not to identify how far legal practices deviate from an ideal model or a formal rule but to describe the modalities of production and reproduction, the intelligibility and the understanding, the structuring and the public character, of law and the many legal activities. Instead of assuming the existence of racial, sexual, psychological or social variables, ethnomethodological and conversational research focus on how activities organize themselves and on how people orient themselves to these activity structures, which they read in a largely unproblematic way. If we are to take law seriously, it is, nevertheless, neither the law of abstract rules nor the law of principles independent of the context in which they are utilized; rather, it is the law of people involved in the daily practice of law, i.e., the law made of the practice of legal rules and of their interpretive principles.

---

[4] Shaham (1997:130).
[5] Sudnow (1976:167).

The attention which ethnomethodology and conversation analysis draws to situated practices sheds light on the mainly routinized nature of the formalizing work which law professionals accomplish. The work of attorneys, magistrates, and prosecutors consists mainly of the formalization of categories that are used in the clients,' offenders' and witnesses' telling of the facts. Conversely, the work of the non-professional parties in a trial often consists in avoiding the blame-implicative inferences that result from the legal characterization of facts. As demonstrated by Rod Watson, the categorizing processes that mark out the path leading to a court decision are as many means for the people concerned to give their act a motivation and, by doing so, to allocate and to negotiate accusation, culpability, motivation, responsibility and, therefore, grounds for excuse and justification.[6]

A Praxeological Account of Causing Harm as Ground for Granting Judicial Divorce

Procedural correctness

Personal status matters are organized in Egypt by a series of laws, mainly Law No. 25 of 1920 and Law No. 25 of 1929, both amended by Law No. 100 of 1985, and Law No. 1 of 2000. In the absence of any statutory provision, Law No. 1 of 2000 stipulates that the judge must refer to "the opinions which are prevalent in the school of *imām* Abū Ḥanīfa." In practice, many judges still make use of Qadrī Pasha's unofficial codification,[7] a compilation of Ḥanafī-inspired legal provisions. Subsequent to the unification of the Egyptian courts in one centralized national system, personal status has been subject to procedural rules that are common to all civil and commercial matters. Cases are adjudicated at the first level by summary courts (*maḥkama juz'iyya*) and courts of first instance (*maḥkama ibtidā'iyya kulliyya*), according to the type of litigation and its monetary value. Courts are divided into circuits, one of which is the personal-status circuit (*dā'ira al-aḥwāl al-shakhṣiyya*). The personal-status circuit of the courts is competent with regard to matters relating to personal status, both financial

[6] Watson (1997); Komter (1998).
[7] Qadrī (1928).

(*wilāya ʿalā al-māl*) and nonfinancial (*wilāya ʿalā al-nafs*), including the granting of judicial divorce on the ground of harm. One provision is particularly relevant, i.e., Article 6 of Law No. 25 of 1929 concerning judicial divorce on the ground of harm.

With regard to judicial divorce on the ground of harm, Article 6 of Law No. 25 of 1929 states:

> If the wife alleges that the husband mistreated her in such a way as to make it impossible for two people of their social standing to continue the marriage relationship, she may request that the judge separate them, whereupon the judge shall grant her an irrevocable divorce if the harm is established and conciliation seems impossible between them. If, however, he [viz., the husband] refuses the petition and she subsequently repeats the complaint without establishing the harm, the judge shall appoint two arbitrators and he shall judge according to the provisions of Articles 7, 8, 9, 10 and 11.

As soon as a woman, represented or not by an attorney, submits a petition that asks the judge to pronounce the divorce on the ground of harm from which she allegedly suffers, the judge's work is, at least formally, constrained by the many stipulations of this statutory provision. A sequential process is initiated in which the case follows a series of successive steps before reaching the stage of the judge's decision. This is reflected in the way the ruling is designed:

"In the name of God the clement, the merciful"

In the name of the people

Gīza Court of First Instance
for the Personal Status for the Guardianship
of the Person
Ruling

At the session held publicly at the palace of the court on Monday . . .
Under the presidency of His excellency Mr . . ., President of the Court
And the membership of Mr . . ., court president, and Mr . . ., judge
In presence of Mr . . ., deputy of the prosecution
In presence of Mr . . ., clerk

The following ruling was issued:

In the case No. . . . of the year 1983, plenary, personal status of Gīza, submitted by:
. . . . against . . .

The Court

After the hearing of the plea, the examination of the documents, and the deliberation:

Considering that the facts of the case and its grounds, as they appear to the Court from the documents, [reveal] that the female petitioner introduced, in pursuance of a form signed by an attorney and deposed at the office of the clerk of this court on . . ., and declared legally the request for a ruling [that would] judicially divorce her [in the form of] an irrevocable divorce, with no right for him to reinstate her, on [the ground of] harm resulting from 1) the impotence that makes it impossible to realize the aims of marriage; 2) his violence against her in the form of beating, insulting, abusing, and formulating accusations against her. . . . [1]

Considering that the petition was put to deliberation as indicated in the records of the sessions; at the session held on . . ., this Court issued a ruling commissioning the forensic physician to conduct a medico-legal inspection of the defendant and the Court made public in its ruling the report issued by the forensic physician. [2]

Considering that His excellency the forensic physician conducted the medical inspection on the defendant and that his report has been put in the case file; it follows that it dated from . . . and it concludes that . . . [3]

Considering that the parties to the case appeared [before the court] after the release of the report and its constitution as one of the documents of the case; none of them petitioned or opposed it. [4]

Considering that the case was deliberated at the subsequent sessions. On the session of . . . this Court issued a ruling transferring it so as to investigate by all the means of proof the existence of the material harm from which she [suffered]; it is up to the defendant to contest it by the same means. [5]

Considering that the court set out to execute the ruling of investigation, whereupon it heard the two witnesses of the petitioner . . .

The court heard also the two witnesses of the defendant . . . [6]

Considering that the court, after the hearing of the witnesses . . ., adjourned the case for the plea to the session . . . [7]

Considering that more than one time the court proposed to the two parties to the litigation a conciliation; [considering] that the representative of the petitioner refused while the defendant accepted. [8]

Considering that the General Prosecution represented in the person of its deputy present to the session presented its opinion to the court. [9]

Considering that the two parties asked for the fixing of [the date of] the ruling; henceforth, the court fixed [the date of] the ruling to the session of . . . and decided to delay the delivery of the motivation of the ruling to the session of today so as to complete the deliberation. [10]

Considering that the petitioner requested the judicial divorce for harm on two grounds, first, sexual impotence, second, blows, insults and abuse. [11]

Considering that, when the court proposed the conciliation to the two parties . . .; this was considered by the court as an impossibility to reconcile . . . [12]

Considering that, with regard to this, the representative of the petitioner refused the conciliation; henceforth, the court was led to proceed. [13]

Considering that, as it emerges from the text of Article 6 of Decree-Law No. 25 of 1929 concerning certain provisions on repudiation, the Egyptian legislature requires, so that the judge may issue the judicial divorce on the ground of harm, that . . . [14]

Considering that the Egyptian legislature has imported (*naqala*) the rule of judicial divorce on the ground of harm from the doctrine of *imām* Mālik . . . [15]

Considering that the Ḥanafī doctrine makes the acceptance of the testimony on the rights of believers conditional upon its congruence with the petition . . . [16]

Considering that, with regard to the first ground of the petition, the forensic physician has established that . . . [17]

Considering that, with regard to the second ground of the petition, namely, the violence against her by the means of blows and insults, her two witnesses testified to the fact that . . . [18]

Considering that, with regard to what precedes, the court realizes that the continuation of their marital life . . . would be an injustice to her. . . . The court has no choice but to grant her a judicial divorce. The General Prosecution does not object to this and, to the contrary, it gave an identical opinion to the court. [20]

Considering that, with regard to what precedes, the court concludes to the judicial divorce of the petitioner from her husband on the ground of harm. [21]

Considering that the expenses . . . [22]

Considering that, with regard to the urgent execution, . . . [23]

For all these reasons

The court rules in the presence [of the litigant parties] the judicial divorce of . . . from her husband . . . [in the form of] an irrevocable divorce and it compels the defendant to [pay] the expenses . . . and it refuses the other demands.

Clerk President of the Court

The statutory provision of Article 6 makes adjudication in matters of judicial divorce on the ground of harm follow the sequential scheme: petition—establishment of the mistreatment—attempt at reconciliation—ruling. Yet further, the ruling discloses an internal structure that can be schematized as follows:

1) introduction
2) petition ["considering" 1]
3) procedures followed by the court ["considering" 2 to "considering" 10]:
   • expertise [2–4]
   • proof of the harm [5]: hearing of the witnesses [6]
   • pleas [7]
   • attempt at reconciliation [8]
   • Prosecution's opinion [9]
   • fixing of the ruling and issuing of the ruling [10]
4) examination of the legal grounds [11–16]
   • reminder of the petitioner's grounds [11]
   • attempt at reconciliation and failure [12–13]
   • concept of harm in Egyptian law [14–15]
   • witnessing in personal-status cases [16–17]
5) application of the law to the facts of the case [18–21]
   • first ground: impotence [18]
   • second ground: violence [19]
   • court's conclusion [20–21]
6) expenses and accessory demands [22–23]
7) ruling

This sequence, although it is formalized by the judge in the shape of a ruling, reflects the actual procedural constraints under which he operates. One of his major tasks, as a professional routinely engaged in his occupation, is to manifest publicly the correct accomplishment of his job. The production of a procedurally impeccable ruling is one of these priorities, and this is demonstrated publicly in the judge's recapitulation of all the necessary steps that must be taken and that were actually performed. At this procedural level, it is obvious that the judge orients exclusively to the technicalities of Egyptian procedural law. These technicalities may include some reference to provisions explicitly relating to Ḥanafī or Mālikī law, but, as in our example and with regard to the testimony of witnesses in cases of judicial divorce on the ground of harm ["considering" 15 to "considering" 16], this is always through the provisions of Egyptian law, as eventually interpreted by the Court of Cassation:

> Considering that the Egyptian legislature has imported (*naqala*) the rule of judicial divorce on the ground of harm from the doctrine of *imām* Mālik—may God be satisfied with him. It is not permitted, in order to establish it [viz., the harm], [to refer] to the same doctrine from which it is imported, and no particular rule was stipulated to establish it. In such a situation, one must go back, so as to prove the harm, to the prevailing opinion in the doctrine of *imām* Abū Ḥanīfa al-Nuʿmān, in pursuance of Article 280 of the Regulation of the *sharīʿa* tribunals to which Article 6 of Law No. 462 of 1955 refers (Cass., Personal Status, Appeal No. 11, 48th Judicial Year, session of 25 April 1979). Henceforth, harm is established by its testimonial evidence (*bi'l-bayyina*), i.e., the testimony of two males or one male and two females. Oral testimony is not accepted to establish it, even if it is authorized in certain matters other than repudiation for harm (Appeal No. 65, 52d Judicial Year, session of 12 March 1984; it [this ruling] also refers to the Compendium of Personal Status for Muslims of Counselor Naṣr al-Gindī, Judges' Club edition, comment on Article 6 of Decree-Law No. 25 of 1929).[8]

Most documents in a file of a trial show the orientation of judges, prosecutors, and other participating professionals to procedural correctness. This is directly linked to the general sequence of a trial, in which every participant eventually addresses people who at a certain time are not physically present in the room but constitute a kind of "over-reading" or "over-looking" audience,[9] whose potential overruling of the participants' procedural accomplishments closely conditions these participants' attitude vis-à-vis the procedures which they are required to follow. These procedural constraints are not attended to by these participants as features imported from whatever external, historical, or overhanging legal system; rather, they constitute the direct, obvious, actual, and practical dimensions of the daily bureaucratic routine of people engaged in the various legal occupations in present-day Egypt. This is exemplified in the general structure of the forensic physician's report:

---

[8] All block quotations are taken from the same ruling: Court of First Instance, Case No. 858, 1998, Personal Status, Giza.

[9] Paul Drew speaks of an "over-hearing audience" in order to designate the silent auditor to whom the participants in a trial address themselves beyond their direct verbal exchange (Drew 1992). I extend the notion and speak of an "over-reading" or "over-looking" audience to encompass the absent people to whom a written document, like a ruling, is addressed.

In the name of God, the clement, the merciful

Ministry of Justice 150, Gīza Forensic Medicine/84

Medico-Legal Report

In case 701, Gīza plenary, year 84

Pursuant to the decision of the Gīza court for personal status (person [viz., the circuit competent with regards to personal matters]), I have examined the case file that has been transferred to us by [the court] in this case and I have examined the defendant . . ., in order to determine whether he suffers from impotence that makes it impossible for him to accomplish of his marital obligations, and in order to evaluate this impotence if it exists, its date and whether it is susceptible of treatment. I report the following:

First: Circumstances of the case . . .

Second: The procedures

We have examined the case file transferred to us by the court in this case and we have fixed the day of . . . as the appointment for conducting it. We gave the two parties to the litigation notice of it by registered notification, which I sent them within the legally required time.

On the fixed day the petitioner . . . appeared . . .

The defendant . . . also appeared.

The two recognized each other in the session. We delivered a report on this.

Third: The Medico-Legal examination . . .

The opinion

According to this, we consider that:

– It emerges from the examination on . . . that he seems to be in a normal health . . .

– It does not emerge from his medical examination that he suffers from any pathological . . . state . . .

– We consider that the defendant . . . may suffer from . . . psychological impotence . . .

– It is well known that . . . it is not possible to determine a precise term for the recovery. . . .

Delivered on . . . Forensic physicians' High Deputy

Apart from the substantial basis of the harm (see below), about which the physician is supposed to testify, the general structure of this document shows that: 1) The report is an achievement in itself: in this report the physician produces all the features that attest to his quality to act and to his mastery of the formal, procedural, and medical technicalities that make it possible for him to produce the document called "medico-legal report"; 2) This report is part of an encompassing procedure: it mentions that it is part of the more comprehensive procedure that is followed in the adjudication of a case that was transferred to the forensic physician by the court, asking him to produce an expert opinion with regard to the alleged impotence of the husband, on the basis of which the court will elaborate its ruling; 3) This report anticipates its further uses by the court: it addresses all the issues that might be deemed relevant by the judge, i.e., the defendant's general health condition, his medical antecedents, etc.; more important, it suggests to the judge the possible characterization of a condition that, in itself, escapes any clinical examination, namely, psychological impotence. It is interesting to note that the forensic physician proposes this characterization as a possible explanation, without concluding as to its certainty, whereas the judge subsequently relies on this opinion as if it was a matter of scientifically established fact.

Legal relevance

Besides the constraining effect of procedural rules, legal issues must be addressed by the many people engaged in the judicial process. These issues mainly consist in giving a factual substance to formal legal definitions. In the case of judicial divorce on the grounds of harm, two questions must be answered: what counts as "harm" and what is the cause of this harm? The two questions are closely related, and all the participants in the judicial process orient themselves to them.

With regard to the harm itself, the statutory provision defines it broadly. Article 6 speaks of the wife alleging that the husband mistreated her in such a manner as to make it impossible for people of their social standing to continue the marriage relationship. Hence, it is up to the judge to characterize the facts under review so as to fit them into the definition of Article 6. Here, the judge is constrained by the definitions given by the Court of Cassation, as it appears explicitly in the following excerpt from the ruling:

> Considering that, as it emerges from the text of Article 6 of Decree-Law No. 25 of 1929 concerning certain provisions on repudiation, the Egyptian legislature requires, in order to allow the judge to issue a ruling of judicial divorce on the grounds of harm, that the harm or the prejudice comes from the husband, to the exception of the wife, and that life together has become impossible. The harm here is the wrong done by the husband to his wife in the form of speech or action,

> or both, in a manner that is not acceptable to people of the same status, and it constitutes something shameful and wrongful that cannot be endured (Cassation, Personal Status, Appeal No. 50, 52d Judicial Year, session of 28 June 1983; its [the Court of Cassation's] standard is here a nonmaterial standard of a person, which varies according to environment, culture, and the wife's status in the society: Cassation, Personal Status, Appeal No. 5, 46th Judicial Year, session of 9 November 1977, p. 1644). The harm also has to be a specific harm resulting from their dispute, necessary, not susceptible of extinction; the wife cannot continue marital life; it must be in the capacity of her husband to stop it and to relieve her of it if he wishes, but he continues to inflict it, or he has resumed it (Cassation, Personal Status, Appeal No. 5, 47th Judicial Year, session of 14 March 1979, p. 798; Cassation, Personal Status, Appeal No. 51, 50th Judicial Year, session of 26 January 1982).

Here again, the Court's formal definition does not totally extinguish the uncertainty that the judge faces when characterizing the facts. This does not mean, however, that the judge's work is utterly problematic or arbitrary. On the contrary, the categories to which the judge refers have, for him, an objective nature, even though it is his characterization that objectifies them. Moreover, the legal process of characterization is thoroughly supported by the sociological process of normalization, i.e., the operations through which the judge routinely selects some of the features of a case that resembles a common, normal, usual type of case.[10] It is to these "normal" categories, which have, beyond their legal definition, a commonsense dimension, that the judge, as well as the prosecutor, the attorney, the victim, the offender, the witnesses, etc., orient themselves.

In the aforementioned case, the wife mobilized two types of reason in order to substantiate the category of harm:

> [The wife requested] a ruling [that would] judicially divorce her [in the form of] an irrevocable divorce, with no right for him to reinstate her, on [the grounds of] harm resulting from 1) the impotence that makes it impossible to realize the aims of marriage; 2) his violence against her in the form of blows, insults, abuse, and formulating accusations against her. . . .

Neither impotence nor violence are explicitly mentioned in Egyptian law. However, impotence is traditionally assimilated with either permanent illness (Article 9 of the 1920 Law) or harm (Article 6 of the

---

[10] Cf. Sudnow, supra.

1929 Law), while violence is considered as the exemplary type of harm. In addition, Ḥanafī law recognizes impotence as grounds for marriage dissolution,[11] and this is confirmed in our case by the judge:

> Abū Ḥanīfa and Abū Yūsuf permitted separation on the grounds of a permanent defect that impedes intercourse between the man and the woman if he is impotent, emasculated, or disabled, because the goal of marriage is the protection of procreation, so that, if the man is not capable of this, it becomes impossible to implement the provision of the contract and there is no good in upholding it. Its upholding despite this [constitutes] a harm for the woman whose prolongation cannot be accepted and which nothing can resolve but separation (The Personal Status of *imām* Abū Zahra, p. 414, par. 297, ed. 1957).

However, this reference to Islamic law is made so as to substantiate a positive-law provision, i.e., Art. 6 of the 1929 Law. Impotence and violence are not presented as Islamic-law provisions that must be directly responded to by the judge, but as two forms of the harm from which the wife suffers and on the basis of which the judge grants a judicial divorce according to Art. 6 of the 1929 Law:

> Considering that, with regard to what precedes, the court concludes to the judicial divorce of the petitioner from her husband on the grounds of harm.

The judge seeks to substantiate the legal category of harm, and what counts as harm for him is not totally dependent on statutorily defined[12] or Islamically defined[13] provisions, even though they may play an important role. This substantiation varies also according to the judge's conception of "normal harm," i.e., the way he typically characterizes a certain type of behavior which he encounters in the performance of his routine activities. As mentioned above, what counts for the judge as harm includes his knowledge of the typical manner in which a wife may suffer prejudice, the social characteristics of given classes of male offenders and female victims, the social and physical features of the settings in which such an event can take place, etc. The judge's conception of harm functions reflexively: he orients himself to a conception which, he thinks, he shares with, and that will be confirmed by, other people participating in the judicial process. At

[11] Shaham (1997:125).
[12] The 1920 and 1929 laws.
[13] The above-mentioned stipulations of Abū Ḥanīfa and Abū Yūsuf.

the same time, these other people lean on the judge's conception, which they are asked to confirm, and produce reports that, in turn, serve as the basis for the judge's final ruling. Unfortunately, this process cannot be properly documented in an empirical way, since most of the judge's work happens in his writing of the ruling, which is not a publicly available phenomenon. The only thing that can be stated with some certainty is that there is a gap between the formal rendering of documents like the ruling and the facts which these renderings claim to document. This gap "is produced through a transformation of locally accomplished, embodied, and 'lived' activities into disengaged textual documents."[14] The ruling operates in a justificatory way, orienting to a body of procedural and substantive rules while hiding the practicalities of its own constitution.[15] Some of these practicalities can be retrieved, however, by a close examination of the many steps that support the judge's work (although these steps are themselves transformed into somewhat disengaged textual documents).

In this judicial procedure, two evidentiary techniques are mobilized in order to establish the types of prejudice that result in the harm. With regard to the husband's impotence, the forensic physician is asked to give a medical report, while the husband's violence is established through the oral testimony of witnesses. As we noted, the forensic physician's report is very much oriented to the accomplishment of its procedural correctness. However, this report is equally oriented to the production of categories of legally relevant facts and

---

[14] Lynch (1993:287).

[15] This justificatory character appears in the conclusion of the ruling: "Considering that, with regard to what precedes, the court realizes that the continuation of their marital life . . . would be an injustice (*ẓulm*) against her. It is up to the judge to stop it in his quality of protector of justice. Although repudiation is the most hated permitted act in the eyes of God, it is equally forbidden to maintain a wife tied by the marital bounds to a husband who inflicts on her harms that make it impossible to continue marital life for women of the same status. The court takes into consideration the words of the Almighty: 'But do not take them back to injure them' [Qur'ān 2:231]; and the words of the Almighty: 'After that, the parties should either hold together on equitable terms, or separate with kindness' [Qur'ān 2:229]; and the words of the [Prophet]—may God pray for him and give him peace: 'Neither harm nor counterharm [viz., a harm inflicted to counter another harm].' It did not belong to the petitioner to ask for a repudiation if she found life with her husband enjoyable. However, she turned to the court, made her public statement and refused the reconciliation on the grounds of the impossibility for them to live together. The court has no choice but to grant her a judicial divorce. The General Prosecution does not object to this; on the contrary, it gave an identical opinion to the court."

people. The forensic physician's medical examination is largely directed at the construction of the record, which, in turn, is largely directed at its future readers. To paraphrase Martha Komter, this record looks backward to establish the medical circumstances of the case and to show its procedural correctness, and it looks forward to its use as evidence in the judicial process, "not only containing 'the facts,' but also displaying those elements that are legally required,"[16] i.e., it establishes that the necessary conditions have been met that can lead to the assimilation of some physical situation to the legal category of "male impotence." This orientation towards legal relevance is reflected in the fact that, despite the absence of any physical disability and of any psychological examination, the report concludes with the probability of psychological impotence, although it is acknowledged that psychological impotence is hard to establish scientifically.

The opinion
According to this, we consider that:

– It emerges from the examination we conducted on . . . that he appears to be in normal health, that his growth and constitution are natural, and that he bears the signs of manliness (*ʿalamāt al-dhukūra*) in a normal way.

– It does not emerge from his medical examination that he suffers from any pathological or constitutional state, either generally or objectively, that would cause him permanent organic impotence.

– We consider that the defendant, even though, from the forensic medical point of view, he is devoid of the causes of organic impotence (*ʿunna ʿaḍawiyya*), is likely affected at the same time by psychological factors that may cause him psychological impotence (*ʿunna nafsiyya*), although we know that it cannot be conclusively determined to the existence of this type of impotence from the clinical examination.

– It is well known that, in cases of psychological impotence, it [the condition] lasts as long as its causes last, so that it is not possible to determine a precise term or a date of recovery, taking into consideration that the necessary period of time depends on the extent of the intrusion of the psychological factor, its type and the sufficient character of the therapy; it also depends on the extent of the wife's readiness to help and to assist in the therapy in particular. If the wife lacks attachment to her husband, respect for him and readiness to assist him in the therapy, this therapy will be either exceptionally long and arduous or simply impossible.[17]

---

[16] Komter (2001).

[17] We must note the authoritative character attributed to medical expertise. Indeed, the judge agrees to the existence of the husband's impotence, as one of the two sources of harm, despite the fact that the physician speaks only in terms of probability.

The second type of evidentiary technique is oral testimony, intended to document the alleged mistreatment of the wife by her husband. As mentioned above, this is one of the few sections of the ruling in which reference is made to Islamic law, although mediated here again by positive law mechanisms, i.e., the Court of Cassation's jurisprudence:

> Considering that the Egyptian legislature has imported (*naqala*) the rule of judicial divorce on the grounds of harm from the doctrine of *imām* Mālik . . . It is not permitted, in order to establish it [viz., the harm], [to refer] to the same doctrine from which it is imported, and no particular rule was stipulated to establish it. In such a situation, one must go back, so as to prove the harm, to the prevailing opinion in the doctrine of *imām* Abū Ḥanīfa al-Nuʿmān. . . . Henceforth, harm is established by its testimonial evidence (*bi'l-bayyina*), i.e., the testimony of two males or one male and two females. Oral testimony is not accepted. . . .
>
> Considering that the Ḥanafī doctrine makes the acceptance of the testimony on the rights of believers conditional upon its congruence with the petition for what it [viz., the testimony] conditions in it [viz., the petition]. Its contradiction is not acceptable [viz., the testimony cannot contradict the petition]. The congruence is complete when what the witnesses testify to is exactly what the petitioner has claimed; the congruence is implicit when it has been testified to part of the case. The latter is accepted as an agreement. The judge considers what the witnesses testified to as the evidence of what the petitioner claimed. The congruence need not be literal; congruence in meaning and intention suffices, whether the expressions are the same or different (Cassation, Personal Status, session of 23 November 1982, published in the Judges' Review; Appeal No. 2, 53d Judicial Year, session of 20 December 1983).

Accordingly, the court decided to collect the testimonies of the witnesses designated by the petitioner and the defendant. Although these testimonies are written documents,[18] they allow us to get closer to the interactional details of the practice of judging. These can be read as follows:[19]

---

[18] Legally, these testimonies made in front of the court are also considered written testimonies.

[19] In these transcriptions, I do not follow any specific system, like the symbols system devised by Gail Jefferson (1979:287–289). However, I try to stick to the mix of vernacular and technical language that is used by the participants. I also decided not to add any punctuation in the material, for two main reasons: first, these are translations of written transcription of *oral* testimonies in which there is no punctuation; second, the original Arabic written transcriptions are devoid of any such punctuation.

[1]

1– The court called the petitioner's first witness and he said:

2– My name is . . . oath

3– Question: What's your relationship to the two parties

4– Answer: My workplace is close to the post office in which the petitioner works

5– Q: What are you testifying to

6– A: The petitioner is the defendant's wife by virtue of a legal marriage contract there were disputes between them and I saw the petitioner's husband whom I know although I don't know the place of his residence he was addressing to her words in front of the post office in which she works calling her I heard him addressing her as you bitch you filthy and other words of this kind for nearly two years and one month ago he called the police against her because there was between them something I don't know

7– Q: For how long have you known the petitioner's husband

8– A: For nearly two years

9– Q: Does he live in your neighborhood

10– A: I don't know

11– Q: For how long has the defendant addressed bad words to the petitioner

12– A: For nearly two years

13– Q: What are the words he's addressed to her

14– A: He told her you bitch you filthy and words of this kind and this was in front of the post office

15– Q: Did any harm affect the petitioner because of this

16– A: Yes she broke down while working at the post office

17– Q: Anything else to say

18– A: No

[2]

19– The petitioner's second witness was called and he said:

20– My name is . . . oath

21– Q: What's your relationship to the case

22– A: The neighbor of the petitioner

23– Q: What are you testifying to

24– A: The petitioner is the defendant's wife by virtue of a legal marriage contract there were disputes between them and I saw him hitting her more than once in front of their home and I also heard him addressing her with words like you filthy you bitch

25– Q: Did you see the defendant hitting the petitioner

26– A: Yes I saw him hitting her in front of their home

27– Q: What's the cause of your testimony

28– A: Because I'm their neighbor and I saw him hitting her

29– Q: Did you hear the defendant insulting the petitioner

30– A: Yes I heard him addressing her with the words you bitch you filthy and other words

31– Q: Did any harm affect the petitioner because of this

32– A: Yes harm affected the petitioner because of this because she's young and a public servant at the post office
33– Q: Anything else to say
34– A: No
[3]
35– The defendant's first witness was called. He said:
36– My name is . . . oath
37– Q: What's your relationship to the two parties
38– A: The defendant lives with me at home
39– Q: What are you testifying to
40– A: The petitioner is the defendant's wife by virtue of a legal marriage contract and the defendant lives with me and he's lived in my home for one year and eight months and nothing like a misunderstanding happened between them and he didn't assault her and he didn't hit her and he didn't insult her and the policeman came and took the defendant and locked him in the station
41– Q: Did you see the defendant assaulting the petitioner
42– A: No
43– Q: Did you hear the defendant insulting the petitioner
44– A: No
45– Q: The petitioner's two witnesses reported that he insulted her and hit her in front of her workplace
46– A: No it didn't happen
47– Q: Anything else to say
48– A: No
[4]
49– The court called the defendant's second witness and he said:
50– My name is . . . oath
51– Q: What's your relationship to the two parties
52– A: The neighbor
53– Q: What are you testifying to
54– A: The defendant is the petitioner's husband by virtue of a legal marriage contract and he lives close to me and she for one year and a half and he didn't hit her and he didn't insult her except once when the policeman came and took her and took him I don't know the cause
55– Q: Did the defendant hit and insult the petitioner
56– A: No
57– Q: The petitioner's two witnesses reported that the defendant had hit her and insulted her
58– A: No I didn't see him hitting her
59– Q: Anything else to say
60– A: No

Even though testimonies are supposed to be transcribed in the witnesses' own words, they clearly appear to have been reformulated, at least partly, by the judge (and his clerk). This is why the witness is always reported to have begun his testimony by stating that the petitioner and the defendant are spouses "by virtue of a legal marriage contract." In addition to this rewriting or editing process, the overall stereotypical nature of the organization of the testimony and the preallocated sequence of turns in the production of the testimony are noteworthy. Both depend on the institutional context in which these testimonies are given. As noted in a seminal study of courtroom interactions, "The talk in each stage of court hearings shares the feature that although it occurs in a multiparty setting . . ., the parties who may participate are limited and predetermined."[20] Moreover, whatever is done in this context is necessarily managed by the participants within the constraining framework of this preallocated turn-taking organization. In other words, unlike ordinary conversations, the order of a speaker's turn in judicial settings is fixed, as is the type of each speaker's turn.

Within this system of turn allocation, both the judge and the witnesses are oriented to the production of information that may be legally relevant and credible. On the judge's side, the credibility of the information provided by each witness is tested by questions directed at the credibility of the witness himself. This is why the interrogation always begins with a question about the witness's "relationship to the two parties" (turns 3, 21, 37, 51). This credibility can be further investigated by asking the witness to produce a first account of his testimony (turns 5, 23, 39, 53) and then assessing the reliability of this global narrative by asking the same witness to confirm his statements piecemeal (turns 7–14, 25–30, 41–44, 55–56). Some of the judge's questions are clearly directed at challenging the witness's version of the facts by confronting him with another witness's testimony (turns 45 and 57): "The petitioner's two witnesses reported that the defendant had hit her and insulted her." Clearly, the judge also seeks to extract some elements of information—nature of demeanor (insulting and hitting: turns 25, 29, 41, 43, 55), temporal dimension of the demeanor (for how long?: turn 11), content of the demeanor (words used by the husband: turns 13, 16, 32), responsibility (who did it?: turns 11, 25, 29, 41, 43, 55), prejudicial nature of the demeanor (what effect on the wife?: turns 15, 31)—that are the constituting features of the legal category of harm. Indeed, together, the spare

[20] Atkinson & Drew (1979): 35.

parts of this query for information are in congruence with the many conditional elements of the notion of harm as defined, in the ruling and according to the Court of Cassation, as "the wrong done by the husband to his wife in the form of speech or action, or both, in a manner that is not acceptable to people of same status, and it constitutes something shameful and wrongful that cannot be endured."

At the same time, the witness attempts to establish his credibility by offering some elements of information that reasonably can be considered to qualify him as a reliable witness—the nature of his perspective (turn 4: workplace; turns 22, 38, 52: neighborhood), duration of his witnessing (turns 8, 12: nearly two years)—or which appear as very plausible—exact wording of the insults (turns 14, 30: "bitch" and "filthy"), effects of these insults (turns 16, 32: her breaking down at the post office). With regard to the content of his testimony, the witness clearly orients himself to what appears to him as the constitutive element of the harm, either denying or confirming its having occurred. Interestingly, the witnesses who deny the existence of any harm directly orient their first global narrative, the elements of which were not elicited by the judge, to the husband's having neither insulted nor hit her. Accordingly, one may conclude that the normal conception of harm is made of either blows or insults, or both, in a manner largely independent of any formal legal definition.

In response to the judge's question confronting them with the petitioner's witnesses who testified to the existence of harm (turns 45 and 57: the petitioner's witnesses reported that the defendant had hit and insulted her), the defendant's witnesses respond with a total denial. This is an indirect way to address the challenge to their testimonies and to defend themselves against the blame-implicative nature of this challenge to their credibility. However, this total denial produces a paradoxical picture: on the one hand, two spouses living in perfect harmony (turn 40: "nothing like a misunderstanding happened between them and he didn't assault her and he didn't hit her and he didn't insult") and, on the other hand, a policeman coming and taking them to the police station (turns 40 and 54). One of the witnesses apparently tries to repair the damage created by this contradiction by saying that he does not know the cause of this police intervention, thereby acknowledging that this intervention occurred, something that contrasts his previous claim that the two spouses lived in harmony. The judge seems to have considered this paradox problematic. Even though he does not directly challenge the sincerity and honesty of the defendant's witnesses, he does not take their testimonies into account in his final ruling.

> Considering that, with regard to the second ground of the petition, namely the assault against her by the means of blows and insults, her two witnesses testified to the fact that they heard him insulting and slandering her in the street; moreover, one of them saw him hitting her more than one time and testified that the words with which he slandered her cannot be accepted. Life together became impossible and she suffered from harm because of this. Pursuant to the above, the testimony of her witnesses is congruent with the petition and is acceptable.

Conclusion

In this essay, I have shown how legal concepts can operate in practical and situated contexts. I argued that it is misleading to characterize "law" in advance as an instance of some general model like "Islamic law." There is no reason to assume that what people refer to as Islamic law is identical to the set of technical provisions that form the idealized model of Islamic law. Nor is there any reason to assume the contrary. To a certain extent, the question is not relevant. It cannot be answered because it is totally disembodied from actual practices, while it fails to address the phenomenon itself—the practice of referring to Islamic law. To the question, What is Islamic law? we should substitute the question, What do people do when referring to Islamic law?

The case examined in this essay reveals what Herbert Hart calls the open texture of law[21] as well as its constrained nature. Hart clearly means that legal provisions are open to interpretation. However, and simultaneously, this open texture of the law is framed by various constraints, among which, as shown, is the orientation of law practitioners toward procedural correctness and legal relevance. This orientation reflects the law practitioners' anticipation of the possible further usages of the official reports which they must produce, their

[21] "Even when verbally formulated general rules are used, uncertainties as to the form of behavior rebuked by them may break out in particular concrete cases. Particular fact-situations do not await us already marked off from each other, and labeled as instances of the general rule, the application of which is in question; nor can the rule itself step forward to claim its own instances." Hart (1961:44).

bureaucratic resistance to the possibility of being overruled, and their preference for conformity. Procedural and substantive provisions are not phrased in self-evident formulations. At least, legal provisions must have been read and understood in order to be implemented. Most often, the reading and understanding of them is not problematic. Sometimes, as in Dworkin's hard cases,[22] their reading implies some interpretation. In both cases, however, law practitioners, in their quest for procedural correctness and legal relevance, manifest the many methods they use in order to produce shared meanings, understandings and characterizations of the law and the facts that are submitted to legal review. In this sense, the study of law can only be the study of law in action, and this can be achieved only through the close examination and description of legal practices in their fine-grained linguistic, textual, and interactional details.

---

[22] Dworkin (1985).

CHAPTER SEVEN

THE CONSTITUTION AND THE PRINCIPLES OF ISLAMIC NORMATIVITY AGAINST THE RULES OF FIQH. A JUDGMENT OF THE SUPREME CONSTITUTIONAL COURT OF EGYPT

Baber Johansen

The Codification of a Jurists' Law

Until the second half of the nineteenth century, Islamic Law existed mainly in the form of what is known as *fiqh*, a system of ethical and legal norms that developed during the course of centuries of discussions among the members of a powerful legal profession. It was a jurists' law: the production of *fiqh* norms was not left to the political legislature, but rather had become the craft of a specialized profession. The *fiqh* norms were accessible only to the specialists who knew the texts and the literary genres in which certain questions were discussed and developed and the issues that divided or united the authors engaged in these debates. There were no codes or law books that would have allowed the laymen to know the actually enforceable norms, the applied law, in their own period or region. Over the centuries, however, the *fiqh* was accepted, in the Muslim world, as a sacred law. The educated, the secretaries of the administration, the merchants and, of course, the religious scholars treated it as an important and, as far as the last are concerned, the most important, form of normative reasoning. The basic principles of the law of inheritance, marriage and divorce and even elements of its specialized terminology were known to the population of all major cities of the Muslim world. In all urban regions of the Muslim world the jurists, "the *fiqh* specialists" as the Arabic term has it, played a major role in adjudication, the administration of property, pious foundations, religious institutions, and local politics. In the Arab world the Sunnī *fiqh* prevailed. The term "*Sunna*" refers to the Prophet's normative life praxis and Sunnī Islam is the Islam of those who consider the Prophet's *sunna* as the basis for the interpretation of the Qur'ān and—together with the Qur'ān and the consensus of the jurists—as the most important material source of the *fiqh* norms.

The Nineteenth Century

The nineteenth century saw the first wave of globalization, i.e., commercial expansion, industrial investment and the spread of European political and economic control over non-European countries in the Ottoman Empire and the Arab world. Law reform was one of the preoccupations of those who ran commercial and industrial ventures and who directed Europe's political expansion. Constitutionalism played no prominent part in their program, which centered on the codification of law. In 1860, Tunisia enacted the first constitution in the Arab world, which was suspended in 1864; it was followed by the even more shortlived Ottoman constitution of 1876. Both constitutions left as their lasting heritage long-lived constitutional movements in the Ottoman Empire and the Arab world. These constitutional movements began to exert a strong influence on the legal and political culture of the Middle East at the beginning of the twentieth century.

The codification of law has a much longer history in the Middle East. Starting in the 1850s and continuing throughout the twentieth century, Ottoman and Egyptian codes spearheaded the movement of codification which has marked the legal development of the Middle East for the last 150 years. Since the 1870s, this movement increasingly was controlled by European powers. From the middle of the twentieth century on, the newly independent states of the Arab world took the matter of codification of law into their own hands.

From the last third of the nineteenth to the middle of the twentieth century, Islamic law in the Arab world acquired a new status as a result of its insertion into national codes of law. Its norms were no longer valid merely because eminent Muslim legists had developed them as their contribution to Islamic normativity and had found support for them in the legal profession. Rather, in the new context, the validity of *fiqh* norms came to depend on the fact that they were state law, legalized by state legislation. As far as substantive law was concerned, the *fiqh* and its representatives lost control of most spheres of law: the new law of the Arab nation states followed models developed in Europe. The law schools and law faculties created since the end of the nineteenth century produced a new type of jurist capable of handling and applying this modern law. The domain that continued to be regulated by the *fiqh* consisted mainly of marriage, family, divorce, and inheritance, that is, personal status law. This sphere of law formed an enclave of the *fiqh* in the modern law books, alongside modern civil, penal and administrative codes. But, as we shall see, this enclave of Muslim norms has, since the 1960s, exerted a strong influence on the way in which the modern courts interpreted the law in other spheres.

The Judges and "the Prevalent Opinion of the Hanafi School of Law" in Egypt

The Egyptian example shows how the legislature, in the period between 1880 and 1955, chose to identify Islamic law with the classical doctrines of one school of Sunnī *fiqh* and how, since the 1960s, this identification of *fiqh* norms with Islamic normativity determined the courts' understanding of state law. Since the nineteenth century, the Egyptian legislature has defined the Hanafi school of *fiqh* as the representative of the *sharīʿa*, the sacred normativity of Islam. This solution was inherited from the Ottoman empire, which controlled Egypt until the end of World War I. In the Ottoman empire the Hanafi school was given official recognition as the dominant school of Sunnī *fiqh*. In 1813, the Ottoman sultan made it obligatory for all Egyptian *qāḍīs* to judge in conformity with Hanafi doctrine and, if there were several Hanafi opinions on a specific matter, to follow the predominant opinion of that school (Borrmans 1977, 80). The Egyptian legislature, in its regulation of the religious courts of 1880,[1] chose to accept this heritage. Until their dissolution in 1955, the religious courts were charged with interpreting Egyptian personal status law in the light of "the prevailing opinion of the Hanafi school" (*arjaḥ al-aqwāl fī madhhab Abī Ḥanīfa*). This formula has had a long career in twentieth century Egyptian law texts. We find it in article 280 of law no. 78/1931 on the organization of the sharīʿa courts, which states: "Judgments [in personal status cases] will be issued in accordance

[1] "Règlement d'organisation judiciaire des Mehkémehs," 17 juin 1880. See Borrmans (1977:80) and Shaham (1997:13).

with what is stipulated in this regulation, and in accordance with the prevailing opinion of the school of Abū Ḥanīfa."[2] Article 6 of law 462/1955, which abolished the *sharīʿa* courts, obligated the state courts, which henceforth were to decide on personal status cases, to base their decisions on the provision of article 280 of law no. 78/1931 in all matters on which the law is silent.[3] The reference to "the prevailing opinion of the school of the Imam Abū Ḥanīfa" as the norm to be applied when legislative texts on personal statute are silent was explicitly reiterated in article 3 of law 1/2000 which—among other things—introduced an important reform of Egyptian divorce law.[4] This order applies only to judges. The legislature is not bound by it and, indeed, throughout the first eight decades of the twentieth century, it often based legislation in personal status matters on the doctrines of other Sunnī schools of law, such as that of the Mālikīs and the Shāfiʿīs.[5] By imposing upon judges the obligation to interpret personal status law in the light of the predominant opinion of the Hanafi school of law, the legislature, obviously, wanted to impose a certain uniformity on the judiciary's interpretation of the law and to prevent the courts from choosing freely among the norms developed by the different schools of *fiqh*. The legislature thus gave the judiciary the right to interpret the classical Ḥanafī law and to integrate their interpretation into Egypt's modern law.

---

[2] If not mentioned otherwise, all twentieth-century Egyptian laws are quoted from Ḥasan and ʿAbd al-Wahhāb (1984). For article 280 of law no. 78 of 1931, see p. 52, and Berger (2001:93).

Berger calls the law a *decree*. The official Arabic text says *marsūm bi-qānūn* which comes very close to the French *décret loi*. This term was used under the third and fourth Republic "pour désigner un décret qui, en vertu d'une habilitation législative, pouvait modifier ou abroger des lois (catégorie qui entre aujourd'hui dans la dénomination d'ordonnance)," Cornu, 1992, s.v. *Décret*, see also s.v. *Ordonnance*. The (decree) law no. 78/1931 abrogates and replaces the regulation of 27 May 1897 (Ḥasan and ʿAbd al Wahhāb, 1984:39, article 1 of the decree).

[3] Ḥasan and ʿAbd al-Wahhāb (1984:68 and 73) for the explanatory memorandum. English translation in Liebesny (1975:101–2).

[4] Qānūn raqam (1) li-sanat 2000 bi-iṣdār qānūn tanẓīm baʿḍ awḍāʿ wa-ijrāʾāt al-taqāḍī fī masāʾil al-aḥwāl al-shakhṣiyya, in *al-Jarīda al-Rasmiyya*, no. 4 (29 January 2000).

[5] Regarding the eclectic choice between the doctrines of various law schools of *fiqh* as a legislative method of reforming personal status law, see Anderson (1976:34–85). On the importance of the Mālikī doctrine on divorce for modern Arab legislation, see Y. Linant de Bellefonds (1965, 2:423–79).

The legislature and the high courts: apostasy trials and ḥisba *actions*

The judiciary has, over the last five decades, used this prerogative to extend its ideological control over the intellectual, artistic and scholarly life of Egypt. Egyptian family law is not extensively codified and its lacunae are many. The judiciary's interpretation of Hanafi law, therefore, plays an important role. Among the institutions developed by the prevailing opinion of the Hanafi school of *fiqh* was a special procedure, a sort of "relator's trial,"[6] called *ḥisba.*[7] Until 1955, articles 89 and 110 of decree law no. 78/1931 had been interpreted by the religious courts as the legal texts upon which to base the application, in personal status cases, of *ḥisba* actions (Sayf 1996: 1–15). The term "*ḥisba*" refers to the obligation incumbent upon every Muslim "to command what is right and to forbid what is evil" (Cook 2000). According to classical *fiqh* norms in all four Sunnī schools, any trustworthy witness who is motivated by the desire "to command what is right and to forbid what is evil" can witness against other persons in order to protect "the claims of God" (Johansen 1979/1999d:38–46/386–94) and to prevent the spread of illicit practices and utterances in Muslim societies. Such a testimony would be sufficient reason for the qāḍī to initiate a procedure against the suspect. The *ḥisba* institution thus became a kind of religious censorship. Law no. 462/1955, which abolished the religious courts, also abolished articles 89 and 110 of law no. 78/1931 and thus, it seemed, withdrew the legal foundation for *ḥisba* trials. In articles 1 and 5, it states that the national courts, which had become competent for personal status cases, must follow the rules of procedure laid down in article 3 of the law on civil and commercial procedures. Neither this law nor the personal status court regulations grant legal standing to persons without a personal and direct interest in cases filed by them with the court. Many Egyptian law professors and lawyers held that, henceforth, *ḥisba* trials were without any legal justification. But the Court of Cassation decided otherwise. On 30 March 1966 it ruled

[6] For the relator's trial see *Black's Law Dictionary* (1990), s.v. "Relator." The dictionary defines the term as follows: "An informer. The person upon whose complaint, or at whose instance certain writs are issued such as information or writ of *quo warranto*, and who is *quasi* the plaintiff in the proceeding; for example, if John Smith is the relator and Jones is the defendant, the citation would read, "State ex rel. John Smith v. Jones."

[7] For *ḥisba* actions in Egyptian codes and adjudication, see Sayf (1996:1–15).

that article 6 of law 462/1955, in combination with article 280 of law 78/1931, entitled a judge to base his judgment on the testimony of *ḥisba* witnesses.[8] The fact that no legislative text mentions such a procedure does not mean, according to the Court of Cassation (*Maḥkamat al-naqḍ* 1996:9–10), that the legislature wanted to contravene basic texts of the revealed law of Islam. The courts are, therefore, obligated to base their judgments on these texts. The Court of Cassation used this argument in order to declare guilty of apostasy a woman who had been accused under a *ḥisba* action filed by plaintiffs who had no personal interest in the case. This judgment, pronounced after the abolition of the religious courts, introduced the classical norms on apostasy into the personal status jurisprudence of the highest national court of Egypt. Under these norms the marriage of an apostate to a Muslim woman is invalid and must be dissolved.

The Court of Cassation's decision of 30 March 1966 conferred legal validity upon the *ḥisba* rules of classical *fiqh*. According to these rules, apostasy cases are filed, not by private plaintiffs or by public prosecutors, but rather by trustworthy witnesses motivated by the desire "to command what is right and to forbid what is evil." The testimony of these witnesses serves both as evidence and originating petition. The status of these witnesses is, for that reason, ambiguous. They are simultaneously plaintiffs and witnesses.

In the 1990s, the Egyptian courts were inundated by *ḥisba* actions against intellectuals, artists, writers and scholars, whose books, articles, images or literary texts were adduced as evidence of their apostasy. According to different sources, between 80 and 200 of these cases were pending before Egyptian courts.[9] Defense lawyers repre-

---

[8] Bälz (1996, 1997), and Court of Cassation (*Maḥkamat al-naqḍ*, al-dā'ira al-madaniyya wa l-tijāriyya wa l-aḥwāl al-shakhṣiyya). Decision dated 5 August 1995:11.

[9] The texts quoted in notes 9–14 are notes of a few pages written by lawyers admitted to plead before the Court of Cassation who acted as defense lawyers for Professor Abū Zayd. These notes, and the newsletters, explain the point of the defense to an Arabic-speaking public.

Dhū l-Fiqār (1996a), a defense lawyer for Professor Abū Zayd, lists personal status actions, civil and penal actions and even commercial actions brought in the name of the *ḥisba* principle. The same author mentions the number of 200 *ḥisba* trials against intellectuals and artists pending before Egyptian courts: see (1996b:1).

Yūsuf al-Badrī, a religious activist, states in an interview in the *Muṣawwar* that he alone prepared forty trials against Egyptian writers. In an interview with *Muṣawwar*, Najīb Maḥfūẓ, Nobel prize laureate of literature, mentions eighty *ḥisba* actions against Egyptian intellectuals.

senting accused intellectuals insisted that these *ḥisba* trials were part of an organized campaign by Egypt's religious right to intimidate liberal intellectuals.[10] The most important instrument of this campaign, according to the lawyers, is article 280 of law no. 78/1931, in combination with article 6 of law no. 462/1955 (Sayf 1996:12–13, sect. 10; Ṣāliḥ 1996:4–5). The defense lawyers maintain that article 280, which entitles judges to decide cases in light of the predominant opinion of Hanafi law, contradicts the constitutional principle of the separation of powers because it gives judges the right to create legal norms through their interpretation of the prevailing opinion of the Hanafi school of law. There is no code which defines the predominant opinions of that school, and judges are free to determine the content of that clause. They thus create their own law. Article 280 of law 78/1931 in its present form thus contradicts the constitution, according to the defense lawyers, insofar as it grants legislative powers to the judiciary (Sayf 1996:12; Ṣāliḥ 1996:4–5). The lawyers, therefore, have called for its abolition or redefinition (Sayf 1996:15; ʿUqba 1996a, 1996b:5–7; al-Sharqāwī 1996).

The most important and best documented apostasy trial—based entirely on *ḥisba* witnesses—was led by six lawyers against Naṣr Ḥāmid Abū Zayd, Professor of Islamic Studies at Cairo University. In 1993, a court of first instance had refused to accept the action because it was based on the testimony of *hisba* witnesses which, according to the court, is not acceptable under Egyptian law. On 14 June 1995, the Cairo Court of Appeal accepted the case against Professor Abu Zayd, declared him guilty of apostasy and ordered his marriage to be dissolved. The Cairo Court of Appeal based its decision on the above-mentioned judgment by the Egyptian Court of Cassation, which, on 30 March 1966, had rendered licit the hearing of *ḥisba* actions by Egyptian courts (Bälz 1996, 1997; Heilmann 1995:61–2). Abū Zayd and his wife brought the matter before the Court of Cassation, which, on 5 August 1996, confirmed the decision of the Cairo Court of Appeal[11]—basing its judgment once again on article 280 of law no. 78/1931, in combination with law no. 462/1955. When it became obvious that the Court of Cassation

[10] Dhū al-Fiqār (1996b:1); (1996a:2); Shalakany Law Office Legal Advisers (1996:1, section 1; 3, section 5); Ṣāliḥ [1996:1, 3]; ʿUqba [1996a:1, 3].

[11] Bälz (1996, 1997), and Court of Cassation (Maḥkamat al-Naqḍ, al-dāʾira al-madaniyya wa l-tijāriyya wa l-aḥwāl al-shakhṣiyya). Decision dated 5 August 1996:11.

would confirm a judgment that held a Muslim professor of Islamic Studies guilty of apostasy, a judgment based only on the accused's books, the legislature promulgated, in January 1996, a law (no. 3/1996) that requires *ḥisba* witnesses to bring their testimony before the public prosecutor, who alone is empowered to decide whether the testimony is sufficient to bring an action before the court.[12] But the Court of Cassation refused to take this law into consideration because it was promulgated after Professor Abū Zayd's case was brought before the court. The defense lawyers, therefore, appealed to the legislature to amend article 3 of the law of civil and commercial procedure so as to definitely rule out *ḥisba* actions: they requested the legislature to declare that a personal and direct interest of the plaintiff is an obligatory condition for all actions in all kinds of trials, not only for the plaintiff's legal standing in suing the defendant but also for his request to execute judgments against the defendant. Although such a law was finally passed in May, 1996, by the People's Assembly (law no. 81/1996), it was not taken into consideration by the Court of Cassation. This law effectively denies all legal validity to *ḥisba* actions.[13] On the strength of this law, in September 1996, a Cairene Court of first instance decided to halt the execution of the judgment passed by the Cairo Court of Appeal against Professor Abū Zayd and confirmed by the Court of Cassation.[14]

Article 3 of law no. 1/2000, which brought about an important reform of the Egyptian law of divorce, still refers to the "prevailing opinion of the Hanafi school of law" as a source of Egyptian personal statute law.[15] The extent to which judges are entitled to create legal norms by interpreting them as the predominant opinion of the Hanafi school of law is not defined by any law nor has there

---

[12] The defense lawyers for Professor Abū Zayd seem to agree on a negative critique of this law. See, for example, ʿUqba (1996b); al-Sharqāwī (1996:1–8); Shalakany Law Office Legal Advisers (1996:3–4, section 7); Dhū al-Fiqār (1996b:1–2).

[13] The Shalakany Law Office, which organized the defense of Professor Abū Zayd, comments on law 81/1996 in its newsletter of 18 September, as follows: "This new law confirmed that any action, appeal or application is not admissible unless it is filed by a person who has a direct and personal interest therein. This Law made this rule a matter of public policy and obligated all Egyptian courts, including the Supreme Court, to observe this rule of public policy and apply it in all pending cases."

[14] See the interviews with Farīd al-Dīb, Fu'ād ʿAbd al-Munʿim Riyāḍ, Monā Dhū al-Fiqār in *Akhbār al-yawm*, 28 September 1996.

[15] See note 4.

been any effort to codify these predominant opinions and to define the matters to which they refer. The reference to these opinions continues to create tensions between liberal intellectuals, high courts, the legislature and politico-religious movements. These tensions form the background against which a decision of the Supreme Constitutional Court, to be discussed below, should be read and understood. This decision limits the extent of the applicability of classical *fiqh* norms under modern constitutional law in Egypt.

Egypt's Supreme Constitutional Court and the "Organic Unity" of the Constitutional Texts

The Supreme Constitutional Court of Egypt (SCC) is a relatively new actor in the legal field. The Egyptian constitution of 1971 announced the establishment of the SCC and charged it with the task of controlling the constitutional character of legislative texts and of giving binding interpretation of legislative texts.[16] Law no. 48/1979, which regulates the functioning of the SCC, added other competencies to it.[17] Articles 29 and 30 of this law entitle all persons engaged in civil, penal or administrative litigation to bring an action against the unconstitutional character of legislative texts under which they are sued or which impede their legal claims. This right is conditional, however. The court before which the trial is pending must confirm that the defendant's argument is relevant. If it does so, the SCC may decide to hear the case.[18] Apart from the constitutional court of Kuwait, established in 1973, the Egyptian SCC is the only constitutional court in the Arab world that allows individual citizens to bring an action of this kind.

Article 2 of the Egyptian constitution of 1971 introduced, for the first time in Egyptian legal history, the notion that "the principles of Islamic normativity (*sharī'a*) are a principal source of the legislation." In 1980 this article was amended and "the principles of Islamic normativity" became "*the* principal source of the legislation." Regarding this text, the SCC had to answer two main questions. Was this

---

[16] See the fifth section of the Constitution, articles 174–8.

[17] See law no. 48/1979, esp. articles 25 and 26. For the text of this law, see the first volume of the court's judgments: al-Maḥkama al-dustūriyya al-ʿulyā (1981:69–99).

[18] Articles 29 and 30 of law no. 48/1979, al-Maḥkama (1981:82).

article addressed to the courts? Did it confer on them the right to define the content of "the principles of Islamic normativity"? Or was it addressed to the legislature, which should translate those principles into legislative texts that bind the courts' interpretation? Against strong opposition from Egyptian judges, the SCC decided unequivocally that article 2 of the Egyptian constitution addresses the legislature only and that it does not empower the courts to treat their understanding of the principles of Islamic law as legal norms (al-Maḥkama 1987:3, 210–24; Johansen 1997b:370–2).

The SCC also had to decide whether article 2 of the constitution stands above all other constitutional texts or whether it should be read and interpreted in light of the constitution's other articles. How, for example, does the constitutional guarantee regarding the freedom of scientific research and artistic creation (article 49 of the constitution) relate to the "principles of Islamic normativity"? Do the Islamic principles take precedence over the freedom of research and cultural creativity? In a number of constitutional decisions issued during the 1980s, the SCC has argued against a hierarchical ranking of constitutional principles. It has decided that legislation dating from the time before 1970 will not be declared unconstitutional even if it contradicts the Islamic principles referred to in article 2 of the Constitution. The SCC obliges the legislature to adapt these texts to Islamic principles gradually. But all new legislation, says the court in a decision from May 1985:

> must conform to the principles of Islamic normativity without transgressing, at the same time, the restraining checks and balances which the other constitutional texts have imposed on the legislature in the context of its exertion of the legislative power. These restraining checks and balances—together with this new limitation [i.e., art. 2]—define the domain in which the Supreme Constitutional Court exercises its judicial control over the constitutional character of the legislative texts (al-Maḥkama 1987, 3:213, 210–1, 221).

The court insists, in many instances, that all constitutional norms form an "organic unity" of mutually interdependent principles, free of any internal contradiction and that they must be interpreted one in the light of the other (Johansen 1997b:364–5). Since the mid-1990s, though, court judgments have stressed the absolute priority of univocal revealed norms, regarded as representations of the fundamental and unchanging principles of Islamic normativity, over all other juristic rules and precepts.[19] It is not entirely clear to me how far this argument modifies the court's attitude towards the "organic unity" of the constitutional texts.

Be that as it may, the concept of the "organic unity" of all constitutional texts is of direct relevance to the case discussed on the following pages. In deciding this case, the SCC focuses on the right of a child to sue his or her father for unpaid maintenance obligations. The court is concerned with harmonizing article 2 with article 9 of the Constitution. Article 9 defines "the family ordered according to religion, values and patriotism" as the foundation on which society is based. Article 9 states further: "The state aspires to preserve the authentic character of the Egyptian family and the values and traditions which it represents, as well as to strengthen and increase this authentic character. . . ." The SCC had to defend the "organic unity" between these two articles of the Constitution against a father who was unwilling to pay the maintenance of his daughter.

The Father's Maintenance Obligation and the Prevailing Opinion of the Hanafi School of Law: A Constitutional Case

Maintenance obligations have been at the core of the modern legislature's concern with the reform of Egyptian personal status law. The norms of the Hanafi school of law concerning family relations, marriage and maintenance obligations were developed between the eighth and the fourteenth century CE, mainly in Iraq and Transoxania. It is thus not surprising that these norms were not always acceptable to Egyptian women and children in the twentieth century. The maintenance obligations of husbands and fathers towards wives, divorcees and children has been one of the most hotly debated points. Modern Egyptian legislation underlines the husband's obligation to ensure the maintenance of his wife or wives and has attempted to adapt this obligation to the conditions of modern society. The

[19] At the same time, the SCC distinguishes between the eternal and unchanging norms of revealed Islam and the legal norms developed by Muslim jurists in past centuries. It gives precedence to the modern legislature's efforts over those of the jurists of past centuries. The argument is developed in detail in al-Maḥkama (1997, 7:656–79) in a decision dating from 18 March 1996. See, esp., 660, 671–2.

first Egyptian law which defined the legal relation between husband and wife, issued in 1920, focuses strongly on the husband's maintenance obligation towards his wife (see articles 1–6 of law no. 25/1920) (Ḥasan and ʿAbd al-Wahhāb 1984:1–2), as does the personal status law of 1929 (see articles 16–18 of law no. 25/1929) (ibid., 8, and the explaining memorandum, 17–19). It is obvious from subsequent legislation that these laws did not solve the problems of divorcees and their children. Law no. 62 of 1976 obligates a state bank[20] to advance to wives, divorcees and children, upon demand, any maintenance payment awarded to them by the courts. By the same law, this bank is entitled to confiscate a percentage of a husband's or father's revenues in order to ensure that he pays his maintenance debts.[21] Law no. 1 of 2000 continues to define the tasks and competencies of that bank in maintenance matters.[22] These laws indicate that the legislature does not rely on the willingness of husbands and fathers to comply with the obligations imposed upon them by the courts.

After decades of struggle, a reform of the personal status legislation was brought about under President Sadat by an emergency decree subsequently approved by the parliament as law no. 44/1979 (El Alami 1994:116–7). For reasons relating to the President's competence to pass emergency legislation in the absence of the parliament, the SCC, in 1985, annulled this law as unconstitutional. In the same year, the People's Assembly passed law no. 100/1985, which restated most of the essential issues of law no. 44/1979. In what follows I focus on the constitutional action brought before the SCC in order to prove that this new law no. 100/1985 was unconstitutional because it contradicted the predominant opinion of the Hanafi school of law.

On 26 March 1994 the SCC dismissed this constitutional action as unfounded. The judgment is published in Arabic in the sixth volume of the SCC's decisions.[23]

---

[20] *Bank Nāṣir al-ijtimāʿī.*

[21] Articles 3,5,6,7,9 of law no. 62/1976. For the text of this law, see Ḥasan and ʿAbd al-Wahhāb (1984:80–2).

[22] Articles 71–76 of law no. 1/2000: Qānūn raqam (1) li-sanat 2000 bi-iṣdār qānūn tanẓīm baʿḍ ʿawḍāʿ wa-ijrāʾāt al-taqāḍī fī masāʾil al-aḥwāl al-shakhṣiyya.

In: *Al-Jarīda al-rasmiyya*, no. 4 (Jan. 29, 2000). See also article 23 of the same law for other methods of putting pressure on the defaulting father or husband.

[23] Maḥkama (1996, 6:231–60). For a French translation, see Dupret (1997).

The following is a summary of events according to the SCC's judgment. In 1989, a man who was a defendant in a maintenance suit pending before the Alexandria personal status court brought a constitutional action against section 4 of article 18b(2), in which law 100/1985 (which modified law no. 25/1929) reforms the maintenance obligation of fathers, thus changing the legal situation that had prevailed in Egypt since 1929. The plaintiff based his action on the fact that Egyptian legislation, in 1931 and 1955, confirmed that decisions in matters of personal status must be decided according to the prevailing opinion of the Hanafi school of *fiqh*. Section 4 of article 18b puts the role of Hanafi law into jeopardy because it radically changes the father's obligation to maintain his children.

The plaintiff had good reasons to fear these changes. His daughter was born in 1973, and in 1974, the mother of his daughter sued him because he was not paying any maintenance for his daughter. The plaintiff denied his paternity of the child—a common strategy in maintenance suits in Egypt (Shaham 1997:156–64). The trial was interrupted so that the questions of filiation could be determined. In 1974, the mother initiated a filiation proceeding against the father in order to have his paternity officially recognized. In 1986, she won her case. Immediately after the judgment was pronounced, the father appealed it, but the court of appeal confirmed his paternity. The father sought legal redress with the Court of Cassation. Three years later, in January 1989, this court turned down his request. By this time, the daughter was sixteen years old and the mother's maintenance suit, brought against the father of her daughter, had been suspended for fifteen years. The maintenance suit resumed in 1989 and the mother won the case, legally and, therefore, morally, but hardly financially: the father was ordered to pay thirty Egyptian pounds to the mother. Both the father and the mother appealed the judgment. Their appeal was negotiated before the court of personal status in Alexandria. It was at this point in time that the father discovered the constitutional dimension of the case. He contested the constitutionality of article 18b, which law no. 100/1985 added to law no. 25/1929. Article 18b had served as the mother's principal legal argument, enabling her to sue her daughter's father for his unpaid maintenance debts. The law states not only that the father is obligated to pay for his daughter's maintenance but also that "Maintenance for children is legally incumbent upon their father from the date on which he refuses to provide them with maintenance." (El Alami

1994:122). The father, therefore, had a clear personal interest in his action against the constitutional character of article 18b(2). The SCC, on 26 March 1994, rejected the father's request. At that moment in time the daughter had reached her twenty-first year and had not yet received a penny from her father.

This case shows how fathers who are unwilling to pay maintenance for their children can circumvent their obligations. The denial of paternity in the first instance, in the court of appeal and in the court of cassation, gave the father a respite of fifteen years. When this remedy failed him, he appealed the maintenance decision and, finally, turned to the SCC. All in all he spent twenty-one years without paying one piaster of maintenance to his daughter.

Hanafi Doctrines on Maintenance Payments

The father based his case entirely on the notion that the "prevailing opinion of the Hanafi school" represents, in Egyptian personal status law, the binding norms of Islam.

As is well known, a jurists' law has a tendency to produce a surplus of legal opinions. Normally, therefore, any long-lived law school has two, three or more opinions on each and every legal topic. Some of these may be more successful in one geographical region than in another, and more acceptable in one social or political context than another. A law school, such as that of the Hanafis, which looks back on a tradition of more than 1200 years and which has been dominant in India, Central Asia, Iraq, in the Balkans and—under the Ottomans—in all parts of the Arab world and the Ottoman empire, has a huge stock of used and unused legal opinions. It is, in fact, very difficult to state with confidence which of the legal opinions produced within the Hanafi school have been dominant among the jurists of the school in a given region at a given historical period. The Egyptian and Syrian Hanafi literature of the Ottoman Period transmits, from the sixteenth century on, three major school traditions concerning the father's obligation for the maintenance of his children. They differ on the question under what conditions are the father's unpaid maintenance obligations transformed into personal debts so that his children or their mother can sue him after he fails to pay in due time. All three doctrines face the same problem: if the father does not deny the child's affiliation to him, he is morally and legally obligated to pay his child's maintenance. The amount of the maintenance payment differs according to the father's social status or the child's wealth. It therefore must be determined by the decision of a judge or by the father's amicable settlement with either his children or their mother. Without such a judgment or amicable settlement, the father's obligation towards his child is unspecified and, therefore, cannot be enforced and does not accumulate as a personal debt that he owes to his child.

One of these three Hanafi opinions, which dates from fourteenth-century Egypt, states that the father's maintenance of his children should be regulated by analogy to the husband's maintenance of his wife. This tradition holds that once the father concludes an amicable settlement with his children or once the *qāḍī* specifies, through his judgment, the amount of maintenance the father owes to his children, the father is obligated—until his sons come of age or his daughters marry—to pay this amount. If he fails to do so, the outstanding maintenance payments accumulate as his personal debt for which his children or their representatives can sue him (Ibn ʿĀbidīn [1889] 2:714, 724, 726, 743; see also ibid., 4:355). This doctrine clearly would not have helped the daughter in our case: the father did not recognize his daughter and he did not conclude an amicable settlement with the mother in her capacity as the latter's representative. Also, during the first fifteen years, no judgment specified the daughter's maintenance claims against her father. Under this doctrine, the father would have been bound to pay his maintenance debts only from 1989 onwards.

A second Hanafi doctrine is mentioned in the Ottoman Hanafi literature from Syria: it states that the father can be obligated to pay the maintenance of his children if he consents unilaterally to do so, even in the absence of a judgment or an amicable settlement. He cannot revoke his consent (Ibn ʿĀbidīn [1889] 2:714). Again, this doctrine would not have been of any help to the daughter in our case because the father never consented to pay his daughter's maintenance.

Both opinions are refuted by the adherents of the third doctrine identified in the Syrian and Egyptian literature of the nineteenth century as the predominant doctrine. It is probably the oldest Hanafi doctrine concerning the maintenance payment for children because we find it fully developed in the Transoxanian legal literature of the eleventh century.[24] It defines the father's maintenance obligation as "a link" (*ṣila*) between him and his children. The term "link" is a technical term used to define a payment for which the recipient can raise a claim that is morally valid but that, with rare exceptions, is not legally enforceable (al-Sarakhsī 1978, 5:184). Only the *traditio* (*qabḍ*) of the payment to the recipient transforms it into her or his legally recognized property.[25] A "link" of this kind is a payment that falls due neither as a contractual obligation nor as a consideration for a specific good or a counter-performance for a specific service.[26]

A wife is entitled to maintenance from her husband on the strength of her marriage contract. Through the amicable settlement which she concludes with her husband, or through the *qāḍī's* judgment, which obligates the husband to pay a certain amount of maintenance to his wife, the husband's maintenance payment becomes a legal obligation. If the husband fails to fulfill it, the overdue maintenance accumulates as his personal debt. His wife can sue him at any moment for the debt which has accrued since the judgment or the amicable settlement. On the other hand, neither the judgment nor the amicable settlement has a retroactive effect: the husband's maintenance obligation towards his wife is enforceable only for the period after its recognition by an amicable settlement or a judgment.

A child has no contract with her or his father nor does the child provide specific services or deliver specific goods. The child's claim to maintenance must, therefore, rest on a different basis. The Hanafi jurists accept two main reasons for a child's claim to maintenance

---

[24] This doctrine was extensively discussed by eleventh and twefth-century Transoxanian authors, such as al-Sarakhsī and al-Kāsānī. The nineteenth-century Syrian Hanafi Ibn ʿĀbidīn traces it to the *Hidāya* of the twelfth-century Transoxanian author Marghīnānī, the *Dhakhīra* of Burhān al-dīn Ibn Māza (1156–1219), the *Adab al-qāḍī* of the ninth-century Iraqi author al-Khaṣṣāf as commented upon by the famous Transoxanian author al-Ṣadr al-shahīd Ibn Māza (d. 1141). He quotes other twelfth-century Transoxanian authors. This genealogy of the prevalent opinion of the Hanafite school in modern Syria and Egypt is impressive proof of the impact which the Transoxanian doctrines have left among the Hanafi jurists of the Arab countries.

[25] al-Sarakhsī (1978, 5:184, 195); al-Ḥaṣkafī [1889] 3:307, 443; Ibn ʿĀbidīn [1889] 3:307, 443. See also 4:355. For the term *traditio* see Black (1990) s.v. *traditio*, p. 1495.

[26] al-Sarakhsī (1978, 5:184, 195; 10:182); al-Samarqandī (1993, 2:160–61); Johansen (1999:119, n. 52, 123–4 and notes 78–9).

against its father. First, the child is part of his father. This "partness" (*juz'iyya*),[27] as the jurists say, distinguishes the father's obligation towards his children from his obligations towards his other relatives. Even a poor father is morally obligated to maintain his needy children, whereas he is obligated to pay the maintenance of other relatives only if he can afford to do so.

The second reason that obliges the father to maintain his children is their need. They cannot support themselves and, therefore, will perish, unless the father—or his relatives—maintain them by paying, at least, for their food, clothing and shelter. At this stage of the discussion the Hanafi jurists discuss a norm that is generally accepted in the school and which shows that, under certain conditions, even moral claims are legally enforceable. The jurists measure the need of the children in units of time, e.g., the maintenance needed for a day, for a week or for a month (artisans pay daily, merchants monthly, landowners yearly, according to Transoxanian authors of the eleventh and Syrian authors of the nineteenth century). If, during this unit of time, that is, on the day or month on which the maintenance is due, the father does not pay, he can be jailed in order to enforce the fulfillment of his maintenance obligations. He may even be subjected to bodily punishment, such as whipping, to insure his compliance. An important Hanafi jurist from eleventh-century Transoxania explains:

> If the father abstains from paying the maintenance for his minor children, he is put into prison (*yuḥbas*) for this reason. This [solution] differs [from the way in which] other debts [are treated]. This difference resides in two aspects: firstly, maintenance is due to satisfy the needs of the time (*al-nafaqa li-ḥājat al-waqt*) and if the father abstains from it [during this time], he deliberately seeks to destroy his child. A father deserves to be punished if he deliberately seeks to destroy his child. It is as if he were attacking him with a sword (*kamā law ʿadā ʿalayhi bi-l-sayf*), as if [the child] was entitled to kill him in order to push him back (*ka'anna lahu an yaqtulahu dafʿan lahu*).[28]

In other words, during the time unit fixed for the maintenance payment, the father's "link" obligation is legally enforceable. The judiciary may intervene to force him to honor his obligation, even by

[27] al-Sarakhsī (1978, 5:208, 222–4, 226); al-Kāsānī (1910, 4:31, 35–7).
[28] al-Sarakhsī (1978, 5:224); see also al-Kāsānī (1910, 4:38).

using corporal punishment.[29] But as soon as the time unit for the maintenance payment elapses, the children's need for food, shelter and clothing during this period also lapses and with it the father's obligation to pay anything for the past time unit. Maintenance debts do not accumulate as the father's personal debt, according to this doctrine, because they do not last longer than the time unit for which they are due.[30] The father can neither be punished nor held responsible for the outstanding maintenance payment. The father's maintenance obligation *vis-à-vis* his children is enforceable only if his children or their mother sue him before the time elapses for which the maintenance falls due. In the case of a daily maintenance payment it is, in fact, difficult to imagine how such a norm could be applied in practice. The maintenance obligation differs from other debts: other debts do not lapse with the passing of time. They accumulate as the personal debt of the defaulting payer. Precisely because maintenance debts lapse into oblivion after the time period set for their payment, the means to enforce them are more important than those accepted for other debts. After the time unit lapses, the children and their mother cannot sue the father in order to recover the overdue maintenance payments.

Since the twelfth century, and perhaps before that, the Hanafi jurists have held that even a qāḍī's judgment[31] obligating the father to pay a certain amount of maintenance is extinguished once the time unit fixed for the maintenance payment passes. The Hanafi doctrine of the Ottoman period teaches that the same holds true for amicable settlements.[32] According to this doctrine, there are only two ways in which the father's maintenance obligation *vis-à-vis* his children can be transformed into a lasting personal debt. If the *qāḍī* orders the mother to borrow money in order to pay her children's maintenance[33] or if he orders her to advance these expenses from

---

[29] al-Sarakhsī (1978, 5:222, 224–5); al-Ḥaṣkafī (1889, 4:346, 355); Ibn ʿĀbidīn (1889, 4:355).

[30] al-Sarakhsī (1978, 5:188, 196, 224–25); al-Kāsānī (1910, 4:38); Ibn ʿĀbidīn (1889, 2:714, 743–44).

[31] al-Kāsānī (1910, 4:38); Ḥaṣkafī (1889, 4:355; Ibn ʿĀbidīn (1889, 2:714, 726, 728; 4:355).

[32] Ibn ʿĀbidīn (1889, 2:714).

[33] al-Sarakhsī (1978, 5:184); al-Kāsānī (1910, 4:33); Ibn ʿAbd al-ʿAzīz (1994:565); Ibn ʿĀbidīn (1889, 2:713–16, 728–30, 745).

her own assets,[34] she is entitled to sue the husband for reimbursement of her debts or monetary advances. The cause for the father's obligation to reimburse his wife is obviously the fact that she contracted debts and effected payments pursuant to a judge's order. Under these circumstances the father's obligation to pay his children's maintenance is transformed into a personal debt that is not extinguished by the passing of time. It is evident that, under this doctrine, the daughter in our case would not have received a judgment endorsing her claims to maintenance from her father for the years that passed between her birth and the judgment of 1986. No judge ever ordered the mother to borrow money or to advance the maintenance payment for her daughter from her own assets so as to acquire a reimbursement claim against the father. She paid everything without such an order.

The Court's Judgment

The plaintiff in our case clearly has very good reasons to identify the prevailing opinion of the Hanafi school with the "principles of Islamic normativity": such an identification allows him to escape his maintenance obligation towards his daughter. Even if he were ordered to pay his daughter's maintenance in 1994, such a judgment, according to the predominant opinion of the Hanafi school, would not have any retroactive effect. Instead of incurring the obligation to pay maintenance for the last twenty years, he would have to pay maintenance payments only from 1994 onwards and only if his daughter had not married in the meantime. Prior to the promulgation of law no. 100/1985, the father would have stood a good chance to find a sympathetic court for his plea. Ron Shaham has found, for the first half of the twentieth century, eight Egyptian court decisions on maintenance suits brought before the court after the time fixed for the maintenance payment had lapsed. He reports:

> A few *qāḍīs* (I counted three cases) applied the general rule of Hanafi doctrine by considering maintenance for a minor as one type of maintenance for relatives. As a result, if the maintenance had not actually

[34] al-Sarakhsī (1978, 5:223); al-Kāsānī (1910, 4:33, 36); Ibn ʿĀbidīn (1889, 2:728–31, 744).

> been obtained from the father within one month (from the date of beginning of entitlement), or if the child had died, the father was exempted from his debts. Other *qāḍīs* (five cases) objected to this line of legal reasoning. . . . Appealing to an alternative Hanafi opinion, these *qāḍīs*, therefore, decided that maintenance for a minor child, similar to matrimonial maintenance, was an accumulating debt of the father from the beginning of the entitlement (Shaham 1997:172).

Until the 1980s, the Egyptian judiciary had the choice among several opinions of the Hanafi school regarding maintenance obligations and could decide whether the one or the other ought to prevail.

That part of law no. 100 of 1985 which modifies law no. 25 of 1929 drastically changed this situation. Section 1 of article 18b states: "If the minor has no wealth [from which maintenance can be provided], then his father is liable for his maintenance." Section 4 of the same article specifies: "Maintenance for children is legally incumbent upon their father from the date on which he refuses to provide them with maintenance" (El Alami 1994:121–2). In other words, the obligation to pay the maintenance of his children becomes the father's personal debt from the moment at which he abstains from honoring his obligation. This would put our plaintiff in a very delicate situation: he is now faced with the unpleasant prospect of paying twenty-one years of accumulated maintenance debt to his daughter. One understands the complex motives that caused him to bring his case before the SCC.

The SCC, which had declared unconstitutional the precursor of law 100/1985, did not follow the plaintiff's reasoning. In the course of its answer to his request, the court elaborated its own understanding of "the principles of Islamic normativity" and their role for the legislature. It first introduced and accepted a classical doctrine of Islamic law according to which norms established by univocal revealed texts, which are interpreted in the same way by all qualified jurists, cannot be changed: they are eternal and are not to be replaced by anything else. This doctrine, which played a major role from the ninth to the twelfth centuries CE in debates on *ijtihād*, that is, individual legal reasoning as a source of norm production, is here used to define the limits which neither the court nor the legislature can transcend (al-Maḥkama 1996, 6:232, 237, 249). The eternal rules of the sacred law in its revealed form are opposed to those norms of the Muslim legal tradition that are the product of the jurists' individual legal reasoning. The *fiqh* norms produced by individual legal reasoning change according to time and place and show a strong degree of plasticity. According to the SCC, there are no eternal and unchanging rules that forbid the retroactive effects of judicial decisions imposing maintenance obligations on a father (ibid., 232, 239) and the legal reasoning of past generations of Muslim jurists produces only changing and modifiable rules that bind neither the jurists nor the political authorities (*walī al-amr*) or the legislature of the twentieth century (ibid., 234, 238–40, 250). The norms promulgated by the modern legislature in this field, says the court, enjoy precedence over all norm suggested by Muslim jurists in the past which, in the final instance, are also based on individual legal reasoning only (ibid., 232–4, 238–40, 250, 254–5). The condition that the legislature has to abide by is respect for the aims and the teleology of the revealed Islamic normativity, not for the individual rules of the jurists' law.

The SCC insisted that not only were the legislators entitled to change the legal norms concerning the maintenance obligation but also that it was their duty to do so. The criticism directed by the Egyptian parliament at the jurisprudence of the country's courts shows, according to the SCC, that such an intervention was necessary. Following the rules of the classical Hanafi doctrine, the Egyptian courts, according to the Egyptian Parliament, had created a situation in which mothers and children must wait for many years before the fathers finally decided to honor their obligation towards their children (ibid., 235, 247).

In pursuit of this reasoning, the SCC did not shy away from attacking the maintenance doctrine of the Hanafi school in the name of the constitution and of Islamic ethics. It focused its criticism of the Hanafi doctrine on four points.

First, the court found fault with the doctrine linking the need of the child to fixed time units in such a way that the expiration of the time unit results in the extinction of the childrens' claims. This doctrine is absurd, the court observed, because it presupposes that a child who does not sue his father in time has no needs (ibid., 233, 239, 241, 243, 251, 253–5). The court underlined the fact that such a doctrine is based neither on the Qur'ān (ibid., 234) nor on the facts of social life.

Second, the court stressed the fact that such a doctrine puts a premium on default: the negligent payer is discharged of his obligation for the simple reason that he does not respect the time limits within which he is supposed to honor his obligations. If a father is ready to disregard the deadlines set by this doctrine, he liberates himself from his financial duties towards his children (ibid., 234, 242–3).

Third, such a doctrine destroys the links between father and child because it encourages the child to become litigious and to sue his father at each new time unit, thus preserving his only chance to recuperate his maintenance payment (ibid., 241, 253).

Fourth, this doctrine puts into jeopardy the rights and the interests of the children, who must wait many years before they can touch the payments which their fathers owe them (ibid., 235, 247). It leads to the impoverishment of the mother who has to bring up the children.

At present, the SCC concluded, it is no longer possible to accept such a doctrine as the law to be applied by the courts. Instead, a sound policy that respects the state's duty to preserve the family, as established in article 9 of the Constitution, must set new and other priorities. It must engage the father's personal responsibility for his children's maintenance. Therefore, any maintenance that the father has failed to pay must be transformed into his personal debt *vis-à-vis* his children (ibid., 233, 236, 241, 248, 253). This is precisely what law no. 100 of 1985 does. There can be no prescription for this kind of obligation (ibid., 234, 236). The defaulting father is answerable for his debts and his obligations until the end of his life and beyond. The children's interest is preserved by the judiciary.

This new family preservation policy which makes fathers legally responsible for the payment of their maintenance debts to their children can only be brought about by political authorities who follow their own independent political and legal reasoning. They alone can guarantee the children's maintenance (ibid., 233, 242); only they are powerful enough to enforce the retroactive effect of the judiciary's decisions on maintenance obligations. And for these—and other—reasons, the independent legal and political reasoning of the political authorities must take precedence over the legal reasoning of earlier generations of Muslim jurists (ibid., 234, 238–9)—so long as the political authorities respect the religious ethics and the teleology of the sacred law (ibid., 239, 250, 254).

The norms of the Hanafi doctrine, therefore, no longer represent "Islamic Law" or the principles of Islamic normativity as far as maintenance is concerned. To the contrary, the court states:

> There is no proof that to defend this [i.e., the Hanafi] doctrine [on maintenance] serves the interest of the family and guarantees the strengthening of mutual compassion between family members. In fact,

> it contradicts the essence of their relations and may lead to the family's destruction. The change of time calls for abandoning this type of legal reasoning in order to keep operational the flexibility that Islamic law encompasses in its practical norms. These are open for development, mindful of the law's ties to the interest of the people and their renewed needs and their changing practices, so long as these do not conflict with a definite revealed rule. This flexibility contradicts [the idea] that the political authorities are fettered by specific legal opinions and not allowed to deviate from them or that their efforts to engage in legal reasoning should stop at a moment in time already left behind by those interests which have to be taken into consideration by the law. This Islamic law, in its roots and sources, develops by necessity, and rejects all deadlock and stagnation (*jumūd*) and the efforts of individual reasoning are not restricted by anything—in the areas in which no revealed texts settle the questions—except by the general rules [of Islamic normativity] and by considerations that do not paralyze the teleology of the sacred law. Within this framework it is a rational duty, a requirement of religious ethics, and it serves the realization of considerable interests to abandon the assumption defended by the Hanafis and their followers (ibid., 252; the translation is mine).

So much for the Hanafi doctrine on maintenance as an incarnation of the principles of Islamic normativity. In the name of the religious ethics of Islam, in the name of the teleology of the Sacred Law, in the name of the Constitution, of reason and of important interests, the judiciary must be emancipated from the Hanafi doctrine concerning the father's maintenance obligation towards his children. The court stresses that section 4 of article 18b is in perfect harmony with article 9 of the Constitution and does not contradict article 2. Article 18b of law no. 100 of 1985 is thus supported by the Constitution and by the principles of Islamic normativity, and all of these are in sharp contradiction with the Hanafi doctrine on maintenance payments.

Conclusion

According to the SCC, the dominant opinion of the Hanafi school of law does not automatically have force of law in the field of family law. The classical *fiqh* norms, even if they were the dominant opinions of the Hanafi school, are no longer ipso facto binding for the legislature or the SCC. They are acceptable only if they are sufficiently flexible and rational to stand the test of functional and constitutional scrutiny. It is true that the legislature still uses the old formulas of 1931 and 1955: in law no. 1/2000—which introduced reforms in divorce law among other things—the legislature decreed once again that judges are required to apply the prevailing doctrine of the Hanafi school. But the meaning of the formula has changed: over the last sixteen years, the legislature, supported by the SCC, has continued to depart from the rules of the dominant opinion of the Hanafi school. Maintenance (law no. 100/1985), divorce on the wife's initiative without the husband's consent (law no. 1/2000), and law 81/1996 on the legal standing of the plaintiffs, are important examples of this tendency to reduce the role of the Hanafi legal tradition as a source for the country's personal status law. The SCC's judgment on the maintenance obligation of fathers is another example. Hanafi legal doctrine thus covers a shrinking field of legal topics in personal status law.

Whereas between the 1920s and the 1970s, the legislature used to invoke the doctrine of other *Sunnī* schools of law in order to justify its departure from the dominant doctrine of Hanafi law, neither the legislature, in 1985, 1996 and 2000, nor the SCC, in 1994, justified their stance with references to the doctrines of other Sunnī schools of *fiqh*. The SCC mentions in passing the doctrine of the Mālikī school, but draws its main argument from Qur'anic ethics, practical needs and the text of the Constitution, not from classical *fiqh* doctrine. According to the SCC the modern legislature's effort to find the right norms takes precedence over that of earlier generations of Muslim jurists. Islamic normativity is not to be found in the historical doctrines of the *fiqh* schools. While the ordinary judge is required to follow the legislature's texts and fill their lacunae by referring to the predominant opinion of the Hanafi school, the legislature can follow its own effort of legal and political reasoning. The constitutional court does not require the legislature to follow *fiqh* norms but to remain within the broad framework of the principles of Islamic normativity. Neither the legislature nor the SCC are bound by the norms developed by Muslim jurists of past centuries. The constitutional court is, according to this line of reasoning, clearly marked off from other branches of the judiciary.

The Islamic law envisaged by the SCC is reconstructed in the form of constitutional principles that direct and orient the work of the legislature. The authors who are empowered to rethink and reformulate Islamic law and Islamic normativity are clearly identified by the SCC: the legislature, political authorities, expert jurists and, of course, the judges of the SCC. The *fiqh* schools and their representatives do not figure prominently in this group. A modern elite composed of intellectuals, politicians, jurists and judges with strong ties to the national political culture plays the leading role. Its members reinterpret, reconstruct and reformulate Islamic normativity and dismantle the classical representations of Islamic law. The court empowers the legislature to enact a modernized version of Islamic law in the form of supra-legislative norms and legislative texts. The court relates norm production directly to political authority. The SCC thus creates a new relationship between the principles of Islamic normativity and the state's legislative texts.

The judgments of the SCC transfer the authority to interpret Islam from a legal profession that specializes in *fiqh* to modern intellectuals, politicians and jurists. Such a transfer of interpretative authority is taking place in many parts of the Muslim world. Whether or not this phenonmenon should be understood as a process of secularization is an altogether different matter. But there is no doubt that the SCC qualifies article 280 of law no. 78/1931 in a way that diminishes the capacity of Egyptian courts to identify institutions of the classical *fiqh* with modern Egyptian legal and constitutional norms.

CHAPTER EIGHT

COMMERCIAL LITIGATION IN A SHARĪʿA COURT

Brinkley Messick

In the month of Rajab 1375 (1956), in the British Crown Colony of Aden, the medieval Indian Ocean emporium turned leading modern port, a Yemeni coffee agent took advantage of the predicament of a foreign buyer. The Yemeni agent had on hand a large quantity of coffee just delivered on consignment from a merchant resident across the border to the North, in the highland town of Ibb. When the coffee arrived in Aden and was unpacked, it was found to be ruined, and the brokers and foreign purchasing agents who had assembled to meet the shipment refused to buy it. A report on these events, quoted verbatim in the case record of a trial that opened in the Ibb sharīʿa court, states that "thanks to his experience and business acumen," the Yemeni agent later "perceived the difficulty of one of the foreign buyers." It seems that this foreigner "was committed for a quantity of coffee to be shipped overseas, with a shipping contract and a specified time limit that was about to be reached, without [his] being able to obtain and buy the quantity that would meet his commitment." This buyer, who may have been French, had been unable to purchase enough coffee to meet his obligations "because it so happened that there was a lag in importations [from the highland producing districts] at that time." According to the report, the Yemeni agent "saw a favorable opportunity to make an effort on behalf of [the Ibb merchant's] coffee, and he went immediately to the foreigner, Denis Lefrateau [*dīnīs līfrātū*], and prepared the way for the subject by conversation on the lag in importations and other matters. Then he presented to him a proposition whereby he would attempt to pressure [the Ibb merchant], owner of 195 cases of coffee, to open all 195 cases for inspection by the foreigner of the whole quantity and for selection of what was possible from that." The report records Lefrateau's reaction: "The foreigner's face beamed. It was as if he had found a ray of hope."

Had the agent in Aden not managed to sell the defective coffee, the Ibb merchant's losses would have been, still in the words of the report, "greater than the mind can imagine." There were significant losses nevertheless, and the Ibb merchant sought compensation for these from the previous owner of the damaged coffee, the state Treasury (*bayt al-māl*). However, the ruling Imām, Aḥmad b. Yaḥyā Ḥamīd al-Dīn (r. 1948–1962), demanded that the issues be tested in the local sharīʿa court. The resulting case centers not on the transaction with the Frenchman but on the prior transaction between the Treasury and the Ibb merchant.

We know little about the handling of commercial cases in sharīʿa courts.[1] In the course of this trial the transaction in question is analyzed as a sale, the paradigmatic bilateral contract in the sharīʿa. The case is instructive both for its substantive contract analysis and also as an exemplification of the doctrinally normative but, in practice, relatively unusual procedural form in which the claimant's side alone presents evidence (see Messick 2002:245). Another unusual feature is that the proceedings terminate with a special type of oath (*yamīn*). Some of the large amount of evidence presented and quoted in the record was obtained by the claimant from government sources, in a period and place approximation of a Freedom of Information Act request in the contemporary United States. As a consequence, this case record represents an important source on the behind-the-scenes activities of bookkeeping and correspondence in the late Imamic-era state, including discussions between the local Ibb Governor and the ruling Imam. The evidence additionally provides extensive detail on prevailing commercial practices and demonstrates the role of commercial "custom" (*ʿurf*) in the judicial process. My presentation will closely follow how evidence of various types is mobilized by the claimant to support his original claim. I will note the care with which both written documents and oral testimony are entered into the record, including the devices used to signal direct quotation and the attention given to such features as handwriting, signatures and seals. In his concluding ruling the judge gives a concise evalua-

[1] H. Gerber (1994:17), for example, states that a contribution of his research is that it shows the applicability of sharīʿa commercial law. In Aden around the turn of the twentieth-century, local merchants posed a faṭwa-seeking question concerning the sharʿī status of western-style freight insurance to the Shāfiʿī Mufti of Singapore, and the matter was later forwarded to Rashīd Riḍā in Cairo (Messick, forthcoming/a).

tion of how the evidence presented relates to the claim and serves as a basis for his judgment.

Addressing this particular relation of theory and practice in Islamic law (see Schacht 1964:76–85), I will comment on how the relevant doctrinal language, according to the official Zaydī school, deals with the right, or option (*khiyār*) to rescind a contract and how that language relates to the claim and to the judge's ruling in the 1956 case. Mainly concerned with sales of defective goods or goods that turn out to be other than described, such option rights may lead to the cancellation of a sale and the return of the sale object and the price money, or to the payment of a monetary indemnity (*arsh*). The specific option to rescind that is at issue in this case is known technically as *khiyār al-ruʾya,* which involves the buyer's "discriminating visual inspection" (*ruʾya mumayyiza*) of the sale object. A closely related type of rescision is called *khiyār al-ʿayb,* which is based on the buyer's discovery of a flaw in the sale object.[2]

Highland commerce in the years prior to the Revolution of 1962 remained intimately connected to agrarian production, the surpluses of which represented the principal trade commodities. Agrarian production was equally fundamental to the economic organization of the state: the in-kind tithe on this production and the border customs taxes on its transport constituted the principal forms of state revenue. Commerce and the state were related not only through taxes collected on the production and circulation of agricultural commodities but also through the transforming of in-kind state revenues into cash, a phenomenon common to pre-modern agrarian societies. In the Indian Ocean, according to Chaudhuri (1985:11), merchants and bankers "remained indispensable intermediaries in converting agricultural surplus into disposable state income."

Yemen's once unique place in the world coffee market had long since been eclipsed, however. Mocha, the famous Red Sea coffee port, declined following its heyday in the seventeenth and eighteenth centuries. Competing production by the Dutch in Java began in the 1720s and, somewhat later, South American production commenced. Yet coffee remained highland Yemen's principal export into the 1950s

---

[2] On the provisions relating to *khiyār al-ruʾya* and *khiyār al-ʿayb* according to the Zaydī school, see al-ʿAnsī (1993, 2:396–404, 412–33). Al-ʿAnsī is a twentieth-century commentator on the school's authoritative, late fourteenth-century manual, *Kitāb al-azhār*. For the Ḥanafī school, see Schacht (1964:152–3).

and the key port for this trade was the venerable Indian Ocean port of Aden, seized by the imperial British in 1839. According to the Aden Census of 1872 (Hunter [1877] 1968:26), there were traders from Arabia, East Africa, India, and Europe, with a smattering of Turks, Persians, Egyptians, Chinese, and Americans. Muslims, Hindus, Jews, Christians, and adherents of numerous other faiths were represented. Among the Arabs, there were important and expanding contingents of traders from both the Ḥaḍramawt and the Yemeni highlands, especially from the Shāfiʿī districts around the Lower Yemen towns of Ibb and Taʿizz. Captain Hunter (1968:28) states that there were three classes of merchants in late nineteenth century Aden: first, the established firms, English, German, French, Italian, American and Indian, which "carry on like in civilized countries"; second, firms that were mostly Arab, and which included some "very wealthy men" whose "principal business is the importation of coffee for sale to the first described class of merchants"; and third, petty traders, Arabs, Somalis, and some Indians.

In the highland Imamic state, the Treasury kept accounts for the other organs of government (except for the administration of Pious Endowments). The main internal function of the Treasury administration (known as the *māliyya*) centered on the management of the state's intake and dispersal of grain, and also of some coffee revenues, all received in the form of *zakāt*, the sharīʿa-based tithe on agricultural production. The Treasury was to the agrarian order of the Imamic state what the Central Bank, created after the Revolution, would be to the commercial order of the succeeding republican state. Like the grain revenues, the *zakāt* on coffee production was paid in-kind, although the amount of tithe coffee recorded in Ibb probably was modest until the famous producing district of al-ʿUdayn, directly to the west, was added to the town's administrative sphere in 1938. From that point on, until after the Revolution, when the tithe itself declined in importance as an official revenue source, coffee accumulated in government coffers. Unlike grain, which constituted the overwhelming portion of the revenues of the old agrarian state, coffee could not be used to feed the garrison, pay administrators, or distribute to the poor. Coffee had to be sold.

Storing agricultural products was a foundational activity in the former Imamic polity, as in many other agrarian states. In the Maghrib, the Arabic term for the Moroccan state was, and is, simply al-Makhzan, literally, "the storehouse." Storage technologies differed from state to state and from place to place. The plural term "stores" (*makhāzin*) is used in the court record; in Ibb, and in much of Yemen, storage mostly involved underground pits (*madfan*, pl. *madāfin*) carved into bedrock. Pits in ordinary houses could hold between one and two hundred *qadah*s, while the capacity of those in some of the older houses and the town warehouses was larger. The pits originally were lined with lime and a fine dark gravel; later, this gravel was mixed with cement. After the Revolution, however, pits gradually were replaced by above-ground storage in metal barrels.

At midcentury storage pits held the surpluses of agrarian production. Within the old walls of Ibb town, where the urban substratum was honeycombed with these storage pits, stored grain constituted the literal foundation of the old state. In the months immediately following the main fall harvest, long lines of donkeys bearing sacks of grain and other in-kind revenues such as pulses and coffee beans streamed into the town. Following the centuries-old stone roads that ascend in long steps from the surrounding valleys and descend from the mountains to the east, the donkeys carried in-kind revenues that would be delivered not only to the Treasury but also to the Endowments Office and to private landlords. In the months following the delivery of the harvest surpluses, the donkeys would complete a cycle by delivering baskets containing night soil from catchments in Ibb houses to the fallow terraces.

In-kind agrarian zakat taxes were delivered to the government's local Collection Room (*shūna*), where grains and other products were measured and sorted in separate bins, prior to being sent to a storage pit. After a delivery had been recorded in a register, the individual who had made the delivery proceeded to the government's in-kind Storage Office (*al-anbār*), where the formal receipt for payment of the zakāt was issued. The office style of this collection and receipt-issuing involved low, slant-topped desks arranged at floor-level and books were kept in in-kind units, in *qadāḥ* and fractions of a *qadāḥ*. Both the Collection Room and the Storage Office were subsections of the Treasury administration.

Coffee case

In 1956, the case was heard in the Ibb Province Sharīʿa Court by Judge Ismāʿīl ʿAbd al-Raḥmān al-Manṣūr,[3] whose signature and court seal appear atop the text, under the *basmala*. Judge al-Manṣūr opens the text by indicating how the case came into his hands. As is revealed later in this record, Imām Aḥmad was apprised of this matter and ordered the Ibb Governor to see it prosecuted in court. There follows the formal *daʿwā*, or claim, presented in person by the merchant claimant, ʿAbd al-Karīm al-Manṣūb, against the defendant, the Treasury, which is represented by a local *wakīl*. Although there is no explicit trace of representation for his side in the judgment, I learned that the claimant had the assistance of another well-known local *wakīl*, named ʿAlī Ḥasan Ṣāliḥ, whom I interviewed in September, 1975. I have read the text from the original judgment record, a vertically rolled document known as a *ḥukm*, that was provided to the claimant's side in the case, one version of which I obtained from ʿAlī Ḥasan Ṣāliḥ and another from the claimant's brother Qāsim, who also discussed the case with me.[4]

The claim both recapitulates the chain of events and makes a series of associated points of legal significance, specifically raising issues related to contract rescission. The basic story is repeatedly narrated, initially in the claim itself; then in the evidence section, in a quoted report prepared by two leading merchants in Aden, in quoted memos to and from the Ibb Governor and the Treasury Office, and in oral testimony; and, finally and decisively, in the judge's ruling.

---

[3] Biography in Aḥmad b. Muḥammad Zabāra (n.d., 1:235), the handwritten expansion of his father's *Nuzhat al-naẓar* (M. Zabāra 1979). Al-Akwaʿ (1995:429) bases his own entry on this "expanded" version. For a biography of this and other Ibb judges of the era, see Messick (n.d.). In his dissertation on the social history of villages southeast of Ibb town, Isaac Hollander (2000: 244–5) presents a 1357/1938 document (#361.20), countersigned by then Ibb Qaḍā' (district) Judge al-Manṣūr, which the local writer describes as involving a "customary judgment with a shariʿa orientation" (*ḥukm ʿurfī wa-wajh sharʿī*).

[4] The *ḥukm* obtained from ʿAlī Ḥasan Ṣāliḥ is in a small hand and consists of 173 lines, excluding an appended Appeal ruling and a final statement by the judge. Of these 173 lines, the opening claim and response together amount to 27 lines and the judge's ruling at the end to 20 lines. A note located above the court seal (which is dated 1370 A.H.) at the top on the front side of the document indicates that a copy of the text was entered in register 11 of the sharīʿa court of Ibb Province (as No. 1016, on pp. 351ff.). I later photocopied this register (which is in the personal archive of Judge Muḥammad b. Ḥasan al-Iryānī, a resident of Ibb) and found the entered copy (*ṣūra*) of the judgment text.

By transfer (*iḥāla*) from the respected Governor, the learned Qāḍī[5] Ṣafī al-Dīn Aḥmad bin Aḥmad al-Sayāghī, may God protect him, in accord with an honored Imamic order, may God strengthen him, ʿAbd al-Karīm bin Muḥammad Ṣaʿīd al-Manṣūb, one of the merchants of Ibb, appeared at this sharīʿa court of Ibb Province, and a claim was issued by him against the individual present with him, al-Qāḍī Muḥammad bin Ghālib al-Muṣannif, *wakīl* for the *bayt al-māl*, appointed by my lord the learned Governor of Ibb Province, may God protect him, saying in his claim,

> In the month of Jumada II, the previous year, 1375, the claimant purchased from the *bayt al-māl*, one thousand four hundred and sixty small *farāsilas*, and thirteen pounds and a half, of clean (*ṣāfī*) [coffee bean] on the order of our Lord the Governor and with the intermediacy of the Treasury Office, for a price per farāsila of fifteen riyāls, for a total value of twenty-two thousand riyāls, and that the contract of sale and purchase was completed before the visual inspection (*ruʾya*) of the sale object and its examination.
>
> Then he had it transported to Aden in a rush due to the opportunity of the availability of trucks for hire, which made it impossible for the plaintiff to visually inspect and to know the flaw (*ʿayb*) in the clean coffee. When he arrived in Aden he delivered it to his agent, al-Ḥājj al-Fāḍil ʿAbd Allāh b. ʿAlī al-ʿAwlaqī. Buyers came to him and the coffee was opened for the viewing of those desiring to purchase. It was discovered that some of it was "weak" (*ḍaʿīf*), since its color had changed and it lacked its smell as a result of remaining in a very humid location in the stores of the Treasury. This portion amounted to a total of one thousand twenty-eight and a half large farāsilas (1028 1/2).[6] And some [of the coffee] was discovered to be ruined since it was permeated with the smell of DDT and had changed its color as a result of the humidity in the stores. This amounted to thirty-seven cases, including two hundred and fifty-eight farāsilas.
>
> The claimant had no knowledge of this, that is, of the flaw in the coffee, either before the purchase or after it, until the discovery

---

[5] In Yemeni usage, the honorific "al-qāḍī" refers to an individual of a non-sayyid descent group with a family reputation for learning. Such descent groups often produced judges, but by no means all men referred to as "al-qāḍī" were members of the judiciary. In the case of Governor al-Sayāghi, the term was more an honorific since, while very talented, he was not trained as a scholar. Al-Muṣannif, the *wakīl* mentioned a few lines below, was an independent scholar who had not served as a judge.

[6] Parentheses in original. My translation follows the number usages found in the text, whether they appear written out or as numbers, or both. For fractions, the document uses the standard symbols of Yemeni accounting rather than the numerical fractions I give in translation.

> of this in Aden. [When] all the buyers refused it, he consigned it to the general agent of the coffee-importing Yemenis in Aden, the aforementioned al-Ḥājj ʿAbd Allāh ʿAlī Sālim al-ʿAwlaqī, and he returned to Ibb to present the matter to our Lord the Governor, inasmuch as he was unable to transport it and return it to Ibb in view of the exorbitant expense.
>
> He petitioned our Lord the Governor, who ordered Shaykh ʿAlī Muḥammad al-Jabalī and al-Ḥājj Aḥmad Ṣāliḥ al-Ṣāyidī to investigate and clarify [the matter] with trusted, religious and reliable individuals, and to examine the coffee to determine if it is completely ruined or if its sale is possible, and [if so] at what price.
>
> When the claimant returned to Aden he found that al-ʿAwlaqī had sold the coffee without the permission of the claimant or [his] knowledge, but rather on his own accord. When he asked him why he sold it, he explained that he feared that it would be completely ruined. The thirty-seven cases were the ones he transported from the stores of the Treasury, sealed, in the presence of the Head of the Storage Office and the porters and others, and these aforementioned cases were not opened until Aden, at [the time of] their presentation for sale by al-ʿAwlaqī. The sale by al-ʿAwlaqī was to the foreigner (*al-khawāja*), Denis Lefrateau, and the foreigner shipped the coffee overseas because he was under pressure to fulfill his obligations. This made it impossible for the claimant to return the coffee.
>
> The loss on the first portion amounted to one thousand ninety-five riyāls, and the loss on the second portion, which was determined to be ruined, was one thousand nine hundred and fifty-eight riyāls. The verified total of his loss on the whole [shipment] is three thousand fifty-three riyāls, excluding his expenses for the entire period in Aden and the roads and the petitions. The amount of that is six hundred riyāls.
>
> For these reasons, and the existence of a manifest flaw attested to, and the denial of his knowledge at the time of purchase, he [viz., the claimant al-Manṣūb] asks the judge for a judgment against the *wakīl* of the Treasury for the share of the decrease associated with the flaw, amounting to 3053 riyāls. He will give evidence for this. This claim is not fabricated to get part of the [i.e., a better] price. The Treasury is richer than I and should not make me carry the loss. The Governor, may God protect him, is the representative of the Imām, and his authorized agent, and he is the one we follow. This is my claim.

This lengthy claim is followed by the second standard segment of a judgment document, the reply (*ijāba*), typical here in its concision, and given by the *wakīl* of the Treasury. Rather than presenting evidence, the defense simply upholds the status quo ante, which is the presumption of the legality, completeness and finality of a concluded sale contract.

> Then, the reply. When the *wakīl* of the Treasury heard [this], he replied by denying the existence of any flaw in the sale object or decrease in the price. The Treasury sold clear to the aforementioned individual, and the buyer was sound in hearing and sight.

Written Evidence

With the legal contest joined by means of diametrically opposed assertions, the segment of the judgment record devoted to evidence begins with a standard formula, and then a reference to what must have approximated our processes of discovery, although the holder of the evidence in this instance was the Imamic state.

> The plaintiff was required to present proof (*burhān*) in accord with his claim, and he brought, first, documents containing the correspondence between the Governor, may God protect him, and the Treasury Office concerning his inquiry about the loss.

Relevant parts of this material obtained from the government by the claimant are entered in the record. In the following line of the judgment record we also see a version of one of the standard devices employed in the management of difficult disputes, namely, the appointment of a committee (coll., *lagna*) of important and/or specially knowledgeable authorities to investigate and, in other cases, to mediate. Most conflicts between merchants were settled out-of-court, informally, expeditiously and at low cost, by respected and knowledgeable individuals from the merchant community. After the Revolution this practice would be institutionalized in the opening of the Ibb Chamber of Commerce (1974), which was primarily devoted to the mediation of merchant disputes. Later still, this specialization would be further institutionalized in (short-lived) commercial courts. The unusual socio-historical view of commercial relations provided in the case at hand ensues from the fact that the second party to this conflict is not another merchant but the local branch of the State Treasury.

Two prominent highland Yemeni merchants resident in Aden were contacted to investigate:

In due course an order was issued [by the Ibb Governor] to al-Ḥājj Aḥmad Ṣāliḥ al-Ṣāyidī and al-Ḥājj ʿAlī b. Muḥammad al-Jabalī or his *wakīl* in Aden for a complete study from numerous sides and from reliable and trusted sources, from their point of view, for clarification regarding al-Manṣūb's complaint and what he claims as a loss in the coffee and the resulting associated expenses.

The judgment record then incorporates verbatim the report prepared by these two leading figures in the Adeni merchant community. Al-Ṣāyidī was an agent for Yemeni migrants, individuals from the northern highlands who used Aden as a jumping off point en route to East Africa, Southeast Asia, England, and the United States. Al-Jabalī, who was a merchant, was also well-known as an agent for Imām Aḥmad's personal business dealings. Their report is quoted in the record as follows:

His honor, exalted master, the very learned and venerable Governor al-Qāḍī Aḥmad b. Aḥmad al-Sayāghī, respected Governor of Ibb, greetings to you and the grace of God and His blessing, and may God guard our master the Commander of the Faithful and his loyal heir al-Badr [Muḥammad], for the protection of the country and the religion. We received your letter written on the 28th of Ramadan, 1375, about ʿAbd al-Karīm Muḥammad Ṣaʿīd al-Manṣūb, one of the merchants of Ibb, and about a quantity of coffee purchased from the Treasury which he transported to Aden, for the settlement of the allegations of the aforementioned [merchant] about a change in the coffee, its ruination, its many measurements, among the many difficulties in the course of dealing with it, etc.

Based upon your excellency's request for an investigation of what was mentioned, the agent al-Ḥājj ʿAbd Allāh ʿAlī Sālim al-ʿAwlaqī, known to us for his energy, his religiosity and his probity, was summoned. He was the one to whom ʿAbd al-Karīm al-Manṣūb had delivered the coffee for sale by him. The interrogation of the aforementioned [agent] and the clarification of the truth from him took place. He stated in his testimony and his report that ʿAbd al-Karīm al-Manṣūb was a well-known Ibb merchant who brought to his store 195 cases of clean coffee on the first day of Rajab 1375, for sale by him, as did others like him among the Yemeni merchants.

At the time of the appearance at his store of the buyers and their brokers on the second of Rajab 1375, for the inspection of the aforementioned coffee, he ordered his porters to open some of the cases and pour it on the ground for inspection by the buyers. [When] the coffee was revealed for inspection, its color had changed, it had lost its appearance and odor, it was permeated with the scent of DDT, and its color had become predominantly white [the normal color of the unroasted clean bean is pale green—BM]. When he saw the buyers withdrawing, he undertook to open other cases and they revealed the same thing as the preceding ones. The buyers withdrew without presenting any offers, disappointment [expressed] in their faces. Then the agent al-ʿAwlaqī told us that he went ten days after the inspection of the coffee and the withdrawal of the buyers without seeing any of the buyers with any desire.

Thanks to his experience and business acumen, however, he perceived the difficulty of one of the foreign buyers, namely, Denis Lefrateau, who was committed for a quantity of coffee to be shipped overseas, with a shipping contract and a specified time limit that was about to be reached without the aforementioned [buyer] being able to obtain and purchase the quantity that would meet his commitment, because it so happened that there was a lag in importations at that time.

The agent al-ʿAwlaqī, who saw a favorable opportunity to make an effort on behalf of al-Manṣūb's coffee, went immediately to the foreigner Denis Lefrateau and prepared the way for the subject by conversation on the lag in importations and other matters. Then he presented to him a proposition whereby he would attempt to pressure al-Manṣūb, the owner of 195 cases of coffee, to open all 195 cases for inspection by the foreigner of the whole quantity and for selection of what was possible from that. The foreigner's face beamed. It was as if he had found a ray of hope.

The foreigner agreed to this proposition with the agent al-ʿAwlaqī, and the appointment was for the second day following. Accordingly, the agent al-ʿAwlaqī ordered the opening of the 195 cases and the foreigner came and inspected them, selecting 80 cases. After all the back and forth, the agreement was completed for the sale of the aforementioned 80 cases to the foreigner for a price of 66, sixty-six rupees. The weighing of it for the aforementioned [foreigner] was completed on 10 Rajab 1375, and the total weight was 557 3/4 Adeni farāsilas and a pound. He then removed the useless weight from it, which amounted to 14 1/4 farāsilas and 1 pound, leaving a weight of 543 1/2 Adeni farāsilas at a price of 66 rupees, giving 35,871 rupees, subtracted from which is the cost of the service and the commission and the wage of the porters, 716 rupees. Thus the net price of the 80 cases after the deduction of the service and the expenses is 35,155 rupees, or 52,732.5 shillings. This is transcribed from the register of the agent al-Ḥājj ʿAbd Allāh ʿAlī Sālim al-ʿAwlaqī.[7]

In addition, since coffee imports remained light and since the foreigner Denis Lefrateau did not find in these imports [an amount] that would complete the remainder of his commitments, the opportunity remained open for the agent al-ʿAwlaqī to play the same role with the foreigner with respect to what remained in his hands of al-Manṣūb's

[7] A doctrinal "choice" (*ikhtiyār*) issued by Imām Aḥmad (d. 1962) permitted the use of trusted merchants' registers as evidence in court.

> coffee. Indeed, the same role as occurred previously occurred again, due to the pressing urgency [on the part] of the foreigner, and he agreed to go down with al-ʿAwlaqī to inspect the remainder of the quantity and to reconsider and select what was possible from it. And luck assisted. . . .

The quoted report from the two Adeni merchants goes on to detail the particulars, omitted here, of this second purchase of 78 further cases at a price of 65 rupees, on the 21st of Rajab 1375, and then to give the total for the two separate purchases. The report then turns to the remaining coffee, which it notes was "whitened" as a result of the humidity in the stores and also "still emitted" the odor of DDT.

> The agent indicated that he made great efforts to offer it and to attempt to sell it at any price, but to no avail; he did not succeed. Al-Manṣūb departed and he [al-ʿAwlaqī] still had it on hand. The agent continued to pay attention and in the course of business an opportunity arose on about the 19th of Ramadan. He found a buyer and after [expending] every effort completed the sale of the mentioned 37 cases for a price of 40 rupees, [i.e.,] forty rupees. . . .

Here the report gives the particulars, again omitted, of this third and final sale of the remainder of Manṣūb's coffee. This sale is different in that, as the report goes on to note,

> The agent declined the service charge and what is associated with it in commission and expenses as participation from him and assistance to the unfortunate ʿAbd al-Karīm al-Manṣūb.

The two reporting merchants conclude their estimation of the efforts of the agent al-ʿAwlaqī on behalf of al-Manṣūb as follows:

> Were it not for his help in evaluating the commitments of the foreigner Denis Lefrateau, and the lag in importations of coffee at the time, which pressured the foreigner with shipping requirements and gave him the idea of taking the 158 cases and mixing them with the large quantity of coffee that he had previously bought, which would cover the damage in the aforementioned coffee, [al-Manṣūb's] disaster would have been [even] more burdensome, greater than the mind can imagine. . . .

The two merchants then mention other sources, stating that what they learned from them conforms with the account given by the agent al-ʿAwlaqī. They then conclude their report and its quotation in the judgment record ends:

> After hearing from the foreigner Denis Lefrateau and his broker (*dallāl*) and other brokers among those present at the importation of the coffee in question, and its inspection and viewing, we find in their declarations support for the evidence provided by the agent al-Ḥājj ʿAbd Allāh Sālim al-ʿAwlaqī in his declarations and his testimony.
>
> This was written with its findings as a service to the truth and to your perspicacious and correct-opinioned excellency. Success resides with God. 23 Shawwal 1375.

Following this lengthy quotation, the judge first reports on the authoritative signatures and seals accompanying the letter from the two merchants, and then he quotes a request written directly upon it by its recipient, the Governor of Ibb. Having been sent from Aden to Ibb, the document from the two merchants now shuttles back and forth from the Governor to the Treasury Office, located in a new building that had been built into the town wall just across the alley from the governor's offices. The judge writes,

> This is the text of the reply, and below it is the seal of Shaykh ʿAlī bin Muḥammad al-Jabalī and ʿAbd al-Qādir Mahbūb, and the seal of al-Ḥājj Aḥmad bin Ṣāliḥ al-Ṣāyidī. On the upper part, in the handwriting and signature of the Governor al-Qāḍī Aḥmad bin Aḥmad al-Sayāghī, God protect him, in its wording:
>
> > To the Treasury Office: clarify the determined amount of the purchase price after the reduction for the service charge, and how much was entered against al-Manṣūb, and the amount of the hiring fees, and the deductions. 28 Shawwal 1375.
>
> Following that is the reply of the Treasury Office, to the Governor, may God protect him, in a list, and they put in it the original of the purchase agreement and the amount of its value and that of the hiring fees claimed by al-Manṣūb, and the amount of the total value of the purchase and the associated customs and town taxes (*khayriyāt*). The summary of all this, against the original sale transaction to al-Manṣūb for 22,000 riyāls, the price of the aforementioned coffee, is the sale of it in Aden for eighteen thousand nine hundred and forty-seven riyāls, and after that the reduction for the service charge, the brokerage commission, the [customs] tithes (*al-ʿushūr*), the deductions, and the hiring fees, 3,000, is exactly the diminution to him, the loss claimed, of three thousand and fifty-three riyāls.
>
> > Below this is the explanation by the Treasury Office, as will be seen, in its wording:

> Our master, the Governor, may God Almighty protect you, here is the clarification of the amount the price was set at after the reduction for the service charge—18,947; clarify how much was entered against al-Manṣūb for the value of the coffee—22,000 riyāls. The buyer has rights vis-à-vis the Treasury, with the clarification of the amount of the hiring fees and the deductions for customs, with the town tax in Taʿizz and al-Rāhida, etc.—3,000 riyāls. And what was established as the sale price in Aden, after the deduction for the service charge, and that is 18,947. This is according to the account list received from Shaykh ʿAlī Muḥammad al-Jabalī and Shaykh Aḥmad Ṣāliḥ al-Ṣāyidī, established by them following your honored order, after investigation and analysis. The accounts for the purchase were transcribed from the register of the agent al-Ḥājj ʿAbd Allāh bin ʿAlī Sālim al-ʿAwlaqī, according to what the two shaykhs found in their investigation attached to this. As for the hiring fees and the customs and the town tax in Taʿizz and al-Rāhida, and the customs in Laḥj, etc., this is on the good faith of ʿAbd al-Karīm al-Manṣūb according to what he submitted for the trucks: eight rupees, or twelve shillings, deducted for each farāsila, with the clarification of what the merchants pay according to the rule and the regulations, as ʿAbd al-Karīm al-Manṣūb stated, and as the deduction for *maṣlaḥa* [tax?], three hundred sixty-two riyāls, according to what you see above. According to what is entered in the Treasury Office of Ibb, the decrease in the sale price in Aden is exactly three thousand and fifty-three riyāls. For your distinguished view. First day of al-Qaʿda 1375, *alif hāʾ* [end of quote].

The judgment text then notes two further brief installments, omitted here, in this exchange between the Governor and the Ibb Treasury Office. As the judgment explains, these take the form of additional lines written above and below the explanation text from the Treasury, the first "written with the pen of our master the Governor." [Governor al-Sayāghī also used a distinctive aquamarine ink].

Then, in "his [viz., the Governor's] handwriting," and "his wording," a final order to the Treasury:

> Draft a telegram to his highness [the Imām], God strengthen him. We have read what has been written. Its wording [should be as follows]:
>
> > Our master the Commander of the Faithful, may God support you, the sale took place of the clean coffee belonging to the Treasury, which was old and ruined. The mice were eating it and it had been sprayed with DDT. Then the buyer took it to Aden and was unable to sell it, except at a loss. There was an order to the Jabalīs and to al-Ḥājj Aḥmad al-Ṣāyidī, who gave a finding on the matter, namely, that the sale transaction in Aden was for the sum of eighteen thousand, nine hundred, and forty-seven riyals;

> that the original price of the transaction to the buyer ʿAbd al-Karīm al-Manṣūb was for twenty-two thousand riyāls; and that the amount of the loss was exactly three thousand and fifty-three riyāls. This according to what was clarified by the Jabalīs and the Ṣāyidīs, and this was after investigation and analysis, and the transcribing of the accounts for the transaction from the register of the agent al-Ḥājj ʿAbd Allāh ʿAlī Sālim al-ʿAwlaqī. This is according to the information from Aden. The cause of the loss was its ruin in a humid place, then the spraying with DDT, until finally its color was changed and it was not salable except at a loss. Your view. Greetings. 19 al-Qaʿda 1375.

The judge appears to be quoting from the telegram document itself, because he now gives the simple, but crucial reply from the Imām, which is written "above this," that is, the telegram text. "In its wording," the Imām's response is:

> God forgive you. Determine what is required by a sharīʿa judgment. The difference is great, and the buyer was sound of hearing and sight. *alif hāʾ* [end]

It is this simple reply from Imām Aḥmad that triggered the court case in Ibb before Judge al-Manṣūr. Had the Imām not taken a hard line, saying, first, the sum in question was large and that, second, the buyer was complete in his sensory capacities, and thus of full legal capacity, the Governor might have been able to respond directly to the original petition of the merchant al-Manṣūb by ordering a compensatory payment. The Imām, however, ordered the Governor to proceed by way of a sharīʿa court judgment. It is with the quotation of these decisive lines from the Imām that all the recapitulated documentation finally results in the reader being brought up to the present voice of the judge writing the record of his sharīʿa decision. As the judgment record notes at this point, all this documentation from the Ibb Treasury Office was provided to al-Manṣūb on the order of the Governor:

> This is what was presented from the Treasury Office by al-Manṣūb according to an order from the Governor, may God protect him.

Oral Evidence

The evidence section of the judgment is not yet concluded. Al-Manṣūb now brings oral testimony from seventeen witnesses, all from Ibb. The testimony includes, first, reports about the circumstances of the nighttime transaction in Ibb by two town merchants, one broker (*dallāl*), five porters (*ḥammāls*), the deputy (*wakīl*) of the Head of the Storage Office, and two other townsmen, and, second, reports by six Ibb men present in Aden about what happened in the port city. There is no need here for supporting witnesses about the witnesses, to establish their identities and their probity, as in some other cases (e.g., Messick 1998). Judge al-Manṣūr, who had resided in Ibb since his posting there in 1934, remarks that all five Ibb porters are "known to us." One witness, nevertheless, testifies only to the fact that he had found the witnesses then present in court present at the weighing and loading of the coffee on the evening in question.

The first group of ten witnesses supports the contention that al-Manṣūb purchased the 195 cases of coffee without knowledge of its flaws. They describe a smaller quantity of coffee, thirty-seven "sacks" (*shuwālāt*, also referred to as thirty seven "cases"), brought in from Shaykh Aḥmad b. ʿAlī al-Ṣabrī. This coffee remained "sewed up," as it had been upon receipt, and it was sold to al-Manṣūb and loaded on the trucks without being opened. These witnesses also describe "weak" and damaged coffee that was spread on the floor to dry in the Ibb government building atop al-Jabāna, the hill (now a neighborhood) extending west of the old town walls. It also is recorded that al-Manṣūb's brother Qāsim (interviewed by me twenty years later) had asked one of the merchant witnesses to bring his scales to weigh the coffee and that this work took place by the light of a battery-powered "electric" light. The other merchant testified that just before the al-Manṣūb purchase, he had contracted with Governor al-Sayāghī to purchase the coffee, but that upon inspection he had found it "weak," ruined and permeated with the odor of DDT and had refused to buy it. He testified, however, that he had not informed al-Manṣūb, or anyone else, of the flaw in the coffee. The deputy of the Head of the Storage Office testified that, "the weighing of the Treasury coffee for al-Manṣūb took place at night by the light of a flashlight, and it [viz., the coffee] had been sprayed with DDT on orders from the Governor, to prevent damage by mice, and the coffee was old." He also distinguishes this, the bulk of the coffee, from that received from the rural shaykh: "And as for the thirty-seven cases that arrived from Shaykh Aḥmad ʿAli al-Ṣabrī, these arrived at the Storage Office sealed and were weighed for al-Manṣūb sealed. [These cases] were not opened, and he did not learn the condition of the coffee inside."

The second set of six witnesses brought by al-Manṣūb were Ibb men who had been in Aden, some of them having traveled with the three trucks carrying al-Manṣūb's coffee. Their testimony buttresses the second part of al-Manṣūb's contention, namely, that when he first learned of the flaw in the coffee he did not give permission for its sale. One witness, riding in a truck with a highland coffee broker, arrived at the store in Aden just as al-Manṣūb's shipment was arriving. When the broker saw the coffee, he exclaimed that it was adulterated to an extent that he had never seen before. When the two men showed samples to a foreign buyer, this individual responded that the coffee could not be Yemeni and that he would not buy it. A man who had traveled from Ibb in one of the trucks describes the arrival scene. He states that when the brokers arrived for the opening of the shipment, they found the coffee germinated, adulterated, and permeated with the odor of DDT. Seeing this reaction, al-Manṣūb reportedly "cried out," and left to return to Ibb to lodge a complaint with the Governor. When another witness arrived at the store several days later, the agent al-ʿAwlaqī said to him, "Look at this coffee from your country [i.e., Ibb], see how they adulterate it!" Still another witness left Ibb four or five days after al-Manṣūb's coffee, and when he arrived in Aden he reproached al-Manṣūb for not offering him a ride down in one of the trucks. Al-Manṣūb is reported to have replied to the witness that he left Ibb at night, that he had received the coffee at night, that he was unaware of its condition, and that when he showed it to the foreigners they refused it. When the witness asked him, "What are you going to do?", al-Manṣūb reportedly replied, "I am going to leave [Aden] to complain to the Governor in Ibb." This same witness said that he also had heard that the eventual foreign buyer had mixed the damaged coffee with a larger shipment of sound coffee.

A last witness, together with one of the already mentioned witnesses, testified about relevant commercial practices, supporting the action taken by the consignment agent. The witness, who had been on one of the trucks, added that al-ʿAwlaqī was a "trustworthy broker (*dallāl amīn*) known to the Yemenis." The witness then explained that if the coffee is sound the broker will not move ahead without having the consent (*riḍā*) of the owner, but if it is adulterated, or if the market is "cold" [weak], he will seek the benefit (*maṣlaḥa*) from selling the coffee and take steps to prevent losses. The other witness, himself a broker in Ibb, testified exclusively to the prevailing commercial practices:

> The custom (*al-ʿāda*) that is known and practiced among the brokers and fiduciaries in Aden and elsewhere is that they seek the benefit for the merchants concerning what is consigned to them. If the goods are excellent, they bargain to the maximum and they will not sell except with the permission of the owner. If [the goods are] weak, or [if] they fear further deterioration, they sell for as much as possible without regard for the permission of the owner.

Ruling

The lines immediately following the *ḥukm* document give the judge's ruling, his *ḥukm* (in the narrow sense, also known as the *jazm*), delivered in 1956. This ruling provides insight into how, within the Zaydī school doctrine on the contract of sale, the right of rescission is exercised and upheld, and how commercial usage is taken into account. Rescission provisions, which are of special importance to merchants, are not so relevant to real estate transactions, the much more typical contractual cases brought before these courts. "It is clear," the judge writes in his concluding opinion,

> . . . that the aforementioned coffee, I mean the clean coffee that was sold to al-Manṣūb, had sprouted due to the length of its storage in the humid stores and its odor had changed due to being sprayed with DDT. But this is not the crux of the controversy, because this much was already clarified in what was determined by the Head of the Storage Office and the people of the Treasury Office, and in what was communicated by the Governor, may God protect him, to the Imām, may God strengthen him.
>
> Rather, the crux of the controversy is the question of visual inspection (*ru'ya*). That is, did the buyer see it [viz., the coffee] in a discriminating visual inspection (*ru'ya mumayyiza*), and did he know with this [viz., the discriminating visual inspection] what flaw (*ʿayb*) it had, or not? The legal representative of the Treasury states that he did, and says that the buyer was sound in hearing and vision.
>
> Al-Manṣūb states that he did not see it [viz., the coffee] at the time of the sale in a discriminating visual inspection, because he purchased it at night and transported it in the trucks. Some of the sacks were received by him before being opened. He did not look carefully at it (*lam yata'ammalhu*) until in Aden, when it was opened there for examination by agents and brokers. And when the aforementioned [agents and brokers] examined it and refused to buy it, he returned quickly from Aden with the intention (*qaṣd*) of making a complaint to the Governor, may God protect him. After his return from Aden, an opportunity arose for his agent al-ʿAwlaqī and he sold, intending by

that to do for him [viz., al-Manṣūb] what was customary (*al-maʿrūf*) and virtuous, even though he had not been given permission to sell. . . .

From the investigation by al-Ṣāyidī and al-Jabalī and from what the Governor, may God protect him, communicated to the Imām, may God strengthen him, and from what witnesses have born witness to, one sees the withholding of consent (*ʿadm riḍā*) of al-Manṣūb due to the flaw apparent upon his visual inspection of the sacks that were opened in his presence in Aden. Added to that, proof (*burhān*) was not brought of his visual inspection of the sale object at the time of the sale in a discriminating visual inspection. As for later, testimony was presented of his visual inspection of the flawed sale object in Aden, but it [viz., the testimony] does not constitute evidence (*bayyina*) of his consent to it, but rather his displeasure and his return to Ibb to make a complaint to the Governor, may God protect him.

Because of the lack of evidence of a discriminating visual inspection, and of the basic fact of its nonexistence,[8] and due to the lack of evidence of his consent to the aforementioned flaw, the plaintiff must take the legal oath, namely, he [must] swear by God Almighty that he did not see the aforementioned clean coffee at the time of the sale in a discriminating visual inspection, and that he did not consent to it after so inspecting it. If he takes this oath, he is to be awarded an indemnity for the loss (*arsh al-naqṣ*), which is [the amount] between the value (*qīma*) of the aforementioned clean coffee, sound [and] unflawed, and its value flawed. This amount of the loss in value should be returned to him from the [original sale] price.

This is what is required and, accordingly, I ruled. Muḥarram 1376 (August 1956).[9] [signature] Ismāʿīl ʿAbd al-Raḥmān al-Manṣūr, Judge of Ibb Province.

---

[8] Or, "and on the presumption of its nonexistence." The text reads, *wa ʿalā anna al-aṣl ʿadamuha.*

[9] Immediately following, there is a further note from the judge concerning the fact that the sum claimed and awarded is less than it ought to be, since the clean coffee came under "the rule of the ruined thing" (*ḥukm al-tālif*). This formulation, which also is used by the litigants, appears in the doctrine on rescission (see al-ʿAnsī 2:321, 435, 442). Al-Manṣūb declines any further remedy, however.

On the back of the rolled document (and also copied in the court register under Judge al-Manṣūr's ruling) is the appeal ruling from the *hayʾa al-sharʿīyya*, a ruling based on the appeal petition and the reply to this petition. This brief ruling, dated 12 Safar 1376 and signed by seven judges, affirms Judge al-Manṣūr's ruling. Above is the seal (and a recording number) of the *hayʾa* and also a confirmation with the seal of the Imām. Below the appeal ruling text is a statement by Judge al-Manṣūr, dated 12 Rabiʿa I, stating that he summoned the two parties and presented the appeal decision to them, whereupon the defendant asked al-Manṣūb to take the oath, and he did so. Below this is a note indicating that a full copy of the judgment and appended notes was entered in the registry of the Treasury Office.

Conclusion

From the opening claim to the judge's ruling the substantive technical language in this case record adheres closely to the Zaydī doctrine on the rescission of contracts. The basic terms—"sale," "sale object," "price," "value," "loss," "ruin," "flaw," "visual inspection" and "discriminating visual inspection"—are shared by the law books and the record of this particular case, although the term for "option" (*khiyār*) does not appear in the court document. Of the three types of rescission rights known to Zaydī doctrine, the *khiyār al-sharṭ*, which involves a time frame stipulated in advance for a mutual option of rescinding, is not at issue in this case.[10] This leaves the *khiyār al-ru'ya*, the rescission right that may be opted for by the buyer upon a "discriminating visual inspection" of the sale object, and the *khiyār al-ʿayb*, the option of rescinding after discovering a flaw. While both of these options appear to be involved in this case, it is the *khiyār al-ru'ya* that is mainly at issue. This is clear from the dual emphasis in the case on (1) the point in time at which a "discriminating visual inspection" occurred, and (2) the buyer's nonacceptance of the flaw and his associated actions to immediately seek redress. The legal doctrine (al-ʿAnsī 1993, 2:395) makes a fundamental distinction between the "visual inspection" and "flaw" option rights: the former must be exercised immediately, the latter not; and the former is a noninheritable right, while the later is inheritable.[11] As with a number of other rights, such as that of pre-emption (*shufʿa*), the option of rescinding a sale based on "visual inspection" must be asserted "immediately following visual inspection" (*ʿaqīb ru'ya*) (al-ʿAnsī 1993, 2:397).

A basic condition of the Islamic contract of a sale is "knowledge" (*ʿilm*) of the sale object (*al-mabiyʿ*) on the part of the buyer.[12] This knowledge normally derives from the proper description of the sale object by the seller and from the physical circumstances of face-to-face transactions. If, however, a routine visual inspection is impossible

[10] On the option known as *khiyār al-majlis*, according to which either party to the sale may rescind before eaving the contract session, see Schacht (1950:159–61, 167).

[11] Cf. Schacht (1964:169).

[12] According to the Zaydī school (al-ʿAnsī 1993, 2:313), there are five conditions for the two *māls* (commodities) that figure in a sale contract, the first of which is that both must be known. If the buyer does not have knowledge of the sale object at the moment of the contract, the sale remains valid but he retains a right of *khiyār* which may be exercised upon gaining the knowledge in question.

or delayed, the purchaser retains the option to revoke the sale until such time as this occurs. The doctrinal text on *khiyār al-ruʾya* states that this right exists when the buyer was absent and "did not see it [viz., the sale object] in a normal visual inspection (*ruʾya mithlihi*), or [if] he was present [and did not see it], or [if] he saw it with a nondiscriminating visual inspection" (al-ʿAnsī 1993, 2:396). Thus the semantic field of "seeing" and "visual inspection" in connection with contracts is opened up to some distinctions, which center on the existence, or not, of a "normal," "equivalent" or "conventional" seeing of the sale object, an event more technically characterized as a "discriminating visual inspection," which also includes the possibility of an inspection that is "nondiscriminating." A "discriminating visual inspection" is further described by the jurists as different from seeing something by means of a mirror, through water or glass (unless one uses a glass to see), or, as in this specific court case, at night. Drawing upon the technical vocabulary of the doctrine on rescinding, the judge, in his final ruling in this case, uses not only the term "discriminating visual inspection" but also the verb *taʾammala*, which I translated above as "to look carefully," and which generally means "to contemplate." For the doctrinal jurists of the Zaydī school, both usages derive from a compound formulation that appears in their authoritative, late fourteenth-century manual: "*ruʾya mumayyiza bi-taʾammul.*" According to the twentieth century commentator al-ʿAnsī, a contemporary of Judge al-Manṣūr, the last element in this formulation, the verbal noun *taʾammul*, refers to an aspect of seeing through by which one "knows a thing and understands . . . its excellences and its demerits, its expensiveness and its cheapness" (al-ʿAnsī 1993, 2:398). Judge al-Manṣūr employs this item of technical language to gloss claimant al-Manṣūb's position with respect to the coffee, writing that "[h]e did not look carefully at it (*lam yataʾammalhu*) until in Aden."

Ordinarily, as part of exercising the option following the visual inspection, the "return" of the sale object occurred. In this case the coffee was not returned and justifications had to be formulated. The immediate justification was prohibitive transport costs and the final one the sales to the foreign buyer. In the doctrine, in connection with a discovered flaw, the return of the sale object is the alternative to monetary indemnity (*arsh*). It is one or the other, as a reciprocally phrased principle held: "Where the return is established, the indemnity is invalidated, and when the return is invalidated, the indemnity is established" (al-ʿAnsī 1993, 2:425n). The doctrine on *khiyār al-ʿayb* also states that the nature of the flaw itself is established when "two just witnesses with expertise (*dhū al-khibra*) in it [viz., the type of flaw] testify" (al-ʿAnsī 1993, 2:413).[13] Such specialized knowledge is called upon by the Ibb Governor when he asks the two prominent Adeni merchants to investigate the matter, and their subsequent report figures prominently in the sharīʿa case record and in the ruling. This report and other evidence brought by the claimant establish both the existence and precise nature of the flaw and the impediments to a return of the coffee.

Determinants according to "custom" are woven through the doctrine on rescinding contracts, and Schacht (1964:78) and Udovitch (1970:13; 1985) have noted that this is a general characteristic of commercial doctrine in the sharīʿa. For example, custom (*al-ʿāda*) determines what is exempt from being visually inspected at the time of a contract, such as the foundation of a house (al-ʿAnsī 1993, 2:398). In the case examined here, the custom of the merchants is at issue, specifically in connection with the handling of the coffee by the Adeni agent al-ʿAwlaqī. This is the subject matter of the report sent by the Adeni merchants, and the claimant also brought witnesses to address this relationship as following prevailing "custom."

Finally, in procedural terms, while the case generally follows the classic model of litigation and judgment set down in the law books, in practice it is unusual in that the defense mounts no counterclaim and presents no evidence. Within the standard framework for the legal process, the voluminous evidence and the often verbatim style of recording are typical of the Yemeni sharīʿa court tradition. But what is the nature of the oath (*yamīn*) with which the trial concludes? Oaths are of two main categories: nonjudicial oaths sworn as vows or undertakings outside the context of legal proceedings, the subject of their own law book chapter; and judicial oaths, which are mainly covered in a section in the chapter on court "Claims."[14] The oath in this case is judicial, but it is not either of the two most common varieties: that taken by the claimant to complement the testi-

---

[13] According to the *khiyār al-ruʾya* doctrine (al-ʿAnsī 1993, 2:398, 402), individuals with specialized knowledge (*dhū maʿarīfa*) may assist the nonexpert buyer in achieving a "discriminating visual inspection."

[14] Al-ʿAnsī (1993, 3:405–33) (*kitāb al-aymān*); al-ʿAnsī (1993, 4:26–38) (a section in *kitāb al-daʿāwī*).

mony of a single witness and that which may be taken, or declined, by the defendant when the claimant cannot produce evidence.[15] This appears to be a further type of oath in which, as in the present case, the claimant is asked by the defendant for the "confirmation of his evidence" (*taʾkīd bayyinatihi*). According to the doctrinal passage on this type of oath (in the chapter on "Claims," al-ʿAnsī 1993, 4:29–30), such a request by the defendant is warranted when the evidence is "not certain" (*ghayr muḥaqqaqa*), that is, when the claimant's witnesses are able to testify only as to what is "manifest" (*al-ẓāhir*), rather than on the basis of their actual knowledge (*ʿilm*).[16]

Best known among the legal principles concerning the judicial oath is the maxim, "Evidence has to be produced by the claimant and the oath has to be taken by the defendant" (Schacht 1950:187). The related law book principle is: "The oath [is required of] every denier (*munkir*)," the position of "denier" being that of the defendant, and this usually refers to the situation where the claimant has no evidence to present (al-ʿAnsī 1993, 4:26). In the present case, however, the twist is that the claimant al-Manṣūb is in the position of denying that he had knowledge of the flaw in the coffee he purchased, until he first visually inspected it in Aden. Judge al-Manṣūr writes that al-Manṣūb must swear that "he did not see the aforementioned clean coffee at the time of the sale in a discriminating visual inspection, and that he did not consent to it after so inspecting it." In the ensuing appeal ruling (which I have not translated here), the higher court affirms "the requirement of his oath as to the non-[existence of his] knowledge of the flaw or [of his] consent to it."

The type of oath in question is also pointed to in the rescission doctrines. The doctrine on *khiyār al-ruʾya* states that "if the seller and buyer differ as to whether he [viz., the buyer] saw the sale object in a discriminating visual inspection, or not" (al-ʿAnsī 1993, 2:404), the decisive statement (*al-qawl*) is that of the buyer, while the doctrine on *khiyār al-ʿayb* envisions the combination of this statement of the buyer with his oath (*yamīn*). In a discussion of the invalidation of *both* the return of the sale object and the right to a monetary

[15] It also is not the sort of oath that may be required by the judge of a suspicious witness, a procedure mentioned in the chapter on "Testimonies" (al-ʿAnsī 1993, 4:71), or evidence—see Messick (2002).

[16] This is the same distinction used to value the single *jarḥ* witness over multiple *taʿdīl* witnesses (see Messick 2002:259–60).

indemnity, eight potential circumstances are sketched, the sixth of which deals with a subsequent transaction by the original buyer, which implies his "knowledge" of the original sale object. To this circumstance, however, there are three exceptions, the second of which concerns the buyer simply presenting the sale object for sale so as "to know its high and low value." This action of merely seeking a valuation of his goods does not comprise the buyer's consent (*riḍāʾ*) to the initial transaction. The relevance of this exception to the present case lies in the conclusion that "the decisive statement is the statement of the buyer concerning his purpose together with his oath, if this [i.e., his purpose] cannot be known except from his perspective" (al-ʿAnsī 1993, 2:417). In this case, as in many others from the period (e.g., Messick 1995, 1998), the court bases its analysis on its assessment of intent and consent. Here this analysis is bolstered by an oath demanded of the claimant by the defendant under the auspices of the judge.

CHAPTER NINE

THE RE-ISLAMIZATION OF CRIMINAL LAW IN NORTHERN NIGERIA AND THE JUDICIARY: THE SAFIYYATU HUSSAINI CASE*

Rudolph Peters
University of Amsterdam

Introduction

Islamic penal law was introduced in twelve states of the Nigerian Federal Republic starting from 2000 and stoning sentences have been pronounced since that time. To date, however, none of these sentences have been carried out. The sentences against Safiyyatu Hussaini and Amina Lawal,[1] both quashed on appeal, have attracted a great deal of international attention, thanks to campaigns launched by international human rights and women's rights organizations. In this article I will analyze the proceedings against Safiyyatu Hussaini in an attempt to show how the Northern Nigerian judiciary is handling the re-Islamization of the penal law.

The re-islamization of islamic criminal law[2]

As in the United States, the states of the Federal Republic of Nigeria have the power to enact their own laws. The re-Islamization of criminal law is, therefore, a choice of the separate states. On January

* I would like to thank Dr. Delfina Serrano y Ruano of the Consejo Superior de Investigaciones Científicas, Madrid, for her comments on the first draft of this essay.

[1] Amina Lawal was sentenced to death by stoning by the Shari'a Court of Bakori, Katsina State on March 20, 2002. On August 19, 2002, this sentence was upheld on appeal by the Upper Shari'a Court of Funtua. The Shari'a Court of Appeal of Katsina State set this decision aside on September 25, 2003, and acquitted Lawal. Although I have not been able to see the appeal sentence, press reports indicate that the reasoning of the Court is very similar to that of the Shari'a Court of Appeal of Sokoto State in the Safiyyatu Hussaini case.

[2] As the Safiyyatu Hussaini case was tried in Sokoto State, I will refer here only to the Sokoto Shari'a legislation, which follows closely the Zamfara Shari'a laws.

27, 2000, Zamfara State enacted the first Shariʿa Penal Code in Northern Nigeria, a few months after Shari'a courts had been established.[3] In response to public pressure, eleven other Northern states followed suit and introduced Shari'a courts and criminal legislation based on the Shari'a.[4] The new Shari'a penal codes are applicable only to Muslims and to those non-Muslims who voluntarily and in writing submit to its jurisdiction. Non-Muslims continue to be governed by the 1959 Penal Code of Northern Nigeria.

The introduction of these new codes has restored the situation that existed before 1960. Until that date, Islamic law was the law applied to all Muslims in the North in civil, personal, and criminal matters. Criminal sentences pronounced under the Shari'a were carried out by the British colonial administration. However, sentences of amputation or death by stoning were commuted into prison sentences, on the grounds that they are "repugnant to natural justice, equity, and good conscience." In 1960 a new Penal Code for the North put an end to the implementation of traditional, uncodified Islamic criminal law. The re-Islamization of criminal law has now restored the pre-1960 situation, but with two major changes: First, Islamic criminal justice is no longer subjected to direct state control, although it must, of course, be compatible with the provisions of the Constitution of the Federal Republic of Nigeria (CFRN).[5] Second, Islamic criminal law has now been codified, as required by Section 36(12) of the Constitution.[6]

The re-Islamization of the legal systems of the Northern states began with changes in the judiciary. Until the year 2000, there were two sets of courts in the Northern States:

• Magistrate Courts applying Common Law, with the State High Court as appellate court.

[3] Zamfara Shari'a Courts Establishment Law, 1999 (Law 5 of 1999).

[4] Bauchi, Borno, Gombe, Jigawa, Kaduna, Kano, Katsina, Kebbi, Niger, Sokoto, and Yobe. Most of these states followed the example of the Zamfara codes with minor changes. Whereas Kano State has enacted an independent Shari'a Penal Code, Niger State has contented itself with adding a few amendments to the 1959 Penal Code for Northern Nigeria. See Peters (2003:81–2).

[5] On the areas of conflict, see Peters (2003:31–43). The Supreme Federal Court has not yet ruled on any of these incompatibilities.

[6] "Subject as otherwise provided by this Constitution, a person shall not be convicted of a criminal offense unless that offense is defined and the penalty therefor is prescribed in a written law, and in this subsection, a written law refers to an Act of the National Assembly or a Law of a State, any subsidiary legislation or instrument under the provisions of a law."

- Area Courts, in two or three levels, applying the Shari'a in civil and personal, and the 1959 Penal Code in criminal cases. In matters of personal law, the State Shari'a Court of Appeal was the appellate court; in other matters decisions of the area courts could be appealed to the State High Court.

Just before the promulgation of Shari'a Penal Codes, the Northern states had set up Islamic courts as a first step towards Islamization. This was done by abolishing the Area Courts (traditionally known as *alkalis* courts, from the Arabic *al-qāḍī*) and replacing them with Shari'a Courts. In fact, only the name Area Courts was changed and the judges sitting in them kept their office. In Sokoto two classes of these courts were established: Lower Shari'a Courts in which only one judge sits and Upper Shari'ah Courts composed of a president and one member. (Section 3 Sokoto Shari'a Court Law, 2000; henceforth SSCL). These judges must be knowlegeable in Islamic Law as shown by diplomas or offices held previously, unless they were already serving on the area courts (Section 4 SSCL). The Shari'a courts have jurisdiction in civil and criminal cases and must adjudicate according to the Shari'a (Section 5(6), 5(7), 10 SSCL). Any law that is enacted will apply only insofar as it is not contrary to the principles of the Shari'a (Section 20 SSCL). This clause is in clear defiance of the Nigerian legal system, in which written, enacted law takes precedence over customary law and Islamic law. Further, the jurisdiction of the State Shari'ah Courts of appeal, which previously could hear appeals only in cases of personal law, was extended to all cases tried before the lower Shari'a courts (Section 5(1), 5(2) SSCL). The new Shari'a Courts are competent in all civil litigation, if both parties are Muslims, and in criminal proceedings, if the accused is a Muslim (Section 5(3), 5(4), 8 SSCL; Section 3 Shari'ah[7] Criminal Procedure Code [henceforth SSCPC]).

The new courts are instructed to apply uncodified Maliki law, in both civil and criminal cases. Section 6 of the SSCL reads:

> The applicable laws in both civil and criminal proceedings before the Shari'a Court shall include: (a) The Holy Qur'an (b) Sunnah and Hadith (c) Ijma; (d) Qiyas; (e) Maslahat Mursala; (f) Istihsan; (g) Istishab; (h) al-urf; (i) Muzhabul—Sahabi [sic! *Madhhab al-Ṣaḥābī* RP]; and (j) Other subsidiary sources.

---

[7] Sokoto State is not consistent in the spelling of the word "Shari'a". It appears without a final "h" in the SSCL and with the final "h" in the SSPC and SCPC.

Section 7 of the SSCL lists sixteen Maliki *fiqh* texts that are authoritative in the Shari'a Courts.[8] Moreover, the law stipulates that practice, procedure, and evidence are to be regulated by Maliki doctrine (Section 10(1.a), 10(1.b) SCL). However, on January 31, 2001, a penal code and a code of criminal procedure replaced uncodified Shari'a when the Sokoto Shari'ah Penal Code (SSPC) and the Sokoto Shari'ah Criminal Procedure Code (SSCPC) came into force. They define the offenses and their punishments and stipulate that the investigation, inquiry, and procedure of Shari'ah offenses shall be governed by the SCPC. However, the introduction of the SSPC has not put an end to the direct enforcement of uncodified Islamic criminal law. Consider the following provision:

> Any act or omission which is not specifically mentioned in this Shari'ah Penal Code but is otherwise declared to be an offense under the Qur'an, Sunnah and *Ijtihad* of the Maliki School of Islamic thought shall be an offense under this code and such act or omission shall be punishable:
>
> (a) With imprisonment for a term which may extend to 5 years, or
> (b) With caning which may extend to 50 lashes, or
> (c) With fine which may extend to N[aira] 5,000.00 or with any two of the above punishments.[9]

The new codes do not contain provisions on a number of crucial issues, as, for example, evidence. This omission was probably delib-

---

[8] In presenting the text of this Section, I have retained its spelling and have added the complete titles in square brackets.

(a) Al-Risalah [by Ibn Abī Zayd al-Qayrawānī (d. 996)]; (b) Muhtasar [by Khalīl b. Isḥāq (d. 1365)]; (c) Tuhfah [*Tuḥfat al-ḥukkām* by Ibn ʿĀṣim (d.1427)]; (d) Al-Adawi [Supercommentary by ʿAlī al-Ṣaʿīdī al-ʿAdawī (d. 1775) on a commentary by Abū al-Ḥasan al-Minūfī (d. 1532) on the *Risāla* of al-Qayrawānī]; (e) Al-Fawakih al-Dawani [*al-Fawākih al-Dawānī* by Aḥmad b. Ghunaym al-Nafrāwī, commentary on the *Risāla* by al-Qayrawānī]; (f) Ibn Ashir [not identified]; (g) Bidayat al-Mujtahid [by Ibn Rushd al-ḥafīd (d. 1198)]; (h) Al-Mudawanah [by Saḥnūn (d. 854)]; (i) Muwattah Malik; (j) Mayyara [Muḥammad b. Aḥmad Mayyāra (d. 1641–2), commentator of the *Tuḥfa* by Ibn ʿĀṣim]; (k) Bahjah [*Al-Bahja*, commentary by al-Tasūlī (d. 1842) on the *Tuḥfa* of Ibn ʿĀṣim]; (l) Jawahir al-Iklil [Jawāhir al-Iklīl by Ṣāliḥ ʿAbd al-Samīʿ al-Ābī on the *Mukhtaṣar* of Khalīl b. Isḥaq]; (m) Dasuki [Super commentary by Ibrāhīm al-Dasūqī (d. 1815) on the commentary by Aḥmad al-Dardīr (d. 1786) on the *Mukhtaṣar* of Khalīl b. Isḥaq]; (n) Al-Khirshi [ʿAbd Allāh al-Khirshī (d. 1689), author of two commentaries on the *Mukhtaṣar* by Khalīl b. Isḥāq]; (o) Bulgatil Salik [Bulghat al-Sālik, supercommentary by Aḥmad al-Ṣāwī (d. 1825) on the commentary on *Aqrab al-masālik li-madhhab al-Imām Mālik* of Aḥmad al-Dardīr]; (p) Mawahibul Hallaq [Abū Shitāʾ b. Ḥasan al-Ṣunhāji (d. 1946), *Mawāhib al-Khallāq ʿalā sharḥ* al-Tāwudī (d. 1700) *li-Lāmiyat* Al-Zaqqāq (d. 1506)].

[9] Sokoto Shari'a Penal Code (SSCP), Section 94.

erate. State legislation on points of evidence would violate the Federal Islamic Constitution, which stipulates that evidence is one of the fields in which the Federation has exclusive power to enact laws.[10] Since the law is silent, the Shari'a courts apply the Maliki doctrine of evidence in cases of homicide and *ḥadd* offenses.

The SSPC, like the other Shari'a Penal Codes enacted in Northern Nigeria, follows a model that was previously introduced in other countries.[11] Like these other Shari'a codes, the SSPC, under the heading *taʿzīr*, contains the penal provisions taken from the previous penal codes (i.e., the 1959 Penal Code for Northern Nigeria in the case of the Northern Nigerian States) to which are added chapters defining the Qur'anic offenses (*ḥudūd*) and the Islamic law of homicide and hurt. In addition the SSPC increased the number of offenses punishable by corporal punishment (caning or flogging).

The chapter on general provisions, section 95, lists the punishments and introduces the new Shari'a penalties, such as retaliation (for homicide and grievous hurt), amputation, caning and the payment of blood money (*diya*) as a compensation for homicide and hurt. The list, however, is not exhaustive. Death by stoning and crucifixion are not listed here, although they are mentioned in Section 129(b) SSPC, Section 231(c) and (d) SSCPC. On the other hand, punishments such as reprimand, public disclosure, boycott, and exhortation, which are mentioned in Section 95, do not occur elsewhere in the code.

Unlawful sexual intercourse in Maliki doctrine

Under Islamic law sexual intercourse is allowed only within a marriage (or, in premodern times, between a slave woman and her owner). Extramarital intercourse is unlawful and may, under certain conditions, constitute a punishable offense, *zinā*, which is one of the *ḥadd* crimes, i.e. crimes mentioned in the Qur'an for which fixed punishments are specified. *Zinā* is to be punished with death by stoning if the offender is *muḥṣan*, i.e., adult, free, Muslim, and one who has previously experienced legitimate sexual relations within a marriage (regardless of whether the marriage still exists) with a person

---

[10] See the Federal Constitution of the Republic of Nigeria (FCRN), Section 4(2), (3) and the Exclusive Legislative List.

[11] See Peters (1994).

who is also *muḥṣan.* A person who is not *muḥṣan* is punished with 100 lashes, which is followed by banishment for one year. The offenders must have acted of their own free will: a woman who has been raped (*mustakraha*) cannot receive the *ḥadd* punishment. However, she must produce some form of evidence to substantiate her allegation of rape. *Zinā* may be established by a confession, the testimony of four eyewitnesses who are Muslim males of good reputation and, exclusive to the Maliki school, by the visible pregnancy of an unmarried woman. The witnesses must have seen the act in its most intimate details, i.e., the penetration ("like the kohl stick [entering] into the kohl container [*mikḥala*]," as the *fiqh* books put it). If the witnesses' testimonies do not satisfy the requirements, they can be sentenced to eighty lashes for an unfounded accusation of fornication (*qadhf*). However, even if the offense has been established, punishment can be averted in the event of *shubha* (uncertainty or doubt about the unlawfulness of the proven act) due to circumstances that cause it to appear as if it were legal, such as intercourse between two parties to a marriage which is null and void, between a master and his female slave of whom he is a co-owner or whom he has acquired on the strength of an invalid purchase, or between a blind man and a woman whom he mistook for his wife or female slave. An unmarried woman who is charged with *zinā* on the strength of her pregnancy can plead in defense that the pregnancy resulted from intercourse with a man who penetrated her while she was sleeping and that she had no knowledge of it, or that the pregnancy resulted from intercourse between her thighs, without penetration. Her statement to this effect is regarded as sufficient grounds for *shubha.*[12] Rape, however, is difficult to establish. Such a plea must be substantiated by circumstantial evidence, for instance, the fact that the woman bled (if she was a virgin) or entered her village screaming for help. If she cannot produce such evidence, her defense is not accepted and, if she identified her attacker, she is also liable to prosecution for defamation (*qadhf*).

[12] See e.g., Ābī (1976, 2:285); Ṣāwī (n.d., 4:455). Ch. on proving *zinā* (*thubūt al-zinā*); Ibn Farḥūn (1986, 2:97) (Ch. 64 on giving judgment on *zinā* on the strength of evidence of pregnancy).

The Case

On March 25, 2002, the Shari'a Court of Appeal of Sokoto State quashed the decision of the Upper Shari'a Court of Gwadabawa that sentenced Safiyyatu Hussaini to death by stoning for unlawful sexual intercourse. As a result she was acquitted. The Appeal Court found that the decision of the lower court could not stand on several grounds: the lower court lacked jurisdiction, had not followed proper procedure, and had erred in the application of the law. In the following several pages I will discuss and analyze this decision, which is a clear illustration of how, after the reintroduction of Shari'a penal law, Shari'a courts deal with it. In the conclusion I will discuss the special features of the Nigerian situation, as Northern Nigeria is the only region in the Islamic world where Islamic criminal law is implemented within the framework of a non-Islamic and essentially secular constitution. Moreover, I will discuss the significance of this decision for future trials of similar cases.

The original decisions were written in Hausa and, to the best of my knowledge, have not been officially published. I have relied on two texts translated into English: one claims to contain the full translation of the sentence[13] and the other contains only a summary.[14] The English of the full translation is defective and sometimes incomprehensible. Moreover, the full translation omits the Arabic texts of legal sources quoted in the Hausa original, and gives references only to these sources, although often in a virtually unrecognizable form (e.g., "Bahjah fi—sharit—tufimam" for *al-Bahja fī sharḥ al-Tuḥfa*). At some points, therefore, my presentation of the case is a product of informed speculation, based on my familiarity with Islamic law and my access to the pertinent Sokoto legislation and the fiqh texts that are quoted. The same holds for quotations from the Arabic sources. I succeeded in tracing most of them in spite of the fact that the translations do not mention the editions that were used. Unless otherwise indicated, the footnotes list the sources of the quotations in the text of the sentence, although in most cases from different editions.

[13] Ladan (2003).

[14] Babaji and Dankofa (2003:103–27). (The summary of the sentence is found on pp. 123–5.)

The trial court and its sentence

On October 9, 2001, the Upper Shari'a Court of Gwadabawa (Sokoto State) pronounced a sentence of death by stoning for unlawful sexual intercourse against Safiyyatu Hussaini of the village of Tungkar Tudu. The execution of the sentence was stayed until the woman finished nursing her infant daughter. At the same time the court acquitted Yakubu Abubakar, who had been accused of the same offense and allegedly was the father of Safiyyatu Hussaini's child. The two had been charged with the offense of *zinā*, illegal sexual intercourse, which Section 128 and 129 SSPC make punishable with a caning of 100 lashes or death by stoning.[15] The charges against Safiyyatu Hussaini were based on the preliminary police investigation, during which Safiyyatu acknowledged that she had had intercourse with Yakubu Abubakar on four occasions, and, as a result, had become pregnant and given birth to a daughter who was now [i.e., during the trial session in July 2001) six-months old. During the police investigation Abubakar denied having had sexual relations with her. Subsequently, four prosecution witnesses testified to the truthfulness of Safiyyatu's acknowledgment and Yakubu's denial. Thereupon Yakubu was given the opportunity to challenge all the testimonies, whereas Safiyyatu was allowed to do so only with regard to two witnesses, both of them police officers. In response to the charges brought against her during the trial, she stuck to her previous statement and declared that to her knowledge it was Yakubu's semen ("water") that entered and made her pregnant, since after she left her husband's house she had three menstrual periods and she has cleansed herself before having sexual contact with Yakubu.

The court took note of Safiyyatu's statement in the presence of two male witnesses and it then formally charged the accused. When they told the court that they did not understand the charges, the court explained them as follows:

---

[15] "Whoever, being a man or woman fully responsible, has sexual intercourse through the genital of a person over whom he has no sexual rights and in circumstances in which no doubt exists as to the illegality of the act, is guilty of the offense of zina." (Section 128) "Whoever commits the offense of zina shall be punished (a) with caning of one hundred lashes if unmarried and shall also be liable to imprisonment for a term of one year; or (b) if married, with stoning to death." (Section 129) It is to be noted that in the text of the code the technical term "*muḥṣan*" is incorrectly translated as "married." The court, apparently, construes "married" as *muḥṣan*.

> What is meant by [the] charge[s] is that the court is suspecting you of *zinā*, [for] which if proved, your punishment will be death by stoning you to death, because you are all Muslims and both have been married before.

Before issuing the sentence, the court asked the accused whether they had any defense that might cause the court to refrain from sentencing them to death. The reports do not mention what the response was. Thereupon the court acquitted Yakubu for lack of evidence and found Safiyyatu Hussaini guilty of the offense of *zinā*, which is punishable by stoning to death as provided by Section 129(b) of SSPC,[16] noting that the sentences shall not be implemented until the woman had finished suckling her baby.

In support of the sentence, the court quoted the *Risāla* (of Ibn Abī Zayd al-Qayrawānī [d. 996]), one of the two leading textbooks of the Maliki school:

> A person who has had unlawful intercourse will not be punished with the *ḥadd* penalty unless there is an acknowledgment, a visible pregnancy (*ḥaml yaẓhar*) or the testimonies of four free adult men of good reputation (*ʿudūl*) who have seen [the male member in the vagina] like the kohl stick [entering] into the kohl container.[17]

In justification of the stay of execution, the court quoted a hadith found in the *Muwaṭṭaʾ* of Mālik:

> On the authority of ʿAbd Allāh b. Abī Mulayka: A woman came to the Messenger of God and told him, while she was pregnant, that she had had unlawful sexual relations. The Messenger of God said to her: "Go away until you have given birth." After she had given birth she came back and the Messenger of God said to her: "Go away until you have finished suckling him." After she had finished suckling him, she came back and he said: "Go away and entrust him [to someone]." She then entrusted him to someone and came back. Thereupon he ordered her to be stoned.[18]

The appeal

Safiyyatu Hussaini engaged a team of eleven lawyers and appealed this sentence to the Sokoto Shari'a Court of Appeal. She now withdrew

---

[16] The translation erroneously mentions section 129(b) of the SSCPC.
[17] Ābī (1976: 592).
[18] Mālik b. Anas (n.d.: 513). Section 253(2) SSCPC contains the same rule.

her confession made during the trial and asserted that the father of her child was her former husband and not Yakubu Abubakar. Her lawyers submitted that the decision of the Upper Shari'a Court of Gwadabawa could not stand and had to be set aside. The Shari'a Court of Appeal found substance in almost all of the grounds presented by the counsel for the appellant and quashed the decision of the trial court. The grounds for appeal related to three aspects of the trial: the trial court's lack of jurisdiction, errors in the procedure followed by that court, and errors in the application of the law. I will deal with the appeal and decision under these three headings, presenting the arguments of the counsel for the appellant (Safiyyatu Hussaini), the state counsel (representing the Attorney General of Sokoto State, who was the respondent) and, finally, the considerations of the Shari'a Court of Appeal.

Jurisdiction of the trial court

The counsel for the appellant argued that the sentence of the lower court had to be set aside because that court lacked jurisdiction to try the case. The appellant was sentenced on the strength of s. 129(b) of the SSPC. This bill had been signed by the Governor of Sokoto State only on January 25, 2001, and was therefore not in force before that date. However, the appellant was arraigned before the trial court on the strength of a police report dated December 23, 2000. The offense of which she was accused must therefore have been committed before that date.[19] Now, neither under Islamic law, nor under the Constitution[20] can a person be punished on the strength of a law that has not been enacted at the time when the offense was committed.

This argument was contested by the state counsel, who referred the court to the provisions of the Sokoto Shari'a Courts Law, which

[19] Since Safiyyatu's infant daughter was six-months old in July 2001, she must have been born in late December 2000 or early January 2001. Although it is not expressly mentioned, it is likely that the police investigation began after Safiyyatu's delivery.

[20] Section 4(9) CFRN stipulates, "Notwithstanding the foregoing provisions of this section, the National Assembly or a House of Assembly shall not, in relation to any criminal offense whatsoever, have power to make any law which shall have retrospective effect." Section 36(12) CFRN reads: "Subject as otherwise provided by this Constitution, a person shall not be convicted of a criminal offense unless that offense is defined and the penalty therefor is prescribed in a written law, and in this subsection, a written law refers to an Act of the National Assembly or a Law of a State, any subsidiary legislation or instrument under the provisions of a law."

had been promulgated in the year 2000. According to this law, the Shari'a courts do have jurisdiction to take cognizance of criminal cases and apply Islamic law.[21] This jurisdiction in criminal cases, the state counsel asserted, is in agreement with Section 38(1)[22] of the Constitution which guarantees freedom of religion, and which includes the right to live under the Shari'a. It is of no consequence that the SSPC, which in Sections 128 and 129 defines the offense of *zinā*, had not yet come into force at the time the offense took place, since the offense was already punishable under the SSCL. Starting from there, the state counsel asserted, the Upper Shari'a Court was competent on the strength of s. 12(1)[23] of the SCPC that was in force at the time of the trial.

The court agreed with the counsel for the appellant and confirmed that the lower court did not have jurisdiction to try the case. It added that the official charge did not mention the date on which the offense allegedly was committed or its location, but that, in any case, this must have been before the coming into force of the SSPC under which the appellant had been sentenced. In addition to the legal provisions cited by the counsel for the appellant in support of the principle that laws do not have retroactive effect, the court referred to Section 36(8) FCRN[24] and Section 7 SSPC.[25]

---

[21] 5(1): "A Shari'ah Court shall have jurisdiction . . . and in criminal cases where the suspect(s) or accused person(s) is/are Muslims." Subsection (4) lists eighteen criminal offenses (among them *zinā*) that the Shari'ah courts are competent to try. Subsection (6) provides that the applicable law shall be Islamic law, whereas subsection (7) gives a list of Maliki authorities (see note 8).

[22] "Every person shall be entitled to freedom of thought, conscience and religion, including freedom to change his religion or belief, and freedom (either alone or in community with others, and in public or in private) to manifest and propagate his religion or belief in worship, teaching, practice and observance." Section 38(1) FCRN.

[23] "Subject to the other provisions of this Shari'ah Criminal Procedure Code, the Upper Shari'ah Courts shall have jurisdiction to try any or all of the offenses listed in 'Appendix A' of this Code." This Appendix lists, among other offenses, *zinā* as an offense to be tried by the Upper Shari'ah Courts.

[24] "No person shall be held to be guilty of a criminal offense on account of any act or omission that did not, at the time it took place, constitute such an offense, and no penalty shall be imposed for any criminal offense heavier than the penalty in force at the time the offense was committed."

[25] "No act or omission committed by a person shall be an offense under the provisions of this law unless such act or omission was committed on or after the commencement date of this law."

Proper procedure

The investigation
The counsel for the appellant submitted that the police did not follow the proper procedure for investigating *zinā* cases and that the case was brought to the lower court in an unlawful manner. During the lifetime of the Prophet and the Rightly Guided Caliphs, it was the offenders themselves, in trials for *zinā*, who presented their cases to the authorities. In this case, however, people had pried into Safiyyatu's affairs and then brought her case to the attention of the authorities on the mere suspicion that she was pregnant out of wedlock. This is unlawful, for *zinā* cases can be brought to court only if there is a confession or four male Muslim eyewitnesses of good reputation.

The state counsel contested this principle, citing the Qur'an and the hadith. First he quoted Q. 16:90:[26]

> Lo! God enjoineth justice and kindness, and giving to kinsfolk, and forbiddeth lewdness and abomination and wickedness. He exhorteth you in order that ye may take heed.

Counsel inferred from this text that Muslims may take action if they are confronted with "lewdness, abomination, and wickedness." He then cited to two hadiths:

1. On the authority of Abū Saʿīd al-Khuḍarī, who said: "I heard the Messenger of Allah say: 'Whosoever of you sees an evil action, let him change it with his hand; and if he is not able to do so, then with his tongue; and if he is not able to do so, then with his heart; and that is the weakest of faith.'" (Muslim)[27]
2. On the authority of Abū Hurayra, who said: A Bedouin came to the Prophet and said: "O Messenger of God, I implore you by God to pass judgment on me in accordance with God's Book." And his adversary, who was better versed in jurisprudence than he, said: "Yes, pass judgment between us and allow me to speak." The Prophet said: "Talk." He said: "My son worked as a laborer for this man and then he fornicated with his wife. I was told that my son deserved to be stoned to death, so I ransomed him for 100

[26] I have made use of the Qur'an translation of M.M. Pickthall, *The Meaning of the Glorious Qur'ān*, except that I have replaced the word "Allah" with "God."

[27] The State counsel refers to hadith No. 37 of the *Arbaʿūn Ḥadīth* of al-Nawawī, which makes no sense in this context, as this hadith deals with the consequences of *niyya* (intention) on the reward or punishment of human actions. He probably meant No. 34, which is the one I quote in the text.

> sheep and a female slave. I then asked the people of knowledge and they informed me that my son deserved 100 lashes and banishment for one year and that the woman deserved to be stoned to death." The Prophet answered: "By the One Who holds my soul in His hand, I shall certainly pass judgment between you in accordance with God's Book. As for the slave girl and the sheep, they must be returned to you. Your son deserves 100 lashes and banishment for a year. Go, Unays, to this man's wife and if she confesses, stone her to death." Thereupon Unays went to the woman and she confessed. Then the Prophet ordered her to be stoned."[28]

The first hadith demonstrates that a Muslim may, indeed, he must take action if he is confronted with an evil deed. The second hadith, according to the state counsel, shows that the Prophet sent Unays to interrogate a woman who was suspected of having had unlawful sexual intercourse.

The court found substance in the submissions of the counsel for the appellant and went to great length to refute the arguments of the state counsel. The court's starting point was that it is forbidden, *ḥarām*, to pry into the affairs of others and to report cases of *zinā* merely on the basis of hearsay. This is based on Q. 49:12

> O ye who believe! Shun much suspicion; for lo! some suspicion is a crime. And spy not, neither backbite one another. Would one of you love to eat the flesh of his dead brother? Ye abhor that (so abhor the other)! And keep your duty (to God). Lo! God is Relenting, Merciful.

Further, the court mentioned (without quoting a source) that Imām al-Shāfiʿī stated that a leader has no right to send someone to a person suspected of the offense of *zinā* in order to interrogate him. Finally, the court referred to texts quoted in *Kitāb al-fiqh ʿalā al-madhāhib al-arbaʿa*.[29] The court concluded that the arrest of Safiyyatu on the mere suspicion of having committed *zinā* was unlawful.

The court dismissed the arguments submitted by the state counsel as inconclusive. The words "and forbiddeth lewdness and abomination and wickedness" in Q. 16:90, quoted by the state counsel, do not specifically refer to *zinā*, but rather, according to the *Jāmiʿ aḥkām*

---

[28] The state counsel refers to the English translation of the *Ṣaḥīḥ* of al-Bukhārī: Bukhārī (1979, 8:536). The translation I give here is based on the Arabic original as found in Ibn Ḥajar al-ʿAsqalānī (n.d.: no. 1031).

[29] Jazīrī 1986, 5: 120–3. (The page number mentioned in the translation 233 is erroneous). Here a number of hadiths are quoted enjoining discretion (*satr*) with regard to the investigation of *zinā*.

al-qur'ān, to all sins.[30] The verse, therefore, does not permit the arrest of anyone who is suspected of *zinā*. The same holds for the hadith about Unays quoted by the state counsel. The *Subul al-salām sharḥ bulūgh al-marām* makes it clear that there is no conflict between the Prophet sending Unays to the woman with whom the Bedouin's son had had intercourse and the Prophet's instruction that fornication (*fāḥisha*) should be kept secret, both by the person who committed it and by others. Nor does this injunction contradict his prohibition of spying on others. The reason that the Prophet sent Unays to the woman was that she had been slandered (*qudhifat*). Therefore, she should either deny the allegation and demand the *ḥadd* punishment for false accusation of unlawful sexual intercourse (*qadhf*), or confess so that the accuser would not be punished. She confessed, thereby exposing herself to the *ḥadd* punishment.[31] This hadith, therefore, does not indicate that the authorities may investigate cases of *zinā* and report them to a court.

Explanation of the charges to the accused

A further procedural ground for appeal submitted by the counsel for the appellant was the fact that the charge frame did not sufficiently explain to the appellant the meaning of a *zinā* charge and its consequences. The counsel for the appellant argued that the trial court should have explained the meaning of the word *zinā*, as is done in s. 128 SSPC, since the appellant is a Hausa village woman and not an Arab. He referred to the hadith of Māʿiz (without giving a source), according to which, after Māʿiz had confessed four times that he had committed *zinā*, the Prophet asked him whether he understood the meaning of the word and explained it to him.[32] Now, Māʿiz was an Arab whereas Safiyyatu does not speak or understand Arabic.

---

[30] al-Qurṭubī (1966, 10:167).

[31] al-Kaḥlānī (n.d., 4:4).

[32] The hadith, which is not quoted in the text, is as follows: On the authority of Abū Hurayra: "A Muslim man [in other sources identified as a certain Māʿiz] came to the Prophet when he was in the mosque and called to him: 'O Messenger of God, I have had illegal sexual relations.' The Prophet then turned away from him. But the man moved in order to face him and said: 'O Messenger of God, I have had illegal sexual relations.' Again the Prophet turned away, until he had repeated it four times. After the man had testified against himself four times, the Prophet called to him: 'Are you perhaps a bit insane?' The man answered, 'No.' Then he asked: Have you ever been married? The man answered, 'Yes.' Then the Prophet said: 'Take him away and stone him.' Ibn Ḥajar al-ʿAsqalānī (n.d.: no. 1033).

Therefore, the court should have made its meaning clear to her. Although the counsel for the respondent submitted that the trial court had sufficiently explained the nature of the offense with which the appellant was charged, the Shari'a Court of Appeal agreed with the counsel for the appellant. In support, the court referred to ʿAbd al-Qādir ʿAwda, *al-Tashrīʿ al-jināʾī al-islāmī*, quoting from the *Subul al-salām sharḥ bulūgh al-marām*:

> For a confession to be accepted it is required that it be detailed and clarify the actual action so that there is no more doubt as to the confession. This is important, especially since the word *zinā* may be used for acts that do not entail the *ḥadd* penalty, such as intercourse without penetration. The requirement of detailed interrogation and explicit clarification goes back to the *sunna* of the Messenger of God (May God bless him and grant him salvation), for when Māʿiz came to him to confess that he had committed *zinā* and repeated his confession, the Prophet asked whether he was insane or whether he had drunk wine, and he ordered someone to smell his breath. Then he questioned him about *zinā*, saying: "Have you perhaps merely kissed her or touched her? In another version: "Did you lie down with her?" He said, "Yes." Then [the Prophet] asked: "Did your body touch hers?" He answered, "Yes." Then [the Prophet] asked: "Did you have intercourse with her (*a-jāmaʿtahā*)?" He said, "Yes." In the hadith of Ibn ʿAbbās [the Prophet asked], calling a spade a spade (*lā yakunn*): "Did you f*** her?" (*a-niktahā*)?" He said, "Yes." Then he asked: "Did that thing of yours enter that thing of hers?" He answered, "Yes." He asked: "Like the kohl stick disappears in the kohl container and the bucket in the well?" He answered, "Yes." Then he asked: "Do you know what *zinā* means?" He said: "Yes, I did with her unlawfully what a man does with his wife lawfully." Then the Prophet said: "What do you intend with these words?" He answered: "That you purify me." Then he ordered him to be stoned.[33]

Taking this hadith into consideration, the court held that the nature of the charge had not sufficiently been explained to the accused. This is both repugnant to the principles of Islamic law and to s. 36(6)(a) of the Constitution.[34] Moreover, the charge did not specify

---

[33] ʿAwda (n.d., 2:433–4). As acknowledged in a footnote, ʿAwda cites this text from the *Subul al-salām sharḥ bulūgh al-marām*. See al-Kaḥlānī (n.d., 4:6–7).

[34] Section 36(6)(a) reads: "Every person who is charged with a criminal offense shall be entitled to be informed promptly in the language that he understands and in detail of the nature of the offense."

when and where the offense took place, which is also contrary to Islamic law (as illustrated by the hadith about Māʿiz) and in conflict with s. 170 of the SSCPC.[35]

Opportunity of defense against testimonies (*iʿdhār*)

The counsel for the appellant further argued that the decision of the lower court had to be set aside because of another procedural error. Under Islamic law, the accused must be given the opportunity to defend himself or bring witnesses in his defense (Hausa *izari*, from Arabic *iʿdhār*). The trial court failed to accord Safiyyatu this opportunity with regard to the four witnesses who testified for the prosecution about the results of the police investigation. The counsel referred to the *Iḥkām al-aḥkām* and the *Bahja*.[36] This was contested by the counsel for the respondent who submitted that *iʿdhār* had taken place. The Court of Appeal, finally, considered that the complaint of the counsel for the appellant was not entirely valid. According to the trial record *iʿdhār* had taken place. However, the lower court did not offer it to the accused immediately before the final sentencing, as is mandatory.[37] Since the *iʿdhār* that took place during the trial was followed by further proceedings, it was nullified and the court had to initiate another one. This entails the nullification of the sentence, as stated in the *Bahja fī sharḥ al-Tuḥfa*.

Advising the accused of his right to legal counsel

The only issue on which the court disagreed with the counsel for the appellant was his submission that the trial court should have advised the accused of her right to legal counsel of her choice. This, the court of appeal held, is not a duty of the trial court.

[35] 170(1) "Every charge under this Shari'ah Criminal Procedure Code shall have a statement of the offense complained of with date and place. . . . (2) The charge shall also as much as possible define the offense so as to give the accused notice of the matter with which he is charged."

[36] The text of the *Tuḥfa* by Ibn ʿĀṣim reads: "Before sentencing the *iʿdhār* must be established by two witnesses of good reputation, which is the preferred opinion." In the two commentaries on this poem to which the counsel refers, the authors lay down that a sentence without *iʿdhār* is null and void and that *iʿdhār* must take place immediately prior to sentencing. If *iʿdhār* is followed by further proceedings, e.g., the testimonies of witnesses, the *qāḍī* must offer a new *iʿdhār*, and his failure to do so entails the nullification of the judgment. See al-Kāfī (1991:21–2), and al-Tasūlī (1977, 1:64).

[37] This is not clear from the translation of the decision of the trial court. RP.

Errors in applying the law

Withdrawal of confession

The counsel for the appellant submitted that the trial court sentence must be set aside because the appellant had now withdrawn her confession, which, according to the *Mukhtaṣar* of Khalīl, is her right.[38] To this the state counsel responded that in *ḥadd* cases a confession may be withdrawn at any time, but that in this case such a withdrawal has no effect due to the pregnancy of the accused. In support of his assertion, he quoted the same passage from the *al-Thamr al-dānī sharḥ risālat al-Qayrawānī* as the trial court did (*vide supra*), and a text from Ibn Rushd's *Bidāyat al-mujtahid*:

> As to the controversy with regard to applying the *ḥadd* penalty [for *zinā*] on the strength of pregnancy in combination with the claim [of the woman] that she has been raped, there is a group that holds that in such a case the *ḥadd* penalty is mandatory on the strength of the hadith of ʿUmar, mentioned by Mālik in the *Muwaṭṭaʾ*.[39] This is the opinion of Mālik. [She is to be stoned] unless she can produce circumstantial evidence (*amāra*) that she was raped.[40]

Counsel also submitted that Safiyyatu could withdraw her confession only in person.[41]

The court did not give an explicit ruling on the merits of this issue. Implicitly it accepted the submission of the counsel for the appellant, as shown from the fact that it discussed the appellant's claim that the child to which she had given birth was her husband's (*vide infra*).

Pregnancy as proof of *zinā* and the effect of doubt (*shubha*)

The counsel for the appellant argued that the trial court erred in law when it regarded the appellant's pregnancy out of wedlock as

---

38 "[*Zinā*] is proven by a confession made once, unless he [the defendant] retracts it." Khalīl b. Isḥāq (1900:230). The counsel for the appellant further referred to the *Ṣaḥīḥ* al-Bukhārī, but he did not give the contents of the hadith, and I, therefore, could not identify it.

39 The hadith, which is not quoted in the text, reads: On the authority of Ibn ʿAbbās: "I heard ʿUmar ibn al-Khaṭṭāb say: 'Stoning is in God's Book, an obligation for men and women who have had unlawful sexual intercourse if they are *muḥṣan* and if there are witnesses, or pregnancy or a confession." Mālik (n.d.: 514).

40 Ibn Rushd (al-Ḥafīd) (1960, 2:440).

41 ". . . unless the person who has confessed having had unlawful sexual relations withdraws his confession, for in that case his withdrawal is accepted and he will not be punished with the *ḥadd* penalty." al-Ābī (1976, 2:284–5).

sufficient proof for the sentence of stoning, since, according to Maliki doctrine, a pregnancy may last for seven years. Therefore, conception may have occurred during her marriage. This constitutes doubt (*shubha*) that stands in the way of convicting a person of a *ḥadd* offense. In support, the counsel quoted the hadith about Māʿiz, related on the authority of Abū Hurayra (*vide supra*) and a passage from *Fiqh al-sunna* by Sayyid Sābiq:

> The majority of scholars is of the opinion that pregnancy alone is not sufficient proof for [applying] the *ḥadd* penalty [for *zinā*] and that either a confession or full evidence by witnesses is required. It has been related on the authority of ʿAlī—may God be pleased with him—that he said to a pregnant woman: "Have you been raped?" She said: "No." Then he said: "Perhaps a man came to you in your sleep." And it has been related from ʿUmar that he accepted the statement of a woman who claimed that she was a heavy sleeper and that a man came to her at night, but that she still did not know who he was.[42]

Departing from the principle that pregnancy out of wedlock is in and of itself sufficient evidence of *zinā*, the counsel for the respondent contested the claim submitted by the counsel for the appellant that in this case doubt prevents the application of the *ḥadd* penalty. He asserted that unlike retaliation (*qiṣāṣ*), the punishment for *zinā*, once it has been established by a confession, by four male witnesses or pregnancy out of wedlock, cannot be waived. Even if a woman claims that the pregnancy was a result of rape, she has to produce witnesses to this claim. In further support of his assertion, he quoted passages from Ibn Juzayy (n.d.: 269),[43] *al-Thamr al-dānī, sharḥ risālat al-Qayrawānī*[44] and the *Bidāyat al-mujtahid* by Ibn Rushd.[45] In this case the judg-

---

[42] Sābiq (1969, 2:421).

[43] "As to what establishes the *ḥadd* offense, that are three things: a confession, the testimonies of witnesses and the appearance of pregnancy." Ibn Juzayy (n.d.: 269).

[44] "A person who has had unlawful intercourse will not be punished with the *ḥadd* penalty unless there is a confession, a visible pregnancy (*ḥaml yaẓhar*) or the testimonies of four free adult men of good reputation (*ʿudūl*) who have seen [the male member in the vagina] like the kohl stick [entering] into the kohl container." Ābī (1976: 592).

[45] "As to the controversy with regard to applying the *ḥadd* penalty [for *zinā*] on the strength of pregnancy in combination with the claim [of the woman] that she has been raped, there is a group that holds that in such a case the *ḥadd* penalty is mandatory on the strength of the hadith of ʿUmar, mentioned by Mālik in the *Muwaṭṭaʾ*. This is the opinion of Mālik, unless she can produce circumstantial evidence (*amāra*) for her having been raped." Ibn Rushd (1960, 2:440).

ment was based on both confession (which, under Maliki law, does not need to be repeated four times) and pregnancy. In addition, he pointed out that the maximum duration of gestation according to the Maliki school is not seven but five years, as mentioned in the *Tuḥfat al-ḥukkām*[46] and by Ibn Juzayy in his *al-Qawānīn al-fiqhiyya*.[47]

The court concurred with the counsel for the appellant. It held that it cannot ascertain the veracity of the appellant's claim that the child to whom she gave birth was fathered by her former husband from whom, according to her statement, she was divorced two years before the lower court trial, because the lower court did not investigate this issue. However, according to the *Tuḥfat al-ḥukkām*, the minimum period of gestation is six months and the maximum period is five years.[48] Therefore, it is possible that the child was fathered by her former husband. This constitutes doubt (*shubha*), which prevents the application of the *ḥadd* penalty, on the basis of the maxim, mentioned in the *Mughnī* of Ibn Qudāma and transmitted on the authority of ʿAbd Allāh b. Masʿūd, Muʿādh b. Jabal and ʿUqba b. ʿĀmir: "If you are in doubt regarding [the enforcement of] a *ḥadd* penalty, avert it as much as you can."[49] If she persists in her claim, she can sue her previous husband before a proper court [for maintenance]. In addition, the court held that the counsel for the respondent apparently was ignorant of the difference between *ḥadd* punishments and retaliation for manslaughter (*qiṣāṣ*), as he seemed to confuse the principle that *shubha*, doubt, averts a *ḥadd* penalty with the principle that retaliation can be set aside by a pardon of one or more of the victim's heirs. No such waiver is possible with regard to a *ḥadd* penalty, which, once pronounced, must be carried out because it is God's judgment and the person who has notified the authorities of the offense cannot waive the punishment.[50]

---

[46] "Five years is the maximum duration of pregnancy and six months the minimum." al-Tasūlī (1977, 1:391–2). (*Bāb al-nafaqa wa-mā yataʿallaq bihā, Faṣl fīmā yajib ʿalā al-muṭallaqāt*), on the margin.

[47] "The authoritative (*fī al-mashhūr*) opinion in the Maliki school is five years, but some scholars fixed it at four or seven years." Ibn Juzayy (n.d.: 179). (Part 2, Book 2, Chapter 7: On *ʿidda* and *istibrāʾ* and related matters.)

[48] See note 46.

[49] *Idhā ishtabaha ʿalayka al-ḥadd, fa-draʾ mā istaṭaʿta.* The maxim is found in the compilation of al-Dāraquṭnī. See Ibn Qudāma (n.d., 8:211).

[50] Here the court refers to Abū Bakr b. Ḥasan al-Kishnāwī, *Ashal al-madārik sharḥ irshād al-sālik fī fiqh imām al-aʾimma Mālik* (by ʿAbd al-Raḥmān b. Muḥammad Ibn ʿAskar (d. 1332)), vol. 3, 188. Unfortunately I have not had access to this work.

Establishing *iḥṣān*

The counsel for the appellant submitted that the trial court erred in complying with the law because it did not establish that the appellant is *muḥṣan*, i.e. an adult, free Muslim who has experienced sexual intercourse within a lawful marriage. This is evident from the following citation from the *Bidāya* of Ibn Rushd:

> There is a difference of opinion about the conditions of *iḥṣān*. According to Mālik, they are: majority, being a Muslim, being free, and sexual intercourse on the basis of a valid contract during a period that intercourse is allowed. The type of intercourse that is forbidden (*maḥẓūr*), according to him, is intercourse during menstruation or during the fast. If someone has unlawful intercourse (*zinā*) after having had lawful intercourse as described above, and if he has the aforementioned characteristics, then, according to him, he must be stoned.[51]

The state counsel denied that *iḥṣān* had not been established and asserted that the lower court, on the strength of the accused's statement that she was divorced two years ago, did in fact ascertain that the appellant was *muḥṣana.*

The court, here too, concurred with the counsel for the appellant. It quoted the *Kitāb al-fiqh ʿalā al-madhāhib al-arbaʿa* on the conditions of *iḥṣān*, for both men and women:

> (a) being free, (b) being of age, (c) being sane, (d) being married (or having been married) with a valid contract to a woman who is also a *muḥṣana*, (e) having had intercourse with her in a period during which this is allowed and when she also was a *muḥṣana*, (f) being a Muslim (according to the Malikis and the Hanafis.[52]

The trial court failed to investigate any of these conditions. The mere fact that Safiyyatu declared that she had been divorced two years ago is not sufficient proof of *iḥṣān*. For it is conceivable that she was married and that her marriage had been consummated, but that she nevertheless was not *muḥṣan* [because, for example, consummation and further intercourse took place during her menstruation or during Ramaḍān. RP]

State counsel introduces a new claim: prosecution for qadhf

Finally the state counsel submitted that if the sentence of stoning to death was not upheld, the accused must be sentenced under Section

[51] Ibn Rushd (1960, 2:435).
[52] Jazīrī (n.d., 5:50).

141–3 SSPC[53] to caning for having defamed (*qadhf*) Abubakar. The court, however, did not agree with this submission, for such a sentence can be pronounced only at the request of the person who is defamed. This does not apply here, since Yakubu Abubakar did not appear in court to seek redress.[54]

Conclusions

The Safiyyatu Hussaini case has many interesting aspects. I will discuss two of them here. First, it illustrates the manner in which the judiciary applies codified Islamic criminal law. Second, it highlights the attitude of the courts towards the Qur'anic penalties.

Prior to the re-Islamization of the law, the area courts in the North would adjudicate civil matters according to uncodified Shari'a, referring to the classical works of Maliki doctrine. When the law was first Islamicized, the legislators, by giving the new Shari'a courts jurisdiction over criminal cases even before the Shari'a Penal Codes had been introduced, apparently envisioned that these courts would follow a similar procedure in criminal matters. This is stipulated in Sections 6 and 7 (for the text, see above, §1.1) of the SSCL, enacted before the Sokoto Shari'a Penal Code. This direct application of uncodified Shari'a law in criminal cases, it seems, was accepted and even welcomed by the lower courts. As we have seen, the Upper Shari'a Court of Gwadabawa applied uncodified Shari'a criminal law in the case and found Safiyyatu Hussaini guilty. Similar sentences (some involving amputation) were pronounced in Sokoto and other

---

[53] The text has Section 183, which is incorrect. The sections of the SSPC dealing with *qadhf* are: *Section* 141: "Whoever by words either spoken or reproduced by mechanical means or intended to be read or by signs or by visible representations makes or publishes any false imputation of Zina or Sodomy concerning a chaste person (Muhsin), or contests the paternity of such person even where such person is dead, is said to commit the offense of *qadhf*, provided that person is deemed to be chaste (Muhsin) who has never been convicted of the offense of Zina or Sodomy." Section 142: "Whoever commits the offense of *qadhf* shall be punished with eighty strokes of the cane; and his testimony shall not be accepted thereafter unless he repents before the court." Section 143: "The offense of *qadhf* shall be remitted in any of the following cases: (a) where the complainant (maqzuf) pardons the accuser (qazif). (b) where the husband accuses his wife of zina and undertakes the process of mutual imprecation (lian). (c) where the complainant (maqzuf) is a descendant of the accuser (qazif)."

[54] The court here cites again from the *Ashal al-Madārik*. See note 50.

states.[55] However, since the Constitution requires that criminal offenses and their penalties be defined by a written law, the Northern states soon realized that they had to draft and enact Shari'a Penal Codes and Shari'a Codes of Criminal Procedure. This was done with great speed. However, important fields of criminal law, such as evidence, were not codified, probably because the legislators realized that the states do not have the power to do so. As a result, uncodified Shari'a again began to play an important role in criminal proceedings. This is clear from the case discussed here. Although the Shari'a Court of Appeal, which must adjudicate according to Islamic law, also refers to the Constitution, the main body of arguments and considerations derive from Maliki legal doctrine. In fact, on those points which the Shari'a Court of Appeal set aside because the decision of the lower court violated constitutional provisions, the Court also argued that there was a conflict with the principles of Islamic law. This was the case, e.g., with regard to the principle that no act can be punished without a previous legal enactment, which, the Court asserted, was also a principle of Islamic law. In general the Court cited a wide array of Maliki *fiqh* works. However, it is not clear why one authority rather than another was being referred to on certain points. In most cases the information that was required was found in several sources.

The second point of interest is that there is an obvious difference between the lower court and the court of appeal with regard to the enforcement of the more severe Qur'anic penalties. The Upper Shari'a Court seemed to be quite willing to pronounce a sentence of death by stoning on the basis of what, even according to classical Islamic standards, are rather thin grounds, by superficially referring to some texts from Maliki compendia. This attitude is perhaps motivated by enthusiasm and zeal for Islamization and a desire to restore an Islamic moral order. The Shari'a Court of Appeal seemed to adopt the opposite attitude, trying to prevent the application of the *ḥadd* punishment for unlawful intercourse insofar as possible. The court used all possible arguments and stretched the classical doctrine to the utmost in order to quash the trial court judgment on as many grounds as possible. Two motives may have played a role. First, as in classical Islam, there was always a reluctance to enforce the stoning penalty. Second, the Court may have been affected by political motives. If

---

[55] See Peters (2003:54–60).

it upheld the trial court judgment (death by stoning), then the case would be submitted to the Supreme Federal Court, which might test the constitutionality of the Shari'a Penal Codes. The constitutionality of the Code is, in fact, questionable on several counts, e.g., the prohibition of cruel, degrading or inhuman punishment, (Section 34 FCRN) and of discrimination on the basis of gender or religion (Section 42 FCRN). Thus, there was a chance that this Supreme Court would find that the new Shari'a Codes are null and void on a number of important points. In order to prevent this, it is likely that the Shari'a Court of Appeal set aside the decision of the lower court, lest the constitutionality of the Shari'a legislation be put to the scrutiny of the Supreme Federal Court.

The decision of the Shari'a Court of Appeal seriously restricts the enforcement of the penalty of death by stoning. The Maliki doctrine that admits as evidence for *zinā* the pregnancy of an unmarried woman has been seriously weakened, since the Shari'a Court of Appeal has ruled that women may rebut such allegations of *zinā*: during the five years following the dissolution of her last marriage, her claim that the child with which she is pregnant was fathered by her former husband constitutes *shubha*, which averts the application of the *ḥadd* punishment, death by stoning. Moreover, the Court has emphasized that the investigation of *zinā* cases on the basis of mere suspicion (e.g., the pregnancy of an unmarried woman) is unlawful and, moreover, that, if a *zinā* case is tried in court, the court must explain to the accused the exact nature of the charge and question the accused in order to ascertain whether he/she might have a valid defense of which he/she was unaware. As mentioned at the beginning of this chapter, the Shari'a Court of Appeal of Katsina has given a similar decision in the Amina Lawal case. It is to be hoped that this will deter lower Shari'a courts from sentencing women to death by stoning solely on the evidence of extramarital pregnancy.

PART II

ORGANIZING LAW

CHAPTER TEN

LAW IN THE MARKETPLACE: ISTANBUL, 1730–1840*

Engin Deniz Akarlı
Brown University

Selim İlkin ağabeye

Studies on Islamic jurisprudence and its history have reached a high level of sophistication.[1] This development, however, is largely based on sources of a theoretical nature. We still know little about how the Islamic legal tradition influenced judicial practice and reasoning in specific historical settings. The present article addresses this gap with the aid of the most detailed sources available to us on Islamic legal practice, namely, the legal documents preserved in the Ottoman archives.

Ottoman legal documents not only provide rich information on legal practice but also demonstrate the significance of law in the Ottoman empire. This should not come as a surprise. The Ottoman state was founded ca. 1300 and dissolved in 1922. It covered far-flung territories and ruled over an ethnically and religiously diverse population. No state could maintain itself over such a broad area, over such a diverse population and for such a long period without a working legal system and notion of legitimacy.

Scope

The sheer quantity of the Ottoman legal documents obliges one to limit the scope of one's research. I focus on the artisans and traders of the four major business districts of greater Istanbul in the period

* I am grateful to David Powers and Baber Johansen for their many helpful comments on this essay.

[1] Baber Johansen and Wael Hallaq have been influential in raising the standards of studies on Islamic jurisprudence and in attracting attention to it. For a sample of their writings, see Johansen (1999) and Hallaq (1997). *Islamic Law and Society* is the major journal where the developments in the field can be observed.

1730–1840. Artisans and traders were religiously and ethnically mixed town-dwellers who worked hard to make ends meet and were vulnerable to the coercion wielded by administrative authorities. They had differences among themselves as well as with other major social groups. The artisans turned to the legal system to defend their interests and became involved in demonstrations calling for justice when they believed that the legal system had failed them.[2]

The period I cover begins with a major popular uprising in which the artisans and traders of Istanbul were actively involved.[3] It ends with a turning point in Ottoman history, when legal and commercial concessions to major European states and the adoption of a policy of bureaucratic and legal reorganization began to transform the Ottoman state and society in ways influenced by West European models. In between, we have a period of relative tranquility and prosperity until about 1775, followed by a phase of internal revolts, successive military defeats, civil war, and economic hardships.[4]

Relying on data reflecting the vicissitudes of this period, the present essay aims at shedding light on the performance of the Ottoman judicial system with a focus on artisans and traders. I argue that the judges acted primarily as moderators in reconciling actual or potential conflicts in an effort to maintain harmony and order in the marketplace. The ultimate outcome of these efforts was the regulation of the marketplace with the active participation of the people to whom the regulations applied. An examination of this participatory judicial process casts light on the place of law in state-society relations during the last stage of Ottoman history, in which the Hanafi school of the Islamic legal tradition remained predominant.[5] Let me begin with a few introductory words about the Ottoman legal system in order to put the Ottoman judges and my sources in perspective.

---

[2] Yi (2004) is the author of the most up-to-date work on Istanbul artisans and traders. Also see Kal'a (1998). Osman Nuri (1922) retains its significance as a seminal work. For *esnaf* customs and traditions, see Gürata (1975).

[3] Aktepe (1958) and Olson (1974).

[4] For a broad introduction to this period see, McGowan (1994). For complementary material see my review in E. Akarlı (1996). On eighteenth-century Istanbul, see Hamadeh (1998). On fiscal problems, see Cezar (1986).

[5] The Ottomans officially adhered to the Hanafi school but recognized other Sunni schools of law as well and appointed judges representing these schools where needed. See Aydın (1999:89–94).

Sites of Dispute Settlement

The Ottoman legal system was three-tiered. First, it allowed a large degree of autonomy to various segments of the population in handling their internal affairs and differences according to local custom (*örf* and *ʿadet*). These groups, segments or "communities" ranged from tribes, villages, residents of the same urban quarters, and artisanal groups in the marketplace to religious communities (*millets*) in general. Normally, disputes within a community were settled under the auspices of its leaders and according to its "custom." When this failed, people came to the regular (kadi) courts and ultimately to the imperial divan (council). The kadi courts constituted the backbone of the Ottoman judicial system. Several branches assisted each major kadi court. The deputy judges (*naʾibs*) who headed these branches were responsible to the kadi of the district (*kaza*). The courts also served as notary publics, registering and thereby providing legal validity to contractual arrangements about the handling of a specific relationship or potential conflict.[6]

The imperial divan, which was the highest executive organ of the Ottoman government, also fulfilled certain judicial tasks. Two of the highest-ranking judges (*kazaskers*) of the Ottoman judicial hierarchy were members of the divan. They advised the divan in legal matters and made up its legal branch, which functioned as a high court. The two judges heard appeals against the decisions of regular courts. They also examined the legal validity of objections to previous decisions of the divan. The litigants presented their respective views, claims, and documentary evidence. The judges checked government records and copies of former divan decisions to verify claims and called in witnesses and experts as needed. Only one of the senior judges, or another senior judge to whom the responsibility was delegated, heard a case. The grand vizier presided over the divan and led discussions on administrative and policy issues, but he did not interfere in the judicial process once the divan turned to judicial issues, although he might be present at the hearings. The judicial section convened separately in the afternoons and on certain days of the week to attend to business that had not been addressed in regular meetings of the divan. The divan's judicial decisions were formulated as recommendations submitted to the palace and put into effect in

[6] Uzunçarşılı (1965:83–143).

the form of a regulation by imperial decree (*emr-i ʿali*) after ratification by the sovereign. The sovereign's ratification was necessary because the review of judicial decisions and the issuance of regulatory decrees to help maintain public peace and order were prerogatives of the sovereign according to the Islamic-Ottoman legal tradition.[7]

Sources

My research relies mainly on the judicial files of the imperial divan.[8] These files are more detailed than the regular court records. Whereas the regular court records usually comprise brief summaries of the court's proceedings, the judicial files of the divan normally include detailed information about the history of each case and documents indicating the evidence on which the judges based their decision. This attention to detail must have been related to the complicated nature of the cases that came before the divan. The regular court records make a better source for legal practice based on the relatively well-established (positive) injunctions of the Shariʿa, such as transactions related to family matters. The divan judges had to deal with cases that often required authoritative interpretation of legal principles and injunctions. Still, the divan judges were subject to the same legal procedure as were the regular kadis and *na'ib*s. Thus, the files of the divan provide rich information not only on complicated and important cases but also on legal procedure and reasoning.

[7] On *kazasker*s, see Uzunçarşılı (1965:151–60). On the divan and its judicial functions, see Mumcu (1986). Mumcu's work covers the period up to the beginning of the seventeenth century. His descriptions apply largely also to the eighteenth century, although Mumcu suggests that the divan became a corrupt institution from the early seventeenth century on. This impression echoes a much-eschewed cliché unsupported by a study of the relevant documents. On the divan and various Ottoman courts, also see Aydın (1994:375–438, esp. 391–404).

[8] The documents I use come from three sources: The first is a register of imperial decrees pertaining to Istanbul artisans and traders that was prepared for Kara Kemal, the minister of provisions in the Ottoman war cabinet of 1915–1918 who was responsible for the organization of the artisans and traders. The register is abbreviated as EEA in the footnotes. The second source is the Cevdet collection of imperial decrees in the Prime Ministry Archives in Istanbul. Most of the documents I use come from the Cevdet-Belediye section of this collection, abbreviated as CB in the notes. I use a few files also from the Cevdet-İktisad section, abbreviated as Cİ, and from the Cevdet-Zabtiye section, abbreviated as CZ. Finally, I use the collection of imperial decisions on Istanbul artisans published by Ahmed Kal'a et al. in two volumes: *İstanbul Ahkam Defterleri: İstanbul Esnaf Tarihi* (Istanbul, 1997–98). I indicate the months of the Islamic lunar calendar by the same abbreviations used in Ottoman documents and archival catalogues.

The Legal Process

The divan files on judicial matters point to the emphasis put on the reconciliation (*sulh*) of differences at all levels of the legal process, at least regarding disputes that affected the marketplace. Clearly, the Ottoman legal system encouraged the parties that disagreed or were likely to disagree to handle their real or potential differences through negotiations and consensual agreements. The courts facilitated these negotiations and saw to the conformity of the consequent agreements to legal norms.[9]

Efforts to build consensual relationships began at the communal or group level. By long tradition, artisans and traders of the same calling tended to form groups (*esnaf*)[10] in order to conduct their affairs as harmoniously as possible and to defend their collective interests as effectively as possible. Conventions and custom (*örf ve ʿadet*) guided the relations within a group as well as its relations with other groups and parties. Artisans justified "custom" as "ancient" or "time-honored" principles of conduct (*usul ul-kadim*), and so it was in certain ways. Yet, nobody supposed that customs remained unchanged and unchangeable. Customs fell into disuse and disappeared, just as they changed incrementally over time. The artisans recognized that when customs and conventions lost their consensual binding power, it was time to renegotiate them. A comparison of the descriptions of the "ancient custom" of any given group of artisans registered by the courts in the period 1730–1840 reveals significant adjustments and changes. Equally significant, these "customs" invariably read as collective agreements reached among the members of the group.

When the members of a group or the representatives of different groups failed to resolve their disputes by their own means, they came to the judges (*naʾib*s and kadis) of the regular courts for help. When the latter failed or when the case transcended their jurisdiction and authority (because it required reinterpretation of principles or revision of public policy), the task fell upon the senior judges of the

---

[9] For general principles governing the concept of reconciliation (*sulh*) and its contractual nature, see the late nineteenth-century compendium *Mecelle-i Ahkam-ı ʿAdliyye*, Articles 1531–1570. (I use the Dersaadet 1308 [Istanbul, 1890–91] edition) and Bilmen (1985), vol. 8, 5–28.

[10] "*Esnaf*" is usually translated into English as "guild." I prefer "group" or "association," because "*esnaf*" were less structured than guilds.

divan.[11] Regular judges as well as the divan judges first tried to reconcile the litigants, unless one side was clearly in the "wrong," for instance, when s/he had persistently breached an agreement or convention to which s/he had consented earlier. Even when the judge had to settle a case by resorting to his decisive legal authority, he still formulated the final sentence in the form of a contractual consensus guaranteed by all the parties involved. A divan judge relied on the same legal procedure in hearing a case and used the same legal concepts in formulating the draft of a "decree" ("*emr-i ʿali*") to be submitted to the palace for ratification.

The Judges

The divan judges were called "*kazasker*" [*ḳażiʿaskar*], a term that literally means military-judge and is often misleadingly translated as such. The Ottoman concept of "*ʿasker*" broadly refers to persons on the government payroll and responsible for the running of the state. The judiciary was on government payroll and had important responsibilities within the state organization. However, the Ottomans made a clear distinction between soldiers ("*ʿasker*" in the strict sense of the term) and the administrative bureaucracy, on the one hand, and the judiciary, on the other. Special laws applied to the military and, to some extent, to the civilian bureaucratic cadres, but not to the judiciary or the civilian population. "Sultanic custom" (*örf-i sultani*) was the source of these martial administrative laws.

The Ottoman judiciary, on the other hand, had developed into an organization expected to maintain the conformity of the overall policies of the government to Islamic norms of legitimacy as well as providing judicial services in keeping with the Islamic legal tradition. All Ottoman judges were trained and held diplomas (*icazet*) in Islamic law (*fıkıh*). Deputy judges in most of the provinces were local people. Some of them were highly reputable legal experts. In order to rise in the judicial hierarchy, however, a judge had to serve in different provinces for many years. Reaching the highest judicial positions also required competence in jurisprudence (*usul ul-fıkıh*) and

[11] Kadis appointed to major provincial centers from Istanbul appear to have played a similar role as appeal judges of sorts. However, appeal to the divan remained open to residents of the provinces as well. Many provincial cases (mostly from the major provincial capitals) may be found among the judicial files of the divan.

qualification to issue a legal opinion (*fetva*). Indeed, many of the senior judges studied and taught Islamic jurisprudence in the leading schools of Istanbul and wrote legal commentaries, as all scholars of repute were expected to do.[12]

Connection to powerful people and nepotism, too, played a role in appointments to senior judicial positions in the eighteenth century. Still, we need to recognize the logic of the system. The *kazaskers* and other senior Ottoman judges were not merely the servants of an imperial state. They were also specialists in a well-established legal tradition that prevailed in a large area, transcending the boundaries of specific states. The law recognized the necessity of states as loci of political and administrative authority and was adaptable to the needs of a specific state. Reaching the senior judicial positions in any given state might necessitate connections as well as extensive training and service within the legal system of that state, as was the case in the Ottoman empire. However, the jurisdiction of the law transcended the jurisdiction of the state. Legal scholars had to and did remain in dialogue with their prominent colleagues elsewhere and read the same classics of their profession.

In short, the Ottoman judiciary constituted a deliberately distinctive branch of the Ottoman government. Its main charge was the peaceful resolution of conflicts. Furthermore, the judges, in general, and the senior judges, in particular, played a crucial role in harmonizing government decisions and customary practices with the norms and principles of an established legal tradition. Their efforts helped legitimize Ottoman rule and smooth the relations between the executive organs of the government and the civilian population. The evidence on artisans and traders illustrates the point.

Cases

The Autonomy of Groups

As already noted, the Ottoman legal tradition respected communal autonomy in settling disputes. Such autonomy called for a degree of

[12] For Ottoman judiciary promotions and organization, see Uzunçarşılı (1965:271–81). Also, see Kahraman, Galitekin, and Dadaş, eds. (1998). Cf. C. Fleischer (1986:257–72) for tension and interaction between the Islamic legal tradition and the Ottoman sultanic custom.

internal organization. A distinctive sign of the existence of a tangible internal organization among a given group of artisans was the designation of a person to serve as its steward (*kethüda*). The steward represented the group in its relations with external parties, including the government, oversaw the management of the internal affairs of the group, and helped settle disputes—in accordance with the consensual conventions or "ancient custom" of the group.[13] In the eighteenth century, artisans and shopkeepers in various lines of economic activity felt a need to streamline their existing associations or to reorganize.[14] To this end, they elected a steward, articulated the "ancient custom" of their trade, and then registered their steward and custom with the courts. As Case 1 below illustrates, however, the courts would also recognize the preference of a group of traders to remain only loosely organized, without either defining their "custom" or electing a steward.

Normally, the master artisans of a group would elect their steward from among their own ranks.[15] In certain lines of activity that directly affected public safety, the government itself might help or force the artisans to become better organized and even appoint the steward (see Case 2). In the last quarter of the eighteenth century, the government also began to hire by contract some of the stewardships to raise additional revenue. Such appointments by government contract often caused grievances among artisans. The judges recognized artisans' complaints and either allowed them to choose their own representatives or warned the steward to observe the contract of his appointment and not to interfere with the group's internal affairs.

> *Case 1*: The government appointed İsmaʿil Ağa, a palace halberdier, as the steward of woolen cloth dealers (*sufçu*). Twenty Jewish shop owners, who sold cashmere shawls imported from Europe or produced in Tosya and who were autonomous affiliates (*yamak*) of the woolen cloth sellers' group, agreed to pay a fee to him, "because we take pride in obeying the sublime government's orders and imperial decrees." İsmaʿil, however, interfered in their affairs, such as the distribution of imported cloth among them, unless they added some cashmere cloth gratis to his fee. In 1795, the cashmere sellers took him to the imperial court [because the government had appointed him], arguing that they needed

[13] See the works mentioned in note 2.
[14] E. Akarlı (2004:166–200) and E. Akarlı (1986:223–32).
[15] For a typical election and registration of a steward with a royal diploma, see İnalcık (1986:135–42).

neither a steward nor a regulation concerning the distribution of their commodities. Any person, including İsmaʿil, could buy cashmere shawls from the merchants who brought them to Istanbul and set up a shop to sell these shawls. The court decided that the shawl sellers should no longer be considered as affiliates of the woolen cloth dealers, and therefore they should no longer pay even the regular fee to İsmaʿil.[16]

Case 2: In 1760, the government appointed stewards over the boatmen of the various quays of the Galata district, apparently to bring some order to this trade, which was important for safe and reliable public transportation in the city, but also to provide some revenue for the Yeni Cami foundation. For a while this arrangement worked fine. In 1782, when one of the stewards began to sell the right to work at the quay under his responsibility, the boatmen took him to the Galata court and obtained a decision for his dismissal. However, the steward challenged the court's decision because he had a lifetime contract (*malikane mukataʿa*) to run the quay. A protracted dispute ensued between the boatmen of the district and their stewards. In 1798, the boatmen brought their case before the imperial court, requesting the right to elect their own stewards, "as once they used to do." The court decided to honor the existing contracts of the stewards, but it also imposed certain restrictions on them in order to protect the boatmen.[17]

Case 3: Seyyid Hacı Mehmed, a cloth dealer with some connections to the palace, had obtained an imperial diploma to become the steward of the hardware dealers (*naʿalbur esnafı*). When the hardware dealers refused to pay Mehmed even the customary stewardship fees, let alone the additional fees apparently mentioned in his appointment document, he took them to the district court and obtained a decision in his favor. When the hardware dealers continued to oppose him, he took them to the imperial court. The dealers pleaded before the court that it was their custom to elect a steward from among their own ranks. One of the main tasks of their steward was to assure that a fair share of the iron that came to Istanbul from the provinces was earmarked for their use and then to distribute it among the members of the group according to its custom. Nowadays, however, argued the dealers, "iron is imported from Europe and sold to whoever pays the highest price. Unable to buy the raw materials of our trade in sufficient quantities, we have become impoverished, but our steward, who knows nothing about our trade and cannot help us deal with our problems, keeps asking us to pay him fees." The court recognized the plight of the dealers and proposed that they elect their own steward as they did in the past but pay the current steward a fixed sum of 55 *kuruş*es per month per shop. Both sides agreed to this solution. The dealers

[16] EEA, pp. 230–2, R 1210 [Oct. 1795].
[17] EEA, pp. 239–41, Ca 1213 [Nov. 1798].

had already decided to choose Mustafa as their steward. Mehmed deputed him as his agent before the court and pledged not to interfere in the affairs of the group. Likewise, the group's representatives present in the court pledged to pay Mehmed the designated fee.[18]

Case 4: *Punç* (or punch) was a warm drink made of rum or brandy, lemon juice, and hot water. A *punççu* was a person who made and sold this drink along with some soft drinks and candies. In 1827, the government encouraged the *punççus* to organize themselves as a distinct group. In return for higher taxes and a registration fee, and also for higher rents for those shops owned by pious foundations, the *punççus* would have the right to control who could practice their trade, to elect their steward, and other advantages. The owners of the fifty-five punch shops that existed in greater Istanbul at the time thus formed the *punççu* group. The warden of Galata, where many of the punch shops were located, appears to have made all these arrangements. Upon his recommendation, the divan issued an imperial diploma to a man called Francisco as the first steward of the *punççus*. Although his document of appointment stated that he was a *punççu*, in fact he was not. Once Francisco assumed his position, he began to sell permits to open a punch shop "to many people, including Muslims and women," without consulting the real *punççus*. Considering this practice a breach of their contract with the government and the custom of the trade, the *punççus* took Francisco to the imperial court. They requested his removal and the cancellation of the new permits issued by him. They also added that they would choose their own steward but did not want the government to issue an imperial diploma for him, for stewards with such diplomas had a tendency to think only of their personal interests. After due investigations, the court agreed to their requests, except that they had to purchase the new stores from their owners, for the latter had invested money into these stores on the basis of legally valid documents. The court confirmed that Francisco was guilty of corruption, although it did not indicate the punishment he deserved other than losing his position as a steward.[19]

Artisans fell into conflict with stewards of their own choice as well and sometimes they themselves wanted the appointment of a trustworthy outsider as the steward of their trade.

Case 5: Forty Muslim and over 100 Armenian bakers took their steward Hacı Ahmed, their colleagues Hacı Said, Mikhail, and Vartan, and the director of the Flour Weigh Station to the imperial court, accusing them of being accomplices in "trampling upon other bakers

[18] EEA, pp. 220–1, Z 1218 [March 1805].
[19] EEA, pp. 150–3, 4 Ca 1247 [11 Oct. 1831].

and turning them into impoverished debtors". The bakers claimed that the steward and his accomplices withheld half of the wheat that came to the weigh station. Since the defendants could not use all this wheat in the twenty-odd bakeries that they controlled, they sold the rest in nearby towns at a profit, while many bakers in Istanbul went out of business. The bakers were unable to cope with Hacı Ahmed, because, backed by the director of the weigh station, he threatened to drive them out of business, indeed, out of Istanbul as well. As a solution to their problem, the bakers requested the appointment of a reliable outsider who could defend them as their steward.[20]

Individual Rights versus Group Rights

(a) *Masters against Senior Apprentices* The masters and the senior apprentices of a trade sometimes fell into conflict with each other over the legal (*şerʿi*) right of the latter to start their own business. These cases came before the divan judges either when the district court failed to reconcile the two sides or because the masters had already obtained from the divan a decision that froze the number of shops in their trade for the best interest of the public. Typically, the masters argued that the uncontrolled expansion of their trade would undermine the ability of the group as a whole to maintain the standards of the trade, thereby causing harm to consumers of their products and services. The judges weighed the arguments of both sides and, when need be, solicited expert opinion to effect a resolution.

Case 6: Some of the silk thread bleachers, affiliates of the dyers, would release their sufficiently experienced apprentices to practice the trade independently. Since the number of the silk bleaching shops was fixed, these people could not set up their own shops. Instead, they worked as itinerant masters, doing whatever bleaching jobs they could find, not only in silk thread but also in any other kind of yarn. In 1759, the dyers took the silk bleachers to the court, accusing them of creating a situation that undermined their business. They demanded that the silk bleachers honor the old customs of the dying business. According to this custom, masters who promoted their experienced apprentices to mastership were obliged to continue to employ them until the latter managed to acquire one of the fixed slots (*gedik*) of independent mastership in the trade. The steward of the silk bleachers, Todori, defended his colleagues by arguing that they did not have sufficient

[20] CB 423. Neither a date nor the court's decision is indicated in this file.

business to hire experienced craftsmen. He requested that their workshops be moved to a more central location in order to enable them to observe the custom. The judge reconciled the parties accordingly.[21]

Case 7: In 1761, experienced apprentices who were qualified to become masters in the brocade weaving trade took their masters to court, because the latter did not allow them to set up their own business without paying a high fee to the established masters. The defendants appealed to an imperial decree dating from 1730–31 (1143 h.) in defense of their position. This decree indeed allowed the masters to collect a fee for the establishment of new looms, but it was clearly a practice intended to facilitate the payment of the brocaders' collective rent to the Fazlı Paşa Khan, a pious foundation (*vakıf*) building, where they worked at the time. In the intervening period, the brocade weavers had left the khan and were practicing their craft in shops located at different places. The court considered the imperial decree in the hands of the masters null and void, determined their demands to be a breach of the Shari'a and warned them that they would be punished if they insisted in their unlawful demands.[22]

Case 8: Master artisans of the Silver Wire Workshop (*Simkeşhane*) had usufruct rights over its looms and could bequeath these rights to their sons by "ancient custom." Their position created a twofold problem. Since the masters did not allow the addition of new looms, the experienced apprentices could not advance to mastership unless they were sons of masters. At the same time, if a master died prematurely, leaving an improperly trained son, no son at all, or a son who did not want to practice his father's trade, then the deceased master's heirs and/or creditors could sell his looms to unqualified people not belonging to the group. Displeased with their prospects, the experienced apprentices forced the masters to make certain concessions through the arbitration of the district judge and the director of the Silver Wire Workshop. According to the new arrangement, masters could allow their experienced apprentices to become partners with them while the latter were simultaneously put, according to seniority, on a waiting list that specified the order of eligibility to purchase a loom (or the time share of a loom) once one became vacant by death, retirement, or sale by an heir. Inheritors of a loom who were not qualified to practice the trade had to sell it to the artisans on the waiting list at a fair price. If the deceased master had a young son, however, he kept the inherited loom, on the assumption that he might grow up to become a silver wire maker himself.[23]

---

[21] EEA, pp. 277–9, Ra 1173 [Nov. 1759].

[22] EEA, pp. 285–6, B 1174 [Feb. 1761].

[23] See CB 411, 8 S 1211 (16 Jan. 1796) along with CB 480, 12 Za 1172 (8 July 1759); CB 44, 9 M 1180 (17 April 1766); CB 381, 1 Ca 1218 (19 Aug. 1803); CB 15, 10 Ra 1224 (25 April 1809); CB 43, 9 S 1228 (4 Feb. 1813), and CB 5534, B 1234 (May 1819).

(b) *One Master against His Colleagues* The judges would rarely back a single master who consistently fell into dispute with his colleagues, so long as the latter made the necessary effort to maintain harmony within their respective group.

> *Case 9*: In 1761, a group of cloth bleachers (*al boyacı*) collectively rented workplaces on a long-term (*icareteyn*) lease in a site in Langa that belonged to the Laleli Mosque Foundation (*vakıf*). As the group expanded its business, it reached a new agreement with the foundation in 1782, increasing the number of their shops from twenty-two to thirty-four. One master, Hristo, emerged as the lone opponent of this new arrangement. He became angry with his colleagues, used "abominable language" against them, and left the group. Soon after, however, he returned to claim his shop. Although his colleagues had already given his shop to someone else, they made room for him after he pledged "to maintain harmonious relations with others in the group." However, he kept annoying his colleagues "with his hand and tongue." His colleagues expelled him from the trade and gave his place to two Yorgis to work in partnership. Hristo, whose real intention was to collect rent from the two Yorgis, tried to settle the issue through the jurist (*müfti*) in charge of the affairs of the Laleli Foundation. When his colleagues ignored his demands, he took them to the imperial court in 1787. The group responded with a counter petition, appearing collectively before the court in defense of the two Yorgis. After hearing the arguments of both sides and inspecting the original documents, the court decided that Hristo's claims were invalid and agreed with the group's view that Hristo's misbehavior merited his expulsion from the trade. He was warned not to disturb his former colleagues.[24]

In certain cases, however, the judges thought the single master had been acting within his rights although his colleagues, too, had a point in opposing his actions. In such cases, the reconciliation of the parties fell upon the judge. In the following case, the judge was trying to balance the objective of maintaining harmonious relations within a group with an individual's right to engage in gainful work in a shop space whose use-right belonged to his wife.

> *Case 10*: The cotton and linen yarn sellers of Istanbul constituted a distinct group that was bound by certain customs that regulated its relations with other groups who sold different kinds of yarn. There were twenty-two of these shops in Zindan Kapısı. One of the owners, Ebubekir, was an independent-minded person who tried to diversify the yarns he sold in his shop. His colleagues warned him against such

[24] CB 787, 27 Ş 1201 (14 June 1787). This file includes copies and summaries of other related documents.

> a practice and took him to the district court, where the judge made him pledge to obey the terms that bound his colleagues. He was "not the type to heed advice," however. He managed to obtain permission to convert the barbershop space owned by his wife in Zindan Kapısı to "another trade." Then, he began to sell yarn imported from Holland and India, along with the regular cotton and linen yarns of his trade, in this new shop in partnership with another person who was an "outsider" (*ecnebi*) to the trade. This time, his colleagues took him to the imperial court and demanded his expulsion from their ranks and the closure of his shops. The judges reconciled the parties. Ebubekir agreed to move his new business to "another place where it would not cause harm to his colleagues," to obey the steward and elders of his trade, and never again to sell imported yarns in Zindan Kapısı. His colleagues agreed to let him stay in the group.[25]

(c) *"Outsiders"* Cases 8 and 10 indicate that established groups opposed people who tried to work in their line of business without joining the group. Typically, the artisans referred to such people as "improperly trained and clumsy outsiders" (*pirperver ve sanʿat ehli olmayan ecanib*) who neither knew nor felt an obligation to honor the custom of the trade. In general, the courts tended to protect the interests of the established artisans against the "outsiders." This was especially the case when the artisans were able to act as a group in defense of their interests.

Typically, an organized group of artisans would claim that "outsiders" cheated consumers and suppliers alike, thereby undermining the integrity and credibility of the group, and discouraging merchants from supplying the necessary raw materials and commodities. Shortages resulted, prices increased, people (*ʿibadullah*, servants of God) suffered, and honest and competent artisans became destitute, unable to feed their families and unable to fulfill their obligations to the government.[26]

One Group against Another

Provisioning Istanbul's large population became a serious problem in the last quarter of the eighteenth and early in the nineteenth century.[27] Unorganized or loosely organized artisans felt disadvantaged in acquiring the raw materials they needed to pursue their trade.

[25] EEA, pp. 145–50, N 1247 (Feb. 1831).

[26] Cases are numerous. For some interesting cases obtained from the records of the Istanbul court in a slightly earlier period, see Aktepe (1958: 27–33).

[27] See Cİ 2131, 29 Za 1208 (26 June 1794), and CB 2020, Za 1225 (Nov. 1810).

This situation contributed to the proliferation of artisanal organizations. Artisans became better organized in smaller groups in an effort to secure their share of the raw materials, merchandise or of the market in a highly competitive environment. The settlement of the consequent disputes between and among the groups became an elaborate task for the courts. The following two cases illustrate that the judges had to consider the relative clout of the groups as much as the economic and legal validity of their arguments.

> *Case 11*: In 1775, the sellers of new shoes (*haffaf esnafi*) took the sellers of old shoes to the imperial court, accusing them of buying new shoes from the cobblers and selling them among their wares, "contrary to the established custom." The new-shoe sellers also claimed [against the basic rules of supply and demand] that the practice of the old-shoe sellers caused a shortage of shoes and an increase in prices. In defending themselves, the old-shoe sellers indicated that in fact the new-shoe sellers intruded into their line of business by selling old shoes along with new ones. The divan referred this case to the kadi of the district court of Istanbul. The kadi made the parties agree that henceforth they would never again intrude into each other's business.[28]

In another incident that involved the old-shoe sellers, however, the courts allowed revisions in business activity upon expert advice.

> *Case 12*: The *na'alçacıs* made a living by tipping boots with iron. There were more than 100 of them in Istanbul in the 1760s. By 1782, however, their number had shrunk to forty, and, according to their claim, they became destitute and indebted, unable to pay even for the raw materials of their trade, because the old-shoe sellers had "come up with the novelty of tipping boots with stout leather." The *na'alçacıs* took the old-shoe sellers to the imperial court, demanding that they stick to the buying and selling of old shoes "in accordance with the established custom" and quit tipping people's boots. The old-shoe sellers admitted that it was not their business to tip shoes, but since they always did some fixing of the old shoes they sold, they also tipped the shoes of their customers if they so desired. The court referred to the expertise of the head cobbler (*dikicibaşı*) to settle this dispute. Following the lines of his advice, the court reconciled the two parties by convincing the *na'alçacıs* that they should leave the old-shoe sellers alone, "since the people of Istanbul had obviously become accustomed to stout leather tips." For the same reason, and in order to avoid further loss of business, the *na'alçacıs*, too, should start offering leather tipping to their customers.[29]

---

[28] CB 6871, 29 C 1189 (27 Aug. 1775).

[29] The decision and decree of B 1196 (March 1782) quoted in CB 525, 16 Ş 1250 (24 June 1834).

Artisans and Proprietors[30]

Most of the work premises in Istanbul belonged to *vakıf*s (pious foundations). Wealthy individuals who contributed to the repair and maintenance of *vakıf* buildings acquired legally valid and government-backed perpetual leases that allowed them to enjoy a good share of the rental revenue of the *vakıf*s. The government encouraged these arrangements at first to help restore dilapidated *vakıf* properties but then also as a means of raising revenue to meet its growing fiscal needs, especially in the case of imperial *vakıf*s that were under indirect government supervision.

Legally speaking, the investors were proprietors of a perpetual use-right over *vakıf* property and entitled to demand rents at the going market rate (*ecr-i misil*). They and the *vakıf* managers began to pressure the artisans and traders to pay higher rents or to vacate the shops. The artisans and traders refused to comply and took their cases to the courts, arguing that they were no ordinary tenants. They emphasized that the shops in which they worked had been reserved for their trade by long custom and therefore could not be rented to others. However, appeal to custom was a weak legal argument against fair rent demands based on a perpetual lease. Consequently, the artisans tried to convince the courts that they, too, were entitled to a legal (*şerʿi*) perpetual use-right over the same property. The artisans argued that their productive activities added to the value of the *vakıf* property. More important, they wanted the courts to register their tools and other tangible investments in a shop as a fixed component of that shop, thus adding to its value and entitling them to perpetual usufruct. Furthermore, the artisans maintained that they kept the premises in good order and renovated them out of their own pockets, thus maintaining and enhancing their value in this way as well.

Finally, the artisans appealed to the logic of public benefit, adding one more layer of legal reasoning to their arguments against the proprietors' claims. The artisans maintained that if they were expelled from their shops or were obligated to pay higher rents, this would disrupt not only their and their families' livelihood but also harm other people. Merchants would encounter difficulty in collecting their

30 The following discussion is a summary of Akarlı (2004).

money and would feel reluctant to supply merchandise. Shortages and price increases would ensue and harm the populace (*ʿibadullah*). For the sake of public benefit (*nafʿan lil-ʿibad*), then, the government ought to prevent proprietors from raising rents.

The courts tried to verify, demarcate, balance and regulate, case by case, the respective rights and obligations of the artisans, *vakıfs*, perpetual lease holders, and the government over the same urban commercial site. The principal legal devices on which the courts relied to fulfill this task were, again, contractual arrangements among the parties involved in each case.

Punishment, Repression and Violence

In eighteenth-century Istanbul, the courts served as the main forum for conflict resolution and hence for the alleviation of tension in the marketplace. Both the courts and the executive organs of the state also employed coercive power to contain conflicts. I call the former "judicial punishment" and the latter "political intervention and repression."

Judicial punishment

Each artisan group was collectively responsible for the preservation of its custom and any agreement it reached with another party through the mediation of the courts. Quite often, these agreements indicated, implicitly or explicitly, the kinds of punishment awaiting those who would "dare to breach" them.[31] Price regulations (*narh nizamları*) constitute a version of such agreements. A price regulation was a periodically renegotiated agreement between the kadi, who represented the government, and the representatives of artisans. The market inspector was authorized to deal with those artisans and shopkeepers who breached the price regulations. He could inflict set fines

[31] See, for instance, CB 7598, Ş 1247 (Jan. 1832), which includes twenty such agreements dating from 12 Ra 1191 (20 May 1777)–25 Ca 1236 (28 Feb. 1821). For similar arrangements, see artisans working for the Imperial Mint (CB 350, 15 Ca 1176 [1 Jan. 1763], and CB 285, 22 C 1183 [23 Oct. 1769]); the snuff sellers (CB 4771, 4 Ş 1196 [15 July 1782]); and owners of taverns and small wine shops (CB 735, 12 C 1222 [17 Aug. 1807]).

and punishments on them if they were caught red-handed or acknowledged their mistake. One of the duties of the district judge was to prevent the market inspectors from abusing their authority.[32]

If an artisan deviated from the agreed-upon custom and regulations, his colleagues would take him to court, unless they brought him into line by their own means. The first time such a person appeared before him, the kadi normally would rebuke him and make him pledge his word of honor not to repeat his mistake but to work in harmony with his colleagues. Repeat offenders, however, were regarded as obdurate people who would heed no advice and therefore deserved to be punished. The stewards and the kadis had the authority to fine such people. In addition, the kadis might sentence them to short terms of imprisonment in Istanbul and/or decide to expel them from the trade if their colleagues agreed on such a measure.[33]

In principle, only the sovereign had the right to mete out severe punishments, such as banishment from Istanbul.[34] In these cases, normally, first the judges of the divan, or another judge authorized by the divan, had to undertake the necessary investigation and interrogations to ascertain the guilt of the accused. The judge reported his decision to the divan, which submitted it to the palace for approval.

> *Case 13*: Flour sellers took their steward, Mustafa, to the district court for oppressing his colleagues. The kadi agreed to expel him from the trade. However, Mustafa managed to rejoin the group and adopted a spiteful attitude toward his colleagues. They took him to the divan this time (in 1733), requesting his unconditional expulsion and banishment from Istanbul "for our well-being and the orderly conduct of our affairs." The divan judge summarized the complaints of the artisans and the previous court decision and submitted his statement, without additional comment, for the sultan's approval. The sultan decided that Mustafa should be banished to Bozcaada.[35]

---

[32] Kütükoğlu (1983); Osman Nuri (1922), 1:327–34; and Heyd (1973:229–34). Also see Osman Nuri (1922], 1:393–470).

[33] See Osman Nuri (1922), 1:637–42 and Cases 9–10 above. Also, the imperial court records provide indirect information on relatively light punishments when they refer to the background of repeat offenders who ultimately deserved a severe punishment.

[34] For a list of the deterrence (*ta'zir*) offenses that were subject to the sultan's approval and discretion, see Cin and Akgündüz (1989:276–82).

[35] CB 1017, 22 Za 1145 (6 May 1733). At this time, Istanbul was still recovering from the confusions of 1730.

Case 14: In 1791, a group of greengrocers petitioned the sultan requesting the punishment of five colleagues who were engaged in black marketeering. The sultan ordered (through the divan) the kadi of Istanbul to summon to his court the petitioners, the steward and other elders of the greengrocers as well as the accused, to inquire into the truth of the matter. One of the accused fled, but the others were brought to the court. They acknowledged the accusations directed against them. In his decision (*iʿlam*) addressed to the sultan, the kadi summarized the results of his inquiries. He recommended the unconditional prevention of the five accused from working as greengrocers in Istanbul again as well as the twisting of their ears and their punishment as a deterrent to others. The sultan ordered their banishment to Bozcaada.[36]

Case 15: Ahmed and Mehmed Sadık Ustas were waterwheel makers who had already been banished to Bozcaada briefly for "oppressing" their colleagues. Upon their return, they continued to act in ways that "disturbed the harmony and order of the group." Their colleagues took them to the divan, where it was decided that the evidence manifested that "discord and mischief making were in the nature of these two individuals." Their punishment and correction were, therefore, in order and important. The sultan approved their banishment to Bozcaada again, as a "deterrent to others."[37]

Political Intervention and Repression

If the persons against whom the judgments were imposed in the cases mentioned above thought of the punishment inflicted on them as unjust, it is unlikely that they would have found many sympathetic ears. Their punishment emerged in a legal process in which their peers actively participated. There were times and cases when the military and administrative authorities resorted to blunt coercive power, or threatened to do so in the name of public peace and order (*maslahat-ı ʿamme ve nizam-ı memleket*) against those who caused discord (*müfsid*) and harmed the people (*muzır lil-ʿibad*).

Case 16: In 1794, the sultan, by his own discretion, ordered the banishment of the steward of the butchers to Rhodes and that of two other butchers to Limnos. In his decree, the sultan speaks thus: "It is manifest to me that there exist among the butchers some avaricious, dishonest, and discordant (*müfsid*) people who defy the ancient custom of their trade and cause shortages of meat for the inhabitants of Istanbul.

---

[36] CB 675, 3 Za 1205 (4 July 1791).
[37] CB 1259, 15 Ra 1218 (5 May 1803).

I have asked the head of my palace doorkeepers, who also oversees the provisioning of meat, to talk to the steward and elders of the butchers and to bring to their attention that it is incumbent upon them to conduct the affairs of their trade properly and to punish their colleagues who defy the custom and regulations of their trade . . . He duly warned them—above all, their steward Hacı Emin—and asked them to convey "my will to every single butcher." However, my investigations indicate that, far from acting accordingly and making an effort to prevent the misdeeds [of his colleagues], this Hacı Emin is himself involved in misdeeds. So I have ordered his arrest and expulsion to Rhodes in order to punish him and to intimidate (*terhiben*) other butchers." In two accompanying decrees, the sultan ordered the banishment of two other butchers to Limnos for similar reasons and to put fear into other butchers' hearts.[38]

Case 17: In 1809, the sultan issued orders for the arrest and banishment of Salih, an olive-oil seller, because it was confirmed that instead of minding his own business like everybody else, Salih caused discord (*ifsad*) among olive-oil sellers and instigated (*tahrik*) them to keep the prices high. He ought to be punished in order to intimidate and chastise (*terhib ü te'dib*) the likes of him. He ordered his banishment to Karahisar-ı Sahib under strict supervision, forbidding him from taking even a single step to go to another place.[39]

Case 18: In 1814, Sultan Mahmud II issued a "blank-sheet imperial decree" [i.e. a decree emanating directly from the palace, without being initiated by any court] that stipulated an administrative solution to a protracted legal dispute among three different groups of cloth dyers concerning the types of cloth they were supposed to dye. In 1812, the sultan had decided on a new arrangement of the affairs of cloth dyers following "long investigations and due consultation with some experts." This arrangement abolished all differences among the subgroups and raised the rents they paid to a pious foundation established to finance military reforms. However, ten of the dyers refused to abide by this administrative decision, thus inviting Mahmud II's fury. In his new decree, he scolded these dyers for claiming the validity of the old legal documents that affirmed their old custom. He added, "What does it mean to act in defiance of my decree . . .? I did not write what is in it off the top of my head, without reflection. I made that arrangement after having examined all [aspects of the issue]. Destroy the documents in their hands and issue them new ones . . . If any of the dyers dares to resist let me know! The new order will surely hold, once a few of them are hanged!"[40]

---

[38] CB 2802 (1–10 C 1208) (4–14 Jan. 1794).

[39] Cİ 1935, 1–10 Ş 1224 (18–28 March 1809). For similar cases, which involved a tailor and three bakers, respectively, see CZ 3710, 1–10 Z 1207 (10–20 July 1793), and CB 4370, 18 B 1252 (9 Nov. 1835).

[40] EEA, pp. 184–7, Za 1229 (Oct.-Nov. 1814).

These cases differ from Cases 13–15 in two ways. First, they represent acts of administrative fiat, although they refer to certain legal concepts, suggesting some adherence to legality. Second, they involve decisions intended to intimidate a particular segment of the civilian population and to strike fear in people's hearts or to coerce them to obey an arrangement in the drafting of which they had not been consulted, contrary to the custom of the marketplace. There were also unusual times when artisans were actually treated summarily and hung as rebels.

> *Case 19*: A case in point appears in a document in which the grand vizier explains to the sultan "the reasons behind the exigent execution of [two] non-Muslims [the other day] (*haklarında icra-yı siyaset olunan zimmilerin sebeb-i katilleri*). This long document involves a dispute between the bakers and the executive authorities over the price, weight and quality of bread. Clearly, the government had demanded conditions that the bakers could not fulfill under the prevailing circumstances. Although the government made some concessions, the bakers remained unsatisfied. Muslim and non-Muslim alike, they gathered to plead their case at the divan. When they were not allowed to do so, they went to the residences of the kadi of Istanbul and the sheikh ul-Islam (chief jurist) to express their grievances. The kadi and the sheikh ul-Islam tried to mollify them, in vain. Hundreds of bakers embarked on large boats to present a petition to the sultan in person when he took his regular walk at the imperial landing site. The bakers just missed the sultan, who had come to the site a little earlier than usual that day. All along, the grand vizier thought that further concessions would spoil the bakers and cause harm to the people (*ʿibadullahı ızrar*). Furthermore, he held that these demonstrations resulted from the agitation (*ifsad ve tahrik*) of only a few instigators (*baʿis-i fesad*). Consequently, he decided to arrest the instigators and to hang two of them summarily as a lesson to others. According to the grand vizier, "Ever since that day there has been neither a complaint nor idle talk. Praise be to God, breads are made like white roses and the people's blessings for your imperial majesty have reached the peak."
>
> The sultan responded to this letter thus: "My [dear] vizier, you are my vizier, the regulator of my state and trusted representative. Pursuit of proper arrangement of the conditions of the people and the attraction of the perpetual prayers of all of them for me are entrusted to you. And my prayers are with you; I accept [the explanation]."[41]

There is no date on this document, as if the incident it records occurred beyond history, beyond the normal flow of life when legal

---

[41] CB 2195, no date.

(*şerʿi*) principles remained the norm. Sultanic custom allowed exigent punishment in order to enforce discipline in military and administrative ranks. The jurists justified the practice as a necessary measure to protect the people from the excesses and oppression (*zulüm, mezalim*) of those who wielded power over them. Their application to the civilian population, except under the unusual circumstances of fighting armed rebels and armed criminals, would undermine the very purpose they were supposed to serve, namely, the protection of the servants of God from oppression at the hands of the servants of the state and the sultan. The vizier in Case 19 circumvented the due legal process and arbitrarily ordered the execution of two individuals to set an example for all protestors. His characterization of the petitioners as rebels causing harm to the public (*ʿibadullah*) represents a testimony to the law's intent. The vizier's action itself, however, was political in nature and verged on *zulüm*, cruel and unjustifiable oppression that was conceived as the opposite of justice. Otherwise, it was religiously and legally incumbent upon the ruler to hear and respond to the complaints of the people, Muslim and non-Muslim alike, so that he might win their blessings, as the sultan himself acknowledged that he should.[42]

Violence

The basic notions of legitimacy that generated a sense of governmental responsibility, however imperfect, also inspired resistance and revolt. Many sultans, not to mention viziers and other top administrators, were deposed and killed amid demands for justice. Whether such murders and depositions were deserved or not, they clearly showed that people did not see the sovereign or his executive representatives to be above the "law." These revolts as well were violent aberrations in the normal flow of life.

The sultan in Case 19 was probably Mustafa IV,[43] who ruled briefly in 1807–1808 amid coups, countercoups, and killings of sultans and viziers. These were difficult times, comparable to the situ-

[42] See Heyd (1973:227); Mumcu (1985), and Aydın (1999:67–77). Cf. Faroqhi (1992).

[43] The cataloguer of CB 2195 suggests that the case might be from Selim III's reign (1789–1807). Mübahat Kütükoğlu, the leading expert of this period, holds that most likely it dates from Mustafa IV's reign (1807–1808).

ation in 1730, when artisans and shopkeepers actively participated in political protests that led to the deposition of the reigning sultan. Whether or not the artisans and shopkeepers of Istanbul had been as actively involved in the events of 1807–1808,[44] the new sultan, Mahmud II (1808–1839), and his advisors adopted generally conciliatory policies toward the artisans. However, this relationship was not always a smooth one. Case 18 illustrates the sultan's eagerness to "regulate" the affairs of the artisans, and not always in full consultation with them. Mahmud's increasingly bureaucratic and efficient administration meant higher taxes and dues for artisans. They organized massive demonstrations to resist a new wave of tax hikes and bureaucratic measures in 1837–38. Mahmud felt obliged to reduce the tax rates but did not compromise the new bureaucratic system that he was building.[45]

Conclusion

These nineteen cases illustrate certain concepts that artisans frequently used in their appeals to the courts as well as the already highlighted features of the Ottoman judicial system. Artisans appealed to the duty of the government to preserve the good (*menfaʿat*) of God's servants—as in the expression of "*nafʿan lil-ʿibad.*" According to the Islamic (and Ottoman) legal tradition, the good of the populace meant a life pleasing to God, which required the protection of religion (*din*), life (*nefis*), reason (*ʿakıl*), progeny (*nesil*), and "property" (*mal*). A legitimate government was expected to sustain and protect these exigencies (*zaruriyat*) of civic life.[46]

The Ottoman documents leave little doubt that all subjects of the state, Muslim and non-Muslim, were cognizant of their basic rights. In other words, "religion" meant all religions recognized by Islam, hence entitling all subjects adhering to these religions to the exigencies

[44] See note 3 above, and Olson (1977). See also Cevdet (1891–2), 8:139–75. Selim III's policies were not always friendly toward the artisans. He sided with proprietors in their rent disputes with artisans, resisted the artisans' efforts to freeze the number of shops in their trade, and tried to curtail their efforts to win fixed usufruct rights over the shops they rented. See Akarlı (2004).

[45] Osman Nuri, 1:335–64, and 375–92.

[46] See Hallaq (1997), 89–90 and 168–74, and Baktır (1982), esp. 175–80, for an introduction and the classical sources.

of civic life. "Property" meant, in the historical context and documents covered here, rightful gain and the basic means of livelihood to assure rightful gain.[47] "Reason," an abstract concept in theory, acquires a quite tangible meaning in Ottoman legal documents, i.e., a reasonably secure and harmonious social order that assured predictability and enabled human beings to live in moderation.

Exigencies could clearly conflict, thereby undermining the desired social harmony. For instance, bequeathing one's property, such as tools or use-right over a shop, was a derivative of the right to progeny. If this right interfered with another person's right to practice a trade in order to earn a livelihood corresponding to his skills (as in Case 8), how should the difference be resolved? Who should decide when one's right to collect fair rent on an investment or to establish one's own business might undermine another person's ability to make ends meet? In short, how should the basic rights be balanced and harmonized?

Judging by the experience of eighteenth-century Istanbul artisans and traders, the fundamental Ottoman response to this inherently political challenge was the cultivation of and adherence to an accommodational legal culture. Recognition of the autonomy of organized groups and a legal process that facilitated negotiated resolution of disputes were manifestations of this culture. The legal process relied on contracts as a major device to assure settlements. Case by case, judges tried to verify, demarcate and balance the respective rights and obligations of each party to a dispute, if the parties had not already done this by their own means and come to the court merely to register their agreement. Even when the judge had to settle a case by resorting to his decisive legal authority, he would formulate the final sentence in the form of an agreement guaranteed by all the parties involved. The *kazasker*s and other commissioned senior judges played a crucial role in this process. They heard cases that required authoritative interpretation of legal principles and injunctions with a view to overall public good and harmony (*maslahat-ı ʿamme*).

Punishment of persistent discord and mischief (*mefsedet, fesad*) was a corollary of the commitment to public good and harmony. In deciding what constituted mischief and how severely such an act should be punished, the Ottoman legal practice allowed, under the

---

[47] Also see Akarlı (2004), which emphasizes the notion of "property."

supervision of judges, a significant degree of responsibility to people to whom such decisions would apply. The contractual arrangements effected through the legal system often involved the terms of punishment that would apply to those who contravened the arrangement to which they agreed.

The ultimate responsibility for protecting and sustaining the social peace and public good belonged to the sovereign. It was his prerogative, therefore, to ratify the contractual legal arrangements that required the interpretation and balancing of the legal principles or the severe punishments decided by the courts. For the sake of "public good," the sovereign could authorize regulations of a broader application than the contractual arrangements made through the legal process. Provincial laws (*kanun*s) that regulated tax and land-tenure relations between the civilian population and the imperial treasury were of this nature. The senior judges and jurists played a leading role in the preparation of such regulations as well, again taking into consideration the Islamic legal principles, on the one hand, and local customs and conditions as established by consultations with the representatives of the local population, on the other.[48]

This often overlooked interactive dimension of the Ottoman laws and legal practice that applied to the civilian population becomes vivid in the imperial decrees concerning the artisans and the shopkeepers of eighteenth-century Istanbul. These decrees, which had the force of a government regulation, were simultaneously self-regulating, albeit in varying degrees. The Ottoman judges oversaw and guided the process. The courts made and remade the laws, in the practical sense of the notion of law as binding provisions, with the participation of those actors to whom the provisions would apply. As such the judges and the courts served as a bridge between the government and the governed and helped maintain the legitimacy of the government.

Intensification of struggles over the distribution of increasingly scarce resources in the last quarter of the eighteenth and the beginnings of the nineteenth century led to cumbersome arrangements, straining the capacity of the courts and the judges to accommodate differences effectively and enduringly. This development, combined

[48] İnalcık's various works make this point clear. A similar example is the city-wide price regulations (see note 32).

with the rise of new notions of government and law, gradually marginalized the interactive judicial processes that helped connect the formulations of public interest to the "public" to which it applied. Administrative decisions began to define public benefit, which became increasingly hard to distinguish from *raison d'état.*[49]

[49] For a broad assessment of developments in the nineteenth century, see Akarlı (2002:261–84). This article summarizes my position, based on detailed research published earlier. For a critical assessment of my position, see H. İslamoğlu and Peter Purdue (2001). For an important assessment of the secularist aspects of legal reforms, see T. Asad (2003, esp. chapter 7).

CHAPTER ELEVEN

ON JUDICIAL HIERARCHY IN THE OTTOMAN EMPIRE: THE CASE OF SOFIA FROM THE SEVENTEENTH TO THE BEGINNING OF THE EIGHTEENTH CENTURY*

Rossitsa Gradeva

The problem of hierarchy and appeal has long attracted the attention of specialists in Islam and Islamic law. Some scholars are concerned mainly with the evolution of the Islamic legal theory during the classical period and in various parts of the Muslim world. Others discuss the formation of appellate institutions in Muslim states across the centuries and the emergence (or not) of judicial hierarchies in Muslim polities. The prevailing view among them, for most of the twentieth century, has been that there are no appellate structures in the Islamic legal system, that a kadi's decisions are final and irrevocable, and that a judgment may not be revised under any circumstances.[1]

The view that Islamic law does not allow for revision of a judgment has been subjected to criticism and modification. One of the first to point to the possibility of judicial review was J. Schacht, who identified three "higher instances" in *fikh* half a century ago. While acknowledging that these "instances" afford certain possibilities for the revision of judgments, Schacht concluded that Islamic legal theory does not allow for such revision (Schacht 1991, 6:1). This view has recently been challenged by B. Johansen, who discusses four ways in which a kadi judgment may be revised. According to Johansen, these procedures were established during the classical period of Hanafi law and one finds mention of them in *fetva* collections of the Ottoman period. In addition, the Ottoman *muftis* seem to have developed new arguments and procedures that made it possible for the parties to a

* I wish to thank Prof. Michael Ursinus, Prof. Leslie Peirce, and the editors of this volume for a critical reading of earlier drafts of this paper.

[1] See Tyan 1955, 236–43; idem 1960, 100–12, 119–55; idem 1973, 4:373; Schacht 1991, 6:1–2; Liebesney 1975, 240. Cf. also the analysis of Western views on judicial review in Islam in Powers 1992, 316–17, 329.

dispute to continue their litigation after the kadi issued his judgment. Thus, the fact that there were no appellate institutions in Islamic law did not mean that the kadi's judgment was final and irreversible (Johansen 1990, 15–17).

According to the Western scholarship, Islamic law never developed formal, hierarchical structures for the purposes of judicial review. Indeed, as early as the ninth century, the Abbasids established the so-called *mazalim* court, headed by the caliph, with his agents or judges specially appointed to it. One of the main functions of this tribunal was to overturn a kadi's decision and it thus may be regarded as a kind of appellate institution. However, since the *mazalim* court existed largely outside Islamic law, Western Islamicists consider it a secular jurisdiction that operated alongside the kadi courts, and, hence, it was not part of a true judicial hierarchy.[2]

Based on the Western scholarship in the field M. Shapiro has approached the problem of appeal in Islam from a different angle. Taking for granted the absence of appeal in Islamic law, he discusses the institutional and cultural reasons why Islamic legal culture did not develop a judicial hierarchy. He argues that there did in fact exist "a system of appeal by trial *de novo* conducted by the delegating authority" (the recorded instances of caliphs reversing decisions of a kadi or sending a case back to him with new instructions). Subsequently, however, this appellate system was disrupted for various reasons (Shapiro 1981, 211). Yet, in those exceptional cases in which Islamic law and a hierarchical government intersected in a relatively stable and long-term way, we encounter appeal in the Muslim world—the *mazalim* court established by the Abbasids and the Imperial Divan of the Ottoman sultans. Shapiro writes that although

> the kadis played an extremely important role in the Ottoman constitution, they were far removed from the central channels of the sultan's authority . . . [because] they were deeply embedded in that portion of Ottoman society mostly insulated from the sultan's absolutist pretensions, namely the traditional Islamic community of notables and learned men. The sultans did, nonetheless, seek to impose their control over the kadis by both a hierarchical personnel system and an appeals system culminating in the person of the sultan. Both of these

[2] Tyan 1973, 4:374; Schacht 1991, 6:2; on the *mazalim* court under the Mamluks, see Nielsen 1985.

> devices seem to have been relatively ineffective, however, precisely because they operated at the farthest and weakest reaches of the sultan's power (Shapiro 1981, 220).

More recently D. Powers has reexamined Islamic legal theory and court practice in fourteenth-century Morocco. He concluded that the Maliki *madhhab* does allow for the reconsideration of a judicial decision and has developed a system of successor review in which a judge might reconsider and overturn a judgment issued by his predecessor, albeit under limited and precisely defined conditions. There is also evidence to suggest that the court of the chief judge of the capital city functioned as a court of review for the decisions of local and provincial judges. Powers discerns the

> outlines of a rudimentary structure comprising at least three levels: provincial courts, the court of the chief judge, and the *mazalim* court. The distinctive characteristic of Islamic judicial review . . . is its relative *informality*, the wide opportunity that it gives to the individual to negotiate with the judicial authorities and to manipulate the system to one's personal advantage, and the instrumental role the *mufti* played in the review process (Powers 1992, 336–7).

While working on the profile of the kadi of Sofia in the sixteenth and seventeenth centuries (Gradeva 2002a, 265–92), I have been surprised by the frequent appearance of officials in the *sicill*s who bear the title of "kadi" but who were not titular holders of the post in Sofia. The cases in which they participated or are mentioned permit us to discern a hierarchical relationship between the kadi in Sofia and his colleagues in the province of Rumili. Here I propose a preliminary study of these "professional" contacts between the *molla* (that is, holder of *mevleviyet*) in the provincial capital city and lower-ranking judges, and of the formation of an embryonic hierarchy among kadis in which the judge located in the centre of a province had some supervisory functions over lower-ranking judges in the same administrative unit. I shall trace the emergence of the *mevleviyet* (jurisdiction of a high-ranking Sharia judge in the Ottoman state) in Sofia, which in all probability was a direct result of the importance of the city as the centre of an Ottoman province. I consider the combination of the importance of the Sofian kadi as an administrative officer and the possibility for cooperation with the governor of Rumili as a major factor that led to the acquisition of additional functions by the Sofian kadi with respect to lower-ranking kadis in the province.

One of the major changes introduced by the Ottomans was the full integration of the *ulema* within the ranks of the state administration.[3] As early as the fifteenth century, teachers and judges were not only regarded as state officials who received upon appointment a patent (*berat*) describing all the prerogatives and functions granted to them by the sultan, but also were graded according to their (honorary) status and salary. Even provincial *mufti*s were considered part of the state apparatus and treated as members of the administration.[4] This is not surprising if we bear in mind that the same applied to *dervişe*s who received a *berat* and hence imperial sanction upon assuming the post of *şeyh* (Gradeva & Ivanova 2001, 324–5). The integration of the *ulema* into the state administration and the elaboration of a hierarchy within its ranks evolved throughout the Ottoman period from the fourteenth till the early twentieth century. Within this hierarchy, according to the standard view, equality in the competencies of kadis of all ranks was maintained and the different grades were honorary designations more than anything else. Higher-ranking kadis, the *molla*s, received (much) higher salaries, and these positions gradually were closed to most "ordinary" kadis. The *mevleviyet*s evolved into almost exclusively family "enterprises" (Itzkowitz 1962, 91–2; Faroqhi 1973, 216–7; Gibb and Bowen 1963, 107). In theory, the development of a judicial hierarchy in the Ottoman state did not entail an expansion of the prerogatives of higher judges at the expense of ordinary ones. The *mevleviyet*, or *mollaship*, found expression in a higher salary and higher prestige, and in access to higher ranks in the Ottoman ruling institution.[5]

---

[3] On the incorporation of the *ulema* into the Ottoman ruling institution, see the classical works of d'Ohsson 1790, 2:268ff; Uzunçarşılı 1964, 96ff.

[4] The status and function of provincial *mufti*s in the Balkans have not received their due attention. See some notes in Walsh 1965, 2:866–7; Masud, Messick, Powers 1996, 12–13; Repp 1986, 62–8. See also Gradeva 2000, 43–4, and the studies mentioned there. Powers points to a similar process in Morocco: "During the second half of the fourteenth century, the office of *mufti* came under the control of the state and began to play an increasingly active role in the administration of justice. By the end of the century, many *mufti*s were appointed by the government, with the result that their power, authority, and prestige came to exceed that of qadis." Powers 1992, 328. The latter process, however, is not witnessed in the Ottoman empire.

[5] See for example El-Nahal 1979, 17, who says: "Internally, the judiciary was organized into a hierarchy of ranks, but for promotional purposes only."

The Kadilik of Sofia

During the period between the fifteenth and seventeenth centuries, the military-administrative and the judicial institutions underwent continuous change, as did the balance of power between new social groups in the provinces and the central authority. Until the early eighteenth century the Ottoman learned institution was repeatedly re-organised and re-structured, and the *kadilik* of Sofia was no exception. R. Repp has convincingly argued that there were no *mevleviyet*s in Sofia, Filibe (Plovdiv, Bulgaria) and Selânik (Thessaloniki, Greece) in the fifteenth century, although he provides no evidence for Filibe and Sofia.[6] Information about the status of the *kadilik* of Sofia prior to the seventeenth century is scanty, scattered in various sources, and often indirect. There is no doubt, however, that once Sofia became the centre of the Rumili *beylerbeylik*/*eyalet* (province), some time in the middle of the fifteenth century, the Sofia judgeship came to enjoy high prestige. For instance, towards the end of the fifteenth century the future Grand Vezir, Piri Mehmed Paşa (d. 1532), began his career in Sofia as a Sharia judge, subsequently moving to Silivri (Turkey), Siruz (Serrai, Greece) and Galata (part of Istanbul).[7]

Unfortunately we have only a few names and even fewer biographies of sixteenth-century Sofian kadis. The biographies of two of the known kadis are relevant to the present investigation. After earning the sultan's favour, Abdi Efendi (d. 1553), who apparently was a member of an eminent family, was appointed as kadi with a salary of 50 *akçe* per day. He was later promoted to the kadiliks of Siruz, Üsküb (Skopje, Macedonia) and, finally, Sofia, where he died while in office (Hammer-Purgstall 1838, 2:268). Hüsrev Efendi (d. 1559–60), also from a family of outstanding scholars, first taught at his grandfather's *medrese* and later became kadi of Selânik, Filibe, Yenişehir (Larissa, Greece), Sofia, Üsküb and, finally, in 1552–3, Galata (Baltacı 1976, 103–4). Fragmentary evidence about an unknown Sofian kadi

[6] Repp 1986, 45. In his extensive study of the Ottoman learned institution, I. H. Uzunçarşılı takes the situation in the seventeenth century as applying also to the fifteenth century. Uzunçarşılı 1964, 96.

[7] Piri Mehmed Paşa (?–1532) was a member of an outstanding *ulema* family from Aksaray which settled in Amasya. For additional biographical details, see *Islâm Ansiklopedisi* 1994, 9:559–61; Süreyya 1996, 4:1335.

reveals a similar career pattern. According to the vita of the Christian neo-martyr, St Nikolay the New of Sofia, his trial in Sofia in the spring of 1555 began without a kadi, because the previous kadi had been recalled to the capital and his successor had not yet made his way to Sofia from Üsküb (Gradeva 2000, 46–7).

Although scanty, these data do support R. Repp's thesis that in the first quarter of the sixteenth century there existed an intermediate grade of *kadilik*s that was lower than the kadiships of the capital cities, Istanbul, Edirne and Bursa, and were *mevleviyet*s in a wider, honorary sense (Repp 1986, 45). It is possible to identify Balkan cities whose kadis belonged to it prior to the decade between 1560–1570: Üsküb, Selânik, Filibe, Yenişehir, Siruz, and Sofia. This list, which may possibly be extended to other Balkan towns, was limited geographically to Rumili. In all probability these *kadilik*s were the highest grade within the provincial hierarchy of judgeships. A kadi did not ascend from one of these posts to a position in Istanbul, Bursa or Edirne, or to the *kadiaskerlik*. In the period between the opening of the Sahn (the highest grade in the Ottoman educational system during the second half of the fifteenth and the beginning of the sixteenth centuries) by Mehmed II (1451–1481) and the middle of the sixteenth century, it seems that only scholars who taught at the Sahn and a few other imperial *medrese*s were promoted to the highest judicial offices in the empire. The known Sofian Sharia judges of that period seem not to have reached such a high level during their teaching careers.

Towards the middle of the sixteenth century, some cities in the newly conquered Arabic lands were elevated to the grade of *mevleviyet*. Other cities were added to the list during the last decades of that century (Repp 1986, 45–8). Beginning in the seventeenth century kadis moved from an ordinary *kadilik* to a *mevleviyet* only occasionally—by special favour of the sultan or as a result of important connections to the high *ulema* and/or the high administration (Gradeva 2002-a, passim). The biographies of judges who lived and worked at the turn of the seventeenth century indicate that the above-mentioned group of Balkan cities had already been divided into two distinct grades. Some of the kadiships became *mevleviyet*s, while others remained ordinary ones. As early as 1575, Selânik (and perhaps other towns) had become the seat of *molla*s (that is, a *mevleviyet*), while Üsküb and Siruz remained ordinary *kadilik*s, albeit in the highest-ranking group among them.[8] It is clear that some change in the status of the Sofian *kadilik* also occurred at that time.

It is difficult to determine exactly when and why Sofia became a *mevleviyet*. The explanation given by Koçu Bey in one of his *Risales* (treatises) of 1640 seems plausible:

> Whatever great provinces (*eyaletler*) there are in the divinely-protected [i.e. Ottoman] dominions, such as Egypt, Aleppo, Diyarbakır, Damascus, Erzurum, Selânik, Budin (Buda, Hungary), Sofia, Bursa, Edirne, Istanbul—[the kadis of] all such as these are 500-*akçe Mollas* (Quoted from Repp 1986, 35).

It is not clear whether the promotion of the city to a *mevleviyet* also meant an enlargement of the territory of the *kadilik*, as was the case with Selânik (Repp 1986, 45). It seems certain that the kadi of Sofia did not combine his functions with those of the *mufti* in the city.[9] Sofia, the administrative centre of Rumili, was probably regarded as a lucrative assignment by high judges. According to the available biographies, the *kadilik* of Sofia was permanently integrated into the *mevleviyet* grade of the judicial hierarchy as early as the first decade of the seventeenth century, probably a little earlier.

The *mevleviyets* themselves were also arranged in a hierarchy. Several lists from the seventeenth century reveal that occasionally one *mevleviyet* rose or declined in this honorary hierarchy, which, however, had a practical manifestation. Kadis who began their judicial careers

---

[8] According to a *ruzname* (daily cash-book) of 1667–8, both Üsküb and Siruz were among the *Menasib-i Sitte-i Aliye*, that is the highest grade among ordinary kadis, the former with 300–*akçe* daily salary, the latter with 499-*akçe* daily salary. Özergin 1976, 259, 271, 292. Another undated, but certainly seventeenth-century, list of the *kadiliks* in Rumeli indicates that the kadis of these two cities were among the best-paid and highest-ranking in the European provinces. Neither list contains *mevleviyets* such as Sofia, Selânik or Filibe. See Natsionalna Biblioteka "Sv. Sv. Kiril i Metodii" (NBKM), Or. Dept., Or 435, the last three folios.

[9] The biographies of several Sofian *muftis* indicate that the *muftis* were usually different persons from the kadis of the town. After a career as a *müderris*, Emini Mehmed Efendi was appointed *mufti* of Sofia (end of 1050/April 1641). Three months later he received his first apointment as *molla* in Lefkoşa (Nicosia, Cyprus) and remained a high judge to the end of his life. Uğur 1986, 295. See also ibid., 470–1: "Sofya *muftisi* Ebussuud Efendi" who received the post after teaching at a 40-*akçe medrese*. Afterwards (in 1081/1671) he joined the judicial institution as kadi of Lefkoşa, and later of Trablus-i Şam. Selânik, too, had a *mufti*, usually a different man than the kadi. See for example, Şerhi Mehmed Efendi. Ibid., 242. So did Üsküb. According to Ata'i, Pir Mehmed, "the best of the provincial *muftis*", served for many years and died there in 1611–2. Quoted from Heyd 1973, 175, n. 6.

at the bottom of the *mevleviyet* hierarchy had little chance of reaching the highest and most respected posts in the judicial institution. The judicial paths of the kadis of Sofia during the seventeenth century reveal that the kadiship of Sofia ranked just below the *mevleviyet*s of Diyarbakır, Kayseri, and Manisa (all in modern Turkey); and just above the *mevleviyet*s of Belgrade, Bosna Saray (Sarajevo) and Sakız (Chios, Greece). All of these *mevleviyet*s, however, were in the lower half of this ladder. Baghdad, Filibe and Izmir were probably the highest-ranking *mevleviyet*s that a Sharia judge in Sofia could hope to obtain. Occasionally the kadis of Sofia received appointments to Kuds-i Şerif (Jerusalem), Medina and Bursa, but these seem to have been the exception rather than the rule. In the seventeenth century, a Sofian kadi could not advance to Edirne or Mecca, although one judge appointed in Sofia had "the *paye* (rank) of Mecca" (Uğur 1986, lix; Gradeva 2002a, passim).

The typical kadi of Sofia was an Ottoman man from any of the extensive provinces—who had received his education in a prestigious *medrese* under the instruction of prestigious professors, and who then pursued a career as a professor in equally prestigious institutions, mainly in the capital, before entering the judiciary. Alternatively, he might owe his career to networks formed by birth, marriage or friendship. The *molla* of Sofia in the seventeenth century might be an authoritative and respected scholar but he could also be a corrupt judge. Whatever his personal qualities and professional qualifications, however, the Sofian kadi, together with his colleagues throughout the empire, maintained the territorial, administrative and legal unity of the Ottoman state (Gradeva 1999a, 177–90). We should add that the kadi, including that of Sofia, was one of the most important provincial officers (Gerber 1994, 16) in the Ottoman Balkans and he was entrusted with a variety of duties that need not be listed here. The Sharia judge embodied the unity of the empire, serving as the "eyes and ears" of the sultan, exercising control over markets and the crafts, the levying of taxes, the *timar* system, *vakıf*s, the mobilisation of soldiers during military campaigns, and the religious institutions of non-Muslims (Gradeva 1999b, 162–204).

Supervisory Functions and Judicial Appeal

From the middle of the fifteenth century until 1836, Sofia was the official seat of the *beylerbey* (governor; towards the end of the seventeenth century this title changed to *vali*) of Rumili, the most important European province of the Empire.[10] The governor of Rumili was generally regarded as one of the highest-ranking officials in the Ottoman state who might even attend sessions of the Imperial Council (Divan) in Istanbul. The combination of Sofia's high judicial rank (*mevleviyet*) and its status as centre of the *eyalet* best explain why the kadi of Sofia developed certain supervisory prerogatives over lower-level kadis in the *eyalet*, particularly those adjacent to Sofia.

My basic sources for the study of the relations between the kadi of Sofia and the local Sharia judges are the *sicill*s of the Sofian Sharia court preserved in Sofia,[11] and the *Mühimme defter*s (registers of important matters),[12] which contain the sultans' orders to the provincial administration. Whenever possible, I compare the situation in Sofia with that in other parts of the empire and attempt to explain why an intermediate judicial rank emerged between the ordinary Sharia judge and the central authority.

1. Documents issued by kadis of other *kaza*s in the province that are recorded in the *sicill* of the kadi of Sofia.

One of the *sicill*s of Sofia contains two *defter*s (registers)[13] of criminals who, "according to an exalted decree (*ferman-i ali*)" (that is, by imperial order) had to be sent from the *eyalet* of Rumili to the capital for punishment. One of them dates from the last ten days of

[10] For the early history of the Ottoman administrative system in the Balkans, see Gradeva 2002–b, 498–507; Ivanova 1997, 9:731.

[11] NBKM, Or. Dept., S 1 bis, of 1617–8; S 308, of 1619; S 12, of 1671–78; S 85, of 1679–80 (containing also a fragment of 14 pages from 1613–4); S 149, of 1683–4.

[12] I wish to thank the authorities at the Başbakanlık Osmanlı Arşivi (BBOA) in Istanbul for their help and friendly attitude during my research there in 1997 and 2001. I also thank the International Center for Minority Studies and Intercultural Relations (IMIR)-Sofia, which supported my stay in Istanbul in 1997, and the Mellon Fellowship, which made possible my three-month research at the Ottoman Archive in Istanbul in 2001.

[13] The two *defter*s raise many problems. Unfortunately they are part of a small 14-page fragment bound together with a volume dating from approximately 70 years later. The rest of the original volume seems to have disappeared or was destroyed during the bombing of the National Library in World War II.

Muharrem 1023/March 1614. Below the heading there follow three pages of documents pertaining to seventeen criminals from the *kaza*s of Berkofçe (Berkovitsa), Iznebol (Trun), Breznik, Sofia, Samokov, Razlok (Razlog), Cuma Pazarı (Blagoevgrad, Bulgaria), Şehirköy (Pirot), Güvercinlik (Golubac, Serbia), Üsküb, and Manastir (Bitola, Macedonia).[14] Of these *kaza*s, the first eight include Sofia and districts that surround it, while the latter three are relatively distant from Sofia. The *defter* contains short annotations of the cases, each referring to the *hüccet* of the respective kadi, which apparently provided a judicial justification for the arrest of the criminal. Each summary states that the case had been recorded in the respective *sicill*. The criminals had been convicted mainly of homicide and banditry, but also battery, theft, and counterfeiting (*ehl-i fesad*).[15] The other *defter*, which is recorded in the same Sharia court register and is contemporaneous with the first, is dated the middle ten days of Zilhicce 1022/January 1614.[16] Its heading reads: "*defter* of the criminals sent from the *kaza* of Sofia to the capital". The criminals, Muslims and Christians, had been convicted of wine-drinking, theft, counterfeiting (or general wrongdoing), homicide, arson, and wounding, and many of them were either residents of Sofia proper or of villages in the same *kaza*. Most of the entries in this register, however, consider criminals from the *kaza*s of Ihtiman, Samokov, Radomir, Siriştnik (a village near Pernik, all in Bulgaria), Şehirköy, and Vranje (Serbia), all near the *kaza* of Sofia. This suggests that these *kaza*s were in some way dependent on the kadi of the capital city of the *eyalet*. Nowhere else in the *sicill*s preserved in Sofia have I come across documents suggesting that criminals from the central part of the vast province of Rumili were sent, with their documents, to the capital city of the *eyalet*, and thence, together with a *defter* compiled in Sofia, to the capital.

These curious registers bring to mind a practice described by U. Heyd. When lawlessness, e.g. murder, robbery, and offences against public morals, increased in a certain region, and the local authorities were unable (or unwilling) to deal with it, the central govern-

---

[14] S 85, pp. 130–2.

[15] On *sa'i bi'l-fesad* and *ehl-i fesad* see Heyd 1973, 195–8. While these terms were generally applied to counterfeiters, it seems that their meaning in the Ottoman context was widened and came to embrace other offences against public order, that is, "wrongdoers".

[16] S 85, pp. 134–5. The date may be read as 1122, but I think that it is 1022, as the document on the verso side of the folio is also from 1022.

ment would send out special commissions (a *beylerbey* or *sancakbey* and a kadi, usually one who was not in office at the time, and, often, a special commissioner *çavuş*), to investigate the situation, arrest, try and punish the criminals. Members of the commission were charged to discover potential or actual criminals by detaining and investigating all persons who, according to the registers of the local Sharia courts or information given by local *imams* and *müezzins*, had a criminal past. If any one of them was found to be actively engaged in mischief, the commission would send him, together with other troublemakers, in chains, to Istanbul or to another port or naval base, to serve in the galleys. Each batch of criminals was accompanied by a register of their names and copies of their criminal records (*suret-i sicill* or *suret-i cerime*).[17] It is not clear whether the Sofian registers were compiled for that or for some other purpose. It is also unclear whether the two *defters* were the result of the work of a commission of the same type. It seems clear, however, that whoever initiated the *defters*, the kadi of the capital city of the province, Sofia, was involved in their preparation, recorded them in his *sicill* and, probably, had to oversee and summarise the work done by his colleagues in the provincial *kazas*.

2. Sultan's orders (*emr, ferman*) to the *paşa* of Rumili, the *molla* of Sofia, and a local kadi in Rumili, relating to events that took place in the district of the local kadi.

Sometimes the *paşa* or the *molla* is missing from the official *elkab* (address); at other times the order is addressed to the *paşa* and the *molla* only, but the content makes it clear that the order is concerned with problems in another *kaza*. Most often the orders pertain to acts of brigandage or to the illegal acts of state functionaries, taxation problems, and disputes over *timars*. The documents apparently were supposed to pass through the hands of the kadi in Sofia and were recorded in his *sicills*. Similar orders can be found also in the *Mühimme defters*.

---

[17] Heyd 1973, 228–9. On penal servitude in the galleys, see ibid., 304–7; Ipşirli 1982, 203–48, Gerber 1994, 73–4. U. Heyd mentions another practice without providing his source. In the sixteenth century, provincial authorities were enjoined to draw up and submit, every four months or every year, a detailed list of the criminal cases they had dealt with, the penalties imposed, especially capital punishments and severe corporal punishments, and the properties seized from the criminals. This was done in order to insure some degree of supervision. Heyd 1973, 269. Unfortunately, I have not seen such documents or similar ones in the Sofia archive.

According to one such order, Ömer, *sancakbey* of Bihor (Transylvania), sent an *arzuhal* (petition)[18] to the central authorities informing them that on his way back from Modon (Peloponnese) he had been attacked by a brigand, an inhabitant of the *kaza* of Bihor, with whom he engaged in a one-hour battle. The order states that the brigand should be forced to appear in court, the case duly investigated and appropriate measures taken.[19] The division of labour among the three functionaries is not indicated. Perhaps the kadi of Bihor had to ensure the appearance of the bandit in court, while the kadi of Sofia and the *paşa* were responsible for the adjudication and punishment. Their involvement probably should be considered as an indication that the battle had taken place within the territory of the province of Rumili. Very similar, but without the *paşa* as an addressee, are two decrees directed to the kadi of Sofia and the kadi of Kratovo (Macedonia).[20] Both are concerned with complaints sent to the capital by the population of "*nahiye-i Kratova* belonging to the *kaza* of Kratova". According to one of the decrees, people complained that the *ehl-i örf* (agents of the sultan's political and executive authority entrusted with policing functions) (Heyd 1973, 169) in their *kaza* charged them with *diyet* in cases in which people had fallen from trees, been hit by carts, or were killed by bandits. The two kadis were called upon to restore order and prevent the oppression of the *reaya*.[21] The other decree was issued in response to a letter from the kadi of Kratova concerning a case which brought the *reaya* to the local court: the *mütesellim* (acting district governor) of Sofia and his troops of *sekban* and *sarıca* (irregular militia) had "committed oppression" in the villages of Kratovo, Kumanovo and Kochani (all in Macedonia). Again both kadis were instructed to prevent any such acts in the future, probably dividing their efforts—the kadi of Kratovo—*in situ*, and the kadi of Sofia, at the seat of the *mütesellim*.[22] We also find in the *sicill* of Sofia an order sent to the kadi of Samokov in connection with a complaint of a *zimmi* from a village in the *kaza* of Samokov. The

---

[18] On the practice of the *arzuhal* in the Ottoman empire, see Inalcik 1988, 33–42.

[19] S 85, p. 153, doc. III-p. 154, Evahir Zilkade 1091/December 1680.

[20] See also an order to the *beylerbey* of Rumili and the kadi of Sofia concerning legal problems in the *kaza* of Kratovo. BBOA, MD 80, p. 58, doc. II, n.d., but the *defter* contains documents from 1613–4.

[21] S 85, p. 168, doc. I, Evasit Receb 1091/August 1680.

[22] Ibid., p. 168, doc. II, Evasit Receb 1091/August 1680. See a similar order in MD 125, p. 58, doc. I, 1128/1716.

man possessed a *tapu* (title deed), a *temessük* (receipt) and a *hüccet* for the right to use summer pastures belonging to *vakıf*s in the *kaza*, but had been prevented from exercising this right.[23]

Similar documents can be found in the *Mühimme defter*s. One of them, addressed to the *vali* of Rumili and the kadis of Sofia and Nevrekob (Gotse Delchev, Bulgaria), was issued in response to a complaint concerning a debt dispute[24] that involved two parties living in the *kaza* of Nevrekob. The dispute had first been taken to the local Sharia court and then to the sultan, who issued the order. But the document makes no reference to the division of labour between the kadis.[25] Another order in the *Mühimme defter*s, this one to the *vali* of Rumili and the kadi of Sofia, treats events that had taken place in the Dukakin *sancak*, *kaza* Gora (Albania). The residents of several *hass* (a fief granted to the highest-ranking Ottoman officials, sultans and their families) villages sent a petition to the sultan complaining about the illegal seizure of their property and oppression (under the pretext of collection of taxes) by the local *mütesellim*s who were accompanied by bandits.[26] The event took place in 1120/1708 and the order dates from 1123/1711, which suggests that the villagers may have tried other legal means before resorting to the highest judicial authority. The *vali* was ordered to enquire into the case in Sofia.[27] A very interesting case is provided by yet another decree in the *Mühimme defter*s. The population of the village of Boboshevo, *kaza* Dupniçe (Dupnitsa, south of Sofia, Bulgaria), belonging to the *vakıf*s of Esmihan Sultan, sent a petition and a man to the capital to complain that a certain Hasan had settled in the said *kaza* several years earlier and ever since had been the *naib* of all the kadis who came to serve as Sharia judges in the district. He, together with the *ehl-i örf*, was accused of oppressing the local people, acting with force and

[23] S 85, p. 137, doc. I, 25 Zilkade 1091/December 1680.

[24] MD 118, p. 225, doc. III, of 1123 (1711–2).

[25] See also ibid., p. 288, doc. II, an order to the *vali* of Rumili and to the kadis of Sofia and Arnavud Belgradı (Berat, Albania) concerning a debt dispute.

[26] Ibid., p. 277, doc. II.

[27] See also an order to the *molla* of Sofia and to the kadis of Timur Hisar (Sidirokastron, Greece) and Siruz, concerning brigands who disrupted tax collection in several villages in these districts. MD 117, p. 181, doc. II, 1123/1711; and two other orders—one to the *vali* of Rumili and the *molla* of Sofia, and the other to the same officials and the kadi of Görice (Korçë, Albania), both about problems in villages belonging to the *vakıf* of Sultan Süleyman and illegal acts of local military men in *kaza* Görice, MD 118, p. 189, doc. I, II, of 1123/1711.

demanding more money and foodstuffs than he was actually due. They demanded that he be banished to another *kaza*. The order for the banishment is addressed both to the kadi of Dupniçe and to the *molla* of Sofia.[28]

Several documents are related to disputes over *timars* (fiefs). In the majority of these, the current *vali* and his *divan* (*Divan-i Rumili*) collaborate with the kadi of Sofia,[29] as decreed in "exalted orders" (*emr-i şerif*). In one case, recorded in March 1680, a dispute over a *timar* village broke out in the *kaza* of Bane-Isfirlig (Soko Bane, Serbia), Vidin *sancak*, between a preacher (*vaiz*) and copyist who served in a mosque in Vidin, and a fortresss guard (*mustahfiz*) from the same *kaza*. The procedure followed is interesting. With regard to the first stages in the dispute, we do not know whether it was brought to the attention of the local kadi or to the kadi in the *sancak* centre. The narrative indicates that the *vaiz* had to go to the capital and check the situation with the Imperial *ruznamçe* (day-book of current financial transactions in government offices). There he was assured that the village was recorded under his name. It turned out that for as long as anyone could remember the village had been a revenue-source assigned to the *vaiz*es and copyists of the same mosque in Vidin. An imperial order was sent to the *vali*, and the kadi of Sofia was invited to the *divan-i Rumili*. The *divan* session was held in the presence of both the *vali* and the kadi, obviously not in the Sharia court.[30] Despite the fact that the *divan* probably maintained a register of its own,[31] the document was recorded in the *sicill*. In another *timar* dispute, an imperial order was addressed to the current kadis of Sofia and Berkofçe. The court session (April 1680) on the subject took place in Berkofçe, to which the kadi of Sofia also sent a representative, while the local kadi was "appointed *naib* of the Sofian

[28] MD 106, p. 50, doc. 159, of 1106/1695.

[29] On cooperation between the *vali* and kadi in the *divan*, see Ursinus 2001, 15–35. The article is based on material from Sofia.

[30] S 85, p. 16, doc. I.

[31] It is widely assumed that provincial governors kept no minutes of deliberations in the governors' councils. See for example Marcus 1989, 82, 114. See, however, Ursinus (forthcoming). See also Ursinus 2001, 17, where the author cites details from the register of the provincial *divan* from the last quarter of the eighteenth century, kept in Manastir; and idem 2002, 359–77. I wish to thank Prof. M. Ursinus for allowing me to use some of his unpublished works on this subject.

kadi".[32] Although the kadi of Sofia is not explicitly mentioned as an addressee, he recorded in his *sicill* an order to the *vali* of Rumili and the kadi of Lofça (Lovech, Bulgaria) concerning the allocation of a *timar* in the *kaza*s of Lofça and Tırnovi (Turnovo, Bulgaria), both belonging to the *sancak* of Niğbolu (Nikopol, Bulgaria), in Rumili.[33]

As mentioned above, judges in the Ottoman Empire became full members of the state administration. Their duties, compared to those of kadis in pre-Ottoman times, had expanded immensely. Among the main obligations of kadis in the Ottoman state was to guard the economic interests of the sultan and the treasury. One of the major tasks of kadis was to exercise control over tax collection, as manifested in the registration of the *berat*s of the tax collectors in the *sicill*s and control over the legal aspects of the tax collection, especially in cases involving the oppression of taxpayers. Some of the documents raise questions about the role of the kadi in Sofia vis-à-vis his colleagues in the smaller *kaza* centers near his seat. Several documents addressed to the kadi of Breznik (a small town to the west of Sofia) are recorded in the *sicill*s of the Sharia court in Sofia. There were, for example, some problems in the registration of the *celepkeşan* (cattle breeders) and, hence, in the payment of the respective tax. We find the order to the kadi of Breznik concerning the settlement of these problems recorded in the Sofia *sicill*s.[34] It is followed by another, this one concerning the *sürsat zahiresi* (forced contributions of grain collected as part of the extraordinary taxes in the Ottoman state) in the *kaza* of Breznik (again addressed to the kadi of Breznik and to other officials in the *kaza*) and a *defter* of the *bedel* (cash equivalent) of the *sürsat zahiresi* for the *kaza*.[35] The *divan* of Rumili and the kadi of Sofia were also involved in a dispute over the collection of the *cizye* (capitation tax collected from non-Muslims) for the *kaza* of

[32] S 85, p. 85, doc. I. See the three verifications at the top of the document belonging to the kadi of Sofia, the kadi of Berkofçe and the officer sent by the kadi of Sofia on that particular occasion.

[33] S 1 bis, p. 172, doc. I, Evasit Cemazi I 1026/May 1617.

[34] S 85, p. 196, doc. I, of 8 Şaban 1091/September 1680. The same problem is treated in ibid., p. 144, doc. I, of 18 Muharrem 1090/March 1679.

[35] Ibid., p. 197, doc. I, of 8 Zilhicce 1091/December 1680, and doc. II, of 5 Cemazi I 1091/June 1680. Similar documents concerning the *bedel-i nüzul* tax (cash equivalent of provisions collected as part of the so-called extraordinary taxes) from *kaza* Breznik are also recorded in that *sicill*, p. 173, doc. I and II, of 8 Ramazan 1091/October 1680.

Razlok.[36] In all these cases, it is not clear whether or not the Sofian judge was acting in his capacity as kadi of the administrative centre of the *eyalet*, and as such was exercising supervisory functions over the kadis of lower rank. His involvement may have been the result of some problems in the *kaza*s of Breznik and Razlok, due to which the orders from the capital had to be carried out by the kadi in Sofia, again as the (administrative) superior of these Sharia judges.

Such an interpretation is probably confirmed by two similar cases from the *sicill*s of the Manastir kadi.[37] One of them, a *tevzi defter* (register for the distribution of local expenses among the inhabitants of the kaza) for the *kaza* of Shtip (Macedonia) for six months in 1796, was signed by the kadi and by the *nazır* of Shtip in the presence of the *ayan* (notables) of the town. The expenses were calculated and checked by the *kaymakam* (lieutenant governor) of the Rumili *vali* who was currently stationed in a village in the *kaza*. The reason for the intervention of the latter official was that the local *ayan* had tried to collect nearly 10% more than the sum to which they were entitled (Ursinus 1980, 181–2). The second is again a *tevzi defter*, but for *kaza* Kolonya (with centre in Ersekë, south of Korçë, Albania), probably caused by the punitive campaign in 1830 of the Rumili *vali* Hurşid Paşa against the Tosks following their siege of Manastir (Ursinus 1994, 49–79). In both cases the involvement of high administrative officials—the *kaymakam* in 1796, and probably the *vali* in 1830, whose seat was Manastir—should be considered the primary factor for the inclusion of the *defter*s of *kaza*s belonging to other *sancak*s in the local *kadi*'s *sicill*s. In our Breznik case of the 1680s we know only that there were some disturbances in tax collection, nothing more. For the time being we can only guess about the role of the *vali*: the Razlok case was first taken to the *vali*'s *divan* and only then to the Sharia court.

[36] Two documents in the Sofian *sicill*s are related to this issue: one apparently describing the session of the *divan-i Rumili*, held in the presence of the *vali* and the kadi of Sofia; the second—only of the Sharia court, the latter actually being the epilogue to the case. The procedure was triggered by an order from the capital requiring that the matter be taken to higher authorities, rather than to the *kaza* where the problem had arisen. S 85, p. 1, doc. I, 2 Zilhicce 1090/January 1680, p. 2, doc. I, Evasit Zilhicce 1090/January 1680.

[37] In the second half of the eighteenth century and until 1836, when it became the official centre of the Rumili *eyalet*, Manastir was the residence of the Rumili *vali*. See Ursinus 1991, 6:372.

The kadi of Sofia was involved not only in problems in the *Paşa sancak*, to which Sofia belonged at the end of the seventeenth century,[38] but also in taxation problems in other *sancaks* of the *eyalet*. According to an order addressed to the kadis of Sofia and Vidin (the capital of a *sancak* in Rumili), the latter, together with three of the local notables in the *nezaret* (tax administration unit) of Vidin, were interfering with the work of the person responsible for collecting the *mal-i miriye* tax for the years 1089 and 1090, and instigating opposition to him among the *reaya*. The three notables were summoned to the capital, and the kadi of Sofia, "being a *molla*", was ordered to deal with the issue, that is, to ensure the payment of the arrears in taxes, so that the treasury did not suffer any losses. The order says nothing about the local kadi's position.[39] The kadis of Sofia and Berkofçe and the *mütesellim* of Sofia were concerned with another problem relating to taxes in Vidin. Many of the *reaya* of the Vidin district had left their old places of residence and settled in villages and *çiftliks* (agricultural estate or farm) in the *kaza* of Berkofçe. The kadi of Berkofçe included them in the *avarız hanes* (tax units for the payment of extraordinary taxes) of the *kaza*. Contrary to an earlier imperial order, the kadi and the *subaşı* (police officer) of the *kaza* prevented the *reaya* from returning to Vidin. The sultan's decree states that the kadi, the *subaşı* and other interested people in Berkofçe should not be allowed to interfere, and the *reaya* should again be included in the *avarız hanes* in their original places of residence in the Vidin *nezaret*, in order to protect the direct interests of the treasury.[40] Another order of the central authorities, this one to the kadis of Gümülcine (Komotini, Greece) and Sofia, responds to a complaint from the *emin* (superintendent) of the imperial kitchen charged with the collection of the alum due for the year 1090/1679–80. The previous officer charged with its collection and merchants from Anatolia were selling alum, while the current officer enjoyed monopoly rights to sell the stores of the product he had. We know from contemporary sources and from the biographies of Sofian kadis that Gümülcine was one of the *mevleviyets*, probably a little lower in rank than Sofia but generally of the same category. The order instructed the two

[38] S 85, p. 169, doc. II, of Evail Ramazan 1091/October 1680: "Paşa sancağında Sofya nahiyesinde Gubislav nam kariye". See also Gradeva 2002, 500.
[39] S 85, p. 165, doc. I, 18 Cemazi II 1091/July 1680.
[40] Ibid., p. 166, doc. I, 8 Receb 1091/August 1680.

kadis to prevent infringements on the *emin*'s monopoly and hence to protect the interests of the treasury, without specifying how the obligations were to be divided or what the role of the Sofian Sharia judge was to be.[41]

3. Cases were transferred from other jurisdictions to the Sofia judgeship, sometimes with an imperial order, sometimes without.

An interesting document, a *hüccet*, was issued by the kadi of Yanya (Yoannina, Greece). Representatives of the non-Muslim *reaya* (the tax-paying population) in the town of Yanya and from several villages and *nahiye*s in the *kaza* of Yanya appeared in the local Sharia court and authorized two non-Muslims from the same *kaza* to be their deputies and to act as their "*naib*s and *vekil*s" in order to look into and take care of matters relating to the district (*vilâyet*) in the capital (*asitane*) of the empire. The two men accepted the appointment, and this was recorded in the kadi records in Yanya. This document, along with a verification of the kadi of Yanya, was also recorded in the *sicill* of the kadi of Sofia.[42] Later in the same document we learn why. A couple of months after the issuance of the *vekâlet*, the two men appeared in the Sharia court in Sofia and made a declaration in front of Ali Ağa b. Mehmed, citizen of Karaferye (Verroia, Greece), who was also to receive the document. According to their declaration, an imperial *ferman* had authorized Ali Ağa to collect the extraordinary taxes (*avarız* and *bedel-i nüzul*) for the *kaza* of Yanya for 1092/1681 and the *cizye* from the infidels (*kefere*) in the same *kaza* for 1093/1682. However, he had collected 709,000 *akçe*s more than the sums indicated in the royal order and the register (*defter*) in the hands of the taxpayers. This dispute reached the sultan and, by imperial order, an agent (*mübaşir*) was appointed to examine the case. The intervention of the latter, together with that of a "master of the judges" (*seyyid ül-ahkâm*),[43] resulted in the following agreement (*sulh*) between Muslims and reconcilers (*müslimin ve muslihun*): in lieu of the disputed sum, the tax collector would pay 600 *guruş*

[41] Ibid., p. 167, doc. III, 28 Zilkade 1090/December 1679. The document is verified by the *mevli-i hilâfeten* of Edirne.

[42] S 149, f. 28v, doc. I, 10 Cemazi I 1095/May 1684.

[43] In the judicial documents I have seen, the term *seyyid ül-ahkâm* appears only rarely, and then in connection with reconciliation and other important issues. More evidence is needed to establish the profile of this official. It is not clear if he was the titular Sharia judge in the *kaza* or a different person of high prestige to whom disputes were referred in difficult cases.

to the representatives of the *reaya*, who, in return, withdrew any further claims against him. Interestingly, the court session was attended by the current *müteselim* and several officers of the *serasker* (military commander), in their capacity as instrumental witnesses (*şuhud ül-hal*), a clear indication of the importance of the case.[44] However, it still is not clear why the case was transferred to the Sofian Sharia court instead of the court in Yanya or Karaferye. No doubt, the decision was based on a combination of factors—the high honorary position of the Sofian kadi and the fact that Sofia was the seat of the provincial governor whose deputy was involved in the court session.

According to a *hüccet* recorded in the *sicill* of the Sofian kadi, a certain Handan Bey b. Abdullah from the *kasaba* (small town) of Şehirköy appeared in the Sharia court in Sofia claiming money from *zimmis* from the village of Temska belonging to the *kaza* of Şehirköy. The court session was held in Sofia, to which the defendants were summoned by an order (*ferman*) of the sultan. According to the plaintiff, five years earlier he had lent 135 *guruş* for the payment of the *cizye* to several *zimmis* (all identified by name) from Temska who stood surety for one another (*kefalet ile kefilleri*). When the debt came due in 1090/1679–80 the villagers acknowledged it in front of the kadi of Şehirköy, and the obligation to pay it was confirmed in the court. Subsequently, however, with the support of some local notables (*ayan-i vilâyet*), the *zimmis* denied having stood surety and being involved in the case. Handan Bey also provided a *hüccet* verified by the signature of the kadi of Şehirköy. The Christians did admit that they had borrowed the money for their *cizye*, but insisted that they had not agreed to be *kefils* and were not involved. Following a demand for further evidence, the claimant produced several witnesses from Şehirköy who confirmed his claim. At the end of the session, the kadi of Sofia announced his decision in favor of the plaintiff.[45]

Another debt problem, this one between a Muslim creditor (Mehmed Ağa, treasurer of Ibrahim Ağa, son of the late Mahmud Ağa, obviously an important local notable, probably the *ayan* of the *vilâyet*),

[44] S 149, f. 29v, doc. I, Evail Şaban 1095/July 1684. Two letters written by a Christian inhabitant of Yanya to his father, a printer in Venice, indicate that in 1682–3 the *paşa* in the district was oppressing the Christian community. I thank Dr. A. Anastasopoulos for providing me with this information.

[45] S 85, p. 16, doc. II, 1 Safar 1091/March 1680.

and a Christian debtor (Rashen son of Peyo) from the village of Dragoshin Yalovası belonging to the Şehirköy *kaza*, again following a court session in Şehirköy, was taken to the court in Sofia. According to the plaintiff's proxy (*vekil*), four years earlier the defendant had borrowed 740 *guruş* for his personal expenditures; subsequently, he paid back 400 *guruş* but another 340 had yet to be returned, as confirmed by the debtor in front of Muslims in the *mahkeme* in Şehirköy. The Christian, however, claimed that he had borrowed 325 *guruş* by way of *mudarabe*,[46] paid back 150 *guruş* in cash, as well as two *vukiye* (a weight of 400 dirhems or 2 lb.) of silver and several heads of oxen and goats, thus clearing his debt. The claim of the plaintiff was again confirmed by witnesses—one from Şehirköy and one from Sofia—who declared that they had been present at the court session in Şehirköy when the debt of 340 *guruş* was acknowledged. The Sofian kadi ruled in accordance with their testimony.[47] In this case, our source provides no indication of why and on what grounds the case was taken to Sofia.

Finally, a case involving fraud that crossed *kaza* boundaries resulted in a correspondence between the judicial authorities of Kutlofçe (Montana, Bulgaria) and Sofia. Mevlâna Elhacc Ebu Bekir Efendi b. Osman, the kadi of Kutlofçe, *kaza* Polomie, in Rumili, informed (probably) the kadi of Sofia[48] by means of a legal copy (*nakl-i şer*) about court proceedings in his court concerning the illegal action of an inhabitant of Sofia (and a member of the *vali*'s staff) who was trying to lay hands on a slave who was part of the inheritance of another person. The local kadi ruled against the *vali*'s officer, but for some reason the case was transferred to Sofia, where witnesses confirmed the authenticity of the document sent by the kadi of

[46] A *mudarebe* or *commenda* is a partnership in which one party acts as the investor and the other as the agent. The capital of the venture is supplied by the investor, who remains a passive partner. The agent works with the money, and any profits are divided according to prearranged proportions. The original capital belongs to the investor and should go back to him. If there is a loss rather than profit, this is borne entirely by the investor. Gerber 1981b, 113–4; Udovitch 1970, 170ff.

[47] S 85, p. 20, doc. I, Evasit Safar 1091/March 1680.

[48] The text does not explicitly mention the kadi of Sofia as an addressee. Indeed, it does not mention any addressee at all. Since the document was included in the kadi *sicill* of Sofia, I assume that the judicial procedure that followed did somehow involve the Sofian kadi. The reason may well have been his ambiguous position as an independent judicial officer but also occasionally a member of the *divan* of the *vali*. See Ursinus 2001, 23–5, 37.

Kutlofçe.[49] Unfortunately, we have no further evidence regarding the judicial procedure that followed and, in particular, we do not know if the *vali* was also involved or if the transfer of the case to Sofia was caused by the fact that the defendant was a high official.[50]

4. The Sharia court in Sofia was a center for other kadis from the same *eyalet*, and even other *eyalet*s.

We frequently find current and former kadis of various *kaza*s in the European provinces of the Empire attending court sessions in Sofia without any obvious reason for that: the kadi of Iznebol,[51] of Hırsova (Hârşova, Romania),[52] Şehirköy,[53] the former kadi of Alaca Hisar (centre of a *sancak*, Krushevac, Serbia),[54] of Ivraca (Vratsa, Bulgaria),[55] the former kadi of Ihtiman,[56] the kadı of Leskofçe (Leskovac, Serbia),[57] the kadis of Bosna (Sarajevo, centre of another *eyalet*, Bosnia) and of Üsküb (centre of a *sancak*),[58] etc. The names of many Sharia judges appear among the *şuhud ül-hal*, bearing the title of "kadi" without any explicit identification.[59] One of them, who attended several sessions of the Sharia court of the titular kadi of Sofia and

[49] S 85, p. 62, doc. II, 16 Muharrem 1092/February 1682.

[50] See also an order to the *vali* of Rumili, the *molla* of Sofia and the kadi of Ipek (Pech, Serbia) concerning a dispute over some property; the kadi of Ipek seems to have been accused by the population of a village in the said *kaza* of having taken a bribe, which may be the reason for the transfer of the case to the centre of the province. MD 121, p. 80, doc. 317, of 1125/1713. See also an order to the *vali*, the *molla* of Sofia and the kadi of Elbasan (Albania), Ibid., p. 362, doc. 1420, of 1124/1712.

[51] S 1 bis, p. 162, doc. III, 11 Şevval 1027/October 1618, in a litigation between two Muslims over a debt; p. 123, doc. II; p. 134, doc. I; S 149, f. 39v, doc. II, 27 Zilhicce 1095/December 1684, manumission of a female slave.

[52] S 1 bis, p. 28, doc. II, Zilkade 1026/November 1617, witnesses to a sale of a vineyard by a Jew to a Muslim; p. 133, doc. I, p. 134, doc. I, Receb 1027/June 1618, where one of the witnesses is identified as the former kadi of Hırsova.

[53] Ibid., p. 36, doc. II, Zilhicce 1026/December 1617, appointment of a *mütevelli*.

[54] Ibid., p. 68, doc. II, Rebi I 1027/March 1618, a case about a slave.

[55] Ibid., p. 99, doc. I.

[56] Ibid., p. 137, doc. VIII, p. 138, doc. I, Receb 1027/June 1618.

[57] S 308, p. 9, doc. I, Şaban 1028/July–August 1619, a dispute between citizens of Siruz over property.

[58] S 4, p. 13, 25 Zilhicce 1120/March 1709.

[59] See, for example, S 85, p. 3, doc. II, Evahir Zilhicce 1090/January 1680 ("fahrulkudat Mehmed Efendi b. Ebu Bekir Ağa"), p. 5, doc. I, Evasit Zilhicce 1090/January 1680 (the same Mehmed Efendi), p. 23, doc. I, 3 Rebi I 1090/April 1679 (a kadi Ibrahim Efendi), p. 68, doc. I, 11 Safer 1092/March 1682 (a kadi Rusul Efendi), p. 80, doc. II, 1 Rebi II 1092/April 1682 (two kadis among the witnesses to a document about a *vakıf*—Yusuf Efendi and Mehmed Efendi b. Abdi), p. 74, doc. I–p. 75, Evail Muharrem 1092/January 1681 (Mehmed *halife* b. Mustafa, kadi); S 149, f. 14v, doc. II, 1 Rebi II 1095/March 1685 (Mehmed Efendi, kadi),

whose name appeared among the technical witnesses, was the *kassam* (law official who fixes inheritance shares) in Sofia; he too bore the title of kadi.[60] At the same time another *kassam*, who specialized in dealing with the inheritances of members of the military institution, also attended court hearings.[61] While the presence of these law officials in the Sofian Sharia court should not be a surprise, the reason for the appearance of so many current and former kadis from the European provinces of the Empire in Sofia remains an open question.

Conclusion

It was not exceptional for the *molla* of Sofia and the ordinary kadis in Rumili to establish relations with one another in the seventeenth century. Although rarely mentioned in studies, such relations existed in other places. Based on his research in kadi *sicill*s from Kayseri (capital of a *sancak* within the province of Karaman with its centre in Konya) in the period 1600–1625, R. Jennings concluded that the *molla* of the town (Uğur 1986, lix) had some influence over the kadis of the Develi, Kara Hisar and Yahyali *nahiye*s. He found in the Kayseri *sicill*s *ferman*s concerning the collection of *avarız*, *nüzul* and other *tekâlif* (all "extraordinary" taxes) or concerning *timar*s in these *nahiye*s, addressed jointly to the Kayseri kadi and to the above-mentioned three kadis. Often *berat*s for the appointment of kadis of the three *nahiye*s were copied in the Kayseri *sicill*s. Even a transfer of

f. 40r, doc. II, Evahir Zilhicce 1095/December 1684; S 4, p. 6, 5 Şevval 1120/ December 1708, where we find a "fahrulkudat Mehmed Efendi" who was also *imam* of the *vali*.

[60] S 85, p. 7, Muharrem 1091/February 1680, p. 94, doc. II, Evasit Cemazi II 1092/June–July 1681. An interesting case is presented in S 12, p. 28, doc. III, Evail Muharrem 1083/1672 where a kadi Şeyh Mehmed Efendi appears in court in his capacity as *vekil* (proxy) of one of the parties in a sale of an inherited house. It turns out that this proxy was most probably the current titular kadi of Sofia—a Parsa Mehmed Efendi (d. 1091/1680), about whom we know with certainty that he belonged to the Mevlevi order, and was earlier in his life *şeyh* of a Mevlevi *tekke*. In fact the first ten folia of the *sicill* S 12 are stamped with his seal and the *sicill* opens with a document declaring his assumption of the position of kadi of Sofia. The date of the document corresponds to the period of his tenure in Sofia (Cemazi II 1082/October 1671—Şevval 1084/January 1674). See more details on him in Gradeva 2002a. It remains an enigma, however, who presided over the court session for that particular case.

[61] See his appointment in S 85, p. 161, doc. II; he appears among the witnesses in ibid., p. 65, doc. I, 23 Muharrem 1092/February 1682.

shares in a mill at Kara Hisar was registered in the Kayseri kadi records (Jennings 1979, 159–61). But Jennings detected no hierarchical relations between the *molla*s of Konya and Kayseri, perhaps because both were of the *mevleviyet* category, that is, almost equal in rank in the personnel hierarchy. Perhaps the kadi of Konya supervised kadis of lower rank in his vicinity, e.g. those in *Paşa sancak* in the province of Karaman (Jennings 1979, 156). Be that as it may, I have not identified any relations of (administrative or judicial) supremacy/subordination between e.g. Sofia and Filibe, both *mevleviyet*s that belonged for most of the period between the mid-fifteenth and end of the eighteenth centuries to the province of Rumili, despite the administrative centrality of the former. The only exception I have seen is the above-mentioned order addressed to the kadis of Sofia and Gümülcine, both of whom held the rank of *molla*. Another indication of the relatively widespread nature of these hierarchical relations is an order from the *şikâyet defter* (containing imperial orders in response to complaints from all parts of the Empire) dating from 1675. It is addressed to the kadis of Ankara (the *sancak* centre) and Çorba, and to the *mütesellim* of Ankara. The three officials are urged to deal with a complaint about bandits sent by villagers from the *kadilik* of Çorba, without any explicit reference to a division of labor between the two judges.[62]

These control functions were not limited to the kadi residing in the centre of a *sancak* or *eyalet*. Several documents from the *sicill*s of the kadi of Rusçuk (of the level of *Ula* among the "ordinary" Sharia judges of an "ordinary" *kaza*, with a daily salary of 300 *akçe*s) (Özergin 1976, 239) reveal that this kadi occasionally was authorised to exercise some sort of control in controversial cases in adjacent *kaza*s. Rusçuk kadis received and recorded decrees addressed to judges of neighboring *kaza*s,[63] and they were instructed to look into problems

---

[62] *Das osmanische "Registerbuch der Beschwerden" (Şikâyet Defteri) vom Jahre 1675*, f. 14v, doc. VI.

[63] See an order to the kadis of Çernova (Cherven, Bulgaria) and Tırnovi concerning *vakıf* villages in their *kaza*s. The order confirmed that the villages were registered as *vakıf* in the state records and exempt from *beyt ül-mal*, *mal-i gaib* and *mal-i mefkud*, which were collected for the primary school (*mektebhane*) founded in Edirne by a certain Cafer Çelebi, father of Ahmed Paşa, *beylerbey*. However, some *sancakbey*s and their men, *subaşı*s, *amil*s and other *ehl-i örf*, continued to interfere and the kadis were ordered to prohibit this practice. B 2919, f. 38v, doc. I, of 4 Zilkade 1070/July 1660, recorded on 9 Rebi II 1074/November 1663. This document is problematic with regard to its date of issuance and recording. Most probably the

there. It should probably be noted here that Rusçuk, though not an important administrative centre, was the seat of the admiral of the Ottoman fleet on the Danube who bore the title of *mirimiran*, that is, provincial governor.

Of particular interest in this respect are two orders. The first is addressed to the *naib* of Tırnovi (but entered in the *sicill* of the Rusçuk kadi) concerning problems raised in a petition submitted by the population of the *kaza* about some *zimmis* identified as brigands and wrongdoers. Below it, is recorded a letter about the same matter by a Mehmed Ağa.[64] The second order deals with problems in Arnaud *köy* (Arbanassi, Bulgaria), a village belonging to the *vakıf* of Rustem Paşa. The kadi of Rusçuk and the *naib* of Tırnovi were commanded to deal with the issue and to prevent the dispersal of the *reaya*. The order specifies that the kadi of Rusçuk was acting in his capacity as *molla* ("ecelden imdi Rusçuk kadısı molla olub mahalinde şeriyle görülüb . . .").[65]

Another example of relations between kadis involves the judges of Yenişehir and Karaferye. In two different instances, in 1613 and again in 1620, the Christian community of Karaferye pressed charges

order was issued earlier, on another occasion when the functionaries interfered with the taxes of the *vakıf* villages; the order was subsequently presented to the local kadi in order to confirm the status of the villagers. Why was the order recorded in the Rusçuk *sicills*? One possibility is that the rank of one (Çernova) or both kadis was lower than that of the kadi of Rusçuk and/or they were under his jurisdiction. The Tırnovi kadi is often referred to as a *naib*, the *kaza* having been granted as an *arpalık*, that is, as an additional salary or pension given to some high religious functionary; in the tax registers Çernova is frequently included in the Rusçuk *kaza*. It is also possible that the compiler of the order used an older title of the kadi of Rusçuk. Çernova was previously the centre of the district, an administrative centre inherited from the Bulgarian state which, over time, declined and, in the second half of the sixteenth century, was replaced by Rusçuk as the military, economic, and then administrative centre of the region. It remained, however, the centre of a *nahiye*.

[64] Ibid., f. 29, doc. I, II, of Evahir Muharrem 1074/August-September 1663.

[65] Ibid., f. 13a, doc. IV, 18 Rebi I 1075/October 1664. No fixed groupings of (three or more) kadis can be discerned in the addresses of the orders of the central authorities which would be used for the purpose of easier communication, in any case no groupings similar to the *tertib-i buyuruldat* (showing the arrangement of the decrees for the districts of the province of Rumili) found by Prof. M. Ursinus in the Manastir *sicills* of the end of the eighteenth or beginning of nineteenth century. It seems that in addition to the geographical proximity, the kadi of Rusçuk was ordered to look into the matters in question mainly because of his higher qualification.

against local *yasakçis* (one who guards an ambassador, high ecclesiastical functionary or other high official), accusing them of exorbitant taxation and abuses and demanding that they be dismissed from office. For unknown reasons, the Christians in the second case turned first to the kadi of Yenişehir. Then, after receiving a decision ordering the dismissal of the wrongdoers, the community took the *yasakçi*s to the Karaferye court where the decision was in fact implemented (Gara 1998, 158). According to Gara, the biases of the local kadi may have motivated the Christians to turn to another Sharia judge, even if the law does not allow for this. I would go further. By the 17th century, the kadi of Yenişehir had joined the ranks of the *molla*s, who may have sought his intervention because of his high position in the judicial hierarchy, which would have made his judgment authoritative and difficult to circumvent.

The hierarchical relations that I have identified between kadis in *eyalet* and *sancak* centres and ordinary kadis lead to the following conclusion. By the seventeenth century there existed a neat classification of kadis in an honorary hierarchy or, as Shapiro puts it, a hierarchical personnel system, with the *mevleviyet*s at the top and the kadis of *nahiye*s at the bottom. This hierarchy was reflected in the daily salary of each kadi. My research on Sofian kadis and *sicill*s, however, shows that there existed another, probably rudimentary, judicial hierarchy that manifests itself in the judicial and administrative subordination of ordinary kadis to the kadis of the *sancak* and *eyalet* centre.[66] In his work, based on kadi *sicill*s, mainly from Bursa, and *şikâyet defter*s, Gerber argues that a kadi's decision, although not sacred, immutable, or irreversible, could be reversed only upon the authority of the sultan. He suggests that this happened only rarely and that no kadi in seventeenth-century Bursa was ever asked to reconsider a case previously decided by another kadi.[67] But this did happen with the Sofian judge.

[66] Gy. Kaldy-Nagy 1973, 375, also mentions such a hierarchy but does not explain its meaning. See also Heyd (1973, 219), who identifies the *vilâyet kadisi*, the kadi of a province, as a grade higher than the "ordinary" kadis, again without further comment.

[67] Gerber 1994, 85. However he points out that complaints of illegal behaviour of kadis were usually re-directed from the capital (the sultan) "to the administrative area superior to or adjacent to the area of the implicated kadi, with orders to investigate and if necessary bring legal action against him." Ibid., 159. Inalcik, too,

During the seventeenth century these hierarchical relations seem to have functioned primarily (perhaps exclusively) in the fields of public order and security, the *timar* system, and the collection of taxes, that is, fields regulated generally by *kanun* (secular law promulgated by the Ottoman sultans) that fell within the prerogatives of secular authorities, namely the sultan, the governor and members of the governor's *divan* on the provincial level. The involvement of kadis in matters relating to *kanun* points to an enhancement of the role of Sharia judges and is generally regarded as a distinctive feature of the Ottoman judicial system (Gerber 1994, 72). But this phenomenon may be explained in another manner, i.e. by the growing integration of provincial kadis within the state administration and into the *divan* of the governors, as has already been noticed (Heyd 1973, 210). The involvement of the kadi in the administration of the *mazalim* court on the provincial level at the turn of the eighteenth century has also been established.[68]

The documents analysed above make it possible for us to go further and to suggest that the involvement of kadis with the *mazalim* on the provincial level had a side effect. It resulted in the extension of oversight responsibility to kadis in the centres of provinces vis-à-vis their colleagues in smaller places, especially in matters regulated by *kanun* and in charges of malpractice levelled against lower-ranking Sharia law officials, and in their occasional functioning as an appellate institution for decisions of local kadis. Since *kanun* matters generally fell within the jurisdiction of the governor (*beylerbey/vali* or *sancakbey*), it seems that the kadi of Sofia frequently was charged by the central authorities to provide a legal justification for the decisions and acts of the governor and to act as a member of the judi-

touches on this issue: "The kadi's decision was in principle final, and there was no provision for appeal in the Ottoman judicial system. However, if the interested party complained directly to the sultan of injustice in a decision, the imperial *diwan*, while not capable of reversing it, could order according to the circumstances either a retrial by the same kadi, a transfer of the case to a nearby *hakim*'s court, or the dispatch of the parties to the imperial *diwan* for a new trial. Governors were strictly forbidden to interfere in the court's activities..." Inalcik 1991, 6:3.

[68] Ursinus 2001, 23–5, 32. Despite the generally accepted opinion that the *mazalim* court disappeared under the Ottomans, it was preserved as an institution in the *divans* of the governors. See Heyd 1973, 224–7.

cial "section" of the *divan* of Rumili. These responsibilities of the kadi of a province were carried out on two levels. Most often they took place on the level of *kaza*s in the immediate vicinity of the provincial centre (perhaps on a *sancak* level). But they also existed on the *eyalet* level, in which case the kadi usually cooperated with the provincial governor, probably in the latter's capacity as representative of the sultan in the province.

It seems clear that during the seventeenth century (and probably even earlier) and at the turn of the eighteenth century, an embryonic hierarchy took shape among provincial kadis. Within this new structure, the kadi of the capital city of a province exercised supervisory control over the Sharia judges in the region. In certain cases, although it is not usually clear exactly when and on what grounds, he also functioned as an appellate instance with regard to the decisions of local kadis. This development was a direct result of the growing integration of Ottoman kadis within the provincial government and the enhanced importance of governors in the provincial administration. The Ottoman example thus confirms Shapiro's argument that judicial hierarchies and systems of appeal serve as instruments of political control. However, his thesis requires some qualification. In the Ottoman state the kadi court was not simply a religious court but also an integral element of the Ottoman judicial system, with the sultan and his *divan* at the top. During the period between the fifteenth and seventeenth centuries, the territorial expansion of the Ottoman empire and the elaboration of the civil administration of the Ottoman provinces resulted in the gradual emergence of an intermediate level between the sultan and the ordinary local kadi. This was the kadi who sat in the centre of a province, usually holding the rank of *molla* in the personnel hierarchy. During this period the *divan* of the provincial governor and the kadi served as appellate institutions, mainly as representatives of the sultan in each province, usually acting in cooperation, but at least during the period we are concerned with, probably also acting on certain occasions independently of one another. But there were further developments. Towards the end of the seventeenth century, the provincial kadi often took part in the sessions of the provincial *divan*, which, at the end of the eighteenth century, began to function as an appellate level in its own right that received petitions for the re-examination of decisions made by lower-ranking kadis, which still left open the option of appealing to the Sultan or the *Divan-i hümayun*.[69] Whether or not this pattern holds also for other provinces of the Ottoman empire, in the core and outlying regions, is a question that requires further investigation.

[69] I wish to thank Prof. M. Ursinus for sharing some of his findings on the issue with me.

CHAPTER TWELVE

ISLAMIC JUDICIAL COUNCILS AND THEIR SOCIOPOLITICAL CONTEXTS: A TRANS-SAHARAN COMPARISON

Allan Christelow

The concern of this essay is with Islamic judicial institutions that have been eliminated: the first one, in Algeria, by a French colonial government in the mid-nineteenth century; the second one by a military regime in Nigeria in the twentieth century (Christelow 1985, 1994). Both of these institutions can be described as councils, in Arabic, *majlis*. "Institution" may not be the best term for them since there were no formal decrees determining the composition of the *majlis* or its rules of operation. Indeed, the lack of formal rules may be the key to understanding their nature: being councils they offered scope for negotiation and consensus formation, for delivering a decision that carried more authority than that of an individual judge, or even a fixed composition panel of judges, however learned they might be.

The concept of *majlis* has received scant attention in academic literature. Halil Inalcik, in his article in the *Encyclopaedia of Islam* on *maḥkama*, for the Ottoman Empire, holds that the terms *majlis* and *maḥkama* were interchangeable. The *qāḍī* was the sole judge, but he might consult with any number of *shuhūd*, expert witnesses who formed "an unbiased and expert body" to help assure the objectivity of the *qāḍī's* decision. But when it comes to actual cases as opposed to legal theory, one person's "objective fact" may appear to another person to be the product of selfish bias. A satisfactory decision may be one that is not the product of expertise in the scientific sense, but rather of what we might term "judicial creativity," the ability to take reports of fact, some of them contradictory, some of them leading, under normal legal logic, to an unsatisfactory conclusion, and forge them into a compelling judicial narrative. Such creativity needs to be founded on a strong knowledge of the law, and insight into the legal players and situations involved. It may involve negotiation, but it may also result in a decision that is a clear, emphatic choice.[1]

A key assumption here is that to understand the realities of law one must study the judicial process in depth at the regional level. It is here that one can best see the interaction between the law and political, social, and economic realities. The regions to be studied here are those of Mascara, in western Algeria, and Kano in northern Nigeria. Both offer fascinating cases for the study of the judicial process, and both were in fact key to the eventual demise of the *majlis* in their respective settings.

In Mascara, in the 1850s, the *majlis* assisted the *qāḍī*, who was appointed by the French colonial administration. But in Kano, it was the emir, the traditional ruler, who presided over the *majlis*. The judicial roles of Muslim rulers have seldom been studied in detail. Those scholars who have paid attention to this question seem to assume that the ruler's jurisdiction is limited to extraordinary matters pertaining to state security, and its decisions guided by principles deemed convenient or necessary by the ruler, which may or may not be in strict accord with Islamic legal principles (Brunschvig 1965). This is sometimes dubbed a *siyāsa* jurisdiction. While this assumption may well hold true for the Bey of Tunis in the eighteenth century, it does not fit very well in Kano. Here, the emir, the local ruler,[2] had jurisdiction not just over extraordinary cases but over a range of types of case. There was a clear division of judicial labor between the emir's judicial council and the *qāḍīs*, in Hausa, *alkalai* (sing.: *alkali*). In many areas, especially in homicide law, the emir's council scrupulously followed Islamic law. In others, it applied what can be described as local custom, and in still others there were legal innovations to meet the exigencies of the new colonial situation, described in the records as *ḥukm zamāninā*, the rule of our era (Christelow 1997).

---

[1] The Islamic *majlis* differs from the Western jury of ordinary citizens, and from the multi-judge court of fixed composition. One might argue that it bears some relation to the western concept of a parliament in that it is in some sense a representative institution, working within an established framework of law. Of course parliamentary institutions in the modern Islamic world are generally termed "*majlis*."

[2] Before the arrival of the British, emirs were appointed by the Sultan of Sokoto but maintained a large measure of autonomy. Under the British, the emir continued to rule, but under the supervision of the British Resident, in the system known as "indirect rule."

It is sometimes assumed that the *majlis* was an appeals court. In Algeria, the French took it to be such. In Northern Nigeria, the British sometimes advised that it be such. This assumption seems to have grown out of a deeply ingrained sense of hierarchy among European colonial administrators. But in both cases, the *majlis* heard perfectly mundane cases concerning such matters as the sale of a donkey or a scuffle in the market. Never is there any mention in recorded cases of appeal from a lower court. Of course, there were also a number of important cases, and at least with the *majlis* of Mascara, we have a rough gauge of this in the form of the number and identity of the *shuhūd* listed at the end of the case.

The legal cultures of these two communities, in both cases clearly Islamic, had important differences. In Mascara, written documents had a key role, especially in disputes over property rights in land. The records of the *majlis* are themselves framed as written documents. In Kano, written legal documents had no role. Oral testimony and oaths were the linchpins of the judicial process, and they lent it a dramatic element, because witnesses, when brought before the council, sometimes decided not to testify, and litigants who were offered the opportunity to take an oath sometimes demurred.[3]

The written records, begun only in 1909 at British instigation, are essentially transcript summaries of an oral process, often employing direct quotation. As well as the facts of the judicial process, these records convey something of its feelings and colors—anger, submissiveness, crude deception, shrewd detection, and even humor. The court proceedings were generally conducted in Hausa, while the records were kept in Arabic (with an admixture of Hausa terms and characteristic Hausa turns of phrase), perhaps to give a sense of formality, perhaps to impede the interference of British officials, few of

[3] The contrast between oral and literate cultures has been emphasized by Goody 1986 and 1987. Other works on this field include Olson and Torrance 1991, and Graff 1987. Literacy in Arabic, and in Hausa and Fulfulde rendered in Arabic letters, was certainly widespread in northern Nigeria, but its use was primarily for religious and literary purposes. Goody would describe this situation as one of "restricted literacy," a concept that perhaps needs refining to deal with different ways in which literacy is restricted, and different reasons as to why it might be restricted. Today, we tend to subscribe to the notion that technology drives change. Considering the use of oral and written communication in Kano, we might be led to ask whether social and political actors might choose to adapt technologies to their own purposes and values.

whom could read Arabic. But the records still convey clearly the oral character of the legal culture.

I examine here the manner in which the two judicial councils dealt with legal issues that would have key roles in their eventual undoing. In the conclusion I will briefly discuss the elimination of regional judicial institutions in both settings and consider why, in one of them, we may be witnessing their reinvention.

Mascara, Algeria—the 1850s

The city of Mascara lies in western Algeria, at the edge of the Eghris Plain, a fertile basin at the southern foot of a small mountain range, the Beni Chougran. It lies some seventy kilometers south of the port city of Mostaganem. Mascara was a natural political center, serving as a base for military garrisons under the Zayanids (1236–1551) and the Ottomans (1551–1830). But other cities in western Algeria usually overshadowed Mascara. Tlemcen served as the Zayanid capital, and even after its fall from political dominance, it maintained cultural and intellectual pre-eminence. The Ottomans did make Mascara capital of a *beylik* administration from 1701 to 1792, but they were quick to move the capital to the port city of Oran when the Spanish abandoned it as a direct result of a local earthquake, and an indirect result of the tremors spreading throughout Europe after the outbreak of the French revolution (Kaddache 1998).

Ottoman authority was never well entrenched in the Mascara region, or more generally, in the Oranais, where Ottoman power was challenged economically and militarily by the Spanish, and in symbolic and political terms by the sharifian monarchy of Morocco. Further east, especially in the region of Algiers, in the Constantinois, and in Tunisia, there had emerged a sort of Ottoman-North African synthesis.[4] But this borderland territory of the west was always open to rejecting Ottoman authority. We see this in a rebellion in the 1820s, and again with the establishment of a new state under the leadership of Amīr ʿAbd al-Qādir in 1832.

[4] For an analysis of the Ottoman-Algerian social synthesis in an urban environment, see Hoexter 1998. There were still boundaries in Algerian cities marked by ethnic identity, neighborhood, and the Hanafi and Maliki ritual-legal traditions. On urban neighborhoods, see Ben Hamouche 1996. On the situation in western Algeria, see Hess 1978.

If western Algeria was rebellious by nature, it was not an easy task to make all the rebellious tendencies coalesce in a unified effort. The sharīfian elite of the Eghris Plain were at odds with the Tijānī order, based at the desert edge in ʿAyn Mādī (Abun-Nasr 1965). Impoverished mountain dwellers, traditionally at the bottom of the political and economic pecking order, preferred the impulsive millenarian style of the Darqāwa Sufi order to the careful strategy and prolonged, concerted effort demanded by ʿAbd al-Qādir. Closer to the coast, the long Spanish presence had left a class of political leaders accustomed to rationalizing collaboration with foreign rulers. By 1847, ʿAbd al-Qādir's resistance effort was exhausted and he surrendered to the French (Danziger 1976). After four years as a virtual prisoner in France, he was allowed to take up exile in the east, first at Bursa, then in Damascus. Napoleon III, who made himself emperor of France in 1851, certainly went out of his way to flatter ʿAbd al-Qādir, and may have toyed with the idea of installing him as ruler of a French protectorate in Algeria. But the relationship between the French and ʿAbd al-Qādir was deeply ambivalent and fraught with distrust. While the former resistance leader might pay visits to France, or support French projects in the Middle East (notably the Suez Canal), there were regular reports that his emissaries encouraged Algerian Muslims to *hijra*, flight from land controlled by the infidel to Muslim lands.

Certainly, the Mascara region had suffered severely during the war of colonial conquest. Many lives had been lost, and many of the region's inhabitants had gone into exile, in Morocco, or, in the case of ʿAbd al-Qādir and his entourage, in Syria.[5] French records give a detailed list of over 500 land owners who had gone into exile during the campaign of military resistance against the conquest, and whose property was thus confiscated and incorporated into the state *Domaine*. At least some of those emigrants did return. They were allowed only to rent their former holdings from the *Domaine*, pending its allocation to French settlers.[6]

[5] On Algerian emigrants in the east, see Hillal 1986. On the spiritual evolution of ʿAbd al-Qādir, see Étienne 1994.

[6] There are two detailed lists of property confiscated, one for the cercle of Mascara, the administrative district in the immediate vicinity of the city, and one for the subdivision, the larger administrative district, published in the Bulletin officiel des actes du gouvernement. On leasing of land by returned emigrants, see

This confiscation reveals two key elements about the legal setting. First, property rights in the Masacara region were already well documented, allowing the French to discover the precise location and description of the property of known exiles. Second, under colonial rule, the state assumed a preponderant role in property matters. But there was a human element to the upheavals as well, revealed by a case in which parents who had returned from exile in Morocco reclaimed their daughter, "a girl who is now called ʿĀīsha," who had been left behind and taken in by another family.[7]

The 1850s mark a critical phase in the history of property rights in the region. Mascara had not yet become synonymous with quality red wine produced for export to France. But French investors had begun to recognize the possibility of acquiring low-cost fertile land only a few days trip by sea from metropolitan markets.[8] Their strategy at this point seems to have been to acquire prime strategic holdings in the area, if possible from *Domaine* holdings, where political influence could be brought to bear, and where there were no legal complications. One investor, for instance, waged an apparently successful campaign to secure rights to a mill site on a creek, the Wād Sīdī Daho, running through the lands of a lineage, the Awlād Sīdī Daho, who had been prime supporters of ʿAbd al-Qādir.

While transactions involving *Domaine* properties are often well documented, we know little in detail concerning how settlers went about trying to buy land from individuals. Fragmentary evidence suggests that some prospective buyers may have preferred an indirect approach, advancing credits to intermediaries who would eventually transfer the land to the settler. The records do in fact indicate that land was often bought and sold within the Muslim community of the Mascara region. But land acquisition was not a simple process. A successful buyer had to be well informed about the complexities presented by Islamic law.

Commandant Subdivision Mascara, 17 juin 1856, in Archives d'Outre-Mer, Aix-en-Provence, 30 JJ 126. On colonial land policy during this period, see Ruedy 1967 and Robe 1864.

[7] Mascara register, Case 5–C, 26 Shaʿbān 1272. The Mascara cases are from the register of the Bureau Arabe qadi covering 1853–56, Archives d'Outre-Mer, Aix-en-Provence, 30 JJ 335. Case numbers are ones I have assigned.

[8] On the development of colonial agriculture in western Algeria, see Yacono 1955–56. Irrigation was a major factor in the intensive colonization of the Oranais. For an analysis of French irrigation development in neighboring Morocco, see Swearingen 1987. On this period in colonial Algeria, see Rey-Godziguer 1977.

By far the most common kind of legal dispute involving land sales were those based on *shufʿa*, preemption by co-owners. According to this principle, if a buyer offers to purchase a piece of real property that is jointly owned, a co-owner of the property may demand to acquire rights to the whole property from the buyer at the price paid. A key condition is that the preemptor not have been aware of the sale when it took place. Thus a buyer had an interest in knowing about the history of the property in question, especially with respect to inheritance rights. The buyer needed a document stipulating that all those with inheritance rights had in some fashion consented to the sale, either putting forth their names as sellers, or stating that they had made a donation of their share to those who did sell it. Although cumbersome, this task was by no means impossible. Many buyers who faced preemption claims successfully defended themselves, documents in hand.

But quite a few *shufʿa* claims were successful, as was the following:

> Al-Sayyid Aḥmad bin al-Majāji and his cousin al-Majāji Walid al-Ḥajj ʿAbd al-Qādir, both from the Awlād al-Baraka Sīdī Aḥmad bin ʿAlī—may Allāh be pleased with him—jointly purchased part of the piece of land called Sakka Bu Ghara in the agricultural territory of the Awlād Sīdī Aḥmad bin ʿAlī—may Allāh be pleased with him—from al-Sayyid al-Najāhī bin ʿAdnāni for twelve Spanish *dūrus*. The *faqīh* al-Bashīr bin al-Sayyid Muḥammad Bin Aḥjada has a share in this which he inherited from his mother, ʿAwda bint al-Sayyid al-ʿAdnānī, which he has never sold. So he asks to buy his share, and the rest of the land, claiming that he didn't know (about the sale when it took place) and that he thus has the right to preempt. So they came before the qāḍī al-Sayyid Ṭāhir Bin ʿAmar—may Allāh strengthen him—whose seal is above. The two buyers explain their case to the qāḍī, saying that the claimant should only get the share of the land which he claims by inheritance from his mother, but that the claim of *shufʿa* should be rejected. Bin Aḥjada summons as witnesses in support of his not knowing [about the sale] al-Sayyid ʿAbdallāh bin al-Ṣaḥrawī, al-Sayyid Muḥammad bin al-Ramasī, al-Sayyid Muṣṭafā bin al-Mukhtār, and al-Sayyid ʿAdnānī bin al-Sayyid Muḥammad al-ʿAdnānī. His opponents ask for confirmation of this in writing so Bashīr shows two documents in the writing of our masters and the shaykhs of our ancestors (*sādātunā wa mashayikh salafinā*), one sealed with the seal of the qāḍī al-Sayyid Ḥashū bin Muḥammad, and the writers of the other being al-Sayyid al-Ḥājj Muḥammad bin Muṣṭafā al-Sharīqī and other men of knowledge. The contents of the first are that the witnesses do not bear the father of the defendant any worldly enmity, and of the second that they have no hatred of the defendant himself, and this is witnessed by

> people of justice (*ahl al-ʿadl*) and others. . . . (After citing some authorities of the Mālikī school) the *majlis* rules in favor of the claimant.[9]

A close examination of cases like this one shows that they had often had two common elements. They were based on the inheritance rights of women, and the claimants were from *awlād sayyid* lineages. Thus these cases offer a prime example of the way law can interact with patterns of social relations.

To understand this phenomenon, we need to look more closely at the social structure of the region and the role of *awlād sayyid.* These were lineages that claimed descent from a notably pious individual in the past, a *sayyid.* Some members of these lineages dominated Islamic religious roles, notably in the domain of law. Nearly all of the thirty individuals who served as *shuhūd* on the Mascara *majlis* came from *awlād sayyid* lineages.

In North African studies, anthropologists preoccupied with finding elegant, intellectually compelling structures, have argued that religious lineages (in the French jargon, *marabouts*), had an interstitial position among competing, structurally opposed lineages. They were, structurally, destined to be neutral, and so they made natural mediators (Gellner 1969, Evans-Pritchard 1949).

This model may work for the High Atlas of Morocco or the desert of Cyrenaica, but it does not help us to make sense of the Mascara region, and much of the rest of western Algeria. Here the *awlād sayyid* lineages comprised a distinct class. They married both within their own lineages and within the larger class of *awlād sayyid*, but they did not marry commoners. It was the marriage links between *awlād sayyid* lineages that were the most likely to lead to successful preemption claims, since the women who married into another lineage, and their spouses and children, were the potential coinheritors who could most convincingly claim to have not heard of the sale. The *awlād sayyid* seem to have owned, at least before the colonial conquest, much of the best land on the Eghris Plain.

In judicial records the scribes referred to members of this class by the title *al-sayyid*, and they inserted honorific formulas after the mention of the founders of their lineages, as in the case above. Most if not all of them claimed descent from the Prophet Muhammad, making them *ashrāf* (sing: *sharīf*). Such claims not only lent them dis-

[9] Mascara register, Case 17 B, 18 Jumādā I, 1272 (26 January 1856).

tinction, but also associated them with the social norms of Morocco, and perhaps hinted at loyalty to that country's sharifian ruler and a lack of enthusiasm for Ottoman sovereignty.

However, these claims of sharifian descent were not accepted with unanimity in the Mascara region. As early as the seventeenth century, a work was composed calling these claims into question. A member of Amīr ʿAbd al-Qādir's lineage had responded with a defense of the claims. A key element in his argument was that sharifian descent could be established by the testimony of two trustworthy witnesses. In the late Ottoman era, the notable scholar and historian Abū Ra'
s al-Nāṣirī, renewed the skeptical approach to the question. Al-Nāsirī was an exponent of Ottoman rule, well known for his literary work celebrating the reconquest of Oran in 1792.[10] Al-Nāṣirī carefully guarded his manuscript questioning the claims of sharifian descent until his death in 1823. His son was persuaded by members of the Awlād Sīdī Daho to lend them the manuscript, which they promptly destroyed. A gauge of the sensitivity of this question is that the Ottoman authorities reacted furiously, imposing a heavy fine on the offenders.

The problematic nature of written documents, as well as of inheritance disputes, is illustrated in the following case:

> Muḥammad walid al-Ḥājj Daho walid Khalīfa from Zūwa [a lineage of the] Awlād al-Baraka Sīdī Daho bin Zarfa (may Allāh be pleased with him), on his own account, and on behalf of his sisters, Khayra, Malḥa, and Khadīja, complain against Mawlūd bin ʿĀshit, the representative for the inheritance of al-Ḥājj Aḥmad bin Khasla al-ʿAṭbī. The complaint of the first party against the second concerns a fruitful place in the land which they inherited from their father, al-Ḥājj Daho, and which he inherited from our sister, his daughter Fāṭima, and she inherited from her husband al-Ḥājj Aḥmad bin Khasla. The grounds are that the inheritance was divided without the immoveable property, and nobody has full rights to it without the participation of the others. The defendants answer that the inheritance was indeed divided, including the immovable property, so that (the plaintiff has) no right to complain. The two parties were called upon to prove their claims, and each displays a document by al-Sayyid bin al-Ṣabr, qāḍī of al-Burjīa. The qāḍī examined it and he found that the text showed division without the immobile property. He also found that the document of the defendant had an erasure, and that this was used to falsify it.

[10] On the writings of al-Nāṣirī, see Saʿadallāh, 1981, vol. 2. On the place of written evidence in Islamic law, see Messick 1993, Chap. 11.

> The document of the Awlād Sīdī Daho party is valid, and they have a right to the price of their share of the land.[11]

Land, especially fertile land as this apparently was, was becoming more valuable. French records of the time indicate a rapid expansion of the area under cultivation around Mascara, representing perhaps a recovery from the devastating conflicts of the 1840s. As noted above, the Awlād Sīdī Daho had lost a good deal of land to sequestration, which might explain, in part, their litigiousness. And it may be that their aggressiveness was further increased by the realization that their opponents were willing to use dishonest legal tactics.

For *awlād sayyid* lineages, holding on to what they had was no doubt crucial at this point, and the device of *shufʿa* was an important legal tool in this task. But it was a tool that involved an element of subjective judgment on the part of the qāḍī and his council. How did one prove that the preemptor did not know about the sale when it took place? As suggested by the testimony concerning lack of malice in the above case, preemption cases had the potential to create serious antagonism. The flexible nature of the *majlis* as it existed in the period before intensive French intervention allowed for a measure of negotiation, but also for a show of solidarity among the region's legists in the face of dishonest tactics, perhaps employed at the behest of an anticipated European buyer. A new system instituted in 1856 left no room for such flexibility.

Kano, Nigeria—the 1910s

When we come to Kano in the early twentieth century, we encounter a very different setting in many respects. Kano was, and remains today the economic hub of northern Nigeria. It is a city whose very physical structure conveys a strong and distinctive identity: massive, ochre-colored earthen walls, and, at the heart of the city, *gidan sarki*, the emir's palace, with its own massive ochre walls.

In the early nineteenth century, Kano, like much of the rest of what would become northern Nigeria, was swept up in an Islamic renewal movement, the *jihād* led by ʿUthmān Dan Fodio.[12] The Shehu,

---

[11] Mascara register, Case 159 A, 16 Ṣafar 1270 (18 November 1853).

[12] Last 1967 and Hiskett 1973 are classic works on the Sokoto *jihād*. Recent

as he is called, roused followers from his own Fulbe ethnic group, and also some Hausa and Tuareg, condemning what he saw as the oppressive policies of the region's Hausa rulers and their tolerance for practices condemned by Islamic law. Yet the new political system that emerged took on many aspects of the old one, in terms of the structure of the ruling institution, the names of the offices, and the rituals surrounding them. For instance, Kano's Fulbe *sarki*, like his Hausa predecessor, always wore a face veil in public appearances.[13]

Several important differences between the Kano and Mascara environments have a bearing on the judicial process. Whereas the organizing principle of Mascara society was kinship and religious status, that of Kano was territory and title in the regional or local hierarchy of offices. Individuals in the records are identified by village, town, or urban ward. Titles, such as *ciroma* or *galadima*, are mentioned in the records. Algeria had been dominated for three centuries by a foreign political military elite, but the pre-colonial state in Kano was of local origin, and the vocabulary and symbols of authority were deeply rooted in local tradition.

Algeria lay on a maritime frontier, raiding and raided by Christian neighbors. Kano, and the Sokoto Caliphate, lay on an African land frontier, bordering people who followed traditional religions. There was frequent raiding to the south, and to the east, in Adamawa, providing large numbers of slaves. While some of these were exported across the Sahara, most went to work on farms within the territory of the Caliphate. Slavery was not only a means of extracting labor but also a mechanism of assimilation. Second generation slaves were called by a different term than those of the first generation. Slave women frequently became the concubines of their masters, and the children of these unions were, by Islamic law, free (Lovejoy 1993, Christelow 1986).

The British did not come to Nigeria seeking land for settlers, but rather commercial opportunities. Kano had its own centuries-old

---

scholarship has focused on the literary production of the Shehu's daughter. See Boyd and Mack 2000. For a guide to the Arabic language literature of the area, see Hunwick 1995, vol. 2.

[13] For a long-term perspective on the political system of Kano, see Smith 1997. (The research for this work was done in the 1950s, and the manuscript essentially complete by the late 1960s.) On political and religious culture in Kano, see Paden 1973.

commercial tradition, producing textiles and leather goods locally, and engaging in trade with the desert, for salt, and with the forest to the south, for kola nuts. Kano quickly adapted to the British presence by becoming a major producer of groundnuts, exported to Europe mainly to make margarine. (Lovejoy 1980, Hogendorn 1978) Kano was conquered by the British in 1903, and only nine years later was linked to the seaport of Lagos by rail.

The Algerians had long used silver currency, either locally minted or of Spanish origin. Long after the French conquest, they continued using Spanish monetary terms (*dūrū, riyāl*) even though the coins might have been French. But in what became northern Nigeria, the only currency in everyday use had been the cowrie shell, a bulky currency kept in strings of 100. Not long after the British conquest (1903), one British pound could fetch 40,000 cowries (Hogendorn 1986). The British quickly worked to introduce much more practicable small silver coins, to facilitate both commerce and tax collection. As we shall see, this also facilitated theft.

The lands of the western Sudan had an Islamic scholarly tradition dating back many centuries. The founders of the Sokoto Caliphate in particular had a prolific literary production to their credit, mainly in Arabic, but also in Hausa and Fulfulde. Many Kano scholars were thus well versed in the various branches of Islamic learning, including the law.

However, prior to the arrival of the British, the people of Kano seldom used written legal documents, in contrast with the situation in Mascara. Legal proof was established either by direct testimony or by oath. We might refer to this as an oral-legal culture. The only written documents that have survived from the precolonial era that might be termed "legal" pertain to slaves.[14] This circumstance may reflect the fact that the main avenue to accumulating wealth had been the acquisition of slaves.

Here again, the British introduced a major change. Compelled by public opinion in Great Britain, the colonial administration abolished the slave trade and required local judges to accept any slave's request for self-redemption. Many slaves, especially young men, had deserted their masters at the time of the British conquest. Suddenly, then,

---

[14] These records are held in the collection of correspondence from the Sokoto Caliphate at Arewa House in Kaduna.

the path to wealth shifted from the acquisition of slaves to the accumulation of silver coins. This economic transformation coincided with a severe drought in 1913–14, made all the more devastating because many people had consumed or sold the food reserves they traditionally kept (Watts 1983).

Algeria and Nigeria thus offer a tantalizing contrast. In Algeria, the colonial conquest brought brutal repression and expropriation, yet there was substantial continuity in terms of the country's social and economic mechanisms. In northern Nigeria, the conquest was quick, and there was no expropriation. Yet colonial rule introduced a profound transformation in the region's internal economic and social mechanisms.

The records of the Emir of Kano's judicial council for 1913–14 suggest a pattern of interaction between major areas of change. As mentioned, many young male slaves had deserted their masters. Yet few, probably, returned to their impoverished mountain villages. Rather, they became a marginal element in local society, prone to crime, especially theft, on their own account, or possibly in collusion with local authorities. Their victims were often traveling merchants. The new silver coins represented a great temptation. Virtually any other item of value, from a horse to a shirt, had its own distinctive features—a spot on its nose, a stain on its sleeve. Such objects were easy to identify and usually hard to conceal. The silver coins were easy to conceal, and they were all the same. The struggle to either maintain or gain possession of coins invited both stealth and violence.

It was the emir's judicial council that presided over cases of theft, assault, and homicide, as well as those involving rights to real property and matters involving slavery. The *alkalai* heard cases involving personal and commercial law. Not long before the cases under study begin, there had been a crisis involving the key position on the council, that of *waziri*, the emir's chief legal adviser. In Kano this office had traditionally been held by a member of the royal family. The British Resident of Kano in 1908, Dr. Cargill, appointed instead a royal slave, Alla Bar Sarki, evidently in the hope that this would enhance his own power. But the loser in the ensuing crisis was Dr. Cargill himself, who was sent back to Britain amid rumors that he had lost his sanity. The new Resident, Charles Temple, was more tactful. Indeed he was one of the chief theorists of the system of Indirect Rule that the British in Northern Nigeria came to pride themselves on. He appointed as *waziri* a legal scholar and former *alkali*, Muhammadu Gidado.[15]

Gidado would remain as *waziri* until his death in 1937. British observers expressed great respect for him, but noted that he was a staunch conservative, refusing for instance to allow *alkalai* to administer British ordinances. It is likely that he played a crucial role in shaping many of the key judicial policies, especially during the reign of Emir ʿAbbās, which would last until 1919. ʿAbbās had been appointed by the British in 1903 to replace his brother Aliyu, who had taken up arms against the British, but had been captured and was now held in Lokoja, the British base at the Niger-Benue confluence. His authority was further weakened by the fact that his branch of the royal family, the Yusufawa, had taken power in 1892, not by appointment of the Sultan of Sokoto, but by winning a civil war against their rivals, the Tukurawa. Emir ʿAbbās needed the assistance of an astute, strong-willed adviser, and he seems to have found this in the person of Gidado.

Unlike the Mascara records, those of the Kano judicial council do not stipulate who sat on the *majlis*. Cases usually conclude with the words, "Thus ruled Emir ʿAbbās," or sometimes with "*wa salām*" indicating that this was the copy of a letter sent to the British Resident to inform him of the decision. Other sources indicate that besides the emir and the *waziri*, the council included the *ma'aji* (the emir's treasurer), a number of Islamic scholars, and various traditional office holders. The tone and style of the records is informal, a feature explained by the fact record keeping was new, a practice imposed by the British.

Cases were heard in a chamber of the emir's palace, and litigants had to follow the deferential etiquette demanded in such a setting. Commoners, at least, would prostrate themselves before the emir throughout the proceedings. This emphasized the emir's ritual authority and may have lent particular solemnity to oaths. Though the setting might seem intimidating, perfectly ordinary people could bring their cases to the emir. The written accounts of cases, as well as containing a legal judgment, often convey the emir's attitude toward

[15] On this episode, and the use of the title "*waziri*", see Lovejoy, Mahadi, and Mukhtar 1993. On the historical context, see Fika 1978. See also the Hausa language history of Kano by Gidado's son: Abubakar Dokaji: Kano ta Dabo Cigari. (Dokaji 1958).

the litigant. For those who were self-effacing and deferential, he had kind words even if he could not provide them with legal redress. With those who were pushy and demanding, he could respond with a snide comment, or even stretch the rules to arrive at a severe judgment against them.

The mixture of shrewd judgment and adherence to Islamic legal principles in response to an everyday complaint is conveyed in the following case involving the theft of a billy goat. It should be noted that Kano goats, like their fellow goats the world over, tend to take care of themselves. In the morning, they amble down the old city's narrow streets and head out the gate to find something to eat. Come evening, they dutifully return home. Gatekeepers were thus bound to be on familiar terms with neighborhood goats.

> Then [there came] Abū Bakr from the community of Darma (ward)—a billy goat was stolen from him. He did not see it until two days later in the possession of Yunka from the community of Fagge. [Yunka] was summoned and the emir questioned him. He said, "I bought it from the Sarkin Kofar Wambai" (the keeper of Wambai Gate). The gatekeeper was summoned and he denied (stealing the billy goat). He said, "I bought it from a man—I don't know where he came from—who brought it to our gate." The upshot was that the emir said, "You are the thief." The case was concluded. The emir jailed him and dismissed him from his position. Then he called for witnesses who knew that the billy goat belonged to Abū Bakr. He mentioned Ḥusayn and Mūsā. They were summoned. They said, "The billy goat is his." They testified as to that. Then the emir ordered Abū Bakr to take an oath. He swore and the billy goat was put in his possession in accordance with Islamic law. Friday, the date of 19 Ramaḍān, the year of the Hijra and the Prophet 1331 (22 August 1913).[16]

We may note here that there were no witnesses to the theft itself, but the gatekeeper had no plausible explanation for his possession of the animal. He should have known that a transaction such as the sale of a goat needed witnesses. Having first betrayed the emir's trust in his capacity as gatekeeper, then having told a bold-faced lie in court, he should not have been surprised at the emir's wrath. Since Yunka, the goat purchaser, lived in the external community of Fagge,

[16] Case 32 G, Thus Ruled Emir Abbas, 103–4. The register, which covers the years 1913–14, is held at the National Archives, Kaduna, Kano Native Authority Series, 1/2/1. Other registers, including the first one, which starts in 1909, are held at the Emir's Palace in Kano.

we might guess that he was a merchant, perhaps a Tuareg from the north. From the timing, it seems likely that he was looking forward to a good feast at ʿĪd al-Fiṭr. As to whether Yunka ever got his money back, we shall probably never know.

Animal theft was a tame affair compared to the theft of goods and money. Assuming the owner could prove his or her claim, the stolen animal was restored to its rightful owner. Animal theft seldom involved breaking and entering, and it seldom let to violence.

The problem of theft of goods and money was most acute for traveling merchants. With the new commerce, new people who may not have belonged to established trade networks were entering the field. Old patterns of ensuring security were breaking down. Traditionally a merchant arriving in a locality was expected to offer *gaisuwa*, greetings, to a local headman. In doing so, he informed the headman of his presence, and also had the opportunity to give him a customary gift, to help insure his security. The trader was expected to stay in the compound of a *fatoma*, a lodging house keeper, who not only provided a place to stay, but also set up business contacts. The *fatoma*, too, needed to be paid. Understandably, some merchants tried to avoid both these expenses, but this had its risks, as seen in the following case:

> Then Hārūn from the community of Kacako—he came to Kano city and stayed in its market. At night a man came up to him and beat him until he lost consciousness. The assailant grabbed his goods and ran away with them. So Hārūn came to the emir with this report. The emir said to him, "You forfeited your property because you did not seek a lodging house owner and you did not stay with an owner." The emir rebuked him for that. Then he said to him, "You have no recourse but to start looking. Perhaps Allāh will help you find your goods in the market."[17]

As the case implies, if Hārūn had stayed with a lodging house owner, his treatment might have been different. Indeed, by this time, he would have had the right to compensation from the *sarkin dogarai*, the chief of the emir's police, as occurred in the following case:

> Then Ṣāliḥ from the community of Daurabaure—he came to Kano city and stayed at the house of Agulle the cotton buyer from the community of Kofar Mazugil (ward). When night fell a thief came to the

[17] Case 179 H, End Dhū al-Ḥijja, 1331 (end of November 1913), *Thus Ruled Emir Abbas*, 184.

> guest and stole from him four pounds, one shilling, and six pence. He left with it and then went to Darma ward and entered the dwelling of Muʿallim and stole from him eleven pounds and six pence. So they complained to the emir. They presented their report to the emir like that. So the emir said to them, "If you take an oath, you will be reimbursed for what was stolen from you." They swore, and the emir ordered the police chief to pay. He paid and it was handed over to Ṣāliḥ and Muʿallim, on the basis of the *ḥukm* of this era of ours. The year of the Hijra 1332.[18]

Here we encounter both an established pattern, the use of an oath to establish theft when conventional proof by testimony was not available (as in the case of the billy goat), but also a new element—the requirement that the police chief pay compensation. This is classified by the legal neologism *ḥukm zamāninā*, the rule of our era, a term also found in cases involving slaves. This is an indication that the rule had been imposed by the British, or at least under the threat of pressure from the British. Not only did they want to protect merchants, but they may have suspected that theft was being used to disguise exactions by the emir or his subordinates from those merchants who had not sufficiently curried the favor of royal authority. It should be noted that more humble theft victims generally desisted from taking this oath, perhaps realizing that to do so would incur the emir's displeasure. For wealthy merchants, such as the ones in this case, the money was more important. This rule seems to have been applied only within Kano city.

I have suggested that former slaves may sometimes have been involved in theft, but the evidence for this is indirect, namely the absence of kin coming forward in cases in which thieves had been killed. This anonymity suggests slave status, although it may also suggest a lone victim of the drought wandering the countryside. But we do find cases of individuals who remained as slaves committing major thefts:

> Then Bila, the slave of the headman of Mafuta—his master summoned him and placed in his custody the money of the *kharāj* tax to take to the city of Kano to deliver to the Sarkin Bai (a title holder and district head). He took it and brought it to a house in Kano and stole seven pounds from it. For this reason the Sarkin Bai brought him to the emir to investigate. The result was that the emir imprisoned him

[18] Case 117 E, End of Jumādā II, 1332 (late May 1914), *Thus Ruled Emir Abbas*, 158.

> for six months on the basis of the accusation. Later he was brought to the emir. He had weakened and was near the point of collapse. Thus he was released, on the basis of *ḥukm.*[19]

This, and other cases, suggest that the bond between ruling class masters and slaves in positions of important responsibility was being seriously eroded, and a new basis for trust between superior and subordinate was needed. There is also a hint, here, and elsewhere, that prison was used not so much to punish as to force a thief to reveal where he had hidden the money.

Perhaps the most dramatic case in the records involves a food theft that occurred in Sabon Gari, literally, the "new town," which had been built outside the old city to accommodate people who had come to Kano from southern Nigeria, most of them to work on the railroad or perform subordinate functions in the colonial administration or in commercial firms. The theft took place in a time of severe food shortage.

> Tafida [a person's name] from the community of Sabon Gari, in the land of the Tafida [title of a royal office holder]—he came to us with their headman, as a prisoner. It was claimed that a man cut open [Tafida's] granary at night with a knife to steal some grain from it. [The thief] came out and was seen. [Someone] screamed. So he came out from the place he had entered. He was followed. People gathered. They beat him and smashed him and castrated him. After that, he stayed here at his house (in the old city). He died nineteen days later. Tafida mentioned Anbu and Yunis. We summoned them but they were not found. We took up once more the cause (of the man's death). We asked them whether they had heard him say anything before his death. Then Tafida's representative told us that he had heard him mention Anbu as the one who had castrated him. We asked for witnesses but none were found. Then we asked for (the victim's) son, Zakariyā, and his brother's son, Sani. They took the fifty-fold *qasāma* oath against Tafida, for it was affirmed that he was the cause (of the death). They swore and so had the right to vengeance. We asked them whether they would let him live. We came back to the blood price. They accepted it and let him live. Thus we write to you (the British Resident of Kano) to inform you that there will be no vengeance against him, only a blood price of one million cowries, and 100 lashes and a year in prison. Thus we write to you to inform you of what he is liable for.[20]

---

[19] Case 22 F, 23 Shaʿbān 1331 (28 July 1913), *Thus Ruled Emir Abbas*, 147.

[20] Case 164 B, 11 Dhū-l-Qaʿda, 1332 (1 October 1914), *Thus Ruled Emir Abbas*, 186.

One element in this case is that under Islamic law, it was not a crime for a hungry man to take food. Here we have a merchant who was evidently storing food to sell to the wage workers of Sabon Gari, at a handsome profit, while people in the old city went hungry. The actual culprits had fled, so the law was stretched to make the granary owner responsible for the death, no doubt a politically popular measure in this time of drought. The granary owner was sentenced to pay what in this context was a quite large sum, the equivalent of £25.

As in the *shufʿa* cases of Mascara, only more clearly here, there was a subjective element in *yamīn al-qasāma* cases.[21] The court had to decide what was necessary to establish *lawth*, the presumptive evidence that paved the way to the oath. *Lawth* was not established in every case, and one can sense political factors behind the determination. Moreover, a murder victim who did not leave behind two agnatic kinsmen to take the oath could never be avenged through the *yamīn al-qasāma*. Even if relatives were available, they might refrain from taking the oath. One final observation should be made concerning these cases. Killings in Kano at this time usually involved beating with a blunt instrument, stabbing, or shooting with a bow and arrow. The wounds were seldom immediately fatal, leaving time for the victim to make a statement as to who had caused his or her death, and leaving us to ponder whether a wound inflicted nineteen days earlier had indeed been the cause of a food thief's death. We might speculate that hunger, too, contributed to ending his life, but on this score again, of course, the granary owner could be considered guilty.

[21] The *qasāma* oath, in the Maliki tradition, allows for two or more of the male agnates of the deceased to share a fifty-fold oath establishing the guilt of the accused, if strong presumptive evidence (lawth) can be established. In Kano, the evidence typically was a statement by the dying person that the accused was indeed the one who had caused his or her death. Since attacks typically were carried out with blunt instruments or knives, victims often lived on for days or even weeks after the attack and had plenty of time to name their killer. Powerful individuals might intimidate witnesses to deter them from reporting the victim's statement to the judicial council. The *qasāma* oath is usually reported in the western scholarly literature to be an "archaic" practice, derived from pre-Islamic Arab tradition and no longer in use. Clearly this was not the case in Kano. For studies of the oath, see Basit 1981, and Peters 2002.

Conclusion

The judicial councils of both Algeria and northern Nigeria were eventually eliminated to make way for hierarchical, centralized systems. The legal issues that contributed the most to their demise were the very ones that appear in the records to have been both frequent and contentious. In Algeria, this was disputes over the right to preemption (*shufʿa*) in land cases, in northern Nigeria, homicide, an issue often linked to theft, and often decided by the device of *yamīn al-qasāma.*

The intensity of these conflicts can be explained in part by their relation to the kinds of economic transformation being carried out in two quite different colonial systems: the large-scale transfer of land to Europeans in Algeria, and the establishment of a new colonial economy in northern Nigeria. There is also a less obvious factor. Both *shufʿa* and the *yamīn al-qasāma* involved elements of subjectivity. Had a plaintiff known about a land sale when it took place? Was there adequate basis for the council to allow the *yamīn al-qasāma* and would agnatic relatives of the deceased actually take the oath?

The regional judicial council appears to have provided a mechanism well adapted to the handling of such cases. The lack of a formal, rigid structure, especially in the case of Mascara, left room for negotiation over who would sit on the *majlis*. The dramatic intensity of cases held before the emir's judicial council, and the emir's skill at invoking the support of public opinion seemed to lend weight to judgments. Yet for all the councils' ability to create judicial narratives that would sway the local regional audience, they lacked the legal rigor and the political weight to withstand challenges from the center. The Algerian *majlis* was first eliminated in 1859, as a result of judicial conflicts in the councils of Oran province, especially in Mascara. Revived in 1866 they were definitively eliminated in 1873.[22] In northern Nigeria, the emirs' councils were first restricted in 1959 with the creation of a Criminal Code in place of Islamic law. Homicide was the key legal issue driving this change. In 1967, the councils were officially eliminated (Christelow 2002).

We might see both cases as a variant on a larger pattern in the Islamic world touched on at many points in this volume. Locally

---

[22] For details, see Christelow 1985. On the Muslim jurisprudence of French courts, see Charnay 1965 and Powers 1989.

based jurisdictions with flexible procedures, guided by the rich and subtle traditions of *fiqh*, were displaced by centralized systems that operated on the assumption that human acts can be objectively described and fit into rigorously defined patterns that must be imposed throughout a sovereign territory.

But there was also a key difference in the two cases. In Algeria, the process of centralization had already begun in the Ottoman era. At least in more densely populated areas, written documents had come to pervade the legal culture. Muslim judges were assimilated into a French-style hierarchical system. But in northern Nigeria, although written *texts* had informed the legal system for several centuries, written legal *documents* were exceedingly rare. While founded on written texts, the legal culture in practice was an oral one. This may explain why the transformation to a centralized system has proven, in critical ways, superficial and ineffective. A little more than three decades after the elimination of the emir's judicial councils, starting in 1999, Islamic criminal law was reintroduced by individual states in the old Northern Region, whose capitals in many cases are those of the major emirates, and whose elected governors were taking on some of the attributes of the region's traditional rulers.

PART III

APPLYING DOCTRINES

CHAPTER THIRTEEN

ILL-TREATED WOMEN SEEKING DIVORCE: THE QUR'ĀNIC TWO ARBITERS AND JUDICIAL PRACTICE AMONG THE MALIKIS IN AL-ANDALUS AND NORTH AFRICA*

Maribel Fierro

Introduction

According to Qur'ān 4:34, a husband whose wife is rebellious may attempt to correct her behavior by first admonishing her, then banishing her to a separate bed, and, as a last resort, beating her—within certain limits established by Muslim jurists. Thus, a husband who uses physical force against his wife does not necessarily commit an offense, as such behavior may fall within the scope of the Qur'ānic prescription. What happens if a husband exceeds those limits? How can his wife prove that her husband's use of physical force against her was excessive? How can a woman in this situation escape from her predicament?

Qur'ān 4:35 provides one remedy. This verse stipulates that if a husband and wife become estranged from one another, two arbiters are to be selected, one from among the relatives of the husband and one from among those of the wife. Muslim jurists disagreed among themselves about the nature of the estrangement, who named the arbiters, and the extent of the latter's powers. These differences, in part, may be traced back to a traumatic episode in the history of the early Muslim community, the battle of Siffin.

---

* This essay is part of a larger study of Muslim women who have been abused by their husbands, and the legal and customary procedures that they used to extricate themselves from such abuse, both in the past and the present. A draft of this essay was read at the International Symposium "Aspects of Islamic Law in the pre-Modern period", The Institute for Advanced Studies at The Hebrew University of Jerusalem, 11–13 January 2000. I thank all the participants for their comments, especially A. Layish, R. Peters and D. Serrano. I also wish to thank Manuel Feria, whose deep knowledge of modern Moroccan law has been most helpful, and David Powers for his careful editing. This essay has been written within the research project BFF2002–00075 financed by the Spanish Ministry of Science and Technology.

Of the four Sunni *madhāhib* or schools of law, only the Malikis allow a wife to request a judicial divorce on the grounds of harm. The doctrinal lawbooks indicate that Maliki jurists understood Qur'ān 4:35 as referring to those cases in which a woman who had been physically abused by her husband sought to be divorced from him. However, other sources suggest that the judicial *practice* in al-Andalus and the Maghrib disregarded the Qur'ānic institution of arbitration and followed instead an institution known as *dār amīn* (alternatively, *dār ʿadl* or *dār al-thiqa*). According to this judicial practice, a woman who had been physically abused by her husband would be sent to live with a trustworthy person, whose main function was to inform the judge of the circumstances surrounding her abuse. This practice, first documented in third/ninth century Cordova, is still referred to in the Moroccan *Mudawwana* (November 22, 1957, reformed in September 1993). In this essay, I shall analyze the origins and geographical scope of this practice, the changes that it underwent over time, and the legal discussion that it generated.

1. *The Qur'ānic Two Arbiters and the Malikis*

In cases of marital discord, Qur'ān 4:35 establishes that two arbiters (*ḥakamān*), one related by kinship to the husband and the other to the wife, should attempt to reconcile them: "And if you fear a breach between the two, bring forth an arbiter from his people and from her people an arbiter, if they desire to set things right; God will compose their differences; surely God is all-Knowing, all-Aware" (*wa-in khiftum shiqāq baynahumā fa-bʿathū ḥakaman min ahlihi wa-ḥakaman min ahlihā in yuridā iṣlāḥan yuwaffiq Allāh baynahumā*).[1] Qur'ānic commentators disagreed regarding who should appoint the arbiters: the sultan or one of his representatives (such as the *qāḍī*), the spouses or the pious people of the community (al-Ṭabarī 1373/1954, 3:70–1, 75–6; al-Rāzī 1990–92, 10:75.)

If we disregard the Islamic law of repudiation and divorce, this Qur'ānic verse may be interpreted as referring to any kind of marital discord, which suggests that two arbiters should be appointed in any case in which a marriage is on the verge of dissolution. Modern legislation in some Muslim countries seems to follow this under-

[1] For Qur'ānic verses I follow the translation of Arberry 1964.

standing, especially when steps have been taken to restrict a Muslim husband's almost unlimited power of repudiation by ensuring that no divorce is effective without court intervention and that every effort has been made to reconcile and to settle the differences of opinion between the parties (see Anderson 1976:127 and 129; Mahmood 1977:185; Jones 1994:246–7; Mir-Hosseini 1993:61–3, 67–70, 75.) Qur'ān 4:35 and more especially Qur'ān 4:128 ("If a woman fear rebelliousness or aversion in her husband, there is no fault in them if the couple set things right between them; right settlement is better; and souls are very prone to avarice," *wa-in imra'atun khāfat min baʿlihā nushūzan aw iʿrāḍan fa-lā junāḥ ʿalayhimā an yuṣliḥā baynahumā ṣulḥan wa-l-ṣulḥ khayrun*) may have influenced this tendency of modern legislation.[2]

Whatever the reasons for modern reformist legislation, in premodern Islamic societies, Qur'ān 4:35 was never understood to refer to every case of marital discord, given the husband's right to repudiate his wife that is clearly established in other Qur'ānic verses. With only a few exceptions, Qur'ān 4:35 is connected with the contents of the preceding Qur'ānic verse (al-Rāzī 1990–92, 10:74; al-Qurṭubī 1935–50, 5:174–9).[3] Qur'ān 4:34 reads: "Men are the managers of the affairs of women for that God has preferred in bounty one of them over another, and for that they have expended of their property. Righteous women are therefore obedient, guarding the secret for God's guarding. And those you fear may be rebellious (*nāshiza*) admonish; banish them to their couches, and beat them. If they then obey you, look not for any way against them." The connection is clear: if after having been admonished, banished and beaten, the rebellious wife still does not obey the husband, then the two arbiters should be appointed. Presumably, it is the husband who asks for arbitration because, for whatever reason, he has no desire to divorce his rebellious wife, using his unlimited right to repudiate her.[4] Now, apart from affection, the most obvious reason for

---

[2] The records of what the modern legislators discussed when providing for conciliation provisions should be studied in order to see if they referred to these Qur'ānic verses. I thank Prof. Ann Mayer for her help on this point.

[3] Ibn Ḥazm 1929, 10:87–8, makes a connection to Qur'ān 4:128.

[4] The Hanafi al-Kāsānī (1910, 2:334) connects Qur'ān 4:35 to the preceding verse: if, after beating his wife, the husband still considers her to be disobedient, he may compel her to appear in front of the *qāḍī*, who may either name the two arbiters mentioned in the Qur'ān or admonish the wife. Al-Kāsānī is exceptional

his not wanting to repudiate her is economic. There are two possibilities: (1) she is a woman of means and the continuation of his marriage to her gives him access to her wealth (Hill 1979:75); (2) by not repudiating her, he is trying to make her ask for a *khulʿ* divorce, in which case he will receive economic compensation from her and will be relieved of providing maintenance (*nafaqa*) (Powers 2003).

As we shall see, however, Muslim jurists understood the resort to arbitration as a mechanism for a wife to seek a judicial divorce on the grounds of harm. This premodern practice is reflected in most Codes of Personal Law in Arabo-Muslim countries, where the Qurʾānic prescription on the two arbiters is always mentioned in the context of a marriage in which the wife has suffered harm or ill-treatment from her husband and she goes to court to ask for a divorce on the grounds that such treatment makes her marital life impossible. One of the grounds on which a Muslim wife at present may claim a judicial divorce or dissolution of marriage in Muslim countries is cruelty or ill-treatment (Anderson 1976:121, 122–3). In modern times, the other schools have borrowed the mechanism of obtaining a judicial divorce on grounds of harm (*ḍarar*) from the Malikis.[5]

We have seen that, according to Qurʾān 4:34, a Muslim husband is allowed to rebuke his wife when she is "rebellious" (*nāshiza*) and, if she persists, he may banish her to sleep in a separate room, and if this is ineffective, he may use physical force against her. There is disagreement between and among the schools of law regarding the definition of the term "rebellious" and also the limits that must be set to the husband's use of physical force (which vary in accordance with the class and background of the parties concerned). To go beyond these limits, whatever they may be, constitutes "injury" or cruelty (*ḍarar*) rather than lawful punishment (Linant de Bellefonds 1975, 2:288–95; Rispler-Chaim 1992; Marín forthcoming.) According to the Malikis, harm is caused when a husband insults his wife, beats her beyond what is acceptable, or commits acts against nature on her (Anderson 1976:130.) This behavior on the part of a man is

---

among the Hanafis in his treatment of the Qurʾānic prescription on the two arbiters, which is usually omitted in Hanafi legal treatises (see note 9 below).

[5] An example is Egypt: until 1929 the Hanafi school of law, which does not allow divorce on the grounds of harm or the sending of two arbiters, was followed. After that year, Maliki doctrine was adopted (Khallaf 1938:120–1, 170–1 and Anderson 1954:313).

sometimes called *nushūz*,[6] a term taken from Qur'ān 4:128. But in *tafsīr* works, a man's *nushūz* is not explicitly linked to physical violence. Qur'ān commentators link this verse to the story of Sawda, one of the Prophet's wives. Fearing that the Prophet wanted to divorce her, Sawda offered to renounce her right to sleep with him and give it to his favorite wife, ʿĀ'isha. Accordingly, a man's *nushūz* signifies distancing (*tabāʿud*) himself from his wife because he dislikes something in her (e.g., she is old) or he prefers another wife. When the husband is responsible for the *nushūz*, it is recommended that the wife agree to reconcile with him. But if the wife is responsible for the *nushūz*, no reconciliation is recommended as a means to solve the problem. A husband's treatment of his wife, defined as *nushūz*, does not have a pejorative meaning;[7] defined as *ḍarar*, it constitutes grounds for divorce in Maliki law.

The Qur'ānic prescription for the two arbiters is recorded in Mālik's *Muwaṭṭa'* in the *riwāya*s of Yaḥyā b. Yaḥyā al-Laythī and Abū Muṣʿab (Mālik b. Anas/Yaḥyā b. Yaḥyā 1981:484–5; Mālik b. Anas/Abū Muṣʿab 1992, 1:646),[8] in a short chapter entitled *mā jā'a fī l-ḥakamayn*, which, in Yaḥyā's *riwāya*, is preceded by the chapter on *jāmiʿ ʿiddat al-ṭalāq*[9] and, in Abū Muṣʿab's *riwāya*, by the chapter on *khulʿ*. The context in which Mālik considered the Qur'ānic verse to be applicable is not clearly spelled out, although Abū Muṣʿab's *riwāya* suggests a connection with the wife's asking for divorce. The main point of the *Muwaṭṭa'* is the extent of the power in the hands of the two arbiters. The text mentions the fourth caliph and cousin of the Prophet, ʿAlī b. Abī Ṭālib, stating that the arbiters have the power to separate the spouses. This is a reference to a tradition reported from ʿAlī, according to which he was approached by an

---

[6] According to the lexicographical dictionaries (al-Zabīdī, Ibn Manẓūr), the *nushūz* of a man means to beat his wife and to treat her with cruelty and violence.

[7] The *nushūz* of the man is not an expression used in Maliki and Shiʿi sources (Mir-Hosseini 1993:47). It is found in al-Shāfiʿī: Rispler-Chaim (1992:315–6) (for the Shafiʿi doctrine see note 10).

[8] See also al-Bājī (1914, 4:113/5); al-Zurqānī (1936, 3:213–4). The section on the two arbiters is absent in the *riwāya* of Suwayd b. Saʿīd al-Ḥadathānī (1994), and of the Hanafi al-Shaybānī (1968). In the latter case, this omission reflects the fact that Hanafis did not usually include the Qur'ānic prescription in their legal manuals, as can be seen in the works by al-Marghinānī (1957) and Abū l-Barakāt al-Nasafī with the commentaries by Ibn Nujaym and Ibn ʿĀbidīn (1893). For a Hanafi exception, see note 4 above.

[9] The chapter on *khulʿ* precedes and is separated from the chapter on the two arbiters by fifteen chapters.

estranged couple, each of whom was accompanied by a group of people. Two arbiters were chosen. ʿAlī asked the arbiters if they knew what was expected of them: if their decision was to divorce the couple, divorce would take place; if their decision was to keep them together, their decision would be binding. This tradition is central to all discussions of Qurʾān 4:35, about which there does not seem to be any Prophetic *ḥadīth* dealing with the implementation of the prescription.

ʿAlī's tradition, however, is not recorded in the canonical collections; rather, it is found in ʿAbd al-Razzāq's *al-Muṣannaf fī l-ḥadīth* (1970–72, 6:511–4), in other noncanonical *ḥadīth* collections, in *tafsīr* works and in some legal texts. The reason for its absence from the canonical collections has to do with the political connotations of the tradition attributed to ʿAlī. As caliph, he was confronted at the battle of Ṣiffīn (37/657) by the Umayyad Muʿāwiya, who was claiming revenge for the death of his kinsman ʿUthmān, the previous caliph. In order to avoid bloodshed among Muslims, it was proposed that the contending parties resort to arbitration. According to some versions, the two arbiters (*ḥakamān*) named concluded that ʿUthmān had been killed wrongfully, thus implicitly supporting Muʿāwiya's claim to the caliphate. This decision was accepted by some, considered to be the forerunners of the Sunnis, who believed that the arbiters' decision was binding and enforceable. But the decision of the Ṣiffīn arbiters was rejected by others, partisans of ʿAlī and the forerunners of the Shiʿis. The deep cleavage in the community caused by the Ṣiffīn arbitration is reflected in the legal discussion of the *ḥakamān* prescribed in Qurʾān 4:35. The ʿAlī tradition referred to in the *Muwaṭṭaʾ* suggests that ʿAlī, who held the decision of the two arbiters regarding the estranged couple to be binding, should have accepted the arbiters' decision at Ṣiffīn as equally binding, even if it went against his own interests. Therefore, when ʿAlī publicly protested against the Ṣiffīn two arbiters, proclaiming their decision to be contrary to the Qurʾān and the *sunna*, and therefore not binding (Hinds 1972), he was going against the doctrine that he had previously upheld. Al-Jāḥiẓ (d. 255/868) speaks of the positions of the *ahl al-Ḥijāz* and the *ahl al-ʿIrāq* regarding the two different views on the Ṣiffīn arbiters and their decision: the former accepted it and the latter rejected it (Pellat 1958:455–8.) This disagreement had an effect on the legal understanding of Qurʾān 4:35 as reflected in the different positions taken by the Malikis (followed by the Hanbalis) and the

Hanafis (and Shiʿis—Ibn Bābawayh al-Qummī 1986, 3:344–5): the former, in a section in their legal works on the *ḥakamān*, treat them as magistrates and regard their decision as binding; the latter in pre-modern times tended to omit any legal treatment of Qurʾān 4:35 and, in any case, they consider the *ḥakamān* to be mere agents of the spouses.[10] This means that, contrary to Maliki doctrine, the arbiters' function is merely consultative and they can never impose their opinion on the spouses,[11] especially on the husband. The diverging doctrines regarding who seeks arbitration (the husband whose wife is rebellious, according to the Hanafi al-Kāsānī, or the wife abused by her husband, according to the Malikis) may also reflect the situation at Ṣiffīn (the caliph ʿAlī fighting the rebel Muʿāwiya or Muʿāwiya trying to obtain satisfaction for the wrong done to his relative). It is even possible that the Maliki acceptance of judicial divorce for the wife on the grounds of harm (*ḍarar*), which is not allowed by the other schools, was also a reflection of the positions taken at Ṣiffīn (Muʿāwiya considered himself to be the injured party and therefore entitled to reject ʿAlī).[12]

In the *Muwaṭṭaʾ*, Mālik commented as follows on the ʿAlī traditions: "This is the best of what I have heard from the people of knowledge. Whatever the two arbiters say concerning separation or joining (of the spouses) is binding." Mālik is here indirectly and implicitly upholding the Sunni version of what happened at Ṣiffīn (this may be one of the reasons why the Umayyads supported the spread of Malikism in al-Andalus.)

We also find a section on the two arbiters in Saḥnūn's *Mudawwana* (1905, 5:49–50),[13] the legal text on which North African Malikism was founded. In it, the Egyptian Ibn al-Qāsim (d. 191/806) is asked: Can the two arbiters be chosen outside the families of the couple?

[10] Shafiʿis tend to follow the Hanafi position that if the two arbiters decide that the couple must divorce, their decision is not binding if the husband does not agree. A minority position within the Shafiʿi school follows the Maliki doctrine. As for al-Shāfiʿī, he expressed his discomfort with the Qurʾānic verse (*wa-Allāh aʿlam bi-maʿnā mā arāda*) and explicitly dealt with the problem of how to establish the context in which the Qurʾānic prescription may apply (al-Shāfiʿī 1903–08, 5:177–8 and al-Muzanī's commentary in 6:47–50, margins.) See also note 7.

[11] The Hanafi doctrine seems to preserve the pre-Islamic concept of *taḥkīm*: see Tyan (1960:49 and 60).

[12] I intend to write a more detailed study on the links between the Ṣiffīn agreement and the legal doctrine on the two Qurʾānic arbiters.

[13] See also the legal question (*masʾala*) on the matter collected by al-ʿUtbī *apud* Ibn Rushd al-Jadd (1988, 5:454–5).

What if the spouses do not have relatives or what if their relatives do not include persons qualified to act as arbiters because they do not satisfy the criteria of competence and probity (*li-annahum laysū min ahl al-naẓar wa-l-ʿadl*)? Ibn al-Qāsim answered: if there are persons among the relatives who are qualified to act as arbiters, they have preference. If there are not or if the spouses do not have any relatives, then one must take recourse to a Muslim who fulfills the required conditions (*alladhī huwa ʿadl min al-muslimīn*). The question is then asked: may the guardians (*wulāt*) of the spouses name just one arbiter instead of two? The answer is positive, so long as certain conditions are fulfilled: the spouses must agree on the chosen person, the person must be qualified to fulfil the role and he cannot be a Christian, a slave, a minor, a woman or a *safīh* (i.e., someone without the required legal capacity).

The presence of a section on the *ḥakamān* became a fixed feature of Maliki *furūʿ*.[14] In later Maliki works, such as Khalīl b. Isḥāq's *Mukhtaṣar* (1900:100; Italian transl. by Santillana 1925–38, 2:66–7), the two arbiters' prescription occurs explicitly in connection with wives ill-treated by their husbands, and, more specifically, in connection with cases in which there is no clear evidence about such ill-treatment. In the case of discord between the spouses or when it is not known which party is responsible, the *qāḍī* should send two arbiters chosen from among the relatives of the couple and, preferably, among those who are also neighbors of the couple (the obvious reason being that such people would be familiar with their daily behavior). If the arbiters reach an agreement, their decision is binding; otherwise, nothing can be done. The two arbiters must first try to reconcile the spouses. If it is not possible to do so, and if the husband is responsible (i.e., for causing harm to his wife), the arbiters must impose repudiation, without the wife having to pay any compensation. If the wife is responsible (i.e., she is rebellious), the arbiters either ask the husband to treat her with patience and moderation or impose a divorce in which the wife must pay compensation (*khulʿ*). If both are responsible, there are two possibilities: a *khulʿ* divorce either with or without compensation by the wife. The arbiters inform

[14] Apart from other Maliki works mentioned below, see Ibn Abī Zayd al-Qayrawānī (1999, 5:282–3); the commentary on Ibn Abī Zayd al-Qayrawānī's *al-Risāla* (where there is no mention of the *ḥakamān*) by al-Manūfī (1963, 2:33–107); Ibn ʿAbd al-Barr (1980, 2:596–7); and (2000, 6:182–4); Ibn ʿĀṣim (1958:68–9).

the judge of their decision, and the judge sees to its execution. If the arbiters were chosen by the spouses without the involvement of a judge, the spouses themselves can dismiss them, but only prior to the moment at which the arbiters reach a decision.[15]

The Malikis emphasize that the arbiters are entitled to impose a divorce on the spouses. According to Ibn Rushd al-Ḥafīd, our Averroes, in his *Bidāyat al-mujtahid* (n.d., 2:80–1; French translation by Laïmèche 1926:245–6), Mālik and his disciples regarded the decision taken by the two arbiters, whatever it might be, as binding, regardless of whether or not they were given a mandate by the couple or obtained their consent. He adds that Mālik treated the arbiters like the *imām* who has the right to pronounce a divorce if ill-treatment (*ḍarar*) has been established, unlike the Hanafis, who consider the arbiters to be mere "agents" (*wakīlān*) chosen by the spouses and with no judicial power. Ibn Rushd emphasizes the scholarly agreement that the two arbiters must be chosen from among the relatives of the spouses, unless persons fulfilling the necessary requirements cannot be found among them, in which case outsiders may be chosen. In sum, the Malikis regard the two arbiters as magistrates whose power derives from the *sulṭān* (al-Wansharīsī 1937:9 and 27), who has the right to dissolve a marriage if harm (*ḍarar*) has been established. Judicial divorces requested by the wife are repudiations (either definitive or revocable) pronounced by the judge in place of the husband. In the case of a judicial divorce on the grounds of harm, the repudiation is definitive, but the spouses may remarry without the wife having to observe the procedure of *taḥlīl* (Linant de Bellefonds 1965–73, 2:308 and 406–7).

2. *The Judicial Practice of Dār Amīn/Amīna in al-Andalus*

To this point we have discussed the doctrine recorded in Maliki legal treatises. However, some of those treatises mention that in al-Andalus the judicial practice (*ʿamal*) did not follow the Qurʾānic prescription of the two arbiters. Rather, judges used to send a couple with marital problems to the house of a trustworthy person, who could be either a man or a woman (*dār amīn/amīna*) (Fierro 1985). This judicial

[15] See also Santillana (1938, 2:286–7). For Khalīl's mention of the related institution of the *dār ʿadl*, see below.

practice is attested in al-Andalus starting in the first half of the third/ninth century. The jurist responsible for the introduction of the *dār amīn* in Maliki legal practice in al-Andalus and the Maghrib was reportedly the Berber jurist Yaḥyā b. Yaḥyā al-Laythī (d. 234/848) (Fierro 1997b), whose *riwāya* of Mālik's *Muwaṭṭaʾ* became canonical in the Islamic West. Although Yaḥyā b. Yaḥyā was never himself a *qāḍī*, he was the most influential mufti of his times and he is reported to have influenced the nomination of Cordovan judges by the Umayyad emir of al-Andalus.

The sources characterize Yaḥyā b. Yaḥyā's introduction of the *dār amīn* into al-Andalus in both negative and positive terms. As for the negative characterization, Yaḥyā b. Yaḥyā was criticized[16] for abandoning the Qurʾānic prescription by failing to dispatch two arbiters when the spouses quarrelled (*lā yarā baʿthat al-ḥakamayn ʿinda tashājur al-zawjayn*) and for departing from the doctrine of Mālik b. Anas himself, as recorded in the *Muwaṭṭaʾ*, by upholding instead that the estranged couple should be sent to *dār amīn.*[17] Yaḥyā b. Yaḥyā did not adduce any known legal precedent in support of *dār amīn* and he is not reported to have provided any explanation for his legal opinion. The famous Maliki jurist Abū ʿUmar b. ʿAbd al-Barr (d. 463/1070)[18] stated that Yaḥyā b. Yaḥyā gave his legal opinion in favor of *dār amīn* in cases that required the dispatch of the two arbiters and that this became the judicial practice (*ʿamal*) in al-Andalus (Ibn ʿAbd al-Barr 1980, 2:597). In fact, the practice of the judges in Cordova during the second half of the third/ninth century was to send the estranged couple to the house of a trustworthy man (*amīn*) or to lodge the *amīn* in the couple's house.[19]

As for the positive characterization, Yaḥyā b. Yaḥyā is reported to have proposed the *dār amīn* when no arbiters could be found among the relatives of the spouses, in what therefore seems to be a

[16] The accusers were "reformed" Malikis such as Ibn Sahl or Abū Bakr b. al-ʿArabī. See on this development Fierro (forthcoming).

[17] This accusation is found in Ibn Sahl (1997, 1:506–17), al-Burzulī (2002, 2:412–26) and al-Wansharīsī (1981, 2:443–4).

[18] This Cordovan jurist was a reformer of Malikism who attempted to adapt its theory and practice to the standards set by the "classical" doctrine of *uṣūl al-fiqh.* In this he was influenced by his previous attachment to Shafiʿism.

[19] The evidence of this third/ninth century practice is found in Ibn Sahl (1997, 1:506–17) (study of this case in Marín 2000:454–5). Ibn Sahl quotes the *Aḥkām Ibn Ziyād,* the court records of a Cordovan judge who served at the end of the third/ninth century. See on the latter work Fierro (1992:124) and Muranyi (1998).

development of the doctrine found in Saḥnūn's *Mudawwana*. Defending Yaḥyā's doctrine, the Cordovan jurist and mufti *mushāwar*, Isḥāq b. Ibrāhīm b. Masarra (d. 352/963 or 354/965), claimed that the practice of *dār amīn* arose for the lack of relatives who could act as arbiters. He explained that all Muslims know that the sending of the two arbiters constitutes a binding precept and that neither the magistrates nor the scholars have rejected such a prescription. However, as time passed, it became more and more difficult to find arbiters among the relatives of the husband and the wife who satisfied all the required conditions and who would reside with the estranged couple for the necessary period of time. Only rarely could one find arbiters who possessed religious and legal knowledge, and who were intelligent, pious and scrupulous. For this reason, when the magistrates could not find arbiters among the relatives of the couple, they chose a qualified person (man or woman) to investigate the reasons for the estrangement and to propose a way to solve it. Often a solution was found without having to decide who was responsible and without separating the spouses. Ibn Masarra added that no judgment was ever issued calling for the separation of a couple on the basis of the testimony of an *amīn* or *amīna*, whose function was to expose the source of the damage to the marriage and who usually succeeded in reconciling the spouses (al-Wansharīsī 1981, 2:443–4; al-Shaʿbī 1992:193–5, nos. 285 and 392, no. 843).[20]

The nonapplication of the Qur'ānic prescription in al-Andalus is also suggested by the absence of documents regarding the two arbiters in the *wathā'iq* work of Ibn Mughīth (1994).[21] Under the Almoravids, the Maliki jurist Ibn al-Ḥājj (d. 529/1135) was asked who should pay for the maintenance of the *amīna*, i.e., the spouse who asked for her services or the spouse who was found to be responsible for the marital discord. Ibn al-Ḥājj's answer was that payment is incumbent upon the former; if the case is unclear, payment is incumbent upon the latter until it is clarified (al-Wansharīsī 1981, 3:414).

[20] This last part reveals the uneasiness at allowing someone to decide to dissolve a marriage without the consent of the husband. For the Malikis, only the arbiters mentioned in Qur'ān 4:35 can make the husband pronounce or accept divorce, if that is the decision reached by both arbiters.

[21] The works of Ibn al-ʿAṭṭār 1983, and al-Buntī (d. 462/1070), *al-Wathā'iq wa-l-masā'il al-majmūʿa* (on which see Aguirre Sádaba 2000:9) do not contain a document on the *ḥakamān*, but no conclusion can be drawn from this, as these texts are preserved incompletely (I thank Javier Aguirre Sádaba for his help on this matter.) On al-Mattītī (d. 570/1174), whose *wathā'iq* work is still unpublished, see below.

This text implies that the judicial practice was still based on the *dār amīn/amīna* institution, in spite of the fact that during the fifth/eleventh century, Abū ʿUmar b. ʿAbd al-Barr and Ibn Sahl, influential Maliki jurists (the latter was also a judge), argued forcefully for Andalusi judges to follow the Qurʾānic prescription. Their stand was also adopted by one of the most important Maliki jurists under the Almoravids. Abū Bakr b. al-ʿArabī (d. 543/1148), famous for his attempt to renew Malikism by adapting it to the classical doctrine of *uṣūl al-fiqh*, complained in his *Aḥkām al-Qurʾān* (s.d., 1:421–7; al-Qurṭubī 1935–50, 5:174–9) of the abandonment in al-Andalus of the Qurʾānic prescription and its substitution by sending the estranged couple to live with an *amīna*. Ibn al-ʿArabī remarked indignantly that he had met only a single Andalusi judge who followed the Qurʾān (he may have been referring to Ibn Sahl). He also explained how, during his qadiship, he judged in accordance with the Qurʾānic verse. Ibn al-ʿArabī's abandonment of the previous judicial practice did not make him popular and this may have been one of the causes of his dismissal as judge of Seville.

Abū Bakr b. al-ʿArabī was in many ways a precursor of the religious revolution of the Almohads, the main aim of which was to renew the Muslim community by bringing it closer to the golden age of the beginnings of Islam (Fierro 1999). The Almohads insisted that the Qurʾān and *sunna* had to be followed and those who had gone astray had to return to the right path. One of the practices to be revived was the Qurʾānic prescription of the two arbiters. Al-Jazīrī (d. 585/1189) (1998:118–20; Marín 2000:455–6) included in his *wathāʾiq* work a document on the two arbiters. The document begins: "The judge Fulan certifies that Fulana came to his *majlis* and told him that her husband Fulan was ill-treating her in her person and possessions. . . . The husband denied [the accusation] and stated that it was [the wife] who ill-treated him in his person and possessions. . . ." The document goes on to record how the two arbiters mentioned in Qurʾān 4:35 should act. The document shows again that the Qurʾānic prescription was understood to pertain to cases of abused wives seeking a divorce, that is, in cases in which the wife takes the initiative in attempting to terminate the marriage. The legal explanation (*fiqh*) that accompanies the document states that the woman took the initiative: if it were determined that the man was responsible, she would be entitled to a divorce and he would not receive any compensation; however, if it were determined that he was not responsible and she was, she must pay him compensation. Although this document clearly aims to apply the Qur'ānic prescription in judicial practice, it also reflects how difficult it was to follow such a prescription in practice, as shown by the fact that it was deemed necessary to specify that if no qualified arbiters were found among the relatives of the spouses, the judge had to name two qualified persons to act as arbiters.

Official Almohad policy apparently sought to apply the Qur'ānic institution of arbitration in the courts. Nevertheless, nonlegal sources refer to the survival of the practice of *dār amīn* under the Almohads. The evidence is found in the biography of an eminent Almohad jurist, Ibn al-Qaṭṭān (d. 628/1230). As chief of the Almohad scholars (*ṭalaba*), he was put in charge of the trial against a young man who had claimed to be a prophet. During the trial, Ibn al-Qaṭṭān censored the young man's father for not preventing his son from making his claim. The father then explained that he had only limited control over the actions of his son, who lived with his mother, not with him. As the result of a quarrel between the husband and wife, the young man's mother resided in a room in the house of a trustworthy man (*hiya sākina li-mushājara baynanā baytan fī dār rajul amīn*) (al-Marrākushī 1984:182).

The Almohads were thus unable to eliminate the judicial practice introduced by Yaḥyā b. Yaḥyā, and Maliki jurists continued to uphold it. The practice of *dār amīn* is referred to by Khalīl in his *Mukhtaṣar* as a precursor to having recourse to the two arbiters: if the husband causes harm to his wife, the judge admonishes him and sends the wife to a trustworthy person, unless the wife is already there. But if the case is difficult, that is, if it is not easy to determine the cause of discord, the judge names two arbiters, chosen from among the relatives of the spouses and, if this is not possible, from among the neighbors.

3. *North African Malikis and the Institution of Dār ʿAdl/Dār al-Thiqa and the Jīrān Ṣāliḥīn*

Qur'ān 4:35 mentions the fear of *shiqāq*, that is, disagreement and enmity (*al-khilāf wa-l-ʿadāwa*) between the spouses. *Furūʿ* works use terms such a *tashājur, nushūz* and *tadāruʿ*. *Tafsīr* works and legal manuals, as we have seen, do not usually explain how the *shiqāq, tashājur* or mutual *nushūz* eventually leads to the intervention of the two arbiters. Information mentioned in Maghribi *fatāwā* collections and court records from both the premodern and modern period confirm the evidence of the Andalusi sources. The fatwas also envision the application of Qur'ān 4:35 in cases in which an ill-treated woman seeks a divorce against her husband's will, while at the same time showing the difficulties of putting into practice the Qur'ānic prescription. A case recorded by L. Milliot (1924:25–32) that took place in Casablanca in the year 1336/1917 illustrates this point. In the legal discussion that accompanies it (which I summarize), one finds extensive reference to precedents in the classical Maliki legal literature.

Amina bint al-Hajj Mustafa Mulin, represented by her brother, explained to the court that her husband had abused her violently and excessively without any reason. She then abandoned the marital house. Amina asked that her husband provide her with maintenance from the moment she left his house. The husband denied having inflicted any harm on her and stated that she left the marital house without his consent, so that he was not bound to pay her any maintenance. However, two female witnesses certified that Amina showed signs of having been beaten before she went to court. The *qāḍī* of Casablanca ruled as follows: (1) the husband must live with his wife among honorable neighbors (*jīrān ṣāliḥīn*), since it had not been conclusively established that he was responsible for her injuries; (2) the husband must provide for his wife's maintenance and lodging for two months, because he did not ask the court to make his wife return and because a wife loses her right to *nafaqa* if she is rebellious, that is, if she runs away without any reason.

But the *qāḍī*'s judgment was revoked for the following reasons. Instead of ordering the husband to live with his wife among honorable people, the *qāḍī* should have asked the neighbors to testify about the husband's behavior, given that the harm allegedly inflicted by him on her had not been established. If the neighbors declared that the husband was in the habit of abusing his wife without any reason, the *qāḍī* should punish and imprison him. If the neighbors merely heard the woman screaming, without actually seeing anything, the husband should be punished (but not imprisoned), because the fact that he did not seek help indicates that he was responsible. This doctrine is based on the precedent established by Saḥnūn as recorded, among others, by the Andalusi Maliki Ibn Salmūn (1884–5:101–6; see also López Ortiz 1927:350–2).

Now, one may argue that the judge ordered the spouses to live among honorable neighbors in order to ascertain if the woman's accusation were true and in order to encourage the husband to mend his ways. However, the wife did not claim that she had been abused on a regular basis, and the *qāḍī* therefore may not act as if she did. Al-Mattītī (d. 570/1174)[22] explained: "If a woman repeatedly claims in front of the judge that she has been harmed by her husband, but without being able to establish the claim, the judge must order them to live among honorable persons charged with witnessing the behavior of the spouses. If the husband already lives in the midst of such honorable persons, the *qāḍī* cannot require him to move to another place."

This opinion was transmitted by al-Mawwāq (d. 894/1489 or 897/1492) (Seco de Lucena 1959:17–8) and the same solution was recorded by Ibn Salmūn. The *qāḍī* should first have checked to determine if the couple lived among honorable persons and, if so, he should have interrogated them. If the couple did not live among honorable persons, the *qāḍī* could have ruled as he did. Assuming that the *qāḍī* did not make this determination, he should have interrogated the neighbors. If they stated that the husband habitually abused his wife without reason, the husband must be punished according to the judge's discretion. If they merely declared that they heard the woman screaming, the *qāḍī* must punish the husband and order the wife to return to the marital house. But if the neighbors declared that the husband did not habitually abuse his wife, the woman should be made to return to the marital house, as the signs of violence on her body do not establish harm on the part of the husband. Ibn Salmūn stated: "According to Ibn Ḥārith,[23] neither a beating nor the traces of a beating, even if its existence has been established, prove harm on the part of the husband. If the woman persists in complaining to the *qāḍī*, without being able to support her claims, the husband should go to live among honorable persons. If the situation remains unclear, the two arbiters mentioned in the Qur'ān must be sent."[24]

---

[22] An Andalusi Maliki jurist, author of a famous *wathā'iq* work, still unpublished.

[23] A jurist from Qayrawān who settled in al-Andalus in the fourth/tenth century. Of his legal production the only book preserved is *Uṣūl al-futyā* (1985) that includes a section on the two arbiters.

[24] The review of the judgment continues, dealing with the issue of whether or not the husband should pay *nafaqa* and provide lodging for his wife.

The legal discussion that accompanies this case shows that the Qur'ānic prescription was not considered very practical, for two reasons: (1) before women went to court, it is likely that the families had already intervened and failed to achieve reconciliation between the spouses; this was the reason one of the spouses went to court; (2) as we have seen acknowledged in the legal manuals, it was not easy to find among the families of the spouses persons who were qualified to act as arbiters: persons who possessed legal knowledge, *ʿadāla*, and were trustworthy.[25] Therefore, recourse to the two arbiters was not the first step, but the last. When a woman seeks a divorce on grounds of harm, the first thing she must do is to prove that harm exists. The most practical thing for the judge to do is to ask the neighbors. If this does not clarify the situation, then the spouses should be placed under observation by trustworthy persons chosen from among honorable neighbors, the *jīrān ṣāliḥīn*. This expression is used by Khalīl b. Isḥāq, an Egyptian Hanafi turned Maliki who lived in the eighth/fourteenth century.[26] Previously and subsequently, another method to determine the cause of marital discord was the institution of *dār amīn*, the existence of which was not limited to al-Andalus. In Tunis, a trustworthy woman (*amīna*) moved into the marital house of an estranged couple in order to observe the problem (al-Burzulī 2002, 2:412–26; Idris 1962, 2:587). This practice was still attested in Tunis in the sixteenth and seventeenth centuries (Largueche 1992:85–112). In more recent times, Anderson reports that in Zanzibar, in cases of matrimonial discord and alleged cruelty, the courts occasionally order the parties to live near an *amīn* (reliable person) whose duty it is to watch over and report on their conduct (Anderson 1954:73–4).[27]

The same practice is referred to as *dār ʿadl* or *dār al-thiqa*. The first expression is found in a number of cases that took place in the Sharīʿa Court of Ajdabiya (northern Cyrenaica, Libya) in the early 1950s (Layish 1995a). In one case, a woman repeatedly complained to the *qāḍī* that her husband was abusing her without an acceptable

[25] Ibn ʿAbd al-Barr (1980, 2:596) establishes that arbiters should be chosen *min ahl al-ʿadāla wa-ḥusn al-naẓar wa-l-baṣar bi-l-fiqh.*

[26] The expression might have been used previously by Malikis such as Ibn Ḥārith (see note 23). The expression *jīrān ṣāliḥīn* also appears in Hanafi law: Meron (1971: 210–11). At the present stage, I do not know which school influenced the other.

[27] The cases recorded by Anderson reflect Ibāḍī (Khariji) law.

reason. The husband accused her of refusing to have intercourse with him (implying that she was rebellious). They discussed divorce, but finally agreed to reside in the neighborhood (*jiwār*) of a well-known *faqīh* from another tribe so that his house might "serve as a house of a virtuous person testifying (to the court) to what was going on between them on the basis of his personal observation."

In another case, the court directed an estranged couple to move to the private house of a man who specialized in hosting spouses with such problems. Some time later, the man was asked in court about relations between the estranged couple. Another estranged couple reconciled after the husband lodged his wife in a dwelling in the vicinity of the *ʿadl*, a tribal shaykh, on whom they had agreed, "in order that he be a witness as to the measure of kindness which they displayed towards each other in living together." Finally, in another case, a wife who complained of abuse asked to be placed in a *dār ʿadl*. Layish explains that the *ʿadl* is an agent of the *sharīʿa* court whose function is to observe the behavior of the couple living near him, and then to assist the *qāḍī* in reaching a decision by providing the necessary information on the nature of the dispute and the party responsible for it. The term *ʿadl* has a normative Islamic connotation: the informant reporting to the court is an eyewitness and, like a professional witness or notary attached to the court, he is therefore expected to possess integrity (*ʿadl*). The function of the *dār ʿadl* is to serve as the temporary residence of the spouses who move there. The *ʿadl*, who is in a position to observe their behavior, then informs the judge of the reasons for their estrangement. The *dār ʿadl*, Layish observes, is a temporary living arrangement that originates in customary tribal law and is intended to serve as a mechanism for handling disputes between spouses by ascertaining the cause of the dispute and the degree of responsibility of each spouse. This information is necessary for the determination of financial consequences at the time of the settlement of the dispute, whether within the marriage or upon its dissolution. For example, in one of the cases, the *qāḍī* decided that the wife had suffered damage (*ḍarar*) and he gave her the option to divorce herself. When she exercised that option, the *qāḍī* ordered the husband to pay the remainder of her dower and other financial obligations.

In two of the cases studied by Layish, it seems to be the woman alone who moves to the *dār ʿadl*. In one of those two cases, however, it is clear that the *ʿadl* was going to observe the marital relations between the spouses, which means that the husband must have visited his wife in the *dār ʿadl*. In the other case it seems that the woman wanted to be moved to the *dār ʿadl* in order to escape her husband's abuse and to live there in safety during the court hearings and proceedings.

The *dār ʿadl* is not mentioned in the Libyan Code of Personal Law, which states that when divorce by mutual agreement is not possible, the court must name two arbiters to attempt a reconciliation. The arbiters must be male, relatives of the spouses, if possible, and if not, they must have knowledge of the spouses and the ability to reconcile them. The court fixes the period of time during which the arbiters must act (no longer than one month, with a possible extension), and if they do not submit a report after that period two other arbiters will be named. If the two arbiters do not succeed in achieving reconciliation, they must report to the court, which then issues a judgment (Ruiz-Almodóvar 1999:175–6).[28] Article 56 of the Algerian Family Code (9 June 1984) states that when marital discord intensifies and the responsibility for it cannot be established, two arbiters must be named to attempt reconciliation. They are to be chosen by the judge from among the relatives of the spouses, one on behalf of each, and they must present a report of their efforts within a period of two months (Pérez-Beltrán 1995:392; Borrmans 1979:315, art. 48). The Tunisian Code of Personal Law (August 13, 1956) states that if one of the spouses declares that the other is harming her/him, but is unable to prove it, and if the judge cannot determine who is responsible, he must name two arbiters, who, after studying the situation, must try to reconcile the spouses, keeping the judge informed (Borrmans 1979:186, art. 25).[29]

In the Moroccan Code (November 22, 1957, reformed in September 1993) known as the *Mudawwana*, the articles on divorce on the grounds of harm (*ḍarar*) establish that if the wife claims that her husband is harming her in such a way that the continuation of marital life is made impossible for people of their status, and if the wife establishes

---

[28] Ruiz-Almodóvar explains that reference to the two arbiters is made in article 36, section 4, chapter 2 of this Code, promulgated in 1984 and modified in 1991. See the English translation (El Alami 1996:181–95). However, article 36 does not appear in the official Arabic text published in *Aḥkām al-usrā fī l-zawāj wa-l-ṭalāq wa-athāruhā*.

[29] The Tunisian Code thus does not connect the arbitration procedures exclusively to abused wives, but interprets Qur'ān 4:35 literally as referring to both spouses.

her claim, the judge is to divorce them if he cannot reconcile them. If the wife's request for a divorce is rejected, and she renews it but is unable to establish harm, the judge names two arbiters who must attempt to reconcile the spouses, looking for the causes of marital discord (*shiqāq*). If reconciliation is possible under certain conditions, the arbiters should specify those conditions. If reconciliation proves impossible, the judge intervenes and makes a decision according to what the arbiters propose (Ruiz-Almodóvar 1995a:432–3; Borrmans 1979:232, art. 56; Ruiz de Almodóvar 1995b:197–207). Arbitration is treated in the Moroccan Code within the context of those cases in which a woman can ask for a judicial divorce for reasons such as the failure of her husband to provide her with maintenance, his illness, the establishment of the husband's abuse or his absence. In all these cases, reconciliation is encouraged by recourse to arbiters.[30] If a wife petitions for the divorce and the spouses are not cohabiting during the court procedures, the woman may be ordered to live in *dār al-thiqa*:

> If that demand is presented in front of the judge and there is no cohabitation of the spouses during the trial, the husband may propose that the woman go and live with one of his relatives of her choice while the judgment takes place. If the woman does not make any choice, her husband may decide with which relative of hers she has to live. If the woman refuses, the judge shall order her to live in the *dār al-thiqa*. In every case, the husband must provide for her maintenance (Ruiz-Almodóvar 1995a:433–4).[31]

Although not explicitly stated, the situation envisaged here is most likely one in which the woman is seeking a divorce and does not want to live in the marital house or has left it for a number of reasons (most probably abuse). It is clear that the *dār al-thiqa* of the Moroccan *Mudawwana* originally was the same institution as the *dār ʿadl* and the *dār amīn*. But the practice recorded in the Moroccan Code appears to be different from that of the premodern period. What is new is that the *dār al-thiqa* is now seen as the final step

[30] For an analysis of cases in Moroccan courts in which women seek a divorce on the grounds of harm, see Mir-Hosseini (1993:106–11). Mir-Hosseini states that arbitration is not observed in practice and that Moroccan courts do not have any arbitration procedures similar to those of Iranian courts (1993:213, note 25).

[31] Cf. Borrmans (1979:232), where it is indicated that in the original version of this article of the *Mudawwana*, *dār al-thiqāf*, "a house of personal arrest," was used instead of *dār al-thiqa*.

among various possibilities offered to the husband in order that he may preserve the power to control his wife outside the marital house. The husband decides where his wife must live and, although she may reject his decision, it is the judge who decides that she must go to *dār al-thiqa*. In the premodern period, it was either the wife who took refuge in the *dār amīn* on her own initiative or the judge who sent her there, apparently without the husband's intervention; this indicates that the *dār amīn* was mostly a place of refuge precisely because it was outside the control of the husband. That the *dār al-thiqa* of the Moroccan Code is not exactly the same institution as the *dār ʿadl/dār amīn* is shown by the fact that in a previous version of the *Mudawwana*, the *dār al-thiqa* was called "house of personal arrest" (*dār al-thiqāf*).

Mir-Hosseini has noted that the grafting of Maliki law onto a modern legal system in Morocco has created a situation in which the patriarchal elements of the *sharīʿa* are reinforced, while the classical leeways are reduced (1993:198).[32] The *dār al-thiqa* is a case in point. Once a custom helpful to women, its long-term incorporation into Islamic law eventually led to its transformation into a place for the control and seclusion of women. The unfolding of this process can be seen in a number of cases.

In a case dated 1367/1948 (Milliot 1924, 4:51), a husband failed to comply with a stipulation in the marriage contract, with the result that his wife asked for divorce. The husband denied that he had violated the stipulation. During the court procedures, the judge treated the woman as still married to the man and put her under the guard of a trustworthy person (*amīn*).[33]

Larguèche has devoted two studies (1992, 1996)[34] to the institution of *dār jawād* (*dar joued*), "house of a noble person," a house of

---

[32] Mir-Hosseini does not mention any case of *dār al-thiqa*, an institution that was still working in 1965: see Ben Talha (1965:92–6). (I owe this reference to M. Marín.) The gradual disappearance of the *dār al-thiqa* in Morocco is documented in al-Fāsī (2000:310–11): Chafi (1996:131); Ibn Maʿjūz (1998, 1:307–9). (I owe these references to M. Feria.)

[33] This may be connected with the following procedure: an unmarried woman who someone claims to have married should be placed in the custody of a trustworthy woman (*amīna*) or be confined at the request of the husband, so that he may establish his claim (Toledano 1981:154–5).

[34] Larguèche (1996:263) states that the institutions of *dār al-thiqa/dār al-iskān/dār al-amāna* had a clear *sharīʿa* basis, although she herself mentions sources that consider it an innovation against the Qurʾānic two arbiters prescription.

arrest and correction, where rebellious and recalcitrant women were confined so as to "bring them around" to the prescribed norms of conduct and morality. This institution flourished in the nineteenth century. Larguèche finds the antecedents of this institution in the *dār al-thiqa, dār al-suknā bi-ḥusnā* and *dār al-amāna* mentioned in *fatwā* collections and court records.[35] According to Larguèche, the movement from one institution to the other is a passage from "a preventive institution to a repressive one." The evolution is from a place in which an estranged couple is placed under the observation of a trustworthy person, that is, a mechanism for regulating marital life, to a place for the control, repression and reeducation of women.[36] This evolution can be documented from the eighteenth century onwards. In the end, the seclusion of women in the *dār al-thiqa* or *dar joued* was ordered by the husband himself, not by the judge. Typically, women are ordered to move to *dar joued* when they reject an undesirable husband or become attached to suitors not acceptable to their families.

4. *On the Origins of the Practice of Dār Amīn*

The material discussed to this point comes from Maliki texts, but not all Maliki texts discuss the *dār amīn* institution. I have not found any reference to it in early Maliki legal literature written outside the Islamic West. At present, I cannot tell whether the Ibadi legal practice in Zanzibar was influenced by Malikism or if the Maliki legal practice was influenced by Ibadism. We have seen how the legal discussion on the Qur'ānic two arbiters can be linked to a major politico-religious event in the history of the early Muslim community, the battle of Ṣiffīn, and the disagreement regarding the arbitration that took place then. When analyzing Qur'ān 4:35, Hanafis, like Shi'is,

[35] Larguèche (1996:266) states: "All the reported cases that finished with an obligated stay by the couple at the *Dar Sukna bi-Husna* are classified under the rubric of 'poor treatment' or 'cohabitation difficulties' (*sū' mu'āshara*), excluding the cases that touch on the intimate life of the couple, including sentimental and sexual relations." She also observes that "*Dar al-Thiqa* or *Dar Sukna bi Husna* were often solicited by women plaintiffs" (1996:267).

[36] Ramírez (1998:61, note 10), compares this process with a similar one that took place during the eighteenth century in La Habana, where the Hospital of San Francisco de Paula provided protection to women who had escaped from their husbands or to women who were alone. Later on, it became a place for the seclusion of women considered to have violated the prevailing social norms.

followed the position taken by the partisans of ʿAlī at Ṣiffīn: they denied that the decision of the two arbiters was binding if one of the parties rejected it, and they did not consider the arbiters to be magistrates, but rather agents of the parties involved. The Malikis, on their part, adopted a position regarding Qur'ān 4:35 that reflects the Sunni understanding of what happened at Ṣiffīn.

There was a third position adopted at Ṣiffīn, that of the Kharijis, who rejected the principle of arbitration (Hawting 1978). Did this Khariji position have any influence on their doctrine regarding the Qur'ānic prescription of the two arbiters?[37] For the moment, I can only say that all Western Maliki legal texts that discuss the origins of the practice of the *dār amīn* state that the practice was established by a famous jurist and mufti living in al-Andalus in the first half of the third/ninth century, the Berber Yaḥyā b. Yaḥyā, and that by the second half of that century the judicial practice of al-Andalus followed his legal view. He is said to have provided no precedent (*riwāya*) for the practice. Whereas later Maliki jurists, struggling to protect the established judicial practice, argued that the *dār amīn* institution was not intended to substitute for the Qur'ānic two arbiters, but was just an earlier step before having recourse to them, earlier jurists clearly stated that Yaḥyā b. Yaḥyā rejected the two arbiters and instead upheld the practice of the *dār amīn*.[38]

As a Berber and a proto-Maliki, Yaḥyā b. Yaḥyā could have been close on this point to the position of either the *ahl al-Irāq*[39] or that of the Kharijis. He may have felt uneasy about Qur'ān 4:35 because of its link with what had happened at Ṣiffīn.[40] Instead of following the Qur'ānic prescription, he followed a practice that may have been rooted in Berber customary law, which would explain why the *dār amīn* institution in pre-modern times was applied in the area of

---

[37] I will explore early Ibadi literature in the forthcoming study mentioned in note 12.

[38] What was at work is the process described by Toledano (1981:21): "When confronted with the innovations of *ʿamal* (which are in clear contradiction to the *Shariʿah*), the Maghribi traditional jurists tend to rationalize them juristically within the framework of the *Shariʿah*, in order to deny *ʿamal* its normative, systematic and independent function."

[39] Hanafism had a noticeable influence in early North African Maliki law: see Fierro (1985).

[40] In Ibn Sahl's text, it is stated that Qur'ān 4:35 was never abrogated, which suggests that some early jurists may have considered it to be a *mansūkh* verse.

Malikism that corresponds to Berber lands. From there, it spread to Egypt and sub-Saharan Africa.

Among Berber tribes studied by Westermarck in Morocco, a woman who does not want to remain with her husband may take refuge in another man's house or tent, where she embraces a pole or takes hold of a handmill and turns it as if she were grinding. The owner of the house or the tent is then obligated to marry her, after making a payment to the husband. This obligation falls upon the man regardless of whether he is single or married; and, in the latter case, regardless of the number of his wives. If he does not marry the woman, she throws an *ʿār* (conditional curse) on him by embracing the pole of his dwelling or turning his handmill; according to popular belief, something terrible would then happen to him (Westermarck 1926, 1:533–4 and 1921:57–8).

Among the Awlad Ali of Cyrenaica (now in the Egyptian Western desert) (Mohsen 1967), an abused woman usually takes refuge with her father or brother. If her husband wants to take her back, he gives her a present as a sign that he misbehaved. If the woman's goal is to obtain a divorce, but she cannot count on the support of her own family, she can initiate a procedure recognized by custom.

> According to this procedure, a woman who does not desire to continue living with her husband can go to a respectable man in the community and "throw herself" over him. By so throwing herself, this man becomes obliged to give refuge to the woman and to start negotiating with her husband to divorce her . . . Due to the nature of his role in mediating, the woman must be careful in selecting the man over whom she throws herself.

Mohsen states that there is no social stigma associated with this procedure or the women who follow it. The procedure of "throwing herself" liberates the woman from her husband and gives her a status close to that of her husband, as far as the ability to dissolve the marriage is concerned (Mohsen 1967:162–5).[41]

An Awlad Ali woman can also divorce her husband without returning the *mahr*, if she establishes that he cannot perform his sexual duties. The husband of course may deny such an accusation. Mohsen writes:

---

[41] The differences between this procedure and that followed by the Sinai bedouins have been analyzed by Stewart (1991).

> If both insist on their stand, one or both may ask to be submitted to *bait el-shanaʿa* or house of the dreadful deeds. Reports are extremely vague about the exact procedures involved in such a case. Some informants stated that the married couple would live in a tent without sidewalls so that everybody can see what goes on inside it. Most informants, however, insist that it merely means that the couple move their tent near to that of a respectable man whose word is dependable and honored. This man is supposed to keep a close watch on the couple's activities, by listening or looking through the holes in the tent. His verdict determines the future of the marriage. If the wife is justified in her claim the husband is forced to divorce her and to forfeit his mahr. If, on the other hand, the verdict is for the husband he not only can divorce his wife and get the mahr back, but he is also entitled to *kabara* or compensation for his injured pride. There was no case of *bait el-shana'a* in the area during the time of the field work, and most people insisted that this practice was obsolete when the mahr was relatively high and was paid in livestock, in which case its return to the husband would have caused great financial inconvenience for the wife's family. (Mohsen 1967:160)

Layish regards "the house of dreadful deeds" as one of the antecedents of *dār ʿadl.* He argues that the expression *bi-jiwār qawm ṣāliḥīn* that is found in some of the documents he has studied should be connected with a customary context. He concludes that the term "*jiwār*" should be understood as "protection," a fundamental institution in tribal law. A violation of protection

> . . . entails a sanction the gravity of which is determined in accordance with the social standing of the guarantor of the protection. In addition the offender must propitiate the injured party. The relationship between the *ʿadl* and the couple is thus primarily one between the guarantor of protection and its recipient. This relationship has an inner logic in tribal society. During the period of observation of their conduct by the *ʿadl,* the spouses are outside their protected natural environment based on agnatic blood relationship. The protection by the *ʿadl* is thus vital in order to provide them an alternative defense against damage to their persons and property during that period. When the *ʿadl* has concluded his task, the spouses return to their natural environment and the protection is no longer required. The *ʿadl* is therefore expected to be—to use Mohsen's mode of speech—a respectable person whose word is believed and honored, or, in other terms, a person whose protection is to be regarded as an honor because of his status and prestige in tribal society (Layish 1995a:207–8).

Layish may be correct in establishing a connection between the *dār ʿadl* and tribal customary law in the form of the "house of dreadful deeds." In my opinion, however, the *dār ʿadl/dār amīn* was also influenced by the practice of abused women who, lacking the support of their families for whatever reason, sought asylum and "threw themselves" at the feet of a respectable man, as described by Mohsen. In some of the cases found in court records and *fatwā* collections, it was the women who sought refuge in the *dār ʿadl/dār amīn* or asked the judge to confine them there. These women had been battered and their lives were in danger. Their reaction was to run away from their husbands and to seek refuge and protection. Whereas the mere protection of a powerful man is sufficient to liberate such a woman from her husband according to tribal customary law (Westermarck, Mohsen), this is not the case under Islamic law. Evidence of harm must be established in order for an abused woman to obtain a divorce without financial loss. The financial implications of divorce were known to the husband and would have motivated him to accept the practice of *dār ʿadl/dār amīn*: if harm could not be established, then the wife, under Maliki law, could obtain a divorce, but had to pay compensation to the husband.

Layish has argued that recourse to *dār ʿadl* by Libyan judges was an attempt to Islamicize local practice (1995:198). By the middle of the twentieth century, however, the *dār ʿadl* had a long tradition within the Western Maliki legal tradition, as shown by the material reviewed in this study. The "Islamicization" of the practice of *dār amīn* (probably a Berber tribal custom) started with the mufti Yaḥyā b. Yaḥyā, whose legal opinion was adopted by Andalusi judges in the third/ninth century. The judicial practice (*ʿamal*) in al-Andalus, in turn, found its way into influential legal works, such as those by Abū ʿUmar b. ʿAbd al-Barr and Khalīl b. Isḥāq,[42] in spite of attempts to eliminate it. *Dār amīn*, also known as *dār ʿadl* or *dār al-thiqa*, thus constitutes an illuminating example of the process by which certain customary practices were incorporated into the body of the *sharīʿa* even when such practices were at variance with Qurʾānic principles (Toledano 1981:10) and given a *sharʿī* rationale.

[42] Layish has informed me (Jerusalem 2000: see Author's note) that there is no mention of the *dār amīn* or *dār ʿadl* in Ibn ʿĀṣim's *Tuḥfa*, the legal manual followed by Libyan judges.

CHAPTER FOURTEEN

THE AWARD OF *MATĀʿ* IN THE EARLY MUSLIM COURTS*

Muhammad Khalid Masud

We have only a limited knowledge of judicial practice in the early Muslim courts, especially during the Umayyad caliphate (41–132/661–750), which is the formative period of the institution of *qaḍāʾ* (judgeship). In the absence of actual court records, historians of Islamic judicial practice rely on the information available in *fiqh* texts and literary sources, such as works on *Aḥkām* (e.g., Amedroz 1910, 761ff., relying on al-Māwardī's *Al-aḥkām al-sulṭāniyya*) and *Adab al-qāḍī* texts (e.g., Nakadī 1923, Ibn ʿArnūs 1934, Mubārak 1977, Zaydān 1983, Āzād 1987, and Fuḍaylat 1991). The *adab al-qāḍī* texts are not reports about actual judicial practice; they were written primarily as guides for qāḍīs (see Introduction). We should therefore keep in mind the warning of E. Tyan, who cautioned that the writings of the jurists describe the ideal rather than the actual practice of Muslim courts (Tyan 1960, 9). In this essay, I use biographical dictionaries as a source, as they provide precious information about the actual judicial practice.

The Umayyad period witnessed the development of *fiqh* and the evolution of the schools of Islamic law; the study of judicial practice in this period helps us to understand the interaction between legal doctrine and judicial practice. I focus here on the judicial practice associated with the legal doctrine of *matāʿ*, a wife's right to receive property from her husband at the time of divorce. Different scholars translate the term *matāʿ* into English as "gift," "maintenance," and "alimony." To avoid confusion, I will use the Qurʾānic term *matāʿ* throughout this essay.

The meaning of the term *matāʿ* and the legal doctrine relating to it have been debated by the jurists over the centuries. I argue here

* I would like to thank David Powers and Ruud Peters for their valuable comments.

that *matāʿ* is not a gift but a right (*ḥaqq*). I take the judicial practice of *matāʿ* in the Umayyad period as my point of departure, using the reports in Wakīʿ (1947) and Kindī (1987) as my source of information about the qāḍīs, their judicial reasoning, and the institution of *qaḍāʾ*. By examining reports about qāḍī judgments relating to *matāʿ*, I hope to shed light on the Umayyad judicial practice and its influence on the development of legal doctrine. The essay is divided into five sections: (1) the sources, (2) the doctrine of *matāʿ* and its practice in early Islam, (3) qāḍīs and the doctrine, (4) the judicial setting under the Umayyad caliphs, and (5) the development of doctrine and differences between the jurists and the qāḍīs.

1. *Sources*

My main sources of information for this essay are Kindī (1987) and Wakīʿ (1947).

Muḥammad b. Khalaf b. Ḥayyān Abū Bakr al-Wakīʿ (d. 306/916), a qāḍī in Ahwāz (Persia), wrote his *Akhbār al-quḍāt* (Masud 1994b) to "report [on] judicial practice in the various cities from the days of the Prophet until his time" (Wakīʿ 1947, 1:4–5). The text was first edited and published in 1947. The book covers all the territories of the Abbasid caliphate in Wakīʿ's time and includes references to qāḍī judgments. In this respect, it differs from other biographies of qāḍīs, which are limited to specific cities or provinces (e.g., Abū ʿUbayd al-Baṣrī's [d. 209/824] *Akhbār quḍāt Baṣra*, and al-Kindī's *Kitāb quḍāt Miṣr*) and focus on biographical details. Noting these features, Schacht observed that the *Akhbār al-quḍāt* "tells us about another phenomenon of legal activity, the development of law in judicial practice" (Schacht 1955:97). Wakīʿ's works served as an important source of information for biographers and historians such as the third/ninth century Ibn Qutayba al-Dīnawarī (Rosenthal 1952:430).

In the introduction to the *Akhbār al-quḍāt*, Wakīʿ expounds on the institution of *qaḍāʾ* and the qualities of an ideal qāḍī; the remainder of the text provides information about qāḍīs in Makkah, Madīna, Ṭāʾif, Baṣra, and the cities of Syria, Ifrīqiya, Iraq and Persia. The *Akhbār al-quḍāt* mentions a broad range of information about qāḍīs, including their judgments, their jurisprudence, and their family and tribal background. Wakīʿ also collected their poetry, *ḥadīth* reports and juristic opinions (Wakīʿ 1947, 1:4–5).[1] For this reason, Wakīʿ's *Akhbār al-quḍāt* is currently our most valuable extant source about qāḍīs in the Umayyad and early Abbasid period. Schacht characterized Wakīʿ's text as "the main source for the study of this period" (Schacht 1955:97).

Abū ʿUmar Muḥammad b. Yūsuf al-Kindī (d. 350/961) is known for his history of the province of Egypt, *Kitāb al-wulāt wa'l-quḍāt*. The book has two parts: the first contains biographies of the governors of Egypt, and the second contains biographies of the qāḍīs. Edited and published in 1912, this work has been used frequently by students of Islamic judicial organization. The book ends in the year 247/861. According to F. Rosenthal, al-Kindī's book "reveals a good deal about legal institutions and practice" (Rosenthal 2003, 5:121).

These two works, by Wakī and by al-Kindī, were subjected to serious criticism by traditional Muslim scholars. Ibn Ḥajar al-ʿAsqalānī (d. 852/1448) and Ibn ʿImād al-Ḥanbalī (d. 1090/1679), both renowned *ḥadīth* scholars and authors of two widely used biographies of *ḥadīth* transmitters, questioned the reliability of Wakīʿ's reports (al-ʿAsqalānī 1912, 5:156; al-Ḥanbalī 1931, 2:249). They characterized Wakīʿ b. Khalaf as an *akhbārī* (chronicler) and considered his knowledge of *ḥadīth* weak. *Ḥadīth* scholars did not regard *tārīkh* and *akhbār* as reliable sources because, as Qasim Zaman explains, the word *akhbārī* was a pejorative term that denoted the uncritical collection of information (Zaman 1997:14–15, e.g., note 45).

Methodological controversies between *ḥadīth* scholars and historians arose because they used different criteria for the evaluation of their sources. Upon examination, however, we find that these scholars could not have found fault with Wakīʿ's series of transmitters. In fact, Wakīʿ's sources and chains of authorities do not differ much from those of the *ḥadīth* collectors. His series of authorities can be divided into two parts. The second part of the chain mentions the same authorities from the first two generations of the first/seventh century as are cited in the *ḥadīth* collections. The first part of the series, closer in time to Wakīʿ, gives three or four names, such as

[1] For instance, Wakīʿ mentions some legal maxims attributed to Shurayḥ as he describes certain practices peculiar to him. Shurayḥ did not accept the testimony of a pilgrim, for example, who came to the court riding on a mount (Wakīʿ 1947, 2:230–31).

Muḥammad b. Ishkāb, Nuʿaym, Sufyān, and Dāʾūd b. Abī Hind. These men reported *ḥadīths* from Jābir and other Companions of the Prophet, on the authority of Shaʿbī, Maḥmūd b. Muḥammad al-Marwazī, Ḥayyān, ʿAbd Allāh and Dāʾūd b. Abī Hind, all known and respected sources.

In my view, *ḥadīth* scholars differed with Wakīʿ because they collected only widely known and frequently transmitted narratives which they regarded as authentic. Wakīʿ, on the other hand, as he tells us, was not interested in collecting what was already known and widely quoted. His main objective, he emphasized, was to fill in gaps in knowledge about qāḍīs about whom information was limited. For instance, he says that very little information was available in his time about qāḍīs like Shurayḥ and Ibn Shubruma, and, for this reason, he collected all the information available on them. This explains why entries devoted to these qāḍīs are longer than those devoted to others (see below).

Modern scholars have criticized Kindī's information on the Umayyad qāḍīs. Analyzing Kindī's reports about the Umayyad qāḍīs Ibn Ḥujayra, Tawba b. Nimr, and Khayr b. Nuʿaym, Schacht (1959:54) comments, "The information on the early judges of Egypt in Kindī can hardly be considered as authentic throughout as far as the first century is concerned, but it agrees with that relating to the first half of the second century in making the judges rely on their personal opinion to the exclusion of traditions" (ibid.: 100). Schacht tends to accept those reports which support his thesis, i.e., the movement for accepting *ḥadīth* as an authoritative source of Islamic law began only in the second century of Islam. He regards any report that attributes a *ḥadīth* to a qāḍī prior to that period as a later addition.

In other words, Schacht holds that judges in this period normally did not cite *ḥadīth*, relying instead on their own opinions. Yet, he dismisses these "personal opinions" as "sweeping interpretation of Koran" and "innovation[s]" (ibid.: 101), "a result of his own discretion" (ibid.: 101) and "irregular by all later standards" (ibid.: 100). In my view, Schacht judges these "personal opinions" according to standards that were developed after the formation of the law schools. In fact, these interpretations of the Qurʾān should not be dismissed as "sweeping" and "irregular" merely because they do not conform to post-Shāfiʿī juristic reasoning. Exclusive reference to the Qurʾān is a very significant feature of judicial reasoning in this period, closely connected with the evolution of the institution of *qaḍāʾ*. In fact, the qāḍīs paved the way for subsequent legal reasoning on marriage and divorce (see below).

Reports

I have found nineteen Reports[2] concerning the award of *matāʿ*, sixteen in Wakīʿ and three in Kindī (see Appendix). Of these nineteen Reports, fifteen recount actual cases in which Umayyad qāḍīs called upon husbands to pay *matāʿ* to their divorced wives; and four mention the opinion or personal practice of the qāḍī about the payment of *matāʿ* or its value.

Sixteen of the nineteen Reports are from Iraq and three are from Egypt. Report 19 claims that qāḍī Khayr's decision to require the payment of *matāʿ* was unprecedented in Egypt. This claim is debatable because Ibn Ḥujayra (Report 1) and Tawba (Report 17) issued judgments for *matāʿ* in Egypt before Khayr did. Although controversial in Egypt, the payment of *matāʿ* seems to have been a common practice in Madinah (see below). I have not found any reports about court cases relating to *matāʿ* from Madinah, which suggests that the matter was not disputed there. The Reports indicate that the disputes arose in Iraq and Egypt, where the qāḍīs referred to the Qurʾān rather than to Sunna or local practice, probably because *matāʿ* was not a common practice there and the qāḍīs had to explain why they awarded *matāʿ*. Apparently, the qāḍīs needed to cite authorities only if the matter was disputed or was not an accepted practice. In these Reports, the qāḍīs frequently cite the Qurʾān.

The Reports suggest not only that the payment of *matāʿ* was controversial outside Madinah, but also that the litigants regarded a qāḍī as if he were a *muftī*, not a judge or a *ḥakam*, because a *muftī* gives advice which they were free to accept or reject. On the other hand, when the litigants chose an arbiter (*ḥakam*) or a third party, they agreed to abide by his proclamation. Another feature of *qaḍāʾ* in these Reports is that qāḍīs, like muftīs, cited the source of their opinion. They relied solely on the Qurʾān, without reference to either *ḥadīth* or the opinion of a jurist.

[2] In this essay, I will refer to these nineteen reports as "Report/s", with a capital "R" to distinguish them from reports other than these. The number of the report refers to the respective number in the appendix.

The Value of these Reports

The Reports examined here are not comparable to a modern "law report" or "court record." As noted in the Introduction to this volume, qāḍī court records are rarely available before the sixteenth century. Some useful information about legal practice and qāḍī judgments may be found in the biographies of the qāḍīs, although this is no substitute for the judgments themselves. The Reports that I have found in these two sources are problematic inasmuch as they are rarely mentioned in early *ḥadīth* collections or works on *tafsīr* and *fiqh*.[3] This may be explained in part as a function of the low estimation of *akhbār* in the eyes of *ḥadīth* scholars, as noted above.

Since the names of the litigants are not mentioned in our Reports, it is difficult to identify and determine the actual number of cases. Nine of the nineteen Reports (nos. 3, 5–11, and 13) repeat each other; they recount similar stories and differ only in their respective chain of transmitters. Thus, it is possible that the number of independent reports is only eleven. Of the nineteen Reports, fifteen are about qāḍī Shurayḥ. In Reports 12, 14 and 15, Shurayḥ awards *matāʿ* but seeks to determine further whether the marriage has been consummated and whether the dower (*mahr*) has been stipulated. The fact that these details, not mentioned in other Reports, are attributed only to Shurayḥ suggests that these reports may reflect attempts by Kufan jurists to authenticate their own doctrines by attributing them to an early source. This suggestion is tempting, but it must be dismissed because, as I discuss below, these details are traceable to the Qurʾān.

I maintain that in the absence of court records, these reports (*akhbār*) are extremely useful as they provide some important information about Umayyad qāḍīs and their judgments.

[3] Wensinck cites other reports that mention Iyās b. Muʿāwiya, another Umayyad qāḍī, in Bukhārī's *Ṣaḥīḥ* in chapters on "lease" and "judgments" (Wensinck 1988, 8:25), Shurayḥ in most of the Ḥadīth collections, e.g., Bukhārī, *Ṣaḥīḥ*; Abū Dāʾūd, *Sunan*; Tirmidhī, *Jāmiʿ*; Nasāʾī, *Sunan* in several chapters, including "cleanliness," "prayers," "funerals," "sales," "complaints," "divorce," "inheritance," and "judgments" (Wensinck 1988, 8:118). In the *Tafsīr* literature, Ṭabarī (1954, 5:128, 129) and Suyūṭī (1983, 1:140) mention Shurayḥ.

2. *The Doctrine of* Matāʿ

The doctrine of *matāʿ* originated in the following Qurʾānic verses:

> For divorced women is a suitable gift [*matāʿ*]. This is a duty [*ḥaqqan ʿalā*] on the righteous [*muttaqīn*] (2:241).[4]
>
> There is no blame on you if ye divorce women before consummation or the fixation of their dower; but bestow on them (a suitable gift) [*mattiʿūhunna*, pay them *matāʿ*]. The wealthy according to his means, and the poor according to his means;—a gift of a reasonable amount is due [*ḥaqqan*, a right] from those who wish to do the right thing [*muḥsinīn*]. And if ye divorce them before consummation, but after the fixation of a dower for them, then the half of the dower (is due to them), unless they remit it (Qurʾān 2:236, 237).

Schacht (1959:101), Asad (1980:54) and ʿAlī (1992:107) translate the term *matāʿ* as "obligatory gift," "alimony" and "suitable gift," respectively. Apparently, the Qurʾānic expression *mattiʿūhunna* does not support the sense of gift, because a gift is voluntary. The verb is in the imperative mood. Similarly, the Qurʾānic phrase *ḥaqqan ʿalā* suggests that the wife is entitled to *matāʿ*, which is qualified as a duty of the pious. ʿAlī translates *ḥaqq* as "due" in this verse and "duty" in the next (2:241). These different contemporary translations, in fact, reflect a longstanding controversy over whether the payment of *matāʿ* is compulsory or voluntary. This controversy, which began in the early Umayyad period, shaped the later development of legal doctrine. Since the controversy originated with the different understandings of the Qurʾān, I will begin with an analysis of the broader context of the Qurʾānic verses on *matāʿ*.

Qurʾān

The payment of *matāʿ* appears to have been a Qurʾānic innovation designed to reform the institution of divorce in pre-Islamic Arabia. The judicial reasoning and social practice in Madinah in the Umayyad period appear to have been closely connected to the reforms that the Qurʾān introduced in the institution of divorce by defining it as a graceful separation (*tasrīḥun bi-iḥsān*, 2:229).

---

[4] In this essay, all translations of the Qurʾān are from ʿAlī 1992, unless otherwise mentioned. I have provided the original Arabic text and an alternative English translation in square brackets in those cases in which I disagree with ʿAlī's translation; the parentheses in the translation are those of the translator.

Divorce (*ṭalāq*) in pre-Islamic Arabia was a prerogative of the husband, who could repudiate his wife repeatedly and retain her at his will (on this point, see Fierro, this volume). The Qur'ānic verses prohibited the practice of repeated repudiations and revocations by husbands and reduced the number of revocable repudiations to two.

> A divorce is only permissible twice; after that the parties should either hold together on equitable terms or separate with kindness (Qur'ān 2:229).

In case of a dispute between the husband and wife, the Qur'ān prescribes a mandatory process of arbitration, appointing *ḥakamān* (two arbiters), one each from the families of the spouses.

> If ye fear a breach between them twain, appoint (two) arbiters, one from his family, and the other from hers; if they seek to set things aright, Allah will cause their reconciliation (Qur'ān 4:35).

The Qur'ānic requirement for arbitration suggests that divorce was not a matter of simple repudiation by the husband in all cases. That is why the Qur'ān required two witnesses for the termination of the marriage contract.

> Thus when they fulfill their term appointed, either take them back on equitable terms or part with them on equitable terms; and take for witnesses two persons from among you endued [sic] with justice, and establish the evidence for the sake of Allah (Qur'ān 65:2).

The Qur'ān also introduced a specified waiting period for a woman divorced after consummation of marriage.

> O Prophet! When ye do divorce women, divorce them at their prescribed periods, and count (accurately) their prescribed periods: and fear Allah your Lord: and turn them not out of their houses, nor shall they (themselves) leave, except in case they are guilty of some open lewdness (Qur'ān 65:1).
>
> Divorced women shall wait concerning themselves for three monthly periods (Qur'ān 2:228).

This waiting period serves two purposes: first, it provides the couple with an opportunity to reconcile, and second, it serves to clear any doubt about the paternity of a child born of the existing marriage. The Qur'ān encourages reconciliation during this waiting period, but insists that husbands should not take their wives back to injure them.

> When ye divorce women, and they (are about to) fulfill the term of their *ʿiddat* [*ʿidda*], either take them back on equitable terms or set them free on equitable terms. But do not take them back to injure them, or to take undue advantage (Qurʾān 2:231).

The Qurʾānic concept of "freedom on equitable terms" is illustrated in 2:229 which admonishes a husband not to recover any property given to the wife.

> It is not lawful for you (men) to take back any of your gifts [*mā ātaytumūhunna*, whatever you gave them] (from your wives), except when both parties fear that they would be unable to keep the limits ordained by Allah. If ye (judges) do indeed fear that they would be unable to keep the limits ordained by Allah, there is no blame on either of them if she gives something for her freedom (Qurʾān 2:229).

It is in the context of this transformation of divorce into a graceful separation (*tasrīḥun bi-iḥsān*) that the Qurʾān prescribes payment of *matāʿ* as a general rule for all divorced wives.

> For divorced women is a suitable gift [*matāʿ*]. This is a duty on [*ḥaqqan ʿalā*] the righteous [*muttaqīn*] (2:241).
>
> O Prophet! Say to thy consorts: "If it be that ye desire the life of this world, and its glitter,—then come! I will provide for your enjoyment [*umattiʿkunna*, I pay you *matāʿ*] and set you free in a handsome manner [*usarriḥkunna sarāḥan jamīla*, I separate from you in a graceful manner] (Qurʾān 33:28).

Citing Ibn Saʿd (d. 230/845), Suyūṭī explains that Qurʾān 33:28 was revealed in connection with the Prophet's wives who complained about maintenance. The Prophet gave them the option of divorce, but only one wife exercised this option (Suyūṭī 1983, 6:593). It is obvious that according to this Qurʾānic verse, the Prophet would divorce his wives at their request and, in this case, it is also clear that the marriages had been consummated. It is important to note this here because in the later development of the doctrine, the jurists subjected the payment of *matāʿ* to certain conditions that are not found in the Prophet's practice. Shāfiʿī, for instance, argued that *matāʿ* is not payable if the divorce is initiated by the wife. We have seen above that the Prophet promised payment of *matāʿ*, even if the divorce was requested by the Prophet's wives. Similarly, the jurists made the payment of *matāʿ* contingent on the nonconsummation of marriage, whereas in the above example the Prophet's marriage was already consummated.

The Qur'ān allows divorce prior to consummation of a marriage, but even in this case it recognizes the wife's right to receive one-half of any dower fixed prior to the divorce.

> There is no blame on you if ye divorce women before consummation or the fixation of their dower; but bestow on them (a suitable gift) [*matti'ūhunna*, pay them *matā'*]. The wealthy according to his means, and the poor according to his means;—a gift of a reasonable amount is due [*ḥaqqan*, a right] from those who wish to do the right thing [*muḥsinīn*]. And if ye divorce them before consummation, but after the fixation of a dower for them, then the half of the dower (is due to them), unless they remit it (Qur'ān 2:236, 237).

Apparently, it is the payment of *matā'*, rather than *mahr*, which properly qualifies a divorce as "a graceful separation." It is with regard to *mahr* that the Qur'ān distinguishes the case in which the *mahr* is fixed at the time of the contract from the case in which it is not fixed; similarly it distinguishes the case in which the marriage is consummated from the case in which it is not. As we shall see subsequently, the jurists argued that the amount of *mahr* to be paid would vary depending on these conditions.

The jurists found the verses about *matā'* and *mahr* to be in conflict with each other. Qur'ān 2:236; 2:241 and 33:28 prescribe *matā'* for all divorcees, while 2:37 mentions *matā'* only in case of divorce prior to the consummation of marriage and fixation of *mahr*. The jurists treated Qur'ān 2:237 as the principal verse, which qualifies the other general verses. Sa'īd b. al-Musayyab (d. 93/711) claimed that Qur'ān 2:237 abrogated Qur'ān 33:28 and 2:241. His contemporary, al-Ḥasan al-Baṣrī, and others rejected the claim of abrogation (Suyūṭī 1983, 1:698, 739), arguing that 2:237 specifies that *matā'* is to be paid only when *mahr* is not due.

As we will see, of the qāḍīs in our Reports, only Shurayḥ linked the payment of *matā'* to *mahr*, whereas four other qāḍīs required payment of *matā'* in all cases of divorce. They too cited 2:236–7, but they did not regard it as qualifying the other verses.

In the Qur'ān, *m-t-'* and its derivatives occur sixty-three times in a general sense, meaning "worldly things," "enjoyment" and "material property." The word *matā'* is used seven times in the context of marriage and divorce; five times with reference to divorced wives, and one time each with reference to widows and married women, respectively. I have already cited the verses about divorced wives (Qur'ān 2:236, 237, 240, 241, and 33:28). Let me turn to the two verses in which this term is used in a general sense with reference to marriage.

In 2:240 *matāʿ* signifies "maintenance."

> Those of you who die and leave widows should bequeath for their widows a year's maintenance [*matāʿan ilā al-ḥawl*], without expulsion; But if they leave, there is no blame on you for what they do with themselves, provided it is reasonable (Qur'ān 2:240).

According to many jurists, this verse was abrogated by Qur'ān 4:11–12, which prescribes a share of the inheritance for the widow (for a detailed analysis of the different views about the abrogation of this verse, see Powers 1986:146–7, 155–7, and 178–85). However, we are not concerned here with either abrogation or inheritance, but rather with the meaning of *matāʿ*. It is significant that whereas the debates about the abrogation or otherwise of 2:240 refer to the waiting period, there appears to be no dispute about the meaning of *matāʿ* as "maintenance." Arguably, the meaning of *matāʿ* in this verse, i.e., "maintenance," can be applied to other verses about the payment of *matāʿ* to divorced women. Even if the jurists regard the *matāʿ* injunction about widows as abrogated because widows now inherit from their husbands, the argument for the divorced woman's right to *matāʿ* is stronger because she is not entitled to inherit. Divorced women should not be left helpless. For this reason, some scholars (e.g., Carroll 1986; Asad 1980:54) identify *matāʿ* with alimony as a settlement between the husband and wife at the time of divorce. Muhammad Asad comments, "The amount of alimony payable—unless and until they marry—has been left unspecified since it must depend on the husband's financial circumstances" (Asad 1980:54).

Matāʿ must be distinguished from *mahr* because the wife is entitled to *mahr* even if she is not divorced, and she frequently receives it before the divorce. The payment of *matāʿ* is neither in lieu of *mahr* nor contingent upon it. *Matāʿ* in the Qur'ān is not necessarily a payment of an outstanding debt, as *mahr* is; it can be a onetime payment or spread over time. Explaining that *matāʿ* (*mutʿat al-mar'a*) can be paid in the form of clothes, a servant, food provision or cash, Ibn Manẓūr cites Abū Manṣūr al-Azharī (d. 370/981), a lexicographer and a Shāfiʿī jurist, who said, "It is not a onetime (*muwaqqat*) payment because God did not limit it in time" (Ibn Manẓūr 1988, 13:15).

The word *mutʿa,* another derivative of the root *m-t-ʿ*, refers generally to "temporary marriage." Muslim jurists, including Shāfiʿī, use the word *mutʿa* in the sense of both divorce payment (*matāʿ*) and temporary marriage. This usage is confusing, and I have not found any explanation for it. Although the word *mutʿa* does not occur in the Qurʾān, *istamtaʿtum*, another derivative of *m-t-ʿ*, is mentioned in Qurʾān 4:24, to which some Shīʿī jurists refer for the justification of *mutʿa.*

> Also (prohibited are) women already married, except those whom your right hands possess: thus Allah ordained (prohibitions) against you: except for these, all others are lawful, provided ye seek (them in marriage) with gifts from your property—desiring chastity, not fornication. Give them their dowry [dower, *ujūr*] for the enjoyment you have [*famā istamtaʿtum*] of them, as a duty [*farīḍa*]; but if, after a dower is prescribed, ye agree mutually (to vary it). There is no blame to you (Qurʾān 4:24).

Abū Jaʿfar al-Ṭūsī (d. 460/1067), who systematized Shīʿī *Fiqh*, argues that the phrase "*istamtaʿtum*" (you enjoyed) can refer only to *mutʿa,* i.e., temporary marriage, because it mentions *ujūr*, (e.g., *ajr*, wages, remuneration) rather than *mahr* (dower). The verse does not refer to *mahr*, which becomes due only upon the conclusion of a permanent marriage contact (Ṭūsī n.d., 7:249). Ṭūsī's argument is based on the distinction between *ajr* and *mahr* and between temporary and permanent marriage. He derives both sets of distinctions from the meaning of "enjoyment" in the phrase *istamtaʿtum.* Unlike a permanent marriage, which has several other objectives, the sole objective of *mutʿa* marriage is *istimtāʿ* (enjoyment), Ṭūsī argues. According to him, temporary marriage (*mutʿa*) is a contract for a specific purpose, in which remuneration (*ajr*) is paid; hence, there is no *mahr* or inheritance. Marriage ends at the appointed term; no *ṭalāq* is pronounced. *Mutʿa* is modeled on a sale contract in which the payment of consideration money and specification of the duration of time are essential conditions.

The debate between the Sunnīs and the Shīʿa over the meaning of *istamtaʿtum* can be traced back to the tenth century. Analyzing the term "*istamtaʿtum,*" the lexicographer Abū Isḥāq al-Zajjāj (d. 311/923) refers to the Shīʿī reliance on Qurʾān 4:24 as justification for *mutʿa* and argues that it is wrong to interpret the term "*istamtaʿtum*" as permission for *mutʿa* (temporary marriage). In Qurʾān 4:24, *istimtāʿ* simply means marriage contract, regardless of whether or not the marriage was consummated (cited in Ibn Manẓūr 1988, 13:14). Al-Zajjāj's explanation suggests that his contemporary Sunnī jurists did not understand the Qurʾānic phrase *istamtaʿtum* as referring to consummation of marriage. Rather, the contracting of the marriage itself constituted *istimtāʿ*.

The Shīʿī jurists distinguish between temporary and permanent marriage, clarifying that a temporary marriage contract comes to an end at the expiration of the appointed time. Regular marriage, on the other hand, is a permanent contract and it is assumed to continue unless the contrary is proven. Hence the Shīʿī jurists insist on two witnesses for divorce to terminate the presumption of the continuity of the contract.

The payment of *matāʿ* to a divorced wife was a general practice in Madinah, even though the value and the form of payment varied. I have not been able to determine whether the practice was pre-Islamic or post-Islamic. Be that as it may, the controversy in Madinah over the nature of the obligation suggests that *matāʿ* was not a pre-Islamic custom.

Practice in Madinah

Ibn Hishām (d. 219/834) mentions two cases in which the Prophet paid *matāʿ* to his wives. In both cases, the divorce took place prior to consummation of the marriage (Ibn Hishām 1955, 2:647). However, Ibn Hishām does not state whether or not the amount of dower was fixed, or whether it was paid in addition to *matāʿ*.[5] The *ḥadīth* literature identifies the Prophet's divorced wives, with some variation in their names, and uses the terms *jahīz* (dowry) and *kiswa* (clothes) along with *matāʿ* for the property transferred to these women. These *ḥadīths* add that the clothes (*kiswa*) were two dresses of a fine Persian

[5] Ibn Hishām (1955, 2:647) gives the names of these divorced wives as Asmāʾ bt. Yazīd al-Kilābiya and ʿUmra bt. Yazīd al-Kilābiya. It is not clear whether these are the names of two different persons. The Ḥadīth collections mention several different names. Bukhārī (1987, 5:2012) cites a report in which the Prophet Muḥammad married Ibnat al-Jawn, who expressed her disapproval of the marriage by taking refuge in God. The Prophet paid her *matāʿ* and divorced her prior to consummation of the marriage. There are two more narrations in this section; one mentions al-Jawniyya; the other mentions Umayma bt. Sharāḥīl. Ibn Ḥajar al-ʿAsqalānī, in his commentary on Bukhārī's *Ṣaḥīḥ*, argues that these are different names for the same person. In his view, it is Ibnat al-Jawn who is mentioned as ʿUmra bt. Yazīd, Umayma bt. al-Nuʿmān, and al-ʿĀliya bt. al-Ẓibyān, and also Kalbiyya, Kilābiyya, and Kindiyya who is mentioned by her tribal name (ʿAsqalānī 1981, 9:357). Different versions of the event are given in Bukhārī 4852, Ibn Mājja 2027, *Musnad Aḥmad* 21799, and Nasāʾī 3364 (*Mawsūʿa al-ḥadīth al-sharīf*, CD-Rom 1997).

cloth (*Razāqiyīn*, Bukhārī, *Kitāb al-Ṭalāq, ḥadīth* no. 4852). The fact that these *ḥadīth* reports mention *matāʿ* but not *mahr* suggests that *matāʿ* was a payment in addition to the *mahr*.

Jalāl al-Dīn al-Suyūṭī (d. 911/1505), a historian and the author of a popular commentary on the Qurʾān, reports that when Ḥafṣ b. al-Mughīra divorced his wife, the Prophet asked him to pay *matāʿ*. Ḥafṣ said that he had nothing in his possession to pay. The Prophet insisted that the payment was obligatory: he must pay even if he possessed only a small quantity of dates (Suyūṭī 1983, 1:740).

Muḥammad b. Abī Shayba reports that ʿAbd al-Raḥmān b. ʿAwf (d. 32/652) and ʿUrwa b. al-Zubayr (d. 93/712) each gave to his divorced wife a female slave in lieu of *matāʿ*. He also reports that Ḥasan b. ʿAlī (d. 49/669) paid 10,000 dirhams as *matāʿ*, and that Anas b. Mālik (d. 179/795), Shurayḥ and Aswad each paid 300 dirhams as *matāʿ* (Ibn Abī Shayba 1995, 4:146).

These reports suggest that the value of the *matāʿ* payment varied and that the husband usually paid the *matāʿ* at the time of divorce. The qāḍīs appear to have followed the practice of Madinah with regard to payment of *matāʿ*.

3. *The Qāḍīs and the Doctrine of* Matāʿ

The qāḍīs of Iraq and Egypt were frequently confronted with the question of whether *matāʿ* is a voluntary payment or an obligation. Keeping in mind the Qurʾānic prescriptions about appointing *ḥakam*s in marital disputes, it is not surprising that marriage and divorce were included within the jurisdiction of the qāḍī. According to Wakīʿ, qāḍīs were frequently called upon to settle marriage and divorce disputes, and they developed certain practices to deal with divorce cases on different levels. They held that a husband must explicitly inform his wife that he had repudiated her or that he had revoked the repudiation before the end of the waiting-period.

Judicial Practice

In a divorce case heard by Qāḍī Shurayḥ, a husband repudiated his wife, who subsequently concluded a marriage after the expiration of her waiting-period. The husband claimed that he had revoked the repudiation, but the wife responded that he had not informed her about it. Shurayḥ rejected the husband's claim (Wakī' 1947, 2:235).[6]

Shurayḥ also declared invalid a triple divorce pronounced by a husband who was on his deathbed, because of the presumption that he wanted to deprive the wife of his inheritance (Wakī' 1947, 2:384; 3:83). Sha'bī ruled that if a husband repudiates his wife on his deathbed, she is entitled to inherit even if she completes the waiting-period of divorce prior to her husband's death. Ibn Shubruma added that a divorced widow is entitled to inheritance from her husband so long as she does not remarry; if she marries after completing the waiting-period, she forfeits the right to inheritance (Wakī' 1947, 3:69). These cases indicate that qāḍīs were solicitous of women's rights in divorce cases.

The fact that the judicial practice conformed to the Qur'ānic reforms is very well illustrated in our nineteen Reports in which Qāḍīs awarded *matā'* to the divorced wife. The following report is typical.

> A husband and his wife brought a legal action to the court of Qāḍī Tawba b. Nimr (d. ca. 120/738) in Egypt. In the middle of the hearing, the husband divorced his wife. The qāḍī then ruled (*fa-qāla*) that the husband should pay *matā'* to his wife (*matti'hā*). Although the husband refused, the qāḍī did not press him (*sakata 'anhu*) because, in his opinion, the payment was not compulsory (*lam yarahu lāziman lahu*). Subsequently, when the same man appeared before the same qāḍī in another dispute, the qāḍī refused to accept him as a witness because, by refusing to pay *matā'* to his divorced wife, he had acknowledged that he was not a pious and God-fearing person, thereby disqualifying himself as a witness (Kindī 1987, 259).[7]

This Report raises several questions about the judicial practice regarding *matā'*, e.g., the nature of the obligation, the power of the qāḍī, and the procedure to be followed. In this Report, the qāḍī regards *matā'* as a consequence of divorce. As soon as the husband repudiates his wife, the qāḍī asks him to pay *matā'*, invoking the authority of Qur'ān 2:241: "For divorced women is a suitable gift; this is a duty

[6] Interestingly, Wakī' (1947, 2:365) reports that some persons told Muḥammad b. Sīrīn that Shurayḥ had himself divorced his wife but did not tell her until the waiting period had expired. Ibn Sīrīn did not believe that Shurayḥ could hide it from his wife. He rejected the report.

[7] Wakī' (1947, 2:327, 347) narrates a similar story about Qāḍī Shurayḥ, on the authority of Muḥammad b. Sīrīn. Unlike the story recorded by Kindī about Qāḍī Tawba, here Qāḍī Shurayḥ scolds the husband, saying, "Don't you deny that you are a kind person! Don't you deny that you are a God-fearing person"!

on the righteous" (*ḥaqqan ʿalā al-muttaqīn*), a phrase that is generally understood as a qualifying clause. The husband refused to pay, claiming that *matāʿ* is obligatory only for the righteous. His refusal constituted an acknowledgement that he was not a righteous person. The qāḍī did not insist that the man pay *matāʿ*, but he took the husband at his word when he subsequently appeared as a witness in another dispute. Tawba refused to accept his testimony because only a righteous person qualifies as a reliable witness.

Wakīʿ narrates similar reports about Qāḍī Shurayḥ (see note no. 7) in which we find more or less the same dialogue between the qāḍī and the husbands of the divorced wives. In these Reports, a husband, either alone or with his wife, appears before a qāḍī in a marital dispute. Usually the husband repudiates the wife in court, whereupon the qāḍī orders the husband to pay *matāʿ* to the divorced wife. In twelve Reports (4–14 and 17) the qāḍīs cite or allude to Qurʾān 2:241, calling for the payment of *matāʿ*, and the husbands insist that the payment is required only of the righteous. Whereas it is reported that Tawba subsequently disqualified the husband as a witness, no such action is attributed to Shurayḥ.

According to the *ḥadīth* collector Ibn Abī Shayba (d. 235/849), a debate over the nature of this obligation had begun already in the 2nd/8th century. Al-Ḥasan al-Baṣrī (d. 110/728) and Ibn Shihāb al-Zuhrī (d. 123/741) regarded every divorcee as entitled to receive this obligatory payment, while Shaʿbī (d. 105/723), Ibrāhīm al-Nakhaʿī, and Muḥammad Ibn Sīrīn (d. 110/728) considered this payment obligatory only in cases in which the marriage had not been consummated and the dower was not fixed (Ibn Abī Shayba 1995, 4:144). As noted above, Qāḍī Shurayḥ also held the latter view, although he regarded this payment as a moral obligation that was not enforceable. Scholars in Madinah generally maintained that the payment is recommended, but not obligatory.

Among the qāḍīs, it is only Shurayḥ who, in connection with the payment of *matāʿ*, raised questions about the consummation of the marriage and payment of the previously agreed upon *mahr*. Four other qāḍīs make no distinction between divorce before and after consummation of the marriage and they do not mention *mahr* (dower) or *nafaqa* (maintenance) in conjunction with *matāʿ*. Other prominent jurists, e.g., Ibrāhīm al-Nakhaʿī, a contemporary of Shurayḥ in Kūfa, expressed similar views. Quite possibly, the legal implications of *matāʿ* and the above-mentioned distinctions were already debated among

Shurayḥ's contemporaries, and Shurayḥ was the first qāḍī to take notice of this debate.

It is also difficult to infer that judicial practice about *matā*ʿ was specific to a territory. Three of our Reports emanate from Egypt (1, 17, and 18), fifteen from Kūfa (2, 16), and one from Baṣra (19). Judgments for *matā*ʿ cannot, therefore, be regarded as a reflection of an exclusively Iraqi or Medinese tradition or doctrine.

Qāḍīs also differed with each other regarding certain details relating to *matā*ʿ. For instance, Shurayḥ and Tawba were reluctant to compel the husband to pay *matā*ʿ. Ibn Ḥujayra and Tawba in Egypt estimated *matā*ʿ at three dinars, Shurayḥ at 500 dirhams, and Iyās at 30 dirhams. In one case Shurayḥ defined *matā*ʿ in terms of clothes, while in other cases, he linked it to the value of the dower. The early qāḍīs agreed that payment of *matā*ʿ is a duty, moral in some cases, that is always supplemental to the payment of dower and maintenance.

4. *Judicial Setting*

The institution of *qaḍā*ʾ (judgeship) underwent structural changes under the Umayyads. Joseph Schacht (1959) regards qāḍīs in the early Umayyad period as traditional Arab *ḥakams*. Baber Johansen[8] (1997c) observes that in the Umayyad period the Muslim judicial system was in its primitive stage of development. As mentioned earlier, information about this important period is limited; hence, our ignorance about the development of the Umayyad judicial administration. I propose here to reconstruct this development from information I find in the Reports.

The nineteen Reports refer to the following five Umayyad qāḍīs: ʿAbd al-Raḥmān Ibn Ḥujayra (d. ca. 83/702), Shurayḥ b. al-Ḥārith (d. ca. 99/718), Tawba b. Nimr (d. ca. 120/738), Iyās b. Muʿāwiya (d. 121/739), and Khayr b. Nuʿaym (d. ca. 127/745).

1. ʿAbd al-Raḥmān b. Ḥujayra al-Khawlānī (d. 83/702) was qāḍī in Egypt from 69–83/689–702, under the Caliph ʿAbd al-Malik (r. 65–86/685–702). During the period in which ʿAbd al-ʿAzīz b.

[8] I am thankful to Baber Johansen for providing a copy of his publication and to Mareike Winkelman for her help in reading this German text.

Marwān was the governor of Egypt, Ibn Ḥujayra held three positions: qāḍī, *qāṣṣ* (record officer) and official in treasury (*bayt al-māl*) (Johansen 1997:679). It appears that historians of Islamic law associate *qāṣṣ* with storytellers (*quṣṣāṣ*) or religious preachers (*wuʿʿāẓ*). Baber Johansen translates the term *qāṣṣ* as "preacher" ("Prediger," Johansen 1997:978), and Coulson describes him as an instructor on religious precepts and precedents (Coulson 1964:29). These translations raise several questions. Was the *qāṣṣ* attached to the court? Coulson's translation suggests that this was the case, whereas Johansen suggests that the position may have been nonjudicial. Why was a "preacher" or a "religious instructor" attached to the court? If we accept Coulson's translation, the *qāṣṣ* would resemble a *muftī* more than a "preacher."

Khaṣṣāf (d. 261/874) makes a remark that may help us to understand the position of *qāṣṣ*. He describes *qiṣaṣ* (sg., *qiṣṣa*, meaning story) as written statements about a case presented to a qāḍī and drafted by a professional in those instances in which a litigant feels that he cannot present his case orally (1978:123). It is possible that the official who wrote these *qiṣaṣ* and kept records held the position of *Qāṣṣ*. Khaṣṣāf makes this remark with reference to a controversy over the "*qiṣaṣ*" (written statements) among the qāḍīs in the Umayyad period; some qāḍīs allowed them, others did not. Shurayḥ, who ignored the *qiṣaṣ*, insisted that litigants present their cases themselves (Khaṣṣāf 1978:123), which suggests that the practice of *qiṣṣa*, although not uncommon, had not yet been institutionalized as a judicial position. Shurayḥ found this practice disadvantageous to litigants who presented their cases orally. Reports about Ibn Ḥujayra, on the other hand, suggest that the position of qāṣṣ was already institutionalized in 1st/7th century Egypt. Ibn Ḥujayra himself had served as qāṣṣ and valued this position over that of qāḍī, perhaps because of the general reluctance of Muslim jurists to accept the position of qāḍī. The position of qāṣṣ was less precarious and less demanding than that of qāḍī. Ibn Ḥujayra was not happy when his son ʿAbd Allāh was transferred from the position of qāṣṣ to that of qāḍī (Wakīʿ 1947, 3:229). Clearly, the position of qāṣṣ must have been different from that of a preacher and storyteller.

2. Abū Umayya Shurayḥ b. al-Ḥārith b. Qays b. al-Jahm (d. 99/718) was qāḍī in Kūfa for a long period (ca. 5–86) during the caliphates of ʿUmar (r. 4–24/634–44) and ʿAbd al-Malik (r. 65–86/685–705). H. Lammens (1930:77–80), E. Tyan (1960, 1:75–6), and J. Schacht (1959:229) dismissed as legendary the reports

about his longevity and service as qāḍī. F. Sezgin and H. Motzki have challenged this view (Kohlberg 2003, 9:513). Conflicting reports about the date of his death are certainly problematic, but long service and long life are not necessarily unbelievable. In this period several other persons are reported to have lived longer than eighty years. For instance, al-Ḥasan al-Baṣrī reportedly died at the age of eighty-nine (Wakīʿ 1947, 2:6).

Wakīʿ dedicates 109 pages to Shurayḥ (Wakīʿ 1947, 2:89–389) in which we find reports from al-Shaʿbī, al-Ḥakam b. ʿUyayna, Ibrāhīm al-Nakhaʿī, Abu'l-Ḍuḥā, and several other scholars from Kūfa and Baṣra. As noted, Wakīʿ gave more attention to those qāḍīs who were less well-known. Certainly, Wakīʿ considered Shurayḥ neither a legend nor an ideal qāḍī. He reports certain common prejudices against Shurayḥ: he or his mother spoke Persian (indicating his non-Arab origins); he ate horse meat and drank *ṭalā*, i.e., wine cooked until it had become thick; and he ate while reclining on cushions (a sign of bad etiquette). Wakīʿ notes that Shurayḥ's date of death was not exactly known (Wakīʿ 1947, 2:199). Several aspects of Shurayḥ's life are disputed. Khaṣṣāf (d. 261/874) refers to a disagreement over whether or not Shurayḥ was literate.[9] Shāfiʿī (d. 205/820) contested the claim that Shurayḥ was a Companion of the Prophet (Shāfiʿī 1987, 5:108). Some scholars in Madinah rejected reports that the caliph Umar I appointed Shurayḥ, on the grounds that the Quraysh would accept only a person from their tribe as qāḍī. Dismissing these criticisms, Wakīʿ gives the names of several qāḍīs who served during the reign of Caliph ʿUmar I but were not Qurashīs (Wakīʿ 1947, 2:190).

Shurayḥ served as qāḍī during a very turbulent period and suffered greatly on account of his suspected political affiliations. Various governors of Kūfa appointed and dismissed him on account of such suspicions. Shurayḥ clashed with Ziyād b. Abīh and Ḥajjāj b. Yūsuf, the Umayyad governors of Iraq in 42–56/662–75 and 75–96/694–714, respectively. They needed support from the judiciary to punish political rebels such as Ḥujr b. ʿAdī, a Companion of the Prophet. Ziyād

[9] It is interesting to note that al-Khaṣṣāf, a Ḥanafī jurist, reports that Shurayḥ said, "I do not read books" (1978:123). He notes, however, that Shurayḥ took that position in a particular case in which one party wanted to present his claim in writing. Shurayḥ refused, saying that he did not know how to read. In fact, he preferred to treat the litigants equally. If he allowed one party to present the case in writing, he would be favoring one litigant over the other.

and Ḥajjāj both wanted Shurayḥ to punish Ḥujr but the qāḍī refused. Balādhurī (1979, 4:255, 276) notes that Ziyād depended on Shurayḥ, in his capacity as qāḍī, to support his administrative actions, but Shurayḥ did not cooperate with him. He also was not popular with opponents of the Umayyads. Caliph ʿAlī called him "*aqḍā al-ʿArab*" (the best Arab judge) but later dismissed him when he decided a case on the basis of his personal knowledge (Khaṣṣāf 1978:405). During their revolts against the Umayyads, Ibn al-Zubayr (64–70/683–89) and Mukhtār al-Thaqafī (66–68/685–87), respectively, dismissed Shurayḥ for his suspected affiliation with the Umayyads. Shurayḥ finally resigned in 77/696 during the governorship of Ḥajjāj b. Yūsuf.

These political conflicts point to a significant aspect of the judicial setting in this period. The office of qāḍī was instrumental in establishing the legitimacy of the new regime, and governors defined the qāḍī as an official of the state, a deputy of the governor. The qāḍīs, however, wanted to retain their independence as *ḥakams*, or arbiters.

3. Tawba b. Nimr (d. 120/738) served as qāḍī in Egypt in the period between 115–20/733–38, under the Caliph Hishām b. ʿAbd al-Malik (r. 105–25/724–43). Wakīʿ calls Tawba the best of the qāḍīs (*khayr al-quḍāt*, Wakīʿ 1947, 3:230). He reportedly was careful about his judicial responsibilities, e.g., he forbade his wife, under pain of divorce, to discuss judicial business with him (Kindī 1987:258, Coulson 1964:33). He began to systematize the office and instituted a register of *awqāf* in 118/736 (Kindī 1987:260). Like other qāḍīs, Tawba felt that the position of qāḍī was precarious, and in order to protect the position from state intervention, he extended the jurisdiction of the qāḍī to include the supervision of *awqāf* properties (Coulson 1964:33).

4. Iyās b. Muʿāwiya b. Qurra al-Muzanī (d. 121/739) was qāḍī of Baṣra between 99–101/718–20, under Caliph ʿUmar b. ʿAbd al-ʿAzīz (r. 99–101/717–20). Numerous stories mention his wit and wisdom. He decided cases more on the basis of his personal insight (*firāsa*) than on the basis of legal texts. *Firāsa* is an Arab science that, like *qiyāfa* (physiognomy), claims to foretell a person's character from his appearance and physical shape (Fahd 2003, 2:916). Experts in this science were often called upon to settle disputes about the paternity of a child. Iyās is reported to have drawn conclusions from the physical appearance of a person about his tribe, trade and moral

conduct. He developed this technique to outwit litigants. For instance, one man came to Iyās complaining that he had entrusted a certain person with some money. The defendant denied the claim. Although the plaintiff had no evidence to present in the court, Iyās guessed that he was right. He instructed the plaintiff to go and search for his money at the spot where he had entrusted it to the defendant. And he instructed the defendant to stay with him while the plaintiff went to that place. When a few hours had passed without the plaintiff's returning, Iyās casually asked the defendant if the plaintiff had reached the place where "you received the money from him." The defendant innocently said no, whereupon Iyās ordered that he be arrested (Wakīʿ 1947, 1:342). Wakīʿ tells several similar stories about how Iyās used *qiyāfa* and *firāsa* in his dealings with litigants (e.g., Wakīʿ 1947, 1:328, 331, 332, 338, and 342). The jurists and the Ḥadīth folk criticized him for this unusual method, which privileged personal knowledge over Qur'ān or Ḥadīth.

ʿAdī b. Arṭāṭ, who was governor of Baṣra under ʿUmar b. ʿAbd al-ʿAzīz, appointed Iyās as qāḍī of Baṣra (Wakīʿ 1947, 1:312–374), but soon a conflict developed between the qāḍī and the governor. ʿAdī wrote to the Caliph suggesting that al-Ḥasan al-Baṣrī be appointed qāḍī in place of Iyās. The Caliph agreed and al-Ḥasan al-Baṣrī was appointed. According to one account, the antagonism between the two men arose when Iyās contradicted the explicit wishes of the governor in a marriage litigation (Wakīʿ 1947, 1:313–6). Apparently, Iyās and al-Ḥasan al-Baṣrī had two different approaches to judicial method, especially with regard to the value of *ḥadīth*. Iyās relied on *firāsa*, which others dismissed as arbitrary opinion (*ra'y*). Qāḍī Khaṣṣāf (d. 261/874) refers to an argument between Iyās and al-Ḥasan al-Baṣrī (Khaṣṣāf 1978:289): when Iyās refused to accept a certain person as a witness, al-Ḥasan al-Baṣrī argued that the Prophet did not discriminate between Muslims as witnesses. Iyās cited Qur'ān 2:282 ("those who you agree to be witnesses") and said that the verse gives the qāḍī the right of discretion to reject a witness (Khaṣṣāf 1978:289). These Reports suggest a shift in judicial procedure from the *ḥakam* who undertook a personal quest to a procedure based on evidence derived from precedents.

5. Khayr b. Nuʿaym (d. 127/745) was a qāḍī in Egypt between 120–27/738–45 under four caliphs, Hishām b. ʿAbd al-Malik (r. 105–25/724–43), Walīd II (r. 125–6/743–4), Yazīd III (r. 126/744), Ibrāhīm (r. 126/744), and Marwān II (r. 127–32/744–50). Khayr

b. Nuʿaym[10] was one of the *Ḥadīth* folk. He heard cases involving Christians in the afternoon at the gate of the mosque. He also held the office of qāṣṣ (Kindī 1987:264).

Like other qāḍīs, Khayr b. Nuʿaym had conflicts with the governor. Although he was initially appointed as a qāḍī, the governor transferred him to the records office. He was later reappointed a qāḍī. During his second term in office, he refused to adjudicate a case according to the wishes of the governor, who remarked, "Perhaps you are angry with us for making you a scribe after you had been a qāḍī?" Khayr continuously resisted the governor's interference and finally resigned (Kindī 1987:269).

The biographies of these five men give us some idea about the judicial setting in this period. Let me highlight three important points.

1. *The Status of Qāḍīs*

It appears that the office of qāḍī emerged against the background of two very important institutions: the *ḥakam* and the *muftī*, both chosen by the disputing parties rather than appointed by the state. The *ḥakam*, a pre-Islamic institution, functioned as a third party chosen by the litigants, and the *muftī*, an Islamic institution, functioned as a teacher and advisor. Whereas a *ḥakam* was not required to explain his decision, a *muftī* had to provide religio-legal reasoning for his opinion. The authority of a *ḥakam* and a *muftī* was not coercive; the parties were free to abide by their advice or choose another *ḥakam* or go to another *muftī*.

In contrast to the *ḥakam*, the office of qāḍī, which was probably introduced by the Umayyads, was a state institution backed by the authority of the state. Wakīʿ remarks that there were no qāḍīs before the Umayyad period and that Muʿāwiya (d. 62/680) was the first to appoint qāḍīs (Wakīʿ 1947, 1:105).[11] This remark is supported by the events of the *taḥkīm* (arbitration) when the two *ḥakam*s appointed

---

[10] We do not find Khayr mentioned in Wakīʿ, who mentions a certain Jubayr b. Nuʿaym as qāḍī Tawba's secretary. Jubayr replaced Tawba when the latter resigned, and Jubayr continued in office until 128/746. This is probably an orthographic error; the scribe mistakenly wrote "Jubayr" instead of "Khayr" (Wakīʿ 1947, 3:231).

[11] This statement apparently contradicts Wakīʿ's other statements about qāḍīs in the Rāshidūn period. Wakīʿ stresses two points. First, the early qāḍīs functioned as *muftī*s, i.e., they had no juridical authority. Second, there were no qāḍīs appointed in Madinah before Muʿāwiya, because the caliph functioned as a qāḍī in the capital.

by ʿAlī and Muʿāwiya in 38/658 failed to reach a mutually agreeable decision, and the institution of arbitration (*taḥkīm*) suffered a great setback (Masud 1999). Subsequently, the office of qāḍī as a state official and a deputy of the governor emerged as a more authoritative office than that of the *ḥakam*. The office of qāḍī developed slowly during this period.

The Umayyad qāḍī was more powerful than the *ḥakam*, but not independent. Wakīʿ observes that he was subject to the authority of the governor because "the governors regarded the administration of justice as their responsibility and appointed qāḍīs according to their choice. A qāḍī could not ride a horse or go anywhere without the permission of the governor because his salary was paid by the governor (*umarāʾ*)" (Wakīʿ 1947, 1:141, 184). Caliphs and governors regarded the qāḍī as an official of the administration. Conflicts between governors/caliphs and qāḍīs often resulted in a qāḍī's resignation or dismissal.

Most of the Umayyad qāḍī were not trained jurists, and some were illiterate.[12] They could also hold other positions, like that of chief of police (Wakīʿ 1947, 3:223).[13] The Muslim community was still not accustomed to the authority of the qāḍī. We hear stories of litigants fighting with qāḍīs and continuing to treat them as *ḥakams*.[14]

---

[12] Such statements about qāḍīs in the early literature need to be seen in the context of the rivalry between *ḥadīth* and *raʾy*. The Ḥadīth group regarded only the knowledge of *ḥadīth* as *al-ʿilm* ("the" Knowledge). They also questioned the authority of the jurists and qāḍīs who do not rely on *ḥadīth*. The early *Adab al-qāḍī* literature indicates that some qāḍīs preferred oral presentations of the case over written statements. Shurayḥ's comment, "I do not read books," reflects his bias against written statements, not his illiteracy. Similarly, ʿĀbis' statement that he did not know the Qurʾān and *ḥadīth* might also mean that he preferred to consult local experts over citation from these sources.

[13] ʿĀbis b. Saʿīd held the posts of chief of police and qāḍī at the same time. He had not memorized the Qurʾān. When the governor Marwān b. Ḥasan asked him how he judged the cases that came before him, he replied that he consulted with knowledgeable persons. The governor let him continue in that position. Ibn Shubruma (d. 144/761) refused the appointment as chief of police (Wakīʿ 1947, 3:118).

[14] The Abbasid qāḍī Ibn Abī Laylā (d. 148/765) remarked, "In the past, people disputed with one another over their rights [*ḥaqq*] because they did not know them. Nevertheless, they believed that title must be restored to the rightful owner. A qāḍī functioned like a *muftī* [telling people what their rights are and which right belongs to which person]. These days, the parties quarrel with the qāḍīs. Now, the people trespass the law frequently" (Wakīʿ 1947, 3:136). Ibn Abī Laylā's remarks also establish that the changes in the role and office of the qāḍīs remained controversial until the early Abbasid period. This remark also explains, at least from a qāḍī's perspective, that the opinion of a *muftī* is not binding.

In this precarious situation, the qāḍīs gradually began to assert their independence. Referring to Khayr b. Nuʿaym's resentment at being transferred from the qāḍīship to a nonjudicial post, N.J. Coulson notes that qāḍīs began to conceive of their office as an exclusive judicial function (Coulson 1964:28). They began to develop other means to exercise their authority, e.g., by developing procedural rules. They also turned away from customary laws and from techniques like *firāsa* (wisdom, personal insight) and *qurʿa* (drawing lots) and began referring to the Qur'ān as a source. By developing judicial practices, the Umayyad qāḍīs contributed to the consolidation of the office.

The position of the qāḍīs changed under the Abbasids, who attempted to exercise control over the judgeship. According to Wakīʿ, it was the Abbasid Caliph al-Mahdī who first began appointing qāḍīs directly (Wakīʿ 1947, 1:227). Baber Johansen regards the centralization of the judgeship as part of the process of Islamization of the qāḍī system under the Abbasids. The advent of law schools (*madhāhib*) facilitated Islamization because these schools ensured the education of the Abbasid qāḍīs (Johansen 1997:976–89).

2. *Procedure*

In the early Umayyad period, the rules of procedure, especially as they relate to witnesses and evidence, were rudimentary. Qāḍīs could issue judgments on the basis of personal knowledge and circumstantial evidence. As noted with reference to Iyās and Shurayḥ, a qāḍī might freely exercise his authority to accept or reject a witness. Gradually, the rule of two witnesses, as prescribed in the Qur'ān, became common.

The litigants were asked to take the oath in the absence of proof. Subsequently, the oath came to be used as a substitute for a witness. Elsewhere, I have argued that Muʿāwiya empowered qāḍīs with new procedural rules in order to restore law and order after the second civil war (Masud 1999). Muʿāwiya encouraged judges to decide murder cases on the strength of only one witness, who could take an oath to compensate for the missing witness. This measure was adopted to settle numerous murders during this period of civil war, in cases in which witnesses were not available.

In Report 4, we find the expression "*lam yaqḍi*" (he did not issue a judgment), which means either that the qāḍī did not issue a judgment or that he did not hold in favor of the plaintiff. Although Shurayḥ was sure about his interpretation of Qurʾān 2:241, he still lacked the power to enforce his decisions. Shurayḥ, therefore, used procedural rules to enforce his authority. He refused to accept as a witness the husband who declined to pay *matāʿ* (see above). In a similar case, however, Qāḍī Ibn Ḥujayra ordered that *matāʿ* should be deducted from the husband's salary because he was a state official.

3. *Judicial Reasoning*

Thirteen of the nineteen Reports mention qāḍīs who cited Qurʾān 2:241 with reference to *matāʿ*. These Reports also point to a controversy over the nature and source of the obligation. Litigants distinguished between moral and legal obligations; the former were not enforceable by the court. This distinction may be related to the controversies in this period between the Ahl al-*Ḥadīth* and Ahl al-Raʾy over the source of obligation and the validity of local practice. The Ahl al-*Ḥadīth* held that only *ḥadīth* and Sunna create a legal obligation. The authority of *Ḥadīth* prevailed over that of local practice, and played a decisive role in resolving differing interpretations of the Qurʾān. The *ḥadīth* scholars regarded judgments that did not rely on *ḥadīth* as nothing more than *raʾy* (personal opinion), which does not create any legal obligation.

Muḥammad b. Sīrīn, one of the Ahl al-Ḥadīth, and a contemporary of Qāḍī Iyās, often criticized Iyās's judgments as arbitrary. He once warned Iyās, saying, "Judge on the basis of precedents (*āthār*), not on the basis of your own opinion" (Wakīʿ 1947, 1:334). The term *āthār* refers not only to the *ḥadīth*, but also to the practice of the first two generations of Muslims. Exclusive focus on *āthār* as a legal source obscured the role of the Qurʾān and local practice in the development of legal doctrine. By emphasizing *āthār*, the Ahl al-*Ḥadīth* apparently sought to discourage arbitrary judgments. Yet, interpretations of the Qurʾān that were not supported by *āthār* were also dismissed as arbitrary. It is in this environment that the jurists and qāḍīs developed several approaches to the doctrine of *matāʿ*.

5. *The Doctrine of* Matāʿ *between Jurists and Qāḍīs*

The jurists of the ninth century CE advanced at least four different approaches to *matāʿ*: a moral obligation, compensation, a substitute for dower, and a supplement to a dower.

1. Matāʿ, *a Moral Obligation*

Malikī jurists in Madinah treated *matāʿ* as a commendable moral obligation; it was obligatory only in specific circumstances. The qāḍīs also distinguished between the legal and moral aspects of the obligation, but for them, one is not free to ignore a moral obligation. Although *matāʿ* is not enforceable in court, one is personally obligated to fulfill it. Shurayḥ and Tawba did not force litigants to pay *matāʿ*, but reproached those who argued that *matāʿ* is only a moral duty and that they were free to ignore it. According to Shurayḥ, for instance, a litigant is not absolved of his moral obligation even though the court cannot enforce it, because a moral obligation is a personal duty. He warned a litigant, "My judgment cannot make permissible to you a thing that God has forbidden" (Wakīʿ 1947, 2:363).

Early Malikī jurists held that moral obligations are beyond the jurisdiction of the court. They are optional and only commendable, if observed. Ibn al-Qaṣim (d. 193/809) stated that although *matāʿ* is prescribed in the Qur'ān, it is not enforceable in a court (Ibn al-Qāsim 1905, 5:15). According to Ibn al-Qāsim, Mālik b. Anas (d. 178/795) recommended payment of *matāʿ* in all cases, but not as an obligation (ibid.). The jurists in Madinah, however, were divided over details; some held that *matāʿ* replaces dower, while others argued that *matāʿ* is merely commendable, unlike dower, which is obligatory. Most Mālikīs preferred ʿAbd Allāh b. ʿUmar's view that *matāʿ* is obligatory only if the dower has not been fixed. Ibn ʿUmar's disciple, Nāfiʿ, held that *mutʿa* (*matāʿ*), not *mahr* (dower), is due only if the *mahr* was not fixed. If it was fixed, then only half of the dower is due. In both cases, the marriage must not have been consummated. Ibn al-Qāsim stated that Ibn ʿUmar's view was accepted among the Mālikīs (Ibn al-Qāsim 1905, 5:16). Saʿīd b. al-Musayyab claimed that Qur'ān 2:237 abrogated Qur'ān 33:28 and 2:241, which prescribe *matāʿ* (Suyūṭī 1983, 1:698, 739).

2. Matāʿ *as Compensation*

The Ḥanafī jurist al-Marghīnānī (d. 593/1196) attributes to Shāfiʿī (d. 205/820) the notion of *matāʿ* as a compensatory payment to the divorcee. He cites Shāfiʿī's argument that *matāʿ* is explicitly obligatory in all cases of divorce (Qurʾān 2:241). It is compensatory because, as Shāfiʿī explains, *matāʿ* is "a consideration to be paid by the husband because he has caused her [viz., the wife] damage by dissolving the contract" (cited in al-Marghīnānī 1936, 1:149).

Matāʿ appears frequently in later *fiqh* texts as compensation for the hardship suffered by a divorced wife. For instance, Ibn al-ʿArabī (d. 543/1148), a Mālikī commentator on the Qurʾān, argued that *matāʿ* is a compensation to the wife for her loss of the marriage contract and for the disgrace that results from the termination of this contract. He explained that a divorce that occurs prior to consummation of marriage may be regarded as a stigma. *Matāʿ*, in this case, means payment of one-half of the dower (Ibn al-ʿArabī 1957, 1:217). N.B.: none of the qāḍīs in our corpus of nineteen Reports describes *matāʿ* as a compensatory payment.

3. Matāʿ *as a Substitute for* Mahr

Dower (*mahr*) was a significant property right created by a marriage contract. In divorce cases, qāḍīs made sure that the husband had already paid the dower. If not, the wife must receive it at the time of divorce. Shurayḥ was very strict in matters of dower. He imprisoned a father who demanded a dower of 600 dirhams for his daughter because it was excessive (Wakīʿ 1947, 2:232). In one case, a husband claimed that his wife had absolved him from the payment of dower, producing witnesses in support of his claim. Shurayḥ rejected the husband's claim, arguing that it is permissible for a wife to exempt her husband from payment of dower only after she has actually seen the amount in cash (Wakīʿ 1947, 2:253).

In general, the marriage contract is incomplete without a dower; and the Ḥanafīs treat such a contract as void. Consequently, they hold that if the dower is not fixed at the time of the marriage contract, *mahr al-mithl* (the fair dower) becomes due. The value of *mahr al-mithl* is estimated on the basis of the dower customarily payable to women of similar social status. In the case of divorce prior to consummation of the marriage, the Qur'ān prescribes payment of one-half of the fixed dower, and *matāʿ*, if the dower was not fixed. The Ḥanafī jurist Abū Bakr al-Sarakhsī (d. 483/1090), author of *al-Mabsūṭ*, defines *matāʿ* (Sarakhsī 1906, 6:63) as a substitute for *mahr al-mithl*. Accordingly, there is no *matāʿ* in cases in which the dower has been fixed. *Matāʿ* also cannot exceed one-half of the proper dower (Sarakhsī 1906, 5:82). Similarly, there is no obligation to pay *matāʿ* when half of the dower is due. Unlike the Mālikīs, the Ḥanafīs regard the payment of *matāʿ* as obligatory because it is in lieu of dower.

4. Matāʿ *as a Supplement to* Mahr

Al-Ṭabarī (d. 310/923), the founder of an early school of law, regarded *matāʿ* as an entitlement, which is supplementary to other payments arising from the act of divorce. He argued that Qur'ān 2:241 declares *matāʿ* to be obligatory in general and absolute terms; payment of one-half of the fixed dower is in addition to *matāʿ* (Ṭabarī 1954, 5:130).

Ibn Ḥazm (d. 456/1064) held similar views. He argued that *matāʿ* is an obligation in all cases and that the qāḍī must impose it in every case, regardless of whether or not the husband agrees to pay it (Ibn Ḥazm 1940, 10:245). He therefore recommended payment of *mutʿa* (*matāʿ*) in addition to dower. After explaining his view in the light of Qur'ānic verses, Ibn Ḥazm observes,

> We find that God has created certain rights of the wife in her husband's property, whether he agrees [with it] or not. They are: dower, maintenance, clothing and accommodation, so long as she remains in the marriage; and *matāʿ*, if he divorces her. God has created no right for a husband in the wife's property (Ibn Ḥazm 1940, 9:508).

Conclusion

Apparently, the jurists and the qāḍīs differed in their perception of *matāʿ*. Most jurists treated it as an entitlement arising from the marriage contract; they regarded payment of *matāʿ* as compulsory mostly in cases in which *mahr* was not due. Among the jurists, Shāfiʿī defined *matāʿ* as a compensation for divorce, which suggests that he saw it as a right arising from divorce. However, this definition was not applicable in all cases because he did not allow it in cases in which the wife caused the divorce. The Ḥanafī jurist al-Marghīnānī (d. 592/1196) criticizes the payment of *matāʿ* as compensation on the ground that divorce is not an offense for which a fine may be imposed. The payment of *matāʿ* is an act of grace (al-Marghīnānī 1936, 1:149). Only a few jurists, e.g., Ṭabarī and Ibn Ḥazm, treated *matāʿ* as a legal consequence of divorce.

The qāḍīs, on the other hand, did not consider dower and *matāʿ* to be mutually exclusive. In the cases in which the husband had fixed the dower but divorced his wife prior to consummation, Shurayḥ (Report 12) held, "She is entitled to one-half as *matāʿ* (*inna lahā fī al-niṣfi matāʿan*)."[15] In other words, the wife receives one-half of the fixed dower as *mahr*, and the other half as *matāʿ*.

The nineteen Reports analyzed here shed light on some other important features of the Muslim judicial setting and its development in its formative phase. Thus, used critically, literary sources such as biographies of qāḍīs, especially the *akhbār* literature, may fill gaps in our knowledge about early qāḍī courts. We have noted that the approaches to the problem of divorce and related issues varied between qāḍīs and jurists; while the qāḍīs stayed closer to the Qurʾān, the jurists developed finer details to qualify the Qurʾānic prescriptions. According to the Reports, the qāḍīs insisted on treating divorce as a graceful separation (*tasrīḥun bi-iḥsān*), as the Qurʾān requires. In these Reports, the qāḍīs raised the following important issues:

> The nature of the obligation: Is the payment of *matāʿ* a moral (personal) or a legal obligation, enforceable in a court of law?
> The value of *matāʿ*: Is the amount of *matāʿ* fixed or related to dower?
> The cause of the obligation: Is it due in all cases of divorce or only in specific cases?

Together with contemporary judicial practice, the jurists defined divorce from four different legal perspectives:

(1). Termination of the contract of marriage by mutual agreement of the parties;
(2). Termination of the contract unilaterally by the husband;

[15] Qāḍī Shurayḥ's ruling may also be interpreted as meaning that one half of the dower was *matāʿ*, and hence no additional payment was due. I find it difficult to accept this interpretation, because in this ruling Shurayḥ is defining *matāʿ*, not dower.

(3). Breach of contract by the husband/wife, resulting in a judicial divorce;
(4). Termination of the contract by the wife.

The Umayyad qāḍīs generally treated the payment of *matāʿ* as a right arising from the act of divorce and insisted on its payment in all divorce cases. The jurists, on the other hand, treated *matāʿ* as a right arising from the marriage contract and made its payment subject to the conditions of the contract. Of the four Sunnī schools of law, only the Shāfiʿīs consider *matāʿ* a right that arises from divorce. However, even the Shāfiʿīs do not regard a husband as obligated to pay *matāʿ* to his wife if she initiates the divorce. The present essay suggests that further studies of the judicial practice in this period when the schools of Islamic law had not yet been established may provide a better understanding of the formation of Islamic law.

APPENDIX: REPORTS

Qāḍī ʿAbd al-Raḥmān b. Ḥujayra (d. 83/702)

Report no. 1. The Qāḍī issued a judgment calling upon the husband, who was a state official [*ṣāḥib al-dīwān*], to pay three dinārs as *matāʿ* to his divorced wife. The qāḍī ordered the payroll office to pay that amount to the wife and deduct it from the husband's salary (Kindī 1987:238; Coulson 1964:31).

Qāḍī Shurayḥ b. al-Ḥārith (d. 99/718)

Report no. 2. No details of the case. The qāḍī assessed the value of the *matāʿ* at 500 dirhams. The statement may also be a report about Shurayḥ's personal practice, i.e., he paid this amount to his divorced wife (Wakīʿ 1947, 2:234).

Report no. 3. No details of the case. Same statement as in no. 2, but with a different chain of authorities (Wakīʿ 1947, 2:262; Ṭabarī 1954, 5:121).

Report no. 4. A husband divorced his wife, and the wife filed a lawsuit in the court. The Qāḍī cited Qur'ān 2:241 and instructed the husband to pay *matāʿ* if he considered himself to be a pious and God-fearing person. He did not issue any judgment [*lam yaqḍi*]. According to Wakīʿ, one of the transmitters of this Report, Shuʿba, saw the Report written in the handwriting of Abu'l-Ḍuḥā (Wakīʿ 1947, 2:266; Ṭabarī 1954, 5:128).

Report no. 5. Same Report as in no. 4, with a different chain of authorities (Wakīʿ 1947, 2:266; Suyūṭī 1983, 1:740).

Report no. 6. Same Report as in no. 4, with a different chain of authorities (Wakīʿ 1947, 2:286).

Report no. 7. Similar to no. 4. The Report adds that the qāḍī instructed the husband not to say that he is not a kind and pious person. No further details (Wakīʿ 1947, 2:327).

Report no. 8. The same as in no. 7, with a different chain of authorities (Wakīʿ 1947, 2:327).

Report no. 9. The same as in no. 7, with a different chain of authorities. Muḥammad b. Sīrīn, the qāḍī of Baṣra, who was present at the hearing, mentions a conversation between the husband and Qāḍī [Shurayḥ]. When the husband refused to pay the *matāʿ*, Shurayḥ told the husband that he should not deny that he was a righteous and kind person. The husband pleaded that he was destitute. The Report does not mention that the Qāḍī declared the payment of *matāʿ* to be obligatory, but the qāḍī did insist that it was the husband's moral duty to pay *matāʿ* (Wakīʿ 1947, 2:343).

Report no. 10. The same as in no. 9, with a different chain of authorities, except that in this Report, the qāḍī twice told the husband that he should not deny that he fears God (Wakīʿ 1947, 2:375).

Report no. 11. The same as in no. 10, with a different chain of authorities (Wakīʿ 1947, 2:377).

Report no. 12. A husband divorced his wife prior to consummation of the marriage. The qāḍī held that the husband must pay the remaining half of the dower to his wife as *matāʿ* [*inna lahā fi'l niṣfi matāʿ an*], because the husband had agreed to pay a specified amount of the dower (Wakīʿ 1947, 2:282).

Report no. 13. Same Report as in no. 7, with a different chain of authorities (Wakīʿ 1947, 2:282; Ibn Abī Shayba 1995, 4:146; Ṭabarī 1954, 5:128).

Report no. 14. No details about the facts. The qāḍī holds that the husband must pay *matāʿ* to his wife, whom he had divorced prior to consummation of the marriage (Wakīʿ 1947, 2:306).

Report no. 15. No details about the facts. The qāḍī held that the husband must pay *matāʿ* to his wife, whom he had divorced prior to consummation of the marriage. This Report differs from no. 9 in that here the husband had not fixed the dower (*mahr*). Muḥammad b. Sīrīn, the reporter, mentions that he was present at the hearing of the case (Wakīʿ 1947, 2:306; Ibn Abī Shayba 1995, 4:144).

Report no. 16. No details about the case. The qāḍī defines *mutʿa* as consisting of a shirt [*dirʿ*], a cloth to cover the head and face [*khimār*], a gown [*jalbāb*], a girdle [*al-minṭaq*] and a wrapper [*izār*] (Wakīʿ 1947, 2:314).

Qāḍī Tawba b. Nimr (d. 120/738)

Report no. 17. A husband and his wife brought a legal action to the qāḍī. The husband divorced her [during the session]. [Qāḍī] Tawba said, "Pay her *matāʿ* (*mattiʿhā*)." He [viz., the husband] said, "I will not pay." He [viz., the reporter] said that he [the qāḍī] did not press him because, in his [viz., the qāḍī's] opinion, it [viz., *matāʿ*] is not obligatory for him [viz., the husband] to pay. This same man [later] came to the qāḍī as a witness [in another case]. Tawba told him, "You are not qualified to appear as a witness." He asked why. The qāḍī replied, "Because you admitted [in a previous appearance in the court] that you are not a person who wishes to do good things, and you denied that you are a righteous person." The qāḍī did not accept him as a [qualified] witness (Kindī 1987:259).

Qāḍī Iyās b. Muʿāwiya (d. 121/739)

18. Replying to a question posed by ʿAbd Allāh b. ʿUmar, the qāḍī specified the value of *matāʿ* at 30 dirhams (Wakīʿ 1947, 1:321). This Report is repeated with a different chain of narrators (Wakīʿ 1947, 1:321).

Qāḍī Khayr b. Nuʿaym (d. 127/745)

19. No details about the facts. The Report states that the qāḍī frequently held for payment of *matāʿ* to the divorced wife. Kindī's source comments that this judgment was unprecedented (Kindī 1987:262).

CHAPTER FIFTEEN

FOUR CASES RELATING TO WOMEN AND DIVORCE IN AL-ANDALUS AND THE MAGHRIB, 1100–1500

David S. Powers

Introduction

Literary sources indicate that qāḍīs have recorded their judgments, and documents relating to those judgments, in their judicial registers since the fifth/eleventh century, if not before (Hallaq 1998). And the documents discovered at the Ḥaram al-Sharīf in Jerusalem point to the careful recording of judgments in the seventh/thirteenth and eighth/fourteenth centuries (Little 1984). It is only with the advent of the Ottomans, however, that the historian encounters true legal archives. For this reason, scholars interested in the work of the qāḍī and the application of legal doctrine in his court in most areas of the Muslim world prior to the tenth/sixteenth century must make use of literary sources such as biographical dictionaries, historical chronicles, *adab al-qāḍī* treatises, legal formularies, and manuals for market inspectors (see Masud, this volume).

One source that is especially useful in this regard is the *fatwā*, i.e., the response of a *muftī* or learned jurist to a question posed by an individual Muslim. The question itself might be about any subject relating to the Islamic way of life, and the person who poses the question (*mustaftī*) is sometimes a layman asking about some aspect of his or her daily affairs. At other times, the question is posed by a qāḍī, who is encouraged to seek the advice of learned experts, especially in cases that raise difficult or unusual issues relating to jurisprudence or legal doctrine. When a qāḍī seeks the advice of a *muftī*, his *istiftāʿ* or request for a *fatwā* invariably includes a written summary of the facts of the case, generally formulated in the abstract, impersonal, and objective language of the law. In this summary, the qāḍī cum *mustaftī* translates the utterances of the litigants and witnesses into the language of legal discourse as he sets down in writing their representations of the events and issues that are the subject of a particular dispute. The *istiftāʾ* may include a transcription of one or more legal documents relating to the case (e.g., a marriage contract, dower agreement, bequest, endowment deed, gift, oath, acknowledgment, or denial), and these transcriptions may preserve details about the names of the parties to a contract or legal transaction, its location, and the date on which it was formulated, details that make it possible to situate a particular dispute in its precise social and historical context.

After receiving the *istiftāʾ*, the *muftī* studies the case, issues a written response (*jawāb*), and returns to the questioner both the *istiftāʾ* and the *jawāb*, which, together, constitute the *fatwā*. Although a *fatwā* was not binding, in those cases in which a qāḍī did rely on it in issuing his judgment (*ḥukm*), it often became part of the documentary record associated with the case, and a copy was inserted in the qāḍī's judicial register (*dīwān al-aḥkām* or *sijill*).

The *fatwā* is an important source for the study of the application of Islamic law in qāḍī courts. Its two components—the *istiftāʾ* and the *jawāb*—are manifestations of the close and reciprocal relationship between the qāḍī and the *muftī*: In the *istiftāʾ*, the qāḍī summarizes the facts of the case and describes the manner in which he went about establishing them, e.g., listening to the claims and counterclaims of the litigants, assessing the credibility of witness testimony, and establishing the legal status of documentary evidence. In the *jawāb*, the *muftī* draws upon his knowledge of the doctrine of his law school (*madhhab*), which he applies to the facts of the case, as formulated by the qāḍī in his question. Thus, the *istiftāʾ* sheds light on the workings of the qāḍī and his court, while the *jawāb* reflects the modes of legal reasoning employed by a *muftī*. The conjunction of the *istiftāʾ* and the *jawāb* marks the meeting point between the work of the qāḍī and that of the *muftī* and between legal practice and legal doctrine. In my view, any analysis of qāḍī courts that focuses on one to the exclusion of the other will necessarily be one-sided and incomplete.

To illustrate how *fatwā*s can help us better to understand the activity of the qāḍī and his court, I will examine here four *fatwā*s dealing with women and divorce that are found in the *Kitāb al-Miʿyār*, a large collection of *fatwā*s compiled by Aḥmad al-Wansharīsī (d. 914/1508; al-Wansharīsī 1981–83). These four cases took place at different points in time in the period between the sixth/twelfth and ninth/fifteenth centuries in Granada (al-Andalus), Tāmasnā (the far Maghrib), and Gafsa and al-Mahdiyya (Tunisia). Each case found its way to a qāḍī court and was then referred to a *muftī* who issued a judicial opinion; the *muftī* returned the opinion to the qāḍī, who presumably used it as the basis of his judgment. The four *istiftā*'s studied here contain summaries of the facts of each case, and, in addition, transcriptions of several legal documents. Together, these four cases illustrate how qāḍīs dealt with plaintiffs and defendants, applied the rules of judicial procedure, and weighed conflicting evidence; how *muftī*s were called upon to clarify the law in hard cases; and how qāḍīs and *muftī*s cooperated in an effort to resolve family disputes in accordance with the teachings of Mālikī legal doctrine.

The Law of Divorce

It is generally acknowledged that the rules of divorce are asymmetrical, favoring men over women.

A Muslim man has the exclusive right to terminate a validly contracted marriage by repudiating his wife three times over the course of three separate menstrual periods, free of sexual intercourse, a procedure known as *ṭalāq*. A husband has the right to repudiate his wife in this manner at will and without cause. Once the divorce takes effect, the man may not remarry his former wife and resume sexual relations with her unless she marries another man, consummates that marriage, and is divorced by him, a process known as *taḥlīl* (Ibn Rushd al-Ḥafīd 1995, 2:71ff.).

A Muslim woman does not have a reciprocal right to initiate a divorce against her husband even if he beats her, fails to provide her with maintenance, or abandons her. The law does, however, make provisions for a wife who finds herself in one of these situations. Using a procedure known as *khulʿ* (literally, "ransom"), she may negotiate her release from the marriage by agreeing to renounce all financial claims against her husband, including the unpaid portion of the dower (*ṣadāq*). In a divorce of this type, which is definite and irrevocable (*bāʾin*), the husband cannot take back his wife during her waiting period (*ʿidda*); and once the waiting period has expired, a new marriage is necessary if the former husband and wife wish to return to each other (ibid., 2:79–83).

It is also possible for a husband to delegate to his wife the power to release herself from his marital power (*ʿiṣma*) by means of a procedure know as *tamlīk*. To do so, the husband must say to his wife, "Your matter is in your hands" (*amruki bi-yadiki*). A husband may stipulate, for example, that if he is absent from his wife for four months without providing her with maintenance, then she has the power to release herself from the marriage. The delegation may either be inserted in the marriage contract itself, in which case any resulting divorce is irrevocable, or it may be conferred upon the wife during the course of the marriage, in which case it is treated as revocable (ibid., 2:84–8; cf. Layish 1991:35 ff.).

A marriage also may be revoked by a qāḍī on the ground of defect (*ʿayb*) in either the husband or the wife. According to Mālikī jurists, four defects can entail revocation: insanity, leprosy, *baraṣ*—a skin disease similar to leprosy—and any disease of the sexual organ that prevents intercourse (Ibn Rushd 1995, 2:59).

Case One: Virginity, Disputed

A. *Version One*

Facts of the Case

Our first case, which took place in or near Granada in the second half of the eighth/fourteenth century, centers on a woman whose name and age are not mentioned in our source (al-Wansharīsī 1981–83, 3:32–5). Let's call her ʿĀ'isha, an orphan subject to the guardianship of her mother (for convenience, Umm ʿĀ'isha; on mothers as guardians, see Powers 2001).

Umm ʿĀ'isha arranged for her daughter to marry. After the groom had paid the dower, he asked the girl's mother for permission to consummate the marriage, but she refused. He then seized his bride and took her to his house against her will (*mukrahat*[an]). The two were alone in the house for several days. Subsequently, the husband claimed that he had sexually penetrated ʿĀ'isha during that time, and that, when he did, he discovered that she was not a virgin (*ghayr ʿadhrā'*), as claimed (ibid., 33, ll. 1–3). If the allegation were true, then it would appear that ʿĀ'isha had lost her virginity prematurely, as a result of illicit sexual relations or some other cause; be that as it may, her mother was—or pretended to be—unaware of the condition of her daughter's hymen at the time of her marriage.

The husband approached the local qāḍī and told him his version of what had transpired. According to the conventions of Mālikī judicial procedure, a qāḍī is required to issue a summons (*iʿdhār*) calling upon the person against whom a complaint has been made to present herself (or himself) in court and explain her (or his) behavior. The qāḍī accordingly summoned ʿĀʾisha to his court and asked her to relate to him her version of what had happened. She insisted that she had never had intercourse with any man, including her husband, and that she was still a virgin (*ʿadhrāʾ*). The qāḍī therefore designated the husband as the plaintiff and the wife as the defendant; and he translated the defendant's oral statement into the language of the law, here, a denial (*inkār*), which was inscribed in a written document. He also sent two midwives to examine the woman. When the examination was complete, the midwives returned to the qāḍī. One of them testified that the woman's hymen had been broken and that she was no longer a virgin, thereby contradicting ʿĀʾisha's testimony. Although our source does not specify what the second midwife said, the qāḍī accepted the testimony of the two women. Curiously, the qāḍī treated ʿĀʾisha's nonvirginity as a defect (*ʿayb*) in the marriage contract (see above), and he accordingly instructed the mother-guardian to return the dower. She complied, although she withheld 25 dirhams, presumably compensation for the man's use of her daughter's vulva. The qāḍī also composed a document in which the husband acknowledged receipt of the aforementioned sum from Umm ʿĀʾisha in the presence of witnesses. In this document the qāḍī declared: "[T]he state of marriage is dissolved on account of the defect, in accordance with the *sunna* on this matter" (*al-zawja* [read: *al-zawjiyya*] *infaṣalat bi-sabab al-ʿayb ʿalā al-sunna fī dhālika*) (ibid., 33, ll. 3–8).

The Mother Appeals

The dissolution of the marriage placed Umm ʿĀʾisha and her daughter in a tight spot. If the dissolution were upheld, it would be difficult to find a man who would agree to marry ʿĀʾisha. Alternatively, Umm ʿĀʾisha may have feared that if her daughter's agnatic relatives learned that she had not been a virgin at the time of her marriage, one of them might decide to remove this blot on the family's honor by killing her—although there is no mention of this in the *fatwā*.

Determined to save her daughter's reputation and, perhaps, her life, the mother-guardian now approached a second qāḍī, the Granadan shaykh and jurist Abū al-ʿAbbās Aḥmad b. Qāḍī al-Jamāʿa Abū al-Qāsim al-Ḥusaynī,[1] to whom she complained that she and her daughter had been the victims of an injustice. She gave the second qāḍī a document containing the testimony of "one of the Ahl Andarash [a city in the province of Almeria], one of the midwives who are expert in what can be observed with regard to the conditions of women." This female expert testified, in response to a written request (*taḥt khiṭāb*) from a qāḍī, that ʿĀʾisha was in fact still a virgin. The mother pleaded with al-Ḥusaynī, "If [my daughter] is divorced (*muṭallaqa*)," she said, "then who will marry her? And if she is not divorced, then issue a judgment on my behalf against her husband in accordance with the requirements of the *sharīʿa*" (ibid., 33, ll. 8–14).

B. *Version Two*

The facts revisited

Seeing merit in Umm ʿĀʾisha's argument, al-Ḥusaynī summoned the husband and interrogated him in the presence of two professional witnesses. Although the general features of the account that the husband gave al-Ḥusaynī were the same as those he had given the first qāḍī, the second version included some important variants.

The husband again acknowledged that he had seized ʿĀʾisha and been alone with her in his house for several days. However, he now explained that he initially had been unable to consummate the marriage because of an unidentified "obstacle"—possibly a reference to sexual dysfunction;[2] be that as it may, as soon as the obstacle disappeared, he did his duty and discovered that ʿĀʾisha was *thayyib*, i.e., not a virgin. At this point, he explained to the qāḍī, he went

---

[1] I have been unable to identify this jurist.

[2] Text: "*annahu iʿtaraḍa dūnahā ghayr mudda wa-annahu zāla ʿanhu al-iʿtirāḍ fa-waṭiʾahā.*" I am grateful to my colleague Roni Shaham for drawing my attention to this reading of the text.

to Umm ʿĀʾisha and told her what had happened: "Give me back [the dower] that you received from me," he demanded, "and hide her." When Umm ʿĀʾisha asked her daughter if her husband was telling the truth, she denied that the marriage had been consummated (ibid., 33, ll. 14–17).

The husband continued his story: In an attempt to save her daughter's marriage and reputation, Umm ʿĀʾisha devised a clever scheme. She now instructed him to return to her daughter and to have sexual intercourse with her—either for the first time, according to ʿĀʾisha's version of events, or for the second, according to his. He complied. Once again, he said, he discovered that she was not a virgin (ibid., 33, ll. 17–18).

It was only at this point in time, the husband explained, that is to say, after he had consummated the marriage not once but twice, that he approached the first qāḍī and submitted his complaint. As in the initial version of the story, the qāḍī sent midwives to examine ʿĀʾisha. Unlike the initial version, we are now told that the second midwife acknowledged that she herself had not seen anything and that she had merely confirmed the testimony of her partner because of the possibility (*iḥtimāl*) that it was the husband who had caused ʿĀʾisha to lose her virginity. In this version of the story, only one of the two midwives testified that ʿĀʾisha was not a virgin at the time of the examination (ibid., 33, ll. 18–23).

C. *The* Fatwā *of Ibn Lubb*

No doubt confused and unsure of how to proceed, the second qāḍī, al-Ḥusaynī, now sent a request for a *fatwā* to the Granadan jurist Abū al-Faraj b. Lubb (d. 782/1381);[3] the *istiftāʾ* contained a summary of the facts of the case and a transcription of the relevant documents.

Ibn Lubb began his response by declaring that the judgment issued by the first qāḍī was a patent mistake (*khaṭaʾ*), that it must be reversed, and that a new judgment should be issued. The *muftī* expressed no interest whatsoever in the condition of ʿĀʾisha's hymen, focusing his attention instead on whether or not the husband had consummated

[3] On Ibn Lubb, see Ibn Farḥūn (1932:220–1); al-Tunbuktī (1932:219–21); Makhlūf (1975, 1:230–1).

the marriage. He explained: A husband pays the dower in return for the right to have intercourse with his wife. In the present instance, the first time that the husband exercised this right, he discovered that his wife was not a virgin. By his own admission, however, he then had intercourse with his wife a second time. If, for the sake of argument, the first act of intercourse did not establish that the two were husband and wife, the second surely did (ibid., 33, l. 24–34, l. 4).

The *muftī* proceeded to refute the two arguments advanced by the husband in defense of his actions: First, he summarily dismissed the husband's attempt to shift blame to the mother and her daughter, i.e., his assertion that he had had intercourse with his wife a second time only out of consideration for her interests and in response to the instructions of his mother-in-law. Second, the *muftī* rejected as inconclusive the husband's reliance on the testimony of the midwife who testified that ʿĀʾisha was not a virgin. His negative assessment of the midwife's testimony was related to the timing of the examination: Such an examination should have taken place shortly after the *initial* act of intercourse, ideally on the morning following the night on which the husband allegedly consummated the marriage. A timely undertaking of the examination is required to ensure that the wound created by the rupture of the hymen is fresh and easy to identify. Custom teaches, the *muftī* added, that such wounds heal quickly. If a midwife testifies that the wound is old, then deflowering may have occurred prior to the husband's initial penetration of his wife, i.e., the woman in question may have lost her virginity prior to the marriage, through an earlier (and illicit-DSP) act of sexual intercourse. In the present case, the midwives did not specify whether the woman had lost her virginity a long time ago (*qadīm*[an]) or only recently (*ḥadīth*[an])—a sign, the *muftī* observes, of a decline in the standards of the profession—and their testimony was therefore inconclusive (ibid., 34, l. 26–35, l. 4).

Thus, the only legally established "fact" was ʿĀʾisha's claim that she was a virgin at the time of the marriage. And since a husband cannot have intercourse with his wife without providing her with compensation (*al-ghurm*), she is entitled to the prompt or immediate dower. In support of his argument, Ibn Lubb cited the *Wathāʾiq al-Majmūʿa* of Ibn ʿAṭṭār (d. 399/1008): "If the husband perseveres in having intercourse with her subsequent to his becoming aware of [the fact that she is not a virgin], then he has no claim" (ibid., 34, ll. 7–8, and 35, ll. 9–10).

It will be remembered that the first qāḍī had dissolved the marriage on account of the alleged defect and had ordered Umm ʿĀ'isha to return the dower to her erstwhile son-in-law. Putting things straight would be no easy matter. Did the husband have any claim against his mother in-law? No, because she was acting on the strength of the initial judgment (despite her disagreeing with it). That judgment was unjust (*ḥukm jawr*) and based upon ignorance. Are the man and woman married or separated? In order to determine their status, it would be necessary to interrogate the witnesses who testified to the mutual separation and dissolution (*al-tafāṣul wa'l-infiṣāl*). If the witnesses understood that the husband intended to divorce his wife (*fa-in kānū fahimū min al-zawj al-ṭalāq*), then so be it. But if they understood that the husband intended to retain his marital power over his wife (*ibqā' al-ʿiṣma*), then he should swear an oath that he did not intend to divorce her; if he swears the oath, the marriage is treated as unbroken and continuous (ibid., 34, ll. 15ff.).

The *muftī* included in his response a sharp rebuke of the qāḍī who had dissolved the marriage "on account of the defect, in accordance with the *sunna* on this matter." He exclaimed, "Would that [the qāḍī] had not mentioned the *sunna*, for how can ignorance and error be a *sunna* in a matter relating to religious practice (*dīn*)? This is extreme carelessness" (ibid., 34, ll. 13–15; cf. Layish, this volume). We do not know whether the qāḍī accepted or rejected Ibn Lubb's opinion.

Case Two: Wife Abandonment

Facts of the Case

Our second case took place in Qafṣa, a port city on the Mediterranean coast 310 km southwest of Tunis (ibid., 3:327–31). We do not know the date of the case or the name of the female litigant. Let's call her Fāṭima.

At a young age and perhaps while still a minor, Fāṭima was married to a certain Aḥmad. The marriage took place in Qafṣa, presumably the residence of both husband and wife. One day, Aḥmad left Qafṣa, heading in the direction of al-Andalus. He did not return.

Our source does not specify the reason for his absence, although it indicates that he had left provisions for Fāṭima and that she had the means to sustain herself. The marriage remained in force, but the wife was effectively husbandless. Eventually, she became involved with another man, causing her family to fear that she might engage in illicit sexual relations, thereby disgracing herself and her agnatic relatives.

In the Qāḍī's Court

Six years after her husband's departure, Fāṭima's father and marriage guardian approached the qāḍī of Qafṣa and asked him to issue a judicial divorce. He brought two witnesses who testified as follows:

> So-and-So b. So-and-So left his wife, So-and-So, in the city of Qafṣa, six years ago, [heading] in the direction of al-Andalus; the aforementioned [sic] Aḥmad is aware of the fact that it is not forbidden for him to enter Qafṣa; that his wife is in need of (*muḥtāja ilā*) a husband; and that she suffers a harm (*maḍarra*) by remaining without a husband (ibid., 327, ll. 12–17).

In addition, two witnesses testified that Fāṭima had "an intense desire" (*raghba shadīda*) to divorce her husband. After examining the witnesses and determining that they were men of integrity, the qāḍī accepted their testimony. Fāṭima's father now asked the qāḍī to release his daughter from the marital power (*ʿiṣma*) of her husband and to impose a judicial divorce (ibid., 327, ll. 17–20).

As noted above, a qāḍī is required to issue a summons (*iʿdhār*) calling upon the defendant to present himself in court and explain his behavior. If circumstances prevent the defendant from responding to the summons in person, he has the right to issue a statement in the presence of witnesses who record his words and convey the resulting testimony to the qāḍī. In the present instance, however, the qāḍī identified four factors that made it difficult if not impossible for him to issue the summons: (1) the great distance between Qafṣa and al-Andalus; (2) the insecurity of travel; (3) the absence of people willing and able to undertake the mission; and (4) the lack of people familiar with the defendant's handwriting who could verify the authenticity of any document that the latter might send (ibid., 327, ll. 20–3).

The First Request for a Fatwā

Would it be proper for the qāḍī to impose a judicial divorce on Aḥmad without giving him an opportunity to defend himself? Uncertain of the answer to this question, the qāḍī consulted with an unnamed *muftī* who issued a *fatwā*, which, as represented by the qāḍī, included the following statement:

> If Aḥmad is absent from that woman, and she is in need of a husband, and if it is feared that she suffers harm (text: *al-maʿarra*; read: *al-maḍarra*), as the testimony indicates, she shall be granted a [judicial] divorce (*tuṭallaqu ʿalā*) from her husband, especially if she is of a tender age (*ḥadīthat al-sin*) (ibid., 327, l. 23–328, l. 1).[4]

The qāḍī accepted the *fatwā* but proceeded with caution. In compliance with the strict requirements of judicial procedure, he did in fact issue a summons calling upon Aḥmad to present himself in Qafṣa, stipulating a deadline for his appearance. When Aḥmad did not respond, the qāḍī granted him several extensions. Again, Aḥmad did not respond. Meanwhile, Fāṭima's father persisted in his demand that the qāḍī issue a judicial divorce on account of a "harm" (*li-maḍarra*) that his daughter was experiencing (ibid., 328, ll. 1–3).

The qāḍī found himself on the horns of a dilemma. He knew that any judicial divorce that he might execute against Aḥmad would be open to challenge on the ground that it had been issued against the husband's will. At the same time, if he did not grant the divorce, Fāṭima might engage in illicit sexual relations. Presumably, the qāḍī attempted to balance the interests of the husband against those of the wife and determined that the scales of justice were weighted in favor of the woman. He explained that after studying the case in the obligatory manner, he "asked God for guidance and executed a single revocable repudiation, by means of which she enters her waiting period."[5] He ordered that two copies of the judgment be produced, one for "my judicial register" (*dīwān aḥkāmī*), in case a need should arise, the other for the woman's legal representative, as security and proof "for that day and the days that followed." Several

[4] The combination of failure to provide maintenance, absence of the husband, and fear for the wife's chastity is commonly found in the Libyan documents studied by Layish (this volume).

[5] If the husband were to appear prior to the expiration of the waiting period, and if he were to provide maintenance, then he would have the right to take back his wife, without going through the formalities of a new marriage.

days later, the judgment was read aloud in the presence of the qāḍī. The resulting document mentioned the day and date of the divorce. Shortly thereafter, the woman remarried (ibid., 328, ll. 3–11).

The Judgment is Appealed

At an unspecified date subsequent to the issuance of the judicial divorce, an unidentified party, perhaps one of Aḥmad's relatives, challenged the qāḍī's judgment and the *fatwā* upon which it was based.

Seeking to have the judgment nullified, the complainant sent a request for a *fatwā* to a second *muftī*. The question itself, although missing in our source, can be reconstructed from the response. The complainant argued that the first *muftī* had deviated from established Mālikī legal doctrine, thereby creating new law, something that only an absolute *mujtahid* has the power to do. (Presumably, the "new law" referred to the qāḍī's execution of a judicial divorce against a husband on the grounds of his wife's inability to engage in sexual relations with him.)

The second *muftī* began his response by addressing the issue of *ijtihād*. At the present time, he observed, there are no absolute *mujtahids*, only *mujtahids* of a lower rank, i.e., *muftīs* within the *madhhab*. When such a *muftī* is asked a question, it is his duty to rely on the opinions of earlier school authorities that lead back in a direct line to the first Imāms, a practice known as *taqlīd*. If such a *muftī* bases his *fatwā* on the views of earlier authorities, then his opinion is sound and immune from criticism. But if a contemporary *muftī* reads the words of the Imāms of the past and contradicts them, "then one of the gates of ignorance has been opened in such a manner that it cannot be repaired." In the present instance, the *muftī* continued, the door of ignorance had been thrown ajar. "I do not know of any Imām," he declared, who has ever issued a *fatwā* in which he stated that a qāḍī can issue a judicial divorce against a man who consummates a marriage and then disappears, but who possesses wealth from which his wife may be maintained; or that a qāḍī may dissolve a marriage bond on the ground that the inability of a wife to engage in sexual intercourse with her husband constitutes "harm" (ibid., 328, ll. 12–24). In support of his opinion, the *muftī* advanced four arguments.

1. *Analogy to* Īlā

Fāṭima's father apparently had compared his daughter's situation to that of a woman whose husband swears an oath—known as *īlā*—not to have sexual relations with her for four months (ibid., 328, ll. 24–5). Herein lies one of the jurisprudential novelties of the case.

Q. 2:226 reads: "For those who forswear their wives, there is a period of waiting of four months; then, if they change their mind, lo!, Allāh is Forgiving, Merciful." This verse establishes the procedure of *īlā*, which makes it possible for a man to divorce his wife by swearing an oath that he will not have intercourse with her for four months in succession. By abstaining from intercourse with his wife for a period of four months, the husband indicates his desire to harm her. If the husband does not resume sexual relations with his wife before the end the four-month time period, then the divorce is accomplished.

Presumably, Fāṭima's father argued that just as a harm is suffered by a woman whose husband swears the *īlā* oath and abstains from sexual relations with her for four months, so too a harm was suffered by Fāṭima, whose husband had not had sexual relations with her for *six years*, albeit, without swearing an oath of continence. And, he no doubt continued, the legal effect (*ḥukm*) of the *īlā* procedure should apply equally to a husband who ceases to have sexual relations with his wife for four months or longer, but does *not* swear an oath to do so. This raises the question: Is the situation of a woman whose husband disappears analogous to that of a woman whose husband swears an oath not to have sexual intercourse with her for four months, with the result that the former is entitled to a divorce on the ground of harm caused by her inability to engage in sexual relations?[6]

No, it does not, the *muftī* responded. In support of his position, he refers, in the first instance, to a "well-known" *ḥadīth* involving the second caliph, ʿUmar b. al-Khaṭṭāb: Two women whose husbands had disappeared were experiencing a high degree of sexual tension, to the point that they composed poetry that included the line, "May

[6] However, Mālik is reported to have held that the legal effect or rule (*ḥukm*) of *al-īlā* does apply to such a man on the ground that his abstention from sexual relations with his wife constitutes a harm, whether he vowed to exercise continence or not. But this is a minority opinion within the school. See Ibn Rushd (1995, 2:123).

this night be long and may its end be black." The matter was brought to the attention of the caliph, who refused to issue a judicial divorce against the two husbands. The *muftī* notes that none of the Companions asked ʿUmar to do so and that no woman expected him to do so. From this the *muftī* concluded that there was a quasi-consensus among the Companions on this point; and, he added, experts in jurisprudence and legal doctrine have drawn a legal deduction (*istiqrāʾ*) regarding this consensus. Now, a fact established on the basis of a legal deduction is of greater epistemological and probative value than a "possibility"—here, the possibility that the woman suffers a harm (ibid., 328, l. 25–329, l. 6).

2. *Definition of "Harm"*

The preceding discussion leads, in turn, to the following question: Does a wife whose husband is unable to have sexual relations with her suffer a harm that may serve as grounds for a judicial divorce?

Again, we now learn that the first *muftī* apparently had asserted that Mālik and his companions held that a woman whose marriage has been duly consummated is entitled to a judicial divorce if her husband has his penis removed. The second *muftī* categorizes the attribution of this opinion to Mālik as "astonishing" and he proceeds to clarify the circumstances in which a woman who suffers a "harm" is in fact entitled to a judicial divorce. He adduces three points. First, although the inability of a wife to engage in sexual relations with her husband may cause a harm, this harm does not necessarily constitute grounds for divorce. Suppose that one or more virile men were to approach the woman whose husband had suffered dismemberment, with the result that she was "flaming with desire." Although no reasonable person would deny that she was afflicted by a "harm," she nevertheless is not entitled to a divorce. Second, in the case discussed by Mālik (dismemberment), there was no expectation that the husband would return to his former state of virility; nevertheless, the second *muftī* maintained, the man may *not* be divorced against his will. Third, although it is well-known that a woman suffers "harm" if she is deprived of sexual intercourse for only four months, the law stipulates that if her husband becomes impotent (note: impotence *is* grounds for divorce), one year must pass before the divorce may be issued (ibid., 329, ll. 14–23).

3. *Justifications for Abstinence*

A man's inability to engage in sexual relations with his wife may be the result of unavoidable causes, some natural (e.g., sickness), others unnatural (e.g., dismemberment).

In the case of *īlā*, if a man expresses hostility to his wife by swearing not to have sexual relations with her for four months, but then is prevented from returning to her as a result of either sickness or imprisonment, the marriage remains intact. The same holds for a man who is unable to return to his home for four months as a result of his falling ill or being arrested. And it also holds for a man who remains with his wife but is unable to have sexual relations with her for an extended period of time as a result of a prolonged illness. In other words, so long as the husband does not manifest hostility towards his wife, his marriage may not be dissolved against his will (ibid., 329, ll. 24–330, l. 5).

4. *Intent*

A husband is not required to live with his wife or to have sexual relations with her, so long as he does not intend to harm her by absenting himself from her and failing to engage in sexual relations with her—on the condition, however, that he provides for her maintenance.

This is because a wife's right to maintenance is absolute so long as she remains obedient to her husband. If the husband provides maintenance for his wife, then it is not sufficient to establish that she suffers a harm by virtue of the absence of sexual relations. Rather, a judge may issue a judicial divorce against such a husband only if it is established that he *intended* to harm his wife by being absent from her, and then only after careful examination of the circumstances (ibid., 330, ll. 6–11).

In the present case, the qāḍī of Qafṣa had failed to take into consideration the fact that the husband did not intend to harm his wife but rather was prevented from returning to Qafṣa by an unspecified obstacle. Had he investigated the matter in the required manner, he would have discovered that the husband did not intend to harm his wife. Surely, the *muftī* continued, husbands and wives cohabit with one another with the understanding that a husband may travel far from home in the pursuit of his livelihood (ibid., 330, ll. 18–20).

For these reasons, the *muftī* concluded, the judgment issued by the qāḍī is null and void, and the *fatwā* upon which it was based is a clear mistake. The judgment must be reversed. Anyone who says that the woman may remain with her second husband condones illicit sexual relations (*zinā*). Whoever is asked to examine this case should fear God and hasten to nullify (*faskh*) the initial judgment. The woman should observe a waiting period with respect to her second husband in order to insure that she is not pregnant, and then be returned to her first husband (ibid., 330, ll. 21–6).

At the end of the *fatwā*, the *muftī* mentions technical problems with two statements in the *istiftā'*.

1. In the first statement, witnesses testified that "So-and-so is in need of a husband, and she suffers a harm by remaining without a husband." The mere existence of a harm, the *muftī* explains, is insufficient. The witnesses also must testify that the woman "complained to us with regard to the harm in that matter, and we knew that she spoke the truth" (ibid., 331, ll. 2–5).
2. In the second statement, witnesses testified that the woman has "an intense desire to divorce her husband." Now, a woman may have a desire to divorce her husband, the *muftī* explains, but not *act* upon that desire, either because of embarrassment or for some other reason. The witness testimony, in its present form, affirms the desire but does not affirm the request for a divorce. Judgments must be based upon explicit statements, the *muftī* concludes, not upon conjecture and allusion (ibid., 331, ll. 6–9).[7]

Again, we are ignorant about the outcome of the case.

Case Three: Delegated Divorce

Facts of the Case

Our third case took place in the Tunisian port city of al-Mahdiyya in the sixth/twelfth century (ibid., 3:311–12).

'Ā'isha bt. 'Uthmān b. Ṭayyib al-Anṣārī, a resident of al-Mahdiyya, was married to 'Abdallāh b. Ṣadaqa al-Anṣārī, who made his living

[7] Cf. Layish (1991:91–2), where fear for a wife's chastity in the absence of her husband *is* a common ground for divorce.

as a ship captain (*ra'īs*), an occupation which, although no doubt lucrative, involved great personal risk. Shipwrecks were not uncommon. And seasonal voyages took ʿAbdallāh away from his wife and home in al-Mahdiyya for months at a time. As we have seen, the consequences of a husband's prolonged absence—or death—might be disastrous: If ʿAbdallāh disappeared somewhere within the abode of Islam, and ʿĀ'isha could not establish that he had divorced her, the law stipulates that proceedings for dissolution of the marriage (and receipt of the unpaid portion of the dower) might not *begin* until four years had passed from the date on which the case was brought before a judge. Alternatively, if she could not establish that ʿAbdallāh had died, the law stipulates that his estate may not be distributed to his heirs (including ʿĀ'isha) until the end of his natural life-span, variously estimated at 70, 80, 90, or even 100 years. In either case, it would be difficult for her to remarry (Ibn Rushd 1995, 2:61–2).

In the year 515/1121, ʿAbdallāh made plans to sail to Sicily on one of the Sulṭān's ships. No doubt concerned about the possibility that he might not return, he took measures to protect his wife. During the last ten days of Muḥarram/middle April, husband and wife approached a local notary and, in the presence of two witnesses, ʿAbdallāh stipulated that if he were to be absent from al-Mahdiyya for more than four months in succession, without sending ʿĀ'isha any subsistence money (*rizq*), he delegated to her the power to release herself from the marriage. The document inscribing the delegated divorce (*tamlīk*) was formulated as follows:

> If (*mattā*) he departs from the city of al-Mahdiyya, leaving his wife ʿĀ'isha, and he is absent from her by necessity (*ghaybat ḍarūra*) for more than four consecutive months, and he does not send to his wife, ʿĀ'isha bt. ʿUthmān b. Ṭayyib al-Anṣārī, any subsistence money (*rizq*), then he delegates to her the power [to obtain a judicial divorce] (*fa-amruhā bi-yadihā*). If he were to travel in the Sulṭān's ships but does not arrive in al-Mahdiyya and Zuwayla in the Sulṭān's ships, he releases the aforementioned ʿĀ'isha. She accepted this acknowledgment fully.
>
> [The witnesses] testified to familiarity with him and to his acknowledgment with respect to himself, to the end of the dating clause in the last ten days of Muḥarram of the year 515 [middle April 1121] (Wansharīsī 1981–3, 3:311, l. 23–312, l. 6).

ʿAbdallāh departed. ʿĀ'isha waited.

In the Qāḍī's Court

ʿAbdallāh reportedly sailed as far as the port town of Ṭarābulus al-Maghrib, i.e., Tripoli in present-day Libya, where he remained for four months, for unspecified reasons, possibly inclement weather or political instability. During that period, he did not send ʿĀʾisha any support, and she apparently had no means to sustain herself.

In Rajab 515/September-October 1121, five months after ʿAbdallāh's departure and one month after the expiration of the stipulated time period, ʿĀʾisha approached the chief qāḍī of al-Mahdiyya, Abū al-Qāsim b. Maymūn,[8] and asked him to grant her a judicial divorce. She summoned two sets of witnesses who gave detailed and seemingly comprehensive testimony on her behalf in the presence of the chief qāḍī. The first set of witnesses stated that they were familiar with both ʿAbdallāh and ʿĀʾisha; that the two were husband and wife; that they had no knowledge of ʿĀʾisha's having left ʿAbdallāh's marital power (*khurūjuhā min ʿiṣmatihi*) until the day on which he had departed for Sicily; that ʿĀʾisha had no knowledge of ʿAbdallāh's return; that ʿAbdallāh was not known to have left any food or maintenance for ʿĀʾisha; that he had not sent her anything; and that he had no wealth by means of which she might support herself. Their testimony was inscribed on the verso of the delegated divorce document, together with the testimony of the second set of witnesses, who stated that ʿAbdallāh "had been absent in the city of Ṭarābulus al-Maghrib for a period of approximately four months" (ibid., 312, ll. 6–12).

The Fatwā

On the one hand, the facts of the case indicated that ʿAbdallāh had violated the terms of the delegated divorce by absenting himself from his wife for four consecutive months without sending her maintenance. On the other hand, it appears that he had not abandoned his wife but rather was prevented from returning to al-Mahdiyya by unforeseen circumstances that were beyond his control.

The qāḍī Ibn Maymūn was reluctant to issue a judicial divorce, and, before taking any judicial action, he consulted with a *muftī*

[8] I am unable to identify this jurist.

(whose name is not specified in our source). In the *istiftā'*, Ibn Maymūn summarized the facts of the case and transcribed the *tamlīk* divorce document and the witness testimony regarding ʿAbdallāh's absence.

The *muftī* examined the documents carefully. As in Case Two, there were technical problems, but, whereas in that case, the *muftī* mentioned the technical problems at the end of his response, in the present case, the *muftī* identified the problems at the very beginning of his response. The *tamlīk* document was flawed, in four respects:

1. The witnesses identified the wife as "ʿĀʾisha" at first mention, but as "ʿĀʾisha bt. ʿUthmān b. Ṭayyib al-Anṣārī" at second mention. Now a Muslim man may be married to up to four women simultaneously, and it may happen that two co-wives have the same name. For this reason, the *muftī* specified that the document is valid only on the condition that ʿAbdallāh does not have another wife also named ʿĀʾisha.
2. The document stipulated that ʿAbdallāh must be absent "by necessity"; thus ʿĀʾisha was entitled to a divorce only if ʿAbdallāh was absent for four months in succession *and* his absence was a result of necessity.
3. The reference to "the sulṭān's ships" was vague (perhaps because the document did not identify a specific ship).
4. The witnesses' testimony regarding ʿAbdallāh's absence was incomplete: It is possible that ʿAbdallāh left for Sicily, returned to al-Mahdiyya, and then left again; the witnesses must specify that the absence in question was the only absence that had occurred subsequent to the composition and certification of the delegated divorce document.

After clarifying these technical issues, the *muftī* stated that ʿĀʾisha was entitled to a divorce on two conditions: First, it is impossible to send a summons (*iʿdhār*) to ʿAbdallāh calling upon him to appear in court and explain his actions, because he is located in a remote location with which communication is difficult (cf. Case Two); and, second, there is no reasonable expectation that he will return in the near future. If these two conditions are satisfied, the *muftī* concluded, then ʿĀʾisha is entitled to a divorce. Our source does not indicate the course of action adopted by the qāḍī.

Case Four: A Woman Flees her First Husband and Marries a Second

Facts of the Case

Our fourth and final case began in Tāmasnā, the coastal plain that serves as a natural passageway between the regions of Fez and Marrakech, some time after the year 482/1089 (ibid., 3:41–3).

A resident of Tāmasnā by the name of ʿĪsā b. Baṭṭān was married and had a daughter named Tāwanzā. When ʿĪsā died, his germane brother became Tāwanzā's legal guardian. At an unspecified date, the guardian arranged for his ward to marry Muḥammad b. Saʿīd al-Janātī. The marriage apparently was concluded without any witnesses being present; and it was unsuccessful, for reasons not specified in our source.

Tāwanzā fled from her husband and moved to another town or village, where she re-married.

In the Qāḍī's Court

To recover his wife, al-Janātī would have to establish the *bona fides* of his marriage to Tāwanzā before the qāḍī of the town in which she currently was living with her second husband.

To this end, approximately two years after the marriage, al-Janātī gathered several witnesses who had knowledge of his marriage to Tāwanzā, even though they had not been present at the marriage itself. Al-Janātī brought these witnesses to the qāḍī of Tāmasnā, in whose presence they testified regarding their knowledge of the marriage. The resulting memorial document (*rasm al-istirʿāʾ*)[9] reads as follows:

> His witnesses are thoroughly familiar with Muḥammad b. Saʿīd al-Janātī by sight and by name, and they have knowledge of the fact

---

[9] Mālikī law accords probative value to a *rasm istirʿāʾ* or memorial document. This is a document in which professional witnesses record the testimony of one or more individuals who have knowledge of a certain topic that may have legal relevance. Such a document is drawn up in anticipation of a subsequent litigation. Its contents remain secret until it is needed, at which time it may be presented to the judge who has been asked to resolve a dispute. The judge's decision to accept or reject the document is conditioned by his assessment of the integrity of the professional witnesses who recorded the testimony. For references to Mālikī sources, see Powers (2002:31, note 35). The *rasm istirʿāʾ* is similar to *shahādat al-naql*, discussed by Layish in this volume.

> that he married Tāwanzā bt. ʿĪsā b. Baṭṭān, who is from the aforementioned tribe [sic]. [The marriage occurred] two years prior to the date [of the document]. [The woman was] under the guardianship of her paternal uncle, the full brother of her aforementioned father, who is known to them [viz., the witnesses] in the same manner as described [above]. [They further stated that] they have no knowledge that the bond of the marriage was dissolved between the two of them until the present time (ibid., 41, ll. 2–42, l. 3).

Al-Janātī took the memorial document, which bore the signature of the qāḍī of Tāmasnā, and set off for the town in which Tāwanzā was living with her second husband. Upon his arrival, he sought out the local qāḍī and showed him the document. Al-Janātī explained to the qāḍī that he had married Tāwanzā two years earlier, that he had never released her from his marital power, and that she therefore was still his wife—even though she apparently had married a second man. He no doubt asked the qāḍī to issue an order instructing Tāwanzā to return to him (ibid., 41, ll. 23–4; cf. Layish 1995b: 488–503).

When the qāḍī examined the memorial document, he discovered that it had several technical defects:

1. The witnesses stated that "they have knowledge of the fact that he married Tāwanzā" but they did not specify the basis of their knowledge. Was this direct and certain knowledge, based upon their presence at the marriage, or indirect and probable knowledge, based upon a widespread rumor?
2. The witnesses stated that Tāwanzā was "under the guardianship of her paternal uncle" but they did not specify whether or not she also had a separate marriage guardian.
3. If someone other than a natural father arranges for a woman to marry, that person must first consult with the woman (the technical term for such consultation is *al-istiʾmār*). The document makes no mention of the required consultation.
4. The witnesses stated that al-Janātī "married Tāwanzā bt. ʿĪsā" but they did not specify whether or not they said that on the basis of certain knowledge (*maʿrifa*) (ibid., 42, ll. 3–14).

The Request for a Fatwā

Did the technical flaws in the memorial document prohibit the qāḍī of the town in which Tāwanzā now dwelt from dissolving her marriage and from ordering her to return to her first husband?

The qāḍī sent a request for a *fatwā* to the *muftī*, Abū ʿAbdallāh Muḥammad b. Abī al-Faḍl al-Ṣabbāgh,[10] to whom he posed several questions. Was the memorial document legally valid in its current form—despite the above-mentioned defects—inasmuch as it may be assumed that the qāḍī who certified the document questioned the witnesses with regard to the uncertainties and was satisfied with their answers? Or is the document invalid in its current form, and does it remain so until such time as it is replaced with a second document in which there are no ambiguities? At the conclusion of the *istiftāʾ*, the qāḍī cum *mustaftī* informed the *muftī* that he did not know how to proceed. Hence the question.

Al-Ṣabbāgh responded that the validity of the memorial document depends on the qualifications of the qāḍī who certified it. If he was a learned and virtuous man (*min ahl al-ʿilm wa'l-faḍl*), then the document has probative value; otherwise, it does not. The *muftī* cited several arguments in support of his view:

1. He referred to the case of a certain Ibn Shammākh, located at the beginning of the *Aḥkām* of Ibn Sahl (d. 482/1089).
2. According to Ibn al-Makwī (d. 401/1010),[11] Ibn ʿAttāb (d. 462/1069–70),[12] and Ibn Sahl himself, the preferred opinion of the Mālikī school is that testimony of this nature is legally effective.
3. This opinion is in conformity with the *Mudawwana*. According to Ibn ʿAṭṭār, it is desirable but not obligatory to have the witnesses specify their testimony. All of this, the *muftī* concluded, is explained at the beginning of the *Aḥkām* of Ibn Sahl.

Conclusion

The four *fatwā*s examined above shed light on certain *general features* of the judicial apparatus of al-Andalus, the Maghrib, and Ifrīqiyā in the period under consideration here.[13]

---

[10] I have been unable to identify this jurist.

[11] Al-Ḥumaydī (n.d. 123, no. 231).

[12] Ibn Baskhuwāl (1966, no. 1194).

[13] It is important to keep in mind several shortcomings of *fatwā*s as a source for the workings of the Islamic judicial system: (1) Our documentation picks up only at the point at which the case reached a qāḍī, and is silent about the preceding stages of individual disputes. (2) We do not know what the final judicial decision

The Qāḍī

All four of the cases deal with the dissolution of marriage. In each instance, the case began when one of the parties approached a qāḍī and asked for his assistance in the resolution of a sensitive family matter. The qāḍīs did not hesitate to intervene in these disputes. Unlike the Moroccan qāḍīs studied by Rosen (1989, 2000), who reportedly resolved similar disputes by attempting to restore the litigants to a position in which they could negotiate the terms of their own relationship, the four qāḍīs who were asked to resolve the disputes followed standard judicial procedure, i.e., they determined the facts of the case, assessed the reliability of witness testimony, and applied Mālikī legal doctrine to those facts, to the best of their ability. In each case, the qāḍī appears to have served as a neutral third party, and each case was a zero-sum game: one litigant emerged victorious, the other defeated (although the reader will recall that we do not know the final outcome of any of the cases).

After receiving the initial complaint, each qāḍī summoned the litigants to his court, heard the complaint and its rebuttal, transformed the oral statements of the parties into the language of the law (acknowledgment, denial, etc.), determined who was the plaintiff and who was the defendant, and instructed the plaintiff to produce evidence in support of his/her claim.

The primary form of evidence presented in court was the testimony of men and women who had knowledge relating to the case, as corroborated by professional witnesses. A high value was placed upon the integrity of the witnesses and the precision of their testimony. Witness testimony that was sufficiently accurate and precise might serve as the basis of a judgment; testimony that was inaccurate or merely imprecise might result in the subsequent reversal of a judgment. Witness testimony typically was inscribed in a written document, which, if properly authenticated, was acceptable as evidence in the qāḍī court and might play a role in the resolution of a dispute. In my experience, written documents played a much more important role in qāḍī courts than is generally recognized (cf. Layish, this volume).

---

was in any of these cases. (3) Four cases do not constitute a significant statistical example and they are not "representative" of either qāḍī courts or Muslim society. (4) In several instances we do not know the names of the litigants, and the underlying social context is usually missing.

If appropriate, the qāḍī summoned expert witnesses and asked them to make a determination of fact, e.g., he might ask a midwife to determine whether or not a woman was a virgin, a handwriting expert to establish the identity of the author of a document, or a water expert to make a determination relating to water usage (on the latter, see Powers 2002:112–17).

Qāḍīs were reluctant to issue a judgment against a defendant who was either unable to appear in court to respond to charges levelled against him or refused to do so. But the inability of a defendant to appear in court did not necessarily stymie the judicial process. A defendant might submit a written statement of his case to the qāḍī. Such a document was acceptable as evidence on the condition that its authenticity could be established by an expert in the analysis of handwriting. Only in extreme cases—i.e., when it was impossible for a defendant either to appear in court himself or to submit a written statement of his position, and, in the case of an absentee husband, if there was no reasonable expectation that he would return—would a qāḍī issue a judgment against a defendant who was not present in court.

The qāḍī kept a written record of the activities of his court, e.g., the notarization of documents, certification of *fatwā*s, and the issuance of judgments. He gave one copy of his judgment to the successful party and placed a second copy in his judicial register (*dīwān al-aḥkām*), where it might be reviewed by his successor. Each qāḍī thus produced a private archive. The fact that most of these private archives are no longer extant is probably a result of the fact that until Ottoman times there was no centralized office for the preservation of qāḍī records (Hallaq 1998).

It was the qāḍī's recording of his judgments in the *dīwān al-aḥkām* that made possible a system of judicial review. Elsewhere, I have demonstrated that Mālikī legal doctrine allows for the reconsideration of a judgment under precisely defined conditions (Powers 1992; cf. Gradeva, this volume). The court of the chief judge of a capital city frequently served as a court of review for the decisions of local and provincial judges. Further, a judge was empowered to reconsider and overturn a judgment issued by his predecessor if it could be demonstrated either that the predecessor lacked jurisdictional authority or that a particular judgment was not in conformity with school doctrine. A distinctive feature of the Mālikī system of judicial review was its informality and the wide scope that it gave to the individual to negotiate with judicial authorities in an effort to manipulate the system to his or her personal advantage (Powers 1992). Two of the cases examined here illustrate how the system of judicial review worked in practice. In Case One, the first qāḍī's dissolution of a marriage on the grounds of defect was overturned by a second qāḍī after the latter consulted with a *muftī*. In Case Two, the qāḍī's decision to issue a judicial divorce on behalf of a woman whose husband had abandoned her six years earlier was, presumably, overturned on the strength of a *fatwā* issued by an unidentified *muftī*.

The Muftī

To fully appreciate the work of the qāḍī and his court, it is essential to consider the role played by *muftī*s, who worked closely with qāḍīs, especially in hard cases.

The issuance of a *fatwā* was a moment when the law was made real, when the principles and rules contained in the Qurʾān and *ḥadīth*, the legal concepts and doctrines set out in treatises on substantive law, and the rules of evidence and procedure, were brought to bear, with greater or lesser force and clarity, upon the facts of a dispute. These cases frequently lay at the edges of established legal doctrine and raised issues that had not been foreseen when the earlier texts were produced or were not understood by the general populace: Is a woman's lack of virginity at the time of her marriage grounds for dissolution? Can a qāḍī issue a judicial divorce against a man who is not present in court and who therefore does not have the opportunity to defend himself? If a man gives his wife the power to divorce herself on the condition that he is absent from her for four consecutive months without sending her any subsistence money, and this condition materializes—albeit, for reasons outside the control of the husband—may a qāḍī issue a judicial divorce against him? If a woman flees her husband, moves to another town, and remarries, how can the first husband establish the *bone fides* of his marriage to the woman in the eyes of the qāḍī of the town in which she is currently living?

In difficult cases, the legal problem posed by the facts of the case did not lend itself to a solution provided by a preexisting formula, but rather was an occasion for thought and argument. The modes of thought and argument employed by the *muftī*s reveal the legal sensibility of the culture in which they lived. When a *muftī* issued his response, he drew upon his knowledge of the layers of the school tradition to which he belonged to identify the legal norms, rules, and categories that properly should govern a particular case. Like jurists in other legal cultures, he turned to the authority of established sources, to wit, Qur'ān and *ḥadīth*, doctrinal law books, legal formularies, and earlier *fatwā*s and judgments. Drawing upon his knowledge of these sources, the *muftī* gave voice to the contemporary position of his law school by selecting the cases and opinions that he considered relevant to the case at hand, carefully arranging them in the narrative that would become his response. Treating earlier doctrine and cases as the relevant sources from which legal rules may be construed, the *muftī* applied the rules that he identified in the sources to the case at hand.

The Division of Labor between Qāḍī and Muftī

The qāḍī was charged to determine the facts of the case, evaluate evidence, assess the testimony of witnesses, apply the rules of judicial procedure, and identify the relevant legal principles. In simple cases, the qāḍī applied the law himself. In difficult cases, he turned to a *muftī*, who drew upon his extensive knowledge of legal doctrine to identify the relevant and appropriate rules and principles.

Considered separately, the qāḍī and the *muftī* represent the poles of practice and doctrine, respectively. But when a qāḍī issued a judgment on the basis of the considered opinion of a *muftī*, doctrine and practice were united to produce a result that became part of an ongoing judicial tradition. If we do not find evidence of legal reasoning in qāḍī judgments preserved in Ottoman *sijill*s and other sources, it does not follow that those judgments were issued in an arbitrary manner without any reference to legal norms; rather, it means only that we do not have access to the legal reasoning that went into the making of a judgment.

Final Observation: On the Character of the Female Litigants

According to a popular stereotype, Muslim women are passive agents who have little or no freedom and whose lives are controlled by their husbands and/or agnatic relatives. It is therefore noteworthy that in all four of the cases examined here, women were active agents who used their wits, savvy and knowledge of the law in an attempt to overcome the powerful asymmetries of the rules of marriage and divorce. In Case One, a mother struggled to preserve the marriage of her daughter to a man who claimed to have discovered that his bride was not a virgin on the night of their wedding, as he expected her to be. In Case Two, a woman whose husband had abandoned her, for unknown reasons, asked a local qāḍī to issue a judicial divorce against him. In Case Three, a woman acted upon a delegated divorce that her husband had formulated for her: she divorced herself on his behalf despite the fact that he had not abandoned her but had been delayed at sea and therefore prevented from returning home prior to the expiration of the four-month time-period stipulated in the delegated divorce. In Case Four, an orphan who was married off at a young age by her paternal uncle, without her consent, fled from her husband, remarried, and resisted her first husband's efforts to recover her.

It appears that these women were familiar with the law and capable of manipulating it in an effort to advance their own interests. Although these cases are not isolated examples (see Powers 2003; Layish 1991:180), additional research needs to be carried out on the role played by women in qāḍī courts.

CHAPTER SIXTEEN

THE APPLICATION OF ISLAMIC LAW IN THE OTTOMAN COURTS IN DAMASCUS: THE CASE OF THE RENTAL OF *WAQF* LAND

Abdul-Karim Rafeq

The adoption of the Hanafi school of law as the official *madhhab* in the Ottoman empire had far-reaching consequences in Syria because the majority of its population were Shafiʿis. The Ottomans, however, allowed judges affiliated to other *madhhab*s to function and sit in the same court with the Hanafi chief judge (*qāḍī al-quḍāt*), to whom they were answerable. The Hanafi chief judge was almost always a Turk (*Rūmī*) appointed from Istanbul. He sat in the main court (*maḥkamat al-bāb*) in Damascus and nominated the judges representing the four *madhhab*s in the six courts that serviced Damascus and its environs, including the Biqāʿ, the Ḥawrān and Tadmor (Palmyra). The chief judge oversaw the administration of justice in the province. His term of office was one year, whereas the local judges of the four *madhhab*s might remain in office for longer periods. The Hanafi chief mufti in Damascus was also a Turk appointed by the Grand Mufti (*Shaykh al-Islām*) in Istanbul. Unlike the Hanafi chief judge, the Hanafi chief mufti remained in office for more than one year. In the seventeenth century he was appointed from among local muftis. Members of the Damascene ʿImādī and Murādī families figured as Hanafi chief muftis in the eighteenth century and some of them remained in office for life.

Several top Shafiʿi *ʿulamāʾ* in Syria switched their affiliation to the Hanafi *madhhab* at the beginning of Ottoman rule in order to retain their judicial positions or acquire new ones. The Damascene biographical dictionaries contain much information about *ʿulamāʾ* who became Shafiʿis. The number of *madhhab*-switchers decreased over time, partly because of the increasing numbers of Hanafi *ʿulamāʾ*, and partly because Shafiʿi judges began to assume a larger role in the judicial administration. One area in which Shafiʿi judges became increasingly involved in the Shari'a courts in Syria was the rental of *waqf* property, initially the domain of the Hanafi judges.

According to Hanafi jurists, agricultural land that has been designated as a *waqf* may not be leased for more than three years, and residential or commercial *waqf* property may not be leased for more than one year, unless the interest of the *waqf* calls for a longer lease period. The lease of state land (*arāḍī bayt al-māl*) and land belonging to orphans (*yatīm*) also should not exceed three years. There is no time limit with respect to the lease of private freehold property.[1] Because lease contracts for land were almost always for three years, the word *ʿaqd* (contract) was understood as referring to a three-year lease. On rare occasions, however, the contract was for two years.

According to the Damascene jurist Ibn ʿĀbidīn, the three-year limitation on the lease of agricultural *waqf* land serves as a precaution in case the lessee is able to cultivate the land only once every three years, or in the event that the land gives produce only once every two or three years.[2] If *waqf* land were leased for a longer period, Ibn ʿĀbidīn adds, this may give the impression that the lessee has become the owner of the land, in which case it would lose its *waqf* status.[3]

The long-term lease of *waqf* property was not completely forbidden by Hanafi jurists, provided certain conditions were met. If a specific *waqf* property was in poor condition and the *waqf* did not possess sufficient resources to maintain it, the property could be leased for a long period so that the lessee might use the rent for maintenance. In such a case, the judge would authorize a long lease (*ijāra ṭawīla*) according to which the lessee would make a large advance payment, to take care of the immediate needs of the *waqf*, and a smaller delayed annual rent. Such a lease is called *ḥaqq al-ijāratayn* (double rent). This arrangement was made in exceptional circumstances to avoid the necessity to sell *waqf* property.[4] The lease of agricultural *waqf* property for long periods without any such justification violates the rules of all four Sunni *madhhab*s.

A person who leases arable *waqf* land enjoys tremendous benefits. The rent is fixed in advance and continues at the same rate for the

[1] Ibn ʿĀbidīn (1853–4, 2:92, 113–4, 117–9); Ibn ʿĀbidīn (1855, 3:397); al-Jazīrī (1986, 3:103).
[2] Ibn ʿĀbidīn (1855, 3:397).
[3] Ibid.
[4] al-Zuḥaylī (1989, 8:228 n. 1).

duration of the lease, notwithstanding inflation. By virtue of a clause in the lease contract, called *muzāraʿa* or *munāsaba*, the lessee has the right to plant fruit trees and construct buildings on the land and to own as freehold one-third to three-fourths of what he plants or builds. The remaining portion goes to the *waqf*. In certain cases, the contract gives the lessee the right to own everything that he plants or builds on the land that he has rented. The lessee thus becomes the owner of real property on the *waqf* land. If the land contains no crops or buildings, it is called *bayāḍ* or *sillikh*. If it does, the lease specifies that it has *qarār* (something resting on it). Another clause in the lease contract, known as *musāqāt* (literally, irrigation contract), gives the lessee the right to tend to the share of the *qarār* that belongs to the *waqf* and to receive as compensation 999 out of one thousand shares (*sahm*) of its revenue; the remaining share goes to the *waqf*. The *qirāṭ* (one unit out of twenty-four) was sometimes used in place of the *sahm*; if so, the lessee would take twenty-three *qirāṭs* of the revenue and leave one *qirāṭ* to the *waqf*. According to these rental procedures, the lessee profits at the expense of the *waqf* beneficiaries. It is no wonder that lessees tried to extend the lease period of *waqf* property.[5]

A person who leases *waqf* land, whether or not it has fruit trees, is also entitled to the usufruct of the land, known as *mashadd maska*. According to Ibn ʿĀbidīn, the term "*mashadd maska*" means to hold fast (*shadda*) to something, literally or figuratively. In agriculture, this involves plowing and turning over the soil and removing mud and sediment from a river bed that irrigates the land, in preparation for its cultivation and irrigation. The *mashadd maska* may not be sold for money, although the holder may cede or transfer it (*farāgh*) to another person for a sum of money called *ʿiwaḍ* (compensation), not price. Ibn ʿĀbidīn adds that according to Ottoman muftis *mashadd al-maska* cannot be inherited, but it may be assigned to the qualified son of the holder. If the holder does not have a son, the *mashadd maska* goes to his daughter, and if he does not have a daughter, it goes to the brother or sister of the holder, and, finally, to his mother.[6]

In the sixteenth century, when the Ottoman administration was strong and the Hanafi chief judge was in a position to enforce Hanafi

[5] Rafeq (1992:295–300).
[6] Ibn ʿĀbidīn (1853–4, 4:18).

law, agricultural *waqf* land was leased for three years and residential and commercial *waqf* property for one year. The first extant court register from Damascus, which covers the period between 11 Shaʿbān 991 and 12 Rajab 993/30 August 1583–10 July 1585, contains fifty rental contracts of freehold, state, and *waqf* property. The Hanafi judge reviewed and authorized the majority of these contracts[7] (see Table 1).

Table 1. *Judges and Lease Contracts*

Type of Property	Number of Contracts	Judges			
		Hanafi	Shafiʿi	Hanbali	Maliki
Residential	11	10	—	1	—
Commercial	7	7	—	—	—
Agricultural	29	26	1	2	—
Mixed	1	1	—	—	—
Water Canal	2	2	—	—	—
Total	50	46	1	3	—
Percentage	100.00	(92.00)	(02.00)	(06.00)	(00.00)

The fact that forty-six of the fifty contracts (92 percent) were referred to the Hanafi judge points to his control over the leases. The involvement of the Hanbali judge in the leasing of property was minimal, although he fared better than his Shafiʿi counterpart, who represented the majority *madhhab* in Syria. Most Hanbalis came to Damascus from the region of Nablus and inhabited the Ṣāliḥiyya suburb overlooking the city. The small number of Malikis in Syria came mostly from the Maghrib as *mujāwirs*, i.e., pilgrims to religious shrines; they also served as watchmen in Damascus and mail carriers between cities. In the eighteenth century, most of the Maghribis were mercenaries.

The data also indicate that the Hanafi judge reviewed the contracts of the most valuable properties. The rent is accounted for in silver *qiṭʿa*, a common term for the Ottoman silver *aqçe*.

[7] See, for example, Law Court Records (LCR), Damascus, vols. 1, 79, 88, 91, 93; see also Rafeq (1987:153–63).

Table 2. *Judges, Contracts, and Rent*

Judges	Number of contracts	%	Total Rent	%
Hanafi	46	(92.00)	108,000	(95.50)
Shafiʿi	1	(02.00)	1,200	(01.06)
Hanbali	3	(06.00)	3,880	(03.44)
Maliki	—	—	—	—
Total	50	(100.00)	113,080	(100.00)

The total rent of the lease contracts reviewed by the Hanafi judge amounted to108,000 *qiṭʿas*, which is 95.5 percent of the total rent of the fifty lease contracts (113,080 *qiṭʿas*). If one compares the number of the contracts reviewed by the Hanafi judge with the total number reviewed by all the judges, the percentage of Hanafi-reviewed contracts is 92.0. If one compares the revenue (rent) from those Hanafi-reviewed contracts to the combined revenue (rent) from all the properties, the total is 95.5%. The reason for this difference is that the values of the leases referred to the Hanafi judge were greater than those reviewed by the non-Hanafi judges.

Of the groups that invested in the real estate market in Damascus at the time, the military occupied first place. A sampling of twenty-five sale and lease transactions reported in the court register of Damascus between 3 Ramaḍān 991 and 3 Ramaḍān 992/20 September 1583 and 8 September 1584 reveals the dominant role of the military in this area. Due to their presence in the countryside, military personnel were in a good position to dominate the lease of agricultural *waqf* land. Of the 200,000 *qiṭʿa*s invested by the military in all types of real estate, 195,880 *qiṭʿa*s (97.9 percent) were invested in agricultural property. Of this figure, 158,240 *qiṭʿa*s (80.7 percent) were invested by the military in the lease of agricultural *waqf* property, typically for long periods and with the approval of Shafiʿi rather than Hanafi judges.

Several lease contracts of agricultural *waqf* land, chosen at random from the court records of Damascus between 1700 and the 1820s, provide details about the ways in which the military and the notables avoided the constraints of Hanafi legal doctrine: they brought their leases to a Shafiʿi and, to a lesser extent, a Hanbali judge, who would approve long leases at fixed rents; these leases were then endorsed and executed by a Hanafi judge.

The investment of the military in agricultural *waqf* land, the number of lease contracts that exceeded the three-year limit, the rent paid for these contracts, and the judges who authorized them are surveyed in three samples from years 1112/1700–01, 1137/1724–5 and 1189/1775–6. Of 104 lease contracts, 37 were leased by the military. The fact that the military paid about one-half of the total rent for leasing these lands points to the large size and productivity of these lands and their ability to exploit them. The length of the leases contracted by the military far exceeded the three-year limit stipulated by Hanafi jurists for the rental of agricultural *waqf* land. Twenty-five leases contracted by the military are for more than three years; only twelve are for three years or less. The other groups contracted forty-one leases that exceeded the three-year limit and twenty-seven leases that fell within the limit. The investors in most of these transactions brought their leases to a Shafiʿi judge for authorization (see Table 3).

Table 3. *Judges, Leases of* Waqf *Land, Length of Leases, and Rent*
Sample of 1112/(1700–01)

Judges	Number of Contracts	%	Length of Lease 1–3 yrs	over 3 yrs	Total Rent	%
Hanafi	2	(10.00)	2	—	594	(17.16)
Shafiʿi	16	(80.00)	8	8	2,672	(77.20)
Hanbali	2	(10.00)	1	1	195	(05.64)
Total	20	(100.00)	11	9	3,461	(100.00)

Sample of 1137/(1724–5)

Judges	Number of Contracts	%	Length of Lease 1–3 yrs	over 3 yrs	Total Rent	%
Hanafi	2	(07.14)	2	—	70	(01.42)
Shafiʿi	25	(89.29)	7	18	4,576	(92.74)
Hanbali	1	(03.57)	—	1	288	(05.84)
Total	28	(100.00)	9	19	4,934	(100.00)

Sample of 1189/(1775–6)

Judges	Number of Contracts	%	Length of Lease 1–3 yrs	over 3 yrs	Total Rent	%
Hanafi	9	(16.67)	5	4	2,063	(07.56)
Shafiʿi	37	(68.52)	10	27	14,244	(52.18)
Hanbali	8	(14.81)	2	6	10,990	(40.26)
Total	54	(100.00)	17	37	27,297	(100.00)

Clearly, by the eighteenth century Hanafi judges had lost control over the length of time that agricultural *waqf* land might be leased. These long leases increasingly were referred to Shafiʿi judges who found ways to allow them and approve them. Hanafi judges either did not contest the leases or rubberstamped them. Hanbali judges also approved long leases, albeit fewer than the Shafiʿis did. Maliki judges do not figure in our data, apparently because there were only a few Malikis in Syria. Thus, fifty-three of sixty-five leases (81.5 percent) that exceeded the three-year limit were approved by a Shafiʿi judge. Hanafi judges approved only four leases that exceeded the limit.

The court records provide detailed descriptions of the legal devices used by Shafiʿi and Hanbali judges to authorize lease contracts of long periods. According to the records, agricultural *waqf* land was leased for 60, 90, and even 200 years.[8] Whenever a Shafiʿi or a Hanbali judge approved a long-term lease of *waqf* land that included a *muzāraʿa* and/or *musāqāt* clause, a professional bidder (*muzāwid*) would come to the court to lodge a formal protest against the irregularities committed by the judge in drawing up the contract. The bidder would object that the lease exceeded the three-year limit, denounce the rent as below the market value (*dūna ajr al-mithl*), criticize the issuance of the lease of agricultural land to non-cultivators, and, finally, assert that the lease contract was in violation of the conditions established by the founder of the *waqf*. In such cases, the judge would recall the witnesses who had been present at the formulation of the lease contract. The witnesses would reiterate that the rent was fair, that it was equal to the market value, and that

[8] LCR, Damascus, vol. 135, 117–22, 220–6. In one of these leases of *waqf* property Asʿad Pasha al-ʿAẓm, governor of Damascus, 1743–57, leased a *waqf* property for 200 years.

the terms of the lease were favorable to the *waqf* beneficiaries. The judge then concluded that the terms of the lease were valid according to his *madhhab* and that any violation of the founder's stipulations was for the sake of the *waqf*.

Frequently, the bidder would offer to rent the *waqf* property himself, usually for one year if the property was residential or commercial (i.e., a shop), and for three years if it was agricultural—and in both cases for a higher rent. If the lessor, who might be the superintendent (*nāẓir*) or the administrator (*mutawallī*) of the *waqf*, agreed that the earlier agreed-upon rent was not equal to the market value, he might ask the lessee to surrender the *waqf* property to the bidder. The judge, who drew up the lease contract, would then call the same witnesses and ask them to restate their position that the rent was fair and equal to the market value. The judge would conclude by saying that the lessor had no right to change his mind about the rent and that the agreed-upon rent was fair and equal to the market value. Thus, there was no reason for him to annul the contract. The Hanafi judge would then certify the contract that had been submitted to him by the Shafiʿi or Hanbali judge. The same bidder appears in a number of lease cases over a long period of time. The judge never ruled in favor of the bidder, which suggests that the bidder's offer was a formality the purpose of which was to doubly establish the legality of the original lease contract by challenging it.

The following case from the Damascus court records illustrates how a Shafiʿi judge authorized a long lease contract and overruled a bidder. The document, found in register 31, pp. 149–50, is dated 3 Muḥarram 1124/11 February 1712. An English translation of the document follows. The names of witnesses occur at the end of the document. The names at the top of the document belong to the preceding case.

> In the presence of our lord the erudite Shafiʿi judge Fayḍ Allāh, may the exalted God support him, the pride of his peers, Bakīr Beshe, son of Yaḥyā Agha al-Mukhmaljī, leased for himself, with his own money, from the pride of the illustrious notables, Sayyid Muḥammad Agha, son of the late Muṣṭafā Agha al-Turjumān, the administrator of the *waqf*s of the Two Holy Sanctuaries in Damascus, the entire piece of land, which belongs to the *waqf* and is not cultivated, located in the village of ʿAyn Tarma, bounded

on the south and the east by property held by the lessee, on the north by the road, and on the west by the field of al-Bawwāb, for a price lawfully known to the parties, for winter and summer farming, and for cultivation, exploitation and usufruct, as customary, for five *ʿaqds*, each of three years, beginning on the day mentioned below, for a yearly rent of three *asadi* piasters, each year's rent to be paid in the month of Rajab. [The lessor] handed over the land [to the lessee] who acknowledged its conveyance, after viewing and cognizance and entering into a legal contract, free of fraud, deception and defect. [The lessor and the lessee] gave their mutual assent to the contract, with due legal consideration. The judge certified the lease on the basis of the testimony of the witnesses mentioned below and their unequivocal acknowledgment of the lease, and also the testimony of ʿUmar, son of Shihāb al-Dīn, and Muḥammad, son of ʿAlī, who identified the leased land and testified that its lease to the lessee for the aforementioned rent and lease period was favorable to the *waqf*. [They also testified] that the rent specified above was equal to the market value and was fair, and even more than fair, which was favorable to the *waqf*. Ḥusayn, son of Muḥammad, then came [to the court] and asked the lessor to lease the land to him for a period of three years for a rent of half a piaster more per year than the agreed-upon rent. The lessor accepted the offer, but the lessee opposed it. [The lessee] sued the lessor and the bidder [before the judge], maintaining that the lease was issued to him at a rent equal to the market value and thus may not be annulled by the increase. He also said that his lease of the land for the aforementioned rent and length of time was favorable to the *waqf* and that the increase offered by the bidder was damaging [to him] and arbitrary. The lessor did not believe him. [The judge] asked the lessee for proof to substantiate his claim. [The lessee] recalled the above-mentioned witnesses, and [the judge] asked them to testify about the matter. They testified before him and in the presence of the lessor and the bidder that they had knowledge of the piece of land located in the village of ʿAyn Tarma that is bounded on the south and the east by property held by the lessee, on the north by the road, and on the west by the field of al-Bawwāb, that its lease to the lessee for the agreed-upon lease period and rent is favorable to the *waqf*, and that the rent specified above is equal to the market value and is fair, and even more than fair, which is favorable to the *waqf*. [They also said] that the rent increase offered by the bidder is damaging [to the lessee] and arbitrary. The testimony was accepted by the judge after due attestation. The lessor then sued the lessee [on the ground] that the lease contract is not valid because it is for a long period and asked him to hand the contract to him. [The lessee] responded that the lease contract had been approved by the aforementioned Shafiʿi judge, who determined that it was valid; he again appealed to the aforementioned Shafiʿi judge to intervene. Our lord the Shafiʿi judge informed the lessor that the lease contract issued by him is valid, even if it was for a long period. He gave a legal ruling establishing the validity [of the contract] and declared it binding throughout the lease period. The lessor then gave legal permission to the lessee to plant on the piece of land during the lease period [stipulating that] whatever he plants will become his own property. The permission was accepted. Indited on the third of Muḥarram 1124/11 February 1712.

Witnesses

kātib al-aṣl (the author of the original copy (*ḥujja*)
that was given to the lessee)
al-Shaykh Shams al-Dīn

muqayyiduhā (the one who wrote it down in the register (*sijill*))
al-Sayyid Yūsuf al-Jalabī

Al-Shaykh Zayn al-Dīn
Al-Sayyid Muḥammad al-Shūwaykī
Muṣṭafā ibn Jumʿa

In this text, an *agha*, or high-military official, who was in charge of the *waqfs* of the Two Holy Sanctuaries in Damascus, leased out *waqf* land to another military official for fifteen years, five times longer than the period allowed by Hanafi legal doctrine. The Shafiʿi judge who authorized the lease contract did not seek the endorsement of the Hanafi judge, perhaps a sign of his growing influence with respect to his Hanafi counterpart. A bidder, Ḥusayn bin Muḥammad, offered to lease the land for three years, according to Hanafi legal doctrine, and, to make the offer more attractive, at a slightly higher rent. This seems to have been a legal strategem to confirm the lease contract as approved by the Shafiʿi judge. The bidder's offer was rejected, as always. The fact that the same bidder appears in several cases of a similar nature suggests that he was a professional whose role was to challenge the lease in order to strengthen its legality. After the Shafiʿi judge certified the lease in accordance with his own legal doctrine and in violation of Hanafi legal doctrine, he gave permission to the lessee to own as freehold all of the fruit trees that he might plant on the *waqf* land during the period of the lease. This generous offer contravenes the common practice of leaving a share of the fruit trees to the *waqf*. The lease contract documents the continuing participation of the military in leasing *waqf* property.

Hanafi judges occasionally intervened in controversial agricultural *waqf* lease contracts, upholding the tenets of their school by invalidating leases that exceeded three years. A *waqf* property in the village of Kafr Sūsiya on the outskirts of Damascus, for example, was leased out simultaneously to two different lessees. One lease, to Ḥajj Aḥmad al-ʿAjamī, for three years, beginning on 29 Jumādā II 1112/11 December 1700, was approved by the local Hanafi deputy judge, Aḥmad Efendi al-Ayyūbī, in *al-maḥkama al-kubrā*; the other, to ʿAbd al-Wahhāb ibn Muḥammad and ʿAlī ibn ʿAlī, for six years, beginning on 1 Muḥarram 1108/31 July 1696, had previously been approved by the Shafiʿi judge Fayḍ Allāh in the same *maḥkama*. The *waqf* superintendent (*nāẓir*) agreed to lease the *waqf* property to Ḥajj Aḥmad al-ʿAjamī, who offered 190 piasters per year for rent, 20 piasters more than the other, plus half a qintar of pomegranates. The superintendent also allowed al-ʿAjamī to take care of the *waqf* fruit trees by *musāqāt* and to take 999 shares of the produce, leaving one share to the *waqf*.

ʿAbd al-Wahhāb ibn ʿAlī and ʿAlī Ibn ʿAlī objected to the new lease given to Ḥajj Aḥmad al-ʿAjamī and appealed to the Hanafi deputy judge Aḥmad al-Ayyūbī. They showed the judge their lease certificate (*ḥujja*), which indicated that their lease period had not expired. The deputy judge overruled the two lessees and certified the three-year lease of al-ʿAjamī, which met the requirements of his *madhhab*.[9]

Many lease contracts of *waqf* land approved by the Hanafi judge were in fact long-term leases spread over three-year periods and

[9] LCR, Damascus, vols. 25, 54, case dated 29 Jumādā II 1112/11 December 1700.

retained by the same lessee or lessees. The lease contract explicitly states that the lessee is already in control of the leased property. For example, on 28 Muḥarram 1112/15 July 1700, an officer leased several pieces of *waqf* land in the village of Kafr Baṭna on the outskirts of Damascus for three years, in the presence of the Hanafi judge. The lease contract describes the officer as already exercising legal control of the land, i.e., as lessee.[10]

A formula used in lease contracts that were renewed before their expiration states that the new lease supersedes the period stipulated for the lessee in the earlier lease (*tāliya li-muddat al-musta'jir*). The renewal of a lease contract before its expiration gave the Hanafi judge a legal pretext to prolong the lease for three-year periods, one period at a time. In one case, a Hanafi judge renewed the lease contract three times, each time for a three-year period, in the same document (*ḥujja*), presumably to satisfy the requirements of his school and accommodate the interests of the lessee, who was an influential person.

As mentioned, according to Hanafi legal doctrine, residential property that had been designated as a *waqf* may be leased for only one year. Like Muslims, Christians leased such property for longer periods by referring the lease to a Shafiʿi or Hanbali judge. For example, before the Shafiʿi judge in Damascus, Mūsā son of Rizq al-Naṣrānī leased a house in the Christian quarter in Hanania (St. Ananias) Street for three years from Khūrī (priest) Shukr Allāh. The rent was paid in advance because the *waqf* needed the money. Two Muslim witnesses confirmed the transaction in court. This lease was a renewal of an earlier lease. Sayyid ʿAlī Agha, the bidder, then appeared in court and paid a higher rent, to which the lessor agreed. The lessor asked the judge to annul the lease and offer it to the bidder because the rent paid by the lessee was below the market value. The judge recalled the witnesses who had testified to the original lease and they again maintained that the rent was fair and favorable to the *waqf*. The lessor also protested that the lease period was long, to which the Shafiʿi judge responded that, according to his *madhhab*, it was legal. The lessor then brought the case before the Hanafi judge, who

[10] LCR, Damascus, vols. 25, 178, case dated 28 Muḥarram 1112/15 July 1700.

ruled that the lease was legal, in accordance with the ruling of the Shafiʿi judge.[11]

In a similar case, a Hanbali judge approved the lease of a *waqf* shop for three years, renewing an earlier lease by the same lessee; this brought protests from the lessor, who objected to the long lease and its continuation. The Hanbali judge nonetheless approved the lease even though it was long and superceded another lease. The Hanafi judge then approved the lease as promulgated by the Hanbali judge.[12]

In 1826, Sultan Mahmud II abolished the Janissaries and, shortly thereafter, he banned the *timar* system. Subsequently, the military cease to figure in the rental of *waqf* property. Further, Shafiʿi judges no longer figured in the authorization of long lease contracts, as demonstrated in the following sample from the court records of Damascus in the year 1245/1829–30. The Hanbali judge occupies first place in authorizing long leases throughout the nineteenth and the early twentieth century. No explanation is given for this shift in responsibility.

Table 4. *Judges, Lease Contracts, Type of Land, Length of Lease, and Rent*

Judges	Number of Contracts	%	Type of Land *Waqf*	*Milk*	*Iqṭāʿ*	Length of Lease 1–3 yrs	over 3 yrs	Total Rent	%
Hanafi	7	(10.14)	—	7	—	6	1	6,215p	(10.76)
Shafiʿi	14	(20.29)	12	—	2	3	11	9,947	(17.21)
Hanbali	48	(69.57)	42	13	3	12	35	41,625	(72.03)
Total	69	(100.00)	54	20	5	21	47	57,787	(100.00)

Of the sixty-nine contracts, the Hanbali judge approved forty-eight (69.5 percent), the Shafiʿi judge fourteen (20.2 percent), and the Hanafi judge seven (10.1 percent). The lease contracts of *waqf* property constitute 78.2 percent of the total contracts. Forty-two of the fifty-four *waqf* property contracts (77.7 percent) were referred to the Hanbali judge; of these the Hanbali judge certified thirty-five contracts

[11] LCR, Damascus, vols. 242, 275–6, case dated 17 Dhu'l-Ḥijja 1212/2 June 1798.

[12] LCR, Damascus, vols. 242, 110, case dated 20 Shaʿbān 1212/7 February 1798.

(74.4 percent) that exceeded the three-year period. Most of the contracts approved by the Hanafi judge were for three years. The rents of the contracts approved by the Hanbali judge accounted for 72 percent of the total rent, whereas the rent of the contracts approved by the Shafiʿi judge accounted for only 17.1 percent of the total. The sample contains many lease contracts that were renewed prior to their expiration.

The Hanbali judge continued to approve the majority of the lease contracts of *waqf* land during the period of Egyptian rule in Syria (1831–1840). The Egyptians did not meddle with the Ottoman judicial system, and the Hanafi chief judge continued to be appointed from Istanbul. However, the Egyptians did establish a Higher Consultative Council, which *inter alia* looked into land problems. The Ottomans created a similar council in Syria in the 1840s.[13]

In the 1850s, during the period of the Tanzimat (Regulations), the Ottomans established European-style courts in Damascus and Aleppo. They also issued regulations organizing the status of *waqf* and the usufruct of state (*mīrī*) land. The Ottoman Land Code of 1858 was an important step in this regard. The Shari'a court, however, retained jurisdiction over the promulgation of lease contracts for *waqf* land, and Hanbali judges retained their domination over Shafiʿi and Hanafi judges in drawing up lease contracts.

On 7 Ṣafar 1284/10 June 1867, the Ottoman government issued a law giving foreigners the right to own real property in the Ottoman empire, with the exception of the Hijaz. Previously, foreigners were allowed to rent real property in Syria according to the same laws that applied to the Muslims. Like Muslims, they turned to either Shafiʿi or Hanbali judges for approval of long-term leases.

Most foreign nationals who purchased real property in Syria in accordance with the law of 1867 were local Christians and Jews who held the nationality of European states that were friendly with the Ottomans (*al-duwal al-mutaḥābba*), as the preamble to the Law states. Although some of the property purchased was residential, most of it was agricultural, i.e., fruit trees on *waqf* land. In theory, these foreign nationals might have purchased this property as Ottoman subjects, but they had chosen instead to acquire foreign citizenship in order to secure the support of a European state so that it might

[13] Rafeq (1999:293–301).

defend them if and when a problem arose. For example, if a "foreigner" loaned money to a villager and the villager defaulted on the loan, the "foreigner" creditor often urged the villager to sell any trees, fields or buildings that he owned. Other foreign nationals, acting through local agents, rented agricultural *waqf* property according to the same regulations that applied to Muslims, such as the right of *muzāraʿa* and *musāqāt,* which enabled them to become owners of property on *waqf* land.[14]

The manipulation of legal doctrine in matters relating to *waqf* property benefited influential groups, such as the military, notables, and foreign nationals, at the expense of *waqf* beneficiaries. Many charitable buildings such as mosques, schools (*madrasas*) and water-fountains (*sabīl*), and many needy groups on behalf of whom the *waqfs* were founded, lost their revenue and suffered as a result. Looking at the sites where *madrasas* and mosques once stood, the Damascene Hanbali Shaykh ʿAbd al-Qāḍīr Badrān (d. 1346/1927–8) saw only ruins and images of the past. Accordingly, he entitled his book, *Munādamat al-aṭlāl wa-musāmarat al-khayāl* (Conversations with ruins and evening chats with phantoms).[15] For example, Badrān blames the disappearance of the Shafiʿi Falakiyya *madrasa,* built in Damascus by Falak al-Dīn Sulaymān in 599/1203,[16] on swindlers (*mukhtaliṣīn*) who had usurped its *waqfs.* A lease contract dated 29 Ṣafar 1213/12 August 1798 of a house in Damascus that was *waqf* for al-Madrasa al-Falakiyya does not refer to the presence of a *waqf* administrator in the court during the lease transaction, as previously had been the rule. The fact that a lessee of the house leased it to another person on his own suggests that the *madrasa* was already in ruins, while its *waqf* properties, which still bore its name, were being leased from one person to another.

[14] Rafeq (2002:175–249).
[15] Badrān (1960:53, 145).
[16] Pouzet (1988:30, 50, 131, 160, 167).

CHAPTER SEVENTEEN

THE *WAQF* IN COURT: LAWSUITS OVER RELIGIOUS ENDOWMENTS IN OTTOMAN ALEPPO*

Stefan Knost

In this essay on the law courts and judges of Ottoman Aleppo ca. 1800, I analyze three lawsuits involving the property of Islamic religious endowments (*waqf*, pl. *awqāf*). I use these cases as an opportunity to consider the organization of the Sharīʿa Courts, judicial procedure and the decision-making process of the judges. Special attention will be given to the use of documents as evidence.

Western perceptions of Islamic law have long been shaped by Max Weber's concept of *Kadijustiz*. This expression was used by Weber to define a certain type of justice that is characterized by "arbitrariness and excessive individualism on the part of the *kadi*; and heavy intervention by the state in the legal process."[1]

Rosen applies the Weberian concept in his discussion of the judge in the contemporary Moroccan town of Sefrou. He develops the aspect that the *qāḍī* is not bound by any fixed legal framework. He sees the judicial process as a "bargaining-for-relationships" between the contesting parties, thus reflecting the mechanisms of the Moroccan society as a whole (Rosen 1989:60f.). He especially follows the concept of *Kadijustiz* concerning the amount of discretionary power that he attributes to the *qāḍī* of Sefrou (ibid., p. 61).

---

* Author's note: I wish to thank Professor David Powers for his invaluable help, both linguistic and methodical, during different stages of my writing this essay. Thanks are also due to Stephen McPhillips, Astrid Meier and Edouard Metenier who read earlier versions of this essay. Needless to say, all remaining errors are the author's own responsibility.

[1] Weber's concept is discussed by Gerber (1994:25ff.). The citation is found on page 28. Max Weber develops the concept of *Kadijustiz* in different parts in his *Wirtschaft und Gesellschaft* (e.g., Weber 1972:486, 563). Although he points out at one point that *Kadijustiz* has little in common with the real principles of Islamic law (Weber 1972:300), he supports the validity of this concept for the Islamic world citing examples from Tunisia and Iran (Weber 1972:477).

Gerber has confronted the Weberian concept and Rosen's analysis of the juridical process with the practice of Islamic law as revealed in Ottoman court records from the major urban centers of Bursa, Edirne and Istanbul. He has shown that the *qāḍī*'s work "was characterized by a substantial measure of real enforcement, rather than free floating bargaining" (Gerber 1994:16). Although it is not unproblematic to compare written court records with an anthropologist's observations from a court room, Gerber concludes that the Ottoman judge applied identifiable laws and rules, rendering *Kadijustiz* in an Ottoman court quite predictable (Gerber 1994:177).

The decision-making process, whether the strict application of procedural law or unconditional bargaining, obviously influences the predictability of the outcome of the court case. Although this study does not propose a quantitative analysis of a substantial number of court cases, the predictability of the judge's decision will be discussed. The documents will equally show in which parts of the procedure the judge might interfere to exercise discretion.

I will argue that the judge in Aleppo was not bound by a fixed doctrine, but decided each case after carefully examining the individual circumstances. In three cases from Aleppo, I will analyze if and to what degree the parties might have "bargained" the result, or if the judge exercised discretion to develop the case in a certain direction.

A translation of the documents is provided at the end of the essay.[2]

The courts of Aleppo in Ottoman times

In 1800, there were five different courts in Aleppo, but not all five were operating simultaneously. The Hanafī chief judge of the province of Aleppo was appointed by the *Shaykh al-Islām* in Istanbul, usually for a one-year term. Aleppan judges ranked in the first category of judges on the sixth and lowest level. Only judges of this category

[2] The documents analyzed here, which originate from the Ottoman court records of Aleppo, are housed in the "Center for Historical Documents" in Damascus. I would like to thank the then director of this center, Mrs. Daʿd al-Ḥakīm, and her staff for their hospitality and support. Documents from the Sharīʿa court records (*Sijillāt al-maḥākim al-sharʿiyya*, SMS) will be cited as follows: number of the register/page number/number of the document.

bore the title "Mollā" (Arab. *mawlā*), mentioned in the court documents. They were recruited from professors of the large *madrasas* in the capital and their first appointments were to posts of this level. Because this was their first appointment outside a teaching position in the *madrasa*, these judges were also called *mahrec mollālarɪ*.[3]

The registers from Aleppo at the end of the eighteenth century refer to the judge as '*qāḍī*' or '*ḥākim sharʿī*', never as *qāḍī al-quḍāt*. His seat was the Maḥkama al-Kubrā, located in a sumptuous Mamluk house (*dār*) in the Suwayqat ʿAlī quarter. This *dār* consisted of three courtyards: one, equipped with a *ḥammām*, served as his personal residence; the middle courtyard was for the *qāḍī*'s court sessions; and in the third courtyard, a deputy judge decided minor cases (Ghazzī 1991–93, 2:155).

Local deputy judges (*nāʾibs*) recruited from the *ʿulamāʾ* families of Aleppo presided over the four other courts that were scattered throughout the city. The historian Ghazzī tells us that the other courts "were for the Shāfiʿīs."[4]

There was a clear judicial hierarchy. Special orders (*murāsalas*) announce that many cases should be treated only in the Maḥkama al-Kubrā. These orders, which appear frequently in the registers of the other courts, instruct the deputy judges to send all important cases to the Kubrā court. An order addressed to the four courts on 4 Rajab 1208/6 February 1794 mentions that ". . . lawsuits whose value is more than 300 piastres, and acknowledgements (*iqrārs*) whose value is more than 500 piastres . . ." should not be treated in the minor courts, either wholly or partly, but should be sent to the

[3] D'Ohsson (1788–1824, 4:530ff.). The first category of judges, that of the *mollās*, is divided into six different levels: I, The *qāżi ʿasker* of Rumelia; II, the *qāżi ʿasker* of Anatolia; III, The judge of Istanbul; IV, The judges of Mecca and Medina (*Ḥaramein mollālarɪ*); V, The judges of Edirne, Bursa, Cairo and Damascus (*bilād-i arbaʿa mollālarɪ*); VI, The judges of Galata, Üsküdar, Eyub, Jerusalem, Izmir, Aleppo, Yenişehir und Saloniki (*mahrec mollālarɪ*).

[4] Ghazzī (1991–93, 2:155). The historian Kāmil al-Ghazzī mentions that all the other courts belonged to the Shāfiʿī school. I cannot determine the extent to which judges applied Shāfiʿī legal doctrine, but when reading the biographies of the *ʿulamāʾ* and *ṣūfī* families (Ṭabbākh 1988–92, vols. 4–7), one notices that the Shāfiʿī school was of great importance in Aleppo throughout the Ottoman period. The name of one of the courts indicates this affiliation, al-Maḥkama al-Shāfiʿiyya. The registers generally do not give any indication of *madhhab* affiliation, except in some cases that were explicitly judged according to Shāfiʿī law, after the chief Ḥanafī judge had issued an authorization to the Shāfiʿī judge, documented on top of the document.

Maḥkama al-Kubrā.[5] This ensured that the Maḥkama al-Kubrā had control of the important cases and, as Nelly Hanna has pointed out, it insured that the chief judge would receive a higher salary, drawn from litigants' fees that were proportional to the sums involved.[6] The three documents to be examined here were registered in the Maḥkama al-Kubrā, even though the value of the objects that were subject to dispute in the second and third cases probably did not exceed 300 piastres. For whatever reason, the litigants decided to present their cases to the Maḥkama al-Kubrā rather than in one of the other courts.[7]

The courts in Ottoman Aleppo had fixed locations. The Maḥkama al-Kubrā, as mentioned, was housed in a Mamluk *dār*. The Maḥkama al-Ṣalāḥiyya was located in the *madrasa* of the same name. The Maḥkama al-Shāfiʿiyya was located in the Masjid al-Nāranjiyya. All three were situated in the Suwayqat ʿAlī quarter in the centre of the old town.[8] This quarter was the transit point between the old central market next to the Umayyad Mosque and the northern suburbs that, in Ottoman times, had developed into the second economic center of the town.[9] The location of the fourth and the fifth court, which were less active and left fewer registers, is less clear. The Maḥkama al-Bānqūsiyya was located next to the market of the Bānqūsā suburb in the northeast. The location of the Maḥkamat Jabal Samʿān is not known. Ghazzī mentions that one court was situated in a *madrasa* in a southeastern suburb (Ghazzī 1991–93, 2:156). These were all public spaces, accessible to anyone who wanted to address the court or who was summoned to appear before it.

Court sessions were sometimes held in other places, such as mosques, dervish convents (*zāwiya*s, *takiyya*s) or *khān*s that were accessible to all. In some cases the court was summoned to a private house, usually that of a notable family, to hear a case in which that family

[5] SMS, 144/92/469.

[6] Hanna (1995:47). The *nā'ib*s generally had a bad reputation; complaints about their incompetence and corruption were frequently addressed to the central Ottoman administration. Cf. Veinstein (2001:251ff.).

[7] Between 1790 and 1810, thirty-six lawsuits over *waqf* property found their way into the court records: of these, twenty-nine were registered in the Maḥkama al-Kubrā; the remaining cases, presented to the other courts, dealt with relatively simple conflicts, such as claims for the payment of the rent.

[8] On this quarter see: David 1998.

[9] On the development of Aleppo in the Ottoman period see for example: Raymond 1979.

was involved, e.g., a sale or the registration of endowments. In the year 1224/1809–10, for example, eight endowments were registered on the same day in a house in the Judayda quarter in favor of the Maronite church.[10]

In Ottoman Aleppo, the activity of *iftāʾ* or *fatwā*-giving, which played an important role in the administration of justice, took place outside the courts. The *muftī*, generally a member of a local *ʿulamāʾ* family, was usually appointed to this office for several consecutive years.[11] We possess different reports about the location of this activity. One document from 1215/1800–01 mentions a *dār al-majd wa al-fatwā* located close to the courts in the Suwayqat ʿAlī quarter.[12] It seems that for a time the *muftī* was located in the Madrasa al-Khusrawiyya next to the citadel.[13] In 1217/1802–03 this institution paid a stipend of 240 piastres to its *muftī*, compared to 47.5 piastres for the mosque's preacher (*khaṭīb*) and 108 piastres for the *imām* and the scribe.[14]

The *muftī* Muḥammad ibn ʿAlī, known as "Ḥājjī Efendī," performed his duties in the *madrasa* and was buried in its garden in 1176/1762–63. Ṭabbākh describes him as a humble man who had no secretary to write down the questions and who usually did not take a fee for issuing a *fatwā*. He lived from the stipend provided by the endowment of the *madrasa* (Ṭabbākh 1988–92, 7:26). He may have been the *muftī* described by Alexander Russell, a physician who spent several years in Aleppo in the middle of the eighteenth century:

> The Mufti is nominated annually by the Porte; but the same person is often continued in office for many years together. He is usually a native of the city, one of the opulent Effendies . . . When the office

---

[10] SMS, 168/142/267f. They were registered into the records of the Maḥkama al-Kubrā.

[11] The *muftī* of the third case, ʿAbdallāh al-Jābirī, remained in office for eighteen years (Meriwether 1981:240).

[12] SMS, 149/41/115. In this document the *muftī*, ʿAbdallāh al-Jābirī, acted as *wakīl* in a sale. The Jābirī family possessed a large double courtyard house in that quarter (David 1998:72). If the '*dār al-majd wa al-fatwā*' mentioned in the document is identical with the house of the family, this *muftī* would have exercised his office at home.

[13] Ghazzī (1991–93, 2:93). The mosque-college of the Khusrawiyya, built and endowed by the governor Khusraw Bāshā in the middle of the sixteenth century, was the first large foundation in Aleppo after the Ottoman conquest and the first building to be constructed as a typical Ottoman central domed mosque.

[14] SMS, 152–I/11/24.

happens to be bestowed on a man of small fortune, and of more religious character, it then assumes a greater appearance of its primitive simplicity. Such a man leads the life of a Dervish, proportioning his expenses to his slender revenue; he engages little in politics; and derives respect only from his supposed sanctity, and incorrupt exertions of his knowledge of the law. The Mufti gives a Fitwa [sic], or law opinion, upon all cases laid before him. The case being briefly stated on a small slip of paper, the Fitwa, comprised in a few words, is written under it. His fee amounts to little more than a shilling, and scrupulously exact, he will accept no higher present. The Cady [sic] sometimes supports his own decision by a Mufti's Fitwa; and a Fitwa is often adduced in place at the Mahkamy [sic]; which is received with deference if agreeable to the Cady, but otherwise, it is easily eluded by showing that, in the detail, circumstances, or facts had been unfairly stated" (Russel 1794, 1:320).

The Use of Documentary Evidence in Lawsuits

Tyan defines a lawsuit (*daʿwā*) as follows: "The action by which a person claims his right, against another person, in the presence of a judge."[15] A valid *daʿwā* requires two contesting parties and a disputed object. The plaintiff is called *muddaʿī*, the defendant *muddaʿā ʿalayh*; in our documents the judge is referred to as *mawlā*, *qāḍī*, or *ḥākim sharʿī* or, in the case of a deputy judge, *nāʾib*.

When the two contesting parties do not reach an amicable agreement, the judge designates one party as the plaintiff and the other as the defendant. Once the roles of plaintiff and defendant have been assigned, the plaintiff formulates his claim. If the defendant denies the claim, the plaintiff is asked to produce evidence. If he does not do so, the defendant can be asked to take the oath and the case is resolved in his favor. The defendant is supported by the apparent facts, so the plaintiff has to establish that these facts should not be accepted. The judge should base his decision only on these apparent facts, supported by evidence. The preferred form of evidence in a lawsuit is oral testimony that confirms the facts of the case.[16] The judge may consider circumstantial evidence, but he does not have to investigate about the facts.[17]

---

[15] Tyan (1965) cites the Ottoman *Madjalla*, art. 1613.
[16] Schacht (1964:189ff.); Tyan (1965); Johansen (1999:435f.).
[17] Schacht (1964:192ff.) says that circumstantial evidence is not admitted. Johansen

Written documents are not treated as evidence, at least in theory. According to Schacht, they are "merely aids to memory, and their contents are evidence only in so far as they are confirmed by the testimony of witnesses" (Schacht 1964:193). But he admits that documents were indispensable in practice, especially in commercial law (Schacht 1964:82f.). Tyan posits a historical evolution that led Muslim jurists in the nineteenth century to a general acceptance of written documents as evidence: "*Et de même, tous les actes que les particuliers rédigent (suivant les formes d'usages) entre eux doivent valoir comme preuve en vertu de la coutume.*"[18] At the same time, citing the seventeenth-century *muftī* Khayr al-Dīn al-Ramlī, he states that legal doctrine concerning written evidence did not change: "*Les preuves légales sont exclusivement au nombre de trois: la preuve (testimoniale), l'aveu, le serment.*"[19]

However, Johansen mentions one important exception to this rule. He notes that, beginning in the thirteenth century, legal textbooks state, regarding endowments whose administration falls under the authority of the judge, the *qāḍī* should treat the court archives as evidence (Johansen 1997:356), when it is in the interest of the endowment.

Be that as it may, both Tyan and Schacht have noted that written documents became indispensable in Islamic law. The existence of notaries (*ʿudūl*), professional scribes whose function was to produce legal documents, attests to the widespread use of documents.[20]

Did the judges of Ottoman Aleppo follow these principles of judicial procedure and were their decisions based upon the legal doctrine or on other factors? It seems that the judge's obligation to apply the rules of Islamic procedural law left him little opportunity to act in an arbitrary manner.[21] By examining three cases from Ottoman Aleppo, I will show how the judge performed his job and reached his decision.

(1999:440), examining Ramlī and Ibn ʿĀbidīn, affirms that the judge may consider the facts, but is not required to inquire into them.

[18] Tyan (1945:91). He cites the nineteenth-century Damascene jurist Ibn ʿĀbidīn (1853–54, 2:18: "*wa ka-dhalika mā yaktubu al-nās fī-mā baynahum yajibu an yakūna ḥujja li-l-ʿurf.*").

[19] Tyan (1945:7), after (Ramlī 1856–57, 2:12). For a presentation of Schacht's and Tyan's arguments, see: Johansen (1997a:333ff.).

[20] Schacht (1964:82ff. and 193), and Tyan (1945:16ff.).

[21] On procedural law, see, for example, Schacht (1964:188ff.), Tyan (1965), and Johansen (1999:435ff.).

The cases chosen for this study concern the property of the Islamic religious endowments (*waqfs*). At the end of the eighteenth century a high percentage of urban property in Aleppo was dedicated to numerous endowments. They are usually divided into public endowments (*waqf khayrī*) for the benefit of religious or welfare institutions and family endowments (*waqf dhurrī*) for the benefit of a lineal descent group. No principal legal distinction exists between these two forms, because the final destination of family endowments also has to be a public one (usually the poor).

The courts played an important role in the administration of these endowments, because the *qāḍī* had a supervisory function over their administration. When the endowment deed did not stipulate a *mutawallīh* (administrator), he could appoint one; he also had the right to dismiss an administrator in case of mismanagement.[22] When it comes to determining the status of a certain property as *waqf*, the *qāḍī* may take the initiative and pursue the case (Krcsmárik 1891:569).

Many of the endowments in Aleppo were quite small. If the endowment was old and the endowment deed was lost or unavailable, it was possible for a third party to challenge the status of the property as *waqf* and to claim that it was private property (*milk*). Nevertheless, disputes relating to *waqf* property are relatively infrequent in the court records. Between 1790 and 1810, 191 new endowments were created in Aleppo and registered in the court records, adding approximately five hundred assets, mainly urban property, to the thousands of assets that already had been designated as endowed property. In the same period only thirty-six lawsuits concerning *waqf* property are mentioned in the records (cf. fn. 7). Although many disputes over *waqf* property no doubt were settled without the help of a judge, this is a remarkably low number and may be explained, in part, by the fact that a lawsuit was a costly affair and usually a last resort.

The Cases

The following three cases were registered in the records (*sijills*) of the Maḥkama al-Kubrā between 1791 and 1800. Each one is pre-

[22] Hoexter (1995:144); Ibn ʿĀbidīn (1994, 6:636).

ceded by the name of the judge who decided the case. In all three cases the judge was the chief *qāḍī* of the province. Each case provides a detailed description of the different stages of court procedure.

Case I: A Family Endowment that was Annulled

In the month Jumādā al-Ūlā of the year 1215/September 1800, the *qāḍī* convened his *majlis shar'ī*, not in the court house (*maḥkama*), but in the *ṣūfī* convent (*takiyya*) of Shaykh Abū Bakr al-Wafā'ī, used as residence by the governor of Aleppo, Ḥājj Ibrāhīm Bāshā.[23] Both the governor and the *qāḍī* were present. This convent is situated to the north, outside of Aleppo, some thirty to forty-five minutes by foot from the Maḥkama al-Kubrā.

This case involved a family endowment that had been created a quarter of a century before the case came to court. In 1189/1775–76, Ḥājj 'Alī al-Madārātī reportedly designated a garden (*bustān*) as a family endowment for the benefit of himself and his descendants. Twenty-six years later, in 1215/1800–01, the garden had become the possession of a certain Ḥājj Muḥammad Āghā who claimed that he had purchased it from the heirs of Ḥājj 'Alī and from a third party and that the garden therefore belonged to him as private property (*milk*); he produced legal documents (*ḥujaj*) that confirmed the sale of the garden. The judge designated a certain Sayyid Arslān, whose ties to the founder, if any, are not specified, as *mutawallī* for the lawsuit (*li-ajl al-da'wā*). From this fact, we may deduce that the foundation did not have a *mutawallī* at the moment and therefore the judge appointed one. This designated *mutawallī* claimed the garden for the endowment, supporting this claim with the original endowment deed. The judge subsequently asked him to produce evidence (*bayyina*) confirming the endowment and its registration. When he failed to do so, the judge dismissed the case.

It is noteworthy that the judge heard this case outside his courtroom. This was rare, and he no doubt attached special importance to this case, probably because it might result in the annulment of an endowment. Yet, as was typical of endowments, the *waqfiyya* contained

---

[23] This *takiyya* is situated on a small hill north of the city. The period in which our documents were written was one of frequent troubles, and the governor preferred to reside outside the town in this *takiyya*, which was equipped with reception rooms for this purpose. For a detailed study of these events, cf. Bodman (1963).

a judgment confirming irrevocability of the endowment (*maḥkūman bi-luzūmihi*), no doubt to protect it against any subsequent claims.

Also noteworthy is the fact that the case was heard in the presence of the governor and that no less than eleven witnesses signed their names to the judgment.[24] The governor may be regarded as the twelfth witness, although his name is not mentioned together with the names of the other witnesses. Court sessions were held in the presence of the governor only in cases relating to the administration of the province. The sensitive character of this particular case probably made his presence necessary.

Here, both parties produced written legal documents supporting their respective claims. Normally, one would expect the descendants of the founder to represent the interest of the *waqf*. The fact that the judge designated Sayyid Arslān as *mutawallī* to represent the endowment in the court procedure suggests that there may not have been any family members left in Aleppo. The judge, who was responsible for the supervision of *waqf*s, as mentioned above, probably opened the case. Indeed, it is possible that none of the beneficiaries was interested in maintaining the endowment and that the case was filed in order to have the endowment annulled.[25] In this case, the

---

[24] Some of these witnesses are clearly from the governor's *entourage* (cf. the list at the end of the first document).

[25] There are other cases in the court records in which the judge designates a *mutawallī* for a lawsuit. This usually happens when the case affects the public interest. In the year 1241/1825–26, for example, Sayyid Abū Bakr Efendī Jābirī Zāda was designated *mutawallī* of the endowment of Sayyid Ismāʿīl al-Ṭībī for the lawsuit that he filed against all living heirs of Sayyid Ismāʿīl. Sayyid Abū Bakr claimed that in 1231/1815–16 Sayyid Ismāʿīl had endowed two houses (*dār*) for Koran recitations and other pious purposes (*jihāt al-birr*). But Sayyid Ismāʿīl died before the endowment was registered and conveyed to the *mutawallī*. The plaintiff asked Sayyid Ismāʿīl's heirs to relinquish possession of their houses, and he produced two witnesses who testified to the establishment of the endowment. The judge decided in favor of the plaintiff; and he dismissed the "*mutawallī* of the lawsuit" (*mutawallī al-daʿwā*) and appointed a "regular" *mutawallī*: Sayyid Muḥammad, the grandson of Sayyid Ismāʿīl. In this case, the plaintiff did not present a document to support his claim, probably because no such document existed (recall that the founder died before the endowment had been registered). SMS, 208/336/515.

In another case, in the year 1224/1809–10 the judge designated Shaykh Aḥmad al-Ashrafī as *mutawallī* of the small abandoned Zujjājīn Mosque next to a *khān* in the Jallūm quarter. Shaikh Aḥmad filed a lawsuit against the *mutawallī* of the *khān* because merchants residing in the *khān* used the mosque as a warehouse and modified the architecture of the building, so that it lost its "character as a mosque" (*maʿālim masjidiyyatihi*). He asked the merchants to leave the place and to restore it to its former state. In support of his claim, he produced two *fatwā*s and twelve witnesses who confirmed the status of the building as a mosque that was used for prayer. The judge decided in his favor. SMS, 165/67/174.

nomination of Sayyid Arslan as *mutawallī* of the *waqf* would only be fictitious to clarify the legal status of the property implied.

Note that the disputed property was a garden (*bustān*) outside of Aleppo that Ḥājj ʿAlī al-Madārātī had endowed in 1189/1775–76. The plaintiff claimed that Ḥājj ʿAlī's heirs had violated the stipulations of the *waqfiyya* by selling the garden. The defendant countered that he had purchased the garden from the heirs of Ḥājj ʿAlī and from a third party, producing written documents (*ḥujaj*) in support of this claim. If the judge did in fact initiate the filing of the lawsuit, it would be interesting to know how the original *waqfiyya* came into the plaintiff's (or the judge's) hands.

The garden was in the possession (*yad*) of the defendant, Ḥājj Muḥammad Āghā. The judge asked the person who had been designated as the *mutawallī* to confirm the establishment of the endowment and its registration. He failed to do so, probably because nearly twenty-six years had passed since the registration of the endowment, and he could not find people who were willing and able to testify to its existence.

Here, both parties produced written legal documents supporting their respective claims. On one hand a sale's document (*ḥujja*) probably certified—as many others we found in the court records—by the judge. On the other hand a *waqfiyya*, also certified as already mentioned. Despite the fact that some jurists (cf. Ibn ʿĀbidin 1994, 6:623 and also Johansen 1997:356) accord special importance to *waqf* documents, the judge in this case obviously considered both documents to have the same legal value, their contradicting content had therefore to be confirmed by testimony.

Concerning written evidence, Ibn ʿĀbidin expressed: "If it is found in the records that, for example, a certain place is *waqf*-property for a certain *madrasa*, this should be accepted without proof. This contradicts the opinion of Ramlī: "The endowment is not confirmed by its mere existence in the imperial records (*al-daftar al-sultānī*), because writing may not be trusted." This last statement reveals the major argument against documentary evidence: written documents can easily be falsified. Both authors mention 'imperial records', like the 16th century Ottoman tax surveys. Some jurists consider these documents to be protected against alterations, because they are issued by order from the sultan, carry therefore his *tughra* and are kept in a save place. Furthermore, for practical reasons, even merchants' commercial records are accepted as proof, for example in case of dispute over a deceased merchant's property (Ibn ʿĀbidin 1853–54, 2:19–20).

The documents mentioned in case I do not belong to these two categories, but Ibn ʿĀbidin states also concerning our documents that when the document's content is confirmed by the *qāḍī*'s records, it should be accepted as proof (*yuʿmalu bihi*) (Ibn ʿĀbidin 1994, 6:622).

The judge might have checked to see if the endowment was registered in the court records. This registration, together with the original *waqfiyya*, would have constituted sufficient evidence to rule in favor of the endowment.[26] Our document does not indicate that he did that; this suggests that the position of the endowment was weak, or, as mentioned above, that the purpose of this lawsuit was to annul the endowment.

The judge's decision contradicts an opinion expressed by Ibn ʿĀbidīn: "If it is found in the records that, for example, a certain place is *waqf*-property for a certain *madrasa*, this should be accepted without proof."[27] But his decision is in accordance with the opinion of Ramlī: "The endowment is not confirmed by its mere existence in the imperial records, because writing may not be trusted."[28]

Despite the fact that the judge is not obligated to follow a particular legal opinion, it was certainly of importance that this endowment was a private one (*waqf dhurrī*), so that no pious institution was harmed by the judge's decision.

Case II: 'The Mosque claimed as Private Property'

Two sisters, Ruqayya and Ṣāliḥa, filed a lawsuit against their brother, Sayyid Hāshim, who was the *mutawallī* of a mosque (*masjid*) in the Farāfra quarter.

The sisters claimed that they had inherited this building as private property (*milk*) from their mother and they therefore demanded their legal share of the inheritance. The brother countered that their father had designated the building as a *waqf* to be used as a mosque. The brother produced a document (*barāʾa sulṭāniyya*) that invested him with the administration (*tawliya*) of the mosque, a position that

---

[26] Ibn ʿĀbidīn (1853–54, 2:19); ibid. (1994, 6:633). Johansen (1997a:356).

[27] Ibn ʿĀbidīn (1994, 6:623: "*law wujida fī al-dafātir anna al-makān al-fulānī waqf ʿalā al-madrasa al-fulāniyya mathalan yuʿmalu bihi min ghayr bayyina.*").

[28] Ibid. He cites Ramlī: "*la yathbitu al-waqf bi-mujarrad wujūdihi fī al-daftar al-sulṭānī li-ʿadam al-iʿtimād ʿalā al-khaṭṭ.*"

his father had occupied before him. The judge did not demand confirmation of this fact, probably because it is mentioned in the *barāʾa*.

The judge decided in favor of the brother on the strength of his argument and the document he produced as evidence. He characterized the evidence contained in the document as *al-mashhūr al-mutawātir* (a generally accepted fact that has been transmitted in an uninterrupted multiple line of transmission). At the end of our court document we find the names of four witnesses: two of them were court employees and one was a member of a notable family (Sayyid Khalīl Efendī Naqīb Zāda).[29]

On what grounds did the judge accept this document as authoritative? Clearly, he was drawing on the twin concepts of *tawātur* and *mashhūr*. These concepts were developed by experts in jurisprudence to explain the authoritative nature of the Koran and the sound *ḥadīth*. They taught that the authoritativeness of a sacred text is based upon two conditions: its transmission must be "multiple and uninterrupted" (*mutawātir*), and the knowledge contained in the text must be "generally accepted" by the community (*mashhūr*). Subsequently, Muslim jurists used these concepts to justify the acceptance of correspondence between judges as evidence.[30]

In our case, the judge used these two concepts to assess the evidentiary nature of the document, concluding that it met the necessary qualifications. He probably had in mind the uninterrupted line of *mutawallī*s who administered the mosque, as confirmed by the *barāʾa* document, and the fact that a building that has been endowed as a mosque and has served that purpose may not subsequently revert to being private property and be transmitted through inheritance.[31]

The two sisters based their claim on their assumption that the building that was disputed had been owned by their mother (or

[29] Meriwether (1981:298). She mentions that members of this family were connected with the courts at the end of the eighteenth century. Sayyid Khalīl appears as a witness in another court case, dated 1222/1807–08, where he is referred to as *ʿumdat al-sādāt* (Senior representatives of the Prophet's descendents) (SMS, 163/84/129).

[30] Johansen has analyzed the modes of reasoning that jurists used to justify the authority of important religious texts, like the Koran and the Prophetic traditions. See Johansen (1997a:338ff.).

[31] For the discussion within the Hanafī school, see, for example, Ibn ʿĀbidīn (1994, 6:545). In the aforementioned case concerning the Zujjājīn Mosque (cf. fn. 25), the *muftī* of Aleppo stated: "a mosque is eternal; even when it is destroyed, it remains a mosque until the day of judgment (. . . *al-masjid yataʾabbadu wa-in khariba wa-yabqā masjidan abadan ilā yawm al-sāʿa* . . .)" (SMS, 165/67/174).

owned jointly by their mother and their father), and that the father had transformed the building into a mosque, despite the fact that he did not own the building in its entirety. It is not mentioned that an endowment was established on that occasion to support this newly created institution. But the mosque itself acquired the status of *waqf* even without a written *waqfiyya*. From this perspective, the sisters were in a weak position.

Rather than formulate a counterclaim, the brother produced the document confirming that he was the *mutawallī* of the mosque. Without asking the two sisters to provide evidence for their claim, the judge dismissed the case.

Elsewhere in the court records, we find the same kind of document employed in court, but with another result: A *barāʾa sulṭāniyya* dated 20 Shaʿbān 1204/6 May 1790 designates Sayyid Muḥammad Efendī as the *duʿājī* (a person who, after the complete recitation of the Koran, prays to God for the well-being of the Muslims, Yediyıldız 1990:304) of the endowment of Bahrām Bāshā. Two years later, on the 14 Jumādā al-Ūlā 1206/9 February 1792, he demanded his salary from the *mutawallī* of the endowment. The *mutawallī* replied the endowment deed makes no mention of the *duʿājiyya* post.[32] The judge demanded that the plaintiff prove that the founder mentioned this position in his *waqfiyya*. Unable to produce the documentation, Sayyid Muḥammad insisted that the position had been registered in the "imperial records" (*muharrara fī al-daftar al-sulṭānī*). The judge dismissed the case, arguing that the plaintiff had no right to claim a salary, because he was unable to prove the "origin" (*aṣl*) of the post.[33]

The defendant did not have to produce the original *waqfiyya* to counter the plaintiff's claim. It was sufficient that the plaintiff could not establish that the founder had created the post in the original *waqfiyya*. To do so, he would have had to produce witnesses who would testify to the creation of such a post, or the original *waqfiyya*. Also, the judge no doubt considered the plaintiff's claim weak, because he had waited almost two years before claiming his salary.

Here, an imperial *barāʾa* was not considered as evidence, despite the fact that Ibn ʿAbidīn refers to a *barāʾa* in his discussion of doc-

---

[32] Ghazzī (1991–93, 2:43ff.). This post is in fact not mentioned in the *waqfiyya* of Bahrām Bāshā.
[33] SMS, 141/4/10.

uments that should be considered as evidence (Ibn ʿĀbidīn 1994, 8:135ff.).

Case III: 'The neglected trees of the Takiyya al-Mawlawiyya'

In 1070/1659–60 a certain Ṣandal Āghā reportedly designated seventy olive trees as an endowment for the benefit of the Takiyya al-Mawlawiyya, an important dervish convent in Aleppo.

The trees reportedly remained in the possession of the *takiyya* until the year 1208/1793–94, when two brothers, Sayyid Ismāʿīl Efendī and Sayyid Hāshim Efendī, took possession of them. Two years later, in 1210/1795–96, Sayyid Muḥammad ʿAlī Dede, one of the most distinguished religious figures of Aleppo (*fakhr al-sādāt wa al-mashāʾikh*) and shaykh of the Takiyya al-Mawlawiyya, filed a lawsuit against the two brothers, claiming that the seventy trees belonged to the endowment. The brothers, who had been in possession of the trees for only two years, responded that they had inherited the trees (the document does not specify from whom). They denied the shaykh's claim that the trees had been designated as *waqf*-property and that he had exercised control (*taṣarruf*) over them in his function as *mutawallī* of the *takiyya*'s endowments.

The judge designated Sayyid Muḥammad as the plaintiff, placing the burden of proof upon the shaykh. Shortly thereafter, the Sayyid Muḥammad produced a *fatwā*: certain trees that had been designated as an endowment were neglected by its *mutawallī*; subsequently someone took possession of the trees. According to the *muftī*, the usurper must pay damages to the endowment.

The judge used this *fatwā* as the basis for his judgment. He asked the plaintiff to produce evidence in support of his claim. Two witnesses testified to the facts, as stated by the plaintiff. After the witnesses gave their testimony, the judge decided in favor of the plaintiff.

The seventy olive trees mentioned here probably had been designated as *waqf*-property to the exclusion of the land on which they stood. They were located near other olive trees that were private property. In the year 1210/1796–96, the endowment was already 140 years old. Although olive trees are long-lived, it is doubtful that all seventy of the trees that had been designated as *waqf*-property in 1070/1659–60 survived until 1210/1795–96. Both the number and, perhaps, the location of the trees varied during that period. This explains why the legal status of the trees might be contested.

Why did the *mutawallī* wait for two years after the two brothers "laid their hands" on the trees before going to court? The trees contributed only modestly to the income of the *takiyya*. In the year 1258/1842–43 they produced fifty piastres whereas the total income of the endowment of the *takiyya* in that year was 34,019 piastres.[34] Thus it is plausible that the *mutawallī* either neglected the trees or forgot to collect the revenue that they produced.

The *mutawallī* produced the endowment deed and presented it to the court, but the judge did not consider it as evidence. Rather, he proceeded in the manner prescribed by the law. The plaintiff had to produce witnesses who would testify to the existence of the endowment. Had he failed to produce witnesses (like the plaintiff in case I), the judge might have annulled the endowment. The *fatwā* presented by the plaintiff established that his claim was valid despite the fact that he waited two years before claiming the trees.

Conclusion

Did the judge in the three cases apply Islamic procedural law or did he base his judgment on personal convictions and arbitrary considerations?

As noted, the judge begins by assigning the roles of plaintiff and defendant. The assignment of roles is important, because, in most cases, it determines which party bears the burden of proof. Unfortunately, our documents do not indicate how these roles were assigned. At this stage of the lawsuit, the judge might interfere in an arbitrary way. But was it the judge who assigned the roles of plaintiff and defendant or did one of the court officers who prepared the case make this decision before submitting the case to the judge? Russell mentions that a deputy judge used to sit in the outer courtyard of the Maḥkama al-Kubrā and decide minor cases (Russell 1794, 1:317). The evidence of our documents suggests that in most cases the litigant who took the initiative to address the court and file the case became the plaintiff and the accused party became the defendant.

How heavy was the burden of proof and was the outcome predictable? The plaintiff seems to have had an advantage over the

[34] Başbakanlık Osmanlı Arşivi, Evkaf Defterleri (EV.), 11687.

defendant, no doubt because he could prepare the case and find witnesses who would support his claim. From a study of eighty-two lawsuits in the records of the Ṣāliḥiyya court in Damascus in the years 1873–78, Toru Miura found that 76.3% were won by the plaintiff. In most of the cases, the ruling was based on the oral testimony of witnesses. Miura mentions that documents were produced in many court cases, but only to support a claim. In no case was a judgment based on documentary evidence alone (Miura 2001:138). These figures suggest that the judge applied the rules of judicial procedure, did not interfere in this procedure, and did not impose his personal views in an arbitrary manner.

The three cases examined here were chosen because they are somehow exceptional and do not represent the daily work of the court. Nevertheless, they show that the judge was able to exercise a certain amount of discretion in making his decision. He used the tools that the law put at his disposal. He was not obligated to follow only one opinion, but could choose between and among the different opinions of his school. Thus, he was able to treat each case in an appropriate manner.

Rosen has argued that judges in the contemporary Moroccan town of Sefrou make inquiries about the social background and financial situation of litigants before issuing their judgments (Rosen 1989:7ff.). Nothing in our sources indicates that the judge in Ottoman Aleppo based his decision on social or financial factors that were not directly relevant to the case. But the historian is not in the same position as the anthropologist, who may observe the judge at work.

The *fatwā* presented in the third case contains extensive legal reasoning, with several references to Hanafī legal literature. The judge himself usually does not engage in legal reasoning; rather, he bases his judgment on a *fatwā*. A *fatwā* may be produced at the request of one of the litigants, as in this case, or at the request of the judge. *Fatwā*s appear in complicated and unusual cases, and the judge generally follows the opinion expressed in the *fatwā*.

The judges had different attitudes about the evidentiary status of documents. Writing certainly played an important role in court procedure: we find legal documents (*ḥujaj*), a written *fatwā*, and the claim of one party presented in writing as a kind of *aide-mémoire*. Following the judge's decision, each case was registered in the court records, creating a growing archive that the judge might consult in future cases. As mentioned, Hanafīs do not consider documents to be evidence. The judges of Aleppo habitually followed this doctrine and asked for testimonial evidence to confirm the content of written documents. Only exceptionally was a document treated as evidence. In the second case, the judge's decision to preserve the mosque as an institution was motivated by his consideration of the public interest. The practice of the courts of Aleppo does not confirm Tyan's conclusion that the Hanafī jurists at the end of the Ottoman period generally accepted writing as evidence. The same judge might accept documentary evidence in one case and refuse it in another. His decision depended on the particular circumstances of the case and, as Johansen has shown, was shaped not only by doctrine, but also by the custom (*ʿurf*).[35]

Judges in Ottoman Aleppo ca. 1800 were neither automatons who applied procedural rules in a mechanical manner nor Weberian *Kadis* who decided cases arbitrarily without reference to any legal rules and principles. Judges were not required to follow a single doctrine. They decided each case according to its particularities, using all the legal tools at their disposal.

Appendix: Translation of the Documents

The original language of the documents has been simplified: the frequent repetitions in the Arabic original have been omitted; also omitted are titles of the judge and other notables that are difficult to translate and that are not necessary for the understanding of the document.

Words in square brackets do not appear in the original document and are intended to make the reading easier. Arabic words and expressions are transcribed in parenthesis.

Document I: "A Family Endowment that was Annulled"[36]

[In the left corner:] Included the interdiction of appeal after the pleading, the poor (*al-faqīr*) servant of God, ʿUthmān Zāda al-Sayyid Maḥmūd,

---

[35] Johansen (1997a:376). He concludes with regard to written evidence: "*C'est donc la relation entre doctrine et coutume qui devrait nous servir de clef pour déchiffrer les dispositions juridiques et les débats sur la doctrine.*"

[36] SMS, 148/150/548.

the *qāḍī* in the city of Aleppo the Grey (*al-shahbāʾ*), may they be forgiven.

In the legal council summoned in the *takiyya* of Shaykh Abū Bakr al-Wafāʾī (may his venerable, noble secret be sanctified), located outside Aleppo, attended by his excellence, Ḥājj Ibrāhīm Bāshā, the present governor of Aleppo (may the exalted Lord preserve him), in the presence of the aforementioned judge.

Sayyid Arslān, son of Ḥājj ʿUmar al-Sammān, the *mutawallī* of the endowment of Ḥājj ʿAlī al-Madārātī, appointed (*manṣūb*) for the complaint.[37] [The endowment is] located in Aleppo. [Sayyid Arslān] accused Ḥājj Muḥammad Āghā, son of Ḥājj Bakrī, known as Ibn al-Dügmeci, of having seized the whole garden (*bustān*), consisting of five *kadnas* and one-third *kadna*,[38] located in the Mazraʿat al-Mubayyaḍ outside Aleppo, known as Bustān al-Ḥājj ʿAlī al-Madārātī. There is no need for its renewal (*al-mustaghnī ʿan al-tajdīd*), because it is widely known. This fact was confirmed by Ḥasan Āghā, son of Muṣṭafā, and Ḥājj Makkī Āghā, son of Ḥājj ʿAbd al-Karīm Āghā.

[The plaintiff] claimed in his lawsuit that the garden was the private property (*milk*) of Ḥājj ʿAlī al-Madārātī, son of Arslān, son of ʿUmar and that during his lifetime, on the nineteenth of Dhū al-Ḥijja 1189/eleventh of February 1776, [Ḥājj ʿAlī] designated it as an endowment for his own benefit, then for his children, his children's children and for their descendants. After their extinction, [the endowment was] for the benefit of the Jāmiʿ Khāṣṣ Bek located in Aleppo; and after the destruction (*indirās*) of the Jāmiʿ, for the poor Muslims of Aleppo, as a sound legal (*saḥīḥan sharʿiyyan*) endowment, certified as being irrevocable (*maḥkūman bi-luzūmihi*), after handing it over to the administrator of the registration (*mutawallī al-tasjīl*), as it is evident from the copy of the *waqf*-document verified (*mushāhad*) in the court.[39] The defendant seized the garden without any legal claim, and therefore I demand that he remove his hands from it and that he hand it over to me for the sake of the endowment.

---

[37] The fact that the judge appointed Sayyid Arslān as *mutawallī* for the complaint suggests that this endowment probably had no *mutawallī*.

[38] A *kadna* represents the land surface that can be cultivated in one day by traditional means, approximately 5000 square meters (Asadī 1981–8, 6:330).

[39] Ibn ʿĀbidīn (1994, 6:527ff.). The plaintiff supports his claim with a short summary of the content of the *waqfiyya*. It contains, like all other *waqfiyya*s registered in the court records of Aleppo at that time, the judge's decision about the *waqfiyya*'s validity and irrevocable character (*maḥkūman bi-luzūmihi*).

When the defendant was asked about the truth of this claim, he answered that the aforementioned garden was the private property of Ḥājj ʿAlī and that he had purchased it after [Ḥājj ʿAlī's] death from his heirs, who are well-known, and from Sayyid Ṭāhā al-Ṣaḥḥān, for a specified amount. He received it from them according to legal documents (*ḥujaj*) verified (*mushāhada*) in the court. He denied that Ḥājj ʿAlī made it an endowment in the manner explained (*ʿalā al-minwāl al-mashrūḥ*).

The plaintiff was asked to produce testimony, confirming the endowment and its registration, as written above. He failed to produce the evidence (*bayyina*).

Then the judge informed the plaintiff that his complaint against the defendant was not accepted without legal proof (*burhān sharʿī*) and he prohibited him from raising any objection to this case.

Written and signed, upon request, on the third of Jumādā al-Ūlā of the year 1215/twenty-third of September 1800.

(11 witnesses: Muḥammad Āghā, Ḥasan Āghā Amīn Jāwūshān Ḥalab, Ḥājj Makkī ibn ʿAbd al-Karīm Āghā, Ḥājj Aḥmad al-Zubaydī, Ḥājj Aḥmad Jalabī ibn Ḥājj Ṭāhā al-Ḥarīrī, Ḥājj Qāsim ibn ʿAbd al-Ghanī Ḥaṭṭāb, Ḥājj Aḥmad ibn Yūsuf Āghā al-Salamatlī, ʿAbdallāh ibn Yūsuf al-Muʿaṭṭish, Ḥājj Amīn ibn Shaikh Yūsuf, Ḥājj Zakariyā ibn Ḥājj Muṣṭafā al-Aiyūbī, Aḥmad Āghā al-Tarjumān)

Document II: "The Mosque claimed as Private Property"[40]

> [In the left corner:] The matter is as follows, written by the poor (*al-faqīr*) servant of God, Kalāhī Zāda al-Sayyid Muḥammad Amīn, the *qāḍī* in Aleppo, may he be forgiven.

The two sisters Ruqayya and Ṣāliḥa, daughters of Sayyid Ṭāhā, made a claim against their brother Sayyid Hāshim, son of the aforementioned Sayyid Ṭāhā, the *mutawallī* according to a *barāʾa sulṭāniyya* of the mosque situated in the Farāfra quarter and known as Masjid QRṢB.[41] They said in their claim:

[40] SMS, 139/104/201.
[41] I am unable to identify this mosque.

> The aforementioned mosque is our inherited property (*milk*) from our deceased mother. Our father transformed [the place] into a mosque (*ittakhadhahu masjidan*) during his lifetime and our brother—his son—took possession of it without any legal claim (*bidūn wajh sharʿī*). We ask him now to remove his hand from our inherited part of it (*ʿan ḥiṣṣatinā al-irthiyya*).

[The defendant] was asked [about the claim] and produced a *barāʾa sulṭāniyya* informing about his nomination as administrator of the mosque, like his father before him.

The claim of the two plaintiffs was against what is generally recognized and transmitted in an uninterrupted chain (*al-mashhūr al-mutawātir*). It became obvious to the judge that their claim is not legal and he informed them that their claim concerning the private property of the mosque (*milkiyyat al-masjid*) is not accepted and prohibited them from raising any objection to the defendant.

Written and signed, upon request, on the tenth of Rabīʿ al-Awwal of the year 1206/eighth of November 1791.

(4 witnesses: Sayyid Khalīl Efendī Naqīb Zāda, Ḥājj ʿAbd al-Karīm Āghā al-Tarjumān, Aḥmad Āghā al-Tarjumān, Muḥammad ibn Aḥmad)

Document III: "The Neglected trees of the Takiyya al-Mawlawiyya"[42]

> [In the left corner:] The matter is as follows, written by the poor (*al-faqīr*) servant of God, Nūr Shaykhī Zāda al-Sayyid ʿAbd al-Raḥīm, the *qāḍī* in Aleppo, may they (sic. *lahumā*) be forgiven.

Sayyid Muḥammad ʿAlī Dede, shaykh of the Takiyya al-Maulawiya, located in Aleppo, and the *mutawallī* of its endowments, made a claim against the two brothers, Sayyid Ismāʿīl Efendī and Sayyid Hāshim Efendī, sons of Sayyid ʿAbd al-Raḥīm Efendī Fanṣa Zāda. In his claim he said:

> All the olive trees, of which there are seventy, located in Mazraʿat Baydūn, which is in the *qaḍāʾ* of Darkūsh,[43] that are bordered in the

[42] SMS, 141–I/54/140.

[43] Darkūsh is a small town situated on the banks of the Orontes river about 100 km to the west of Aleppo.

> direction of the *qibla* in the east and in the north by open country (*falaḥ*), and in the west by the possession (*yad*) of Rustum Zāda, belong to the endowments of the *takiyya*. Ṣandal Āghā, son of ʿAbdallāh, designated them as an endowment for the benefit of the *takiyya*, as is evident from the *waqf* document that was verified (*mushāhad*) in the court and that dates from the year 1070/1659–60. The *mutawallī*s of the *takiyya* have had free possession (*taṣarruf*) of [the trees] since the date on which the endowment was established until the administration (*tawliya*) of the endowment passed to me, under the eyes of the ancestors the defendants. I myself had possession of [the trees] for a period of twenty years, under the eyes of the defendants. Two years ago they seized the trees without any legal claim. I am asking that they be ordered to return them and not to oppose me in the possession of [the trees]."

When the two defendants were asked about this, they acknowledged that the trees were in the possession (*yad*) of the plaintiff, that two years ago they had seized them, and that they are their inherited private property. They denied the plaintiff's claim that they are *waqf*-property and [they denied] his free possession (*taṣarruf*) for the aforementioned period.

The plaintiff produced a distinguished *fatwā* in response to the following question: Certain trees are *waqf*-property in favor of certain beneficiaries. The custodians [of the endowment] have possessed them from ancient times until now, under the eyes of Zayd and his son, who were silent [about that]. Next to them were trees held in private property (*milk*). Someone claimed that some of the *waqf* trees are private property, because there is no mention of them in the *waqf* document. [Zayd] took possession of [the trees] on the mere basis of his claim, without any proof. The *mutawallī* did not challenge this act. Then clarification (*muṣarraḥa*) was found in the *waqf* document. Should the case be treated on the basis of the claim, without any proof, and is [Zayd's] taking possession of [the trees] as mentioned before [i.e. legal]?

The answer: it should not be treated on the mere basis of the claim and his seizing [the trees], as mentioned. In *Al-Durr al-mukhtār*; a right is not established merely by a claim (end of quotation).[44] The best indicator of private property (*milk*) is possession (*yad*) over it. There is no difference in that respect between *waqf* and private

[44] Muḥammad ibn ʿAlī al-Ḥaṣkafī, (1025–1088/1616–1677), *muftī* of Damascus, author of *al-Durr al-mukhtār*, on which Ibn ʿĀbidīn wrote his commentary, *Radd al-muḥtār*. See Ziriklī (1979, 6:294).

property, as [stipulated] in the *Khayriyya*;[45] only the rightful possession is to be validly recognised "(*Al-yad al-muʿtabara hiya yad al-muḥaqqa*), and God knows best."[46]

On the copy:[47] If ʿUmar collected the fruit of the trees for a period of time, can the *mutawallī* ask him to pay [the profit] back, or not?

Yes, the *mutawallī* can ask him to pay that back because he is a usurper (*ghāṣib*), and rule (*ḥukm*) of usurpation is the obligation to return [the property], if it is [still] in the hands of the [usurper] and compensation for the damage (*ghurm*) if it was spent, as [stipulated] in *Al-Durr al-mukhtār*. The benefits of the endowment are guaranteed, either collected by it or given to it (*fīhi manāfiʿ al-waqf maḍmūna istawfaha wa aʿtāha*). God knows best. Signed and written by *al-faqīr* Sayyid ʿAbdallāh al-Jābirī, the *muftī* in Aleppo, may he be forgiven.[48]

The aforementioned judge studied [the *fatwā*] and then asked the plaintiff to produce evidence supporting his claim, as explained. Two witnesses, Shaykh Muḥammad Sharīf Efendī, shaykh in the Takiyyat al-Arbaʿīn, and Muḥammad, son of Yūsuf, from Dārat ʿIzza,[49] who were legally authorized to testify, testified against the two defendants:

> We testify that the olive trees whose number is seventy, located in the *mazraʿa* known as Mazraʿat Baydūn, in the *qaḍāʾ* of Darkūsh, delimited by the above mentioned borders, are *waqf*-property within the *awqāf* of the Takiyya al-Mawlawiyya. They were designated as *waqf*-property by Ṣandal Āghā, son of ʿAbdallāh. The shaykhs and *mutawallīs* of the *takiyya* have possessed them from the moment the endowment was established until the supervision of the endowment passed to the plaintiff. He also had free disposition over them for a period of twenty years, under the eyes of the two defendants. We know that and testify to it.

[45] The *fatwā*-collection, *al-Fatāwā al-khayriyya* of Khayr al-Dīn ibn Aḥmad al-Ramlī (993–1081/1575–1671). See Ziriklī (1979, 2:327).

[46] The significance of this phrase is probably that mere possession without a legal title is not valid, especially when a claim is supported by legal evidence.

[47] In the document: *wa fī al-ṣūra*, probably another *fatwā* on the same sheet of paper.

[48] ʿAbdallāh al-Jābirī (1169–ca. 1216/1755–56–1801–02) was a member of a distinguished *ʿulamāʾ* family of Aleppo. His father, Muṣṭafā al-Jābirī, occupied the position of the "head of the notaries and scribes" (*raʾīs al-ʿudūl wa al-kuttāb*) at the Maḥkama al-Kubrā. ʿAbdallāh al-Jābirī was appointed to that same position, when his father became *muftī* of Aleppo. ʿAbdallāh himself was appointed as *muftī* in 1201/1786–87. See Ṭabbākh (1988–92, 7:151ff.).

[49] Dārat ʿIzza is a small town about 30 km west of Aleppo.

Then the judge informed the two defendants since the possession (*taṣarruf*) of the plaintiff (the *mutawallī*), and [the free disposal of the other *mutawallīs*] before him, over the aforementioned trees by means of the supervision of the endowment is confirmed, in particular the possession of the plaintiff under the eyes [of the defendants] during [the aforementioned] period and their silence [about that], they do not have the right to oppose him in his possession [of the trees].

Written and signed, upon request, on the twenty-fifth of Rajab 1210/fifth of February 1796.

(3 witnesses: Zakariyā Āghā al-Muḥḍirbāshī, Aḥmad Āghā al-Tarjumān, Sayyid Ibrāhīm Jalabī al-Tarjumān)

CHAPTER EIGHTEEN

SHOPPING FOR LEGAL FORUMS: CHRISTIANS AND FAMILY LAW IN MODERN EGYPT

Ron Shaham

Introduction

Orientalists have studied extensively the recourse of the "Protected People" of the Islamic state (henceforth dhimmis) to Islamic courts, starting from the early medieval period and extending to the modern period. Although in principle the dhimmis enjoyed judicial autonomy, some legal issues, such as penal law and some aspects of civil law, were under the exclusive jurisdiction of the *sharīʿa* (henceforth shariʿa) courts, being the state courts. For settling such issues, resorting to Islamic courts was obligatory for the dhimmis. Still, there were instances in which applying to a Muslim court resulted from a free choice of the dhimmis, in an effort to obtain material gains. My study adds to this field of research the case of modern Egyptian Christians who maneuvered between their religious family laws and the family laws of the Islamic majority. The Egyptian case is presented by a detailed analysis of a decision by the shariʿa court of Bani Sueif from 1926. In the last part of the study, I suggest that legal shopping was not unique to dhimmis but was also practiced to some extent by Muslims, who maneuvered between the four Orthodox Sunni schools of law. Forum shopping of dhimmis should therefore be perceived as part of a broader Islamic cultural phenomenon, and this Islamic phenomenon is in its turn part of a universal phenomenon.

Part One: The Judicial Setting-Courts, Judicial Personnel and Litigants

In the public session held at the Shariʿa Court of First Instance in Bani Sueif, on Tuesday, 11 Jumādā al-Awwal 1345 (November 16, 1926), under the chairmanship of the honorable scholar al-Sheikh Aḥmad Ṣalāḥ, deputy of the court, and the membership of the honorable

> scholars, al-Shaykh ʿAbd al-Raḥmān Ḥasan and al-Shaykh Maḥmūd Mubārak, *qāḍīs* (s. *qāḍī*, henceforth qadi) of the court, and in the presence of al-Shaykh Aḥmad Muṣṭafā Ḥamīda, the court clerk, the following judgment was given in the appeal case no. 130, years 1925–1926, filed by Yūnān Sharābīn Daqash, a peasant from the Abwān county in Markaz Samālūṭ, al-Minyā province, against Qadīsa bt. Ḥannā Daqash, having no profession and residing in Nazlat Ḥannā Masʿūd, attached to the above-mentioned Abwān, requesting to appeal the decision of the Shariʿa Court of Summary Justice in Samālūṭ, in case no. 542, years 1925–1926, which turned down the demand of the appellant to cancel the entitlement of the respondent to maintenance (*nafaqa*).

The court document includes three parts.[1] In the first part (translated above), bearing no title, the qadi presents the name of the court, the date of the decision, his own name, the name of the court clerk, the case's serial number, the names of the plaintiff and the defendant (usually without any further data on their place of residence, occupation, or social status), and in some cases the names of their legal representatives.

The shariʿa courts—jurisdiction

During the Ottoman period, the jurisdiction of the shariʿa courts included personal status and pious endowment (*waqf*), as well as civil, criminal, and administrative affairs. Starting in the early nineteenth century, Egypt reformed its legal system along Western lines. One aspect of this reform was the gradual restriction of the jurisdiction of the shariʿa courts. The 1897 Ordinance on the Organization of the Shariʿa Courts (*Lāʾiḥat tartīb al-maḥākim al-sharʿiyya*)[2] restricted the

---

[1] *Al-Muḥāmāt al-sharʿiyya* (henceforth, MS), vol. 1 (1929), pp. 303–6, decision no. 87. This periodical (26 vols., Cairo 1929–1955, henceforth MS) was published by the Egyptian shariʿa Bar. It contains thousands of decisions on disputes relating to personal status and *waqf* issued by all three instances of the shariʿa courts located throughout Egypt. For a methodological evaluation of this source, see Shaham (1997:18–21). For a similar logic of presentation in Ottoman Yemeni court documents, see Messick (1993:191). Throughout the translation of the document, I use three types of brackets: { } for brackets located in the Arabic original text; ( ) for transliteration of Arabic terms or phrases; and [ ] for my explanatory additions.

[2] This Ordinance had later amendments and versions. Throughout this study, I refer to the later versions by using the following formats: the "1910 Ordinance," the "1931 Ordinance," etc. The text of the 1910 Ordinance appears in *Majallat al-aḥkām al-sharʿiyya*, vol. 9:193–233. The text of the 1931 Ordinance appears in MS, vol 2:707–62.

jurisdiction of these courts to personal status and *waqf.* In 1955, the shariʿa (and the non-Islamic sectarian) courts were abolished and their jurisdiction was transferred to special courts for personal status established in the framework of the National Courts. For the regime, this was the final step in the long-standing policy of creating a unified and centralized national legal system.[3]

The present study examines the jurisdiction of the shariʿa courts with respect to non-Muslims. This jurisdiction is a result of the legal setting of Egypt, which is characterized by a plurality of religious family laws (*taʿaddud al-sharāʾiʿ*).[4] Legal sociologists developed the model of legal pluralism as an anti-thesis to the model of legal centralism, which places the state legal system in an exclusive position. A legal system is pluralistic when the sovereign tolerates the application of different legal systems for different groups, according to ethnic, religious or geographical criteria, and when the operation of the parallel legal systems is dependent upon the state (Merry 1988:871). One example for "internal pluralism of state law" is a situation in which the latter recognizes a variety of family laws, derived from different religious or customary laws. Each of these family laws forms part of state law through its endorsement by state's authority (Woodman 1999, especially 14).

In modern Egypt, until the abolition of the shariʿa and the sectarian courts in 1955, the Muslim population was judged by the shariʿa courts, while the recognized non-Muslim sects (*ṭawāʾif*, s. *ṭāʾifa*)[5] enjoyed, as the continuation of the Ottoman practice, judicial autonomy

---

[3] On this reform process, see Shaham (1997:11–12) and the sources mentioned there.

[4] Berger (2001:88, 123) prefers to use the term inter-religious duality instead of plurality of religious laws because, in Egypt, the division is between Islamic law, on the one hand, and the totality of the non-Islamic laws, on the other hand. Moreover, the term pluralism implies equality between the laws, while in Egypt Islamic family law is first among equals, because it serves as the general family law of the land.

[5] Egyptian legal texts use three terms for this matter: the most general is "religion" (*dīn* or *diyāna*), distinguishing between Judaism, Christianity and Islam; a narrower term is "rite" (*milla* or *madhhab*), distinguishing between Rabbanites and Karaites in Judaism, and between Catholics, Orthodoxs and Protestants in Christianity. The narrowest term is "sect" (*ṭāʾifa*), referring to the communal distribution among each rite. See Berger (2001:96). In Modern Egypt there are twelve recognized Christian sects: Orthodox-Copt, Greek-Orthodox, Armenian-Orthodox, Syrian-Orthodox, Catholic-Copt, Greek-Catholic, Armenian-Catholic, Syrian-Catholic, Maronites, Chaldeans, Roman-Catholic and Protestants.

in family affairs, in the framework of the religious court of each sect.[6] According to Egyptian judicial practice, the sectarian courts had exclusive jurisdiction over the majority of personal status matters, in which both parties belonged to the same non-Muslim recognized sect, and in which at least one of them insisted on the case being tried by their sectarian court. In such circumstances, the shariʿa court had to declare itself incompetent and to refer the parties to the appropriate sectarian court. However, if one party was a Muslim and the other non-Muslim; if the parties belonged to different non-Muslim sects; if they belonged to the same unrecognized sect; and in inheritance cases between non-Muslim parties, even if they belonged to the same sect, by default only the shariʿa courts had jurisdiction, on the grounds that Islamic law was the general family law of Egypt (Shaham 1995:121, and the sources mentioned in notes 33 and 34). Practically speaking, the division of jurisdictions between the shariʿa, the sectarian and the civil courts was not clear-cut and the different courts continuously competed for jurisdiction (Shaham 1995, 122–125).

Legal pluralism creates a variety of complicated legal problems, such as the need to determine to which transactions or disputes the family law of a particular group applies, to which sect an individual belongs, how an individual can change the law applicable to him, and which law applies to disputes involving individuals from different groups. My case study demonstrates these various problems.

The shariʿa courts—the applicable positive law[7]

Although the majority of the Muslim population in Egypt adheres either to the Shāfiʿī school (in Lower Egypt) or to the Mālikī school (in Upper Egypt), the dominant school in the Egyptian shariʿa courts was the Ḥanafī (henceforth Hanafi), a legacy of Ottoman rule. In the early nineteenth century, the Hanafi school acquired exclusive status in the courts, regardless of the personal affiliation of the litigants.

Formal codification is unknown to the shariʿa. In the premodern period qadis had to find their way through the voluminous legal lit-

---

[6] On the historical development of the jurisdiction of the non-Muslim communal judicial bodies in the Ottoman state in general and in Egypt in particular, see Shaham (1995:117–22).

[7] The following survey is based on Shaham (1997:12–15) and the sources mentioned there.

erature of their respective schools of law, although compendiums (*mukhtaṣars*) may have served as quasi-codes (Fadel 1996). A first codification of Hanafi personal status regulations, composed by Qadrī Pasha, was published by the Egyptian government in 1875 and supposedly enjoyed semi-official status (*EI*², *s.v.* Maḥkama, 23). From my own experience, however, Egyptian qadis of the shariʿa courts rarely mentioned Qadrī Pasha's code as a source for their judgments. They preferred to consult Hanafi *fiqh* works (see below).

Egyptian legislation in family matters in the first half of the twentieth century included a number of laws that codified certain aspects of personal status: Law No. 25 of 1920 and Law No. 25 of 1929, dealing mainly with marriage and divorce; Law No. 77 of 1943 on intestate succession; and Law No. 71 of 1946 on testamentary dispositions. These laws deviated from Hanafi doctrine by adopting elements from the other three schools of law in an eclectic manner (*takhayyur*), or by combining elements from various schools into a patchwork (*talfīq*) that, in its final form, is not recognized by any of the schools. The shariʿa courts, as a first priority, had to apply the above-mentioned legislation. According to article 280 of the 1931 Ordinance, if the subject matter of the case was not covered by legislation, the courts had to judge according to the preponderant Hanafi opinion (*arjaḥ al-aqwāl fī madhhab Abī Ḥanīfa*).

The shariʿa courts—organization[8]

In the late nineteenth century, the organization of the shariʿa courts in Egypt was reformed as well. The 1897 Ordinance introduced the concept of institutional hierarchical appeal, by organizing the shariʿa courts into three levels: Courts of Summary Justice (*maḥākim juzʾiyya*), Courts of First Instance (*maḥākim ibtidāʾiyya*) and a Supreme Court (*maḥkama ʿulyā*). The authority of the Courts of Summary Justice (headed by one qadi) to hand down final decisions was restricted in terms of both the subject matter and the monetary value of the suit. In certain matters their decisions were not final and could be appealed to the Courts of First Instance (staffed by three qadis), which were spread out in the large cities and provincial towns. The decisions of these courts, in turn, were subject to appeal before the Supreme

[8] For the following survey, see Shaham (1997:12) and the sources mentioned there.

Court of Cairo (usually staffed by three qadis).[9] The decision of an appeals court does not enjoy the formal status of a binding precedent for the lower courts, but it enjoys practical authority.

The training of qadis and their school (madhhab) *affiliation*

The general theme that runs through my analysis of the development of the Egyptian legal system so far is the institutionalization and bureaucratization of the legal profession and the legal system under the central authority of the Egyptian nation-state. One of the best demonstrations for this process was the state's attempt to control the training of qadis and of other court personnel which was until then exclusively controlled by the autonomous al-Azhar. An outstanding development took place with the establishment of the training school for qadis (Madrasat al-Qaḍā' al-Sharʿī) in 1907, modeled on an Austrian school established in Sarajevo.[10] The training program of the school was a liberal one. The curriculum naturally included *fiqh* and Arabic, but it also included mathematics, geometry, astronomy, biology, chemistry, geography and history, as well as practical proficiencies, such as knowledge of the court's procedures, the writing of decisions and administrative law.[11] The first teaching staff included many prominent scholars recruited by al-Azhar and by the Ministry of Education.[12] The school operated under the supervision of various state ministries until al-Azhar's faculty of law absorbed it in 1929. It nevertheless was responsible for producing a generation of legal practitioners who acquired a broader legal training and world outlook than that of al-Azhar graduates and who later occupied high positions in the religious-legal system, such as head-muftis of Egypt.[13]

---

[9] The procedures of the appeal appear in articles 305–326 of the 1910 Ordinance.

[10] For the school's history, see Shaham (1997:15) and the sources mentioned there; Skovgaard-Petersen (1997:62–3) and the sources mentined there; and Mudhakkira (1919).

[11] See Mudhakkira (1919:14) with respect to ʿAbduh's proposals for the teaching program, and ibid., (pp. 15–17) with respect to articles 7 and 13 of the 1907 statute for the establishment of the school, which contains the curriculum.

[12] See a partial list in Mudhakkira (1919:19–20). ʿAbd al-Razzāq al-Sanhūrī, the most famous modern Egyptian jurist, and the creator of the 1949 civil code, taught in the school for one year in 1920, before he left for France to undertake his doctoral studies. See Hill (1987:2).

[13] A few examples follow: Ḥasanīn Muḥammad Ḥasanīn Makhlūf (d. 1990), the chief mufti of Egypt between 1946–50 and 1952–54, who graduated from the school

Since the Hanafi school was the official school of the Ottomans, and the Ottoman chief qadi of Egypt was Hanafi as well, during the nineteenth century there was a strong tendency to exclude non-Hanafis from judgeships. This preference for the Hanafi school is reflected in a decree of the Minister of Justice from December 10, 1891, according to which all qadis, official muftis and employees of the Public Prosecution (Niyāba) had to be Hanafis (this decree was abolished by the 1910 Ordinance; the last version of the Ordinance, from 1931, does not mention this topic). The administrative practice to exclude non-Hanafis from the judgeship remained prevalent well after Egypt became an independent nation-state.

Representation of litigant by proxy

Each party may nominate a proxy (*wakīl*) to represent him or her in court. The proxy must be a professional lawyer, or be related by blood or by marriage to the person he represents (art. 76 of the 1910 Ordinance). Law No. 15 of 1916 organized the sharʿī lawyers (*al-muḥāmūn al-sharʿiyyūn*) in a special Bar, similar to that of the civil lawyers, and defined the qualifications required of them as well as their rights and duties. The new Bar accepted graduates of the Cairo law school, ulema from al-Azhar and qadis from the shariʿa courts.

I do not have reliable statistics about the percentage of lawsuits in which the parties were represented. My general impression, however, is that such representation was widespread and became more necessary as the work of the courts became more formal and sophisticated. It seems that a non-Muslim who resorted to a shariʿa court needed a professional proxy more than a Muslim, because such a proxy possessed the required legal knowledge. Moreover, non-Muslims were reluctant to appear in court in person, for two possible reasons: first, the shariʿa court was a relatively unfamiliar arena and the prospect of meeting the qadi face-to-face might have been frightening and threatening; second, a non-Muslim may have been interested in hiding from his or her co-religionists the fact that he was breaking

in 1914. The same is true with respect to three other chief muftis: ʿAllām Naṣṣār (graduated 1917; mufti 1950–52; d. 1966); Ḥasan Ma'mūn (graduated 1918; mufti 1955–64; d. 1973); Aḥmad Muḥammad ʿAbd al-Huraydī (probably graduated in 1936; mufti 1960–70). See Skovgaard-Petersen (1997:171–2, 193–4).

the bonds of sectarian solidarity. For all these reasons, representation by proxy was the rule in most cases for non-Muslims.

Application of non-Muslims to Islamic courts

Recourse by non-Muslims to the shariʿa courts in family matters is a well-known phenomenon, which started in the early Islamic period. In premodern Egypt, some Christians registered their marriage contracts at the shariʿa courts in order to enjoy the right of unilateral divorce, in order to insert stipulations in the contract, or in order to contract a marriage between Christian spouses affiliated with different churches. Moreover, Christians applied to the shariʿa courts in marital and divorce disputes.[14] Scholars differ about the scope of this kind of recourse and about the severity with which the religious and secular leaderships of the non-Muslim sects viewed this breaking of sectarian autonomy (Qattan 1999:435, 442 (note 30); Hanna 1995: 54–55; Afifi 1996: 204–207).

The availability of unilateral divorce (*ṭalāq*, henceforth talaq) has been the main motive for the resort of Christian husbands to the shariʿa. Such a divorce, easily obtainable according to the shariʿa, is recognized neither by Christian Orthodox law nor by Catholic law. Orthodox-Coptic law recognizes various grounds for dissolution of marriage,[15] but dissolution of marriage involves a complex and sometimes a long judicial process, while unilateral divorce is a speedy act and does not have to involve the court at all. In 1941, the supporters of divorce within the Coptic community applied to King Fārūq and demanded that the state guarantee the Coptic right to divorce according to Islamic law (Afifi 1996: 210).

[14] For the pre-Ottoman period, see Goitein (1978, 3:83); and Jirjis (1999:47–53). For the Ottoman period, see ʿAfīfī (1992:230–40); Afifi (1996:203–7); and Jirjis (1999:60–2). Compare to the use that Christians and Jews made of the Muslim *waqf* in late Ottoman Palestine, Shaham (1991:467–71); and the recourse that Egyptian Jews had to the shariʿa courts during the first half of the twentieth century, Shaham (1995: especially 125–32).

[15] These grounds were included in the Orthodox-Copt internal codification of personal status from 1938 but it was resented by the Coptic religious establishment. See Fawzī (1994:86–7); and Ghattas (1991).

Part Two: The Court in Session—The Case is Presented and Discussed

The second part of the court document is the protocol of the lawsuit (*al-waqāʾiʿ*, or *waqāʾiʿ al-daʿwā*). This is a summary, probably dictated by the qadi to his clerk, of all court discussions that took place prior to the issuance of the decision. This summary includes the arguments of the parties, the evidence brought by each of them to support his or her claim, the inquiries of the qadi, and the intermediate decisions made by the court during this stage. From the social historian's point of view, this is the most promising part of the document, but at the same time it is to some extent disappointing, for the qadi does not usually reveal the full factual and social background of the case. He does so only to the extent that is needed for handing down his decision. For example, the memoranda presented to the court by each party, containing the full background of the dispute and the arguments, sometimes phrased in the litigants' own language, are missing. In his own concise and dry legal language the qadi paraphrases the expressions of the parties. In this process of "translation" a lot of social data are lost. The second part of our court document follows now:

> In the Shariʿa Summary Court of Samālūṭ, the appellant {Yūnān Sharābīn} claimed against the respondent {Qadīsa bt. Ḥannā} that she had been his wife by a valid marriage; on February 18, 1926, he had triply divorced her by way of a declaration in front of the abovementioned court. Then, on March 7, 1926, the same court ordered him to pay her maintenance. He asked the court to cancel this obligation on the grounds that both of them were dhimmis, and that through the talaq she was irrevocably repudiated from him and did not have to observe a waiting period (. . . *wa-biʾl-ṭalāq bānat minhu wa-lā ʿidda ʿalayhā*) [henceforth, I use "w.p." for "waiting period"]. Her representative[16] asked [the court] to turn down the lawsuit on the grounds that [1] it contradicted the rules of the Islamic shariʿa, because the parties had not converted to Islam and therefore the rules of talaq were not applicable to them; and [2] it contradicted Christian law (*al-sharīʿa al-Masīḥiyya*), in which talaq is prohibited except for specific reasons; [he quoted . . .] "we [Muslims] were ordered to judge [between the dhimmis] according to their own law (*wa-qad umirnā biʾl-ḥukm bi-mā yuwāfiqu sharīʿatahum*)." Then, he [viz., Qadīsa's representative] turned away from this [statement] by saying that the talaq had not canceled the

[16] The name of the proxy and his religious affiliation are not mentioned in the document.

prescribed maintenance. The court, on August 22, 1926, turned down the plaintiff's claim, arguing that the fact that the parties had applied to the court was an indicator that they agreed to [the application of] Islamic law [to their case] (. . . *dalīl al-riḍā bi-aḥkām al-Islām*). [The court continued that] the Ṣāḥibān [Abū Ḥanīfa's disciples, Abū Yūsuf and Muḥammad al-Shaybānī, henceforth Sahiban] held that a dhimmi's wife [i.e., divorcee] has to observe the w.p. under any circumstances, while the Imam Abū Ḥanīfa [henceforth, Abu Hanifa] holds that it [the w.p.] is required [only] with respect to the continuity of maintenance. The one who lost the case [Yūnān] appealed the verdict on September 4, 1926, and the appeal was registered on the following day. As a justification for the appeal, he said that the respondent was a dhimmi and therefore did not have to observe a w.p. following the talaq and was not entitled to maintenance. He [further] said that she was not pregnant, that both of them were Orthodox-Copts, and that they were persisting in their religious [Christian] belief and in their [Orthodox] rite (. . . *lā yazālāni muṣirrīna ʿalā dīnihimā wa-madhhabihimā*); [On these grounds] he asked to cancel the appealed verdict and to hand down a decision cancelling the prescribed maintenance.

Part Three: The Court Hands Down the Decision

The third part of the court document is the judgment, titled "the court" (*al-maḥkama*). In its first part, the longer one, the qadi presents the legal reasoning and the legal authorities on which he has based his decision. The absence of such reasoning renders the judgment void (art. 279 of the 1910 Ordinance). Following the decision's reasoning is the verdict, usually very short, which starts with the phrase "For these reasons" (*fa-li-hādhā*). The third part of our case study follows now:

Following the proceedings at law, the inspection of the documents and the legal deliberation concerning this:

Since the appeal has been submitted and registered before the statutory deadline;

And since the appealed verdict concerns the subject matter and it is permissible to appeal it;

And since it is agreed that the parties are Orthodox Christians, that they married each other according to their religion, and that the appellant subsequently divorced the respondent unilaterally on the abovementioned date by way of a declaration in front of the Shariʿa Summary Court of Samālūṭ;

And since it is agreed that the sect to whom the parties belong is dhimmi. There is a dispute among the Hanafi imams concerning the obligation of a dhimmi's divorcee to observe a w.p.: the Sahiban held that the w.p. is incumbent upon her because *ahl al-dhimma* took upon themselves our [viz., Islam's] laws through the dhimma contract and therefore it is required that these laws apply to them; the Imam [Abu Hanifa] agreed with them with respect to the pregnant divorcee. He obligated her to observe the w.p. until she gives birth, because the marriage-bed exists (*al-firāsh qā'im*);[17] if she did not have to observe the w.p., she would have been permitted to marry [another husband], and the paternity of her child would be questioned as a result of this marriage. He [viz., Abu Hanifa] therefore made the w.p. obligatory in order to protect the right of the child. He [however] opposed them [viz., the Sahiban] in the case in which she [the dhimmi's divorcee] is not pregnant; he held that if, according to their [viz., the dhimmis'] religion, she [the divorcee] does not have to observe a w.p., then she does not have to observe it, because the meaning of the w.p. is of worship (*ʿibāda*) and closeness [to Allāh] (*qurba*); it is impossible to make [the w.p.] obligatory as the husband's right because [as a dhimmi] it is not part of his belief; [it is impossible to make the w.p.] obligatory as the right of Allāh (*ḥaqqan li-Allāh*) because they [the dhimmis] were not addressed [by Allāh] with anything which is worship or closeness [to Allāh], and we [Muslims] were ordered to leave them [the dhimmis] [judge among themselves] according to their belief. The preponderant opinion (*rājiḥ*) in the [Hanafi] school is that of the Imam and the school texts follow his opinion (*wa-ʿalayhi mutūn al-fiqh*) {consult *al-Durr*; Ibn ʿĀbidīn, part II, the section on the marriage of an infidel (*Bāb nikāḥ al-kāfir*) and part III, towards the end of the section on the w.p. (*Bāb al-ʿidda*); *al-Badā'iʿ*, part II, the section on "any marriage permissible to Muslims is permissible to *ahl al-dhimma*" and part III, the section on "as for one who is one of the subordinates" (*tawābiʿ*)};

And since, following this clarification, it is necessary to investigate whether the talaq pronounced by the appellant was a valid divorce, causing an irrevocable repudiation without an obligation to observe a w.p., or was a void divorce, carrying no legal consequences;

And since the Islamic jurists did not clarify what is meant by [the phrase] "talaq[18] of a wife by her dhimmi husband": Is this a divorce that is valid according to his [the dhimmi's] religion and belief, or is this a talaq that is recognized by the Islamic shariʿa? According to the principle of the Sahiban, i.e., that by the dhimma contract he [viz.,

[17] According to the principle that "the child belongs to the marriage bed" (*al-walad lil-firāsh*), any child born to a married woman is affiliated to her husband.

[18] An adequate translation of the term "talaq" in the decision is problematic, since in some places it denotes the Islamic unilateral form of divorce and in other places it denotes other, not unilateral and non-Islamic, forms of divorce. I left the term "talaq" as it is whenever the context is the Islamic use, and used "divorce" for the other contexts.

the dhimmi husband] takes upon himself the laws of Islam, it is required to understand the term "talaq" as the talaq recognized by the Islamic shariʿa, the rules of which he took upon himself through the dhimma contract; [on the contrary,] according to the principle laid down by the Imam, i.e., that the rights of Allāh were not addressed to the dhimmis and that we [Muslims] were ordered to leave them [the dhimmis] [judge among themselves] according to their belief, it is required to understand the term "talaq" as a divorce that is recognized by their own religion. This [conclusion] is [based] on the grounds that the Imam—if he holds that the divorcee does not have to observe the w.p. {If they [viz., the dhimmis] believe that there is no w.p. after divorce} since it is impossible to make it [the w.p.] obligatory as the husband's right, because it is not part of his belief, or as the right of Allāh, because the rights of Allāh were not addressed to them [viz., the dhimmis]—it is required to interpret his [Abu Hanifa's] understanding of the term "talaq" as the [form of] divorce that is part of their belief, because this is the divorce that, they believe, is not followed by a w.p. As for the [Islamic] talaq, which is not part of their religion and which they do not consider as divorce, they regard it as null and void, resulting in neither a w.p. nor the absence of a w.p. This conclusion is supported by the fact that the Imam based the rules regarding them [viz., the dhimmis] on their own beliefs, in the sections on marriage and divorce, as attested by *al-Mabsūṭ, al-Fatḥ, al-Badāʾiʿ*, and the respected works of the school (*muʿtabarāt kutub al-madhhab*);

And since, by consulting the opinions of the scholars of the Christian religion and their books, it has become known that the principle of Christian belief is the absence of divorce, except on the grounds of adultery; the husband, however, absolutely does not have the right to unilaterally divorce his wife because the divorce is the right of the church, represented by the religious spiritual head. Later, their scholars extracted from the texts of their sacred books principles that permit divorce under circumstances different from adultery; it is, however, absolutely forbidden that a divorce takes place without the knowledge of the religious spiritual head. If a man divorces his wife, the divorce is null; if the divorce was declared by the religious head, the wife is separated from her husband, she does not have to observe a w.p., and she is permitted to marry another man, unless the divorce was on the grounds of adultery, and the divorcee is not pregnant. If she is pregnant, she has to observe the w.p. until she gives birth {consult the issues related to divorce in *Kitāb al-aḥwāl al-shakhṣiyya lil-ṭawāʾif al-Urthūdhuksiyya*; the studies on divorce and its consequences in *al-Majmūʿ al-Ṣafawī* by Ibn al-ʿAssāl; the statutes (*qawānīn*) of the Church; and the New Testament};

And since the parties acknowledge that they still adhere to their religion, the talaq pronounced by the husband has no effect because it is not included in his religion and belief; this divorce does not effectuate either a w.p. or the absence of a w.p., because the belief in it [i.e., in unilateral divorce] according to his religion is nonexistent;

And since, on top of that, the court holds that the appellant's lawsuit (*kaydiyya*) is malicious, and that he designed it in order to cause harm to the respondent without having a right [to that], since according to his religion she is still his wife; what he pronounced is not a divorce carrying any effect according to his religion and belief, to which he still adheres. It is required to turn down a malicious suit;

And since, on the basis of the above-mentioned [arguments], the decision of the Court of Summary Justice to turn down the suit was essentially a correct decision, for the reasons mentioned [by the appeal court] and not for the reasons mentioned by the Court of Summary Justice. The understanding of the Court of Summary Justice was that the opinion of the Imam—that the divorcee of a dhimmi does not have to observe a w.p.—refers only to the permission given to her to remarry immediately after the divorce, and does not refer to the cancellation of the divorcee's maintenance. The [appeal] court does not agree with the understanding of the Court of Summary Justice because the legal texts deny this understanding.[19]

For all these reasons, we decided, in the absence of the parties, to accept the appeal formally, and substantially to confirm the appealed decision and to turn down the appeal.

The qadis' reference to Hanafi sources on talaq of a dhimmi wife and its legal effects

As mentioned before, according to article 280 of the 1931 Ordinance, every personal status matter that is not covered by Egyptian statutory legislation must be judged according to the preponderant Hanafi opinion. The first and only direct reference by Egyptian codification to the non-Muslims' divorce took place in the framework of the 1931 Ordinance and was a procedural regulation rather than a point of positive law.[20] As a result, when a case involving a divorce between

[19] In other words, the Court of Summary Justice held that, according to Abu Hanifa, the dhimmi's divorcee was entitled to marry another man immediately after the divorce, but if she did not remarry, she was entitled to maintenance from her ex-husband until the expiration of the w.p. On the contrary, the appeal court (the Court of First Instance) held that, according to Abu Hanifa, the dhimmi's divorcee was entitled to remarry immediately, and did not have a right to maintenance from her ex-husband under any circumstances.

[20] Paragraph seven of article 99 of the 1931 Ordinance states that the shariʿa courts are not authorized to entertain a divorce suit (*daʿwā al-ṭalāq*) submitted by a

non-Muslims was submitted to a shariʿa court prior to 1931 (as in our case study), the qadi, as a default, had to apply the preponderant opinion of the Hanafi school. The preponderant Hanafi opinion on family matters involving Christians is not always clear, due to differences of opinion between the Imam, who represents a tolerant and permissive attitude towards the dhimmis, and the Sahiban (especially Abū Yūsuf), who held a strict attitude in favor of a broad application of Islamic law to the dhimmis (Libson 2002). As a result, we find different approaches and opinions on these topics among twentieth-century Egyptian jurists and qadis.[21]

Our case study raises two disputed legal questions. The first concerns the meaning of the term talaq, as applied to dhimmis: does this term mean the Islamic talaq, that is, a unilateral divorce of a wife by her husband, or other forms of divorce that are recognized by the laws of the dhimmis? The second dispute within Hanafi sources concerns the question of whether a dhimmiyya who has been divorced by a dhimmi (or has become a widow) is obligated, like a Muslim divorcee, to observe the w.p., and, as a result, is entitled to maintenance during that period.

Regarding the first question, the Sahiban argued that divorce among dhimmis must be treated as if it is the Islamic talaq. Abu Hanifa, however, used the term talaq in this context as meaning

---

non-Muslim against his spouse, unless divorce was recognized by the religious laws of both spouses (. . . *illā idhā kānā yadīnāni bi-wuqūʿ al-ṭalāq*).

The explanatory memorandum of the 1931 Ordinance states that this piece of legislation was made necessary by the fact that, prior to the promulgation of this law, the shariʿa courts used to affirm the validity of talaq between non-Muslim spouses. This judicial strategy caused prejudice to Christian women, whose communal law did not recognize divorce. Such divorcees (the memorandum implicitly referred to Catholics) were not permitted by their churches to remarry, and consequently were left in a desperate situation unable to remarry, on the one hand, and not entitled to maintenance, on the other. The legislation was intended to prevent the occurrence of such social evils.

The ways in which this piece of legislation is applied by the shariʿa courts are beyond the scope of the present study. Suffice it to say that article 99 has left unclear the question how the term "talaq" should be understood by the courts when it refers to non-Muslims. This continuing ambiguity resulted in a variety of interpretations given to article 99 by different courts, similar to the situation which prevailed prior to 1931, as our case study demonstrates (see below).

[21] For essays in legal periodicals concerning these debates, see Bakhīt (1930), al-Najjār (1930), and al-Marāghī (1936). Bakhīt and al-Najjār say specifically that they wrote their essays as a response to the demands of Coptic clergymen to prohibit the shariʿa courts from judging divorce cases of Christians and consequently to punish qadis who did so.

only the forms of divorce that existed in the laws of the dhimmis. The Samālūṭ Court of Summary Justice, which gave the first ruling in the case, followed the opinion of the Sahiban.[22] However, the Bani Sueif Court of First Instance, when it discussed Qadīsa's appeal, held that the view of Abu Hanifa is the preponderant one in the school and rejected that of the Sahiban.[23] Following Abu Hanifa's reasoning, the qadis referred to Christian legal texts,[24] to see what forms of divorce existed there. They found that the only grounds for divorce mentioned in the Old Testament is adultery (*zinā*), and that in later Christian legal literature additional grounds were added.[25] For a Christian divorce to be valid, the court argued, the church authorities must issue it and the husband may not perform it unilaterally. Since Yūnān and Qadīsa were Copts, the unilateral divorce initiated by Yūnān was void and did not carry with it any legal consequence. Reversing the decision of the lower court, the appeal court regarded Yūnān and Qadīsa as being still legally married. Yūnān's suit was rejected and he was required to continue providing for Qadīsa, as her husband.

Regarding the second question, Abu Hanifa and the Sahiban concurred that, if the Christian divorcee is pregnant, she must observe

[22] For additional cases in which qadis followed the opinion of the Sahiban, see Anon. 1918. *Majallat al-Aḥkām al-Sharʿiyya*, 12:186–7; anon.1930. ibid. MS 2:656–60.

[23] For an example of another court who followed the same approach, see MS 1:30–1 no. 8—Qalyūb, March 16, 1929.

[24] The Christian legal sources cited in our court case appear in a descending chronological order. In chronological order, after the New Testament, the most important compilation of Coptic family law is *al-Majmūʿ al-Ṣafawī* (dated 1239), written by al-Ṣafī ibn al-'Assāl at the request of the 74th Patriarch, Kyrillos (or Cyril) the 3rd, known as Ibn Laqlaq. The period of Ibn Laqlaq was generally characterized by legislative activity. One of its products was *Kitāb al-qawānīn al-khuṣūṣiyya*, ascribed to Ibn Laqlaq himself. *Al-Majmūʿ* of Ibn al-ʿAssāl remained the most authoritative compilation until the late 19th century. In the 1890s, the Egyptian Ministry of Justice required the Patriarch Kyrillos the 6th to submit anew the personal status code of his community. Asked by the Patriarch to complile the code, Hegumenos Jirjis Philutawus (ʿAwad), the head of St. Mark church in Cairo, wrote in 1896 the code known as *al-Khulāṣa al-qānūniyya fī'l-aḥwāl al-shakhṣiyya li-kanīsat al-aqbāṭ al-Urthūdhuksiyyīn*, which was substantially based on al-*Majmūʿ* of Ibn al-ʿAssāl. On the development of the sources for the Coptic family law, see Nimmar and Ḥabashī (1957:90–3); Salāma (1958:110); Ṣādiq (1998:9–12); Ghattas (1991:1941–43). Prior to the promulgation of the 1938 internal codification, the Coptic communal courts based their decisions on *Al-Majmūʿ* and on *al-Khulāṣa*. See Askarus (1966/67:531).

[25] The Coptic late legal sources, mainly *al-Majmūʿ* and *al-Khulāṣa*, refer to additional grounds for divorce, for example: abandonment of Christianity by a spouse; absence or imprisonment; disease; danger for life and physical damage. See Jundī 1993, 66–7, 73–4, 77, 80, 85, 96–8, 115, 119–20.

the w.p. until she gives birth (and, as a result, she must be supported by her former husband during this period), out of concern for the paternity of her child. They differed, however, with respect to a non-pregnant divorcee or a widow. Abu Hanifa exempted her from the obligation to observe a w.p. if her sectarian law does not require that (which implies that she is not entitled to w.p. maintenance). By contrast, the Sahiban, according to their principle of comprehensive application of the shariʿa to dhimmis, argued that she must observe a w.p. as if she were a Muslim, and therefore is entitled to w.p. maintenance. In our case study, the Samālūṭ court followed the opinion of the Sahiban, while the appeal court followed that of Abu Hanifa.[26] We find this splitting up of opinions in many similar cases appearing before the shariʿa courts.[27]

Two of the Hanafi fiqh works to which Egyptian qadis resorted in our case study are classical[28] works: *al-Mabsūṭ*, i.e., *Kitāb al-mabsūṭ* by al-Sarakhsī (d. ca. 1096); and *al-badāʾiʿ*, i.e., *Kitāb al-badāʾiʿ waʾl-ṣanāʾiʿ fī tartīb al-sharāʾiʿ* of al-Kāsānī (d. 1191). Three of the works are postclassical: *al-Fatḥ*, i.e., *Fatḥ al-qadīr* by Ibn al-Humām (d. 1457); al-*Durr*, i.e., *al-durr al-mukhtār* by Ḥaṣkafī (d. 1677); and Ibn ʿĀbidīn, i.e., *Radd al-muḥtār ʿalā al-durr al-mukhtār* by Ibn ʿĀbidīn (d. 1836). The use of postclassical Hanafi works was prevalent among contemporary Egyptian qadis.[29]

Conclusion—Shopping for Legal Forums in Pluralistic Settings

Judicial disputation is an interactive process in which litigants maneuver in order to maximize their advantages and to best serve their interests. This process is not harmonious due to the fact that liti-

---

[26] For the differences between Abu Hanifa and Abū Yūsuf concerning the w.p. of a dhimmiyya, see Libson (2002:355–6, 366–8, 370–1).

[27] For other examples of qadis who hold that the dominant opinion of the school is that of Abu Hanifa, see MS 4:776–8 no. 246—Qinā, April 9, 1932; MS 12 (9–10):56–61 no. 15—Cairo Court of First Instance, May 22, 1941. For qadis who hold the alternative opinion or who engage in compromising the apparently contradictory opinions, see MS 17 (1–2):26–9 no. 5—Cairo Court of First Instance, August 31, 1942; MS 21 (7–8):395–7 no. 75—Asyūṭ, January 9, 1947; MS 26:127–31 no. 22—Cairo Court of First Instance, May 31, 1955; MS 26:132–49 no. 23—Rūḍ al-Faraj, December 25, 1951.

[28] I follow here the periodization of Hanafi sources used by Libson (1997:141–2).

[29] See, for example, the works used by the prominent Egyptian qadi-jurist Aḥmad Muḥammad Shākir (d. 1958), in Shaham (1999:448–9).

gants have to take into consideration contradictory interests. Availability of various legal forums empowers the litigants, who practice forum shopping, but weakens the state and its legal system.[30] Anthropological studies conducted on judicial strategies in situations of legal pluralism have established that litigants create hierarchal order of their preferences. The first preference is to settle the dispute at the local level. The litigant who threatens to transfer the conflict from the local to the national level puts pressure on his or her adversary in order to get a better settlement at the local level. Before transferring the conflict from the local to a higher level, the litigant has to consider the implications of his or her move in terms of social relationships, availability of resources, psychological factors and economic cost.[31]

The Egyptian Christian case study fits well into this pattern. The local level for settling familial disputes among Copts was the sectarian court. The party who took the dispute to the shariʿa court escalated the confrontation and thereby pressured his or her adversary. It should be emphasized that the sharʿi legal system was not foreign to Christians. They demonstrated impressive knowledge of Islamic legal practices. Moreover, their cultural-legal norms and visions of familial structures and gender relations were close to those of the Muslim majority (Qattan 1999:433; Tessler 1978:368). On the one hand, the resort to the shariʿa courts promised material advantages, namely laws which were more convenient than Christian laws and an efficient enforcement of court verdicts. On the other hand, a Christian who applied to a shariʿa court had to consider the negative religious, social and political implications of his or her strategy. Applying to a Muslim court signified the infringement of Christian religious law, the breaking of communal consensus and the encouragement of state intervention in the autonomy of the Christian community. My impression is that considerations of personal benefits were often stronger than moral, religious, or social commitments. Egyptian Copts took from the shariʿa what best suited their needs without obliging themselves to the shariʿa as a whole (Afifi 1996:207).

[30] For a definition of forum shopping, see Dupret (1999:34–5). See also Nader and Todd (1979:16, 22–3).

[31] Nader and Todd (1979:23–4, 26–9). Nader studied Mexican Indians from the Zapotec tribe who were colonized by the Spanish. They maneuver between the village court, which applies local customs, and the district court, which applies the national Mexican law. See Nader (1990:244).

My suggestion for further study is to consider forum shopping among Christians in the wider context of forum shopping among Muslims, for example, between the four Sunni schools of law. Writing on the administration of courts in Ottoman Cairo, Hanna, basing her discussion mainly on court records, says:

> The familiarity between the people and the courts worked both ways. On the one hand, the qadi was part of the culture of the people around him, and, on the other hand, the general public—not only the "educated" class of shaykhs with specialized knowledge—had some familiarity with the system, how it worked, and what to expect from it . . . Even the legal doctrines of the four schools of law seem to have been understood by the people. What we regard today as a very formidable and specialized area of knowledge—the various distinctions between the Hanafi, Shafi'i, Maliki, and Hanbali schools of law, in matters, for instance, of personal status or transactions—seems to have been common knowledge at that time. It was not unusual for one person to buy a house one day according to Hanbali law and get married next day according to Maliki or Shafi'i law. By assessing the specific differences between the schools of law with regard to property, marriage, or other matters, people deliberately chose the school that best defended their interests in any particular case or transaction.[32]

Forum shopping between the Sunni schools is certainly not identical to the Christian case. Indeed, maneuvering between the schools did not carry the same negative image, because all four schools are equally Orthodox. Crossing the borders between the schools was not a severe breaking of religious, moral or social taboos, except for cases in which this practice was exaggerated to cynical degrees. What I do wish to suggest however is that this atmosphere of shopping for legal forums among the Muslim majority had its effect on the

[32] Hanna (1995:53). Marcus (1989:109), studying the shari'a court records of 18th century Aleppo, also speaks about ". . . the interplay of jurisdictions and the wide range of practices that existed within the community." For additional examples of forum shopping during the Mamluk period, see Jackson (1996:150–2); Winter (2001:204); Escovitz (1984:39 [note 127], 136–7, 139, 150–2, 158, 160); and, during the Ottoman period, see Sonbol (1996:237 [especially note 3]); Nahal (1979:46–7); Imber (1997:186–7, 208); Peters (forthcoming/b), especially p. 9. More recent findings are those of the French scholar Henry who, on the basis of his anthropological studies in the Maghreb, developed the notion of "variance juridique," namely that litigants make use of various inter-related legal systems, according to their political and social strategies. See Thielmann (1999:49–50). Another good example is Ido Shahar's recent study on Palestinians in the Jerusalem area who shop between the Israeli and the Palestinian family law courts. See Shahar (2000:67, 71, 73–6).

non-Muslim minorities, who formed part of the same legal culture. If we assume that minorities are usually affected by the legal practices of the majority, we should not be surprised to find that Christians considered their sectarian family law as one 'madhhab', while Islamic family law was considered as an alternative 'madhhab', ready for utilization according to considerations of convenience.

PART IV

RECORDING PROCEDURES AND EVIDENCE

CHAPTER NINETEEN

TWELVE COURT CASES ON THE APPLICATION OF PENAL LAW UNDER THE ALMORAVIDS*

Delfina Serrano

The purpose of my essay is to explore legal practice in matters of penal law during the period of Almoravid rule over al-Andalus and the far Maghrib (last quarter of the 11th–first half of the 12th centuries). Only a few studies have been published on the application of penal law in this region of the Islamic world. Much of this work has focused on the Cordovan judicial administration of the Caliphate and Taifa periods (10th–11th centuries), as well as the Nasrid kingdom of Granada (13th–15th centuries) and caution must be exercised as we attempt to extend the results of previous research to other geographical and chronological settings in the Muslim West.

Court records from the Muslim West are scarce but a wide range of sources to study legal practice is available, e.g., fatwā collections, model *shurūṭ* formularies, manuals for the instruction of *qāḍīs*, commentaries on early sources of the Mālikī school, treatises on market inspection (*ḥisba*), etc. Fatwā collections provide rich information about legal procedure and the circumstances in which litigation took place. One must bear in mind, however, that these sources were compiled with the aim of instructing the jurists, not of preserving documents; we encounter a certain level of subjectivity on the part of their authors and find few references to judgments. Together with commentaries, model *shurūṭ* formularies and manuals for the instruction of *qāḍīs*, fatwās are useful for the study of doctrine and change.

This essay draws upon twelve legal cases involving penal law excerpted from two sources: *Madhāhib al-ḥukkām fī nawāzil al-aḥkām* and *al-Taʿrīf bi-l-qāḍī ʿIyāḍ*. The author of these texts was the Mālikī jurist Muḥammad b. ʿIyāḍ (b. Ceuta, ca. 1130; d. Granada or Ceuta,

* This paper is part of my participation in the research project "Violencia y castigo en sociedades islámicas pre-modernas (al-Andalus y el Magreb)," ref. BF 2002–00075. The author thanks D. Powers, the editors and M. Fierro for their comments on a previous version of this work.

1179), son of Qāḍī ʿIyāḍ (b. Ceuta, 1083; d. Marrakech, 1149.) The cases shed light on how ʿIyāḍ, the father, performed the functions of *qāḍī* and mufti. The *Madhāhib al-ḥukkām* is a collection of fatwās, issued at the request of, or by, ʿIyāḍ on actual legal cases (*nawāzil*), most of which took place during the period of Almoravid rule over al-Andalus and the far Maghrib. Muḥammad b. ʿIyāḍ compiled these fatwās in the first decades of Almohad domination (ca. 1160–1179).[1] Compared to other sources of the same genre, the *Madhāhib* represent an effort to adapt the compilation of fatwās to the requirements of the legal policy of the Almohads,[2] e.g., the need to explain the legal basis for an opinion and the legal discrepancies (*ikhtilāf*) affecting a certain legal subject. This concern is reflected in Ibn ʿIyāḍ's commentaries on the legal cases that he transmits. The *Taʿrīf* is dedicated to the personal and "professional" aspects of Qāḍī ʿIyāḍ's life. Together with al-Maqqarī's *Azhār al-riyāḍ fī akhbār ʿIyāḍ* (Rabat: 1978–1980, 5 vols.), the *Taʿrīf* is the richest available source of information on the biography of Qāḍī ʿIyāḍ.

The *Madhāhib al-ḥukkām* contains eleven cases dealing with penal law. Seven appear in the chapter on Qur'ānic sanctions (*ḥudūd*): there are three on slander (*qadhf, shatam, najah*), one on blasphemy (*istikhfāf bi-l-muslimīn wa-nabiyyi-him wa-kitābi-him*), one deals with rape (*ghaṣb*) and there are two on murder (*qatl*). Two cases appear in the chapter on ordinary crimes or torts (*jināyāt*)—one on corporal wounds to persons and one on damage to a beast.

A slander case appears in the chapter on testimonies (*al-shahādāt*); and a theft case (*sariqa, akhdh*) is found in the chapter on "claims and oaths" (*al-daʿāwī wa-l-aymān*). An additional case on wine-drinking (*sharb al-khamr*) has been excerpted from *Taʿrīf al-qāḍī ʿIyāḍ* (see appendix.) I have organized the analysis of the cases in four sections plus a concluding summary. Data drawn from other legal sources, which I consider helpful in explaining my main two sources, appear enclosed in brackets.

The court cases analyzed in this essay do not answer the question of variations in the competencies of different magistrates, either in the adjudication of the case or in the application of the penalty. Whereas similar sources (e.g., *al-Aḥkām al-kubrā* of Ibn Sahl, the

[1] On the history of the Almoravid and Almohad periods see Viguera (1997). On law and theology see Fierro (1997a). On the judiciary see Rodríguez Mediano (1997); Lagardère (1986) and El Hour (2000).

[2] On this policy see Fierro (1999:226–48).

Fatāwā of Ibn Rushd al-Jadd, al-Wansharīsī's *Mi'yār*) contain references to civil authorities, our two sources mention only the *qāḍī* and the judge (*ḥākim*), perhaps because Almoravid provincial and judicial administration did not respond to one and the same pattern. However, this is a question that requires further research.

According to the evidence that I have examined, Almoravid jurists were not concerned with the problem of who enjoyed judicial and executive powers in matters of penal law.[3] Rather, they questioned whether or not judges in charge of injustice, recusal, heritage, etc. (*naẓar . . . al-maẓālim wa-l-radd wa-l-tarika wa-ghayri-hā*) and a *qāḍī* who had been appointed by the local military governor but not appointed by the ruler (*qāḍī qaddama-hu qā'id al-balda wa-lam yuqaddim-hu al-amīr*) had the right to issue a judgment on matters falling under the "*qāḍī*'s exclusive competence" (*qaḍā' al-khuṣūṣ*).[4] The evidence of the *Madhāhib al-ḥukkām* shows that the application of penal law in the Almoravid period posed a series of problems that were connected, on the one hand, with the intricacies of Islamic procedural law and, on the other, with the difficulties created by certain restrictions and special rules that governed the criminal process. Judges knew that there was a difference between the "civil" and the penal process. However they were not sure how these differences operated in practice.[5] The problem became more complicated when equally valid but conflicting legal rules applied to a single case (*ikhtilāf*).

The fatwās contained in *Madhāhib al-ḥukkām* are organized according to their legal subject matter. As mentioned, Muḥammad b. 'Iyāḍ placed murder cases in the chapter on *ḥudūd*, instead of in the chapter on *jināyāt*. In this respect, he deviated from the practice of a majority of his colleagues—at least those I have consulted—who, when dealing with penal law, made a clear distinction between *ḥudūd* and *dimā'* on the one hand, and crimes subject to *adab* and *ta'zīr* punishments on the other.[6] Perhaps the murder cases that Ibn 'Iyāḍ

---

[3] Al-Wansharīsī, however, echoes this concern in his time: see *Mi'yār*, 2:411.

[4] See *Madhāhib al-ḥukkām*, 35.

[5] Similar uncertainties are documented among 12th century Ḥanafī jurists. See Johansen (1999b:400).

[6] Some authors divide *ḥudūd* into those affecting the rights of God and those affecting the rights of men. The first include neglect of religious duties such as prayer, fasting and pilgrimage and the commission of forbidden acts such as *zinā*, wine-drinking, theft, and brigandage. The latter include false accusation of fornication and *jināyāt* punished by retaliation or blood money; see al-Māwardī (1978), chapter "*fī aḥkām al-jarā'im*." For Averroes, *jināya* encompasses blood crimes (*dimā'*),

placed in the chapter on *ḥudūd* were actually *ḥirāba* cases in which the killer's intention to acquire the victim's property was deemed not worthy of mention.[7] Perhaps Muḥammad was trying to differentiate between public and private concerns, murder being considered a crime whose public character prevails.[8] This might be a personal stance or the result of the legal policy of his time, but this is a hypothesis that, in the present state of research, I cannot confirm.[9]

Institutional and Jurisdictional Considerations

The *qāḍī*, whose territorial jurisdiction is referred to by the term "*balad*," was responsible for cases of slander, blasphemy, rape, wine-drinking, murder, and wounds. A judge (*ḥākim*), whose territorial jurisdiction is referred to by the term "*jiha*," presided over a case of theft (see case no. 8). The question of what was the relationship between territorial jurisdiction and the presiding magistrate and between a *qāḍī* and a judge is difficult to answer. The term "*balad*" refers to ʿIyāḍ's area of competence, either the city of Ceuta or Granada, with their respective districts (*aʿmāl*). In our source, *jiha* signifies a rural district under the jurisdiction of a judge, encompassing one or several villages (*qarya*), while in the collection of fatwās of Ibn Rushd al-Jadd, *jiha* designates the territorial jurisdiction of a *qāḍī*, who was in charge of "two *jiha*s inhabited by more than 1000 men."[10] Our texts do not indicate that the rural judge was dependent on any judicial authority other than the chief *qāḍī* (*qāḍī al-jamāʿa*),

ḥudūd and offenses punished with *taʿzīr* and *adab*. Some modern writers such as Abū l-ʿAlāʾ al-Mawdūdī (Pakistan, 1903–1979) assert that crimes that affect the security of an Islamic order should be punished with prescribed penalties (*ḥudūd*), see Siddiqi (1981:202, n. 57). In the opinion of A.F. Bahnisi (1965:17), in *qadhf* and crimes subject to *talio*, the rights of God and those of men merge. In the former, the rights of God prevail, while in the latter the private character dominates.

[7] Mālik's definition of *ḥirāba* includes murder with the intention of taking the victim's property, independent of whether the crime takes place on a highway or in a town. See Safwat (1982:165), drawing on *Sharḥ al-Zurqānī*, 8:109. On *ḥirāba* see now Abou El-Fadl (2001: esp. 135–8).

[8] On murder as a crime in which private and public interests merge see al-Māwardī (1978:268) and Johansen (1999:378–86, 394–409). Also see F. Rodríguez Mediano (1996:614–5).

[9] On the state of this research see Fierro (1997a:460–6).

[10] See *Fatāwā Ibn Rushd*, 3:1609.

although it might be that the *ḥākim* in case no. 8 was ʿIyāḍ's deputy.[11]

Our texts shed light on the role played by *qāḍī*s in the exercise of their "ordinary" and "extraordinary" competences in the application of penal law. An example of the latter was the "redress of injustices" committed by state officials (see no. 4). This competence was not performed by *qāḍī*s directly; rather, the Almoravid *amīr*s granted special audiences in order to hear the complaints of their subjects against personnel attached to their service, either military, judicial or administrative. The prince did not issue a judgment on the matter but submitted the case to one of his *qāḍī*s.[12]

The *qāḍī* normally acted on his own, except in *ḥadd* cases that might require the application of the death penalty. These cases, according to Ibn Rushd al-Jadd, had to be reported to the *qāḍī al-jamāʿa*.[13] The sultan had to be notified only if the sentence was crucifixion or amputation [as punishment for banditry].[14] When there was a disagreement as regards evidence, e.g., which party should bear the burden of proof in a case of slander (see no. 1), and the *ḥadd* did not entail a death sentence, a fatwā might be solicited from the *qāḍī al-jamāʿa*. If he recommended the application of a *ḥadd* punishment, his opinion was submitted to the muftis attached to the presiding *qāḍī*'s court (*majlis*). If they agreed with the opinion of the chief *qāḍī*, they would endorse it with the statement: "The answer of the *qāḍī l-jamāʿa* is correct". Obviously, a *ḥadd* punishment in the aforementioned circumstances could not be issued without the agreement of the chief *qāḍī*; that his *fatwā* had still to be endorsed by the *mushāwarūn* shows that matters of statutory penal law were handled with extreme care.

Composition of the Court

Courts were made up of the presiding *qāḍī*, the muftis of his *shūrā*, professional witnesses and the *qāḍī*'s assistants. Professional witnesses served as "public prosecutor" in a case on wine-drinking (see no. 7);

---

[11] On the Almoravid *ḥākim* as a magistrate subordinate to the *qāḍī*, see Müller (2000:69–71).

[12] See Serrano Ruano (2000:215–6).

[13] See Ibn Rushd al-Jadd (1987, 3:1394–5).

[14] See al-Khushanī (1914:220); Ibn ʿAbdūn (1948:77); and Peláez (2000:394–5 n. 50 and 396 n. 59).

we do not know how many such witnesses there were in ʿIyāḍ's court. Our sources do not provide any information regarding the exercise of the functions of the judicial secretary (*kātib*), although we know that during ʿIyāḍ's qadiship in Granada, his nephew, al-Zāhid Abū ʿAbd Allāh, fulfilled this function.[15] *Qāḍīs* had assistants (*aʿwān*) who, besides sending messages and judicial summonses, were in charge of bringing the accused to court (see no. 10).

Together with their role as legal advisers to the *qāḍī*, muftis appear as legal advisers of individuals (see no. 6). With respect to the judge (*ḥākim*), we have no details about the composition of his court.

Court Procedure

Claims

In cases involving slander, claims were made by private initiative. Usually the person who had been slandered would denounce the slanderer in the presence of the *qāḍī*. In case no. 2 this meant appearing before the *qāḍī* with a document in which testimony against the defendant had been written down and signed, i.e, the making of a claim and simultaneously producing evidence in support of this claim. Once the *qāḍī* had certified the document (*wa-thabata ʿalay-hi ʿaqd bi-hādhihi l-mathāla ʿinda qāḍī l-makān*), the claim was accepted and the defendant summoned to court (*iʿdhār*). Unfortunately, the procedure followed in order to certify the document is not described.

Likewise, nonlethal corporal wounds, nonviolent theft (*akhdh*) and damage to livestock were prosecuted by private initiative.

The party who denounces is called the *ṭālib*. It seems that the term *muddaʿī* was avoided in order to prevent any misunderstandings if and when the defendant became the plaintiff (*muddaʿī*) for the fact that had to be legally established, i.e., to avoid confusion between what a modern Spanish jurist would call the "material plaintiff" (*ṭālib*) and the "formal plaintiff" (*muddaʿī*).

Blasphemy and wine-drinking were prosecuted through public initiative. In case no. 5, a group of persons whose connection with the judiciary is probable, although not clearly stated, testified:

---

[15] See ʿIyāḍ (1989:74/206) and ʿIyāḍ (1982:11, 106, 108 and 114).

> that a *dhimmī* had insulted (*istakhaffa*) the Muslims, their Prophet and their Book.[16] However, the local *qāḍī* (*qāḍī baladi-hi*) did not certify anything against him (*lam yuthabbit shay' 'alay-hi*) nor did he investigate the issue. Indeed, the *dhimmī*'s protectors appeared in order to defend him (*ẓaharat muḥāmatu-hu la-hu*). Subsequently the man moved to a different area (*fa-waqa'a fī balad ākhar*) whose *qāḍī*, presumably 'Iyāḍ, ordered the man's detention (*thaqafa-hu*) as well as an inquiry into the matter, disregarding (*lam yaltafit*) the action taken by the aforementioned *qāḍī*.[17] [The grounds on which this detention took place—witness testimony or circumstantial evidence—is not specified.] As a result of the judicial investigation, a group of trustworthy people from the area (*thiqāt al-balad*) of the provenance of the *dhimmī*, sent a letter to the *qāḍī* (*khāṭaba-hu*). They told him that they possessed common knowledge (*istifāḍa*) regarding the *dhimmī*'s conduct, and that some of them had borne witness thereto. This was mentioned to the *qāḍī* by one of the persons whom he accepted, who had written it down [viz., an account of the facts] in a document (*wa-dhakara dhālika la-hu man waththaqa-hu mimman yaqbalu-hum qāḍī dhālika l-balad.*)

I infer (1) that the document was not a *kitāb al-qāḍī ilā l-qāḍī*,[18] and (2) before certifying it, the receiving *qāḍī* (a) established the rectitude of the witnesses whose testimonies had been recorded in the document and (b) had the man who had written down the document and submitted it to him "mention" [i.e., attest] that the content of the document corresponded to the facts, i.e., that it was common knowledge that the *dhimmī* had insulted (*istakhaffa*) the Muslims, their Prophet and their Book.

In case no. 6, a group of Muslims "from among people of integrity and others" submitted to questioning a woman who disappeared from her family and was absent for several days. Subsequently, in front of the *qāḍī* the woman denounced a man for having raped her. It seems to me that she was obliged to do so to avoid a *zinā*-accusation from the "people of integrity and others" who questioned her. The *qāḍī* who heard this case was aware of the special restrictions of statutory penal law according to which declarations made during the questioning are not binding. 'Iyāḍ clarified this point as

---

[16] The version of this fatwā collected in al-Wansharīsī (1981–83, 2:526–27) specifies that he had insulted (*sabba*) the Book.

[17] Cf. Johansen (2002:178–9): "According to classical Sunni doctrine, the *qāḍī* should establish the facts on the basis of the testimony of witnesses and the acknowledgments of the defendant. He is not entitled to initiate an investigation: he has no power of *inquisition*."

[18] On which see Hallaq (1999).

follows: The woman's accusation would be inconsistent if, [before the questioning], she arrived crying and shouting that she had been raped by one man but later, in the presence of the *qāḍī*, she said that she had been raped by another man.

Murder could be claimed either on public or private initiative[19] (see nos. 9 and 10).

Pretrial detention

Claims relating to rape, blasphemy, nonviolent theft (*akhdh*) and murder, if accepted as valid by the *qāḍī*, resulted in the imprisonment of the accused. In the case of murder, the accused could avoid imprisonment if, in the absence of conclusive proofs against him, he was able to establish an alibi and give assurance of his good reputation, e.g., he had witnesses that "on the night of the murder he had performed the prayer of the first quarter of the night (*ʿatama*) with them (viz., the witnesses) at their local mosque and that he did not deserve that accusation (*wa-anna-hu mimman lā yalīq bi-hi mā rumiya bi-hi min dhālika*) (see no. 10).

Once the accused had been imprisoned, however, even when he could present testimonies of his good conduct, release was dependent on consultation with muftis, at least when the accusation involved murder and nonviolent theft (see no. 10 and 8).

No other coercive measures are cited.

Testimonies, Oaths and Legal Presumptions

Mālikī jurists debated the probative value of the declaration of a single witness.[20] According to ʿIyāḍ, a judge was entitled to accept it as evidence of slander or not. In the former case, the bearer of the right (*ṣāḥib al-ḥaqq*) was not required to swear an oath in order to complete the declaration of a single witness. He had to swear an oath only when the declaration of one witness was accepted as a valid proof in favor of the defendant, given that the plaintiff was not required to swear an oath by virtue of a mere claim.[21] If the

[19] Cf. Schacht (1964:177).

[20] On Mālikī jurists' disagreement with regard to this question see ʿIyāḍ (1989:79–81/210–2). Also see Carmona (1998:75–8) and Masud (1999).

[21] According to the majority opinion, the doctrine practiced by Mālik, his companions and the seven *faqīh*s of Medina was that oath for the mere claim is not

testimony of one witness strengthened the argument of the plaintiff, then the defendant was obliged to swear an oath. If he refused, he was imprisoned until he swore. This rule was difficult for some judges to apply and led to procedural errors (see no. 3).

Likewise, Almoravid jurists had reached no consensus regarding the question of who bore the burden of proof, the slanderer or the slandered. These discrepancies caused judges to hesitate before passing judgment and might require the agreement of the chief *qāḍī* when the application of a *ḥadd* punishment was at stake (see no. 1). According to the seven muftis who intervened in case no. 1, if someone slandered an Arab of Ummayad lineage by saying that he was a slave, the burden of proof fell on the slanderer. The person slandered was required only to present witnesses to reject a substantiated claim that he was of slave origin.[22] In accusations of a crime such as inciting other people to burn a building, the reputation of both the accused and the accuser was essential for some jurists, while for others, the case depended on the accuser's ability to substantiate his claim (see no. 3).

There were also differences of opinion regarding the level of evidence required to disqualify (*tajrīḥ*) a person of exemplary uprightness (*mubarriz*). For those who followed the opinion of Aṣbagh b. al-Faraj, a *mubarriz* may not be disqualified on the grounds of slander (*isfāh*) and personal enmity (*al-ʿadāwa fī ḥaqq alladhī yushhadu ʿalayhi khāṣṣat*[an] *lā fī l-amr al-ʿāmm*). Another group of Mālikīs held a "different opinion" (*qawl ākhar*) according to which a man possessing exemplary uprightness cannot be disqualified, nor can someone with a higher level of integrity, for he is free from rivalry and envy. The fact that the second opinion is presented as different from the first suggests that for Aṣbagh, exemplary uprightness was not equivalent to an immunity that could not be challenged at all. The mufti consulted by ʿIyāḍ opted for the opinion of Aṣbagh and dismissed the claim on the condition that the defendant could establish that the plaintiffs acted out of rivalry and enmity (*idhā ṣaḥḥat al-munāfasa wa-ʿurifa min al-ṭāʿinīn al-ḥasāda*), not on the grounds of immunity (see case no. 4, and nos. 2 and 3).

---

due except in cases in which suspicions (*shubuhāt*) exist, in accusations of murder (*luṭkha*) and when there is a business relationship (*khulṭa; mukhālaṭa*) between the plaintiff and the defendant: see *Madhāhib*, 71/200–1.

[22] For an example of a substantiated claim of slavery see al-Wansharīsī (1981–83, 2:427).

Also debated was the question of whether or not a strong suspicion (*lawth*) could trigger the *qasāma* procedure, and consequently, either *qiṣāṣ* or blood money. According to Ibn al-Ḥājj, a strong suspicion is equivalent to the deposition of an upright witness (*al-shāhid al-ʿadl*), although this was also a matter of disagreement among jurists (see no. 9). [That a strong suspicion is equivalent to the deposition of an upright witness was the opinion of Ibn al-Qāsim. The reverse is also true, i.e., if a single impartial witness declares that someone has perpetrated a crime, this produces *lawth* and thus the right to *qasāma*. *Lawth* may also be established on the grounds of "strong" hearsay evidence (*idhā qawiya al-samāʿ*).[23] Likewise, if one or two upright witnesses give imprecise testimony regarding a *tadmiya* accusation[24] against someone, that yields the right to *qasāma*. Whether this also applies to a group of unauthorized witnesses (*shahādat lafīf al-nās*) is debated.][25]

If a strong suspicion existed about a suspect in a murder, and no relatives of the deceased appeared at the outset of the case, the suspect received the *taʿzīr* punishment. If the deceased's relatives appeared after the penalty had been applied, demanding the *qasāma* oath, there was a difference of opinion as to whether or not the application of a *taʿzīr* (i.e., a public claim) rendered the right of the deceased's relatives (i.e., a private claim) void (see no. 9). Our source does not specify whether both the public and the private claim were adjudicated by the *qāḍī*, or rather the public claim before the political authority and the private claim before the religious magistrate.

---

[23] See al-Wansharīsī (1981–83, 2:281, 318 and 269–70).

[24] See an example of a document containing a *tadmiya* accusation in *Fatāwā Ibn Rushd*, 2:1212–3 and model *tadmiya* formularies in Ibn al-ʿAṭṭār, Ibn Mughith and al-Jazīrī.

[25] See al-Wansharīsī (1981–83, 2:270 and 287). Subsequently, the *lafīf* testimony was accepted as constitutive of *lawth*, see Arévalo (1939:19). For a definition of *lawth* and the conditions under which it confers the right to *qasāma*, see al-Wansharīsī (1981–83, 2:292 and 311–2), and *Fatāwā Ibn Rushd*, 2:868–9. These definitions stem from Mālik. Some Mālikīs, like Khalīl b. Isḥāq, emphasize that—contrary to the opinion of jurists in other schools—the mere fact that a corpse is found in a place inhabited by a group of people or in one of their houses does not produce *lawth* (see *Mukhtaṣar* [trans. E. Fagnan], 39) unless it is known for certain that enmity existed between them and the victim (see Arévalo [1939:20 n. 1]; the latter was an exception made by Ibn Juzayy).

Only a minority of Mālikī jurists discuss the validity of *qasāma* as proof to put someone to death, see *EI*², *s.v.* "*Ḳasāma*" [J. Pedersen-Y. Linant de Bellefonds] and *EI*², *s.v.* "*Ḳiṣāṣ*" [J. Schacht].

Common knowledge produced by hearsay testimony may not serve as the basis of a *ḥadd*-punishment, but it may produce suspicion and thus, grounds for an *adab* punishment. In eleventh century al-Andalus, some jurists recommended punishing with beating and long imprisonment a *dhimmī* against whom there existed "strong hearsay evidence," i.e., strong suspicion of blasphemy. In contrast, Almoravid jurists recommended long imprisonment, until he repented, for an alleged blasphemer against whom "hearsay evidence" existed (see no. 5). In the absence of a strong suspicion of murder, the accused could not be punished with beating.[26]

As for accusations of rape, in the Almoravid period ʿIyāḍ had to stress that (1) the argument that a woman is not bleeding cannot be used to reject her claim of rape, unless she is a virgin, (2) the verbal form "she bleeds" (*tadmī*) refers [not only to the blood of the virgin] but [also] to the rush of the attack and the suffering that points to the absence of consent (*wa-inna-mā hādhā l-lafẓ ʿibāra ʿan surʿat al-qiyām wa-l-tashakkī al-dāll ʿalā ʿadam al-ṭawʿ*); (3) the requirement that a woman appears before the *qāḍī* "seizing" the accused (*mutaʿalliqa [bi-hi]*) is not a prerequisite to accepting her claim, for not all women are able to seize the man who has raped them; (4) circumstantial evidence of rape is that the victim appears crying, shouting and mentioning the name of the perpetrator, and that she immediately and spontaneously denounces the crime (see no. 6).

In accusations of wine-drinking, the testimony of the *majlis*' witnesses regarding the perpetrator's breath was accepted as sufficient proof for the application of the *ḥadd* punishment. [Mālikis—unlike Shāfiʿīs, Ḥanafīs, a majority of the jurists of Iraq, a group of jurists of the Ḥijāz and most of the Basrans—admitted the smell of *khamr* established by the testimony of two upright (*ʿadl*) witnesses as proof of wine drinking].[27]

[If there is a strong suspicion against the culprit, the *qasāma* serves to establish the accused's guilt and, therefore, it is offered to the relatives of the victim.[28] However, when strong suspicion is established

---

[26] Al-Wansharīsī (1981–83, 2:351). See also Lagardère (1995:72), who mentions the case of a *dhimmī* blasphemer who was sentenced to death. On the legal assessment (*ḥukm*) on insulting or scorning the Prophet see al-Wansharīsī (1981–83, 2:327 and 521–2).

[27] See Averroes, *Bidāya*, *Kitāb al-qadhf*, *bāb fī shurb al-khamr*.

[28] In the Mālikī school, *qasāma* may also operate as a compurgation oath. See Ibn Rushd al-Jadd (1988, 15:484–5); Khalīl b. Isḥāq, *Mukhtaṣar* (trans. E. Fagnan) 39–41; and Arévalo (1939:21). Cf. *EI*², *s.v.* "*Ḳasāma*" [J. Schacht].

on the grounds of a single witness' testimony but the witness does not possess integrity (*ghayr ʿadl*), the right to *qasāma* may or may not be offered to the relatives, depending on the discretion of the *qāḍī*.[29] If it is not offered, the culprit may be required to swear fifty oaths that he is innocent of the crime. Subsequently, he may be punished, depending on the quality of the witnesses who testified against him. If it is known for certain, or presumed, that they lack integrity (*maʿrūfīn bi-l-jurḥa aw tutawahham fī-him bi-l-jurḥa*), the culprit may be imprisoned for a long period if the suspicion against him is strong (*qawiyat al-tuhma*), in the hope that upright witnesses will appear. Strong suspicion of a lesser extent than *lawth*, however, may not be the basis for a punishment of beating. If, after long imprisonment, the suspicions (*shubuhāt*) are not confirmed, the accused may be required to swear fifty oaths that he is innocent and then be released from prison. When the right to *qasāma* oath is conferred but either the integrity or lack of integrity of the witnesses is uncertain (*al-majhulīn lā yuʿrafūn bi-jurḥa wa-lā ʿadāla*), the accused should be punished with a hundred lashes[30] and imprisoned for one year if the victim's relatives either decline the oath, forgive the culprit in exchange for the blood money, or negotiate a monetary compensation with him before, or after the *qasāma* oath has been pronounced.[31] When the conditions to swear the *qasāma* oath are not met, the aforementioned punishment may not be implemented. The transmissions regarding Mālik's opinion in this respect are contradictory.[32] Nevertheless, no disagreement affected the binding force of the declaration of a single upright witness as regards the enactment of the *qasāma* procedure. According to Ibn Rushd, not to judge accordingly was to transgress school doctrine.[33]

---

[29] That the declaration of a witness not possessing integrity could not establish *lawth* was the doctrine of Ibn al-Qāsim. See al-Bājī (1990:420). On the disagreement with respect to the value of the declaration of a non-*ʿadl* witness in order to create *lawth*, see also Ibn Rushd al-Ḥafīd (1995, 2:519–21).

[30] A penalty which in tenth-century Cordova was carried out by [agents of] the sultan. See Ibn al-ʿAṭṭār (1983:291).

[31] If the perpetrator had already received a beating as *taʿzir* punishment, he could not be beaten a second time. See Ibn al-ʿAṭṭār (1983:291). According to Schacht (1983:148–9 and 151–4), imprisonment for one year and a hundred lashes was not *taʿzīr* but *ʿuqūba*.

[32] Some of Mālik's disciples transmitted from him that *lawth* might be established by a non-*ʿadl* witness. However, Ashhab transmitted from Mālik that "in blood questions" the testimony of a non-*ʿadl* witness may not be accepted. The latter was also the opinion of Ibn al-Qāsim, as we have seen. See al-Bājī, *Fuṣūl*, 420.

[33] See al-Wansharīsī (1981–83, 2:288 and 312–3 and *Fatāwā Ibn Rushd*, 2:869–71,

Suspicion (*shubha, tuhma*) of a lesser degree than *lawth* entailed preventive detention of varying duration, unless the suspicion was strengthened by the declaration of one or two upright witnesses, in which case the plaintiff had the right to *qasāma*. If this lesser degree of suspicion was strong (*idha qawiyat al-tuhma*), long imprisonment without beating was recommended as a preventive measure.

Presumptions regarding the reputation of the defendant came into play in the absence of conclusive evidence or strong suspicion against him (see cases 2, 3 and 4). [A person who had a bad reputation should be detained for approximately one month, a person with a "neutral" reputation two or three days, and a person who was above suspicion "not a single day".][34] The judge in our theft case (see no. 8), however, kept two detainees in prison for two months.

In claims of theft, some *qāḍīs* required the plaintiff to swear an oath, although they gave him the right to defer the oath to the defendant.[35] When a group of people was accused of theft, if one or more of them acknowledged the theft and agreed either to return the stolen item or to pay his share of its entire value (*ghurm*), (a) they incurred no penal liability; and (b) those who did not acknowledge the theft could be placed in preventive detention. However, if the latter had a good reputation and the claimant could not otherwise substantiate his claim, they had to be released after swearing that they did not take part in the theft (see no. 8).

In *qiṣāṣ* claims for the loss of incisor teeth, when the plaintiff did not substantiate his claim with witness testimony, and the defendant had no defense other than his declaration, the plaintiff was required to swear that the teeth were lost because of the deliberate action of the defendant. If he swore, he won the case.

It is significant that in the four cases relating to slander transmitted in the *Madhāhib al-ḥukkām*, the plaintiff was a mufti, a *qāḍī*, the guardian of an orphan and an Arab of Umayyad lineage, respectively.

3:1364–6. For a case in which *qasāma* applied on the basis of a strong suspicion established with non-*ʿadl* witnesses, see al-Wansharīsī (1981–83, 2:319 and 321).

[34] That a man who was above all suspicion could not be put into prison when conclusive proofs were lacking was the opinion of the Cordovan muftis of the eleventh century such as Ibn Lubāba, Ibn Walīd, Yaḥyā b. Sulaymān, Ibn Ghālib, Yaḥyā b. ʿAbd al-ʿAzīz, Aḥmad b. Yaḥyā, Ayyūb b. Sulaymān and ʿUbayd Allāh b. Yaḥyā. See Molina López (1991:174, no. 19). On the role of moral qualities in presumption see also Johansen (1999b:396–400 and Heyd (1973:250–1). Cf. Schacht (1964:178).

[35] See ʿIyāḍ (1989:66/196).

The question arises whether, leaving false accusation of fornication apart, common people were also concerned with slander, addressed other judicial instances, or were deemed subjects capable of committing slander but not objects of slander.

Judgments and Punishments

During the Almoravid period the muftis unanimously agreed that accusing an Arab of Umayyad lineage of being a slave without evidence was equivalent to *qadhf* and thus merited a *ḥadd*-punishment of whipping. This legal assessment had been issued by Ibn al-Qāsim.[36]

Slander could also be classified as *shatam* and punished with a "painful corrective" consisting of whipping and imprisonment. Some, however, wanted such cases to be settled with a *ḥadd*[37] (see nos. 2, 3 and 4). There was a certain vacillation in the use that Mālikī jurists made of the terms *shatam* and *qadhf*, however.[38] [For some jurists,[39] *shatam* encompasses (a) *qadhf* or false accusation of fornication, (b) false accusation of other crimes, e.g., theft, wine-drinking, lying (*kadhab*), treason (*khiyāna*), and usury, and (c) dishonoring someone with the name of a humble craft or commerce, e.g., calling him "Hey, son of the blacksmith," "son of the wood dealer," "son of the olive oil dealer" or "son of the barber."[40] That the Ẓāhirī jurist Ibn Ḥazm used the expression *al-qadhf bi-l-zinā* implies that he understood *qadhf* as calumny in general.[41] The Granadan jurist Ibn Juzayy provides a definition of *qadhf* which corresponds to the meaning of the term that appears in our cases: *Qadhf* is, besides a false accusation of fornication against the alleged perpetrators, telling someone that he is not the son or the grandson of someone. Also *qadhf* may

---

[36] This textual evidence is provided by Muḥammad Ibn al-Jadd, one of the intervening muftis. The "shouting of evil words" with no grounds is condemned in Qur'ān 4:148, see Safwat (1982:175).

[37] Probably for concerns similar to those of Ibn al-ʿAṭṭār, who complains about the proliferation of malicious accusations, especially by debtors against their creditors. See Ibn al-ʿAṭṭār (1983:294–5).

[38] Contrary to the idea that one infers from the sources used by Arévalo (1939:97–8) and Arcas (1994).

[39] See al-Wansharīsī (1981–83, 2:422–3).

[40] On the bad image of urban labor in medieval islam see Brunschvig (1962) and Shatzmiller (1989).

[41] See Ibn Ḥazm (1966, 1:300). L. Peirce (1998:317) observes that in Ottoman Aintab, the term *qadhf* was used in court by the local community for calumnies other than false accusation of *zinā*.

be committed indirectly, e.g., telling an Arab that he is a barbarian or making any other allusion of the kind.][42] For ʿIyāḍ, *qadhf* was a calumny subject to *ḥadd* punishment while *shatam* was an abuse punishable with an *adab* penalty (see no. 3).

In case no. 6, a man accused of rape was imprisoned. Because his culpability could not be fully established, he was sentenced to an *adab* punishment of scourging. Unlike *ḥadd, adab* allows for negotiation of a settlement with the plaintiff. Therefore, to avoid the punishment, the defendant paid a certain amount of money to the plaintiff on the condition that she waived her claim.

In the wine-drinking case, the testimony regarding the culprit's breath was accepted as valid proof and taken as the basis of the corresponding *ḥadd* punishment, apparently without resort to the *shūrā*. The compiler's specification that a "complete" *ḥadd* (eighty lashes) was applied suggests that Mālikī *qāḍī*s had the option to apply a less severe sanction (forty lashes).[43]

Strong suspicion of murder was accepted as a valid basis for imposing a *taʿzīr*. The punishment by *taʿzīr* was not considered grounds to nullify the rights of the deceased's relatives, notwithstanding the jurists' disagreement on this point. If a strong suspicion against the accused existed, the plaintiffs were entitled to swear the *qasāma* oath, again notwithstanding difference of opinion in this respect. First, however, the relatives had to establish that they were the legitimate heirs of the victim. Additionally, the accused had the right to defend himself (see no. 9). We do not know whether in case no. 9 *qiṣāṣ* was actually applied or if the payment of blood money was negotiated with the culprit. The important point is that the public punishment imposed for the crime does not nullify (*yusqiṭ*) the rights of the relatives; conversely, if the relatives pardon the defendant, the governmental authorities might still punish him with imprisonment and flogging.[44]

---

[42] See Ibn Juzayy (1982:362).

[43] Notwithstanding that Mālikīs are counted among those who advocate eighty lashes as *ḥadd* for wine-drinking. See Mālik b. Anas, *al-Muwaṭṭaʾ*, *Kitāb al-ḥudūd, bāb taḥrīm al-khamr* and Ibn Rushd al-Ḥafīd, *Bidāya, kitāb al-qadhf, bāb fī shurb al-khamr*. See also Safwat (1982), who records 160 lashes, drawing on Ibn Sharīf al-Nawawī, *Minhāj al-ṭālibīn* (trans.), 450.

[44] See also Heyd (1973:254).

[In the opinion of al-Qarāfī, *taʿzīr* varied across time and space. Because *taʿzīr* is intended to dissuade the culprit, the number of lashes should correspond to this aim, no less and no more. If beating or whipping are deemed not useful, an adult perpetrator should be imprisoned until he repents.[45]

There was legal disagreement as to whether *talio* should be carried out by decapitation with the sword or by the same kind of death inflicted upon the victim. In al-Andalus, the practice was death with the sword when the crime had been established by means of *qasāma*, and the same kind of death inflicted upon the slain when the crime had been established by confession or complete testimonial evidence.[46] The blood money for a sane Muslim was one thousand dinars or twelve thousand dirhams.][47]

In order to obtain the right to *qiṣāṣ* for his incisor teeth, the defendant was invited to present his arguments. Since he could not produce anything in his defense and the arguments of the claimant were accepted, the defendant was sentenced to *qiṣāṣ* after the claimant had sworn the oath. I infer this from the agreement of the two muftis, Ibn Rushd al-Jadd and Ibn al-Ḥājj (see no. 11).

[That *talio* was applied for the loss of teeth was the opinion of Mālik. If the implementation of a *talio* was complicated, an "expert" should be called (*yusʾal ʿan dhālika man yaʿrifu-hu fa-yaqtaṣṣ min-hu*).[48] Blood money for a tooth was five camels (*ibl*), fifty dinars or 600 dirhams.[49]

According to Ibn Rushd al-Jadd, the *qasāma* oath must be pronounced in the mosque, standing up in front of the *qibla* wall, after the Friday midafternoon (*ʿaṣr*) prayer. In the Almoravid period this was the *qāḍīs*' practice (*ʿamal al-quḍāt*),[50] a practice which was already established a century before[51] but not yet in the tenth century.[52]

---

[45] See al-Wansharīsī (1981–83, 2:416–8).
[46] See al-Wansharīsī (1981–83, 2:303) and Arévalo (1939:32).
[47] On the recommendation to give up *talio* and juristic disagreement in this respect, see al-Wansharīsī (1981–83, 2:305–7).
[48] See Saḥnūn (1986: question *fī l-rajul yukassir baʿḍ sinn rajul fa-yuqtaṣṣ min-hu*).
[49] See al-Bājī, *Fuṣūl*, 424.
[50] See al-Wansharīsī (1981–83, 2:302–3); Lagardère (1995:64). The Madinans used to swear next to the pulpit, see Saḥnūn (1986: *kitāb al-diyāt*, question "*mā jāʾa fī taqsīm al-yamīn fī l-qasāma*").
[51] See al-Wansharīsī (1981–83, 2:324–5) and Lagardère (1995:59).
[52] See Ibn al-ʿAṭṭār (1983:291).

Qasāma had to be sworn by at least two of the deceased's relatives and no more than one person could be executed by means of *qasāma*.][53]

The *Mi'yār* of al-Wansharīsī shows that uncertainty over the definition of *lawth* and the applicability of *qasāma* continued for the next three centuries. I have found no evidence of any further discussion regarding the conflict between public and private prosecution in murder cases. This may mean either that the opinions of Ibn Rushd al-Jadd and Ibn al-Ḥājj (i.e., that the application of *ta'zīr* did not nullify the rights of the deceased's relatives) created jurisprudence, or that the circumstance under which *ta'zīr* and *qiṣāṣ* merged was not frequent.

Persons responsible for injuries to animals were subject to a monetary fine as compensation for the damage, with respect to which two different rules, both attributed to Mālik, were in force. The jurists also disagreed with regard to how this fine should be calculated.[54] Mistreatment of a beast incurs financial liability but no penal liability. Such a behavior is considered blameworthy[55] and is classified by Muḥammad b. 'Iyāḍ as a *jināyā* rather than a damage (*ḍarar*).

Nonviolent theft (*akhdh*) was settled according to the rules of usurpation (*ghaṣb*), not *sariqa* (theft punished by *ḥadd*) or *ta'zir*.[56] If the defendant acknowledged that he had "seized" the stolen item, he was required either to return it or, if this was no longer possible, to pay compensation (*ghurm*). Al-Wansharīsī mentions a couple of cases in which Andalusī *qāḍī*s ordered the amputation of the hand of a person who forged a document in order to acquire properties.[57] These cases, however, have the appearance of being exceptional[58] and the legal sources do not clarify whether the excessive recourse to mutilation attributed to the first Almoravid rulers[59] corresponded to reality or was a means to discredit them. Be that as it may, the fact that the historian Ibn Ḥayyān (second half of the tenth–first quarter of the eleventh century) had formulated a similar accusation against

---

[53] See al-Wansharīsī (1981–83, 2:296 and 322); also Chalmeta (1999:49–51).

[54] See 'Iyāḍ (1989:86–7, 219–20).

[55] See Santillana (1938, 1:14 and 380).

[56] See Santillana (1938, 2:452–54ff.) and Schacht (1983:149–51).

[57] See al-Wanasharīsī (1981–83, 2:414; 10:225–26); and Lagardère (1985:72, 131 n. 1, 453).

[58] The practice of cutting off the hand for forgery seems to have survived in Northern Nigeria. See R. Peters, this volume, section 3.2.4.

[59] See Fierro (1997a:444–5).

the Umayyad caliphs[60] shows that by his time, moderation in matters of *ḥudūd* had became a moral imperative which rulers were expected to meet.

I cannot determine whether the terms *ʿuqūba* and *adab* are used synonymously, or whether *ʿuqūba* refers to *ḥadd* and *adab* to discretionary punishment. The corrective punishments most commonly applied appear to have been life imprisonment without beating, beating and subsequent imprisonment, and beating and subsequent release from prison. No fines are cited. Unlike imprisonment, the application of a beating invalidated a suspect's right subsequently to claim innocence.

Imprisonment was used for the purpose of pretrial detention as well as a corrective punishment, at times combined with whipping.

The term *ijtihād* appears in connection with the *qāḍī*'s discretionary power to determine the appropriate punishment for a particular crime or to assimilate this crime to another one for which a fixed penalty is laid down in the sources. In case no. 12, a jurist put forward a solution obtained by *qiyās*, but this reasoning was judged unnecessary by his colleagues, provided that authoritative opinions issued by earlier Mālikī authorities could be applied to the case. Although the muftis knew these opinions, only one, ʿIyāḍ, was able to locate them in the sources (or at least this is the message that his son wanted to convey).

Appeal

Case no. 6 illustrates the stage prior to an appeal. The defeated party wanted to obtain exoneration from an accusation of rape, to retrieve a certain amount of money that he had paid to the plaintiff in order that she waive her claim, and to have her punished for a false accusation of fornication. The advice of a legal expert about the proper strategy to make the appeal successful was sought. The mufti, ʿIyāḍ, recommended that the defendant concentrate on the lack of an immediate and spontaneous claim of rape. On the other hand, the mufti used the verb *tashakkā* instead of *iddaʿā* to refer to the claim of the plaintiff. My impression is that ʿIyāḍ wanted to

---

[60] See Peláez (2000:396, n. 54), which draws on Ibn ʿIdhārī's *al-Bayān al-Mughrib*.

avoid the possibility that the woman who had claimed the rape be punished should the defendant's demand for revision be successful, since a "complaint," unlike a false "accusation" of fornication, does not incur the *ḥadd* punishment prescribed for the false accusation of fornication.[61] Probably, the mufti suspected—as one does when one examines the case in detail—that the woman had been pressed to denounce rape in order to avoid an accusation of *zinā*.[62]

Conclusion

The examination of twelve legal cases cannot provide a comprehensive and representative picture of the application of penal law in al-Andalus and the far Maghrib. Rather, the examination of these cases in the light of other legal and nonlegal sources qualifies and expands our knowledge of aspects of the application of penal law in *qāḍī* courts, e.g., the difference between the "civil" and the penal process, the problem posed by legal disagreement, and the role of suspicion and judicial discretion.

Public and private offenses could be reported to the *qāḍī* and judged according to the rules of *fiqh*. A quantitative evaluation of the cases transmitted in *Madhāhib al-ḥukkām* would indicate that slander was denounced before the *qāḍī* more frequently than other offenses. This assumption, however, is not confirmed by the voluminous *Miʿyār* of al-Wansharīsī; of approximately three hundred cases recorded in its chapter on *nawāzil al-dimāʾ wa-l-ḥudūd wa-l-taghrīrāt* (*al-taʿzīrāt?*), only twenty-nine are connected with abuse and slander.

In cases of murder and bodily wounds, it seems that the *qasāma* and *qiṣāṣ* procedures were common practice.[63]

Our texts confirm that *qāḍī*s enjoyed a considerable degree of freedom with respect to the application of *adab* and *taʿzīr* punishments. *Qāḍī*s also exercised some discretionary powers in the domain of *ḥudūd*, e.g., they might choose between lesser and more severe penalties; likewise *qāḍī*s engaged in analogical reasoning in order to assimilate

---

61 See Ibn Hazm (1929–40, 11:291–3).

62 See D. Serrano Ruano (2003), 125–48.

63 See Christelow (this volume); R. Peters (2002). Compare with *EI*², *s.v.* "*ḳasāma*" [J. Pedersen-Y. Linant de Bellefonds], who assert that "it does not appear that this institution functioned much, even in the past when the penal law of Islam had a certain application."

certain crimes to crimes subject to Qurʾānic sanctions. Freedom of action, however, should not be equated with arbitrariness. Some jurists, like Ibn Rushd al-Jadd, recommended that discretionary punishments (*adab*) be established for each particular case by means of *ijtihād*.[64] However, there was a tendency to apply standard *adab* and *taʿzīr* punishments for which a basic proportionality was established with the level of suspicion against the accused.[65]

Several interrelated factors, like the discretionary powers of *qāḍīs*, the legal weight assigned to suspicion, and the admission of the testimony of a single upright witness as complete proof, made for difficulty in that the restrictions used to prove crimes subject to *ḥadd* might result in exempting the criminal from punishment. In murder cases, divergent opinions like those advocating that *lawth* (strong suspicion) might give rise to the *qasāma* (fifty oaths) procedure, and that the declaration of a non-*ʿadl* witness or a group of unexamined witnesses (*lafīf*) might produce *lawth* were not rejected. No doubt difference of opinion (*ikhtilāf*) made the adoption of decisions more difficult. The very fact that divergent opinions like the aforementioned were not rejected, however, allowed *qāḍīs* to opt for them and to circumvent restrictions regarding testimonial evidence which might hinder the application of prescribed legal penalties like *qiṣāṣ*.

A gap between doctrine and court practice occurs in cases of nonviolent theft, which was adjudicated according to the law of obligations. *Qāḍīs*' hesitation about the rules of penal procedure, together with *ikhtilāf*, complicated and surely slowed down the final resolution of litigations. The institution of *iftāʾ* as well as judicial review, however, increased the probability that the rules of *fiqh* were strictly observed.

---

[64] See al-Wansharīsī (1981–83, 2:419).

[65] I ignore the grounds on which B. Johansen (2002:176, note 22) asserts that Mālikī jurists systematically exceeded the limits of *taʿzīr*.

APPENDIX

List of Cases

I number the cases according to the order in which they appear in *Madhāhib al-ḥukkām* and classify those cases that do not appear in the chapters on *ḥudūd* and *jināyāt* according to their subject matter.

Case no. 1, slander (*qadhf*), *Madhāhib al-ḥukkām*, 75–7. See also *Miʿyār*, 2:514–5.
Case no. 2, slander (*shatam*), *Madhāhib al-ḥukkām*, 77. See also *Miʿyār*, 2:515.
Case no. 3, slander (*najah*), *Madhāhib al-ḥukkām*, 77–9. See also *Miʿyār*, 2:515–6.
Case no. 4, slander (*jarḥ*), See *Madhāhib al-ḥukkām*, 43. See also *Miʿyār*, 10:164–5.
Case no. 5, blasphemy (*istikhfāf bi-l-muslimīn wa-nabiyyi-him wa-kitābi-him*), *Madhāhib al-ḥukkām*, 81. See also *Miʿyār*, 2:526–7.
Case no. 6, rape (*ghaṣb*), *Madhāhib al-ḥukkām*, 81–2. See also *Miʿyār*, 10:235–6.
Case no. 7, wine-drinking, *Taʿrīf*, 112. See also *Miʿyār*, 2:410, and Lagardère (1995), 65.
Case no. 8, theft (*akhdh*), *Madhāhib al-ḥukkām*, 67. See also *Miʿyār*, 10:240.
Case no. 9, homicide (*qatl*), *Madhāhib al-ḥukkām*, 84. See also *Fatāwā Ibn Rushd*, 2:1149 and *Miʿyār*, 2:302.
Case no. 10, homicide, *Madhāhib al-ḥukkām*, 84–5.
Case no. 11, *qiṣāṣ* for incisor teeth, *Madhāhib al-ḥukkām*, 85–6.
Case no. 12, damage to livestock, *Madhāhib al-ḥukkām*, 86–7. See also *Miʿyār*, 2:532–3.

CHAPTER TWENTY

SHAHĀDAT NAQL IN THE JUDICIAL PRACTICE IN MODERN LIBYA[1]

Aharon Layish

In memoriam Jeanette A. Wakin

I. *Introduction*

The cases under review were recorded in the Sharīʿa Court of Ajdābiya,[2] a district center in the plain near the Mediterranean coast. The people of this area are part of the Saʿādī confederation. The principal tribes of this confederation are the Maghāriba and Majābira (Davis 1987:7–8, 80ff., 84–5, 94, 169, 189; idem 1998:7–13). Prior to the abolition of the *sharīʿa* courts in Libya in early 1970s, the local *sharīʿa* court had sole jurisdiction in matters of personal status, succession and *waqf*; and it also dealt with civil claims, contracts and property, homicide, assault, and more—matters that formally were amenable to the civil court. This extensive jurisdiction may have been a carryover from the period before the Ottoman reform of the judicial system. The material law applicable in the *sharīʿa* court in the period under review was the uncodified *sharīʿa* in its Mālikī version (Layish 1991:14–15; idem 1998:14–20).

Shahādat naql (attestation of the conveyance of evidence) is a document, attested to before a qāḍī, that contains a statement of fact pertaining to matters such as conjugal rights, succession, and property. The qāḍī endorses the corroborating testimony of the witnesses.

---

[1] The Libyan documents were placed at my disposal by John Davis of Oxford University. I am most grateful to him. Wael Hallaq read an early version of this essay and made generous, valuable comments for which I express my profound gratitude. I am also indebted to Delfina Serrano for her comments and to Alexander Borg and David Powers for their expert editorial assistance. The research was supported by the Israel Science Foundation.

[2] For this spelling, see Yāqūt (1866–76, 1:131–2).

The proceeding is authenticated by the court notaries (*shuhūd al-ḥāl, ʿudūl*) and registered in the minutes of the *sharīʿa* court (*maḥāḍir*). A copy of the written testimony is given to the claimant so that it may be conveyed to a qāḍī of another locality for the purpose of accomplishing the legal proceedings required for handing down a decision, or (more often) so that the written testimony may be used by the claimant for any practical purpose at an unspecified future date as the need arises.

II. *Written Documents in Doctrine and Practice*[3]

The Qurʾān rules explicitly (2:282):

> When you contract a debt for a fixed term, record it in writing. Let a scribe record it in writing between you. . . . Be not averse to writing down [the contract], whether [the amount] be small or great, with its term.

The *ḥadīth*, too, supports the use of written documents. The rulings of the Qurʾān and the *ḥadīth*, however, were reduced by doctrine to a recommendation rather than a binding injunction. Written documents (*ṣakk, wathīqa*) were nevertheless admitted, especially in the Mālikī school, as valid evidence once they had been attested by qualified witnesses.

Indeed, written documents proved so indispensable in practice that they remained in constant use, became a normal accompaniment of every transaction of importance, and gave rise to a highly developed branch of law with a voluminous literature of its own.[4] Formally, attestation of witnesses remained the ultimate requirement in classical Islamic legal theory; doctrine continued to reason as if there were no documents but only the oral testimony of witnesses, possibly supported by private records; practice, on the other hand, acted as if documents were essential and "witnessing" only a formality to make

---

[3] Unless otherwise indicated, the following survey is based on: Wakin (1972:4–10); Schacht (1964:82–3, 193); Tyan (1960:239–41); idem (1986); Coulson (1964:125, 146, 173); Peters (1995:208); Toledano (1981:11 [and the reference to Tyan 1945], 13–14).

[4] The branch of legal science that deals with documents is called the science of *shurūṭ*, "formularies," (or *wathāʾiq*, "documents," in the Mālikī school). See Schacht (1964:82 fn. 1; Wakin 1972:1 fn. 1, 13). On the relations between doctrine and practice, see Hallaq (1995).

them fully valid. Professional witnesses (*ʿudūl*), whose integrity (*ʿadāla*) had been established by the court, came to exercise the functions of notaries public. They had legal training and were appointed and dismissed by the qāḍīs.[5]

The authors of the manuals of legal formularies were specialists in *fiqh*; they provided forms of documents for all possible practical needs and safeguards against all contingencies; these had only to be "witnessed" in order to become legally valid.

In Andalusia, the judicial practice (*ʿamal*) was reflected in formulary manuals (*wathāʾiq*). Much of this material was later incorporated in *al-ʿĀṣimiyya* or *Tuḥfat al-ḥukkām* by Ibn ʿĀṣim (d. 829/1426) (See References. Cf. Serrano 2000), the Qāḍī al-Jamāʿa of Granada. The science of *wathāʾiq* was first and foremost a practical outcome of customary law in the Maghrib. The *wathāʾiq* works became closely connected with the judicial practice, the terms of the documents being drafted in accordance with this judicial practice (Wakin 1972:13–14; Toledano 1981:13–14).

In the modern period, during which the application of Islamic law and the organization of its tribunals have been modified by independent Islamic governments, written documents have been generally admitted as valid proof, and sometimes the competence of the qāḍīs has been restricted to cases in which documentary evidence is produced. The introduction of written documents (*tawthīq biʾl-kitāba*) in modern Egypt was approved by Muḥammad ʿAbduh (ʿAbduh 1900:34; Anderson 1976: Index, s.v. *ʿadam al-samāʿ*.).

The phenomenon of *shahādat naql*, as reflected in the Libyan *sijill*, appears to be a variation of, or deviation from, the institution of *kitāb al-qāḍī ilā ʾl-qāḍī* (conveyance of testimony from one qāḍī to another) caused by the judicial practice and justified by considerations of public interest (*maṣlaḥa*). The communication of *kitāb al-qāḍī ilā ʾl-qāḍī* took place when "a qāḍī of a particular locale writes to a qāḍī of a different locale regarding a person's right that he, the first qāḍī, established against another person, so that the receiving qāḍī might carry out the effects of the communication in his locale" (Hallaq 1999:438 and fn. 6 there). The *raison d'être* of this communication was to avoid the injustice that might be caused to the plaintiff

[5] Hallaq maintains that at least some notaries operated independently, drafting and authenticating documents for individuals outside the boundaries of the court (personal communication).

due to geographical distance between the two locales, that is, the hardship involved in bringing witnesses, whose testimony is essential, to the court of the receiving qāḍī.[6]

It was probably as a result of this hardship that the Mālikī judicial practice, sometime during the eleventh century, deviated from the procedure regarding written communications. The Andalusī and Maghribī qāḍīs began to admit the validity of written instruments without the testimony of the witnesses. Instead, the authentication of the document by the attestation of the qāḍī's handwriting (*al-shahāda ʿalā 'l-khaṭṭ*) was sufficient to validate it. If the receiving qāḍī could not identify the handwriting of the sending qāḍī, he had to procure two just witnesses, experts in handwritten documents and knowledgeable of the handwriting of the qāḍī in question, to identify the handwriting in order to verify the authenticity of the document. Immediate registration and attestation of the document's validity is required for reasons of legal certainty that may arise in case the sending or the receiving qāḍī—or both—died. The new practice was justified on the basis of *ḍarūra* (necessity), the authoritative basis of which was found in the Q. 2:185 (Hallaq 1999:453–4, 457–8).

Evidence suggests that the institution of *shahādat naql* was adopted by Ibn ʿĀṣim in his treatise *al-ʿĀṣimiyya* or *Tuḥfat al-ḥukkām*, commonly used by some of the Libyan qāḍīs (Layish 1998:18 fn. 26). The *shahādat naql* is discussed in this treatise under the section "*Khiṭāb al-Quḍāt* and Related Matters."[7] The procedural similarities between *Khiṭāb al-Quḍāt* and *kitāb al-qāḍī ilā 'l-qāḍī* leave no doubt as to the source of the former, despite differences in details. The *Khiṭāb al-Quḍāt* is a mechanism whereby the sending qāḍī notifies the receiving qāḍī of the established facts in the case under review on the basis of a court decision. The key word in this context is "*aʿlama*" and its derivatives. *Al-ʿĀṣimiyya* states explicitly that "notification" by means of this word is legally admissible (*qabūl*) in "contemporary judicial practice" (*wa 'l-ʿamal al-yawm*) (line 86). If the sending qāḍī dies or is dismissed, his notification is unacceptable unless it has been registered (line 89). Registration implies that the notification has been properly authenticated by witnesses. A notification issued by a qāḍī of good reputation (*ʿadl*) by virtue of his judicial authority should be

[6] Hallaq (1999, 444, 449, 451); Santillana (1938, 2:604–5 [*naql al-shahāda*:] and the reference to Khalīl in fn. 283).

[7] See Ibn ʿĀṣim (1958:14, 16 and the French translation and annotation).

executed (line 91). Once the decision becomes executable, the qāḍī must register it upon the plaintiff's request (line 95). The qāḍī may perform the registration on his own initiative (line 96). At the plaintiff's request, the qāḍī may register documents, provided these are not disputable, as in the case of old charters of *waqf*, the handwriting of which can be authenticated by witnesses (line 97). Following the pronouncement of a decision, the plaintiff may request the qāḍī to rule that the defendant is prohibited from advancing any claim in the future (*taʿjīz*), subject to exceptions in matters relating to *waqf* (*ḥabs*), divorce (*ṭalāq*), paternity (*nasab*), homicide (*dam*), or manumission of a slave (*ʿitāq*) (lines 98–9).

III. Shahādat naql *in Judicial Practice*

Shahādat naql is a common practice in the Libyan *sijill*. The present study is based on a casual sample of a dozen documents, all issued by the Sharīʿa Court of Ajdābiya between 1951 and 1954.

The documents are usually written in stereotyped phraseology and formulaic language. The most common introductory formula is the utterance of an invocation and a prayer for the soul of the Prophet, his family and Companions, intended to invoke divine guidance in the processes of justice and to reinforce the validity and binding character of the qāḍī's legal pronouncements. Tribute is also paid to Muḥammad Idrīs al-Mahdī al-Sanūsī, the Emir of Barqa, the region of Eastern Libya (Cyrenaica), who was proclaimed king of independent Libya in 1951.

The introductory formulas are followed by the definition of the subject matter of the document: "*shahādat naql* in favor (*li-ṣāliḥ* or *li-maṣlaḥa*) of [so and so]," a reference to the page and number of the protocol in the court minutes (*maḥḍar*), the location of the Sharīʿa Court, and the name of the qāḍī or *nāʾib* presiding over the specific case, "may Allāh, the Exalted, grant him success."

Next the document provides details that accurately identify the claimant (Cf. Wakin 1972:50–1): his private name, the names of his father, grandfather (up to three generations), lineage (*ʿāʾila*), tribal affiliation (*qabīla*), age, place of birth and residence. Usually, it is stated that the claimant has been "identified by his person and name" (*maʿrūfan dhātan wa-isman*) (Layish 1998: e.g., doc. 48, line 6; doc. 57, line 5; doc. 61, line 5; doc. 67, line 5), a formula that refers to the *sharʿī* procedure of identification (*taʿrīf*). In one case there is a clear indication to this effect: *wa-baʿd maʿrifatihā ʿalā al-manhaj al-sharʿī* (Layish 1998, doc. 14, line 5). The possibility, however, that the claimant was identified by the qāḍī on the basis of personal knowledge cannot be ruled out. Thus, in one case, it was stated: *al-maʿrūf ladaynā* [i.e., the qāḍī] *isman wa-dhātan* (Layish 1998, doc. 58, lines 5–6).

Subsequently, the claimant presents his case before the qāḍī. Generally, the narrative is written in the past tense. The claim is cast in personal subjective style, quite often in first-person statements (Cf. Wakin 1972:42), at the end of which the claimant asks the qāḍī to summon his witnesses to the court and hear their testimony. The qāḍī complies and asks the claimant to produce witnesses who will corroborate the alleged facts of the case. Usually, the primary witnesses testify to a fact or event that they themselves witnessed or about which they had personal knowledge (Layish 1998, doc. 4, line 6; doc. 54, lines 9ff.; doc. 48, lines 11–12). Occasionally, witnesses testify on the basis of hearsay. Thus, in one case, the witnesses met the claimant's husband out of town and heard him say that he had divorced his wife sometime previously. In a case pertaining to an inheritance dispute, the witnesses' testimony was based on a "widespread rumor."[8]

In two cases the primary witnesses' credibility was tested (*tazkiya*) by the *imām* and *mukhtār* of the town and by *shaykh*s of the same tribe (Layish 1998, doc. 14, line 14; and doc. 57, line 12). The witnesses usually use formulas calculated to reflect their credibility. The most common formulas are: "[He] gave testimony [the truthfulness of which he deemed to be] beyond any shadow of doubt, corroborating in letter and spirit the statement of [. . .]" (Layish 1998, doc. 61, line 9. Cf. doc. 14, line 12; doc. 48, 11; doc. 67, line 10). The witnesses conclude their testimony with a pious expression: "This is our testimony. Let Allāh be our pledge [lit. agent] (*wakīl*) to what we have said."[9]

The qāḍī authenticates the content of the document. The usual formula for this purpose is: "On the basis of [the statement] endorsed

[8] Layish (1998: doc. 14, lines 11–14; and doc. 67, lines 10–11, respectively). Hearsay evidence is admissible in court in litigations relating to inheritance. See Ibn ʿĀṣim (1958:28–9, lines 177ff.).

[9] Layish (1998: doc. 4, line 13; doc. 48, lines 12–13; 48, lines 16–17; doc. 61, line 10; doc. 67, lines 11–12). Cf. Layish and Shmueli (1979:41).

by the aforementioned witnesses, both of whom were in a state of legal competence (*ḥāla jāʾiza*) in *sharʿī* terms, as duly certified before the aforementioned judge, the latter endorsed (*ajāza*) this testimony, given on the account of both witnesses,[10] signed it, and had the undersigned [notaries] testify to it, and instructed that it be registered." Occasionally he makes the primary witnesses sign the witnessed document (Layish 1998, e.g., doc. 54, lines 22–4; doc. 58, line 14). In one case, the qāḍī added, as a gesture of credibility, that the testimony of the five witnesses to a testamentary *waqf* was "free from any hint of collusion (*tawāṭuʾ*) among them." Their signatures appear alongside those of the professional witnesses (Layish 1998, doc. 54, lines 17, 22–4).

The professional witnesses, that is, notaries, present in court sign the written testimony. Their names and court functions[11] are mentioned at the bottom of the document, their task being to witness the entire proceedings that transpired in court.

In fact, four kinds of witnesses may be distinguished in the witnessed documents: (1) witnesses required to identify (*taʿrīf*) the claimant or the primary witnesses; (2) primary witnesses enlisted by the claimant for the purpose of corroborating his contention; their testimonies are expected to be based upon their knowledge of the facts; (3) witnesses required to ascertain the primary witnesses' credibility (*tazkiya*); and (4) court notaries (Cf. Wakin 1972:65–70).

The notaries' signatures are followed by the qāḍī's endorsment of the legal validity of the proceedings. The usual formula for this purpose is: "The matter is as indicated above." Upon the claimant's request, the qāḍī gives him a copy of the witnessed document (Cf. Wakin 1972:45–7) that bears the date of its registration, which usually coincides with the date on which the document was drawn up or witnessed. The date is recorded by the day, month, and year of the Hijrī calendar, followed by the corresponding Gregorian date (Cf. Wakin 1972:47–8).

[10] Layish (1998: doc. 4, line 14; doc.14, line 16; doc. 48, line 14; doc. 57, line 11; doc. 61, line 11; doc. 67, line 13).

[11] Ibid. (doc. 57, line 19 [*mubāshir*, court usher]; doc. 61, line 14 [*nāʾib*, deputy *qāḍī*]).

Case 1[12]

I have come across only one instance in which *shahādat naql* corresponds to the procedure of *kitāb al-qāḍī ilā 'l-qāḍī*. A small boy, Ismāʿīl, from the Maghāriba tribe was run over by a car and, as a result of the accident, his right leg was severely injured. The injury caused a highly visible physical disability. A date was set for a meeting, at the Sharīʿa Court of Benghazi, between the boy's agnates and the driver involved in the accident in order to determine the amount of financial compensation. Since the boy's father could not travel there, he asked the Sharīʿa Court of Ajdābiya to hear the testimony of his witnesses, who were tribal assessors, so that their testimony could serve as a factual basis for the court in Benghazi to determine appropriate compensation.

The Sharʿī Nā'ib granted his request and, after ascertaining the witnesses' credibility according to *sharʿī* procedures, ordered the assessors to testify regarding the injured leg. Their assessment appears to have been based on criteria pertaining exclusively to tribal customary law. The Nā'ib—without interfering with the principles underlying the assessors' procedures—gave the boy's father a certified copy of the testimony for his use at any eventual legal proceedings in Benghazi. The translation of this document follows:

Translation

[1] In the name of Allāh, the Merciful, the Compassionate. May Allāh bless our Lord Muḥammad, his family and Companions and grant them peace.
[2] In the reign of his Excellency *sayyid*[13] Muḥammad Idrīs al-Mahdī al-Sanūsī, Emir of Barqa [Cyrenaica].
[3] ATTESTATION OF THE CONVEYANCE OF EVIDENCE (*shahādat naql*) IN FAVOR OF SHAYKH AL-LĀFĪ AL-MUFTĀḤ AL-ṢUBḤĪ
Entered in register no. 5/314, p. 5/214
[4] In the Sharīa Court of Ajdābiya, presided over by Muḥammad al-Mabrūk Abī Jāziya, the Nā'ib of his honor the *sharʿī* Qāḍī, and in

[12] For the Arabic text, see Layish (1998: doc. 57). For an annotated translation of this document with introduction, see idem (2005: doc. 57). Cf. Hallaq (1999:441 fn. 21).
[13] The title implies the status of a *sharīf*, that is, a descendant of the Prophet Muḥammad. Cf. Evans-Pritchard (1949:83, 117).

Charge of the Qāḍī's Affairs. May Allāh the Exalted grant him success. [5] Shaykh al-Lāfī b. Muftāḥ from the al-Shaykhī lineage [*ʿāʾila*] of the Ṣubḥ [subtribe] (De Agostini 1922–23:323–4) belonging to Maghāriba tribe [*qabīla*], identified by name (*maʿrūf*) appeared [in court] accompanied by his son Ismāʿīl, [6] who is about 10 years [old], and made the following statement:

> Fifteen months ago, my son Ismāʿīl, present here, was run over by a car that crushed his right leg. [7] After [the bones] were set and medically treated, [the leg technically] healed but a highly visible physical defect due to permanent mutilation (*ʿadam*)[14] remained which reduced [the leg] to the state of utter disability; [8] [the leg] ceased to function as a healthy limb. Since a date has been fixed for a meeting between me and the perpetrator (*jānī*)[15] concerning my son and his kinsmen[16] before the Qāḍī of Benghazi, and since I am unable [9] to travel there with the child, I ask [the court] to hear the testimony of the witnesses [present here] who are fully qualified[17] to testify to the fact that my son's leg has been reduced to a state [10] of disability.[18]

His request was granted and he was permitted to produce his witnesses. He brought Shaykh Muḥammad Bū al-Bughayyiḍ al-Zuwayyī al-Sudaydī[19] and Ḥājj [11] Yūnus b. Ṣāliḥ al-ʿĪdiyya of the aforementioned [Zuwayya] tribe, both of whom are known by name. Each of them gave testimony on his own account, corroborating his claim, [12] after due examination of the boy's leg, on the basis of

[14] In determining the amount of compensation due for bodily injury, tribal law among the Awlād ʿAlī in the Western Desert makes a distinction between wounds that heal (*al-ḍarb al-salīm*) and wounds that cause permanent mutilation (*al-ḍarb al-ʿadīm*). The case under review belongs to the second category. See al-Ḥabbūnī (1960:31, 34); al-Jawharī (1961:187ff.); Maḥjūb (n.d.: 183, 200, 314–5, 318 [definition of *ʿadam*]); Mohsen (1975:149); Murray (1935:205); Stewart (2000:890–1); cf. Abū Ḥassān (1974:230); Ghayth (1990:137).

[15] The unintentional nature of the motor accident does not exempt the perpetrator from the financial liability for the injury caused. Davis notes that the victim's agnates in road accidents receive double compensation: i.e., both from the state insurance company, and from the driver involved in the accident and his kinsmen in conformity with tribal law. This phenomenon has also been observed in Jerusalem. See Davis (1987:176, 223–4); Zilberman (1991:70).

[16] The injured boy and his solidarity group (*ʿāqila*), i.e., male agnates up to a certain degree of relationship, share the financial compensation paid for the injury caused to him. Cf. al-Qusūs (1972:83–4).

[17] Tribal assessors for bodily injuries are intended here. See Mohsen (1975:148ff.); cf. Stewart (1988:19, 83–5, 110–1 (*qaṣṣāṣ*), Index, s.v. injury assessors); idem (1990: Glossary, s.v. *qaṣṣāṣ*); Kressel (1996:79 [*qaṣṣāṣīn al-dam*]).

[18] Attestation of conveyance is not admitted in Islamic criminal procedure (Schacht 1964:198); however, homicide and bodily injury are considered, under both *sharʿī* and tribal law, as instances of damages within the domain of private law.

[19] In other words, he belongs to the Sudaydī branch of the Zuwayya tribe. See De Agostini (1922–23:407).

their expertise. Subsequently, Shaykh Saʿīd b. Yūnus Shalabī and Shaykh [13] ʿAlī b. al-Fūl, both from the Hayba lineage of the Naṣr [subtribe] belonging to the Maghāriba (De Agostini 1922–23:316, 323) [tribe] were summoned for the purpose of ascertaining [the assessor's] credibility (*tazkiya.*). They both testified that the aforementioned witnesses were persons of good reputation and that their testimony [14] completely corroborated the established facts. All this transpired and was registered on the date stated below, and upon his [i.e., the claimant's] request [the court] gave him a copy [of this document][20] bearing the date of the 21st day of Dhū [15] 'l-Qaʿda 1370 corresponding to August 23, 1951.

[16] Witnesses to the proceedings (*shuhūd al-ḥāl*)
[17] The Court ushers (*mubāshir*)
[20] ʿImrān Manṣūr al-Magharī
Muḥammad ʿAbd al-Salām[21]

[17] The matter being as indicated above
[18] The Deputy-in-Charge of the Affairs
of the Qāḍī of Ajdābiya,
the Sharʿī Nāʾib
[21] Muḥammad al-Mabrūk Abī Jāziya

Case 1 corresponds to the pattern of *kitāb al-qāḍī ilā'l-qāḍī* in the sense that the written testimony is addressed to a certain *qāḍī.* All the other cases entitled "*shahādat naql* in favor of [. . .]" in the Libyan *sijill* deviate from this pattern in the sense that they can be classified—to use Hallaq's wording—as an "open communication," that is, a communication addressed to any qāḍī, even one in the same locale.[22] The original rationale for the written testimony, i.e., to avoid the

[20] The qāḍī's role is here reduced to the hearing and registration of the testimonies of the assessors brought by the claimant without interfering with the principles of tribal law underlying the assessors' procedures. Under the *sharīʿa,* the qāḍī may resolve dispute of blood money (*diya*) in cases of unintentional injuries (*jirāḥ al-khaṭaʾ*). See Ibn ʿĀṣim (1958:232f. [the chapter on injuries, *jirāḥāt*]). Nonetheless, it is worth noting that the test of the assessors' credibility is carried out in accordance with *sharʿī* procedures. The registration of testimonies is intended to serve the interests of the boy and his kinsmen at proceedings pertaining to damages to be held in Benghazi.

[21] He acts concurrently or intermittently in two capacities: as a court usher and as a notary or professional witness. See Layish (1998: Name Index, 103–4).

[22] Hallaq (1999:452). Cf. *rasm istirʿāʾ* in Powers (1990:245 and fn. 97); idem (2002:31–7 [for definition, see 31 note 35] 43, 50, 120–1, 128, 130, 136, 221–2, 225, 227).

hardship of enlisting witnesses caused by geographical distance—is replaced here by the desire to avoid the hardship of enlisting witnesses at some future unspecified date when their testimony may be required to ensure the realization of some right or goal. In other words, the dimension of distance as the cause of hardship is replaced by the dimension of time. The witnessed document before the qāḍī is deposited in his *sijill* for safekeeping (Cf. Wakin 1972:9 and the reference to Tyan 1945 in fn. 2); it is intended to achieve legal certainty on the spot so that it may be used for some purpose at some unspecified date in the future. As will be seen from the cases below, the qāḍīs implicitly justify the deviation from the normative pattern of written testimony on the basis of the doctrine of *maṣlaḥa* (public interest).

Case 2[23]

ʿAbd al-Karīm appeared in the Sharīʿa Court of Ajdābiya, presided over by Shaykh Muḥammad al-Aḥlāfī. He acted as his wife's proxy concerning her deceased father's estate. The couple belonged to the Zuwayya tribe. ʿAbd al-Karīm made the following statement:

> [6] The [property of the] late Ḥasan, father of [7] Balāʾil, whom I am representing, and of his brother Muḥammad [. . .], within their [joint] ownership, be it immovable property, livestock, merchandise convertible into cash [8] and [other] goods, was not divided (*qisma*)[24] between the two before their successive deaths. They [continued] to own the entire [patrimony] that they left behind in al-Kufra and Jikharra [See Evans-Pritchard, map facing p. 35] oases and in Maṭrūḥ in equal shares until [9] the present.[25] I have brought with me a witness who will testify regarding what I have said; he is [. . .]. I ask [10] the noble Sharīʿa Court to question him, to register his testimony and to give it to me [so that it will be available to me] when the need arises (*ʿinda al-luzūm*).[26]

---

[23] For the Arabic document, see Layish (1998: doc. 48). For annotated translation of the entire document, see idem (2005: doc. 48).

[24] On the mechanisms for allotment (*qisma*) of immovable and other property in Mālikiī law, see Ibn ʿĀṣim (1958:140–6).

[25] In other words, no succession order was issued in regard to the estate that was inherited by the two brothers. Instead of dividing it between them as required by *sharʿī* apportionment, they chose to retain their joint ownership—a kind of family *mushāʿ*—and to administer the household on a cooperative basis.

[26] I.e., when a succession order is issued in which his wife's *sharʿī* share in her

The *qāḍī* endorsed this testimony, affixed his signature thereto, had the notaries testify to this effect, and instructed that it be registered in the *sijill*.

The written testimony here was intended to facilitate the issuance of a court order enabling Balā'il to secure her share of her father's estate. The fact that the estate of the two brothers remained undivided even after their deaths implies that Balā'il was deprived of her personal share in the estate. The representation of a married daughter by her husband here suggests the possibility of exerting structural pressures in the division of the patrimony. As an outsider, the husband is not guided by concern for the integrity of the agnatic patrimony.

Case 3[27]

Two brothers, ʿAbdallāh and ʿAbd al-Qādir, from the Ibn al-Ruways lineage of the Qabā'il tribe, worked a land in their joint ownership, with the understanding that they would equally share the expenses involved. Following a dispute between them, they appeared in the Sharīʿa Court of Ajdābiya, presided over by Shaykh Muḥammad al-Sanūsī al-Ghazzālī. ʿAbdallāh made the following statement:

> [6] My brother ʿAbd al-Qādir and I own [in common] livestock and other movable property (*manqūlāt*). We have dissociated ourselves from each other [with respect to the common property] (*tafāṣalnā*) (Cf. Lane 1984:2406ii) today in the presence of the witnesses who are present: [. . .] [7] I call upon the honorable Sharīʿa Court to register their testimony.

Two witnesses testified that ʿAbdallāh spent nothing on the purchase of the seeds and that it was ʿAbd al-Qādir who solely financed their purchase. Hence it was agreed that ʿAbdallāh should pay the sum

father's estate will be secured. Although the written testimony here sounds like "open communication," it stands to reason that the document was meant to be delivered to the *qāḍī* of the Sharīʿa Court of Kufra when the time would be appropriate for issuing a succession order. As indicated in line 8, the entire patrimony of the two brothers was located in Kufra and other places while the witness and the claimant were residing in Ajdābiya. In this respect, the written testimony here is closer to the pattern of *kitāb al-qāḍī ilā'l-qāḍī*.

[27] For the Arabic document, see Layish (1998: doc. 4). For annotated translation of the entire document, see idem (2005: doc. 4).

of fifteen pounds to ʿAbd al-Qādir towards the end of the harvest period of that year.

> [12] ʿAbd al-Qādir had borne the responsibility for all their debts, except for that relating to the dower, [concerning which an agreement had already been reached to the effect that]: Each of them would pay his own dower independently [13] for his respective wife.[28] We have borne witness to this effect.

On the basis of what has been established, the qāḍī endorsed the testimony given, had the witnesses testify to its validity and registered their testimony.

It seems that the written testimony in the case under review was intended to safeguard the payment of fifteen pounds to ʿAbd al-Qādir at the end of the harvest, the settlement of debts against the family estate by ʿAbd al-Qādir and, most important, the payment of the dower independently by each of the brothers for his respective wife at an unspecified date in the future. The document precludes any attempt in the future on the part of either brother to obtain the dower out of the family estate.

Case 4[29]

Sālima bint Ṣāliḥ from the al-Harash lineage of the ʿUjaylāt tribe appeared in the Sharīʿa Court of Ajdābiya, presided over by Shaykh Ḥusayn Muḥammad al-Aḥlāfī. She made the following statement:

> [6] A paternal cousin of mine called Maḥmūd al-Harash married me and [subsequently] divorced me about ten months ago. [7] I have brought witnesses with me who will testify to what I have stated

---

[28] In other words, for the time being, until the patrimony is divided between the two brothers; they seem to run the joint estate on the basis of partnership (*shirka* or *mushāraka*). The exclusion of the dowers from the partnership is a significant indication of their intention to bring about a total division of the patrimony at some future date. See Colucci (1927:27 [The landed property remains united within the *bayt* even after the death of the head of the family], 29); Peters (1980:154). (The cooperative farm usually breaks after the brothers have married); cf. Rosenfeld (1968).

[29] For the Arabic document, see Layish (1998: doc. 14). For an annotated translation of the entire document, see idem (2005: doc. 14). Cf. Sharīʿa Court of Ajdābiya, p. 27 no. 52 of September 8, 1951 (ill-treatment of a wife in a polygamous marriage); p. 218 no. 363 of July [?], 1953 (nonprovision of maintenance to a grandson).

> concerning the divorce from my aforementioned husband. Their [names] are: [. . .] [8]—all belonging to the ʿUjaylāt tribe. I ask the honorable Sharīʿa Court [9] to question them, to record their testimony, and to grant me permission to [re]marry and thus safeguard my honor (*karāma, sharaf*), since I am young and still a minor, and I am afraid [10] of falling into temptation (*ʿanat*).[30]

When the aforementioned witnesses were questioned, the first two said:

> We all met with [11] ʿAlī al-Kawnī, the Shaykh of our tribe, who told us: "I heard Maḥmūd al-Harash say that he had divorced his aforementioned wife Sālima [12] bint Ṣāliḥ." ʿAlī [. . .] gave testimony, regarding which he had no doubt whatsoever, that he had definitely met the aforementioned Maḥmūd [13] al-Harash in the town of al-ʿUjaylāt, where the latter had told him: "I have divorced my wife Sālima bint Ṣāliḥ," and this meeting [14] with Maḥmūd occurred in the month of Muḥarram 1373. Afterwards, all [the witnesses] said: "This is what we know and testify to."

After the witnesses corroborated Sālima's claim regarding the divorce and their credibility had been established (*tazkiya*), the qāḍī endorsed the testimony given, had the witnesses testify to its validity and registered their testimony.

The written testimony here was meant to serve Sālima's interests by authenticating her marital status as divorcee, thus removing legal bars to any future remarriage. It is worthwhile mentioning in this connection that the wife's fear of committing adultery is a common ground for divorce in Libyan judicial practice (cf. Layish 1991:91–2). The sanctions against illicit intercourse (*zinā*) are very stringent, both in customary law (cf. Abū Ḥassān 1974:242; Kressel 1981) and *sharīʿa*.

Case 5[31]

The *shaykh* and administrator of Zāwiyat Sīdī ʿAbd al-Salām (a Ṣūfī saint) in Ajdābiya, Shaykh ʿAbdallāh al-Jīlānī from the Ben Gharīb

---

[30] Cf. D'Emilia (1946:25) (*yukhshā ʿalayhā al-fasād*); Mohsen (1975:116–9); Powers, this volume. The woman's honor here should be evaluated in terms of her good name (*ʿirḍ*), as understood by an agnatic society.

[31] For the Arabic document, see Layish (1998: doc. 54); for an annotated translation of the entire document, see idem (2005: doc. 54).

lineage of the Maṣwāna tribe, born in Benghazi and residing in Ajdābiya, appeared in the Sharīʿa Court of Ajdābiya, presided over by the Qāḍī, *sayyid*[32] Muḥammad al-Sanūsī al-Ghazzālī al-Khaṭṭābī. He made the following statement:

> [6] In my capacity as guardian of the Zāwiya[33] known as Zāwiyat Sīdī ʿAbd al-Salām[34] in Ajdābiya, [I have been informed] that the woman [7] called Mabrūka [. . .] bequeathed (*awṣat*) one-third[35] of her immovable property [in favor of a certain *zāwiya*; see below] in the presence of a group of Muslim witnesses, and subsequently died. I ask that the noble Sharīʿa Court [8] hear the testimony of the following witnesses: [. . .] [9], and register [their testimony] in favor of the aforementioned Zāwiya.

His request was granted. We [the qāḍī] questioned each of the five witnesses, who concurred that

> [10] Mabrūka [. . .] summoned us to her house, where [11] she held a session while in her bed, and had tea served to us and drank with us. Subsequently she said:
>
> > I am very ill and apprehensive concerning my health. You are my witnesses that I have no claim [12] against anyone; nor does anyone have a claim against me.[36] I own two goats, and I would like to have them slaughtered and given away as charity (*ṣadaqa*) [to the

---

[32] I.e., *sharīf*, a descendant of the Prophet Muḥammad.

[33] The *shaykh* of the *zāwiya* fulfills both a spiritual-ritual function and an administrative one. Sometimes the founder of the *waqf* stipulates that the *shaykh* should also act as the *mutawallī* of the *waqf*. Mohsen (1975:73–4). Cf. Layish (1994:161–2).

[34] The reference is to Sīdī ʿAbd al-Salām al-Asmar al-Fīṭūrī from Zliten; see Albergoni (1993:128); cf. Layish (2002:107n., 87, and the sources indicated there concerning saints' worship); al-Sūrī (1984:395–6).

[35] The testamentary *waqf* is subject to the *ultra vires* doctrine which is meant to safeguard the legal heirs' *sharʿī* rights to the estate; it is not legally permissible to bequeath by will more than one-third of one's estate. See Ibn ʿĀṣim (1958:202, lines 1374, 1381); Coulson (1971:235–6). On testamentary *waqf*, see Layish (1983:2ff.).

[36] In Mālikī law, a testamentary disposition within the limits of one-third of the estate is valid regardless of whether the testator is in good health or in a state of "death-sickness" (*maraḍ al-mawt*) (see Ibn ʿĀṣim [1958:202, line 1374]; Zaydān [1993, 10:383, § 11195]). Similarly, a *waqf* in death-sickness is valid provided it is within one-third of the estate and not in favor of a legal heir (see Zaydān [1993, 10:457–8, § 11403]). In contrast, a charitable gift made in death-sickness or where the object of the gift is subject to heavy debts—is not valid (see Ibn ʿĀṣim [1958:176, line 1191]; Zaydān [1993, 10:369, § 11159]; cf. Coulson [1971:269]). There is no information here as to whether the testamentary *waqf* and the charitable gift were made in death-sickness. There is, however, a clear statement to the effect that the woman's property was not subject to debts.

> poor] after my death.[37] I have a building complex bordering on [. . .]. [15] I have designated (*awqaftu*) [by means of testamentary disposition] one-third of my building complex as a *waqf* in favor of Zāwiyat[38] Sīdī ʿAbd al-Salām currently presided over by Shaykh ʿAbdallāh al-Jīlānī. The chest in the house is the private property of my husband Abī Bakr.
>
> [16] This is her testimony and bequest of her own free will and choice and without coercion or compulsion. Though sick in body she was mentally in a state of a full legal capacity.[39]

On the basis of the testimony of the five witnesses, the qāḍī endorsed the witnesses' testimony relating to the testamentary *waqf* in favor of the Zāwiya, signed it, had the undersigned notaries testify thereto and instructed that it be registered [in the *sijill*].

The written testimony here was required to prevent any attempt in the future to invalidate the testamentary *waqf* on some legal grounds such as the testatrix's incompetence to engage in transactions or that her property was subject to debts.

Case 6[40]

ʿAlī b. Faraj from the Zuwayya tribe appeared in the Sharīʿa Court of Ajdābiya, presided over by the Qāḍī Ḥusayn Muḥammad al-Aḥlāfī. He claimed that fifty years previously his late mother, Fuṭayma, had purchased a female slave from ʿAlī b. Masʿūd from the same tribe, in return for a camel owned by her.[41] He said:

---

[37] This pious gesture is performed by the testatrix in order to ensure the salvation of her soul; cf. Layish (1994:147); Reiter (1996:109). Sacrifice is practiced among the Bedouin of Cyrenaica. See Peters (1984:214); cf. Stewart (1998: Index, s.v. sacrifice).

[38] On *waqf* in favor of a *zāwiya*, see Baer (1997:266–71); Reiter (1996:107). This form of pious activity is particularly common among women. See Layish (1994:156); Baer and Layish (1971:21). In Cyrenaica, the propensity for founding *waqf* in favor of *zāwiyas* was no doubt intensified on account of the special status enjoyed there by the Sanūsī order. See Layish (1991:5, 12, 16–17, 204–5, and the sources indicated there).

[39] On the testator's legal capacity, see Coulson (1971:216–7).

[40] For the Arabic document, see Layish (1998: doc. 61). For an annotated translation of the entire document, see idem (2005: doc. 61).

[41] Under the *sharīʿa* a slave is considered as property (*māl*) that can be disposed of in a legal transaction provided that the owner's rights over the slave are not restricted in any way. On the sale of slaves in Mālikī law, see Ibn ʿĀṣim (1958:110, lines 737ff.); Ibn al-ʿAṭṭār (1983:33ff.); on slaves in Libya see Davis (1987:111); cf. Abū Ḥassān (1974:255–6 [aggressors are liable to pay fines by giving slaves]).

> [7] I have brought with me two witnesses called [. . .], both [8] from the Zuwayya tribe. I [hereby] ask that the noble Sharīʿa Court question them [on this matter], register their testimony and give me [a document pertaining to] their testimony [that I can use] as the need arises.[42]
>
> When the aforementioned witnesses, identified in person and name, were questioned, [9] they both gave testimony [whose truthfulness the witness deemed to be] beyond any shadow of doubt, corroborating in letter and spirit the statement of the aforementioned ʿAlī b. Faraj.

The qāḍī sanctioned (*ajāza*) their testimony and instructed that it be registered in the *sijill.*

The reason for the written testimony is indicated explicitly in the document: It is to be used "as the need arises." As a legal heir ʿAlī was anxious to ensure that no one dispute his mother's ownership of the female slave. Since the sale of the female slave had taken place fifty years earlier, he felt that it was important to enlist the testimony of the witnesses to that sale before they died. Such a document would be necessary in the event of any transaction pertaining to the slave girl.[43]

Case 7[44]

A dispute arose concerning the estate of a deceased woman between Mabrūka, the deceased's daughter-in-law through her deceased son Ādam, and Maryam, daughter of the deceased, both of them belonging to the Sudaydī lineage of the Zuwayya tribe. The case was heard in the Sharīʿa Court of Ajdābiya, presided over by the Qāḍī Ḥusayn Muḥammad al-Aḥlāfī. Mabrūka, the claimant, denied Maryam's right

---

[42] Such as in the event he decides to sell the female slave.

[43] Cf. Sharīʿa Court of Ajdābiya, p. 224 no. 371 of July 15, 1953 (A woman belonging to the Maṣrāta tribe claimed that she, her father and sister together bought a house in Ajdābiya, each of them having one-third of the house; the claimant shared her portion with her late husband. She brought her father to testify to this effect, and asked the court to issue a "*shahādat naql* in my favor [to be used] when the need arises"); p. 230 no. 380 of July 23, 1953 (A man belonging to the Zuwayya tribe claimed that he owned a house in the Ajdābiya. He brought his witnesses to testify that he had built the house with his private money); p. 342 no. 581 of July 6, 1954 (*shahādat naql* pertaining to sale of land); p. 346 no. 590 of July 4, 1954 (sale of land).

[44] For the Arabic document, see Layish (1998: doc. 67). For an annotated translation of the entire document, see idem (2005: doc. 67).

to inherit a certain she-camel belonging to her mother since, according to the former, the mother had, in her lifetime, gifted (*wahabat*) this same camel to Ādam. In her version, since the time of the gift, Ādam

> [7] proceeded to dispose of it and of its issue, so that they [the camel and its issue] passed into his property (*milk*).[45] After the death of the mother[46] and her son [Ādam, [8] the camel and its issue] became part of his [Ādam's] estate [by virtue of the gift].[47] [. . .] I have produced witnesses to testify [to the truth] of my statement, and they are [. . .]. [9] I ask that the noble Sharīʿa Court interrogate them and register their testimonies.

Mabrūka's witnesses testified that according to "widespread" rumor that had reached them, the aforementioned camel had been transferred to Ādam by gift rather than intestate succession. The qāḍī endorsed their testimony and instructed that it be registered in favor of Mabrūka.

The written testimony was requested here because Ādam's right to the camel by virtue of the gift was contested by Maryam, daughter of the deceased, who had been deprived of her share in the camel and its issue by this gift as an instrument for circumventing the *sharʿī* rules of inheritance, and the qāḍī endorsed the transaction on the basis of hearsay evidence.[48]

Occasionally, the differences between a regular judicial decision and a *shahādat naql* are blurred. The same phraseology and legal formularies are used in both cases and the documents are intended to serve the same purpose, namely, to avoid the necessity of enlisting witnesses to a specific right or event when that necessity constitutes a hardship. In both cases the qāḍī appears to have been guided by the doctrine of *maṣlaḥa* (public interest).

---

[45] On gifts and other means for circumventing the *sharʿī* rules of inheritance, see Layish (1983); idem (1997); Powers (2002:207–10).

[46] Mention of the mother's death is irrelevant in a case of a gift, since the camel did not constitute part of her estate. Cf. fn. 48 below.

[47] The daughter-in-law bases her claim to the she-camel on her right to her husband's estate.

[48] Cf. Sharīʿa Court of Ajdābiya, p. 344 no. 587 of July 11, 1954. (Shortly after the issuance of a *sharʿī* order of succession on her mother-in-law's estate, a woman claimed in court that three she-camels out of this estate had been given as a gift to her late husband by his mother thirty years earlier and that since then he had been disposing of the progeny of these she-camels freely as his own private property rather than part of his mother's estate. She asked the court to issue a *shahādat naql* in her favor.)

Case 8[49]

Al-Sāʿidī, belonging to Julūlāt, a branch of the Zuwayya tribe, born and residing in Ajdābiya, appeared in the Sharīʿa Court of Ajdābiya, presided over by the Deputy Qāḍī, the Nāʾib Muḥammad al-Ṭālib al-Hammālī. Al-Sāʿidī claimed that his daughter Fawziyya, aged eight, while playing with her sister at home, fell down on the sharp handle of a handmill and, as a result, broke her hymen. A woman, probably a practitioner of popular medicine, examined the girl immediately after the accident, while she was still bleeding, and confirmed the girl's loss of virginity as a result of the accident. Al-Sāʿidī made the following statement:

> [10] [. . .] Since this accident has been ordained [11] by Allāh the Exalted, I [al-Sāʿidī] request that it be registered at the Sharīʿa Court so that I may resort to [the document] whenever the need arises and testify to its contents.[50]

All this occurred [12] in the presence of witnesses [i.e., the notaries] listed below.

On the basis of what has been established by the aforementioned al-Sāʿidī [. . .] while he was in a state of legal competence in *sharʿī* terms, as duly certified [13] in the presence of the aforementioned Nāʾib, the latter issued a judgment endorsing what has been

[49] For the Arabic document, see Layish (1998: doc. 58). For an annotated translation of the entire document, see idem (2005: doc. 58).

[50] Loss of virginity out of wedlock is tantamount to illicit intercourse which under customary law implies disgrace to the bride's agnates and may entail severe sanctions. Bedouin would stipulate in the marriage contract that the bride should be a virgin. If on the day of the marriage the virginity test shows that the bride is not a virgin the marriage may be canceled or (if concluded) revoked and the bride (or her father) be requested to return the prompt dower. Dissolution of the marriage under such circumstances seriously diminishes the woman's chances to remarry. Moreover, due to the disgrace caused to the bride's agnates she may be exposed to death threats. See Peters (1965:121–2 [virginity test], 129); D'Emilia (1946:38); Powers (this volume); Mohsen (1975:107); Obermeyer (1968:122); Abū Ḥassān (1974:241–2). The *sharīʿa* takes a more lenient attitude in this matter. In the case under review, the girl's father was fully aware of the consequences under customary law of loss of virginity and this may well be the reason why he presented the case as an accident attributable to an irrevocable "act of God." In his distress he resorted to the Sharīʿa Court, rather than to tribal proceedings, to obtain a document certifying that the girl's ruptured hymen did not imply disgrace to her agnates. The recourse to the Sharīʿa Court rather than to tribal justice may have been prompted also by considerations of discreteness. This document would presumably serve to forestall misunderstandings with a future husband and the resort to severe sanctions on the part of the girl's agnates.

established above, and had the undersigned [professional witnesses] testify to it. He then signed and endorsed it [14] and had it registered [in the *sijill*].

Because the accident occurred in the absence of witnesses, this legal document was meant to establish, at the time of Fawziyya's marriage, that her loss of virginity did not occur in circumstances liable to disgrace her agnates. Fully cognizant of the father's delicate predicament, the Nā'ib accepted the father's version without even requiring the testimony of the woman who had examined the daughter immediately after the accident. The expert's report may be regarded as circumstantial evidence. Formally, we have here a judicial decision. In practical terms, however, the procedure was equivalent to *shahādat naql*. The Nā'ib complied with al-Sāʿidī's request to issue the document even though there were no witnesses to the event. He was probably motivated to do so by regard for Fawziyya's welfare.

IV. *Summary and Conclusions*

Hallaq's main conclusions with respect to the institution of *kitāb al-qāḍī ilā 'l-qāḍī* are that the written instrument is indispensable in daily life and that practice, through the coercive power of custom and social reality, modified and redefined legal doctrine to the point of bridging the gap between doctrine and practice, the ideal and the real (Hallaq 1999:464–6). These conclusions seem to be valid also with respect to the institution of *shahādat naql*, although there are some differences deriving from the nature of the source which deals with the written testimony (legal treatises vis-à-vis judicial practice) and the period in which the written testimony took place (premodern vs. modern). The justification for both institutions lies in the need for written documents in daily social and economic life. In the case of Libya this is reflected in the qāḍīs' awareness of the necessity to adapt practical norms to the exigencies of changing circumstances. Naturally, the sophistication manifested by the qāḍī in his attempt to bring about a synthesis of orthodox *sharʿī* rules of evidence and day-to-day pressures is less evident here than it is in the *adab al-qāḍī* literature. This, however, does not detract from the qāḍīs' contribution to narrowing the gap between doctrine and practice. The qāḍīs seem to be motivated in the first place by pragmatic considerations. This approach displays itself also in their efforts to bring sedentary tribal society within the orbit of normative Islam (Layish 2002:90–3). The doctrine of *ḍarūra* (necessity) in *adab al-qāḍī* treatises (Hallaq 1999:457) has been replaced in the Libyan judicial practice by variants of *maṣlaḥa*, both being, in effect, two sides of the same coin. This trend manifests itself in the qāḍī's admitting into his court decisions the claimant's request to register his testimony so that the written testimony is issued in the claimant's favor to be used "when the need arises."

We have noted earlier that the Libyan qāḍīs do not often invoke the legal literature. It is, however, important to mention that some of them do refer to Ibn ʿAṣim's *al-ʿAṣimiyya*, which incorporates the judicial practice (*ʿamal*) of al-Andalus.[51] This suggests that the qāḍīs are aware of the power of custom as an informal source of law that molds legal norms in daily life and are ready to compromise with it, at the expense of the traditional rules of evidence.[52] In this respect we witness here a realistic form of Islamic jurisprudence, though the main burden in our case lies on the shoulders of the qāḍīs rather than those of the jurists (Cf. Coulson 1964:147).

The widespread practice of *shahādat naql* in the Libyan *sijill* is in conformity with the modern trend of admitting, by means of statutory legislation, written documents as valid proof (See above, 497). As already observed, the *raison d'être* of *kitāb al-qāḍī ilā 'l-qāḍī*, dating back to premodern times, remained intact. However, the hardship of enlisting witnesses has shifted from geographical distance, of less significance nowadays due to the modernization of communications, to legal certainty, which meets the requirements of present-day exigencies. From this perspective, written documents are regarded as an indispensable instrument for securing legal and financial rights in the unforeseen future. In this respect, *shahādat naql* may be regarded as an extension of the Mālikī judicial practice (*ʿamal*) that seeks to accommodate the *sharīʿa* to the present-day circumstances. All the qāḍīs in the abovementioned cases seem to share the same approach towards written documents.[53]

---

[51] See above, 498; Layish (1998: doc. 1, line 23; doc. 31, lines 25–6).

[52] Cf. Layish (1984:41 {The Qāḍī of Bethlehem: "Since reconciliation is stronger than the qāḍī (*al-ṣulḥ yuqawwī al-qāḍī*), because it is based on agreement between the parties, it affects the *sharʿī* decision}).

[53] Unfortunately, no information on the Libyan qāḍīs' *sharʿī* education and legal training is available to me.

As noted earlier, all the cases of *shahādat naql* were registered in the Sharīʿa Court of Ajdābiya, a district center in the plain near the Mediterranean coast, and none in the Sharīʿa Court of Kufra, which is located in the southern tribal region of Cyrenaica, far from governmental administrative centers (Davis 1998:7). It seems that the process of integration of sedentary Bedouin into normative Islam is largely facilitated by the pragmatic judicial practice of the *sharīʿa* court as manifested *inter alia* in mechanisms such as *shahādat naql.*

CHAPTER TWENTY-ONE

PAKISTAN'S EVIDENCE ORDER ("QANUN-I-SHAHADAT"), 1984: GENERAL ZIA'S ANTI-ISLAMIZATION COUP

Lucy Carroll

Introduction

Many of the major statutes, long in force (and generally still in force) in the South Asian subcontinent, were originally enacted during the British period. One such statute is the Evidence Act, 1872. Based on English law of the time, this statute continues in force in India and Bangladesh, and was in force in Pakistan until 1984, when it was repealed and its terms, with very few changes, were reenacted by General Zia ul-Haq through a Presidential Order as the Qanun-i-Shahadat Order (Evidence Order). This paper focuses on the latter event.

Among the topics dealt with by the Evidence Act is the presumption of legitimacy of the child born of a valid marriage. This particular provision figures in two of the three decisions discussed below, and was one of two major sections which were altered by the Evidence Order of the Zia regime. Section 112 of the 1872 statute declares:

> 112. *Birth during marriage conclusive proof of legitimacy.*
> The fact that any person is born during the continuance of a valid marriage between his mother and any man, or within two hundred and eighty days after its dissolution, the mother remaining unmarried, shall be conclusive proof that he is the legitimate son of that man, unless it can be shown that the parties to the marriage had no access to each other at any time when he could have been begotten.

Some of the propositions incorporated in this section differ significantly from the terms of Muslim, and particularly Sunni, law. Hanafi law does not recognize proof of nonaccess, or even of nonconsummation of the marriage, as sufficient grounds for refuting the ascription of paternity to the husband of the child's mother, as long as birth occurs six months or more after the marriage. Sunnis recognize quite extended periods of gestation (Hanafis twenty-four months). Most particularly, Muslim law of all schools regards six months as the minimum period of gestation and insists that this period should elapse between the marriage and the birth in order for paternity to be conclusively and automatically established in the husband of the mother.

Although Muslim writers frequently call attention to the latter discrepancy, remarking that under section 112 the child is presumed legitimate no matter how soon after marriage it may be born, it should be appreciated that the innocent bridegroom would presumably have little difficulty (particularly in a culture where pre-nuptial courtship and "dating" are unknown) in establishing nonaccess prenuptially, and thus asserting that the early-born child was not his. On the other hand, Hanafi law permits the husband to acknowledge as his the child born to his wife within six months of the marriage. The difference between section 112 of the Evidence Act, 1872, and Hanafi law could be summarized by stating that in Hanafi law, the husband has to *act to affirm* paternity of the early-born child (by acknowledging that it is his, without admitting that it was conceived in *zina*), while under the Evidence Act, he has to *act to rebut* the presumption of paternity (by proving nonaccess). However, even this statement exaggerates the difference, since the husband may acknowledge the child simply by treating it as a legitimate child would ordinarily be treated; it is repudiation of the child that requires some specific statement or overt action (e.g. turning the wife and child out of the house), and this action must take place immediately.

Section 112 is actually more generous to the betrayed husband than Hanafi law, since under the Act, proof of nonaccess will rebut not only paternity of the early-born child, but also paternity of the child born during, but more than six months after, the marriage; and the child born after dissolution of the marriage. In Muslim law, the former child can only be repudiated through the (spiritually dangerous) procedure of *lian*; and even that procedure, which (in Hanafi law) can only take place between parties who are at the time husband and wife, is not available after dissolution of the marriage. (Lian for repudiation of paternity is not recognized in South Asian law.)[1] Further, Muslim law requires that the repudiation of the child

[1] The Qazf Ordinance (Offense of Qazf [Enforcement of Hudood] Ordinance) was promulgated simultaneously with the draconian Zina Ordinance (Offense of

be immediate; delay is equivalent to acknowledgment of paternity, and a child once acknowledged, even implicitly, cannot subsequently be repudiated.[2]

The 1872 statute and the "1938 repeal-revival" hypothesis

More than a century and a quarter ago, in order to clear the ground for the application of the Evidence Act, 1872, section 2 of that Act repealed, in addition to the various provisions found in preexisting statutes, "all rules of evidence not contained in any Statute, Act or Regulation in force in any part of British India." This phrasing included rules derived from the uncodified Muslim law which dealt with any of the matters specifically covered by the Evidence Act (including, e.g., allocation of the burden of proof, the definition of admissible evidence, and the presumptions raised by section 112).

Section 2 of the Evidence Act, 1872, was itself repealed in a routine operation in 1938. The repealing and/or amending of acts (or sections of acts amending or repealing another statute or sections of a statute) are done routinely simply to keep the bulk of the official code from growing unnecessarily and to facilitate access to the up-to-date statutes.[3] Section 2 had accomplished its purpose; the sections of preexisting statutes which had been repealed had been stricken

---

Zina [Enforcement of Hudood] Ordinance) in 1979. The former, which provides for punishment of a false accusation of *zina*, was undoubtedly intended as a brake on careless and frivolous charges being brought under the latter Ordinance, but (poorly drafted and very limited in scope) it most emphatically did not have that effect. The immediate point is that while the Qazf Ordinance provides for a corrupted form of *lian* for *qazf* if the accusation of unchastity is made by a husband against his wife, it does not permit denunciation of the child born of any such alleged adultery.

[2] Repudiation of a child in circumstances where the child cannot be bastardized nonetheless constitutes *qazf* against the mother of the child and exposes the husband to the eighty lashes decreed by the Qur'ān, unless he undergoes the ritual of *lian*, which will dissolve his marriage with the child's mother but cannot bastardize the child or free himself from his obligations toward the child presumed to be his. As noted in fn. 1, the Qazf Ordinance in Pakistan does not provide for bastardization of the child in any case.

[3] When a statute is amended by the omission or rewording of any section, or by the addition of a new section, etc., the terms of the amending act are included in the official version of that statute; there is no need to search through the entire collection of statutes to find if and when the statute in question might have been amended. Once the changes have been incorporated in the main statute, there is no need to retain the amending act itself.

from the text of those statutes; the uncodified rules of Muslim or Hindu law repealed by section 2 had likewise ceased to have legal effect more than half a century previously; there was no further need for section 2 to remain on the statute books. The repeal of an amending or repealing act (or part of an act performing these functions) does not affect the continuation of the change made by the repeal or amending act.[4] Surely in 1938 no one could possibly have anticipated the legal argument which would, a quarter of a century later, be based on what those who carried it out would have seen as a routine bureaucratic task.

The "1938 repeal-revival"[5] hypothesis contended that the repeal of section 2 of the Evidence Act in 1938 had had the effect of bringing *all* the uncodified Muslim law rules, previously repealed in 1872, back into force. Thus, so the argument went, after 1938 these formerly repealed and now "revived" Muslim law rules existed, side by side with the contrary terms of the Evidence Act, and the court functioning in the Islamic Republic had the option of applying them (or any one of them), instead of the comparable provision of the Evidence Act, in litigation involving Muslims. This is obviously a very radical position—a much more radical position than either of the courts which accepted it appear to have realized. It is also an erroneous position; both courts which endorsed the "1938 repeal-revival" hypothesis focused on the provisions of the General Clauses Act concerning "enactments" which had been amended or repealed, and guaranteeing the continuation of such amendments and repeals in spite of the repeal of the amending/repealing act which had brought the changes into being; the Muslim law rules which had been repealed were uncodified and were not to be found in any "enactment." Thus the courts held that since the situation was not covered the General Clauses Act, the relevant Muslim law rules had been "revived." Unfortunately, in reaching this conclusion the courts completely overlooked the provision of the General Clauses Act which did govern the situation.

The "1938 repeal-revival" hypothesis was raised and considered in three Pakistan cases—*Ghulam Bhik*, West Pakistan High Court 1957; *Abdul Ghani*, West Pakistan High Court 1962; and *Hamida Begum*, Pakistan Supreme Court 1975.

---

[4] General Clauses Act, 1897, relevant provisions of which are discussed below.

[5] My term.

Ghulam Bhik, West Pakistan *High Court 1957*

The wife in *Ghulam Bhik*[6] had obtained a *lian*-divorce[7] on the grounds that her husband had falsely accused her of adultery; the appellate court had upheld the decree. Before the Single Judge (in second appeal) and the Divisional Bench (in Letters Patent appeal), the husband urged that such an accusation could not lead to a dissolution of marriage except through the procedure of *lian* (i.e., swearing the mutual oaths; see Qur'ān, 24:4–9). These further appeals were also dismissed. Neither Justice Kayani nor Justice Kaikaus (who constituted the Divisional Bench; each wrote a separate opinion) accepted the appellant's contention that the Muslim law rules of procedure and evidence were applicable. (Reference here is to the manner of proving a false and reckless accusation of *zina* by a husband against his wife—by his refusal to swear the oaths of *lian*, or by his inability to prove the truth of his statement by any evidence admissible under the Evidence Act.)[8] Justice Kayani reiterated that section 2 of

---

[6] *Ghulam Bhik v. Hussain Begum*, All Pakistan Legal Decisions (hereafter "PLD") 1957 (West Pakistan) Lahore 998.

[7] Although *lian* as such was not available in British India, the principle that a chaste wife who had been falsely or recklessly accused of adultery by her husband had been grievously wronged and was entitled to relief was recognized. *Lian* was converted into a wife's suit for divorce (which I term *lian*-divorce) on the grounds that her husband had falsely accused her of adultery. This was one of the very few grounds on which a Muslim woman in British India could obtain a judicial divorce prior to 1939. After the Dissolution of Muslim Marriages Act, 1939, *lian*-divorce continued to be available and was brought within the parameters of that statute either under section 2(ix), which permits the court to dissolve a marriage solemnized under Muslim law "on any other ground which is recognized as valid for the dissolution of marriages under Muslim law;" or under clause (viii)(a), which entitles a wife to sue for divorce on the grounds of cruelty.

The Pakistan Qazf Ordinance, 1979, introduced *lian* for *qazf* (scandalous accusation) in Pakistani law. *Lian*-divorce remains an option, and is preferable because it offers the wife the best chance of clearing her name; *lian* proceedings leave her reputation under a cloud. Further, the Qazf Ordinance only applies in circumstances where the accusation is made "before a Court," with the result that any extrajudicial accusation no matter how reckless and false, and no matter how publicly made, can be retracted merely by failing to repeat it "before the Court" when summoned by the complaining wife. *Lian*-divorce is available if the wife can prove that the accusation was made, and the husband cannot prove that the accusation is true. *Lian* for repudiation of paternity is not available, even in Pakistan.

[8] Since the *hadd* for *qazf* was not enforceable in British India or in pre-1979 Pakistan, the husband, were his position accepted, could painlessly decline to swear the oaths, leaving the wife without a remedy prior to 1939. After 1939, if a false accusation of adultery would only result in a dissolution of marriage if her husband agreed to swear the oaths of *lian*, the wife would have to prove one of the specified

the Evidence Act "had repealed 'all rules of evidence not contained in any Statute, Act or Regulation in force in any part of British India,' including obviously, the rules of Muhammadan Law relating to evidence."

What is of particular interest here is the argument raised by counsel for the husband, and Justice Kayani's response to it:—

> Mr Mahmud Ali's [husband's counsel's] contention that section 2 [of the 1872 Evidence Act] having itself been repealed in 1938 revived the rules of Muhammadan Law is without force, because these rules did not exist in 1938 (having been repealed by section 2 in 1872), and nothing can come back to life which does not exist, unless it is revived by a legal fiction. Far from being revived by an express provision, their continued demise was ensured by a general provision in section 6 of the General Clauses Act that the repeal of an enactment "shall not revive anything not in force or existing at the time at which the repeal takes effect."[9]

Relying on *section 6 of the General Clauses Act*, 1897, the High Court rejected the "1938 repeal-revival" hypothesis. And indeed, section 6 of the General Clauses Act constitutes a complete and conclusive answer to the contention: the Muslim law rules in conflict with the provisions of the Evidence Act had been repealed in 1872; they were consequently "not in force" in 1938 when section 2 was itself repealed; section 6 of the General Clauses Act clearly states that repeal of any enactment [e.g., repeal of section 2 of the Evidence Act] "shall not—(a) revive anything not in force or existing at the time at which the repeal takes effect."[10]

---

grounds available under the 1939 Act in order to obtain a divorce in the face of such refusal; among such grounds is the fact that the husband "makes her life miserable by cruelty of conduct even if such conduct does not amount to physical ill-treatment." A malicious and false accusation (i.e., an accusation which the husband could not prove to be true) of unchastity would undoubtedly constitute "cruelty of conduct" sufficient to make the woman's life "miserable."

[9] *Ghulam Bhik*, PLD 1957 (West Pakistan) Lahore 998, 1011.

[10] Section 6 of the General Clauses Act, 1897, reads (as far as is relevant here):— "Where this Act, or any Central Act or Regulation made after the commencement of this Act [e.g., the Repealing Act, 1938], repeals any enactment hitherto made [e.g., section 2 of the Evidence Act, 1872] or hereafter to be made, then, unless a different intention appears, *the repeal shall not—(a) revive anything not in force or existing at the time at which the repeal takes effect*; . . ." (Emphasis added.) The Muslim legal rules, which had been repealed and superseded by the Evidence Act, were obviously "not in force" at the time section 2 was repealed.

Abdul Ghani, *West Pakistan High Court 1962*

Five years later the same argument was made in regard to legitimacy and section 112 of the Evidence Act in the *Abdul Ghani* case.[11] P died in 1936 subject to customary law, which, in the absence of a son, and any near collateral male agnates, passed his property to his daughter in life-estate.[12] Some seventeen years later, one sister and the children of the other (who had by then died) attempted, very belatedly, to oust the daughter by contending that she was illegitimate.[13] At the commencement of the decision the High Court concurred in the finding of the lower court that the suit was barred by limitation; if the daughter were legitimate, she was sole heir of her father; even if she were illegitimate, she had held possession of the property for more than twelve years and thus had prescribed title by adverse possession.

Nevertheless, the court proceeded to consider the arguments of the appellants, and dealt with the case on merits (although the conclusion on merits would be of no consequence in this particular case, given the finding on limitation). The *Abdul Ghani* court concluded that the 1938 repeal of section 2 of the Evidence Act had "revived" the Muslim laws concerning (e.g.) legitimacy of the child born of a valid marriage,[14] which had been repealed by that same section in

---

[11] *Abdul Ghani v. Taleh Bibi*, PLD 1962 (West Pakistan) Lahore 531.

[12] The property was in fact the entire property previously held by P's father, although P was one of four siblings. His brother, who had inherited half of his father's property along with P (daughters being excluded under customary law by the presence of sons), had predeceased P, who was his brother's sole heir. In the event, all of the father's land had ended up in the hands of the surviving son, who then died leaving a daughter as his sole heir, plus his mother and two sisters, who were not heirs under customary law in the presence of P's descendant.

[13] The litigation only makes any sense at all if the absence of any male agnatic heir is postulated; the delay in filing suit only makes sense on the assumption that shortly before the suit was filed, the last surviving male agnate, who would have barred the married sisters (who only take precedence over cognates) had died. The sisters were now in the immediate line of succession, and would take absolutely (i.e., not in life-estate); but at the same time, given the absence of a male agnate, the daughter's life-estate would be converted into an absolute estate, and she would oust the sisters. If the daughter were removed, the sisters would take as absolute heirs (after a life-estate held by P's mother, an elderly woman); the sons of the deceased sister would represent her, taking with the surviving sister.

[14] Note that *all* the rules of Muslim law concerning legitimacy were not repealed by the Evidence Act; only the rules in conflict with section 112 of the Evidence Act were repealed and superseded by that statute. These were the rules concerning the child born during the subsistence of a valid marriage, and within a certain period following its dissolution.

1872, and that these "revived" rules were (and, although nobody had previously noticed it in the preceding quarter of a century, had been since 1938!) available for application to Muslim litigants. The daughter was found to be illegitimate on the grounds that she had been born within six months of the marriage of her parents; she was not an heir; she was merely a trespasser who had perfected title through adverse possession.

While Justice Kayani in *Ghulam Bhik* had (correctly) invoked section 6 of the General Clauses Act to rebut the "1938 repeal-revival" hypothesis, the *Abdul Ghani* court did not refer to this section at all. The *Abdul Ghani* court (incorrectly) assumed that *section 6–A of the General Clauses Act* was the relevant section, and held that since section 6–A *did not prevent the revival* of the (previously repealed) Muslim law rules following the repeal of section 2 of the Evidence Act, the Muslim law rules had been "revived" by the repeal of section 2.

Section 6–A of the General Clauses Act is totally irrelevant to the situation; it deals with the repeal of a statute amending (or repealing) "the text of any Central Act or Regulation;" the Muslim legal rules repealed by section 2 of the Evidence Act were part of the uncodified Muslim law, and were not found in "the text of any Central Act or Regulation."[15] The fact that section 6–A does not deal with the specific situation of the uncodified Muslim legal rules repealed by section 2 of the Evidence Act, does not mean that another section of the General Clauses Act might not be applicable to the situation. The *Abdul Ghani* court did not even consider whether the situation might be covered by another section, and specifically by section 6, of the General Clauses Act.[16]

The fact that two Benches of concurrent jurisdiction and equal weight had reached contrary conclusions on the effect of the repeal

---

[15] Section 6–A of the General Clauses Act, 1897, reads: "Where any Central Act or Regulation made after the commencement of this Act [e.g. the Repealing Act, 1938] repeals any enactment by which *the text of any Central Act or Regulation was amended* by the express omission, insertion or substitution of any matter, then unless a different intention appears, the repeal shall not affect the continuance of any such amendment made by the enactment so repealed and in operation at the time of the repeal." (Emphasis added.)

[16] The *Ghulam Bhik* decision is not cited in the judgment. The daughter did not appear to defend the appeal (against the decision in her favor), and it was heard *ex parte*. Had she chosen to defend the appeal and retained counsel, he almost certainly would have brought up *Ghulam Bhik*. In the event, it is perhaps unfortunate that she didn't retain counsel. (See discussion of the *Hamida Begum* case below, in which both sides were represented by counsel.)

of section 2 of the Evidence Act, 1872, would ordinarily mean that the Supreme Court would undoubtedly consider the question at the earliest opportunity. That opportunity came in the 1975 *Hamida Begum* case.

Hamida Begum, *Pakistan Supreme Court 1975*

Hamida Begum[17] was another legitimacy case. P's widow and her children alleged that Hamida, the daughter of the deceased by his first (and predeceased) wife, was illegitimate. The issue had been complicated and the litigation prolonged by an abundance of forged documents and perjured testimony;[18] by the time the matter reached the Supreme Court, Hamida had spent more than twenty-five years in litigation attempting to establish her status as a legitimate child of her father and an heir to his estate.

Before turning to the facts of the actual litigation before it, the Supreme Court dealt with the "1938 repeal-revival" hypothesis—as one would expect it to do, given the conflict of opinion between the Divisional Benches of the High Court. Amazingly, however, again *Ghulam Bhik* is neither discussed nor cited.[19] The Supreme Court only referred to *Abdul Ghani* and dealt with the "1938 repeal-revival" hypothesis simply because it was appropriate that this argument (accepted by the West Pakistan High Court in *Abdul Ghani*) be considered by the apex court, and because the point needed to be decided in order to determine what law was applicable to the appeal immediately before it.

Surprisingly, the Supreme Court accepted the "1938 repeal-revival" hypothesis. The Supreme Court considered section 6–A of the General Clauses Act (relied upon by the High Court in *Abdul Ghani*), and (correctly) realized that it did not apply to the situation. However, the Supreme Court (incorrectly) assumed that *section 7 of the General*

---

[17] *Hamida Begum v. Murad Begum*, PLD 1975 Supreme Court 624.

[18] The Supreme Court observed (ibid., 663): "Many of the documents produced by the defendants appear to be forged, and would have ordinarily called for penal action, but for the fact that the main actor in the drama, namely, Mst. Murad Begum [P's second wife] who went to such lengths to exclude her stepdaughter from her rightful share in the property of her father, has since died [during pendancy of the appeal to the Supreme Court]."

[19] The more surprising, since Hamida Begum was the appellant and was represented by counsel.

Clauses Act was the relevant section, and held that since section 7 *did not prevent the revival* of the (previously repealed) Muslim law rules following the repeal of section 2 of the Evidence Act, the Muslim legal rules had been "revived" by the repeal of section 2. In support of the latter contention, the Supreme Court invoked the pre-1850 rule of English common law (superseded in England by the Interpretation Act, 1850), that, in the absence of a clear manifestation that the repeal effected by the now-repealed repealing enactment was to continue, the effect of the repeal of a repealing act was to restore the law has it had existed before the repeal. This rule (of no force in England for more than a century by 1962 and a century and a quarter by 1975) could have no effect in South Asia if the matter were covered by the terms of the (South Asian) General Clauses Act; and this precise proposition was clearly and emphatically negated in general terms by section 6 of the General Clauses Act (and with specific reference to the repeal or amendment of statutory law by section 6A and section 7).

Section 7 of the General Clauses Act, assumed by the Supreme Court to be the applicable clause, is, again, totally irrelevant to the situation; it deals with the "revival" of a repealed "enactment"; the Muslim legal rules repealed by section 2 of the Evidence Act were part of the uncodified Muslim law, and were not found in any "enactment."[20] The Supreme Court did not even consider whether the situation might be covered by another section of the General Clauses Act.

Neither the High Court in *Abdul Ghani* nor the Supreme Court in *Hamida Begum* gave any thought at all to section 6 of the General Clauses Act, which, as Justice Kayani had realized in 1957, is the applicable section of the General Clauses Act, and precluded the "revival" of the Muslim legal rules after the repeal of section 2 of the Evidence Act. Section 6 of the General Clauses Act constitutes a complete rebuttal to the argument the High Court and the Supreme Court were, respectively, persuaded to accept.

Having held that the Muslim law rules concerning legitimacy of the child born of a valid marriage had been "revived," and were

---

[20] Section 7 of the General Clauses Act, 1897, reads (in the section that is relevant here): "(1) In any Central Act or Regulation made after the commencement of this Act [e.g. the Repealing Act, 1938], it shall be necessary, for the purpose of *reviving*, either wholly or partially, *any enactment wholly or partially repealed*, expressly to state that purpose." (Emphasis added.)

equally available to the court as was the alternative provision found in section 112 of the Evidence Act, the Supreme Court made a policy decision that the former should be applied in litigation involving Muslim parties. The defendants contended that Hamida had been born within six months of the marriage of her mother and the deceased, and that the latter had repudiated paternity. It is clear from the Supreme Court judgment that in order to succeed, the defendants would have had to establish both of these propositions; they established neither.

> The defendants have failed to prove that the plaintiff was born within six months of the marriage. They have also failed to prove . . . that her paternity was repudiated by . . . [the deceased] soon after her birth or within a reasonable time thereof. . . . Mst. Hamida Begum is . . . a legitimate daughter of . . . [the deceased], and thus entitled to succeed to his property.[21]

Hamida Begum overruled *Abdul Ghani* on what the necessary requirements are to prove a person illegitimate. Even assuming that in *Abdul Ghani* the sisters of P had proved that his daughter was born within six months of the marriage,[22] they certainly had not proved that her paternity had been repudiated immediately by her mother's husband. The latter proposition would appear to be not only impossible to prove but conclusively rebutted, given the facts (apparent from the decision itself) that the girl's father had died in 1936 when she was less than four years old; that she had apparently lived with her father (until his death) and paternal grandmother; that in the immediate aftermath of her father's death, she was recognized by his family as his heir; that the suit was not filed until some seventeen years later in 1953; and that in the meantime the girl had been regarded as a member of her father's family, and raised by her paternal grandmother. If her father had not repudiated her at birth, his heirs cannot belatedly repudiate her legitimacy more than a decade and a half later.

---

[21] PLD 1975 Supreme Court 624, 663–4.

[22] By my calculations the child was born only four days less than six lunar months from the date of the marriage. Reliance was placed on a birth registration to establish a birthdate for the girl; particularly if the birth were registered late (as births of girls frequently are, if registered at all), four days is certainly not beyond the range of human error. (The birth of a daughter is not a particularly memorable occasion.)

The Evidence Order, 1984

In the interval between the *Hamida Begum* decision in late 1975 and the 1984 Evidence Order, General Zia ul-Haq seized control of the country in the military coup of July 1977. Initially promising elections within ninety days, Zia prolonged his rule for eleven years; the end came with his death in a plane crash in 1988. Anxious to create a "constituency" to give his reign at least the appearance of legitimacy and some popular support, Zia patronized the Islamic parties,[23] promised reform and revitalization of the country through "Islamization," and justified the continuation of his dictatorship by his commitment to the "Islamization" program and the necessity of his leadership to see it through.

The question of amending the Evidence Act arose early in the Zia regime. During the lengthy consultation process preceding promulgation of the Evidence Order, the Council of Islamic Ideology[24] had insisted that the Evidence Act of 1872 be scrapped and replaced by a new Islamic Law of Evidence based on the Qur'ān and Sunnah; mere patchwork alterations would not be sufficient to eradicate the 1872 Act's Anglo-Saxon roots and character. The Law Commission had maintained that very little contained in the Evidence Act could be criticized as contrary to Islam, and that a few amendments would be sufficient to deal with the situation.

As a result a new statute, with a new name ("Qanun-i-Shahadat"),[25] which suggested that it was a new codification undertaken from an Islamic perspective, was promulgated and heralded by the government as evidence of the regime's commitment to "Islamization." But the contents belied what was implied by the title and claimed by the government. The text merely reenacted the Evidence Act of

---

[23] Particularly the Jamaat-i-Islami (JI) and the Jamiat-i Ulama-i Islam (JUI). Insignificant in electoral politics, these parties achieved during the Zia regime power and influence far beyond anything their popular support justified.

[24] This was a constitutional body, comprised of members appointed by the President from among persons having "knowledge of the principles and philosophy of Islam as enunciated in the Holy Qur'ān and Sunnah, or understanding of the economic, political, legal or administrative problems of Pakistan." (Constitution of Pakistan, 1973, Article 228.) The functions of the Council of Islamic Ideology are purely advisory.

[25] At the time and to this date, it is the only central or provincial statute which does not bear an English name. Curiously, the "Qanun-i-Shahadat" itself was in English, and its translation into even Urdu was (again, curiously) long delayed.

1872, with only a very few (and only two major) departures from the century-old statute it replaced: a very strange compromise between the positions of the Council of Islamic Ideology and the Law Commission!

One of only a couple dramatic changes from the 1872 statute is the new section 128, equivalent to section 112 found in its predecessor.[26]

> 128. *Birth during marriage conclusive proof of legitimacy.*
> (1) The fact that any person was born during the continuance of a valid marriage between his mother and any man and not earlier than the expiration of six lunar months from the date of the marriage, or within two years after its dissolution, the mother remaining unmarried, shall be conclusive proof that he is the legitimate child of that man, unless
> (a) the husband had refused, or refuses, to own the child; or
> (b) the child was born after the expiration of six lunar months from the date on which the woman had accepted that the period of *Iddat* had come to an end.
> (2) Nothing contained in clause (1) shall apply to a non-Muslim if it is inconsistent with his faith.

(This very ineptly drafted section is considered further below.)

Why go to all the trouble of enacting a completely new statute? The few changes made in the Evidence Act, 1872, could easily have been accommodated in a simple amendment act. Why arbitrarily

---

[26] The second is found in section 17 (equivalent to section 134 of the 1872 statute, which simply stated: "No particular number of witnesses shall in any case be required for the proof of any fact"):

> "17. *Competence and number of witnesses.* (1) The competence of a person to testify, and the number of witnesses required in any case shall be determined in accordance with the Holy Qur'ān and Sunnah.
> "(2) Unless provided in any law relating to the enforcement of *Hudood* or any other special law—
> "(a) in matters pertaining to financial or future obligations, if reduced to writing, the instrument shall be attested by two men, or one man and two women, so that one may remind the other, if necessary, and evidence shall be led accordingly; and
> "(b) in all other matters, the Court may accept, or act on, the testimony of one man or one woman, or such other evidence as the circumstances of the case may warrant."

Reference to the Hudood laws is to a series of laws General Zia promulgated in 1979, purportedly introducing Islamic criminal law as regards the offenses for which punishment has been ordained in the Qur'ān: Offenses Against Property (Enforcement of Hudood) Ordinance; Offense of Zina (Enforcement of Hudood) Ordinance; Offense of Qazf (Enforcement of Hudood) Ordinance; and Prohibition (Enforcement of Hadd) Order.

rearrange the order of the chapters, thus (a) deliberately making it difficult to compare the two statutes; and (b) needlessly making it necessary for lawyers, judges, court officials, etc. to learn new section numbers for the statutory provisions with which they were already familiar? Why the inordinate delay in making an Urdu translation of the statute available, with the result that the only official text was in English? And why disguise the reenacted 1872 Act under a title like "Qanun-i-Shahadat," which suggests that it was a new codification undertaken from an Islamic perspective?

It is impossible not to relate the promulgation of the Evidence Order to the *Hamida Begum* decision, in which the Supreme Court had (surprisingly) accepted the radical position of the "1938 repeal-revival" hypothesis. As the law of Pakistan stood after the *Hamida Begum* decision, all those uncodified rules of Muslim law which dealt with topics covered by the Evidence Act and which had been repealed more than a century previously by section 2(1) of the Evidence Act, had been "revived," and were again in force, side-by-side with the contrary rules of the Evidence Act, 1872.[27] To identify precisely all the rules which might be claimed, under the dictum of the Supreme Court in *Hamida Begum*, to be Islamic rules of evidence "revived" and in force in Pakistan, to anticipate all the questions that might arise, was impossible. There was, of course, a theoretical limitation in that the only rules which could have been "revived" were those which had been repealed in 1872. The previous Evidence Act (1855), the Civil and Criminal Procedure Codes (1859 and 1861), the Limitation Act (1859), the Penal Code (1860), and various other acts and regulations had superseded much of Islamic judicial practice, including rules of evidence and procedure, but whether a particular rule had been explicitly "repealed" before 1872 would often be an open question. The question of whether any particular "rule of evidence" derived from Muslim law had been repealed in 1872 would require not only an examination of *fiqh* to identify the appropriate rule but also an essay in legal history to determine its precise status in 1872. Answers on both questions might differ from court to court; litigation would be complicated and prolonged.

---

[27] Given their focus on the matter of legitimacy, it is possible that neither the High Court in *Abdul Ghani* nor the Supreme Court in *Hamida Begum* had seriously thought the matter through and envisaged all the possible repercussions.

Once the "revived" rule had been identified, the decision whether to apply the "revived" rule or the alternative rule laid down by the Evidence Act would itself considerably influence, if not actually determine, the outcome of the litigation. Appeals would mean that a final decision on the content and status of each "revived" rule would await decision by the apex court, a process that could drag out literally for decades while uncertainty and confusion persisted.

To take a very simple and obvious example, the trespasser in possession of the property of a missing person would obviously contend for application of the "revived" Muslim law rule (death cannot be presumed until ninety years have passed since the birth of the missing person),[28] while the heir-presumptive would equally obviously contend for application of the rule laid down by the Evidence Act (death can be presumed after seven years if the missing person "has not been heard of . . . by those who would naturally have heard of him if he had been alive").[29] The decision as to what law was applicable would determine the result—and that decision would be totally in the hands of the individual judge, dependent upon his ideological position, or his sense of justice, or his personal whim or prejudice.

Acceptance by the Supreme Court of the radical "1938 repeal-revival" hypothesis had created a potential problem of massive and uncharted dimensions.[30] Rather than leaving the overburdened courts to deal with each of these issues as and when they came up, one

---

[28] Muslim law rules concerning succession to and by a missing person were applied until the Evidence Act, 1872; see e.g., *Kalee Khan v. Mst. Jadee*, 1873 North-Western Provinces, High Court Reports 62, a case decided before (and reported after) the Act of 1872 came into force. Repealed in 1872, this rule was unquestioningly "revived" by the dictum of the Supreme Court in *Hamida Begum*.

[29] Evidence Act, section 108; now found in section 124 of the 1984 Evidence Order. I.e., "revived" by the Supreme Court decision in *Hamida Begum*, the rule concerning presumption of death laid down by the 1872 Evidence Act was reinstated verbatim by the 1984 Evidence Act.

[30] It needs to be appreciated that Zia was determined to keep firm control of "Islamization" in his hands; the post-*Hamida Begum* situation was one which could easily spin out of control. Significantly, a particular area of law which Zia was determined to keep out of the hands of the "Islamists" and the "Islamization" program was that concerning judicial procedure (including evidence). The Federal Shariat Court (and the appellate body, the Shariat Bench of the Supreme Court)—created by Zia and endowed with the authority to examine any "any law or provision of law" and to strike down any found "repugnant to the Injunctions of Islam"—was explicitly denied jurisdiction to pronounce on "any law relating to the procedure of any Court or tribunal." (Presidential Order 22 of 1978, 4 Dec. 1978; see now Constitution of Pakistan, Article 203B(c).)

by one, and waiting for each case to work its way slowly to the apex court, it would clearly be far more efficient to overrule *Hamida Begum* by a new statute. However, a short, simple enactment overruling *Hamida Begum* and voiding the "1938 repeal-revival hypothesis" would not do.[31] Explicitly overruling the *Hamida Begum* decision would have been considered too blatant an "anti-Islamization" posture for the self-styled leader of the "Islamization" program to assume. Another consideration would have been the need to get rid of the notation recalling section 2—"2. [Repealed by Repealing Act, 1938, s. 2 and Schedule]"—which remained in the 1872 Act after the repeal of section 2. The "1938 repeal-revival" hypothesis was built on the fact that section 2 had once been part of the Evidence Act, 1872, and had been repealed. Only a new statute, in which there was not (and had never been) a section comparable to section 2 of the old Act would get rid of the remnant of section 2 and the history associated with that section, and ensure that the "repeal-revival" hypothesis could not again be raised.

At the same time that part of the *Hamida Begum* decision reintroducing the Muslim law rules concerning legitimacy of the child born of a valid marriage had to be maintained; that was the part of the decision the public, particularly the constituency General Zia was cultivating, understood.

In the event, the Evidence Order was promulgated in 1984.[32] And in so doing the Zia regime not only carried out a tremendously

---

[31] The *Hamida Begum* decision was well known; it had been enthusiastically received in the very quarters whose opinion was important to Zia. However, what was known about the decision was that it had resulted in the Muslim law of legitimacy becoming applicable to Muslims instead of section 112 of the Evidence Act. Little attention was paid to precisely how this result had been obtained. Sooner or later lawyers would take a closer look at the decision, and begin to realize that the argument underlying the decision was applicable in other contexts—that *all* other Muslim law rules (not merely those concerned with legitimacy of the child born of a valid marriage), repealed in 1872, had been "revived" by the 1975 decision and were presently in force. (Indeed, it is more than probable that somebody in the Ministry of Law had figured this out pretty quickly; somebody, somewhere obviously did. And realized that pre-emptive action was necessary!) Explicit statutory negation of the "1938 repeal-revival" hypothesis together with any and all Muslim law rules which had been revived by the *Hamida Begum* decision could never have been passed off as "Islamization."

[32] Although the immediate connection between the need to statutorily overrule the *Hamida Begum* decision and the need to promulgate the Evidence Order, 1984, appeared obvious to me from the beginning, I have not found any discussion directly relating the promulgation of the Evidence Order with the "1938 repeal-revival"

important preemptive "anti-Islamization" coup, but managed to disguise the fact under the heading of "Islamization." In the same way, the fact was disguised that the 1984 Order was essentially merely the reenactment of the 1872 Act but under the title "Qanun-i-Shahadat." Although it did little else, the Evidence Order (with all the curiosities of its promulgation) overruled *Hamida Begum*; voided the "1938 repeal-revival" hypothesis, and made sure it could not again arise; ousted (with the couple of exceptions specifically covered by the altered terms of the new statute) all those Muslim legal rules which had been, or which it might have been, "revived" by the repeal of section 2 of the 1872 statute in 1938; and it very largely restored the *status quo ante.*

The Evidence Order, 1984, of course, repealed the Evidence Act, 1872, wiping out the remnant of section 2 and the history associated with the fact that section 2 had been part of the 1872 statue until it had been repealed in 1938. More importantly, the phrase "any other law" in section 165—which (apparently so innocuously) states: "The provisions of this Order shall have effect notwithstanding anything contained in any other law for the time being in force"—includes the law as laid down by the Supreme Court in *Hamida Begum,* both the "1938 repeal-revival" hypothesis (from 1975 until 1984 the law of Pakistan) and any rules of Muslim law which it might have been contended had been "revived" as a result of the dictum in *Hamida Begum.* Since the new Evidence Order contains nothing comparable to section 2 as found in the 1872 statute, and no indication that such a section had once been part of the statute and had subsequently been repealed, there is absolutely no scope for any "repeal-revival" hypothesis to arise under the Evidence Order, 1984. All this was achieved, covertly and in a manner which would not attract attention, as effectively and conclusively as if there had been a short statute explicitly overruling *Hamida Begum* and the "1938

hypothesis. Nevertheless, the facts remain (1) that the radical and problematic proposition that the Muslim rules of evidence which had been repealed in 1872 had been "revived" in 1938 and were now part of the law of Pakistan was itself the law of Pakistan after the Supreme Court decision in 1975; and (2) that this radical and problematic proposition was statutorily overturned and all the "revived" rules (unless specifically endorsed by the new statute) were again ousted, by the 1984 Evidence Order. Rather than endorsing and building upon the dramatic "Islamization" inadvertently accomplished by the Supreme Court in *Hamida Begum,* the "victory" was deliberately (and covertly) negated. This must be something more than mere coincidence.

repeal-revival" hypothesis. The 1984 Order made it clear that, with only a couple of exceptions (e.g., the rule concerning legitimacy of the child born of a valid marriage, which section 128 sets out so inadequately), the Muslim law rules which had been repealed in 1872 were not to be "revived"; and if any had been, they were no longer in force.

A Comment on Section 128, Evidence Order

Section 128 is one of a couple of significant changes made by the Evidence Order in the direction of incorporating rules of Muslim law. Recognition of Muslim law as providing the governing rule in the matter of legitimacy of the child born of a valid marriage is, however, more directly attributable to the *Hamida Begum* decision. The Zia regime (even had it wanted to) could not overrule *Hamida Begum* on the legitimacy question without very seriously compromising its "Islamization" credentials.[33] Indeed, the problem was how to statutorily negate *Hamida Begum* as regards the means through which the Supreme Court had managed the "revival" of, for example, the Muslim legal rules concerning legitimacy of the child born of a valid marriage, while leaving intact the conclusion that legitimacy was a matter to be determined according to Muslim law.

The new section 128 incorporates the notion that legitimate birth must result from conception within marriage, limiting the conclusive presumption of legitimacy to the child born after the expiration of the minimal period of gestation reckoned from the date of the marriage. As regards the maximum period of gestation, the Pakistan legislation is curiously out of step with developments in other parts of the Muslim world, where the trend has been in the direction of establishing a maximum gestation period of one year.[34] Pakistan, to the contrary, has now replaced the presumption of a normal gestation

---

[33] Although actually, in fact, it did so; the grossly ill-drafted section 128 supersedes the decision in *Hamida Begum* (see further on this aspect of the decision below). The immediate point is that the Zia regime had to concede that this matter was to be decided according to Muslim law, although the terms of that Muslim law are very ineptly detailed in the new statute.

[34] Egypt (1929), Tunisia (1956), Morocco (1957), Iraq (1959), Somalia (1975), Syria (1975), Jordan (1976), and Kuwait (1976) have an established maximum gestation period of one year; Algeria (1984) opted for ten months.

period of 280 days laid down by the Evidence Act, 1872, with the traditional Hanafi maximum of twenty-four months. During the consultation process preceding the promulgation of the Evidence Order, the Law Commission had commented negatively on this proposal:

> [T]he Members [of the Law Commission] are unanimously of the view that the provision relating to legitimacy of a child within two years after dissolution of his parent's marriage, the mother remaining unmarried, is neither based on the Holy Qur'ān or Sunnah nor on any physical possibility. Continuity of a pregnancy for two years is physically and medically impossible and the provision, at present included in the proposed [Evidence] Ordinance, will certainly encourage immorality and create serious complications in the matters of inheritance.[35]

The Zia regime ignored such advice. Something dramatic was necessary to give an "Islamic" color to the Evidence Order; the two year gestation period, insisted upon by the Islamists, was a token to evidence progress on the "Islamization" front.[36]

Beyond recognizing the minimal and maximum periods of gestation as laid down by the classical Hanafi law, the new section has been poorly thought out and is very badly drafted. On the one hand, it might appear that section 128 reflects Hanafi law in refusing to recognize proof of nonaccess (or even nonconsummation of the marriage) to rebut the presumption of paternity. At the same time, clause (1)(a), which (particularly given the use of the term "husband") appears applicable to the first part of the main clause,[37] produces the shocking

---

[35] Pakistan Law Commission, *Report No 9, Re Draft of the Evidence Ordinance*, 29 December 1983. Two years previously the Law Commission had suggested that the wording of the revised section be: "The fact that any person was born during the continuance of a valid marriage between his mother and any man, *but not before the expiry of six lunar months from the date of marriage*, or within two hundred and eighty days after its dissolution, the mother remaining unmarried, shall be conclusive proof that he is the legitimate son of that man, unless it can be shown that the parties to the marriage had no access to each other at any time when he could have been begotten." (*Report No. 4, Law of Evidence*, 12 January 1982; emphasis added.) This formulation merely inserted the italicized phrase in the sentence comprising section 112 of the 1872 Act. Both the presumption of a normal gestation of 280 days and the availability of proof of nonaccess as a rebuttal to the presumption of paternity were retained. Neither of these latter provisions was accepted by the draftsman of the new section 128.

[36] See also fn. 26.

[37] Subclause (b), with its reference to the period of *iddah*, clearly applies to the second part of the main clause (concerning the child born "within two years after ... dissolution [of the marriage], the mother remaining unmarried") and relieves the husband from liability for the child "born after the expiration of six lunar months

result that the husband is apparently given a blanket right to "refuse to own" a child born to his wife "during the continuance of a valid marriage . . . and not earlier than the expiration of six lunar months from the date of the marriage."

While under classical law, simple denial of paternity would render the child born in less than six months of the marriage illegitimate,[38] section 128 is explicitly and solely concerned with the child presumed legitimate because of being born "not earlier than the expiration of six lunar months from the date of the marriage." Mere "refusal to own" such a child would not have the effect of bastardizing the child in the classical law. A child, born six months or more after marriage and legally presumed to be legitimate, could only be bastardized by the procedure of *lian*. While *lian* for *qazf* (scandalous accusation) has been available in Pakistan since 1979,[39] no provision has been made for *lian* as a basis for repudiation of paternity.

Subclause (a) makes no more sense if (ignoring the term "husband") it is held applicable only to the second part of the main clause, with the result that the *former* husband is given the right to "refuse to own" a child born to his divorced wife within two years of the dissolution of the marriage (the woman remaining unmarried). Again, mere "refusal to own" would not, under the classical law bastardize the child in such a situation; further, such a child could not in Hanafi law be bastardized by *lian*.[40]

---

from the date on which the woman had accepted that the period of *Iddat* had come to an end." This is in accordance with Muslim law. (Given the six month period of minimal gestation, the woman was obviously in error when she announced the conclusion of the *iddah* if the child were born within six months of that announcement.)

[38] Because there is no legal presumption that it is legitimate. For such a child to be legitimate, the mother's husband must acknowledge the child as his, without admitting that it had been conceived in *zina*. Since he may so acknowledge the child simply by treating it as a legitimate child would ordinarily be treated, it is repudiation of the child that requires some specific statement or action. A child once accepted by the father as legitimate cannot subsequently be disowned by anything short of *lian*.

[39] Offense of Qazf (Enforcement of Hudood) Ordinance, 1979, section 14. The oaths set out in the statute for husband and wife, respectively, are the oaths for *lian* for *qazf*; the effect of the procedure is merely a dissolution of the marriage. *Lian* for repudiation of paternity requires different oaths and produces a severance of lineage between the husband and the specifically identified child, as well as well as a dissolution of the marriage.

[40] This is so because the parties have to be married to each other both at the time of the accusation which leads to the *lian* proceedings, and at the time of the proceedings themselves.

Pakistan's new rules as set out in section 128 of the Evidence Order fail to accurately and coherently reflect the classical law; and fail to give women and children the protection which the classical law provides, while at the same time denying them the protection heretofore available under section 112 of the Evidence Act 1872.

Further, section 128 of the Pakistan Evidence Order applies to *all* litigants; the non-Muslim may plead that it is "inconsistent with his faith," but absolutely no guidance is given as to the rule which would then be applied in such a situation. Much more serious is the fact that section 128 imposes Hanafi law on Shiʿis, and does not offer the Shiʿi litigant the opportunity of pleading that the new law is "inconsistent with his faith." Shiʿi law presumes a normal gestation period of nine lunar months, considerably less than the twenty-four months now incorporated in the Evidence Order.

Hamida Begum *on Legitimacy*

It is particularly interesting to compare the terms found in section 128 of the 1984 Evidence Order with the law of legitimacy as expounded by the Supreme Court a decade previously, representing the law of Pakistan at the time when the Evidence Order came into force. Having held that the rules of Muslim law repealed in 1872 had been "revived" in 1938 by the repeal of section 2 of the Evidence Act, the Supreme Court of Pakistan further held that the Muslim legal rules concerning legitimacy (rather than the rule laid down by section 112) would apply in litigation concerning legitimacy to which the parties were Muslims.

Since the parties in *Hamida Begum* were Hanafis, the Supreme Court took the occasion to summarize Hanafi law on the point, relying on such sources as the *Fatawa-i-Alamgiri; Radd-ul-Muhtar*; Abdur Rehman, *Institutes of Mussalman Law*; Ameer Ali, *Mahommedan Law*; Abdur Rahim, *Muhammadan Jurisprudence*; and Dinshah Fardunji Mulla, *Principles of Muhammadan Law*. The following propositions are taken from that summary.

> 1. "[T]he paternity of a child born in lawful wedlock is presumed to be in the husband of the mother without any acknowledgment or affirmation of parentage on his part [when birth takes place at least six months after the marriage]."
> 2. "[T]he presumption of legitimacy is so strong that in cases where a child is born after six months from the date of marriage and within

two years after dissolution of the marital contract, either by the death of the husband or by divorce, a simple denial of paternity on the part of the husband would not take away the status of legitimacy from the child."

3. The presumption of legitimacy "is subject to the right of disavowal on the part of the husband for want of access."[41]

4. The husband disowning a child must act immediately, "either on the day of the child's birth or at the time of purchasing articles necessary in view of its birth or during the period of rejoicing."

5. "If . . . a child is born within six lunar months of the marriage, no affiliation would take place unless the man acknowledges it to be his issue."

6. "[I]t is the right of the man to legitimate a child born within . . . [six months of the marriage] by acknowledging expressly or impliedly that the conception took place within wedlock."

7. The husband can repudiate a child born more than six months from the date of the marriage "only . . . by the procedure of *lian*, that is to say, if he swears before the Qadi that the child is illegitimate and the fruit of adultery."[42]

The new terms of Pakistan's Evidence Order fail to properly reflect and explicitly endorse (2), (3), (4), (5), (6), and (7) in the enumeration above. Section 128(1)(a) appears to confer upon the husband a blanket right to "refuse to own the child," even when born six months after marriage or within two years of the divorce. How this is to be done remains unclear: what does "refuse to own the child" mean? Is a simple verbal statement, made any time and under any circumstances, sufficient?[43] In the classical law, repudiation of a child whom the law ascribes to the woman's husband, can only be accomplished through *lian*. Further, the denial of paternity must be made

[41] Although this proposition is part of Shiʿi law, it does not find a place in the classical Hanafi law. It had, however, been part of South Asian law (section 112 of the 1872 Evidence Act) for more than a century at the time of this judgment. Given the fact that the Supreme Court did not question the two-year period of gestation and the interval between impregnation and birth may be anywhere from six to twenty-four months, proof of nonaccess for the entire period when conception might have occurred would often be extremely difficult (if not impossible), particularly when the child is born two years or more after the marriage.

[42] Summarized from PLD 1975 Supreme Court 624, 651–2.

[43] For example, one that was made many years after the birth when the separated or divorced mother sues the father for maintenance for the child? (Under Muslim law, a man is not required to maintain his illegitimate issue. South Asian secular law, on the contrary, had long rendered a man liable for the maintenance of his offspring, legitimate or illegitimate; this provision was repealed in Pakistan in 1981.)

immediately; although a belated repudiation of the child would render the husband liable to the *hadd* for *qazf*, and render *lian* for *qazf* necessary to avoid that punishment, *lian* for repudiation of paternity would not be available. At the time of the *Hamida Begum* decision in 1975, neither *lian* for *qazf* nor *lian* for repudiation of paternity was available in Pakistan;[44] perhaps both would have been covered by the "revived" rules of evidence; see *Ghulam Bhik* discussed above.

At the same time the Evidence Order does not allow the husband to refute the presumption of paternity by proof of nonaccess (point (3) in the list above), a right long recognized in South Asia (under section 112 of the 1872 statute), found in Shiʿi law, and endorsed by the Supreme Court in *Hamida Begum.*

Since the parties in *Hamida Begum* were Hanafis, the Supreme Court in *Hamida Begum* summarized the *Hanafi* law concerning legitimacy. Clearly, a similar exercise would have taken place if the litigants were Shiʿis. The Evidence Order not only makes no provision for Shiʿi law, it fails explicitly to confer upon the Shiʿi party (as opposed to the non-Muslim party) an opportunity to contend that the rule laid down "is inconsistent with his faith."

Hamida Begum left section 112 of the Evidence Act (which continued in force side by side with the "revived" Muslim law rules) applicable to non-Muslims; the "revived" Muslim law rules would apply only to Muslims. The terms of the new Evidence Act apply to all Muslim Pakistanis (Hanafi, Shiʿi, etc.); and to non-Muslim Pakistanis unless the non-Muslim establishes that the rule in question "is inconsistent with his faith."

The draftsman of section 128 of the 1984 Evidence Order might well have paid closer attention to the summary of Hanafi law provided so conveniently in *Hamida Begum*, and have given closer consideration to the position of both Shiʿis and non-Muslims under the new dispensation.[45] In the event, a tremendous responsibility has

---

[44] Although *lian* for *qazf* was subsequently introduced by the Qazf Ordinance, 1979, *lian* for repudiation of paternity was deliberately not introduced.

[45] Note the brief (and grossly inaccurate) comment on the 1984 Evidence Order contained in a recent textbook: "These significant changes [i.e., section 128 of the Evidence Order], part of the process of Pakistan's islamisation, re-introduce Muslim rules of evidence, apply the position developed in the case law, as well as making [sic] an appropriate saving clause for the non-Muslim citizens of Pakistan." (Pearl and Menski: 1998:404.)

been placed on the Courts in interpreting and applying the ill-drafted statutory provision. One may hope that the provisions as summa-

---

The Evidence Order was *not* "part of the process of Pakistan's [I]slamisation;" section 128 did *not* "re-introduce Muslim rules of evidence;" it did *not* even "re-introduce" Hanafi rules concerning legitimacy of the child born of a valid marriage; it did *not* "apply the position developed in the case law;" it did *not* apply the position laid down by the Supreme Court in *Hamida Begum* (the authoritative "case law" in 1984); it did *not* make appropriate provision for "non-Muslim citizens of Pakistan;" and did *not* make appropriate provision even for non-Hanafi Muslim citizens of Pakistan!

The same "textbook" dismisses the simple "1938 repeal-revival" hypothesis, which the compilers encounter in their hopeless attempt to say something about the *Abdul Ghani* decision, as "*a highly technical argument*," a "*complex argument*" in "this *complex case*." Unable to comprehend either the argument or its importance, they merely insert a footnote reading: "This is a highly technical argument, found at pp. 541–543 of the judgment." (Actually, the relevant pages are 542 to 545.) The student/reader is left to look up the decision and make what sense he can out of something the compilers themselves cannot understand and present. Needless to say, the compilers fail to realize that the same argument was considered in both the *Ghulam Bhik* and the *Hamida Begum* decisions (both of which they attempt, grossly unsuccessfully, to address), and that as a result of the latter decision this "highly technical"and "complex" proposition, apparently unworthy of discussion and analysis, was actually the law of Pakistan for nearly a decade. Similarly, the compilers completely fail to appreciate the fundamental fact that *Hamida Begum* overruled *Abdul Ghani* on everything they *think* that case decided, while at the same time upholding (albeit on a different basis) the *Abdul Ghani* court's position on the "1938 repeal-revival" hypothesis.

The "textbook" compilers consider the *Abdul Ghani* decision important (and thus waste much space and uninformed waffle in an attempt to discuss it) because of some supposed determination of the (long-dead) question of whether the rules of Muslim law concerning the legitimacy of the child born during the subsistence of a valid marriage were rules of "substantive law" or rules of "evidence" *in the context of South Asian jurisprudence.* (Part of the problem is that they do not appreciate the nature of the question in the first place: the question was *not* how these rules might be classified in the classical law, but how they are classified in the scheme of South Asian jurisprudence after the Evidence Act of 1872.) However, even assuming that *Abdul Ghani* decided what the compilers think it did, any such conclusion was clearly and emphatically overruled by the Supreme Court in *Begum Hamida*:

> . . . . It appears to us, therefore, that the Evidence Act adopts an elaborate scheme of its own by treating the subject of presumptions and the burden of proof as regards the question of legitimacy as a part of the law of evidence. . . . It follows, therefore, that although under the classification adopted by writers on Muslim law, the subject of legitimacy and paternity is treated as a part of the substantive law, yet *in view of the scheme underlying the Evidence Act, 1872, the rules governing legitimacy must be regarded as rules of evidence,* for otherwise the legislative intent underlying the promulgation of the Evidence Act, namely, "to consolidate, define and amend the law of evidence," was likely to be defeated, by excluding from its purview several subjects which have been specifically dealt with in this Act, but are not described as rules of evidence under other systems of law which were then in operation under the Punjab Laws Act of 1872 and corresponding laws obtaining in other Provinces of India. On this

rized and set forth by the Supreme Court in *Hamida Begum* will influence and assist the courts in this task.[46]

---

view of the matter, *we consider that the rule enunciated by the Punjab Chief Court as early as 1884 . . . and since followed in a large number of cases* [i.e. followed without dissent—lc], *was indeed correct, namely, that for the purpose of section 2(1) of the Evidence Act the rules of Muslim law on the question of legitimacy must be treated as rules of evidence,* and accordingly repealed by it, with the consequence that the matter would be governed by section 112 of the Evidence Act even in those cases where the parties were Muslims. [*Hamida Begum,* PLD 1975 Supreme Court 624, 647–8; emphasis added.]

(The Supreme Court then proceeded to consider the effect of the 1938 repeal of section 2 of the Evidence Act, with the results detailed in the text above.)

Unfortunately (but typically) the "textbook" compilers read no more of the long and important *Hamida Begum* decision than the head notes, and even skipped most of these. (For the Pearl & Menski "textbook" and case-law see, e.g., Lucy Carroll [2001].) It would be as difficult, if not impossible, to find a single statute which has been read with such minimal comprehension as it is to find a single judicial decision which has been so read.)

[46] And during the more than a decade and a half since I first made these statements, there is clear evidence that this is occurring; see, e.g., *Maqbool Hussain v. Abdur Rehman,* PLD 1995 Peshawar 124. Having quoted extensively from the summary of Hanafi law provided by the Supreme Court in *Hamida Begum* (which it termed "a monumental judgment"), the High Court held that those denying the legitimacy of the plaintiff had failed to prove that he had been born within six months of the marriage or more than two years after the divorce. The court further held that the repudiation of the child by the father in the course of maintenance proceedings was of no consequence: "A *legitimate* child could not be bastardized . . . by means of denial in the criminal Court with a view to get rid of the maintenance allowance." (emphasis added.)

This decision implies that (contrary to the inept wording of section 128), the "refusal to own the child" referred to in section 128(1)(a) encompasses only the child born within six months of marriage or more than two years after its dissolution, i.e., a child who is not automatically legally defined as legitimate. Further reliance on the *Hamida Begum* decision would lead to the conclusion that the child born within six months of marriage could only be repudiated immediately, and that a belated repudiation (e.g. in the context of maintenance proceedings) could not undo a implicit acknowledgment at or about the time of the child's birth. I consider it also probable that "nonaccess" will come back in as a ground for "refusal to own the child;" e.g., that a husband who had been incarcerated for two years or more (without conjugal access) when his wife gave birth would be permitted to "refuse to own the child" on the ground that he had not had access to his wife at any time when the child could have been conceived.

REFERENCES

Archives

Aintab Sicilli, National Library, Ankara, Registers 2 and 161.
Başbakanlık Osmanlı Arşivi: Evkaf Defterleri (EV.), 11687.
Center for Historical Documents, Damascus: Sharīʿa Court Records of Aleppo (Sijillāt al-Maḥākim al-Sharʿiyya), vols. 139, 141, 141–I, 148, 149, 152–I, 163, 165, 168, 208. (Cited as SMS in notes.)
Esnaf Emr-i ʿÂlîleri (Imperial decrees on artisans and traders). In the private collection of Selim İlkin, Istanbul,Turkey. This collection comprises the register of a selection of Ottoman imperial decrees about Istanbul artisans and traders compiled for Kara Kemal, Minister of Provisions in the Ottoman War Cabinet of 1915–18. Abbreviated EEA in notes.
History Museum-Ruse: Sicill: B 2919, of 1663–4. Başbakanlık Osmanlı Arşivi (BBOA)—Istanbul: Mühimme Defteri: MD 80, of 1613–4; MD 106, of 1694–5; MD 117, of 1710–13; MD 118, of 1711–2; MD 121, of 1713–4; MD 125, of 1715–6.
Law Court Records (LCR), Damascus.
National Library-Sofia (Natsionalna Biblioteka "Sv. Sv. Kiril i Metodii", NBKM), Oriental Department: Or 435 (manuscript). Sicills: S 1 bis, of 1617–8; S 308, of 1619; S 12, of 1671–8; S 85, of 1679–80 (containing a fragment of 14 pages from 1613–4); S 149, of 1683–4; S 4, of 1709–10.
T.C. Başbakanlık Osmanlī Arşivi (The Republic of Turkey Prime Ministry Ottoman Archives). Istanbul, Turkey. Muallim Cevdet Tasnifi (Muallim Cevdet collection). From this collection, material was used from three specific subsections: Muallim Cevdet Tasnifi—Belediye (Files on municipal matters—abbrev.: CB); Muallim Cevdet Tasnifi—İktisad (Files on economic matters—abbrev.: CİO); Muallim Cevdet Tasnifi—Zabtiye (Files on public security matters—abbrev.: CZ).

Published Works

ʿAbd al-Razzāq al-Ṣanʿānī. *See* al-Ṣanʿānī, ʿAbd al-Razzāq.
ʿAbduh, Muḥammad. 1900. *Taqrīr fī iṣlāḥ al-maḥākim al-sharʿiyya.* Ed. Muḥammad Rashīd Riḍā. Cairo: Maṭbaʿat al-manār.
Ābī, Ṣāliḥ ʿAbd al-Samīʿ al-Azharī al-. N.d. [1976?]. *Jawāhir al-iklīl sharḥ mukhtaṣar Khalīl.* 2 vols. Cairo: ʿĪsā al-Bābī al-Ḥalabī.
——. N.d. *al-Thamar al-dānī sharḥ risālat Ibn Abī Zayd al-Qayrawānī.* Tunis: Maktabat al-manār.
Abou El-Fadl, Khaled. 2001. *Rebellion and Violence in Islamic Law.* Cambridge: Cambridge University Press.
Abū Ḥassān, Muḥammad. 1974. *Turāth al-badw al-qaḍāʾī.* Amman: Dāʾirat al-thaqāfa wa'l-funūn.
Abun-Nasr, Jamil. 1965. *The Tijaniyya: a Sufi Order in the Modern World.* London: Oxford University Press.
ʿAfīfī, Muḥammad. 1992. *al-Aqbāṭ fī Miṣr fī 'l-ʿasr al-ʿUthmānī.* Cairo: al-Hayʾa al-Miṣriyya al-ʿĀmma lil-Kitāb.

——. 1996. "Reflections on the Personal Laws of Egyptian Copts," in *Women, the Family, and Divorce Laws in Islamic History*, ed. by Amira El Azhari Sonbol. Syracuse: Syracuse University Press.

Agostini, E. De. 1922–23. *Le Popolazioni della Cirenaica.* Bengasi: Governo della Cirenaica, Azienda Tipo-Litografica della Scoula d'Atri e Mestieri.

Aguirre Sádaba, Javier. 2000. "Notas acerca de la proyección de los *kutub al-wathā'iq* en el estudio social y económico de al-Andalus." *Miscelánea de Estudios Árabes y Hebraicos*, 49:3–30.

Aḥmad, Sa'īd, trans. 1987–2001. *Sharḥ adab al-qāḍī.* Commentary by Burhān al-A'imma Ḥusām al-Dīn 'Umar b. 'Abd al-'Azīz b. Māzza al-Bukhārī. 4 vols. Islamabad: Islamic Research Institute. *See also* al-Khaṣṣāf. 1978.

Akarlı, Engin D. 1986. "Gedik: Implements, Mastership, Shop Usufruct and Monopoly among Istanbul Artisans, 1750–1850." *Wissenschaftskolleg Jahrbuch 1985/86.* Berlin: N.p., 223–32.

——. 1996. "Ottoman Historiography," *MESA Bulletin*, 30:33–6.

——. 2002. "The Tangled Ends of an Empire and its Sultan," in L. Fawaz and C. Bailey (eds.), *Modernity and Culture from the Mediterranean to the Indian Ocean.* New York: Columbia University Press, 261–84.

——. 2004. "Gedik: A Bundle of Rights and Obligations for Istanbul Artisans and Traders, 1750–1840," in Alain Pottage and Martha Mundy (eds.), *Law, Anthropology and the Constitution of the Social: Making Persons and Things.* Cambridge and New York: Cambridge University Press, 166–200.

Akgündüz, Ahmet. 1990. *Osmanlı Kanunnâmeleri ve Hukukî Tahlilleri II. Bâyezid devri kanunâmelari.* Istanbul: Fey Vakfı Yayınları.

Aktepe, Münir. 1958. *Patrona İsyanı (1730).* Istanbul: İstanbul Üniversitesi Edebiyat Fakültesi.

Akwa', Ismā'īl b. 'Alī al-. 1995. *Hijar al-'ilm wa-ma'āqiluhu fi'l-Yaman.* 5 vols. Beirut: Dār al-fikr al-mu'āṣir.

Alami. *See* El Alami.

Albergoni, G. 1993. "Droit coutumier, ethos tribal et économie moderne: un *'urf* bédouin de 1970." *Études Islamologiques*, 27:109–136.

'Alī, 'Abdullāh Yūsuf, trans. 1992. *Qur'ān.* English Translation. Madinah: Ministry of Ḥajj and Endowments.

Amedroz, H.F. 1910. "The Office of the Kadi in the *Aḥkām Sulṭāniya* of Māwardī." *Journal of the Royal Asiatic Society*, 2:761–96.

Anderson, J.N.D. 1970 [1954]. *Islamic Law in Africa.* London: Cass.

——. 1976. *Law Reform in the Muslim World.* University of London: The Athlone Press.

'Ansī, Aḥmad b. Qāsim al-. 1993 [1938–47]. *al-Tāj al-mudhhab li-aḥkām al-madhhab.* 4 vols. Ṣan'ā': Dār al-ḥikma al-yamanīyya.

Antoun, Richard. 1980. "The Islamic Court, the Islamic Judge, and the Accommodation of Traditions: A Jordanian case Study." *International Journal of Middle East Studies*, 12:455–67.

Arberry, J.A., trans. 1964. *The Koran Interpreted.* London: Oxford University Press.

Arcas, M. 1994. "La penalización de las injurias en el derecho malikí." *Boletín de la Asociación Española de Orientalistas*, 30:209–17.

Arévalo, R. 1939. *Derecho penal islámico.* Tánger: Tipografia P. Erola.

Asad, Muhammad. 1980. *The Message of the Qur'ān.* Gibraltar: Dār al-Andalus.

Asad, Talal. 2003. *Formation of the Secular: Christianity, Islam, and Modernity.* Stanford: Stanford University Press.

Asadī, Khayr al-Dīn al-. 1981–8. *Mawsū'at ḥalab al-muqārana.* 7 vols. Aleppo: Jāmi'at ḥalab.

'Asalī, Kāmil J. al-. 1983–5. *Wathā'iq maqdisiyya ta'rīkhiyya ma' muqaddima ḥawla ba'ḍ al-maṣāḍir al-awliyya li-ta'rīkh al-quds.* 2 vols. Amman: N.p.

Askarus, William. 1996–7. "Daʿwā al-ḥabs li-dayn al-nafaqa." *al-Muḥāmāt*, 47:528–36.
ʿAsqalānī, Ibn Ḥajar. See Ibn Ḥajar al-ʿAsqalānī.
Asyūṭī, Shams al-Dīn Muḥammad b. Aḥmad al-Manhājī al-. N.d. *Jawāhir al-ʿuqūd wa-muʿīn al-quḍāh wa'l-muwaqqiʿīn wal-shuhūd.* Ed. Muḥammad Ḥāmid al-Fiqqī. 2 vols. Cairo: N.p. Repr. Riyāḍ: N.p. 1955.
Ata'i, Nevʿizade Ataula. 1851–2. *Hada'ik ül-haka'ik fi tekmilet üş-şaka'ik.* Istanbul: Darü't-ṭabāʿati'l-ʿĀmire.
Atkinson, J. Maxwell and Paul Drew. 1979. Order in Court: The Organisation of Verbal Interaction in Courtroom Settings. London: Macmillan.
ʿAwda, ʿAbd al-Qādir. N.d. *al-Tashrīʿ al-jinā'ī al-islāmī*. 2 vols. Cairo: Dār al-turāth.
Aydın, M. Akif. 1994–8. "Osmanlıda Hukuk," in E. İhsanoğlu (ed.), *Osmanlı Devleti ve Medeniyeti Tarihi.* 2 vols. Istanbul: Research Center for Islamic History, Art, and Culture, vol. 1, 375–438.
——. 1999. *Türk Hukuk Tarihi.* 3rd ed. Istanbul: Beta.
Azad, Ghulam Murtaza. 1987. *Judicial System of Islam.* Islamabad: Islamic Research Institute, International Islamic University.
Azharī, al-. See Ābī.
Babaji, B. and Y. Dankofa. 2003. "Assessing the Performance of the Lower Courts in the Implementation of Shari'a Penal Laws in Northern Nigeria," in J.N. Ezeilo, M.T. Ladan and A. Afolabi-Akiyode (eds.), *Sharia Implementation in Nigeria: Issues and Challenges on Women's Rights and Access to Justice.* Enugu: Women's Aid Collective, 103–27.
Badrān, ʿAbd al-Qādir. 1960. *Munādamat al-aṭlāl wa-musāmarat al-khayāl.* Damascus: al-Maktab al-islāmī.
Baer, G. 1997. "The Waqf as a Prop for the Social System (Sixteenth–Twentieth Centuries)." *Islamic Law and Society*, 4:264–97.
Baer, G. and A. Layish. 1971. *Waqf ba-hevra ha-ʿaravit ha-modernit. Leqeṭ teʿudot* [Waqf in Modern Arab Society. A Selection of Documents]. Jerusalem: Academon.
Bahnisi, A.F. 1965. *al-Ḥadd wa'l-taʿzīr.* Faggala: Maktabat al-waʿy al-ʿarabī.
Bājī, Abū al-Walīd Sulaymān b. Khalaf al-. 1914 [1332H]. *Kitāb al-muntaqā: sharḥ muwaṭṭa' imām dār al-hijra sayyidnā Mālik b. Anas.* 7 vols. in 6. Cairo. Matbaʿat al-saʿāda.
——. 1990. *Fuṣūl al-aḥkām wa-bayān mā maḍā ʿalay-hi al-ʿamal ʿinda al-fuqahā' wa'l-ḥukkām.* Ed. al-Bātūl ben ʿAlī. Rabat: Wizārat al-awqāf wa'l-shu'ūn al-islāmiyya.
Bakhīt, Muḥammad. 1930. "Quḍāt al-Islām: Hal lahum an yaḥkumū bayna ghayr al-muslimīn fī masā'il al-aḥwāl al-shakhṣiyya wa-ghayrihā? baḥth hādhā al-mawḍūʿ wa-taḥqīquhu wa-muqāranat al-madhāhib baʿḍihā bi-baʿḍin fī dhālik." *al-Muḥāmāt al-Sharʿiyya*, 2:484–98.
Bakhit, Muhammad Adnan. 1982. *The Ottoman Province of Damascus in the Sixteenth Century.* Beirut: Librarie du Liban.
Baktır, Mustafa. 1982. *İslam Hukukunda Zaruret Hali.* Ankara: Akçağ.
Balādhurī. 1979. *Ansāb al-ashrāf.* Wiesbaden: Franz Steiner Verlag G.B.H.
Baltacı, Cahid. 1976. *XV.–XVI. Asırlarda Osmanlı Medreseleri.* Istanbul.
Bälz, Kilian. 1996. "Eheauflösung aufgrund von Apostasie durch Popularklage: der Fall Abu Zayd." *IPRax: Praxis des Internationalen Privat- und Verfahrensrechts.* 1996:353–56.
——. 1997. "Submitting Faith to Judicial Scrutiny through the Family Trial: The 'Abû Zayd' Case." *Die Welt des Islams*, 37:135–55.
Basīt, Muḥammad Ismaʿīl. 1981. *al-Qasāmah fi'l-fiqh al-islāmī.* Beirut: Mu'assasat al-risālah.
Ben Hammouche, Mustapha. 1996. "Les quartiers résidentiels et les organisations populaires à Alger à l'époque Ottomane." In *Mélanges Charles-Robert Ageron.* 2 vols. Zaghouan, Tunis: Fondation Temimi pour la recherche scientifique et l'ínformation, vol. 2, 515–30.

Ben Talha, Abdelouahed. 1965. *Moulay-Idriss du Zerhoun. Quelques aspects de la vie sociale et familiale*. Rabat: Éditions Techniques Nord-Africaines.

Benson, Douglas and John Hughes. 1991. "Method: Evidence and Inference—Evidence and Inference for Ethnomethodology," in G. Button (ed.), *Ethnomethodology and the Human Sciences*. Cambridge: Cambridge University Press.

Berger, Maurits. 2001. "Public Policy and Islamic Law: The Modern *Dhimmi* in Contemporary Egyptian Family Law." *Islamic Law and Society*, 8:88–136.

Berkes, Niyazi. 1998. *The Development of Secularism in Turkey*. Repr. New York: Routledge.

Bilmen, Ömer N. 1985. *Hukuk-i İslamiyye ve Istılahat-ı Fıkhiyye Kamusu*. 8 vols. Istanbul: Bilmen Yayınevi.

Black, Henry Campbell. 1990. *Black's Law Dictionary Centennial Edition (1891–1991)*. 6th ed. St. Paul, Minn.: N.p.

Bligh-Abramski, Irit. 1992. "The Judiciary (*Qāḍīs*) as a Governmental-Administrative Tool in Early Islam." *Journal of the Economic and Social History of the Orient*, 35:40–71.

Bodman, Jr., Herbert L. 1963. *Political Factions in Aleppo, 1760–1826*. The James Sprunt Studies in History and Political Sciences, 45. Chapel Hill: University of North Carolina Press.

Borrmans, Maurice. 1977. *Statut Personnel et Famille au Maghreb de 1940 à nos jours*. Paris: Mouton.

——. 1979. "Documents sur la famille au Maghreb de 1940 à nos jours. Avec les textes legislatifs marocains, algériens, tunisiens et égyptiens en matière de status personnel musulman." *Oriente Moderno*, 59 (1–5), 1–438.

Bosworth, C. Edmund. 1970. "An Early Arabic Mirror for Princes: Ṭāhir Dhū al-Yaminain's Epistle to his Son ʿAbdallāh (206/821)." *Journal of Near Eastern Studies*, 29:25–41.

Bowen, John R. 1998. "'You May Not Give It Away': How Social Norms Shape Islamic Law in Contemporary Islamic Jurisprudence." *Islamic Law and Society*, 5:382–408.

——. 1999. "Legal Reasoning and Public Discourse in Indonesian Islam," in Dale R. Eickelman and Jon W. Anderson (eds.), *New Media in the Muslim World: The Emerging Public Sphere*. Bloomington: Indiana University Press, 80–105.

——. 2000. "Consensus and Suspicion: Judicial Reasoning and Social Change in an Indonesian Society 1960–94." *Law and Society Review*, 34:97–128.

——. 2003. *Islam, Law, and Equality in Indonesia: An Anthropology of Public Reasoning*. Cambridge: Cambridge University Press.

Boyd, Jean and Beverly Mack. 2000. *One Woman's Jihad: Nana Asma'u, Scholar and Scribe*. Bloomington: Indiana University Press.

Brison, Karen J. 1999. "Imagining a Nation in Kwanga Village Courts, East Sepik Province, Papua New Guinea." *Anthropological Quarterly*, 72:74–85.

Brockelmann, Carl. *Geschichte der arabischen Litteratur*. Original edition: 2 vols. Weimar: E. Felber. 1898–1902. 3 suppl. vols. Leiden: E.J. Brill. 1937–42. Rev. ed. of vols. I–II. Leiden: E.J. Brill, 1943–49.

Brown, Nathan J. 1997. *The Rule of Law in the Arab World: Courts in Egypt and the Gulf*. Cambridge: Cambridge University Press.

Brunschvig, Robert. 1962. "Métiers vils en Islam." *Studia Islamica*, 16:41–60.

——. 1965. "Justice religieuse et justice laïque dans la Tunisie des beys jusqu'au milieu du XIXe siècle." *Studia Islamica*, 23:27–70.

Bukhārī, Muḥammad b. Ismāʿīl al-. 1979. *The Translation of the Meanings of Sahih al-Bukhari*. 8 vols. Lahore: Kazi Publications.

——. 1990 [1987]. *Ṣaḥīḥ*. Ed. Muṣṭafā Dīb al-Baghā. 6 vols. + indices. Beirut: Dār Ibn Kathīr.

Burzulī, Abū al-Qāsim Aḥmad al-. 2002. *Fatāwā*. Ed. Muḥammad al-Ḥabīb al-Hīla. 7 vols. Beirut: Dār al-gharb al-islāmī.

Button, Graham. 1991. "Introduction: Ethnomethodology and the Foundational Respecification of the Human Sciences," in G. Button (ed.), *Ethnomethodology and the Human Sciences*. Cambridge: Cambridge University Press.
Cammack, Mark. 1997. "Indonesia's 1989 Religious Judicature Act: Islamization of Indonesia or Indonesianization of Islam?" *Indonesia* 63:143–68.
Caplan, Pat. 1995. "'Law' and 'Custom': Martial Disputes on Northern Mafia Island, Tanzania," in Pat Caplan (ed.), *Understanding Disputes: The Politics of Argument*. Oxford: Berg Publishers.
Carmona, Alfonso. 1998. "Las diferencias entre la jurisprudencia andalusí y el resto de la escuela de Mâlik: el texto es atribuido a Abû Isḥâq al-ârnâṭî." *Al-Qanṭara*, 19:67–102.
Carroll, Lucy. 1986. "Muslim Women in India and England: Divorce and Alimony." *Islamic Quarterly*, 30:20–30.
——. 2001. Review of *Muslim Family Law* (3rd ed.), by David Pearl and Werner Menski. *Journal of Muslim Minority Affairs*, 21:391–403.
Çelebi, Evliya. 1935. *Evliya Çelebi Seyahatnamesi*. 10 vols. Istanbul: Devlet Matbaası.
Cevdet, Ahmed. 1891–2. *Tarih-i Cevdet*. 12 vols. 2nd. ed. Istanbul: Matbaa-i Osmaniyye.
Cezar, Yavuz. 1986. *Osmanlı Maliyesinde Bunalım ve Değişim Dönemi*. N.p.: Alan Yayıncılık.
Chafi, Mohamed. 1996. *Code du statut personnel annoté: textes legislatifs, doctrine et jurisprudence*. Marrakech. Imprimerie Walili
Chalmeta, P. 1999. "Acerca de los delitos de sangre en al-Andalus durante el califato," in J.M. Carabaza and A.T.M. Essay (eds.), *El saber en al-Andalus. Textos y Estudios, II*. Sevilla: Universidad-Fundacion El Monte, 45–64.
Charnay, Jean-Paul. 1965. *La vie musulmane en Algérie d'après la jurisprudence de la première moitié du vingtième siècle*. Paris: Presse Universitaire de France.
Chaudhuri, K.N. 1985. *Trade and Civilization in the Indian Ocean*. Cambridge: Cambridge University Press.
Christelow, Allan. 1985. *Muslim Law Courts and the French Colonial State in Algeria*. Princeton: Princeton University Press.
——. 1986. "Slavery in Kano: Evidence from the Judicial Records." *African Economic History*, 57–74.
——. 1994. *Thus Ruled Emir Abbas: Selected Cases from the Emir of Kano's Judicial Council*. East Lansing: Michigan State University Press.
——. 1997. "In Search of One Word's Meaning: *Zaman* in Early Twentieth Century Kano." *History in Africa*, 24:95–115.
——. 2002. "Islamic Law and Judicial Practice in Nigeria: an Historical Perspective." *Journal of the Institute of Muslim Minority Affairs*, 22:185–204.
Cin, Halil and Ahmet Akgündüz. 1989. *Türk Hukuk Tarihi*. Vol. 1. *Kamu hukuku*. Konya: Selçuk Universitesi.
——. 1990. *Türk-Islam Hukuk Tarihi*. 2 vols. Istanbul: Timas Yayınları.
Cohen, Amnon and Elisheva Simon-Piqali (eds.). 1993. *Yehudim be-veit ha-mishpat ha-muslemi: hevrah, kalkalah ve-irgun qehilati bi-yerushalayim ha-ʿothmanit* [*Jews in the Moslem Court: Society, Economy and Communal Organization in Sixteenth Century Jerusalem*]. Jerusalem: Yad Izhak Ben-Zvi.
Colucci, Massimo. 1927. "Il diritto consuetudinario della tribù della Cirenaica." *Revista Coloniale*, 22:24–37.
Constitutional Court of Egypt. *See* Maḥkama al-dustūriyya al-ʿulyā al-.
Cook, Michael. 2000. *Commanding Right and Forbidding Wrong in Islamic Thought*. Cambridge: Cambridge University Press.
Cornu, Gérard. 1992. *Vocabulaire Juridique. Troisième Edition revue et augmentée*. Paris: Presses Universitaires de France.
The Coptic Encyclopedia. 1991. 8 vols. New York: Macmillan.
Coulson, N.J. 1964. *A History of Islamic Law*. Edinburgh: Edinburgh University Press.
——. 1971. *Succession in the Muslim Family*. Cambridge: Cambridge University Press.

Crone, Patricia and Martin Hinds. 1986. *God's Caliph, Religious Authority in the First Century of Islam.* Cambridge: Cambridge University Press.
D'Emilia, Antonio. 1946. "La giurisprudenza del Tribunale superiore sciaraitico della Libia in materia di fidanzamento matrimonio e divorzio (1929–1941)." *Revista degli Studi Orientali,* 21:15–50.
D'Ohsson, I.M. 1788–1824. *Tableau général de l'Empire othoman.* 7 vols. Paris: Imprimerie de Monsieur Firmin Didot.
Dannhauer, Paul Gerhard. 1975. *Untersuchungen zur frühen Geschichte des Qāḍī-Amtes.* Bonn Inaugural-Dissertation zur Erlangung der Doktorwürde der Philosophischen. Bonn: Fakultät der Rheinischen Friedrich-Wilhelms-Universität.
Danziger, Raphael. 1976. *Abd al-Qadir and the Algerians.* New York: Africana Press.
David, Jean-Claude. 1998. *La Suwayqat ʿAlī à Alep.* Avec la collaboration de Fawaz Baker, Thierry Grandin et Mahmoud Hreitani. Damascus: Institut Français de Damas.
Davis, J. 1987. *Libyan Politics: Tribe and Revolution.* London: I.B. Tauris.
——. 1998. "A Social Perspective," in A. Layish (ed.), *Legal Documents on Libyan Tribal Society in Process of Sedentarization. Part 1: The Documents in Arabic.* Wiesbaden: Harrassowitz, 7–13.
Departemen Agama. 1996/1997. *Kompilasi Hukum Islam di Indonesia* [Compilation of Islamic Law in Indonesia]. Jakarta: Direktorat Jenderal Pembinaan Kelembagaan Agama Islam, Departemen Agama R.I.
Dhū l-Fiqār, Monā. 1996a. *Bayna qānūn al-ḥisba wa-ḍarūrat taʿdīl al-mādda al-ṭāliṭa min qānūn al-murāfaʿāt.* Maktab al-Shalaqānī li'l-istishārāt al-qānūniyya wa'l-muḥāmāt. Cairo, 2 p.
——. 1996b. *Taʿlīq ʿalā mashrūʿ al-qānūn al-muqaddam li-tanẓīm al-ḥisba.* Maktab al-Shalaqānī li'l-istishārāt al-qānūniyya wa'l-muḥāmāt. Cairo, 4 p.
Dokaji, Abubakar. 1958. *Kano ta Dabo Cigari.* Zaria: Northern Nigeria Publishing Company.
Drew, Paul. 1992. "Contested Evidence in Courtroom Cross-Examination: The Case of a Trial for Rape," in P. Drew and J. Heritage (eds.), *Talk at Work. Interaction in Institutional Settings.* Cambridge: Cambridge University Press.
Dulong, Renaud. 1998. *Le témoin oculaire. Les conditions sociales de l'attestation personnelle.* Paris: Editions de l'EHESS.
Dupret, Baudouin. 1997. "A propos de la constitutionnalité de la sharīʿa: Présentation et traduction de l'arrêt du 26 mars 1994 (14 Shawwāl 1414) de la Haute Cour Constitutionnelle (*al-maḥkama al-dustūriyya al-ʿulyā*) égyptienne." *Islamic Law and Society,* 4 (1):91–113.
——. 1999. "Legal Pluralism, Normative Plurality, and the Arab World," in B. Dupret, M. Berger, and L. al-Zwaini (eds.), *Legal Pluralism in the Arab World.* The Hague: Kluwer Law International, 29–40.
——. 2000. *Au nom de quel droit.* Paris: Centre d'Études et de Documentation économique, juridique et sociale.
Dworkin, Ronald. 1985. *A Matter of Principle.* Oxford: Clarendon Press.
El Alami, Dawoud S. 1994. "Law no. 100 of 1985. Amending Certain Provisions of Egypt's Personal Status Law." *Islamic Law and Society,* 1 (1):116–7.
El Alami, Dawoud S. and Doreen Hinchcliffe. 1996. *Islamic Marriage and Divorce Laws of the Arab World.* London, The Hague, and Boston: Kluwer Law International.
El Hour, R. 2000. "The Andalusian Qâḍî in the Almoravid Period: Political and Judicial Authority." *Studia Islamica,* 90:67–83.
El-Nahal, Galal H. 1979. *The Judicial Administration of Ottoman Egypt in the Seventeenth Century.* Minneapolis and Chicago: Bibliotheca Islamica.
Ergene, Boğaç A. 2003. *Local Court, Provincial Society and Justice in the Ottoman Empire: Legal Practice and Dispute Resolution in Çankırı and Kastamonu.* Boston and Leiden: E.J. Brill.

Escovitz, Joseph H. 1984. *The Office of Qāḍī al-Quḍāt in Cairo Under the Baḥrī Mamlūks.* Berlin: Klaus Schwarz Verlag.

Étienne, Bruno. 1994. *Abdelkader: isthme des isthmes.* Paris: Hachette.

Evans-Pritchard, Edward E. 1949. *The Sanusi of Cyrenaica.* Oxford: Clarendon Press.

Fadel, Mohammad. 1996. "The Social Logic of *Taqlīd* and the Rise of the *Mukhtaṣar.*" *Islamic Law and Society,* 3:193–233.

Fahd, T. 2003. "Firāsa," in *The Encyclopaedia of Islam.* New ed. Leiden: Brill.

Faroqhi, Suraiya. 1973. "Social Mobility among the Ottoman Ulema in the Late Sixteenth Century." *International Journal of Middle Eastern Studies,* 4:204–18.

——. 1992. "Political Activity among Ottoman Taxpayers and the Problem of Sultanic Legitimation (1570–1650)," *Journal of the Economic and Social History of the Orient,* 35:1–39.

Fāsī, ʿAllāl al-. 2000. *al-Taqrīb. Sharḥ mudawwanat al-aḥwāl al-shakhṣiyya.* 2nd ed. 2 vols. Rabat: Maṭbaʿat al-risāla.

Fawzī, Maḥmūd. 1994. *al-Bābā Shanūda wa-muḥākamat al-qasāwisa.* 2nd ed. Cairo: al-Maktaba al-miṣriyya al-faransiyya.

Feridun Beg. 1880–1. *Mecmua-ı Münşeat üs-Selatin.* Istanbul: Mahmud Bey Matbaası.

Fierro, Maribel. 1985. "Los mālikíes de al-Andalus y los dos árbitros (*al-ḥakamān*)." *Al-Qanṭara,* 6:79–102.

——. 1992. "Tres familias andalusíes de época omeya apodadas Banu Ziyad," in M. Marín y J. Zanón (eds.), *Estudios Onomástico-Biográficos de al-Andalus 5.* Madrid, 85–142.

——. 1997a. "La religión," in *El retroceso territorial de al-Andalus. Almorávides y almohades. siglos XI al XIII.* Historia de España Menéndez Pidal, VIII–II. Madrid: Espasa Calpe, 435–546.

——. 1997b. "El alfaquí beréber Yaḥyà b. Yaḥyà, 'el inteligente de al-Andalus,'" in M.L. Avila and M. Marín (eds.), *Estudios Onomástico-Biográficos de al-Andalus 8.* Madrid and Granada: CSIC, 269–344.

——. 1999. "The legal policies of the Almohad caliphs and Ibn Rushd's *Bidâyat al-mujtahid.*" *Journal of Islamic Studies,* 10 (3):226–48.

——. Forthcoming. "Proto-Malikis, Malikis and reformed Malikis," in *The Islamic School of Law: Evolution, Devolution, and Progress.* Cambridge: Harvard University Press.

Fika, Adamu. 1978. *The Kano Civil War and British Overrule.* Ibadan: Oxford University Press.

Findley, C.V. 1990. "Maḥkama. 2 (ii). The Ottoman Empire," in *The Encyclopaedia of Islam.* New ed. Leiden: E.J. Brill.

Fleischer, Cornell. 1986. *Bureaucrat and Intellectual in the Ottoman Empire: The Historian Mustafa Âli (1541–1600).* Princeton: Princeton University Press.

Frenkel, Yehoshua. 2002. "Is there an Islamic Space? Urban and Social Issues, as Reflected in the Qadi (Cadi) Courts of Egypt and Syria (13th–16th Centuries)," in Yaacov Lev (ed.), *Towns and Material Culture in the Medieval Middle East.* Leiden: E.J. Brill.

Fuḍaylat, Jabr Maḥmūd. 1991. *al-Qaḍāʾ fi'l-islām wa-adab al-qāḍī.* ʿAmmān: Dār ʿāmm.

Fyzee, Asaf A.A. 1964. "The *Adab al-Qadi* in Islamic Law." *University of Malaya Law Review,* 6:406–16. Reprinted in *Compendium of Fatimid Law.* Simla: Indian Institute of Advanced Study, 1969.

Gara, Eleni. 1998. "In Search of Communities in Seventeenth-Century Ottoman Records." *Turcica,* 30:135–61.

Gellner, Ernest. 1969. *Saints of the Atlas.* London: Weidenfeld and Nicolson.

Gerber, Haim. 1981a. "*Sharia, Kanun* and Custom in the Ottoman Law: The Court Records of 17th-Century Bursa." *International Journal of Turkish Studies,* 2:131–47.

——. 1981b. "The Muslim Law of Partnerships in Ottoman Court Records." *Studia Islamica,* 53:109–19.

——. 1994. *State, Society and Law in Islam: Ottoman Law in Comparative Perspective.* Albany: State University of New York Press.
Ghattas, Iskandar. 1991. "Personal Status Law," in *The Coptic Encyclopedia.* 8 vols. New York: Macmillan.
Ghayth, Muḥammad Ḥasan Abū Ḥammād. 1990. *Qaḍā' al-ʿashā'ir fī ḍaw' al-sharʿ al-islāmī.* 2nd ed. Jerusalem: al-Maṭbaʿa al-ʿarabiyya al-ḥadītha.
Ghazzī, Kāmil b. Muḥammad al-. 1991–3. *Nahr al-dhahab fī tārīkh Ḥalab.* Ed. Maḥmūd Fāḥūrī and Shawqī Shaʿth. 2nd ed. 3 vols. Aleppo: Dār al-qalam al-ʿarabī.
Gibb, Hamilton A.R. and Harold Bowen. 1963. *Islamic Society in the Eighteenth Century.* In *Islamic Society and the West.* Vol. 1, parts 1 and 2. London and New York: Oxford University Press.
Goitein, Shlomo D. 1978. *A Mediterranean Society.* 5 vols. + indices. Berkeley: University of California.
Goody, Jack. 1986. *The Logic of Writing and the Organization of Society.* Cambridge: Cambridge University Press.
——. 1987. *The Interface between the Written and the Oral.* Cambridge: Cambridge University Press.
Gradeva, Rossitsa. 1999a. "The Activities of a Kadi Court in Eighteenth-Century Rumeli: The Case of Hacioğlu Pazarcik," in *Oriente Moderno,* n.s. XVIII (LXXIX), no. 1:177–90.
——. 1999b. "Kadiyskiyat sud v bulgarskite zemi (XV–XVIII v.)" [The Kadi Court in Bulgarian Lands, 15th–18th centuries], in Maria Radeva (ed.), *Bulgarskoto obshtestvo, XV–XVIII vek (Bulgarian Society, 15th–18th centuries).* Sofia: Universitetsko Izdatelstvo "Sv. Kliment Ohridski," 162–204.
——. 2000. "Apostasy in Rumeli in the Middle of the Sixteenth Century." *Arab Historical Review for Ottoman Studies,* 22:29–73.
——. 2002a. "On Kadis of Sofia, 16th–17th centuries," *Journal of Turkish Studies,* 26:1, 265–92.
——. 2002b. "Administrative System and Provincial Government in the Central Balkan Territories of the Ottoman Empire, 15th century," in H.C. Güzel, C.C. Oğuz, and Oğuz (eds.), *The Turks.* Vol. 3, *Ottomans.* Ankara: Yeni Türkiye Publications, 498–507.
Gradeva, Rossitsa and Svetlana Ivanova. 2001. "Researching the Past and Present of Muslim Culture in Bulgaria: The 'Popular' and 'High' Layers." *Islam and Christian-Muslim Relations,* 12:317–37.
Graff, Harvey. 1987. *The Labyrinths of Literacy.* London: Falmer.
Gürata, Mithat. 1975. *Unutulan Adetlerimiz ve Loncalar.* Ankara: Tisa Matbaacılık.
Habbūnī, ʿAbd al-Salām al-. 1960. *Ansāb qabā'il al-ʿarab.* Cairo: Dār al-zaynī li'l-ṭibāʿa wa'l-nashr.
Ḥājjī Khalīfa. 1893. *Kitāb kashf al-ẓunūn.* 2 vols. Istanbūl: Dār al-saʿāda.
Hallaq, Wael B. 1995. "Model *Shurūṭ* Works and the Dialectic of Doctrine and Practice." *Islamic Law and Society,* 2:109–134.
——. 1997. *A History of Islamic Legal Theories: An Introduction to Sunnī* uṣūl al-fiqh. Cambridge and New York: Cambridge University Press.
——. 1998. "The Qāḍī's Dīwān (*Sijill*) before the Ottomans." *Bulletin of the School of Oriental and African Studies,* 61 (3):415–36.
——. 1999. "Qāḍīs Communicating: Legal Change and the Law of Documentary Evidence." *Al-Qanṭara,* 20:438–66.
——. 2001. *Authority, Continuity and Change in Islamic Law.* Cambridge: Cambridge University Press.
——. 2004. *The Origins and Evolution of Islamic Law.* Cambridge: Cambridge University Press.
Hamadeh, Shirin. 1998. "The City's Pleasures." Ph.D. diss., Massachusetts Institute of Technology.

Ḥamawī, Yāqūt b. ʿAbdallāh al-. 1866–76. *Muʿjam al-buldān*. Ed. F. Wüstenfeld as *Jacut's Geographisches Wörterbuch*. 6 vols. Leipzig: F.A. Brockhaus for the deutsche Morgenlandische Gesellschaft.

Hammer-Purgstall, Joseph von. 1838. *Geschichte der osmanischen Dichtkunst bis auf unsere zeit*. 4 vols. C.A. Hartleben, Pest.

Ḥanbalī, Ibn ʿImād al-. 1931. *Shadharāt al-dhahab fī akhbār man dhahab*. Cairo: Maktabat al-qudsī.

Hanna, Nelly. 1995. "The Administration of Courts in Ottoman Cairo," in N. Hanna (ed.), *The State and Its Servants: Administration in Egypt from Ottoman Times to the Present*. Cairo: American University in Cairo Press, 44–59.

Hart, Herbert L.A. 1961. *The Concept of Law*. Oxford: Oxford University Press.

Ḥasan, Ḥilmī ʿAbd al-ʿAẓīm and Muḥammad Raṣṣād ʿAbd al-Wahhāb (eds.). 1984. *al- aḥwāl al-shakhṣiyya li'l-muslimīn ṭibqan li-aḥdat al-taʿdīlāt*. Cairo: al-Hayʾa al-ʿāmma li-ṣhuʾūn al-maṭābiʿ al-amīriyya.

Haṣkafī, ʿAlā al-dīn Muḥammad b. ʿAlī al-. N.d. [1889]. *al-Durr al-mukhtār sharḥ tanwīr al-abṣār*. 5 vols. Cairo: al-Maṭbaʿa al-maymaniyya (on the margin of Ibn ʿĀbidīn, *Radd al-Muḥtār*).

Hawting, Gerald. 1978. "The Significance of the Slogan *lā ḥukm illā lillāh* and the References to the *ḥudūd* in the Traditions about the *Fitna* and the Murder of ʿUthmān." *Bulletin of the School of Oriental and African Studies*, 41:452–63.

Heilmann Annette. 1995. "Der Koran zwischen Gegenwart und historischem Kontext." Inamo Beiträge. *Informationproject Naher und Mittlerer Osten Berichte und Analysen zu Politik und Gesellschaft des Nahen und Mittleren Ostens*, 3:61–2.

Hess, Andrew. 1978. *The Forgotten Frontier: a History of the Sixteenth Century Ibero-African Frontier*. Chicago: University of Chicago Press.

Heyd, Uriel. 1973. *Studies in Old Ottoman Criminal Law*. Ed. Victor L. Ménage. Oxford: Clarendon Press.

Hill, Enid. 1979. *Mahkama!: Studies in the Egyptian Legal System*. London: Ithaca Press.

——. 1987. *Al-Sanhuri and Islamic Law*. Cairo: The American University in Cairo Press.

Hilāl, ʿAmmār. 1986. *al-Hijra al-jazāʾiriyya nahwa bilād al-shām (1847–1918)*. Algiers: Lafawmayk.

Hinds, Martin. 1972. "The Ṣiffīn Arbitration Agreement." *Journal of Semitic Studies*, 17:93–129.

Hirsch, Susan F. 1998. *Pronouncing and Persevering: Gender and the Discourse of Islamic Courts in an African Islamic Court*. Chicago: University of Chicago Press.

Hiskett, Mervyn. 1973. *The Sword of Truth: The Life and Times of Shehu Uthman Dan Fodio*. London: Oxford University Press.

Hoexter, Miriam. 1995. "*Ḥuqūq Allāh* and *Ḥuqūq al-ʿibād* as Reflected in the *Waqf* Institution." *Jerusalem Studies in Arabic and Islam*, 19:133–56.

——. 1998. *Endowments, Rulers, and Community: Waqf al-Ḥaramayn in Ottoman Algiers*. Leiden: E.J. Brill.

Hogendorn, Jan S. and Marion Johnson. 1986. *The Shell Money of the Slave Trade*. Cambridge: Cambridge University Press.

Hollander, Isaac. 2000. "Protection, Politics and the End of the Jewish-Muslim Experience in Lower Yemen, ca. 1918–1949." Ph.D. diss. Hebrew University.

Hour. *See* El Hour.

Ḥumaydī, Muḥammad b. Fattūḥ al-. N.d. *Jadhwat al-muqtabis fī dhikr wulāt al-Andalus*. Ed. Muḥammad b. Tāwīt al-Ṭanjī. Cairo: Maktabat al-thaqāfa al-islāmiyya.

Hunter, Capt. F.M. 1968 [1877]. *An Account of the British Settlement of Aden in Arabia*. London: Frank Cass.

Hunwick, John O. 1995. *Arabic Literature of Africa*. 2 vols. Leiden: E.J. Brill.

Ibn ʿAbd al-ʿAzīz, ʿUmar. 1994. *Sharḥ adab al-qāḍī*. Ed. Abu l-Wafāʾ al-Afġānī and Abū Bakr Muḥammad al-Hāṣimī. Beirut: Dār al-kutub al-ʿilmiyya.

Ibn ʿAbd al-Barr, Yūsuf b. ʿAbdallāh. 1980. *Kitāb al-kāfī fī fiqh ahl al-Madīna al-mālikī*. 2 vols. Riyad. Maktabat al-Riyāḍ.
——. 1987. *al-Kāfī fī fiqh ahl al-madīna al-mālikī*. Beirut: Dār al-kutub al-ʿilmiyya.
——. 2000. *al-Istidhkār al-jāmiʿ li-madhāhib al-amṣār wa-ʿulamāʾ al-aqṭār*. 9 vols. Beirut: Dār al-kutub al-ʿilmiyya.
Ibn ʿAbdûn. 1948. *Sevilla a comienzos del siglo XII*. Trans. E. García Gómez. Madrid: Moneda y Credito.
Ibn Abī al-Dam[m], Shihāb al-Dīn Abū Isḥāq Ibrāhīm. 1982 [1975]. *Kitāb adab al-qaḍāʾ wa-huwa al-durar al-manẓūmāt fī al-aqḍiya wa'l-ḥukūmāt*. Ed. Muḥammad Muṣṭafā al-Zuḥaylī. Damascus: Majmaʿat al-lugha al-ʿarabiyya.
Ibn Abī Shayba, ʿAbd Allāh b. Muḥammad. 1995. *al-Kitāb al-muṣannaf fī'l aḥadīth wa'l-āthār*. 9 vols. Beirut: Dār al-kutub al-ʿilmiyya.
Ibn Abī Ṭāhir al-Ṭayfūr, Abū al-Faḍl Aḥmad. 1949. *Kitāb Baghdād*. Cairo: Maktabat nashr al-thaqāfa al-Islāmiyya.
Ibn Abī Zayd al-Qayrawānī. 1980. *La Risala: ou, Epitre sur les elements du dogme et de la loi l'Islam selon le rite malikite, texte arabe et traduction française avec un avant-propos, des notes et trios index, par Leon Bercher*. Alger: J. Carbonel.
——. 1999. *al-Nawādir wa'l-ziyādāt ʿalā mā fī'l mudawwana min ghayri-hā min al-ummahāt*. Ed. ʿAbd al-Fattāḥ Muḥammad al-Ḥulw. 15 vols. Beirut: Dār al-gharb al-islāmī.
Ibn ʿĀbidīn, Muḥammad Amīn. 1853–4. *al-ʿUqūd al-durriyya fī tanqīḥ al-fatāwā al-ḥāmidiyya*. Ed. Ḥāmid Efendi al-Imādī. 2 vols. in 1. Cairo: N.p.
Repr., Beirut: Dār al-maʿrifa. 197–?.
——. 1855. *Radd al-muḥtār ʿalā al-durr al-mukhtār*. 5 vols. Cairo: Bulāq. Repr. Beirut: Dār iḥyāʾ al-turāth al-ʿarabī. 1987.
——. 1307H [1889]. *Radd al-muḥtār ʿalā al-durr al-mukhtār*. 5 vols. Cairo: al-Maṭbaʿa al-maymaniyya.
——. 1893. *Minḥat al-khāliq ʿalā al-baḥr al-rāʾiq*. 8 vols. Cairo: n.p.
——. 1994. *Radd al-muḥtār ʿalā al-durr al-mukhtār sharḥ tanwīr al-abṣār*. Ed. ʿĀdil Aḥmad ʿAbd al-Mawjūd and ʿAlī Muʿawwaḍ. 12 vols. Beirut: Dār al-kutub al-ʿilmiyya.
Ibn al-ʿArabī, Muḥammad b. ʿAbdallāh Abū Bakr. 1957. *Aḥkām al-qurʾān*. Ed. ʿAlī Muḥammad al-Bajāwī. 4 vols. Cairo: Dār iḥyāʾ al-kutub al-ʿarabiyya.
——. N.d. *Aḥkām al-qurʾān*. 4 vols. Beirut: N.p.
Ibn ʿArnūs, Muḥammad. 1984 [1934]. *Tārīkh al-qaḍāʾ fī'l-Islām*. Cairo: Maktabat Kulliyat al-Azhar.
Ibn ʿĀṣim, Abū Bakr Muḥammad b. Muḥammad al-Mālikī al-Gharnāṭī. 1958. *Al ʿAcimiyya ou Tuh'fat al-h'ukkam fi nukat al-'uqoud wa'l ah'kam* [*Tuḥfat al-ḥukkām fī nukat al-ʿuqūd wa'l-aḥkām*]: "le présent fait aux juges touchant les points delicats des contrats et des jugements." Ed., trans., and annot. L. Bercher. Alger: Insitut d'Etudes Orientales, Faculté des lettres, Université d'Alger. N.d. *Tuḥfat al-ḥukkām fī nukat al-ʿuqūd wa'l-aḥkām*. Beirut Dār al-fikr. 1882–93. French trans. by O. Houdas and F. Martel. *Traité de droit muselman, la tohfat d'Ebn Acem; texte Arabe avec traduction français, commentaire juridique et notes philologiques*. Alger: N.p.
Ibn al-ʿAṭṭār, Muḥammad b. Aḥmad al-Umawī al-maʿrūf bi-. 1983. *Kitāb al-wathāʾiq wa'l-sijillāt* (Formulario Notarial Hispano-ʹArabe). Ed. P. Chalmeta and F. Corriente. Madrid: Academia Matritense del Notariado Instituto Hispano-Arabe de Cultura.
Ibn Bābawayh al-Qummī, Muḥammad b. ʿAli. 1986. *Kitāb man lā yaḥḍuruhu al-faqīh*. Ed. Ḥusayn al-Aʿlamī. 4 vols. Beirut: Muʾassasat al-aʿlamī li'l-maṭbuʿāt.
Ibn Bashkuwāl, Khalaf b. ʿAbd al-Malik. 1966. *Kitāb al-ṣilah fī taʾrīkh al-Andalus*. 2 vols. Cairo: al-Dār al-miṣriyya li'l-ta'līf wa'l-tarjama.
Ibn Farḥūn, Ibrāhīm b. ʿAlī. 1932. *Kitāb al-dībāj al-mudhahhab fī maʿrifat aʿyān ʿulamāʾ al-madhhab*. Cairo: Dār al-turāth.
——. 1986. *Tabṣirat al-ḥukkām fī uṣūl al-aqḍiya wa-manāhij al-aḥkām*. 2 vols. Cairo: Maktabat al-kulliyyāt al-azhariyya.

Ibn Ḥajar al-ʿAsqalānī. N.d. *Bulūgh al-marām min adillat al-aḥkām*. Cairo: Dār al-kitāb al-ʿarabī.
——. 1912. *Lisān al-mīzān*. Hyderabad: ʿUthmāniyya.
——. 1981. *Fatḥ al-bārī*. Lahore: Dār nashr al-kutub al-islāmiyya
Ibn Ḥanbal, Aḥmad b. Muḥammad. 1969. *Musnad al-imām Aḥmad b. Ḥanbal*. 6 vols. Beirut: al-Maktab al-islāmī li'l-ṭibāʿa wa'l-nashr.
Ibn Ḥārith al-Khushanī. 1985. *Uṣūl al-futyā*. Ed. M. al-Majdūb, M. Abū l-Ajfān, and ʿU. Battīkh. Tunis: al-Dār al-ʿarabiyya li'l-kitāb.
Ibn Ḥazm, ʿAlī b. Aḥmad. 1929–40. *al-Muḥallā*. 11 vols. Cairo: Idārat al-ṭibāʿa al-munīriyya.
——. 1966. *Muʿjam fiqh Ibn Ḥazm al-Ẓāhirī*. 2 vols. Damascus: Maṭbaʿat jāmiʿat Dimashq.
Ibn Hishām. 1955. *al-Sīra al-nabawiyya*. Cairo: Muṣṭafā al-bābī.
Ibn Juzayy, Muḥammad b. Aḥmad. 1982. *al-Qawānīn al-fiqhiyya*. Libya-Tunis: al-Dār al-ʿarabiyya li'l-kitāb.
——. N.d. *al-Qawānīn al-fiqhiyya*. New rev. ed. N.p.
Ibn Khaldûn. 1958. *The Muqaddimah: An Introduction to History*. 3 vols. Trans. Franz Rosenthal. Princeton: Princeton University Press.
Ibn Maʿjūz, Muḥammad. 1998 [1983]. *Aḥkām al-usra fi'l sharīʿa al-islāmiyya wifqa mudawwanat al-aḥwāl al-shakhṣiyya*. Casablanca: Maṭbaʿat al-najāḥ al-jadīda.
Ibn Manẓūr. 1988. *Lisān al-ʿarab*. 18 vols. Beirut: Dār iḥyā al-turāth al-ʿarabī.
Ibn Mughīth al-Ṭulayṭulī, Aḥmad. 1994. *al-Muqniʿ fī ʿilm al-shurūṭ*. Ed. F.J. Aguirre Sádaba. Madrid: Consejo superior de investigaciones científicas.
Ibn al-Qāsim, ʿAbd al-Raḥmān. *See* Saḥnūn.
Ibn Qudāma. 1964. *al-Mughnī*. 10 vols. Cairo: Maktabat al-imām.
——. N.d. *al-Mughnī*. 11 vols. Beirut: Dār iḥyāʾ al-turāth al-ʿarabī.
Ibn Rushd al-Ḥafīd. 1926. *Bidāyat al-mujtahid*. French trans. of the section on marriage by A. Laïmèche. Alger: Imprimerie La Typo-Litho.
——. 1960. *Bidāyat al-mujtahid wa-nihāyat al-muqtaṣid*. 2 vols. 3d ed. Cairo: Muṣṭafā al-Bābī al-Ḥalabī.
——. 1975. *Bidâyat al-mujtahid wa-nihâyat al-muqtaṣid*. 2 vols. Ed. ʿAbd al-Ḥalīm Muḥammad ʿAbd al-Ḥalīm and ʿAbd al-Rāmān Ḥasan Muḥammad. Cairo: Dār al-kutub al-ḥadītha.
——. 1995. *The Distinguished Jurist's Primer*. Trans. I.A.H. Nyazee. 2 vols. Reading-Berkshire: Garnet Publishing.
——. N.d. *Bidāyat al-mujtahid*. 2 vols in 1. Cairo: al-Maktaba al-tijāriyya.
Ibn Rushd al-Jadd, Muḥammad b. Aḥmad. 1987. *Fatāwā Ibn Rushd*. Ed. Mukhtār b. Ṭāhir al-Talīlī. 3 vols. Beirut: Dār al-gharb al-islāmī.
——. 1988. *Kitāb al-bayān wa'l-taḥṣīl*. Ed. M. Ḥajjī. 20 vols. in 19. Beirut: Dār al-gharb al-islāmī.
Ibn Sahl, Abū al-Ābagh ʿĪsā. 1973; 1980–83; 1983. *al-Aḥkām al-kubrā*. Partial eds. T. Azemmouri (*Hespéris-Tamuda*, 14) and Muḥammad ʿAbd al-Wahhāb Khallāf. Cairo: N.p.
——. 1997. *Dīwān al-aḥkām al-kubrā*. Ed. Rashīd al-Naʿīmī. 2 vols. Riyāḍ: al-Ṣafaḥat al-dhahabiyya
Ibn Salmūn, Abū al-Qāsim. 1884–5. *al-ʿIqd al-munaẓẓam li'l-ḥukkām*. 2 vols. Cairo (on the margins of Ibn Farḥūn, *Tabṣirat al-ḥukkām*).
Idris, Hady Roger. 1962. *La Berbérie Orientale sous les Ẓirides. Xᵉ–XIIᵉ siécles*. 2 vols. Paris: Maisonneuve.
Imber, Colin. 1997. *Ebuʾs-suʿud: the Islamic Legal Tradition*. Stanford, CA.: Stanford University Press.
İnalcık, Halil. 1986. "The Appointment Procedure of a Guild Warden (*Kethuda*)." Festschrift Andreas Tietze. *Wiener Zeitschrift für des Morgenlandes*, 76:135–42.

——. 1988. "Şikâyet Hakkı: Arz-ı Hal ve Arz-ı Mahzarlar." *Osmanlı Araştırmaları. The Journal of Ottoman Studies*, 7–8:33–53.
——. 1991. "Maḥkama, 2(i)," in *The Encyclopaedia of Islam*. New ed. Leiden: E.J. Brill.
——. 2000. *Osmanlı'da Devlet, Hukuk, Adalet*. Istanbul: Eren Yayıncılık.
İpşirli, Mehmet. 1982. "XVI. Asrın İkinci Yarısında Kürek Cezası ile İlgili Hükümleri." *Tarih Enstitüsü Dergisi*, 12:203–48.
İslamoğlu, Huricihan and Peter Purdue. 2001. "Introduction," "Empire and Nation in Comparative Perspective," and "Modernities Compared: State Transformations and Constitutions of Property." Special issue, *Journal of Early Modern History*, 5:271–304 and 353–86.
Itzkowitz, Norman. 1962. "Eighteenth Century Ottoman Realities." *Studia Islamica*, 16:73–94.
Ivanova, Svetlana. 1997. "Sofia," in *The Encyclopaedia of Islam*. New ed. Leiden: E.J. Brill.
ʿIyâḍ, Muḥammad b. 1982. *al-Taʿrīf bi'l-qâḍī ʿIyâḍ*. Ed. M. Bencherifa. Muḥammadiyya: Wizārat al-awqāf wa'l-shu'ūn al-islāmiyya.
——. 1989. *Madhāhib al-ḥukkām fī nawāzil al-aḥkām*. Ed. M. Bencherifa. Beirut: N.p. Spanish trans. D. Serrano. 1998. *Madhāhib al-ḥukkâm fī nawāzil al-aḥkām* (*La actuación de los jueces en los procesos judiciales*). Madrid: Consejo Superior de Investigaciones Científicas-Agencia Española de Cooperación Internacional.
ʿIyāḍ b. Mūsā. 1967. *Tartīb al-madārik wa-taqrīb al-masālik li-maʿrifat aʿlām madhhab Mālik*. Ed. Aḥmad Bakīr Maḥmūd. 4 vols. Beirut: Dār maktabat al-ḥayāt.
Jackson, Sherman A. 1996. *Islamic Law and the State: The Constitutional Jurisprudence of Shihāb al-Dīn al-Qarāfī*. Leiden: E.J. Brill.
Jarīda al-Rasmiyya, al- (The Official Gazette of Egypt).
Jaṣṣāṣ, Abū Bakr. 2000. *Aḥkām al-qurʾān*: Bāb al-Mutʿa. In Ḥarf, *Jāmiʿ al-Fiqh al-Islāmī*. CD Version 2.0. Cairo: Ḥarf Information Technology.
al-Jawharī, Rifʿat. 1961. *Sharīʿat al-ṣaḥrāʾ: ʿādāt wa-taqālīd*. Cairo: al-Hay'a al-ʿāmma li-shuʾūn al-maṭābiʿ al-amīriyya.
Jazīrī, ʿAbd al-Raḥmān al-. N.d. [1986]. *Kitāb al-fiqh ʿalā al-madhāhib al-arbaʿa*. 5 vols. Beirut: Dār iḥyāʾ al-turāth al-ʿarabī.
——. 197–?. *Kitāb al-fiqh ʿalā al-madhāhib al-arbaʿa*. 5 vols. Cairo: Dār al-irshād li'l-ṭibāʿa wa'l-nashr.
al-Jazīrī, ʿAlī b. Yaḥyā. 1998. *al-Maqṣad al-maḥmūd fī talkhīṣ al-ʿuqūd*. Ed. A. Ferreras. Madrid: Consejo superior de investigaciones científicas.
Jefferson, Gail. 1979. "The Transcript Symbols" in G. Psathas (ed.), *Everyday Language: Studies in Ethnomethodology*. New York: Irvington.
Jennings, Ronald C. 1975. "The Office of *Vekil* (*Wakil*) in 17th Century Ottoman Sharia Courts." *Studia Islamica*, 42:147–69.
——. 1978. "*Kadı*, Court, and Legal Procedure in 17th c. Ottoman Kayseri." *Studia Islamica*, 48:133–72.
——. 1979. "Limitations of the Judicial Powers of the *Kadı* in 17th c. Ottoman Kayseri." *Studia Islamica*, 50:151–84.
Jirjis, Majdī. 1999. *al-Qaḍāʾ al-qibṭī fī miṣr: Dirāsa taʾrikhiyya*. Cairo: Mīrīt.
Johansen, Baber. 1979. "Eigentum, Familie und Obrigkeit im Hanafitischen Strafrecht. Das Verhältnis der privaten Rechte zu den Forderungen der Allgemeinheit in hanafitischen Rechtskommentaren". *Die Welt des Islams*, 19:1–73. (Reprinted in Johansen, *Contingency*, 1999:349–420).
——. 1981. "Sacred and Religious Element in Hanafite Law—Functions and Limits of the Absolute Character of Government Authority," in E. Gellner and J.-C. Vatin (eds.), *Islam et Politique au Maghreb*. Paris: Éditions du Centre national de la recherche scientifique, 281–303.
——. 1990. "Le jugement comme preuve. Preuve juridique et vérité religieuse dans

le Droit Islamique hanéfite." *Studia Islamica*, 72:5–17. (Reprinted in Johansen, *Contingency*, 1999:434–45).
——. 1993. "Legal Literature and the Problem of Change: The Case of the Land Rent," in Chibli Mallat (ed.), *Islam and Public Law. Classical and Contemporary Studies.* London/Norwell Ma: Graham and Trotman, 29–47.
——. 1997a. "Formes de langages et fonctions publiques: stéréotypes, témoins et offices dans la preuve par écrit en droit musulman." *Arabica*, 44:333–76.
——. 1997b. "Supra-Legislative Norms and Constitutional Courts: The Case of France and Egypt," in Eugene Cotran and Adel Omar Sherif (eds.), *The Role of the Judiciary in the Protection of Human Rights.* London: Kluwer Law International, 347–76.
——. 1997c. "Wahrheit und Geltungsanspruch: Zur Begründung und Begrenzung der Autorität des Qadi-Urteils im Islamischen Recht." *La Giustizia Nell'Alto Medioevo (Secoli IX–XI).* Spoleto: Presso la Sede del Centro, 975–1074.
——. 1999. *Contingency in a Sacred Law. Legal and Ethical Norms in the Muslim Fiqh.* Leiden: E.J. Brill.
——. 2002. "Signs as evidence: the doctrine of Ibn Taymiyya (1263–1328) and Ibn Qayyim al-Jawziyya (d. 1351) on proof." *Islamic Law and Society*, 9 (2):168–93.
Jones, Gavin W. 1994. *Marriage and Divorce in Islamic South-East Asia.* Kuala Lumpur: Oxford University Press.
Jundī, Aḥmad Naṣr al-. 1993. *al-Taṭlīq wa'l-tafrīq ʿind al-masīḥiyyīn min al-miṣriyyīn.* N.p.: Maṭbaʿat al-kharbūṭlī.
Kaddache, Mahfoud. 1998. *L'Algérie durante la période Ottomane.* Algiers: Office de Publications Universitaires.
Kāfī, Muḥammad b. Yūsuf al-. 1991. *Iḥkām al-aḥkām sharḥ tuḥfat al-ḥukkām li-Ibn ʿĀṣim.* Casablanca: Dār al-rashād al-ḥadītha.
Kaḥlānī, Muḥammad al-. N.d. *Subul al-salām sharḥ bulūgh al-marām li-Ibn Ḥajar al-ʿAsqalānī.* 4 vols. Cairo: Dār al-fikr.
Kahraman, Seyit Ali, Ahmet N. Galitekin, and Cevdet Dadaş, eds. 1998 [1916]. *İlmiyye Salnamesi:Osmanlı İlmiyye Teşkilatı ve Şeyhülislamlar.* Istanbul: İşaret Yayınları.
Kal'a, Ahmet. 1998. *İstanbul Esnaf Birlikleri ve Nizamları.* Istanbul: İstanbul Arastırmaları Merkezi.
Kal'a, Ahmet et al., eds. 1997–8. *İstanbul Ahkam Defterleri: İstanbul Esnaf Tarihi.* 2 vols. Istanbul: İstanbul Arastırmaları Merkezi.
Kaldy-Nagy, Gyula. 1973. "Ḳāḍī," in *The Encyclopaedia of Islam.* New ed. Leiden: E.J. Brill.
Karadeniz, Feriha. 1996. "Complaints against the Kadis and Abuses of Their Authority." Master's thesis. Ankara: Bilkent University.
Karibi-Whyte, A.G. 1993. *History and Sources of Nigerian Criminal Law.* Ibadan: Spectrum Law Publishers.
Kāsānī, ʿAlāʾ al-dīn Abū Bakr b. Masʿūd al-. 1910 [1327–48]. *Kitāb badāʾiʿ al-ṣanāʾiʿ fī tartīb al-sharāʾiʿ.* 7 vols. in 6. Cairo: Sharikat al-maṭbuʿāt al-ʿilmiyya. Repr. Cairo: Dār al-kutub al-ʿilmiyya. N.d.
Keay, E.A., and S.S. Richardson. 1966. *The Native and Customary Courts of Nigeria.* London: Sweet and Maxwell.
Kennedy, Hugh. 1981. "General Government and Provincial Élites in the Early ʿAbbāsid Caliphate." *Bulletin of the School of Oriental and Asian Studies*, 44:26–38.
Khalīl b. Isḥāq. 1900. *Mukhtaṣar.* Paris: Maṭbaʿat al-dawla al-jumhūriyya. Trans. by D. Santillana as *Il "muhtaṣar" o Sommario del Diritto Malehita di Halīl ibn Isḥāq.* 2 vols. Milan. 1919. Trans. by G.H. Bousquet as *Abrégé de la loi musulmane selon le rite de l'imâm Mâlik.* Alger: Editions algériennes en-Nahdha. 1956.
Khallāf, ʿAbd al-Wahhāb. 1938. *Aḥkām al-aḥwāl al-shakhṣiyya fi'l sharīʿa al-islāmiyya ʿalā madhhab al-imām Abī Ḥanīfa wa-mā ʿalayhi al-ʿamal al-ʾān bi'l -maḥākim al-sharʿiyya al-miṣriyya.* 2nd ed. Cairo: Maṭbaʿat dār al-kutub al-miṣriyya.

Khaṣṣāf, Abū Bakr Aḥmad b. ʿAmr al-. 1978. *Kitāb adab al-qāḍī*, with the commentary of Aḥmad b. ʿAlī al-Rāzī al-Jaṣṣāṣ. Ed. with Introduction by Farhat Ziyāda. Cairo: American University Press. *See also* Aḥmad Saʿīd, trans. 1987–2001.

Khushanī, Muḥammad b. Ḥārith al-. 1914. *Historia de los jueces de Córdoba por Aljoxaní.* Ed. and trans. J. Ribera. Madrid: Junta para Ampliacion de Estudios e Investigaciones Cientificas-Centro de Estudios Historicos.

Kindī, Abū ʿUmar Muḥammad b. Yūsuf al-. 1987. *Tārīkh wulāt miṣr*. Beirut: Muʾassasat al-kutub al-thaqāfiyya.

Kohlberg, E. 2003. "Shurayḥ," in *The Encyclopaedia of Islam.* New ed. Leiden: E.J. Brill.

Komter, Martha. 1998. *Dilemmas in the Courtroom. A Study of Trials of Violent Crime in the Netherlands.* Mahwah, New Jersey: Lawrence Erlbaum Associates.

——. 2001. "La construction de la preuve dans un interrogatoire de police," in "Le droit en action et en contexte. Ethnométhodologie et analyse de conversation dans la recherche juridique," ed. B. Dupret, special issue, *Droit et Société*, 48:349–366.

Krcsmárik, J. 1891. "Das Waîfrecht vom Standpunkte des Šariʿatrechtes nach der ḥanefitischen Schule. Ein Beitrag zum Studium des islamitischen Rechtes." *Zeitschrift der Deutschen Morgenländischen Gesellschaft*, 45:511–576.

Kressel, G.M. 1981. "Sororicide/Filiacide: Homicide for Family Honour." *Current Anthropology*, 22:141–58.

——. 1996. *Ascendancy through Aggression.* Wiesbaden: Harrassowitz.

Kütükoğlu, Mübahat. 1983. *Osmanlılarda Narh Müessesesi ve 1640 Tarihli Narh Defteri.* Istanbul: Enderun Kitabevi.

Ladan, Ibrahim, trans. 2003. *Safiyyatu's Case.* Enugu: Women's Aid Collective.

Lagardère, V. 1986. "La haute judicature à l'époque almoravide en al-Andalus." *Al-Qanṭara*, 7:135–228.

——. 1995. *Histoire et Société en Occident Musulman au Moyen Âge. Analyse du Miʿyâr d'al-Wansarîsî.* Madrid: Consejo Superior de Investigaciones Cientificas.

Laïmèche. 1926. See Ibn Rushd al-Ḥafīd. 1926.

Lammens, H. 1930. *Études sur le siècle des Omayyades*. Beirut.

Lane, E.W. 1984. *Arabic-English Lexicon.* Rev. format. 2 vols. Cambridge: Islamic Texts Society.

Largueche, Dalenda. 1992. "Dar Joued ou l'oubli dans la mémoire," in D. Largueche and A. Largueche, *Marginales en terre d'islam.* Tunis: Cérès, 85–112.

——. 1996. "Confined, Battered, and Repudiated Women in Tunis since the Eighteenth Century," in A. El Azhary Sonbol (ed.), *Women, the Family, and Divorce Laws in Islamic History.* Syracuse: Syracuse University Press, 259–76.

Last, Murray. 1967. *The Sokoto Caliphate.* London: Oxford University Press.

Layish, A. 1975. *Women and Islamic Law in a Non-Muslim State.* New Jersey: Transaction Books.

——. 1983. "The Mālikī *Waqf* according to Wills and *Waqfiyyāt.*" *Bulletin of the School of Oriental and African Studies*, 46:1–32.

——. 1984. "The Islamization of the Bedouin Family in the Judean Desert as Reflected in the *Sijill* of the *Sharīʿa* court," in E. Marx and A. Shmueli (eds.), *The Changing Bedouin.* New Brunswick, N.J.: Transaction Books, 39–58.

——. 1988. "Customary *Khulʿ* as Reflected in the *Sijill* of the Libyan *Sharīʿa* Courts." *Bulletin of the School of Oriental and African Studies*, 51:428–39.

——. 1991. *Divorce in the Libyan Family: A Study Based on the Sijills of the Sharīʿa Courts of Ajdābiyya and Kufra.* New York: New York University Press and Jerusalem: The Magnes Press.

——. 1994. "The Muslim *Waqf* in Jerusalem after 1967: Beneficiaries and Management," in F. Bilici (ed.), *Le waqf dans le monde musulman contemporain (XIXᵉ–XXᵉ siècles).* Institut Français d'Études Anatoliennes. *Varia Turcica*, 26:145–66.

——. 1995a. "*Dār ʿadl*—Symbiosis of Custom and *Sharīʿa* in a Tribal Society in Process of Sedentarization." *Jerusalem Studies in Arabic and Islam*, 19:198–213.
——. 1995b "*Sharīʿa* and Tribal Custom in Libya: Was Tajdīda Married to Two Husbands?" *Archív Orientální*, 63:488–503.
——. 1997. "The Family *Waqf* and the *Sharʿī* Law of Succession in Modern Times." *Islamic Law and Society*, 4:352–88.
——. 1998. *Legal Documents on Libyan Tribal Society in Process of Sedentarization. Part 1: The Documents in Arabic*. Wiesbaden: Harrassowitz.
——. 2002. "The Qāḍī's Role in the Islamization of Sedentary Tribal Society," in M. Hoexter, S.N. Eisenstadt, and N. Levtsion (eds.), *Public Sphere in Muslim Societies*. Albany: SUNY Press, 83–107.
——. 2005. *Sharīʿa and Custom in Libyan Tribal Society. An Annotated translation of Decisions from the Sharīʿa Courts of Ajdābiya and Kufra*. Leiden: E.J. Brill.
Layish, A. and A. Shmueli. 1979. "Custom and *Sharīʿa* in the Bedouin Family according to Legal Documents from the Judaean Desert." *Bulletin of the School of Oriental and African Studies*, 42:29–45.
Lee, John. 1991. "Language and Culture: The Linguistic Analysis of Culture," in G. Button (ed.), *Ethnomethodology and the Human Sciences*. Cambridge: Cambridge University Press.
Lev, Daniel S. 1972. *Islamic Courts in Indonesia: A Study in the Political Bases of Legal Institutions*. Berkeley: University of California Press.
Libson, Gideon. 1997. "On the Development of Custom as a Source of Law in Islamic Law." *Islamic Law and Society*, 4:131–55.
——. 2002. "Legal Autonomy and the Recourse to Legal Proceedings by Protected Peoples according to Muslim Sources during the Gaonic Period." *The Intertwined Worlds of Islam: Essays in Memory of Hava Lazarus-Yafeh*. Jerusalem: Ben Zvi Institute, 334–92 [in Hebrew].
Liebesny, Herbert. 1975. *The Law of the Near & Middle East. Readings, Cases and Materials*. Albany: State University of New York Press.
Linant de Bellefonds, Y. 1965–73. *Traité de Droit Musulman Comparé*. 3 vols. Paris: Mouton.
Little, Donald P. 1982. "Two Fourteenth-Century Court Records from Jerusalem Concerning the Disposition of Slaves by Minors." *Arabica*, 29:16–49.
——. 1984. *A Catalogue of the Islamic Documents from al-Ḥaram aà-'arīf in Jerusalem*. Wiesbaden/Beirut: Franz Steiner Verlag.
——. 1998. "Documents Related to the Estates of a Merchant and His Wife in Late Fourteenth Century Jerusalem." *Mamlūk Studies Review*, 2:93–193.
——. 2001. "Two Petitions and Consequential Court Records from the Ḥaram Collection." *Jerusalem Studies in Arabic and Islam*, 25:171–94.
López Ortiz, José. 1927. "Algunos capítulos del formulario notarial de Abensalmún de Granada." *Anuario de Historia del Derecho Español*, 4:319–75.
Lovejoy, Paul. 1980. *Caravans of Kola: The Hausa Kola Nut Trade, 1700–1900*. Zaria: Ahmadu Bello University Press.
——. 1993. *Transformations in Slavery: A History of Slavery in Africa*. Cambridge: Cambridge University Press.
Lovejoy, Paul, Abdullahi Mahadi, and Mansur Ibrahim Mukhtar. 1993. "C.L. Temple's Notes on the History of Kano." *Sudanic Africa*, 4:7–76.
Lutfi, Huda. 1983. "A Study of Six Fourteenth-Century *Iqrār*s from al-Quds Relating to Muslim Women." *Journal of the Social and Economic History of the Orient*, 26:246–94.
Lynch, Michael. 1993. *Scientific Practice and Ordinary Action: Ethnomethodology and Social Studies of Science*. Cambridge: Cambridge University Press.
Maḥjūb, Muḥammad ʿAbduh. N.d. [Ca. 1974]. *Muqadimma li-dirāsat al-mujtamaʿāt al-badawiyya (manhaj wa-taṭbīq)*. Beirut: Dār al-qalam.

Mahkama al-dustūriyya al-ʿulyā al-. 1981. *Wathāʾiq inshāʾ al-maḥkama; al-aḥkām wa'l-qarārāt allatī aṣdarathā ḥattā 30 yūnyō sanat 1981.* Vol. 1. Cairo: Maṭābiʿ dār al-shaʿb.

al-Maḥkama al-dustūriyya al-ʿulyā. 1987. *al-Aḥkām allatī aṣdarathā al-maḥkama min yanāyir 1984 ḥattā dīsambar 1986 m.* Vol. 3. Cairo: Dār al-hanā li'l-ṭabāʿa.

——. [1996]. *al-Aḥkām allatī aṣdarathā al-maḥkama min awwal yūlō 1993 ḥattā ākhar yūnyō 1995.* Vol. 6. Cairo: Maṭābiʿal-ahrām al-tijāriyya.

——. [1997]. *al-Aḥkām allatī aṣdarathā al-maḥkama min awwal yūlō 1995 ḥattā ākhar yūnyō 1996.* Vol. 7. Cairo: Maṭābiʿal-ahrām al-tijāriyya.

Mahmood, Tahir. 1977. *Muslim Personal Law. Role of the State in the Subcontinent.* New Delhi: Vikas Publishing House.

Mahmud, Abdulmalik Bappa. 1988. *A Brief History of Sharīʿah in the Defunct Northern Nigeria.* S.l.: s.n.

Majallat al-aḥkām al-sharʿiyya. 1902–23. Cairo.

Majer, Hans Georg., Ed. 1984. *Das osmanische "Registerbuch der Beschwerden" (Şikâyet Defteri) vom Jahre 1675.* Wien: Verlag der Osterreichischen Akademie der Wissenschaften, Bd. 1.

Makhlūf, Muḥammad b. Muḥammad. 1975. *Shajarat al-nūr al-zakiyya fī ṭabaqāt al-mālikiyya.* 2nd ed. 2 vols. in 1. Beirut: Dār al-kitāb al-ʿarabī.

Mālik b. Anas. 1968. *Muwaṭṭaʾ, riwāya of al-Shaybānī.* Ed. ʿAbd al-Wahhāb ʿAbd al-Laṭīf. Cairo: N.p.

——. 1981. *Muwaṭṭaʾ, riwāya of Yaḥyā b. Yaḥyā.* Beirut: N.p.

——. 1992. *Muwaṭṭaʾ, riwāya of Abū Muṣʿab.* Ed. Bashshār ʿAwwād Maʿrūf and Maḥmūd Muḥammad Khalīl. 2 vols. Beirut: N.p.

——. 1994. *Muwaṭṭaʾ, riwāya of Suwayd b. Saʿīd al-Ḥadathānī.* Ed. A.M. Turki. Beirut: Dār al-gharb al-islāmī.

——. N.d. *Muwaṭṭaʾ.* Ed. Muḥammad Fuʾād ʿAbd al-Bāqī. Cairo: Dār al-shaʿb.

Mandaville, Jon. 1966. "The Ottoman Court Records of Syria and Jordan." *Journal of the American Oriental Society*, 86:311–19.

——. 1969. "The Muslim Judiciary of Damascus in the Late Mamluk Period." Ph.D. diss., Princeton University.

Manūfī, ʿAlī b. Muḥammad al-. 1963. *Kifāyat al-ṭālib al-rabbānī li-risālat Ibn Abī Zayd al-Qayrawānī.* 2 vols. Cairo: Maktabat Muḥammad ʿAlī Ṣabīḥ.

al-Marāghī, ʿAbd Allāh Muṣṭafā. 1936. "Rūḥ al-tashrīʿ fi'l islām (part 11)." *al-Muḥāmāt al-Sharʿiyya*, 8:25–31.

Marcus, Abraham. 1989. *The Middle East on the Eve of Modernity. Aleppo in the Eighteenth Century.* New York: Columbia University Press.

Marghīnānī, Abu'l Ḥasan ʿAlī al-. 1936. *al-Hidāya.* Cairo: Muṣṭafā al-bābī. Repr., Karachi: Dārul Ishāʿat Urdu Bazar.

——. 1957. *The Hedaya or Guide: A Commentary on the Mussulman Laws. Translated, by order of the Governor-General and Council of Bengal.* Transl. Charles Hamilton. 2nd ed., with preface and index by Standish Grove Grady. Lahore: New Book Company/ Premier Book House.

Marín, Manuela. 2000. *Mujeres en al-Ándalus. Estudios Onomástico-Biográficos de al-Andalus 9.* Madrid: CSIC.

——. Forthcoming. "Disciplining Wives: A Historical Reading of Qurʾān 4:34." *Studia Islamica.*

Marrākushī, Muḥammad b. Muḥammad Ibn ʿAbd al-Malik al- . 1984. *al-Dhayl wa'l-takmila.* Ed. Muḥammad b. Sharīfa. Rabat: Publisher. [Vol. 8]

Masud, Muhammad Khalid. 1994a. "Qāḍī Wakīʿ b. Khalaf kī taṣnīf *Akhbār al-quḍāt*: tārīkh Islām kī ēk aham dastāwīz." *Fikr-o-Nazar*, 32:19–48.

——. 1994b. "Theory and Practice in Islamic Law: A Study of Wakīʿ's (d. 306/917) *Akhbār al-Quḍāt.*" Paper presented at Joseph Schacht Conference on Islamic Law, Leiden.

——. 1999. "Procedural Law between Traditionists, Jurists and Judges: The Problem of *yamîn ma' al-shâhid.*" *Al-Qanṭara*, 20 (2):389–416.
Masud, Mahmud Khalid, Brinkley Messick, David S. Powers. 1996. "Muftis, Fatwas, and Legal Interpretation," in M.Kh. Masud, B. Messick, and D.S. Powers (eds.), *Islamic Legal Interpretation: Muftis and their Fatwas.* Cambridge, MA.: Harvard University Press, 3–32.
Masud, Muhammad Khalid, Brinkley Messick, and David S. Powers (eds.). 1996. *Islamic Legal Interpretation: Muftis and Their Fatwas.* Cambridge: Harvard University Press.
Māwardī, Abu'l Ḥasan. 1915. *Les status gouvernmentaux ou règles de droit public et administrative.* Ed. and trans. Edmond Fagnan. Alger: Adolphe Jourdan.
——. 1978. *al-Aḥkām al-sulṭāniyya.* Ed. Muḥammad Fahmī al-Sirjānī. Cairo: al-Maktaba al-tawfīqiyya
——. 1971–2. *Adab al-qāḍī.* Ed. Muḥyī Hilāl Sirḥān. Baghdad: Ri'āsat dīwān al-awqāf.
——. 1994. *al-Ḥāwī al-kabīr.* 23 vols. Beirut: Dār al-fikr.
Mawsū'at al-Ḥadīth al-Sharīf. 1997. CD-Rom. Second Edition. Cairo: al-Sharika al-barāmij al-islāmiyya.
al-Mawsū'a al-fiqhiyya. 1986. 34 vols. Kuweit: Wizārat al-awqāf wa'l-shu'ūn al-islāmiyya.
McGowan, Bruce. 1994. "The Age of Ayans, 1699–1812," in H. İnalcık and D. Quataert (eds.), *An Economic and Social History of the Ottoman Empire, 1300–1914.* Cambridge and New York: Cambridge University Press, 637–743.
Mecelle-i Ahkam-ı Adliyye. 1308. Dersaadet. Istanbul. 1890–91.
Meriwether, Margaret L. 1981. "The Notable Families of Aleppo, 1770–1830: Networks and Social Structure." Ph.D. diss., University of Pennsylvania.
Meron, Ya'akov. 1969. "The Development of Legal Thought in Ḥanafī Texts." *Studia Islamica*, 30:73–118.
——. 1971. *L'obligation alimentaire entre époux en droit musulman hanéfite.* Paris: Librairie Générale de Droit et de Jurisprudence R. Pichon et R. Durand-Auzias.
Merry, Sally E. 1988. "Legal Pluralism." *Law & Society Review*, 22:869–96.
——. 1990. *Getting Justice and Getting Even: Legal Consciousness among Working Class Americans.* Chicago: University of Chicago Press.
Messick, Brinkley. 1990. "Literacy and the Law: Documents and Document Specialists in Yemen," in D. Dwyer (ed.), *Law and Islam in the Middle East.* New York: Bergin and Garvey.
——. 1993. *The Caligraphic State: Textual Domination and History in a Muslim Society.* Berkeley: University of California Press.
——. 1995. "Textual Properties: Writing and Wealth in a Shari'a Case." *Anthropological Quarterly*, 68 (3):157–70.
——. 1998. "L'écriture en procès: les recits d'un meutre devant un tribunal shar'i." *Droit et Société*, 39:237–56.
——. 2002. "Evidence: From Memory to Archive." *Islamic Law and Society*, 9 (2):231–70.
——. Forthcoming/a. "*Madhhabs* and Modernities." In *The Islamic School of Law.* Cambridge: Harvard Law School, Islamic Legal Studies Program.
——. Forthcoming/b. "Provincial Judges: The Sharī'a Judiciary of Mid-Century Yemen," in Ron Shaham (ed.), *Law Custom, and Statute in the Muslim World.*
Milliot, Louis. 1924. *Recueil de jurisprudence chérifienne.* 7 vols. Paris: Éditions Ernest Leroux. Publications de l'Institut des hautes études marocaines.
Mir-Hosseini, Ziba. 1993. *Marriage on Trial: A Study of Islamic Family Law: Iran and Morocco Compared.* London and New York: I.B. Tauris.
Miura, Toru. 2001. "Personal Networks Surrounding the Ṣāliḥiyya Court in 19th-Century Damascus," in Brigitte Marino (ed.), *Etudes sur les villes du Proche-Orient, XVIe–XIXe siècle. Hommage à André Raymond.* Damascus: Institut Français d'Etudes Arabes de Damas, 113–50.

Mohammed, Khalil. 2001. "Development of an Archetype: Studies in the Shurayḥ Traditions." Ph.D. diss. McGill University.

Mohsen, Safia K. 1967. "The legal status of women among Awlad 'Ali." *Anthropological Quarterly*, 40 (3):153–66.

——. 1975. *Conflict and Law among Awlad 'Ali of the Western Desert.* Cairo: National Center for Social and Criminological Research.

Molina López, E. 1991. "L'attitude des jurises de al-Andalus en matière de droit pénal. A propòs d'une publication récente sur le thème," in *Actes du VII Colloque Universitaire Tuniso-Espagnol sur Le patrimoine andalous dans la culture arabe et espagnole.* Tunis: Centro d'Etudes et de Recherches Economiques et Sociales, 155–91.

Moors, Annelies. 1995. *Women, Property and Islam: Palestinian Experiences, 1920–1990.* Cambridge: Cambridge University Press.

Motzki, Harold. 2002. *The Origins of Islamic Jurisprudence: Meccan Fiqh before the Classical Schools.* Trans. Marion H. Katz. Leiden: E.J. Brill.

Mubārak, Aḥmad b.'Abd al-'Azīz. 1977. *Niẓām al-qaḍā' fi'l-Islām.* Damascus: Maktabat dār al-qalam.

Mudhakkira. 1919. *Madrasat al-qaḍā' al-shar'ī fī ithnay 'ashar 'āmman: Mudhakkira marfū'a ilā al-hay'āt al-niyābiyya fī miṣr wa-ilā wuzarā' al-ḥukūma wa'l-ra'y al-'āmm bi-munāsabat mā ushī'a min tafkīr al-ḥukūma fī ilghā' al-madrasa.* N.p.

al-Muḥāmāt al-shar'iyya. 1929–55. Cairo.

Müller, Christian. 1999. *Gerichtspraxis im Stadtstaat Córdoba: Zum Recht der Gesellschaft in einer mālikitisch-islamischen Rechtstradition des 5.11. Jahrhunderts.* Leiden: E.J. Brill.

——. 2000a. "Administrative Tradition and Civil Jurisdiction of the Cordoban *ṣâḥib al-aḥkâm* (I)." *Al-Qanṭara*, 21:57–84.

——. 2000b. "Judging with God's Law on Earth: Judicial Powers of the *Qāḍī al-jamā'a* of Cordoba in the Fifth/Eleventh Century." *Islamic Law and Society*, 7:159–86.

——. 2001. "Constats d'héritages dans la Jérusalem mamelouke: les témoins du cadi dans un document inédit du Ḥaram al-Sharīf." *Annales Islamologiques*, 35:291–319.

Mumcu, Ahmet. 1983. *Osmanlı Devleti'nde Siyaseten Katl.* Ankara: Ankara Üniversitesi Hukuk Fakültesi.

——. 1985. *Osmanlı Hukukunda Zulüm Kavramı.* 2nd ed. Ankara: Birey ve Toplum Yayınları.

——. 1986. *Divan-ı Hümayun.* 2nd ed. Ankara: Birey ve Toplum Yayınları.

Muranyi, Miklos. 1998. "Das *Kitāb Aḥkām Ibn Ziyād.* Uber die Identifizierung eines Fragmentes in Qairawān (Qairawāner Miszellaneen 5)." *Zeitschrift des Deutsches Morgenländisches Gesellschaft*, 148:241–60.

Murray, G.W. 1935. *Sons of Ismael. A Study of the Egyptian Bedouin.* London: George Routledge and Sons.

Muslim b. Ḥajjāj al-Qushayrī. 1998. *Ṣaḥīḥ.* Riyāḍ: Dār al-salām.

Nader, Laura. 1990. *Harmony Ideology: Justice and Control in a Zapotec Mountain Village.* Stanford: Stanford University Press.

Nader, Laura and Harry F. Todd. 1979. "Introduction: The Disputing Process," in L. Nader and H. Todd (eds.), *The Disputing Process: Law in Ten Societies.* New York: Columbia Universiy Press, 1–40.

Nadīm, Muḥammad b. Isḥāq al-. 1970. *The Fihrist of al-Nadim: A Tenth Century Survey of Muslim Culture.* 2 vols. Trans. and ed. by Bayard Dodge. New York and London: Columbia University Press.

Nahal El-, Galal H. *See* El-Nahal, Galal H.

Najjār, 'Abd al-Wahhāb. 1930. "al-Maḥākim al-shar'iyya: Hal lahā an taḥkuma bi-ṭalāq al-masīḥiyyīn?" *al-Muḥāmāt al-shar'iyya*, 2:414–15.

Nakadī, 'Ārif. 1923. *al-Qaḍā' fi'l-islām.* Damascus: N.p.

Nasafī, Abū al-Barakāt 'Abdallāh b. Aḥmad al-. 1894. *Kanz al-daqā'iq*, with the commentaries by Ibn Nujaym, *al-Baḥr al-rā'iq*, and by Ibn ʿĀbidīn, *Minḥat al-khāliq*. 8 vols. Cairo: N.p.

Nielsen, Jorgen S. 1985. *Secular Justice in an Islamic State: Mazalim under the Bahri Mamluks, 662/1264–789/1387*. Istanbul: Nederlands Historisch-Archaeologisch Instituut.

——. 1991. "Maẓālim," in *The Encyclopaedia of Islam*, New ed. Leiden: E.J. Brill.

Nimmar, Muḥammad Maḥmūd and Alafī Baqṭar Ḥabashī. 1957. *al-Aḥwāl al-shakhṣiyya li'l-ṭawā'if ghayr al-islāmiyya min al-miṣriyyīn*. Cairo: Maṭābiʿ dār al-nashr li'l-jāmiʿāt al-miṣriyya.

Obermeyer, G.J. 1968. "Structure and Authority in a Bedouin Tribe: The ʿAishibat of the Western Desert of Egypt." Ph.D. diss., Indiana University.

Obilade, A.O. 1979. *The Nigerian Legal System*. Ibadan: Spectrum Books.

Ocak, Ahmet Yaşar. 1991. "Idéologie officielle et réaction populaire: un aperçu général sur les mouvements et les courants socio-religieux à l'époque de Soliman le Magnifique," in G. Veinstein (ed.), *Soliman le magnifique et son temps*. Paris: La Documentation Française, 185–92.

Olson, David R. and Nancy Torrance. 1991. *Literacy and Orality*. Cambridge: Cambridge University Press.

Olson, Robert W. 1974. "The *Esnaf* and the Patrona Halil Rebellion of 1730: Realignment in Ottoman Politics?" *Journal of the Economic and Social History of the Orient*, 17:329–44.

——. 1977. "Jews, Janissaries, Esnaf and the Revolt of 1740 in Istanbul." *Journal of the Economic and Social History of the Orient*, 20:185–207.

Osman Nuri [Ergin]. 1922. *Tarih-i Teşkilat-ı Belediye*. Vol. 1 of *Mecelle-i Umur-i Belediye*. Istanbul: Matbaa-i Osmaniyye.

Özdeğer, Hüseyin. 1988. *Onaltıncı Asırda Ayıntâb Livâsı*. Istanbul: Bayrak Matbaacılık.

Özergin, M. Kemal. 1976. "Rumeli Kadılıkları'nda 1078 Düzenlemesi," in *Ord. Prof. İsmail Hakkı Uzunçarşılı'ya Armağan*. Ankara: Türk Tarih Kurumu, 251–309.

Paden, John. 1973. *Religion and Political Authority in Kano*. Berkeley: University of California Press.

Pearl, David. 1987. *A Textbook on Muslim Personal Law*. 2nd ed. London: Croom Helm.

Pearl, David and Werner Menski. 1998. *Muslim Family Law*. London: Sweet and Maxwell.

Peirce, Leslie. 1998. "Le dilemme de Fatma: crime sexuel et culture juridique dans une cour ottomane au début des temps modernes." *Annales: Histoire, Sciences Sociales*, 53 (2):291–319.

——. 1999. "'The Law Shall Not Languish': Social Class and Public Conduct in 16th-century Ottoman Legal Discourse," in A. Afsaruddin (ed.), *The Hermeneutics of Honor: Negotiation of Public Space in Islamicate Societies*. Cambridge: Harvard University Press, 140–58.

——. 2003. *Morality Tales: Law and Gender in the Ottoman Court of Aintab*. Berkeley and Los Angeles: University of California Press.

Peláez, D. 2000. *El proceso judicial en la España musulmana (Siglos VIII–XII)*. Cordoba: El Almendro.

Peletz, Michael G. 2002. *Islamic Modern. Religious Courts and Cultural Politics in Indonesia*. Princeton: Princeton University Press.

Pellat, Charles. 1958. "Une *risāla* inédite de Ǧaḥiẓ sur l'arbitrage entre ʿAlī et Muʿāwiya." *al-Mashriq*, 52:417–90.

Pérez Beltrán, Carmelo. 1995. "El código argelino de la familia: estudio introductorio y traducción," in C. Pérez Beltrán and C. Ruiz-Almodóvar (eds.), *El Magreb coordenadas socioculturales*. Granada: Grupo de Investigación Estudios Árabes Contemporáneos Universidad de Granada, 375–411.

Peters, E.L. 1965. "Aspects of the Family among the Bedouin of Cyrenaica," in M.F. Nimkoff (ed.), *Comparative Family Systems*. Boston, Mass.: Houghton Mifflin, 121–46.
——. 1980. "Aspects of the Bedouin Bridewealth among Camel Herders in Cyrenaica," in J.L. Comaroff (ed.), *The Meaning of Marriage Payments*. London: Academic Press, 125–60.
——. 1984. "The Paucity of Ritual among Middle Eastern Pastoralists," in Akbar S. Ahmad and David M. Hart (eds.), *Islam in Tribal Societies. From the Atlas to the Indus*. London: Routledge and Kegan Paul, 187–219.
Peters, Rudolph. 1990. "Murder on the Nile: Homicide Trials in 19th Century Egyptian Shariah Courts." *Die Welt des Islams*, 30:95–115.
——. 1994. "The Islamization of Criminal Law: A Comparative Analysis." *Welt des Islams*, 34:246–74.
——. 1995. "Shāhid," in *The Encyclopaedia of Islam*. New ed. Leiden: E.J. Brill.
——. 1997. "Islamic and Secular Criminal Law in 19th Century Egypt: The Role and Function of the Qadi." *Islamic Law and Society*, 4:70–90.
——. 1999. "Administrators and Magistrates: The Development of a Secular Judiciary in Egypt, 1842–1871." *Die Welt des Islams*, 39:378–97.
——. 2002. "Murder in Khaybar: Some Thoughts on the Origins of the *Qasāma* Procedure in Islamic Law." *Islamic Law and Society*, 9 (2):132–67.
——. 2003. *Islamic Criminal Law in Nigeria*. Ibadan: Spectrum Books.
——. Forthcoming/a. *Crime and Punishment in Islamic Law*. Cambridge: Cambridge University Press.
——. Forthcoming/b. "What Does it Mean to be an Official *Madhhab*? Ḥanafism and the Ottoman Empire," in P. Bearman, R. Peters and F. Vogel (eds.), *The Islamic School of Law: Evolution, Devolution, and Progress*. Cambridge, MA: Harvard University Press.
Pickthall, M.M., trans. N.d. *The Meaning of the Glorious Qur'ān*. New York: Penguin Books.
Pouzet, Louis. 1988. *Damas au VIIe–XIIIe Siecle, Vie et structure religieuses dans une metropole islamique*. Beyrouth: Dar El-Machreq.
Powers, David S. 1986. *Studies in Qur'ān and Ḥadīth: The Formation of the Islamic Law of Inheritance*. Berkeley: University of California Press.
——. 1989. "Orientalism, Colonialism and Legal History: The Attack on Muslim Family Endowments in Algeria and India." *Comparative Studies in Society and History*, 31:535–71.
——. 1990. "A Court Case from Fourteenth-Century North Africa." *Journal of the American Oriental Society*, 110:229–54.
——. 1992. "On Judicial Review in Islamic Law." *Law and Society Review*, 26 (2), 315–41.
——. 1994. "*Kadijustiz* or Qāḍī-Justice? A Paternity Dispute from Fourteenth-Century Morocco." *Islamic Law and Society*, 1:332–66.
——. 2001. "Parents and Their Minor Children: Familial Politics in the Middle Maghrib in the Eighth/Fourteenth Century." *Continuity and Change*, 16:177–200.
——. 2002. *Law, Society, and Culture in the Maghrib, 1300–1500*. Cambridge: Cambridge University Press.
——. 2003. "Women and Divorce in the Islamic West: Three Cases." *HAWWA: Journal of Women of the Middle East and the Islamic World*, 1:29–45.
Pulaha, Selami, and Yaşar Yücel. 1995. *I. Selim Kanunnâmeleri (1512–1520)*. Ankara: Türk Tarih Kurumu.
Qadrī, Muḥammad. 1875. *Kitāb al-aḥkām al-shar'iyya fī al-aḥwāl al-shakhṣiyya 'alā madhhab al-imām Abū Ḥanīfa al-Nu'mān*. Cairo: al-Maṭba'a al-'uthmāniyya al-miṣriyya.
Qalqashandī, Aḥmad. 1913–19. *Ṣubḥ al-a'shā fī ṣanā'at al-inshā'*. 14 vols. Cairo: Dār al-kutub al-khadīwiyya.

Qattan, Najwa al-. 1999. "*Dhimmīs* in the Muslim Court: Legal Autonomy and Religious Discrimination." *International Journal of Middle East Studies*, 31:429–44.
al-Qaysī, Abū Muhallab Haytham. 1972. *Adab al-qāḍī wa'l-qaḍā'*. Ed. Farḥāt al-Dashrāwī. Tunis: al-Sharika al-tūnisiyya li'l-tawzī'.
Qummī, Abū Ja'far al-. *See* Ibn Bābawayh al-Qummī, Muḥammad b. 'Ali.
Qurṭubī, Muḥammad b. Aḥamd al-. 1935–50. *al-Jāmi' li-aḥkām al-qur'ān*. 20 vols. Cairo: Dār al-kutub al-miṣriyya.
——. 1966. *al-Jāmi' Aḥkām al-qur'ān*. 24 vols. Beirut: Dār iḥyā' al-turāth al-'arabī.
al-Qusūs, 'Awda. 1972. *al-Qaḍā' al-badawī*. 2nd ed. Amman: al-Maṭba'a al-urduniyya.
Rafeq, Abdul-Karim. 1987. "Aspects of Land Tenure in Syria in the Early 1580s," in Abdeljelil Temini (ed.), *Les provinces arabes à l'epoque Ottomane*. Zaghwan: Centre d'Etudes de Recherches Ottomanes et Morisco-Andalouses, 153–63.
——. 1992. "City and Countryside in a Traditional Setting: The Case of Damascus in the First Quarter of the Eighteenth Century," in Thomas Philipp (ed.), *The Syrian Land in the 18th and 19th Century*. Berliner Islamstudien, Bd. 5. Stuttgart: Franz Steiner Verlag, 295–331
——. 1999. "Injustice and Complaint (*zulm wa-shikayet*) in Mid-Nineteenth-Century Syria (the case of the *I'ana* tax)," in Markus Köhbach, Gisela Prochazka-Eisl, and Claudia Römer (eds.), *Acta Viennesia Ottomanica*. Wien: Im Selbtverlag des Instituts für Orientalistik, 293–301.
——. 2002. "Ownership of Real Property by Foreigners in Syria, 1869–1873," in Roger Owen (ed.), *New Perspectives on Property and Land in the Middle East*. Harvard Middle Eastern Monographs. Harvard: Cambridge, 175–249.
Rahim, Abdul. 1968. *The Principles of Muhammadan Jurisprudence*. Lahore: Indus Publishers.
Ramírez, Angeles. 1998. *Migraciones, género e islam. Mujeres marroquíes en España*. Madrid. Cultura Hispánica.
Ramlī, Khayr al-Dīn al-. 1856–7. *al-Fatāwā al-khayriyya li-naf' al-barriyya*. Collected by Ibrāhīm Sulaymān al-Ramlī. 2 parts in 1 vol. Cairo (Būlāq): Maṭba'at Muḥammad Sa'īd Bāshā.
Raymond, André. 1979. "Les grands *waqfs* et l'organisation de l'espace urbain à Alep et au Caire à l'époque ottomane (XVI°–XVII° siècles)." *Bulletin d'Etudes Orientales*, 31:113–28.
Rāzī, Fakhr al-dīn al-. 1990–2. *Mafātiḥ al-ghayb*. 30 vols. Beirut: Dār al-kutub al-'ilmiyya.
Rebstock, Ulrich. 1999. "A Qāḍī's Errors." *Islamic Law and Society*, 6:1–37.
Reiter, Y. 1996. *Islamic Endowments in Jerusalem under British Mandate*. London: Frank Cass.
Repp, Richard. 1986. *The Mufti of Istanbul. A Study in the Development of the Ottoman Learned Hierarchy*. London: Ithaca Press.
Rey-Goldziguer, Annie. 1977. *Le Royaume Arabe de Napoléon III*. Algiers: Société Nationale d'Édition et de Diffusion.
Rispler-Chaim, Vardit. 1992. "*Nushūz* between Medieval and Contemporary Islamic Law: the Human Rights Aspect." *Arabica*, 39:315–28.
Robe, Eugène. 1864. *Les lois de la propriété fonçière en Algérie*. Algiers: Imprimerie de l'Akhbar.
Roded, Ruth. 1999. *Women in Islam and the Middle East: A Reader*. London: I.B. Taurus & Co. Ltd.
Rodríguez Mediano, F. 1996. "Justice, crime et châtiment au Maroc au 16e siècle." *Annales, Histoire, Siences Sociales*, 51 (3):611–27.
——. 1997. "Instituciones judiciales: Cadíes y otras magistraturas," in *El retroceso territorial de al-Andalus. Almorávides y almohades. siglos XI al XIII*. Historia de España Menéndez Pidal, VIII–II. Madrid: Espasa Calpe, 169–86.

Rosen, Lawrence. 1989. *The Anthropology of Justice: Law as Culture in Islamic Society*. Cambridge: Cambridge University Press.
——. 2000. *The Justice of Islam*. Oxford: Oxford University Press.
Rosenfeld, H. 1968. "Change, Barriers to Change and Contradictions in the Arab Village Family." *American Anthropologist*, 70:732–52.
Rosenthal, Franz. 1952. *A History of Muslim Historiography*. Leiden: E.J. Brill.
——. 2003. "al-Kindī, Abū ʿUmar Muḥammad," in *The Encyclopedia of Islam*. New ed. Leiden: E.J. Brill.
Ruedy, John. 1967. *Land Policy in Colonial Algeria: The Origins of the Rural Public Domain*. Berkeley: University of California Press.
Ruiz-Almodóvar, Caridad. 1995a. "El código marroquí de estatuto personal," in C. Pérez Beltrán and C. Ruiz-Almodóvar (eds.), *Magreb coordenadas socioculturales*. Granada, 413–85.
——. 1995b. "Estudio comparado de los Códigos magrebíes del Estatuto Personal," in G. Martín Muñoz (ed.), *Mujeres, democracia y desarrollo en el Magreb*. Madrid: Editorial Pablo Iglesias.
——. 1999. "El código libio de estatuto personal," in C. Castillo, I. Cortés, and J.P. Monferrer (eds.), *Estudios árabes dedicados a D. Luis Seco de Lucena (en el XXV Aniversario de su muerte)*. Granada: University of Granada, Grupo de investigación Ciudades andaluzas bajo el Islam, 165–87.
Russell, Alexander. 1794. *The Natural History of Aleppo*. 2nd ed. 2 vols. London: G.G. and J. Robinson.
Saʿadallāh, Abū al-Qāsim. 1981. *Taʾrikh al-jazāʾʾir al-thaqāfī*. 2 vols. Algiers: Société Nationale d'Édition et de Diffusion.
Sābiq, Sayyid. 1969. *Fiqh al-sunna*. 2 vols. Beirut: Dār al-kitāb al-ʿarabī.
Ṣādiq, Mūrīs. 1998. *Mawsūʿat al-aḥwāl al-shakhṣiyya li-ghayr al-muslimīn: al-khuṭba waʾl-zawāj waʾl-ṭāʿa waʾl-ṭalāq lil-ṭawāʾif al-masīḥiyya al-aqbāṭ*. Cairo: Maktabat dunyā al-qānūn.
Saḥnūn. 1905. *al-Mudawwana al-kubrā*. 16 vols. in 7. Cairo. Maṭbaʿat al-saʿāda.
——. 1986. *al-Mudawwana al-kubrā*. 4 vols. Beirut: N.p.
Safwat, S.M. 1982. "Offences and Penalties in Islamic Law." *Islamic Quarterly*, 26:149–81.
Salāma, Aḥmad. 1958. *al-Aḥwāl al-shakhṣiyya liʾl-miṣriyyīn ghayr al-muslimīn wa-liʾl-ajānib*. 2 vols. Cairo: Dār al-fikr al-ʿarabī.
Ṣāliḥ, Ibrāhīm ʿAlī. N.d. [1996]. *Ḥawla mashrūʿ al-qānūn al-khāṣṣ bi*-daʿwā al-ḥisba al-muqaddam ilā majlis al-shaʿb. Cairo, 5 p.
Samarqandī, ʿAlāʿ al-Dīn al-. 1993. *Tuḥfat al-fuqahāʾ*. Beyrut: Dār al-kutub al-ʿilmiyya.
al-Ṣanʿānī, ʿAbd al-Razzāq. 1995 [1970–2]. *al-Muṣannaf fīʾl-aḥadīth*. Ed. Ḥabīb al-Raḥmān al-Aʿẓamī. 11 vols. Beirut: Manshūrāt al-majlis al-ʿilmī.
Santillana, D. 1925–38. *Istituzioni di diritto musulmano malichita con riguardo anche al sistema sciafiita*. 2 vols. Rome: Istituo per l'Oriente.
Sarakhsī, Abū Bakr Muhammad b. Aḥmad al-. 1906–13. *Kitāb al-mabsūṭ*. Cairo: Maṭbaʿ al-saʿāda. 3rd ed. (photomechanical repr. of 1906–13 ed.). Beirut: Dār al-maʿrifa. 1978.
Sāwī, Aḥmad b. Muḥammad al-. N.d. *Ḥāshiyat al-ṣāwī ʿalā al-sharḥ al-ṣaghīr*. 4 vols. Cairo: Dār al-maʿārif.
Sayf, Aḥmad. 1996. *al-Ḥisba bayna al-dawla al-madaniyya waʾ l-dawla al-dīniyya*. Cairo: Markaz al-musāʿada al-qānūniyya li-ḥuqūq al-insān, 15 p.
Schacht, Joseph. 1955. "Thalāth muḥāḍarāt fī tārīkh al-fiqh al-islāmī," in Ṣalāḥ al-Dīn al-Munajjid (ed.), *al-Muntaqā min dirāsāt al-mustashriqīn*. Cairo: Lajnat al-tālīf.
——. 1959 [1950]. *The Origins of Muhammadan Jurisprudence*. Oxford: Oxford University Press.

——. 1983 [1964]. *Introduction to Islamic Law*. Oxford: Clarendon Press. Translated as *Introduction au droit musulman*. Paris: Maisonneuve et Larose.
——. 1991. "Maḥkama," in *The Encyclopaedia of Islam*. New ed. Leiden: E.J. Brill.
Schneider, Irene. 1990. *Das Bild des Richters in der "Adab al-Qāḍī" Literatur*. Frankfurt: Peter Lang.
——. 1993. "Die Merkmale der idealtypischen *qāḍī-Justiz*-Kritische Anmerkungen zu Max Webers Kategorisierung der islamischen Rechtsprechung." *Der Islam*, 70:145–59.
Seco de Lucena, Luis. 1959. "La escuela de juristas granadinos en el siglo XV." *Miscelánea de Estudios Árabes y Hebraicos*, 8:7–28.
Serrano, Delfina. 2000. "Legal practice in an Andalusī-Maghribī Source from the Twelfth Century CE: The *Madhāhib al-Ḥukkām fī nawāzil al-aḥkām*." *Islamic Law and Society*, 7:187–234.
——. 2003. "La violación en derecho malikí: doctrina y práctica a partir de tres fetuas de los siglos X a XII d. C." *Mélanges de la Casa de Velázquez*, Nouvelle Série, 33:125–48.
Shaʿbī, Abū l-Muṭarrif ʿAbd al-Raḥmān b. Qāsim al-. 1992. *al-Aḥkām*. Ed. al-Ṣādiq al-Ḥalawī. Beirut. Dār al-gharb al-islāmī.
Shāfiʿī, Muḥammad b. Idrīs al-. 1903–8. *Kitāb al-umm*, 7 vols. in 5. Būlāq: al-Maṭbaʿa al-Amīriyya (with al-Muzanī's *Mukhtaṣar* on the margins).
——. 1987. *Kitāb al-Umm*. 7 vols. Ed. ʿAbd al-Razzāq Muṣṭafā. Cairo: al-Hayʾa al-miṣriyya al-ʿāmma li'l-kitāb.
Shaham, Ron. 1991. "Christian and Jewish *Waqf* in Palestine during the Late Ottoman Period." *Bulletin of the School of Oriental and African Studies*, 54:460–72.
——. 1995. "Jews and the *Sharīʿa* Courts in Modern Egypt." *Studia Islamica*, 82:113–36.
——. 1997. *Family and the Courts in Modern Egypt: A Study Based on Decisions by the Sharīʿa Courts, 1900–1955*. Leiden: E.J. Brill.
——. 1999. "An Egyptian Judge in a Period of Change: Qāḍī Aḥmad Muḥammad Shākir (1892–1958)." *Journal of the American Oriental Society*, 119:440–55.
Shahar, Ido. 2000. "Falastinim be-veit din israeli: Tarbut, shlitah ve-hitnagdut be-veit ha-din ha-sharʿī be-maʿarav yerushalayim" ["Palestinians in an Israeli Court: Culture, Control, and Resistance in the Shariʿa Court of Western Jerusalem"]. MA Thesis, The Hebrew Univ.
Shalakany Law Office Legal Advisers. 18/9/1996. *The Case against Dr. Nasr Hamed Abu Zeid*. Cairo, 5 p.
Shapiro, Martin. 1981. *Courts. A Comparative and Political Analysis*. Chicago and London: The University of Chicago Press.
Sharqāwī, ʿAbd al-Munʿim al-. 1996. *Taʿlīq ʿalā mashrūʿ al-qānūn alladhī yunaẓẓim ijrāʾāt rafʿ daʿwā al-ḥisba*. Cairo, 8 p.
Sharrock, Wes and Bob Anderson. 1991. "Epistemology: Professional Scepticism," in G. Button (ed.), *Ethnomethodology and the Human Sciences*. Cambridge: Cambridge University Press.
Shatzmiller, M. 1989. "The image and social status of urban labour in al-Andalus," in M.J. Viguera (ed.), *La Mujer en al-Andalus; reflejos de su actividad y categorías sociales*. Madrid and Seville: Universidad Autonoma-Editoriales Andaluzas Unidas, 61–70.
Siddiqi, M.S. 1981. "The Concept of *Ḥudûd* and its Significance." *Islamic Culture*, 55:191–207.
Sijpesteijn, Petra Marieke. 2004. "Shaping a Muslim State: Papyri Related to a Mid-Eighth Century Egyptian Official." Ph.D. diss. Princeton University.
Skovgaard-Petersen, Jakob. 1997. *Defining Islam for the Egyptian State: Muftis and Fatwas of the Dār al-Iftā*. Leiden: E.J. Brill.
Smith, Michael G. 1997. *Government in Kano, 1350–1950*. Boulder: Westview.

Sonbol, Amira al-Azhari. 1996. "Adults and Minors in Ottoman Shari'a Courts and Modern Law," in A. Sonbol (ed.), *Women, the Family and Divorce Laws in Islamic History*. Syracuse: Syracuse University Press, 236–56.
Starr, June. 1978. *Dispute and Settlement in Rural Turkey: An Ethnography of Law*. Leiden: E.J. Brill.
——. 1992. *Law as Metaphor: From Islamic Courts to the Palace of Justice*. Albany: State University of New York Press.
Stewart, Frank H. 1988–90. *Texts in Sinai Bedouin Law. Part 1. The Texts in English Translation. Part 2. The Texts in Arabic*. Wiesbaden: Harrassowitz.
——. 1991. "The woman, her guardian, and her husband in the law of the Sinai Bedouin." *Arabica*, 38:102–29.
——. 2000. "*'Urf*. 2. Arab Customary Law," in *The Encyclopaedia of Islam*. New ed. Leiden: E.J. Brill.
Sudnow, David. 1976. "Normal Crimes: Sociological Features of a Penal Code in a Public Defender's Office." *Social Problems*, 12:251–76.
Supreme Constitutional Court (of Egypt). *See* Maḥkama al-dustūriyya al-ʿulyā al-.
Süreyya, Mehmed. 1996–. *Sicill-i Osmani*. 6 vols. Istanbul: Kültür Bakanlığı.
Sūrī, Ṣalāḥ al-Dīn Ḥasan al-. 1984. "Lībiyā wa'l-ghazw al-thaqāfī fi'l-iṭālī," in Ṣalāḥ al-Dīn Ḥasan al-Sūrī and Ḥabīb Wadā'a al-Ḥusnāwī (eds.), *Buḥūth wa-dirāsāt fī 'l-ta'rīkh al-lībī 1911–1943*. Tripoli: Markaz dirāsat jihād al-lībiyīn ḍidda al-ghazw al-īṭālī, vol. 2:393–431.
Suyūṭī, Jalāl al-Dīn al-. 1983. *al-Durr al-manthūr fi'l-tafsīr al-ma'thūr*. Beirut: Dār al-fikr.
Swearingen, Wil. 1987. *Moroccan Mirages: Agrarian Dreams and Deceptions, 1912–1986*. Princeton: Princeton University Press.
Ṭabarī, Abū Jaʿfar al-. 1954–68. *Jāmiʿ al-bayān ʿan ta'wīl āy al-qur'ān*. 2nd ed. 30 vols. in 12. Cairo: Muṣṭafā al-Bābī al-Ḥalabī.
——. 1954. *Tafsīr al-Ṭabarī: Jāmiʿ al-Bayān ʿan ta'wīl āya al-Qur'ān*. Ed. Maḥmūd Muḥammad Shākir. 16 vols. Cairo: Dār al-maʿārif.
Ṭabbākh, Muḥammad Rāghib al-. 1988–92. *Iʿlām al-nubalā' bi-tārīkh Ḥalab al-shahbā'*. Ed. Muḥammad Kamāl. 2nd ed. 7 vols. + index. Aleppo: Dār al-qalam al-ʿarabī.
Tabi'u, M. 1991. "The Impact of the Repugnancy Test on the Application of Islamic Law in Nigeria." *Journal of Islamic and Comparative Law* (Zaria), 18:53–76.
Ṭarābulusī, ʿAlī b. Khalīl al-. 1892. *Muʿīn al-ḥukkām fī mā yataraddad bayn al-qismayn min al-aḥkām*. Cairo: N.p.
Tasūlī, ʿAlī b. ʿAbd al-Salām al-. 1977. *al-Bahja fī sharḥ al-tuḥfa li-Muḥammad b. ʿĀṣim*. 2 vols. Beirut: Dār al-maʿrifa.
Tate, Jihane. 1990. *Une waqfiyya du XVIIIe siècle à Alep. La waqfiyya d'al-Ḥāğğ Mūsā al-Amīrī*. Damascus: Institut Français de Damas.
Tessler, Mark A. 1978. "The Identity of Religious Minorities in Non-Secular States: Jews in Tunisia and Morocco and Arabs in Israel." *Comparative Studies in Society and History*, 20:359–73.
Thielman, Jorn. 1999. "A Critical Survey of Western Law Studies on Arab-Muslim Countries," in B. Dupret, M. Berger, and L. al-Zwaini (eds.), *Legal Pluralism in the Arab World*. The Hague: Kluwer Law International, 41–54.
Toledano, H. 1981. *Judicial Practice and Family Law in Morocco: The Chapter on Marriage from Sijilmāsī's* al-ʿAmal al-Muṭlaq. New York: Columbia University Press.
Torgerson, W. 1958. *Theory and Method of Scaling*. New York: Wiley.
Tsafrir, Nurit. 2004. *The History of an Islamic School of Law: The Early Spread of Hanafism*. Cambridge, MA.: Islamic Legal Studies Program, Harvard Law School.
Tucker, Judith E. 1998. *In the House of the Law: Gender and Islamic Law in Ottoman Syria and Palestine*. Berkeley: University of California Press.
Tunbuktī, Aḥmad Bābā al-. 1932. *Nayl al-ibtihāj bi-taṭrīz al-dībāj*. On the margin of Ibn Farḥūn, *Kitāb al-dībāj*. Cairo: Dār al-turāth.

Ṭūsī, Abū Jaʿfar, al-. N.d. *Tafsīr al-tibyān.* Najaf: Maktabat al-amīn.

——. N.d. *Kitāb al-khilāf.* Qum: Dār al-maʿārif al-islāmiyya.

——. N.d. *Tahdhīb al-aḥkām.* Tehran: Dār al-kutub al-Islāmiyya.

Tyan, Émile. 1945. "Le Notariat et le régime de la preuve par écrit dans la pratique du droit musulman." Université de Lyon. *Annales de l'Ecole Française de Droit de Beyrouth,* 2:3–99. Repr. Harissa, Lebanon: St. Paul Publishers. 1959.

——. 1955. "Judicial Organization," in Majid Khadduri and Herbert J. Liebesny (eds.), *Law in the Middle East.* Vol. 1. *Origin and Development of Islamic Law.* Washington D.C.: The Middle East Institute, 236–78.

——. 1960. *Histoire de l'organisation judiciaire en pays d'Islam.* 2nd rev. ed. Leiden: E.J. Brill.

——. 1965. "Daʿwā," in *The Encyclopaedia of Islam.* New ed. Leiden: E.J. Brill.

——. 1973. "Ḳāḍī," in *The Encyclopaedia of Islam.* New ed. Leiden: E.J. Brill.

——. 1986. "ʿAdl," in *The Encyclopaedia of Islam.* New ed. Leiden: E.J. Brill.

Udovitch, Abraham L. 1970. *Partnership and Profit in Medieval Islam.* Princeton: Princeton University Press.

——. 1985. "Islamic Law and the Social Context of Exchange in the Medieval Middle East." *History and Anthropology,* 1:445–56.

Uğur, Ali. 1986. *The Ottoman Ulema in the mid-17th century. An Analysis of the Vakā-i ʿÜ'l-Fużalā of Mehmed Şeyhi Ef.* Berlin: Klaus Schwarz Verlag.

ʿUqba, Maḥmūd (Mustashār). N.d. [1996a]. *Mulāḥaẓāt ʿalā mashrūʿ daʿwā al-ḥisba.* Cairo, 6 p.

——. N.d. [1996b]. *Wajhan li-wajhin amāma tashrīʿ al-ḥisba.* Cairo, 7 p.

Ursinus, Michael. 1980. "Shtipskiot kadilak vo 1796 godina. Prilog kon istoriyata na makedonskite sela vrz baza na turski dokumenti od kadiskite sidjili" (The Shtip kadilik in 1796. A Contribution to the History of the Macedonian Villages on the Basis of Turkish Documents from the Kadi Sicills). *Glasnik. Institut za natsionalna istoriya-Skopje,* 24 (1):179–87.

——. 1991. "Manāstër," in *The Encyclopaedia of Islam.* New ed. Leiden: E.J. Brill.

——. 1994. "Das Qaza Qolonya um das Jahr 1830. Ein Beitrag zur regional Geschichte des Osmanischen Reiches nach einheimischen Quellen." In *Quellen zur Geschichte des Osmanischen Reiches und ihre Interpretation.* Istanbul: Isis Verlag, 49–79.

——. 2001. "Razdavane na pravosudie ot edno provintsialno upravlenie: Rumeliyskiyat divan v kraya na XVII-nachaloto na XVIII vek" (Dispensation of Justice by a Provincial Government: The Divan-i Rumili in the late 17th and early 18th century) In R. Gradeva (ed.), *Istoriya na myusyulmanskata kultura po bulgarskite zemi* (History of Muslim Culture in Bulgarian Lands). Sofia: IMIR, 15–35 (in Bulgarian, with English summary.)

——. 2002. "Das Rechnungsbuch des kağıd emini Mustafa Çavuş vom Jahre 1613: Zum osmanischen Petitionswesen vor Beginn der Şikayet Defterleri," in I. Hauenschild, C. Schönig, and P. Zieme (eds.), *Festschrift für Barbara Kellner-Heinkele zu ihrem 60 Geburtstag.* Veröffentlichungen der Societas Uralo-Altaica. Bd. 56.

——. Forthcoming. "Grievances Heard at Manastir: a Provincial "Book of Complaints" from the Late Eighteenth Century", in *Festschrift Halil Inalcik.*

ʿUtbī, Muḥammad al-. 1984–7. *al-Mustakharaja min al-asmiʿa mimmā laysa fī l-Mudawwana apud Ibn Rushd al-Jadd, Kitāb al-bayān wa'l-taḥṣīl.* Ed. Muḥammad Ḥajjī et al. 20 vols. Beirut: Dār al-gharb al-islāmī.

Uzunçarşılı, Ismail H. 1988 [1964, 1965]. *Osmanlı Devleti'nin İlmiye Teşkilâtı.* Ankara: Türk Tarih Kurumu.

Veinstein, Gilles. 2001. "Sur les *nâ'ib* ottomans (XVème–XVIème siècles)." *Jerusalem Studies in Arabic and Islam,* 25:247–67.

Veselý, Rudolf. 1972. "Die Hauptprobleme der Diplomatik arabischer Privaturkunden aus dem spätmittelalterlichen Ägypten." *Archiv Orientální,* 40:312–43.

Viguera, M.J. 1997. "Historia política," in *El retroceso territorial de al-Andalus. Almorávides y almohades. Siglos XI al XIII.* Historia de España Menéndez Pidal, VIII–II. Madrid: Espasa Calpe, 1–123.
Vogel, Frank. 2000. *Islamic Law and Legal System: Studies of Saudi Arabia.* Leiden: E.J. Brill.
Wakīʿ, Abū Bakr Muḥammad b. Khalaf b. Ḥayyān. 1947. *Akhbār al-quḍāt.* Ed. ʿAbd al-ʿAzīz Muṣṭafā al-Maraghī. 3 vols. Cairo: Maṭbaʿat al-saʿāda.
Wakin, Jeanette A. 1972. *The Function of Documents in Islamic Law: The Chapters on Sales from Ṭaḥāwī's* Kitāb al-Shurūṭ al-Kabīr. Albany: State University of New York Press.
Walsh, J.R. 1965. "Fatwā," in *The Encyclopaedia of Islam.* New ed. Leiden: E.J. Brill.
Wansharīsī, Aḥmad al-. 1937. *Kitāb al-wilāyāt.* Ed. and trans. Henri Bruno and Gaudefroy-Demombynes as *Le Livre des Magistratures d'el Wancherisi.* Rabat: Éditions Félix Moncho.
——. 1981–3. *al-Miʿyār al-muʿrib wa'l-jāmiʿ al-mughrib ʿan fatāwī ʿulamāʾ ifrīqiyā wa'l-andalus wa'l-maghrib.* 13 vols. Rabat: Ministry of Culture and Religious Affairs.
Watson, Rod. 1997. "The Presentation of Victim and Motive in Discourse: The Case of Police Interrogations and Interviews," in M. Travers and J.F. Manzo (eds.), *Law in Action: Ethnomethodological and Conversation Analytic Approaches to Law.* Aldershot: Dartmouth/Ashgate.
Watts, Michael. 1983. *Food, Famine and Peasantry in Northern Nigeria.* Berkeley: University of California Press.
Weber, Max. 1959–69. *Max Weber on Law in Economy and Society.* 2nd ed. Trans. Edward Shils. Cambridge: Harvard University Press.
——. 1972. *Wirtschaft und Gesellschaft. Grundriß der verstehenden Soziologie.* Tübingen: Mohr.
Welchman, Lynn. 2000. *Beyond the Code: Muslim Family Law and Shariah Judiciary in the Palestinian West Bank.* Boston: Kluwer International.
Wensinck, A.J. 1988. *Concordence et indices de la tradition musulmane.* Leiden: Brill.
Westermarck, Edward. 1921. *Les cérémonies du mariage au Maroc.* Trans. J. Arin. Paris: Éditions Ernest Leroux.
——. 1926. *Ritual and Belief in Morocco.* 2 vols. London: Macmillan and Co.
Winter, Michael. 2001. "Inter-*Madhhab* Competition in Mamluk Damascus: al-Ṭarsūsī's Counsel for the Turkish Sultans." *Jerusalem Studies in Arabic and Islam,* 25:195–211.
Wizārat al-awqāf. See *al-Mawsūʿa al-Fiqhiyya.* 1986.
Woodman, Gordon R. 1999. "The Idea of Legal Pluralism," in B. Dupret, M. Berger, and L. al-Zwaini (eds.), *Legal Pluralism in the Arab World.* The Hague: Kluwer International, 3–19.
Würth, Anna. 2000. *ash-Shariah fī Bāb al-Yaman: Recht, Richter und Rechtspraxis an der familienrechtlichen Kammer des Gerichts Süd-Sanaa [Republik Jemen] 1983–1995.* Berlin: Duncker and Humblot.
Yacono, Xavier. 1955–6. *La colonisation des plaines du Chélif.* 2 vols. Imprimerie E. Imbert.
Yāqūt b. ʿAbdallāh al-Ḥamawī. *See* Ḥamawī, Yāqūt b. ʿAbdallāh al-.
Yediyıldız, Bahaeddin. 1990. *Institution du vaqf au XVIII° siècle en Turquie. Etude socio-historique.* Ankara: Editions Ministère de la Culture.
Yi, Eunjeong. 2004. *Guild Dynamics in Seventeenth Century Istanbul: Fluidity and Leverage.* Leiden and Boston: Brill.
Yngvesson, Barbara. 1993. *Virtuous Citizens, Disruptive Subjects: Order and Complaint in a New England Court.* New York: Routledge.
Zabāra, Aḥmad b. Muḥammad. N.d. *Nuzhat al-naẓar.* 4 vols. (handwritten expansion)
Zabāra, Muḥammad b. Muḥammad. 1979. *Nuzhat al-naẓar fī rijāl al-qarn al-rābiʿ ʿashar.* Ṣanʿāʾ: Markaz al-dirāsāt wa'l-abḥāth al-yamaniyya.

Zaman, Muhammad Qasim. 1997. *Religion and Politics under the Early ʿAbbāsids: The Emergence of the Proto-Sunnī Elite*. Leiden: E.J. Brill.
Zaydān, ʿAbd al-Karīm. 1983. *Niẓām al-qaḍāʾ fi'l-sharīʿa al-islāmiyya*. ʿAmmān: Maktbat al-bashāʾir. Wiesbaden: Harrassowitz.
——. 1993. *al-Mufaṣṣal fī aḥkām al-marʾa wa'l-bayt al-musallam fī 'l-sharīʿa al-islāmiyya*. 11 vols. Beirut: Mu'assasat al-risāla.
Zilberman, I. 1991. "ha-Mishpaṭ ha-minhagi ke-maʿarechet ḥevratit" ["Customary Law as a Social System"]. *Hamizrah Hehadash*, 33:70–93.
Ziriklī, Khayr al-Dīn al-. 1990. *al-Aʿlām. Qāmūs tarājim li-ashhar al-rijāl wa'l-nisāʾ min al-ʿarab wa'l-mustaʿrabīn wa'l-mustashriqīn*. 9th ed. 8 vols. Beirut: Dār al-ʿilm li'l-malāyīn.
Zuḥaylī, Muḥammad al-. 1995. *Taʾrīkh al-qaḍāʾ fi'l-islām*. Damascus: Dār al-fikr.
Zuḥaylī, Wahba al-. 1996 [1989]. *al-Fiqh al-islāmī wa-adillatuhu*. 8 vols. Damascus: Dār al-fikr.
Zurqānī, Muḥammad b. ʿAbd al-Bāqī al-. 1936. *Sharḥ muwaṭṭaʾ al-imām Mālik*. 4 vols. Cairo. Maṭabʿat Muṣṭafā Muḥammad.

INDEX

In this index, a number of frequently used words have been normalized, despite the various spellings used by individual authors. Among these are *Hanafi, Hukm, Mufti, Qadi, Quran, Quranic,* and *Sharīʿa.*

Abbāsid dynasty, court, 13; establishment of *mazalim* court by (ninth century), 272; period 11, 351
ʿAbd al-ʿĀzīz b. Marwān, 365
ʿAbd Allāh b. ʿUmar, 374
ʿAbdallāh Jābirī, 448
ʿAbd al-Malik, 10, 365
ʿAbd al-Qādir, Amīr, 302–4
ʿAbd al-Raḥmān, 15
ʿAbd al-Raḥmān b. ʿAwf, 362
ʿAbd al-Raḥmān, caliph, 15
Abdi Efendi, 275
Abdul Ghani v. Taleh Bibi, 523–24
ʿĀbis b. Saʿīd, qadi, 371
Abū Ḥanīfa, 16, 29, 159, 162, 172, 461, 464–5
Abū Muṣʿab, *Riwāya* of, 327
Abū al-Qāsim b. Maymūn, qadi, 400
Abū Ra'Ras al-Nāṣirī, 307
Abū Yūsuf, 12, 17, 29, 159, 459–60, 464, 466
Abū Zayd, Naṣr Ḥāmid, 175ff.
Adab, 475, 492
Adab punishment, negotiable, 487; suspicion as a basis of, 483; *Adab* vs. *taʿzīr* punishments, 491
Adab treatises, early examples of, 17
Adab al-Qadi, 16, 17–32, 383, 514; agency, 23; authority of, 17–18; circumstantial evidence, 28; court, 21; dhimmīs, 23; documents, 21; judgment, 29–30; letter of qadi, 27; literature, 16–17; litigation, 22–3; oath, 27; out of court settlement, 24; procedure, confession, 24–5; *qaḍā'*, 19–20; qualities of a qaḍi, 20; successor review, 30–2; value of, 16; witness, 25–7; women, 23
Adab al-Qadi (al-Khaṣṣāf), 184n24
ʿAdāla, 497
Adat, 119, 136, 13; Gayo *adat*, 137
Adatrecht, 140–1
Aden, 196, 198
ʿĀdil, 18, 227. *See also* Witness
ʿAdl, 339, 483. *See also ʿAdāla*
Adultery, and fornication, in Süleyman's law book, 81; by one who is not *muḥṣan*, 224. *See also Zinā*
Agency. *See Wakāla*
Agricultural products, storage of, a foundational activity of early Imamic state (Yemen), 198
al-Aḥkām al-kubrā (Ibn Sahl), 2, 402
al-Aḥkām al-sulṭāniyya (al-Māwardī), 17
Ahliyya, defined, 62
Aḥmad b. ʿAlī al-Ṣabrī, qadi, 210
Aḥmad b. Yaḥyā Ḥamīd al-Dīn, Imām (Yemen), 196ff.
Aḥmad Efendi al-Ayyubi, 421
Ahmet Yaşar Ocak, 90
Aintab, appointment to, of judge from Istanbul, 72–3; breakdown of order in, 91; corruption in, 91; enhanced jurisdiction of, 73; increase of police surveillance in, 91; integration of, into Ottoman Empire (sixteenth century), 72; local origin of judges in, before Ottoman conquest, 76; local families in judicial offices of, 76; Ottoman surveys of, 72; public court records of, 72; as regional economic and cultural center, 71
Akhbār, 350, 354, 377
Akhbārī, 351
Akhbār al-quḍāt (Wakīʿ), 2, 350
Algeria, acquire French property rights in, 304
ʿAlī b. Abī Ṭālib, 327–8
Alkali (Hausa), defined, 40, 300, 311
Almohads, courts, 333–4, 474; divorce, 335; objectives of, 334; use of arbiters for divorce, 335

Almoravid rule, appeal, 491; composition of the court, 477; differences between civil and penal processes, 491; frequency of *qasāma* and *qiṣāṣ* procedures in, 478–80, 491; judgments and punishments, 486–90; judicial considerations, 476–7; legal cases from sources of information on penal law, 473; list of cases, 493; and maintenance payments, 333, 473–93; testimonies, 480–6
ʿAmal, 2, 331, 497, 513, 515
Amīn, 21
Amina Lawal. *See* Lawal, Amina
Amr, 57
Anbārī, ʿUbaydullāh b. al-Ḥasan, al-, 12
Anderson, J.N.D., 96
Anglo-Muhammadan Law, 39
Anṣārī, Abu'l-Ruḥ, qadi, 49, 51, 52, 55, 58, 69
Anshary, Judge, decision of, in inheritance case (Aceh), 135
Anthropologists, in Islamic studies, 4
Apostasy, cases, 74; guilty verdict in, 175
Appeal, to appellate court (Aceh), of case on land division, 137; a higher court, 124, 137; in asserting consensus within family on land division, 137; dismissal of grounds for (Nigeria), 228
Appeal, Court of (Tanzania), primacy of, 40; controls Zanzibar qadi courts, 42
Arbaʿūn ḥadīth (al-Nawawī), 230
Arbitration, requirement of, during divorce, 356. *See also Ṣulḥ*
Archives, qadis and court records, 4
ʿĀrifs, 9. *See also ʿUrf*
Arrest, illegality of, on basis of hearsay, 231
Arsh (Yemen), 197
Artisans, and apprentices, disputes involving (Istanbul), 255–8; vs. artisans, cases involving (Istanbul), 259; groups of, autonomy of, 251; and outsiders (Istanbul), faults of the latter, 258; revolt of, in 1730 (Istanbul), 266–77; and shopkeepers, in political protests, 267; treatment of, as rebels, 265
Arzuhal, 282
Asesbaşi, as morals police, 86
Ashʿarī, Abū Mūsā, 9
Aṣl, 440
Asmā' bint Yazīd, 361
Asyūṭī's manual, 52, 56
Aṭā'ī, Nevʿizāde, 78
Averroes, 475n6. *See also* Ibn Rushd
Awlād sayyid, lineage of, 306
Ayan, 286
Ayyūbid, 57
al-Azhar, as autonomous school for training of qadis, 456

Badrān, Shaykh ʿAbd al-Qādir, 425
al-Bahja fī sharḥ al-Tuḥfa (Ibn ʿĀṣim), 234
Banda Aceh, provincial capital, 134
Banishment, sentence of, as judicial punishment (Istanbul), 262–3
Basmala, 123, 200
al-Baṣrī, al-Ḥasan, qadi, 10
Bāṭin, 30
Bayt al-māl, 19, 412
Bayyina, 48, 435. *See also* Evidence
Bengal, British control of, 37
Bequest (Indonesia), lack of substantiation of, 133; to caretaker son, 136; to son, unfairness of, 139; validity of, 138. *See also Wasiat*
Berber customary law and protection of women, 347
Beylerbey, 279
Bibi Mosa v. Bwana Juma (Zanzibar), 105–15; verdict in, 109, 112; written settlement of, 112
Bidāyat al-Mujtahid (Ibn Rushd), 235, 238
Biographical, dictionaries, early Islamic, 1; encyclopedias, contents of, 77
Bismillāh. See Basmala
British Resident (Nigeria), extensive legal power of, 40
Brocade weavers (Istanbul), conflict with apprentices, 256
Burden of proof, judge's latitude in assigning (Indonesia), 130; uncertainty in assigning (under Almoravids), 481
Burhān, 203
Bwana Machano v. Bibi Aisha, divorce case of, 98–105

Caliphs, Four Righteous, 8; powers of, 8; Umayyad, 8

Cankari, 4
Careers, judicial, in Istanbul, bias toward, 78
Cassation of a ruling, 134
Celebi, Gulamsahi Ahmed, 75
Certification, of claim by defendant (Ḥaram documents), 57; judicial, determining purpose of, 48
Chief Kadhi (Zanzibar), 96
Christians, 8, 451–69; use of shariʿa, *ṭalāq* the main motive for, 458; al-sharīʿa al-Masīḥiyya, 459; *ṭalāq* of a dhimmī wife, 463
Circumstantial evidence, allowability of, 28; criteria for validity of, 28; inadmissibility of, in *ḥadd* cases, 28; strong, 28. *See also* Evidence
Civil court (Indonesia), judges in, 119
Civil law code, 131
Claims, of bequests (*wasiat*), 127; of division according to Islamic law (*fara'id*), 127; of incompatibility with husband, denial of, 107; of verbal abuse, denial of, 107
Cloth bleachers, dispute involving, 257
Code of Civil Procedure (Indian), introduction of, 38
Codification, of Islamic criminal law, 220; of law, importance of, in nineteenth century, 170; of shariʿa, in Ottoman Empire, 36; movement toward, in Ottoman and Egyptian codes, 170
Coercion, threats of, 263
Coffee, beans, no visual inspection of, 201; market, Yemen's importance in, 197; merchants, in nineteenth-century Aden, 198; sale, requirements for broker to act, 211; damaged, 205, 211; commercial practices in sale of, 211; compensatory payment for, 207, 209; court litigation concerning, 203; denial of permission for sale of, 211; illegality of sale of, 202; Imam's determination in case of, 209; impediments to return of, 216; inspection of, by potential buyer, 205; investigation of sale of, 202; litigation concerning sale, 212; rescission of contract in sale of, 200
Colonial India, reform of qadi courts in, 37–9
Colonial Nigeria, court system of, 39–40
Colonial rule, jurisdiction of qadi courts under, 36
Commercial doctrine in the shariʿa (Yemen), determination of, 216
Communal-level negotiation, Ottoman encouragement of, 249
Commutation of harsh sentences, British issuance of regulations for, 37
Compilation of Islamic Law (1991), instituted by Suharto (Indonesia), 118, 127
Concepts, legal, functioning of in practical and situated contexts, 167
Confession, conditions of, 25; of *zinā*, withdrawn, 235. *See also Ḥadd* cases; *Zinā*
Conflict, among merchants, institutionalization of in Chamber of Commerce, 203; among merchants, settlement of, out-of-court, 203; containment of, through punishment, 261; dispute between cotton and linen sellers, 257–8; resolution of, in eighteenth-century Istanbul, 261
Consensual agreements (*musyawarah*), 127, 132
Consensus, contractual, use of, in settling of disputes, 250 (Ottoman regime); failure of, in *Samadiah v. Hasan*, 137
Constitution (Egyptian), Article 2 of, 178
Constitution (Nigeria), violation of, 233
Constitutional principles, hierarchical ranking of, 178
Constitutionalism, in globalization of Arab world, 170
Contract, means of settling disputes (Istanbul), 268; right of rescission, 197
Contractual consensus (Ottoman regime), use of, in settling of disputes, 250
Corruption, in legal administration, Ottoman concerns about, 91; susceptibility of qadis to, 20
Cotton and linen sellers, dispute between, 257–8
Council of Islamic Ideology (Pakistan), 528

Court, 13; composition of (Almoravid period), 477–8; fairness of, 84; growing political strength of (Aceh, Indonesia), 136; as public forum, 93; role in weighing allegations of accuser and of accused, 84; Sharīʿa courts, jurisdiction, 452; support of authoritarian government in (Aceh, Indonesia), 136; trial, jurisdiction of, 228; two classes of (Sokoto, Nigeria), 221
Court cases, from Ḥaram documents, 51–2; divorce proceedings (transcription), 61; individual circumstances of, as a determining factor, 428; judgment in divorce proceedings (transcription), 161; legal relevance in, 157; majority opened by women (Mkokotoni), 96; questioning of defendant in, 100; resolution of, by qadi's judgment (*ḥukm*), 52; role of emir in deciding (Kano, Nigeria), 313; role of psychological impotence in divorce, 161; settlements of (Aceh, Indonesia), 140; structure of (Indonesia), 125–6; utilization of two evidentiary techniques in divorce proceedings, 160; women favored in settlements of (Aceh, Indonesia), 140; in Zanzibar, 95–115
Court certification, to resolve dispute, 29. *See also Thubūt*
Court claim, conformity with school of law, 54; examples of, by public initiative (Almoravid period), 478–80; legal qualification of *ḥukm* recorded in, 54
Court clerks, division of labor among (Aceh, Indonesia), 120; education of, 120; interrogation of clients by, 120
Court complaint, inadequate maintenance (divorce case), 105
Court costs, assignment of, 134
Court decisions, absence of, in juridical literature, 48; importance of moral and social ideas in (Aceh), 140; role of clerks in, 113; without a judgment, in *Ḥaram* collection, 58
Court documents, as partial reconstructions, 84; best source for qadi legal deeds, 49; problems with use of, 49; representing an "act of judgment", 52
Court ethnography, 113
Court judges, identification of, 134
Court judgment, validity of, 54. *See also Ḥukm*
Court of Cassation, appeal of paternity suit to, 181; compendia summarizing rulings of, 148; divorce, and, 155; refusal of, to consider new law, 176; ruling of, in *Ḥisba* case, 173–4
Court of First Instance (Egypt), 455–6
Court of law, staffed by local men, under Sukarno (1945–65), 118
Court of Mughal governor, transformation of, into high court for appeal, 37
Court of Summary Justice, authority of (Egypt), 455
Court registers, appearance of, in sixteenth century, 47
Court ruling, primary importance of oral testimony in, 442; secondary role of documentary evidence in, 442
Court session, call to order by pronouncing the *Basmala*, 123
Court system, dissolution of in 1955 (Egypt), 171; importance of elders in, 105; Indonesian, 117; unification of Indian, 38
Court work, broadened scope of under Hüsameddin Efendi (Aintab), 74
Crimes, community liability for, 83
Criminal cases, uncodified Shariʿa law in (Nigeria), 239
Criminal law, implementation of severe measures by British (India), 38; re-Islamization of, in Nigeria, 219
Criminal offenses, constitutional requirement of written law for (Nigeria), 240
Criminal residents, collective right for expulsion of, 83
Cuckold tax, 81
Custom, Ancient, 252. *See also ʿUrf*
Customary law, Berber, protection of women, 347; role of in judicial decision, 443. *See also Adat, ʿUrf*

Dallāl, 210
Dār ʿadl, 339; as attempt to Islamicize divorce proceedings (Libya), 347; no

mention of in Libyan law, 340; practice of, in Libya, 338–40, 346
Dār amīn, 324; development of, as alternative for lack or arbiters, 332–3; introduced by Yaḥyā b. Yaḥyā into Maliki legal practice, 332; origin of, in Berber customary law, 344–5; variations on, from Berber customary law, 345; widespread practice of, 338
Dār jawād (dar joued), purpose of, 342–3
Dār al-thiqa, 338, 341ff.
Ḍarar, 144–7, 326ff., 331. *See also* Harm
Ḍarūra, 498, 515
Daʿwā, 52, 200, 430. *See also* Court Claim
Death sentence, reason to refrain from issuing, 227
Decision, judicial, flexibility in, 443; judicial, retroactive effect of (Egypt), 189
"Decision" (*putusan*), as name of court document, 125
Decision-making, by qadi, 48
Deductive reasoning, reliance on, by Indonesian Islamic judges, 127
Defamation (*qadhf*), prosecution for, 238–9. *See also Qadhf*, Slander
Defective goods, applicability of right of rescission with, 197; establishment of, in court, by two expert witnesses, 216
Defendant, counterclaim, contents of, 101; deposition of, concerning plaintiff's claim, 56–7
Defter, 3, 279; availability of, 4; contents of (Sofia), 280; criminals listed in, 279; *Mühimme*, 283; Tevzi, 286
Denier, 217
Deputy judges, Ottoman. *See Nāʾib*
Dervish affiliations, moral rectitude and, 82
Desertion of husband without explanation, 108
Dhimmīs, 24; judicial autonomy of, 451. *See also* Christians Protected People
Didong, Gayo poetic tradition of, 141
Difaraʾid, 129
Dimāʾ, 475, 475n6
Discord, punishment for (Istanbul), 268
"Discriminating visual inspection," broad interpretation of, in court, 215
Dispute resolution, 203; importance of elders and local kadhis in (Tanzania), 105; in Indonesia, 132; failure, 249; and Pancasila (Indonesia), 132
Dissolution of marriage, procedures involved in (Maghrib, 1100–1500), 405. *See also* Divorce
Divan, files, 249; governor's, 296; imperial, 247; of Rumili, 297; senior judges of, 249–50. *See also Dīwān*
Division of estates, Islamic law not dominant in (Indonesia), 138; unfairness of, 132
Divorce, 98ff., 122, 383–409; abandonment as reason for, 389–96; Aceh Islamic court, 122; appeal to overturn, due to abandonment, 395; arbiters, 329; bias toward men in, 385; buying of, mandated, 111; confusion between doctrine and practice, 145; cost of buying, 105, 111; defect or disease as grounds for, 146, 386; by delegation, validity of, according to *muftī*, 398–401; desertion as grounds for, by women (Zanzibar), 96; frequency of (Zanzibar), 96; and Hanafi law, 146; impotence of husband (Egypt), 158; imprecision of term *ḍarar* in, 146; judgment (*hukūma*) in, 103; judicial, granting of, 150; judicial, ruling in, 154; judicial, substantiating *harm* as grounds for, 148; judicial, wife's initiative in, 144; the law of divorce, 385–6; and the 1929 Law (Egypt), 146; literature about, 144; *matāʿ* as a right arising from, according to Shāfiʿīs, 378; on one's own initiative (Zanzibar), 100; out-of-court, validity of, 114; payment to husband for, 100–1; prevention of, through use of arbiters, 325; pronouncement, inner structure of, 154; pronouncement, verbatim account of, 151–3; and public interest, 146; Quranic prescriptions on, 377; as a result of harm to a woman, 144, 326; by repudiation (*ṭalāq*), 96, 144, 356, 385; treatment of, among dhimmis,

456–66; treatment of, conflicting ideas about, 114; understanding of, by laymen and professionals, 95; violence against wife, 158; wife abandonment, 391–8; wife flees and marries a second husband, 402–4
Divorce arbiters, decisions of, 329; role of, only consultative, 329
Divorce case, circumstances of (Zanzibar), 100, 102, 104; harm claimed in, due to impotence of husband (Egypt), 158; harm claimed, due to violence against wife, 158; judgment (*hukūma*) in, 103; preponderance of, in Central Aceh Islamic court, 122; reason for, desire for remarriage (Zanzibar), 104; unqualified witness in, 102
Dīwān, 21. *See also Divan*
Diya, 7, 223
Document, written, as formulation of qadi's judgment, 55; inadmissibility of, as legal proof, 299; indispensable for future exigencies, 514; modern practice of use of, 515; of a trial (Egypt), orientation of participants in, 155; use of, recommended by Quran and *hadith*, 496; validity of, without testimony of witnesses, 498
Dominant opinion in Hanafi school, identification of, 182
Doubt of paternity, reason for inapplicability of *ḥadd* penalty, 237

Ebu Suʿūd, fatwas issued by, 89, 277
Edda, 98, 100, 113; dismissal of case, by Kadhi (Zanzibar), 104–05; incomplete, as reason for court case, 104; observance of, 103; violation of, 98–9, 101. *See also ʿIdda*
Education, of judges (Indonesia), 117
Egypt, 3, 43; authority of *fiqh* schools, 192–3; constitution and Islamic law as legal norm, 178; dissolution of religious courts 1955, 171; preservation of family, 179
Emir ʿAbbās, 312ff.
Emirs, 40
Emr-i ʿālī, 248, 250
Esnaf, 249
Eternal rules of sacred law vs. norms of Muslim legal tradition, 188
Ethnographic issues, role of, 113
Ethnomethodology and conversation analysis, role of, 150
Eujeong Yi, 246n2
Evidence, 519–41; admissible, written communication between qadis, 29; circumstantial evidence, 28; criteria for validity of, 28; English law as basis of, 517; *ḥadd* cases, 28; indispensability of documents in legal cases, 433
Evidence Act, 1872 (India), English law as basis of, 517; and Muslim law, discrepancies between in proving paternity, 517–8
Evidence Order (Pakistan 1984), 528; reasons for promulgation of, 530–3; similarity to Evidence Act of 1872, 533
Executions of sentences, staying of (Nigeria), 226
Expulsion (Istanbul), punishment by, 264
Extramarital intercourse, unlawfulness of. *See Zinā*
Eyalet, 275, 277, 291
Eyewitness testimony, 25

Fāḥisha, 232
Falak al-Dīn Sulaymān, 425
Family endowment. *See* Waqf
Family preservation policy, political authorities, responsibility of, 179, 190
Faraʾid, 127
Farāsila, 201, 205
Fāsiq, 26
Faskh, 144; distinguished from *ṭalāq*, 145. *See also* Divorce
Fatāwā. *See Fatwā*
Fatāwā Ibn Rushd (Ibn Rushd al-Jadd), 477
Fāṭimids, 15
Fatwā, 47, 251, 383, 393, 400ff., 403ff., 431, 443; collections of, 2; issuance of, by mufti, 431; usefulness of, as early sources of legal judgments, 383. *See also Iftāʾ*, *Istiftāʾ*
Fayḍ Allāh, qadi, 418, 421
Federal Constitution of the Republic of Nigeria (FCRN), 223n10
Federal Shariat Court (Pakistan), purpose of, 42–3

Female litigants, use of law by, in achieving desired results, 408–09
Fetva. See Fatwā
Fikih. See Fiqh
Filiation proceeding, 181
Fines, excessive, 91
Fiqh, 47, 169, 250, 349; books, 39; corpus of, as grounds for divorce laws, 146; dominance of Hanafi school in, 171; incompatibility of, with State law, 127; as jurists' law, 169; norms, accessibility of, 169; norms, new validity of, as state law, 170; predominance of personal status law in, 171; schools, Islamic normativity not found in, 192; specialists, role of, 169
Fiqh al-sunna (Sayyid Sābiq), 236
Firāsa, 368, 372
Forensic physicians' report, content and structure of, as evidence, 156
Forum shopping among Sunni schools, frequency of, 468
Freedom of religion, Constitutional guarantee of (Nigeria), 229; precedence over shariʿa injunctions, 41
Furūʿ, Maliki, 330; works, 335

Ghalaṭ, 63
Garden of Truth (Nevʿizade Ataʾi), 78
Gayo (Indonesia), application of *adat* in, 137; highlands of, 118; social norms and loss of women's right to family estate, 136
Ghulam Bhik v. Hussain Begum (Pakistan), rejection of appeal of verdict, using "repeal-revival" hypothesis, 521–2
Globalization, 170
Governor, provincial (Aintab), elevation in rank of, 75

Ḥadd, cases, 25, 40, 477; crimes, 26, 86; offenses, 223; penalty, 236–7; punishment 237, 240. *See also Ḥudūd*
Ḥadīth, 221, 227, 373, 496; of Māʿiz, 232; No. 37, *Arbaʿūn*, 230
Haji, Shaykh, 102, 104–05, 109, 114
Ḥajjāj b. Yūsuf, 367ff.
Ḥājjī Efendī, 431
Ḥakam, 6, 8, 353, 365; as pre-Islamic institution, role of, 370
Ḥakamān, dual of *Ḥakam*, 330, 333n21
Ḥākim sharʿī, 432
Ḥāl, 62
Hamida Begum, applicability of "1938 repeal-revival" hypothesis in case of, 525; contradictions in applying Hanafi law and provisions of Pakistan's Evidence Order, 537–8; determination of legitimacy of daughter in case of, 525–6
Ḥaml yaẓhar, 227
Ḥammāls, 210
Hanafis, Aleppo, 427–49; assumptions, necessity of abandoning, 191; judges, intervention of, in *waqf* lease, 421; judges' latitude, in divorce cases, 176; law, impotence in, 159; law, supremacy of, in court challenge, 181; legal doctrine, documents not considered evidence in, 443; legal tradition, reduction in contemporary role of, 192; *madhhab*, 16, 411; opinions as source of tensions, 177; preference for, in judgeships and related offices (Egypt), 457; qadi judgment based on doctrines of, 14; school, 14, 71–93, 171–2, 179–93, 182–3, 187, 191, 246–70, 271–98, 344, 411–25, 454, 457, 460–4; school of *fiqh*, dominant in Egypt and Ottoman Empire, 171
Hanbalis, 14
Hanging, by vizier's orders, 266; punishment by (Istanbul), 264–5
Ḥaqq ādamī, defined, 30
Ḥaram al-Sharīf, 49
Ḥaram documents, 3, 47–68; distinction between judgment and certification in, 67
Ḥaram records, request for *ḥukm* in, 56
Ḥarām, 231
Harm, 339; conception of, 160; confirmation of existence of, 166; defined by Mālikī legal sources, 149; definition of, statutorily or Islamically, 159; denial of, in testimony, 166; as grounds for divorce, 144, 326; judge's conception of, 160; judicial definition of, 157–8; judicial determination of, 158; praxeological account of causation of, 150; substantiation of, 159; syllogistic reasoning in determination of, 149

Hārūn al-Rashīd, 12
Ḥaṣkafī, al-, 184n25, 186n29, 186n30
Havale, 75
Hearing, judge's, before sentencing, 92
Hearsay, use of, in court, 25; illegal use of, in court, 231
Hiba, 125
Hidāya (al-Marghinani), 184n24
Hierarchies, judicial, and systems of appeal (Ottoman), as instruments of political control, 297
Higher Islamic Court (Indonesia), 134
Hijra, 6
Ḥirāba, 476, 476n7
Ḥisba, actions of, ruled invalid, 176; defined, 173; development of, as a result of Hanafi law, 173; purpose of, 173; trials, argument for abolition of, 175; trials, lack of legal justification for, 173; use of, for religious censorship, 173; use of, to control intellectual activity, 173; use of, to declare apostasy, 174
Hishām b. ʿAbd al-Malik, 10, 369
Histoire de l'organisation judiciare en pays d'Islam (Tyan), 1
History, Islamic. *See* Islamic history
Homosexual conduct, regulation of, under rubric of *zinā*, 87
Homosexual rape, reference to, in court record, 87
Ḥudūd, 476; as equivalent to crime, 13n3; crimes, dealt with in *Madhāhib al-ḥukkām*, 474; definition of, in penal code, 223; moderation in, during period of Umayyads, 489–90
Ḥujr b. ʿAdī, 367
Ḥukm, 29, 47, 200, 384; *amr* and *fiʿl*, distinguished from, 57; appeal for God's guidance in, 55; attestation to truthfulness of, by witnesses, 54; case ending without, 63–4; court decisions without, 58; deciding litigation without, 57; distinction between *thubūt* and, 66; evidence of failure to issue, 57–8; as explanation of sale of slaves, 53; formulas pertaining to issuance of, 53; frequent absence of, in settlement of legal cases, 57; inadmissibility of deciding case without, 57; in description of court events, 50; in orders, 50; issuance, determination of, 48; issuance of, necessary, 68; lack of need for, in some domains of the law, 68; lack of requirement of, 62, 66; legal and judicial characteristics of, in Ḥaram documents, 50; legal characteristics of, in Mamluk period, 50; as legal document set by religious school, 53; litigation ending without, 63–5; mention of, in deeds, 50; necessity of, for additional security in certification, 66; by qadi, only by request, 67; request for, 56; and *tawqīʿ* orders, 67. *See also* Judgment
Hukuma (Zanzibar), 98, 103; assistance to secular judge and kadhi, 98; number of, in each primary court, 98; training of, 98
Hurşid Pasa, 286
Hüsameddin Efendi, 71, 73–6, 78, 85, 92
Ḥusayn Muḥammad al-Aḥlāfī, qadi, 505, 507, 510, 511
Ḥusaynī, Abū al-ʿAbbās Aḥmad b Qāḍī al-Jamāʿa Abū al-Qāsim al-, qadi, 388
Hussaini, Safiyyatu, acquittal of, 225; application of uncodified Shariʿa criminal law to, 239; charges against, 226; sentence of, death by stoning, 219
Hüsrev Efendi, 275

Ibāḍī school, 343
Ibb merchant (Yemen), suit of, for damages from state treasury, 196
Ibn ʿAbd al-Barr, 332, 334
Ibn Abī al-Dam[m], 17, 52, 63
Ibn Abī Laylā, 371
Ibn Abī Ṭāhir al-Ṭayfūr, 1
Ibn ʿĀbidīn, 183, 184n24, 184n25, 186n29, 437, 440
Ibn ʿArabī, 334
Ibn ʿĀṣim, 497–8, 515
Ibn Farḥūn, 17
Ibn Ḥajar al-ʿAsqalānī, 351
Ibn al-Ḥājj, 333
Ibn Ḥārith, 337
Ibn Ḥazm, 376
Ibn Hishām, 361
Ibn Ḥujayra, qadi, 352, 365–6,
Ibn Kemal, *fatwa*s issued by, 89
Ibn Lubb, 389ff.
Ibn Masarra, 333
Ibn Qāsim, 329, 374

Ibn Qaṭṭān, 333
Ibn Qudāma, 31, 32
Ibn Qutayba al-Dīnawarī, 350
Ibn Rushd, 235, 238, 399. *See also* *Bidāyat al-Mujtahid*
Ibn Sahl, 2, 332, 334, 474
Ibn Salmūn, 336
Ibn Samāʿa al-Tamīmī, 17
Ibn Sīrīn, 373
Ibn Ṭulūn, 2
Icazet, 250
Iʿdhār, 57, 64, 232, 234, 392, 401
ʿIdda, 356, 385. *See also* Edda
Idhn, 61
Iftā', 431; role of, in increasing strict observance of rules of *fiqh*, 492. *See also Fatwā, Istiftā'*
Iḥkām al-aḥkām, 234
Iḥṣān, conditions for, 238; failure to establish in trial, 238
Ijāba, 202
Ijmāʿ, 29
Ijtihād, 18, 20, 29, 394, 490, 492
Ikhtilāf, 55
Īlā', 395
Illicit sex, false accusation of, 26; new penalties for, Sultan Süleyman's law book, 73; suspicion of, 80; unreported, no punishment for, 82. *See also Zinā*
Imām, 14, 500
Imamic state (Yemen), role of treasury in, 198
Impotence, argument for legal proof of, in divorce case, 161; as cause for divorce, 343–4; as grounds for dissolution of marriage, 159; psychological. *See also* Medico-legal report
Imprisonment, uses of, as punishment (Almoravid), 490
Inen Maryam v. Aman Mas, 127; burden of proof in, 130–1; cause of, 128; claims in, 128; ruling in, 128; unfairness of, 138
Inheritance case, analysis of, 127; domination of men in, 135; inequality of land division in, 135; judgment in, 133, 135; nonlegal social norms in decision on, 127; testimony of witness in, 129
Indian judiciary, British reform of, 37
Informants, opposition to, 80, 83
Institut Agama Islam Negeri (IAIN), course of study at, 117
Iqrār, 24–5, 66
Iqṭāʿ, 11
Ishhād, 50, 55, 64
Islamic courts, compared to civil courts, 126; difficulty in staffing with judges (Takèngën), 119; increase in number of divorce cases heard (Takèngën), 121; judges appointed by Indonesian government, 117; judges dependent on broad social norms, 117; jurisdiction of (Indonesian), 117; modeled after Western-style civil courts (Indonesian), 117; Muslim marriage and divorce cases heard in, 121; non-Muslim individuals in, 121; primary and appellate (Zanzibar), 96; restricted jurisdiction of (Takèngën), 121; types of cases heard in, 121
Islamic criminal justice, lack of state control of (Nigeria), 220
Islamic history, formative period of, 1
Islamic Judicial Councils, 299–319
Islamic law, absence of appeal in, reasons for, 272; ambiguities of, 147; conflict in principles of, 240; daily social practice as normative ground for, 141; flexibility of, necessity of maintaining, 191; interpretations of, in equality and fairness, 141; interpretation of, clerk's role in, 113; irrational, 5; and Islamic normativity (contemporary), reformulation of, by Supreme Constitutional Council (Egypt), 192–3; and its schools, 147; jurisprudence, legal doctrine, and local practice in, 4; last stronghold of personal status statutes in, 143; new status of, in twentieth century, 170; policy on maintenance, not identical with Hanafi doctrine, 190; rational and consistent, 5; rejection of stagnation in, 191; search for origins of, 147; variation in British application of, 39; Zanzibari norms in, 95
Islamic learning, Kano (Nigeria) scholars well versed in, 310
Islamic normativity, basis of, not found in *fiqh* schools, 192; precedence of, since 1983, 178; principles of, main

source of legislation, 177; principles of, not eternal and unchanging, 188–9
Islamic rights, lack of agreement, in *Samadiah v. Hasan*, 137
Islamist regimes, shariʿa courts dominant in, 43
Islamization of law (Nigeria), 239; of legal system (Pakistan), 42; of Nigeria, initial steps in, 221
Istanbul, appointment of judges from, 73; business districts of, artisans and traders in, 245; history of, in archival sources, 248n8; judges as moderators in the marketplace of, 246; maintenance of harmony and order in, 246; performance of judicial system in, 246; political, legal, economic events of 1730–1840 in, 246
Istiftāʾ, 3, 383. *See also Fatwā, Iftāʾ*
ʿIyāḍ, Muḥammad b., 2, 473–5
Iyās b. Muʿāwiya, 368–9, 381

Jāḥiẓ, al-, 328
Jāmiʿ aḥkām al-qurʾān (al-Qurṭubī), 231–2
Janissaries, abolition of, coincidental with military involvement in *waqf* property, 423
Java, 197, Javanese residents, in Aceh province, 119
Jawāb, 384
Jawāhir al-ʿuqūd (Shams al-Dīn Muḥammad al-Manhājī al-Asyūṭī). *See also* Asyūṭī's manual
Jerusalem, 50, 51, 55, 58
Jews, 8
Jiha, 476
Jihād, 308
Jilwāz, 21
Jināyāt, 472–3, 475, 489
Judges, allocation of, according to case type (Aceh), 123; and deductive reasoning (Indonesia), 127; in religious sciences, prejudice against, 78; normal appointment of, 75; presiding, rarely named in court records, 77; provincial, bias against, 78; provincial, historical records of, 79; provincial, salary of, 78; right of, to create legal norms, 175
Judgeship, expansion of, 10
Judging, activity of, 144
Judgment, based on consensus of qadi and jurists, 29; claimant's request for, 53; equal to estimate of estate value divided evenly (Indonesia), 133; errors in, 30; in maintenance case, stipulated attempt at reconciliation mandated, 109; nonfulfillment of terms of, (maintenance case), 110; nullification of, criteria for, 32; personal knowledge not allowable in, 30; predominant role of rules of procedure in, 442; qadi's consultation with jurists on, 29; qadi's qualification for issuance of, 29; qadi's role in issuing, 408; reversals of, due to improper reasoning, 31; reversals of, due to incompetent judge, 31; stock phrasing used in request for, 53; successor review of, 31–2; use of Islamic legal framework in, 140; value of fairness in, 29–30; against *wakīl*, for loss of money (Yemen), 202; written formulation of, 55. *See also Ḥukm*
Judgments (Aceh court), governance of equality and fairness in, 140; rejection of written agreement for, 140; use of Gayo *adat* in, 140
Judicial practice in Modern Libya, 495–516
Judicial process. *See* Process, judicial
Jurisdiction, in homicide cases, shared between niẓāmiye and shariʿa courts (Ottoman), 36
Jurisprudence, Islamic, effect of, on judicial practice, 245; studies of, 245
Justice, in Muslim societies, 1

Kadhis (Zanzibar), 95; appointed by state, 97; basis of selection, 97; dependence on local kadhis, 105; interrogation of, 117; training and education of, 97; followers of Shafiʿi *madhhab*, 97. *See also* Kadi, and Qadi
Kadhi's Act, structure of legal system described in, 96
Kadi (Ottoman), courts as backbone of Ottoman judicial system, 247; duties of, 285; education of (Sofia), 278; expanded duties of, 285; importance of, in Ottoman Balkans, 278; Sultan's orders to, concerning

criminal activity in province (Rumili), 281–8
Kadijustiz, 5, 427; as more predictable than discretionary, 428
Kadilik, 275–6
Kal'a, Ahmet, 246n2
Kalāhī Zāda, al-Sayyid Muḥammad Amīn, Qadi, 446
Kano (Nigeria) and Mascara (Algeria), colonial conquest of, results compared, 311; cultural differences between, 309; judicial process in, 301
Kanun, Sultanic, 86; *Kanunname*, 73
Kasam, 292
Kāsānī, al-, 186n30, 186n31
Kasim, judge, 137–9, 141
Kātib, 21
Kaza, 247, 282
Kazasker, 247, 250; role of, in settling debts, 268
Kazf, 79–85. *See also* Qadhf
Kethüda, 252. *See also* Steward
Kharijis, 344
Khaṣṣāf, al-, 17, 30, 31, 367n9
Khayr b. Nuʿaym, qadi, 352, 369–70, 381
Khayriyyāt, 207
Khiṭāb, 27
Khiyār, 197; *Khiyār al-ʿayb*, 216; *Khiyār al-ruʾya*, 197, 214; *Khiyar al-sharṭ*, 214
Khulʿ, in which wife is at fault, 326, 330. *See also Khuluu*
Khuluu, 97n2, 100; court-ordered, 111; hadith of Prophet Mohamedi concerning, (Zanzibar), 112; negotiation of cost, 111n15; and out-of-court settlement, 111; validity of divorce through, 103. *See also Khulʿ*
Khuṣūmāt, 48
Kindī, 2, 350ff.; historical work of, 252
Kitāb adab al-qaḍāʾ (Ibn Abī al-Damm), 17
Kitāb al-fiqh ʿalā al-madhāhib al-arbaʿa, 231, 238
Kitāb al-kharāj, 12
Kitāb al-miʿyār (Aḥmad al-Wansharīsī), 384
Kitāb al-qāḍī ilā ʾl-qāḍī, in case involving injury to a child (Libya), 502–05; use of, to secure rightful inheritance of estate (Libya), 505–06
Kitāb al-wulāt waʾl-quḍāt (al-Kindī), 351
Koçu Bey, 277
Kontramemorie, as answer to *memorie*, 134
Kuandikia pesa. *See* Writing for money
Küçük Ali, qadi, 77
Kufr al-Māʿ, 4

al-Lāfī b. Muftāḥ, qadi, 503
Land transfer, corroboration of, 56
Lawal, Amina, sentence of, death by stoning, 219, 241
Law, assumptions about, 143; determination of Islamic part of, 143; of divorce (Egyptian) and Hanafi school, 176; as general model, 167; in the marketplace (Istanbul), 148; normative, 74; as object of interpretation, 148; of the land, 41; open texture of, 167, 167n21; personal status, 143; praxeological respecification of, 149; secular, imported from the West, 143; sources of knowledge of (Istanbul), 248; study of enforcement of, 91; uniformity in interpretation of, 172; Western orientation of, 41
Law book, imperial (Ottoman), 91
Law of 1929 (Egypt), grounds for divorce outlined in, 149
Lawth, 28, 317, 492
Legislation (Egyptian), constitutionality of, 178; source of, 177–8
Legislature and Supreme Constitutional Council (Egypt), boundaries of, 192
Legislature, modern, precedence over all norms of past jurists, 189
Legitimacy, 537–41; of a child, 517
Letter, admissibility as evidence, 27
Liʿān, 518
Libya, 43, 495–516
Litigation, concluded without judgment, 58–65; of conflicting claims, 58; and out-of-court settlement, 24; Protected People and, 24; resolution of, by judicial certification, 67; resolution of, by qadi's order (*amr*) or action (*fiʿl*), 67; in shariʿa court (Ibb, Yemen), 195; women and, 23–4
Local courts (Ottoman), as instrument to achieve local order, 90
Local moralities, normative laws in the context of, 90

Lower court and court of appeal (Nigeria), difference in severity of Quranic penalties, 240

Madai (the plaintiff's claim), 99, 104, 106
Madhāhib al-ḥukkām fī nawāzil al-aḥkām (Muḥammad b. ʿIyāḍ), as source of cases involving penal laws, 2, 473–4, 475
Madhhab, 11, 13, 384; doctrine in Ottoman Empire, 36; Maliki and judicial reconsiderations in, 273; replacement of, under colonial rule, 36; in Zanzibar, 97
Madrasa, 42, 431, 437
Madrasat al-Qaḍāʾ al-Sharʿī, 456
Mafia Island, 105
Mahari, 100, 108, 111. *See also Mahr*
Maḥḍar, 21, 23, 42, 64, 65, 66; court minutes, 499
Mahdī, al-, 11–12, 372
Maḥkama. See Court
al-Maḥkama al-Kubrā, 429–30
Mahkamah Syariah, 118
Maḥkamat al-bāb, 411
Mahr, 345, 358, 359. *See also Mahari*
Maintenance, child's "partness" as reason for, 185; for children from previous marriage, 108; debts of father, 186; exemption from payment of, 187; father's responsibility for his children, 106; inadequacy of, 105; postponement of payments for children, 190; present faults in policy of, 189; purpose of policy, 190; right of child to sue for, 179; suit ruling in favor of mother (1989), 181; termination of obligation, 186; unreasonableness of rules for, 189
– obligation, annulment of, 180; avoidance of, 187; bank's cooperation in ensuring payment of, 180; denial of, 181; early development of, in Iraq and Transoxania, 179; elapse of, 186; enforcement of, 180; extension of, 186–7; Hanafi doctrine on, 187, 191–2; history of, 179; legal measures to ensure payment of, 180; modern Egyptian advocacy of, 179; mother ordered to pay, 186–7; partial success in upholding of, (Egypt), 180; punishment for failure to fulfill, 185; SCC's judgment on, 192; upholding of constitutionality of, 180
– payment, amount of, 183; by father, 187; children's need for, 185; circumvention of, through successive court appeals, 182; father agrees to or qadi specifies, 183; father consents to, unilaterally, 183; and Hanafi doctrines, 182; legal right of wife to, 184; morally valid but not enforceable legally (Hanafi opinion), 183–4; not retroactive to wife, 184; overdue, 186
Māʿiz, hadith of, 232
Majlis, 131, 299, 477; comparison with Western jury, 300n1; composition of (Nigeria), 312; elimination of (Algeria), 318; elimination of (Nigeria), 318; role of, in Kano (Nigeria), 300; role of, in Mascara (Algeria), 300
Male-female contact, increase in number of cases, 73, 89; legitimate versus idle, 89; monitoring of, 79–83; new regulation of, 87; prohibition of, 81; public scrutiny of, 87
Male-female relationship, illicit, *sicill* concerning, 80
Male-female segregation, among elite classes, 89; failure to maintain, 89
Mālik, 155
Maliki doctrine, applicability to countries in North Africa, 335–43; application of, 223; *fiqh* texts in Shariʿa Courts (Nigeria); qadi judgments based on, 14; *qasāma* procedure and British deference to, 40; two interpretations of divorce procedure in, 324
Maliki School, 219–41, 324ff.
Mamlūks, chancery usage, 63; content of chronicles, 47; documents, nature of, 49; reign of, 15
al-Manṣūr, Ismāʿīl ʿAbd al-Raḥmān, qadi 200ff.
al-Marghinani, 184n24
Marital discord, responsibility for, 112; property cases and women's advantage in, 125

Market, 246; market rate (*ecr-i misil*), 260
Market inspector, work of, performed under court authority, 75
Marriage, of an apostate to a Muslim, invalidity of, 174; cultural norms affecting (Zanzibar), 114; dissolution due to personal status law, 145; grounds for dissolution of, 144–5; negotiation for release from, 385; nonfulfillment of terms of judgment concerning, 110; second, of a woman, *fatwā* concerning, 404; temporary, 360
Marriage law of 1974 (Indonesia), significance of, 127
Marsūm, as opposed to *ḥukm*, 61–2
Mascara (Algeria), judicial process in, 301; political history of, 302
Mashhūr, 438
Maṣlaḥa, 84, 512, 515
Matāʿ, 349–81; compensation for damage caused by divorce, 375; conditions under which paid, 357; conflict in Quranic interpretation of, 358–9; debate over payment as obligatory or recommended, 364; as supplement to *mahr*, 376; jurists on, 359; moral obligation, 374; origin of concept, 355; payment of, at time of divorce, 362; payment of, by the Prophet, 361; payment of, as voluntary or compulsory, 355; practice in Madina, 361–2; Qur'an and, 355–9; qadi's role in settling disputes concerning, 362–5; as replacement for dower, 374–5; supplement to payment of dower and maintenance, 365; Umayyad judicial practice concerning, 362–5
Mattītī, al-, 337
*Maulvi*s, 37
al-Māwardī, 17
al-Mawwāq, 337
Maẓālim, 11, 21
Mecelle, 35
Medico-legal report, discussion of psychological impotence in, 157; inquiry into relevant issues brought up by, 157; verbatim transcription of, 156
Mehmed Efendi, qadi, 291
Mehmed II, 276
Memorie, arguments concerning, 134
Mengadili, third part of formal Decision, 126
Merchants' benefit, brokers' practice of seeking (Yemen), 212
Mevlana Elhacc Ebu Bekir Efendi, qadi, 273–6, 278
Mevleviyet, 273–6, 278
Miḥna, 12
Milk, 434, 438
*Millet*s, 247
Mimbar Hukum, journal of Ministry of Religion, 120
Ministry of Religion (Indonesia), 118
Mirimiran (Ottoman), 294
Mixed courts for commerce and crime (1840s), presence of Christian judges in, 35
Miʿyār (al-Wansharīsī), 3
Mkokotoni (Zanzibar), 96; role of clerks in cases from, 113
Molla, 273–4, 292; category of, 429
Money, theft of, by slave (Kano, Nigeria), 315–16
Morocco, control and seclusion of women in, 342; grafting of Maliki law onto modern legal system of, 342
Mosque, as *milk* or *waqf* (Aleppo), 438
Muʿāwiya, 8–9, 32–9, 370, 372, 381
Muʿāyana. *See* Eyewitness testimony
Mudawwana (Saḥnūn), 329–30
Muddaʿā ʿalayh, 22, 432. *See also* Defendant
Muddaʿī, 22, 430. *See also* Plaintiff
Muftī, 19, 21, 383; role of, 370; role of in difficult cases, 407–08. *See also* *Fatwā*, *Iftā'*, *Istiftā'*
Mughal Empire (India), 37; qadi system under, 15
Muhammad, the Prophet, 6, 7; as ideal judge, 7
Muḥammad b. ʿAlī, Muftī, 431
Muḥammad b. ʿIyāḍ, 473–5
Muḥammad al-Sanūsī al-Ghazzālī, qadi, 506, 509
Muḥammad al-Ṭālib al-Ḥammālī, qadi, 513
Muḥammadu Gidadu, qadi, 31
*Mühimme defter*s, contents of, 283; defined, 279
Muḥṣan, 223, 238
al-Muhtadī Billāh, 18
Muhtasip, 75, 86–7. *See also* Market Inspector

Muʿīn al-ḥukkām (al-Ṭarābulusī), 17
Mujtahid, 14, 29, 394
Muqallid, 14
Murder, strong suspicion of, 487; reason for imposition of *taʿzīr*, 487; murder case, community surveillance as a part of, 83
Muṣannif, Muḥammad b. Ghālib al-, qadi, 201
Mushāwar, 477
Muslim countries, limitations on Shariʿa jurisdictions in, 42
Muṣṭafā IV, 266
Mustaftī, 383. *See also Fatwā, Iftā', Istiftā'*
Musyawarah, 127, 131–2; absence of, 135; as evidence, 136; lack of free agreement in, 132; validity of, 135
Musyawarah mufakat, 128, 134
Mutʿa, 359–60. *See also* Temporary marriage
al-Muʿtaḍid, 13
Mutawallī, 435–6, 438
Mütesellim, 282; bandits accompanying, 283
Mutilation, as punishment, 489
Muwaṭṭa' (Mālik), 327; hadith found in, 227
Muzakkī, 21
Mwalimu Simai, purpose as witness, 102

Nā'ibs, 12, 247, 249, 285–6, 429, 432
National legal system, Shariʿa as part of, 41
National supreme court, shariʿa justice controlled by, 42
Native Courts Ordinance of 1933 (Nigeria), power of British Resident confirmed by, 40
al-Nawāwī, 230n27
Negotiation of settlement (divorce case), allowance of, 114
Nigeria, *alkalis* courts (Area Courts), abolition of, 221; Northern states, re-Islamization of, 220; Penal Code, pre-1960, commutation of sentences, 220; post-conquest changes, 311; Shariʿa Penal Code, modeled after other countries, 223; Supreme Court, protection of freedom of religion by, 41
Niẓāmiye courts, 35; and civil cases, 35; French influence on, 35; nonreligious nature of, 35
Nonviolent theft, punishment for, 489
Norms, legal, and Hanafi doctrine, 189; socio-cultural, 6; Gayo social norms and loss of women's right to family estate, 136; normative laws, 90
Nūr Shaykh Zāda al-Sayyid ʿAbd al-Raḥīm, qadi, 447
Nuri, Osman, 246n2
Nushūz, 327

Oath, 218; in case of damaged coffee, unorthodox use of, 216–17; in civil cases, taking of, 27; judicial, 217; by merchant, as part of final court judgment, 213; as proof in court, 27; in rescission doctrines, 217; swearing of, requirement under Almoravids, 480; taking of, allowable as proof in property cases, 27; taking of, requirement in theft cases, 27; taking of, not required in *ḥadd* cases, 27
Ottoman Empire, communal-level negotiation in, 249; integration of qadis in provincial government, 297; judicial administration of, 72; judicial principles of, 267; judicial reform in, 34; justice in, 90; legal documents in, 245; legal innovations, 71n1; legal system, imperialization of, 71; legal system, structure of, 247–8; modernization of judiciary in, 34–6; public court record in, 72; promulgation of Gülhane Decree (1839), 34; qadi system under, 15; rebelliousness of tribal groups in, 90; rebelliousness of soldiers in, 90; training of judges in, 250–1; use of judicial arm in, 90
Ottoman judiciary, and nepotism, 251; responsibility of, 250
Ottoman law, interactive nature of, 269; transcendent jurisdiction of, 251
Ottoman civil code. *See* Mecelle
Out-of-court settlement, arbiter's limitation in, 24

Pakistan, 42, 43; Islamization of, 528; repeal of Muslim law rules (1872), 534
Pancasila, 132

Panitera, 120
Peace, sovereign's ultimate responsibility for, 269
Pematang, 136; valid only by consensus, 137
Pemba, 96
Penal code, Nigerian, pre-1960. *See* Nigeria
Penal law, re-Islamization of in Nigeria, 219–29; under Almoravids, role of suspicion in preventive detention, 485
Pengadilan Agama, 117
Pengadilan Negeri, 117
Personal status, adjudication of cases (Egypt), 150; law, codification of (Egyptian), 147; law, Egyptian, and shariʿa courts, 144; law, error in *a priori* characterization of, 143–4; law, examples of, 171; law, *fiqh,* control of, 171; law, and schools of Islamic law, 147; law, subject to civil and commercial rules, 150; legislation, use of by President Sadat to enforce maintenance obligation, 180; matters, in pre-revolutionary Egypt, 147; matters, organized by laws, 150
"Pimp", slanderous use of the word, 84; use of in innuendo, 85
Piri Mehmed Paşa, 275, 277
Plaintiff, advantage of, in legal cases, 442; claim, of abuse with bad language, 106; claim, contents of, 99; claim, of inadequate maintenance, 106; personal and direct interest of, 176
Pluralism, legal, problems with, 454; in legal system (Egyptian), 453
Political authorities, responsibility for maintenance policy, 190
Political intervention, cases of punishment by, 263–6; by sultan (Istanbul), with banishment as result of, 263–4; by sultan, with hanging as a result of, 265
Positive claim, 130; applicability in *Inen Maryam v. Aman Mas,* 131; in defense statement, 130; system of, 131
Positive-law provision, substantiation of, 159
Praxeology, in study of law and courtrooms, use of, 149
Precedents, lack of, in juridical literature, 48
Pregnancy as proof of *zinā,* doubtful as evidence, 236
Pretrial detention, causes for, 480; role of, in court procedures (Almoravid), 485
Procedure, judicial, appellate level, 124; colonial-era style of, 124; format of decision in, 124; shift from dependence on *ḥakam*s to evidence-based, under Umayyads, 368–9; routine of (Aceh), 124; in *zinā* case, 230
Process, judicial, dependence on oral testimony (Nigeria), 301; marginalization of (Istanbul), 270
Process, legal, derivation from European civil law tradition (Indonesia), 126; in marketplace, negotiation (Istanbul), 249
Proof, standards of, 130. *See also Thubūt*
Property case (Aceh), division of estate in, 125; frequency of types of, 124; limited witness acceptability in, 25
Property settlements, men favored in, 140
Prosecution, role of local residents in, 83
Protection, legal, of subjects (Ottoman), 92
Protected People, 24. *See also* Dhimmīs
Punç, Punççu, 254
*Pundit*s, 37
Punishment, administration of, 262; by banishment, 262–3; caused by accusations of illicit sex, 82; judicial, authorization of by divan, 262; judicial, fines or imprisonment as example of, 262; judicial, of steward, 262; judicial, role of court in (Istanbul), 261; judicial, types of 261–2; provision for under Maliki school (Nigeria); use of, in eighteenth-century Istanbul, 261
Putusan. See "Decision"

Qaḍāʾ, 10, 19, 249; changes in the office of, under the Umayyads, 363; early expansion of, 10; limitations of, 19; as right of God, 19; *Qaḍaʾ tark* (temporary judgments), 61
Qadāh, unit of measure for agrarian goods, 199

Qadhf, unfounded accusation of fornication, 26, 224; punishment of whipping for, 486. *See also* Slander
Qadi, Abbasid, 11–4; and colonial rule, French, Dutch, Italian, British, 36–41; and court records, 4; duties of, 10; emergence of the office of, 8; extrajudicial functions of, 14, 15; female as, 20; the four righteous caliphs as, 8; freedom from *madhhab* doctrine, 14; historical records of, before advent of Ottoman archives, 383; jurisdiction of, 8–9; literature on, 1–6; local functions of, 4; modern period, 32–41; modernization of judiciary in Turkey, 34–6; Mughals, Safavids, Fatimids, Mamluks, 15; and *muftī*, 48; office of, introduced by Umayyads, 368; origin of, 8; Ottoman, 15–6; in the period of prophecy, 6–7; qualities of, 20; responsibility of, in settling divorce disputes, 362; role as administrator, 4; role of, in modern period, 32; salary of, 19; as state functionary under ʿAbbāsids, 13; and Shari'ah justice today, 41–4; as state official, in early Umayyad period, 368; supervisory functions of, 434; training of, 20; in the Umayyad period, 9–11; undesirability of accepting office of, 18. *See also* Kadi and Kadhi
Qadi ʿaskar, 15. *See also Kazasker*
Qadi courts, abolition of, 36; colonial supervision of, 36–7; bureaucratization of, in Ottoman Empire, 35; determination of plaintiff and defendant in, 22; failure of defendant to appear in, 22; frequency of sessions of, 22; interrogation of litigants in, 23; jurisdiction of, under colonial rule, 36; litigation in, 22–4; location of, 21; personnel of, 21; procedures in, 24–9; as single judge courts, 21; treatment of litigants in, 23; Western influence on, 33–44
Qāḍī ʿIyāḍ, 2
Qāḍī al-jamāʿa, 15
Qāḍī al-jund, 9
Qāḍī al-quḍāt, 12
Qadiship, ʿAbbāsid transformation of, 13; historical survey of, 6–16; as patronage, 11; procedures and duties of, 18–19; qualifications for (Hanafi), 18
Qadrī Pasha, 455; codification of laws by, 150
al-Qalqashandī, 17
Qānūn, 15. *See also Kanun*
Qanun-i-Shahadat, as relacement for Evidence Act, 528
Qarīna, 28
Qasāma, 28, 480n25, 482; oath, 316, 317n21; use of, in determining sentences, 483–4
Qāṣṣ, 366
Qiṣāṣ, 487, 492; right to, as a result of loss of incisor teeth, 485, 488
Qur'ān, revelation of, 6
Quranic ethics, 192
al-Qurṭubī, 232n30

Rape, claim of, conditions considered for (Almoravid period), 483; proof of, 224
Rashīd, Hārūn al-, 12
Rasm al-istirʿāʾ, 402
Raʾy, 11, 373
Reasoning, social norms underlying (Indonesia), 117
Reaya, 288; dispersal of, 294; oppression of, 282
Reconciliation, mandated by judge, 109
Reform, dual legal system resulting from (Ottoman), 36
Regulation, broader application than contracts (Istanbul), 269
Re-Islamization, of legal system, 43; of Northern Nigerian states, 220
Religious and legal terms, Kiswahili forms of, 95
Remarriage, of defendant, in divorce case, 101; proof of legality of, 104; valid because of *khuluu*, 103
"Repeal-revival" hypothesis of 1938, effect on 1872 Evidence Act (Pakistan), 519; voided by Evidence Order, 533
Repudiation, divorce by, 97. *See also* Divorce
Reputation of family, male's responsibility for, 84

Responsa literature, 47
Revenue from criminal acts, 92
Riḍā, 211, 218
Right of rescission, circumstances under which applicable, 215; commercial applications in, 212; exercise of, 212
Risāla (Ibn Abī Zayd al-Qayrawānī), 227
Rizq, 399
Rosen, Lawrence, 4–5
Rules, legal, application of by judges, 88; of procedure, in Umayyad period, 372
Rumili, importance of, 279
Russell, Alexander, 431
Rusul Efendi, qadi 291
Ru'ya, 201
Ru'ya mumayyiza bi-ta'ammul, 215

Saadeddin and Ayşe, case of, 79–85
Sacred normativity of Islam, 171
Safavid Iran, 15, 90
Ṣafī al-Dīn Aḥmad b. Aḥmad, al-Sayāghī, qadi, 201, 204, 207
Safiyyatu Hussaini. *See* Hussaini, Safiyyatu
Ṣāḥib al-masā'il, 21
Sale, contract, conditions of, 214; of slaves, document explaining, 53–4
Samadiah v. Hasan, 136–7
Sancakbegi, 86
al-Sanūsī, Muḥammad b. Idrīs al-Mahdī, 499
al-Sarakhsī, 184n25, 186n29, 186n30
Saudi Arabia, shariʿa dominant in, 43
al-Sayyid bin al-Ṣabr, qadi 307
Sayyid Muḥammad, ʿAlī Dede, 438
SCC. *See* Supreme Constitutional Court
Schacht, J., 352, 433
"Science of the shares", neglect of, 132; validity of, 135. *See also* Inheritance
Scientific research vs. Islamic normativity, 178
SCPC (Shariʿah Criminal Procedure Code) (Nigeria), 229; applicability of provisions of, 229
Scribe, qualities of, 21. *See also Amīn*
Sectarian courts, jurisdiction of, personal matters for non-Muslims, 454
Section 128 of Evidence Order (Pakistan, 1984), errors of writing and thinking in, 535–6; Hanafi law rules in, 535
Secular courts, emergence of, 33
Self-defense in court case, documentation of, 92
Selim I, judicial structure created by, 15
Separation of powers, constitutional principle of (Egypt), 175
Şerhi Mehmed Efendi, 277
Settlement of land case, division of, declared invalid, 139
Sexual relations, inability to have, 397; permissibility of, 223
Seyyid Cafer, qadi, 77
Shaʿbī, 10
al-Shāfiʿī, 17, 231, 375–6
Shafiʿis, qadi judgments, based on doctrines of, 14; school, 47–68, 95–115, 117ff.; Syrian population, majority of, 411
Shahāda bi'l-khabar, 25
Shahādat naql, defined, 495; format of, 499–501; historical development of, 497–9; institution of, adopted by Ibn ʿĀṣim, 498; institution of, adopted from *Kitāb al-qāḍī ilā 'l-qāḍī*, 497; purpose of, 495–6
Sharʿī, 512
Shariʿa, 171, 451; applied in special courts, 42; codification of, 33, 42; in India, administered by British judges, 37; justice, in present-day nations, 41–4; as law of the land (Northern Nigeria), permanence of, 41; legal issues under jurisdiction of, 451; limited implementation of, 41; as part of national legal system, 41; primacy in civil law, replacement of, 38; primacy in India, abolition of, 38; tribunals of, 43
Shariʿa Courts, abolition of in 1955 (Egypt), 453; bureaucratization of, 33; case heard in Yemen, background records on, 196; commercial litigation in, 195; emergence of, 33; enthusiasm for death sentence in (Nigeria), 240; jurisdiction limited by Ministry of Justice (1886, Ottoman Empire), 35; jurisdiction, limitation of, 35;

jurisdiction of (Nigeria), 221; jurisdiction of (Ottoman period), 452; jurisdiction of criminal law in, 229; jurisdiction of, for Muslims only (Egypt), 453; and national courts, integration of, 33; reform of, in late nineteenth century (Egypt), 455; replacement of, with National Courts (Egypt), 453; representation for non-Muslims in, by proxy, 457; restriction of jurisdiction of (Egypt, 1897), 452–3; role of commercial practice and custom (*ʿurf*) in (Yemen), 196; transaction involving defective coffee analyzed in, 196; use of law codes for adjudication in, legal requirement of, 35
Shariʿa Court of Appeal (Nigeria), 240
Shariʿa criminal law (Indian), British modification of, 38
Shariʿa Penal Code, first enactment of (Nigeria), 220; questionable constitutionality of, 241; restoration of to pre-1960 status, 240
Sharīf, 306
Sharṭ, 473, 496n6
Shaykh, 438, 500
Shaykh al-Islam, Grand Mufti in Istanbul, 15, 411, 428
Sheha (Zanzibar), 97, 102, 109–10, 115
Shiqāq, 335
Shopping, for legal forums, by Muslims, 451; in litigation, consequences of, 466–7; practice of among dhimmīs, 451
Shubha, 224, 236
Shufʿa, 305
Shuhūd, 299, 301, 306
Shūrā, 477
Shurayḥ, qadi, 9, 362, 364, 366–7, 374, 379–380
Sicill. *See Sijill*
Signatures, suspicious, 139n7
Sijill, 21, 80, 83, 273, 279, 494
Silk bleachers, conflict with dyers concerning master Apprentices, 255–6
Silver Wire Workshop, masters vs. apprentices on rights of succession, 256
Siyāsa, 12, 15, 32, 34, 300
Slander, 80–1, 87. *See also Qadhf*
Slave trade, abolition of in Nigeria, 310
Slavery, in pre-colonial Kano (Nigeria), 309–10
Social order, preservation of by judges, 88
Sociological process of normalization, in judicial determination, 158
Sofia, as official seat of governor of Rumili, 279; reason for rise to status of *mevleviyet*, 277; Shariʿa court of, as center for Kadis from same and different *eyalet*s, 291; *sicill*s of, use of for historical data, 279
Sokoto, Shariʿa Court Law (SSCL), 221; Shariʿa Criminal Procedure Code (SSCPC), 222; Shariʿa Penal Code (SSPC), 222–3
State courts, and assumption of powers from shariʿa courts, 172; role of Hanafi doctrine in, 172
Steward (of artisans' group), appointment of by government, 252–3; court appointment overturned, 253; designation of, as sign of group's existence, 252; request for removal of, due to corruption, 254–5; role of, 252
Stewardships, government hiring of (Istanbul), 252
Stoning, as punishment, 227; introduction of sentences of, in 2000 (Nigeria), 219. *See also Ẓinā*
Su'āl, 63, 65
Subaşi, 86
Ṣubḥ al-aʿshā (al-Qalqashandī), 17
Subjects' rights, universal knowledge of (Istanbul), 267
Substantive law, European models of, 170
Subul al-salām sharḥ Bulūgh al-marām, 232, 233
Successor review, discretionary right of, 31; informality of, 273
Süleyman I, 15; law book, 73, 88
Ṣulḥ, 249
Sultan Mahmud II, 264, 267, 423
Sunna, 11, 169, 373, 387
Sunni Islam, 169
Sunni schools, 192, 378
Support of children. *See* Maintenance
Supreme Constitutional Court of Egypt (SCC), 43, 177; and Hanafi school

of law, 191; not bound by classical *fiqh* norms, in family law, 191; powers of, 177; regulation of, by law no. 48/1979, 177; tasks of, 177
Supreme Court (Indonesia), authority of, 124; judges overseen by, 118
Surveillance, social, by community (Ottoman Aintab), 80; covert aims of, 90; and harassment, narrow line between, 87; male-female, increase in, 88; as part of legal process, 83
al-Suyūṭī, 363
Syamsiah binti Mudali v. Aji Aman Sarana, 138
Syariah as basis of laws (Aceh province), 118

Tabṣirat al-ḥukkām (Ibn Farḥūn), 17
Taḥkīm, 370
Takèngën (Indonesia), civil court judges in, 119; Islamic court judges in, 119; structure of court in, 119
Takiyyat al-Mawlawiyya, 440
Ṭalāq. See Divorce
Talfīq, 455
Talio, 57, 488. *See also Qiṣāṣ*
Tamlīk, 399, 401
al-Ṭarābulusī, 17
al-Taʿrīf bi'l-qāḍī ʿIyāḍ, 473
al-Tashrīʿ al-jināʾī al-islāmī (ʿAbd al-Qādir ʿAwda), 233
Taslīm, 56
Tawātur, 438
Tawba b. Nimr, qadi 352, 363, 368, 374, 381
Tawliya, 438
Tawqīʿ, 50, 64–5
Tax-farm, 86
Tax-farmers, disciplining of, 75
Taʿzīr, 487–8
Testimony, revocation of, is unacceptable, 26–7. *See also Shahāda*
Testimony, written, endorsed by Nāʾib, attesting to accidental loss of virginity, 513–14; endorsed by qadi, affirming a camel had been transferred to son of a deceased woman, 511–12; endorsed by qadi, attesting to bequeathal of property to a *zāwiya,* 508–10; endorsed by qadi, attesting to purchase of a slave, 510–11; endorsed by qadi, authenticating a woman's marital status as a divorcee, 507–8; endorsed by qadi, to insure future payment of a dower, 506–7
al-Thamr al-dānī sharḥ risālat al-Qayrawānī, 235
Thubūt, 29, 47, 64–5; same as a *ḥukm* 66–7
Timar, defined, 284; disputes over, 284–5; *sicills* concerning, 292
Traders, and artisans, disputes involving conflicts with stewards, 252–4; loose organization of, 252; stewards of, appointment by government, 252–3. *See also* Artisans
Training, legal, demand for (Indonesia), 118
Transoxanian authors, 185
Treasury (in Imamic state), equivalent to Central Bank, 198
Trial, by judge, advantage of, 92; as negotiation, 92
Tuḥfat al-ḥukkām (Ibn ʿĀṣim), as source for judicial practice, 497
Tuhma, as ground for discretionary punishment, 28
Turkey, Republic of, foundation, 36
Turkish Code of Commerce (1850), influenced by French *Code de Commerce,* 35
Tyan, E., 1

ʿUdūl. See ʿĀdil
ʿUlamāʾ, 274, 276, 409, 411, 429, 457
Ulema. See ʿUlamāʾ
ʿUmar I, 9, 367
ʿUmar II, 10
Umayyad, caliphs, 8, 10; caliphate, 349; period, early, 265; period, legal developments during, 349; period, rules of legal procedure in, 372; period, source of information of, 351; qadis, lack of training of, 371; qadis, power of, 371; qadis, subject to governor's authority, 371
Umm (al-Shāfiʿī), 17
Umma, 7
Uncodified Islamic criminal law, after introduction of Sokoto Sharia Penal Code, 222
Uncodified Maliki law in new courts (Nigerian), 221
Uncodified Muslim law, and Evidence Act of 1872 (Pakistan), 520

Unconstitutional legislative texts, individuals' right to bring action against, 177
Unlawful intercourse, acquittal of charge, 225; confession of, 228; proof of, by testimony, 227. *See also* *Zinā*
'Urf, 196, 444; *örf* (custom), 247, 249; Örf-i Sultani, 250; and documentary evidence, 432ff.
Usufruct of the land, entitlement to, 413
'Uthmān, 9, 328
Uthman dan Fodio, 308
'Uthmān Zāda al-Sayyid Maḥmūd, qadi, 444

Vakıf, artisans' occupancy of as a public benefit, 260; artisans' rights to perpetual use of, 260; defined, 260; investor/proprietors of, 260; as source of revenue for government or individuals, 260. *See also* *Waqf*
Violence (Istanbul), instigation of, 266; participation of artisans in, 266–7
Virginity, loss of, before marriage 386–7; disputed as a valid cause for divorce, 386–91; treated as a defect in divorce case, 387
Vizier, replacement of chief qadi by, 13; Grand, function of, 247

al-Wafā'ī, Shaykh Abū Bakr, 433
Waiting period, after divorce, 356. *See also Divorce, Edda, 'Idda*
Wakāla, limitations on, 23
Wakī', Abū Bakr Muḥammad, 2, 350, 367; historical work by, 351–2
Wakīl, 200, 202, 210, 431n12, 457
Waqf, 62, 427; administration of by qadi, 434; in Aleppo, 427–49; annulment of family endowment, 435–7; Christian, 422; in Damascus, 411–25; Hanafi judges, 417; Maliki judges, 417; lease of, 422–3; maintenance of, 436; property, advantages of extended lease of, 412–13; property, conditions of lease of, 412; property, loss of, due to legal manipulation by foreign owners, 424–5; Shafi'i judges, 417; supervision of, 436 supervision of, 436; *waqf dhurrī*, 434; *waqf khayrī*, 434. *See also* *Vakıf*
Waqf land, extended lease of, 418–20; Hanafi domination of, 414; long-term leases through three-year periods, 421–2; military domination of, 415–16; ownership by foreign nationals of, 424
Wasiat, 128, 133, 139; lack of proof of, 133. *See also* Bequest
Wathā'iq, 22, 497. *See also* Document
Weber, Max, 5, 427
Wine-drinking, imposition of *ḥadd* punishment for, 483
Witness(es), conditions causing exclusion as, 26; disqualified, 28, 481; husband of, as opponent, 134; number of, required in legal proceedings, 372; relationship to litigants, 165; reliability of, 166; requirement of four, in cases of illicit sexual relations, 26; requirement of personal integrity, 26; requirements applicable to, 25; testimony, contradictory, 166–7; testimony, elements of, 166
Witness testimony, institutional context of, 165; speakers' turns fixed during, 165; stereotypical nature of, 165; editing and rewriting of, 165
Women and divorce, *fatwā*s dealing with, 384
Women's rights, judge's view of (Aceh), 136
"Writing for money," as a common misunderstanding of divorce, 114; unlawful out-of-court divorce, 104

Yaḥyā b. Yaḥyā al-Laythī, 327, 332, 344; *Riwāya* of, 327
Yakubu Abubakar, acquittal of, 226
Yamīn, 196, 216–7
*Yasakçı*s, 295
Yazīd II, 10
Yazīd III, 369
Yemen, eclipse of commerce in coffee, 197; revenue of, dependent on coffee, 197

Ẓāhir, 30
Zakāt, 198–9,
Zamfara, 219

Zanzibar, 42, 95–6; family law issues in, 95; qadi courts, 42; town, 96
Zanzibari courts, claimants' perceptions of issues in, 95; documents and records in, 95
Zayanids, 302
Zaydī, doctrine on rescission of contracts, 214; legal ruling on inspection of merchandise (coffee), 214n12, 215; school of law, 195–218
Zia ul-Haq, 517
Zinā, 25, 81, 223, 229n23; charge of, 226; conviction and appeal of, 236–67; establishment of, 224; illegal procedure in prosecution of, 230; illegal use of hearsay in case of, 231; insufficient explanation of charges, 233; insufficient opportunity to defend against testimony, 234; new regulation of homosexuality under rubric of, 87; nullification of withdrawal from confession of, 235; offense of, not in effect, 229; penalty for married woman, 81; punishment for, 226; requirement of witnesses, 230; right of withdrawal of confession, 235; suspicion of, 232. *See also* Adultery, Stoning
Zorastrians, 8
al-Zuhrī, 10